BEYOND THE COURTROOM

RESOLVING DISPUTES THROUGH AGREEMENT

Touro University Press Books

Series Editor
MICHAEL A. SHMIDMAN, PhD (Touro College, New York)
SIMCHA FISHBANE, PhD (Touro College, New York)

TOURO UNIVERSITY PRESS

BEYOND THE COURTROOM

RESOLVING DISPUTES THROUGH AGREEMENT

Collected Articles
and Book Chapters
by **Hal Abramson**

NEW YORK
2020

Library of Congress Cataloging-in-Publication Data

Names: Abramson, Harold I., author.
Title: Beyond the courtroom : resolving disputes through agreement /collected articles and essays by Hal Abramson.
Description: New York : Touro University Press, 2020.
Identifiers: LCCN 2019037848 (print) | LCCN 2019037849 (ebook) | ISBN 9781644692547 (hardback) | ISBN 9781644692554 (adobe pdf)
Subjects: LCSH: Dispute resolution (Law) | Mediation.
Classification: LCC K2390 .A915 2020 (print) | LCC K2390 (ebook) | DDC 347/.09--dc23
LC record available at https://lccn.loc.gov/2019037848
LC ebook record available at https://lccn.loc.gov/2019037849

Published by Touro University Press and Academic Studies Press.
Typeset, printed and distributed by Academic Studies Press.
ISBN 978-1-64469-254-7 (hardback)
ISBN 978-1-64469-255-4 (adobe pdf)

Touro University Press
Michael A. Shmidman and Simcha Fishbane, Editors
320 West 31st Street, Fourth Floor,
New York, NY 10001, USA
tcpress@touro. edu

Academic Studies Press
1577 Beacon Street
Brookline, MA 02446, USA
press@academicstudiespress. com
www.academicstudiespress. com

Book design by PHi Business Solutions Limited.
Cover design by Ivan Grave.

To my other family,
the community of dispute resolution academics and practitioners
who have inspired and taught me*

* My other books have been dedicated to members of my immediate family.

Contents

Acknowledgements

I want to express my deep appreciation for the support of Touro College and its law school throughout my career at Touro that made this lifetime of scholarship (so far) possible. I want to give special thanks to Dr. Bernard Lander, the founding and visionary President of Touro College and University System, and his visionary successor Dr. Alan Kadish. I also want to thank the deans at the law school who were supportive during each of their tenures-Howard Glickstein, Larry Raful, Patricia Salkin, Harry Ballan, and our new dean, Elena Langan.

A book project like this one would not have gone forward without considerable encouragement, and for that I want to thank Simcha Fishbane and Michael Shmidman, Editors of Touro University Press. I also want to thank Academic Studies Press, and especially the professional staff that labored behind the scenes and did magnificent editorial and design work, including Production Editor Kira Nemirovsky, Production Editor Associate Daria Pokholkova, and Editorial Director Alessandra Anzani. Finally, I want to give my personal thanks to two superb Research Assistants who came to the rescue at the right time to help move this project forward and to closure, Touro Law Students Meaghan Caltabiano and Yasmine Dieudonne.

Hal Abramson
June 18, 2020

Copyright Permissions

I want to gratefully acknowledge the permissions by these publishers for permitting me to reprint in this book the following articles and book chapters that they originally published:

Chapter 2. *Acknowledgements,* MEDIATION REPRESENTATION—ADVOCATING AS A PROBLEM-SOLVER (Aspen 3rd Edition, 2013). Reproduced with the permission of CCH Incorporated from Mediation Representation (ISBN 9781454831075) by Harold I. Abramson © 2013.

Chapter 3. *Problem-Solving Advocacy in Mediations: A Model of Client Representation 10 Harv. Neg. L.R. 103* (Sp. 2005).

Chapter 4. *Table of Contents and Introductory Chapter,* MEDIATION REPRESENTATION—ADVOCATING AS A PROBLEM-SOLVER (Aspen 3rd Edition, 2013). Reproduced with the permission of CCH Incorporated from Mediation Representation (ISBN 9781454831075) by Harold I. Abramson © 2013.

Chapter 5. *Are Legal Disputes Just About Money? Answers from Mediators on the Front Line,* with Birgit Sambeth Glasner, Bill Marsh, Bennet G. Picker, and Jerry Weiss, *Alternatives* 35 (9 October 2017).

Chapter 6. *Mediation Representation: Representing Clients Anywhere,* in *ADR in Business,* Volume II, Chapter 14 (Editor Arnold Ingen-Housz, Kluwer Law International, 2011).

Chapter 8. *Protocols for International Arbitrators Who Dare to Settle Cases,* 10 *Am. Rev. of Intl. Arb.* 1 (1999).

Chapter 9. *Mining Mediation Rules for Representation Opportunities and Obstacles,* 15 *Am. Rev. of Intl. Arb.* 103 (Sp. 2005) This article originally appeared in the American Review of International Arbitration. 15 *Am. Rev. of Intl. Arb.* 103 (Sp. 2005).

Chapter 10. *Selecting Mediators and Representing Clients in Cross-Cultural Disputes,* 7 *Cardozo J. of Confl. Resol.* 253 (2006).

Chapter 12. *Crossing Borders into New Ethical Territory: Ethical Challenges When Mediating Cross-Culturally,* 49 *S. Tex. L.R.* 921 (2008).

Chapter 13. *Outward Bound to Other Cultures: Seven Guidelines for U.S. Dispute Resolution Trainers,* 9 *Pepperdine Dispute Resolution Law Journal* 437 (2009).

Chapter 14. *The New Singapore Mediation Convention: The Process and Key Choices, Sing. Ref. Bk.,* 20 *Cardozo J. Conflict Resol.* 1037 (2019).

Chapter 15. Ch. 1, *Negotiating in Mediations,* MEDIATION REPRESENTATION —ADVOCATING AS A PROBLEM-SOLVER (Aspen 3rd Edition, 2013). Reproduced with the permission of CCH Incorporated from Mediation Representation (ISBN 9781454831075) by Harold I. Abramson © 2013.

Chapter 16. *Fashioning an Effective Negotiation Style: Choosing Between Good Practices, Tactics and Tricks,* in *The Negotiator's Desk Reference* (Andrea K. Schneider and Christopher Honeyman, eds., DRI Press/Mitchell Hamline School of Law and NDR Books LLC, 2017).

Chapter 17. *Nelson Mandela as Negotiator—What Can We Learn from Him?,* 31 *Ohio State Journal of Dispute Resolution* 19 (2016).

About the Author

Professor Hal Abramson is a full-time faculty member at Touro Law Center, New York, where he has taught, trained, and written on negotiations, mediation, mediation advocacy, and resolving intercultural and international disputes for more than thirty years. For his contributions to the field of dispute resolution, he received the 2013 Peace Builder Award from the New York State Dispute Resolution Association.

He has taught or trained on dispute resolution in nineteen countries on six continents. While at Touro, he has visited full-time at other schools. He visited at Cardozo Law School in NYC and UNLV Law School in Las Vegas. He also visited for a year as a Distinguished Visiting Professor at the U.S. Air Force Academy where he assisted in building their negotiation program, including teaching negotiations and training negotiation teachers. He still is assisting the Air Force in different capacities on negotiation training and program design. He also serves on the adjunct faculty at La Trobe University Law School in Melbourne.

Abramson's numerous publications include the leading treatise on representing clients in mediation entitled *Mediation Representation: Advocating as a Problem Solver* (received the annual book award of the CPR Institute for Dispute Resolution). In addition, he co-authored the textbook *International Conflict Resolution: ADR Consensual Processes* (West). His article on "Nelson Mandela as Negotiator" received the CPR Institute for Dispute Resolution award for the best professional article of 2016.

For the International Academy of Mediators (IAM), he created a Scholar-in-Residence program in which academics contribute to the organization on a rotating basis. He also served as its first scholar and was given an award by IAM for his contributions and leadership. UNLV Law School in Las Vegas also selected him as one of its first two Saltman Senior Scholars in ADR.

Abramson served as Chair of the ABA Committee of the Section for Dispute Resolution that drafted the mediation representation rules for its national competition and received an ABA special service award for his work.

He also served as a member of the inaugural committee that launched the International Chamber of Commerce's global mediation competition in Paris.

He chaired an IMI (International Mediation Institute) task force that designed the first ever program for certifying intercultural mediators. He also chaired the Post-Summit Initiatives Committee for the ABA-UNCITRAL International Mediation Summit in Delhi.

Abramson participated in the three-year UN (UNCITRAL) drafting initiative that resulted in the new Singapore Mediation Convention to enforce cross-border mediated settlement agreements. He assisted IMI, IAM, and the U.S. State Department, participated in drafting sessions, and designed and moderated for UNCITRAL three mediation educational programs for the UN Delegates and public. He also co-chaired a symposium on the new Convention three months after the UN approved it. The symposium included presentations and written contributions by UN delegates that were published in a book entitled *Singapore Mediation Convention Reference Book* for use by countries contemplating adopting the convention and for parties using it.

After Hurricane Sandy, he assisted FEMA (Federal Emergency Management Agency) in designing a system for resolving disaster relief claims.

Abramson is an experienced domestic and international commercial mediator. He has been selected for the International Who's Who of Commercial Mediation since its inaugural year in 2011 and has mediated cases involving parties from more than a dozen countries. He also serves on the Association of American Law Schools' twenty-person panel that facilitates faculty retreats and has conducted strategic planning processes for law schools.

At Touro, he served for nine years as vice dean responsible for academic programs, faculty development, and international programs and was one of the first two faculty members inducted in the Law Center's Builders Society. He also has taught online courses and a range of business-related courses, including contracts, sales, business organizations, international business transactions, and anti-trust. He established the law school's first summer abroad program at Russia's premier university, Moscow State University, and he worked as an ABA CEELI (Rule of Law) Specialist in Russia on two law reform projects during Russia's early transition to democracy. In 2020, Professor Abramson received the Touro College Presidential Award for Scholarship.

Prior to joining the Touro faculty, he worked in private practice and state government for seven years, where he litigated contract disputes in a civil legal services office and then helped formulate business regulatory policies and litigated complex regulatory cases for a New York State agency.

For a full biography and list of publications, see Tourolaw.edu/faculty/abramson.

Forewords

Cliff Hendler

As an early pioneer in the field of commercial mediation, I have found Hal Abramson's research and writings valuable for informing and improving my mediation practice, now in its 30th year. In Abramson's newest book, *Beyond the Courtroom*, he brings together in a single source for practitioners like me many of his most illuminating publications over his more than thirty years of work in the field of dispute resolution.

I first met Hal in 2006 at the inaugural year of the International Chamber of Commerce Mediation Competition in Paris. He was a member of the committee that launched this global competition and helped design its rules. It was clear to me then, as it is for all of those who have interacted with him over the past decades: Hal is dedicated to identifying and promoting best practices that are not just theoretical. He focuses on practices that are realistic and practical for disputants, their advocates, and mediators, for preparing and participating in mediations.

Hal has taught students, advocates and mediators around the world. His seminal book, *Mediation Representation*, is used world-wide. I use the book as guidance for the advocates in my mediations and for insights into the hundreds of mediations I conduct annually.

Because of his thoughtful and enduring contributions to improving practice, I approached Hal in 2014 to design for the International Academy of Mediators (IAM) a program that would engage academics with the membership of this peer-selected organization of full-time mediators from around the world. He proposed various options to the IAM Board, and it ultimately adopted a Scholar in Residence Program (SIR) with rotational academic appointments. Hal served as the inaugural SIR for two years. The purpose of the program is to create a mutually beneficial dialogue between academics and practitioners. There is often a tension between theory and practice, and through this robust exchange the SIR program has been able to bring about understanding and growth between academics serving as SIRs and the membership of senior mediators who handle complex disputes.

Hal has had a profound impact on the establishment and growth of the ADR field and profession during his academic career. This new book, *Beyond the Courtroom,* compiles his top publications as a ready and useful reference for negotiators, advocates and mediators.

Cliff Hendler
Mediator
Founder and Past President of the International Academy of Mediators
Toronto, Ontario
January, 2020

Jeremy Lack

As a practitioner who has been involved in many international negotiations, mediations and other dispute resolution processes as an advocate and neutral, I have benefited greatly from the publications and trainings of Hal Abramson, who is the consummate "pracademic." He brings together a rare combination of highly regarded academic scholarship (as evidenced by his award-winning publications) and practical experience (as evidenced by having been selected every year since its inauguration by the *International Who's Who of Commercial Mediation*).

As demonstrated in this book, Hal excels in taking complex processes, analyzing them, and distilling what he learns into practical insights and techniques that can be readily applied by students, scholars, or professionals, whether in Common Law or Civil Law jurisdictions.

I first met Hal in Paris in February 2007 at the second ICC International Commercial Mediation Competition. What initially struck me about Hal was his dedication to learning and education, as illustrated by his chance encounter with a two student team without a coach from the National Law School of India, Bangalore. After the team passed the first round without a coach, Hal offered to help them if they were interested. They welcomed his support, having self-funded the trip to come alone to Paris. It was impressive to see the working relationship that quickly developed between Hal and these students as they prepared for each of the subsequent rounds. They knew nothing about Hal's background as a professor and practitioner, and he did not want these talented students to know and risk feeling they should be deferential to him. The team reached the finals and took the second place by a split vote. Their prizes included a copy of Hal's book, *Mediation Representation.* It was only then that they learned who Hal was and the erudition that had accompanied his coaching.

As a partner to a Swiss law firm, I subsequently invited Hal to Zurich and Geneva to give trainings to seasoned lawyers and in-house counsel. Within one day, he taught us new practical skills in negotiation and mediation advocacy that will remain with us for the rest of our careers. What was particularly noteworthy was Hal's ability to induce us to revisit our engrained patterns for resolving disputes and to open our minds to new ways for improving our skills. The trainings also involved a different approach to preparing for negotiations and mediations, which included formulating a representation plan and actively working with clients. His advice to "always keep your eye on the 3 i's" (interests, impediments, and information) has proven to be a simple and memorable encapsulation of three key ideas that has been extremely helpful to me on many occasions.

I subsequently convinced Hal to become actively involved in the International Mediation Institute (IMI) and to co-chair its new task force on cross-cultural mediation. I served as a member. The task force was set up to foster mediation as a global profession and to design standards for certifying cross-cultural mediators. Here too Hal's ability to approach a complex topic by breaking it into simple and useful concepts was invaluable, especially in formulating "Cultural Focus Areas" or "CFAs" as guides for possible interventions in multicultural mediations (*see* Chapter 11). Hal went on to advise IMI on several more projects, most recently on the drafting of the Singapore Mediation Convention, which opened for ratification in August 2019. His recent article and edited book on the challenges and choices made in drafting the Convention shed illuminating light on this important new treaty (*see* Chapter 14).

Finally, a key finding of the Global Pound Conference Series in 2016 (an international project in 22 countries on access to justice and how to improve the future of dispute resolution) illustrates once again how Hal is forward-thinking. He had already thought through and written about one of the most important saliences to emerge from that project—the growing interest in "mixed mode" processes for combining mediation, conciliation and arbitration to generate bespoke, cost-effective dispute resolution processes. Seventeen years earlier, Hal had published an article entitled *Protocols for International Arbitrators Who Dare to Settle Cases* (*see* Chapter 8). This article and the appendices on final offer arbitration and minitrial procedures in his *Mediation Representation* book were prescient. They are likely to continue to influence academics and practitioners for years to come.

This collection of publications highlights Hal's vocation and "superpower"—to translate his vast understanding of the ADR field into simple, elegant and easy-to-remember insights that can be used in practice and remain fresh for all levels of experience. This book enriches the professional lives not only of newcomers, but seasoned lawyers and practitioners as well. It is a welcome compendium for everyone interested in studying or practicing ADR.

Jeremy Lack
Attorney-at-Law & ADR Neutral
Geneva, Switzerland,
January, 2020

Lela Love

As an academic, I have been impressed with how Hal Abramson's academic work speaks to multiple worlds. His work reaches practitioners looking for foundational ideas and best practices in negotiations, mediation advocacy, and mediations, including those interested in navigating cultural differences in international negotiations and mediations.

To take one of his foci, representation in mediation, discussed in Part I of this book, his published work grew out of and then informed his practice as a law school professor, a trainer of lawyers and neutrals, and a widely popular speaker at conferences and professional organizations. While legal academics must face the fact that their written work—in textbooks and law journals—are not inherently popular beyond those who are assigned to read them in the classroom or those looking for additional footnotes, in the case of Hal Abramson, his fate has been different. He has combined his written work (the stuff of academia) with practice, speaking and training, which has given his published work a reach and impact that are not typical of many academics.

I have had the privilege of co-teaching with Hal for over ten years an intensive course on Representation in Mediation at Cardozo Law School. It was "intensive" because it involved 28 hours of teaching in one week. It was also intense. Hal became deeply involved—one could say obsessed—with the theories he was working on, and that quality of focus and passion was translated into his written work. In the case of Representation in Mediation, his text *Mediation Representation: Advocating as a Problem Solver* won the 2004 coveted CPR Award for best book and has survived into a 3d edition and into the minds and hearts of both law students and professionals taking continuing educational programs and attending conferences.

The development of the book, in turn, provided fuel for the development of national and international mediation representation competitions, especially for the American Bar Association and the International Chamber of Commerce. The book also fueled the creation of a whole other dimension in law school teaching—courses on Representation in Mediation to parallel the longstanding focus in law schools on Moot Court and Trial Advocacy. As the academic world shifts to serve new fields, the world of practice is also influenced—and vice versa.

His other works also have had a practical impact. Hal's work on cultural competence for mediators has impacted international standards. His work on negotiations have been used for teaching students and training practitioners and most recently as a basis for building a negotiation program at the US Air Force Academy.

If this book is a compilation of Hal's top written contributions to date, then it is evident that he has influenced law schools and academia—while also influencing the real world of practitioners and organizations. He has made many meaningful contributions to the field of dispute resolution. I look forward to seeing the next chapter of his work.

Professor Lela P. Love
Cardozo School of Law
New York City
January, 2020

CHAPTER 1

Introduction and Overview of the Three Parts*

(summary of publications)

First a disclaimer. I did not want to write this book. This is what others do—they compile selections of their writings. I initially ignored the request and resisted it until I succumbed as a favor.

I now must admit that I learned much about myself and my career path preparing this manuscript. It turned into a personally rewarding period of self-reflection, although much of that learning is not suitable for this book, which I suspect will be a relief to others.

My publications, I discovered, can be naturally grouped under three subjects: mediation representation, intercultural and international mediation, and negotiations. Even though the book is so subdivided, the three parts are connected and interdependent, as will be highlighted in this introductory and overview chapter.

As any academic knows, our individual contributions to a field are part of a larger tapestry fashioned by many contributors. No one scholar can claim to dominate a field, and I surely do not in this book. We learn from each other while trying to add to the corpus. It is for these reasons that I acknowledge many of the contributors who helped shape my thinking (*see* Part I, Ch. 2). Because my journey was accompanied by so many fellow travelers, I have dedicated this book to them, my other family—my dispute resolution family that has provided me much personal and intellectual nourishment.

When I look back at my publications, *so far,* I noticed that they are connected by one thread: how disputing parties can effectively resolve their own disputes. Thus the book title. I now suspect that an arbitration case induced me to focus my writings on settlement. In a commercial arbitration case early in my academic career, I was serving as the sole arbitrator. When I met with the

---

* I want to thank my diligent Touro Law research assistant, Meaghan Caltabiano, for the thorough and timely work she did reviewing and formatting each chapter and the book.

two attorneys, I inquired facetiously whether they were able to resolve the legal dispute while waiting for me. The attorneys said they could have, but not their clients. When I asked whether they considered mediation, they welcomed the idea and agreed to convert the arbitration into a mediation. They settled on terms that were strikingly better for both parties than what arbitration could have offered. After that case, I found it confining to stay within an arbitrator's role. I kept spotting opportunities to uncover better results for the parties if I could only switch to mediate. That experience combined with other experiences as a mediator and facilitator inspired me to focus primarily on how parties can improve resolving their own disputes.

Nevertheless, I have written on adjudicatory processes where a third-party neutral resolves a dispute.[1] That work has helped inform my understanding of consensual processes. Comparative studies can help make differences salient and therefore improve our understanding of our primary subject.

In my writings, I also have tried to achieve one overarching professional goal—to produce publications useful to practitioners. I have viewed the opportunities afforded by my position as a tenured faculty member as a privilege. I have tried not to live in an ivory tower. I did not want to squander my career by publishing works that would be of interest to only a small group of specialists and family members whose interest may end after reading the dedication.

I tried to build bridges between the worlds of practice and theory that often operate on separate paths. I have striven to ground my work in practice while moving beyond simply describing. I have read plenty of valuable descriptions of custom and usage. I wanted my work to be *practically aspirational*, which means to me, informed by practice, practical to do, and reflective of improved practices based on theories and studies for achieving better and optimum settlements.

In an effort to learn how to link the two worlds, I have not resided safely in front of my computer, although I have spent much time there. I have devoted considerable time in the practice world, as an academic, in order to learn personally what was happening on the front line. I have conferred frequently with practitioners and have experienced and navigated practice realities as a neutral, consultant, administrator, and chair of professional committees. I also have

1 *See* Nolan-Haley et al., *International Conflict Resolution* (2005). For example, the chapter I drafted on multi-step ADR clauses for this co-authored book on *International Conflict Resolution* included provisions on arbitration. The arbitration comparison (the third step) helped to clarify the distinctive nature of the consensual-based processes of negotiation and mediation (the first two steps).

subjected my observations and ideas to the sharp and sometimes harsh critique of colleagues and practitioners.

Here is a summary of my practice exposure. A fuller description can be found in the Preface on "About the Author":

- Served on national and international neutral panels that afforded the opportunity to arbitrate and mediate business disputes. Selected for International Who's Who of Commercial Mediation since its inaugural year.
- For AIG, trained their U.S. in-house lawyers in mediation advocacy.
- Helped FEMA (Federal Emergency Management Agency, Homeland Security Department) design a system for handling disaster relief claims.
- Chaired a task force for the International Mediation Institute (IMI) that designed criteria for certifying intercultural mediators and tested the materials in pilot programs in Paris, Brisbane, and Singapore.
- Engaged regularly with practitioners when training attorneys and law students in nineteen countries on six continents and as the first "Scholar-in-Residence" for the International Academy of Mediators, an international organization of the top commercial mediators around the world.
- Active with the American Bar Association (ABA) Section on Dispute Resolution since it was formed over twenty years ago and attended every annual meeting because of the contact the meetings afforded with practitioners.
- Designed student mediation representation competitions that involved practitioners as judges and mediators. Chaired the committee that created rules for the ABA Competition on Mediation Representation and served on the inaugural committee that launched the global mediation competition for the ICC (International Chamber of Commerce) in Paris.
- Served for nine years in administration at Touro Law Center, as vice dean. Negotiating was part of the daily routine when was responsible for faculty development, academic programs, and international programs, including setting up Touro's first summer abroad program (at Moscow State University.)
- This past year (2017–2018),
    - Finished working on a three-year treaty drafting project with IMI, IAM, the U.S. State Department, and the UN (UNCITRAL-United Nations Commission on International Trade Law). The resulting

new Singapore Mediation Convention, approved by the UN General Assembly, facilitates enforcing cross-border mediated settlement agreements.

- Helped build a negotiation program suitable for the military context when visiting full-time for a year as a distinguished visiting professor at the U.S. Air Force Academy. Continue to serve as Negotiation Advisor to the program at the Air Force Academy.

During some of these front-line engagements, I also learned from being criticized, as many academics encounter when leaving the safety of the academy. I have been accused of "not getting it," "you are only an academic," and "you do not understand what is happening in practice and what markets demand," among other charges. Although these reproaches are not pleasant to hear, and can sting, I have listened and learned from them.

These diverse experiences over the years have informed my efforts to produce practically aspirational publications. I have gained much from others although my writings in this book ultimately reflect my best judgment. Even though I suggest the substantive areas where I tried to make meaningful contributions, I leave to others to judge their value and significance.

Finally, I want to apologize for the use of the first person throughout the book. This is a book about my works, so first-person references are unavoidable although personally uncomfortable. But here goes.

INTRODUCTION TO PART I: MEDIATION REPRESENTATION

If I am known for anything in the dispute resolution field, it is for my book on mediation representation (how attorneys can effectively represent clients in mediation). It received the CPR Institute for Dispute Resolution annual book award when the first edition was published in 2004, and has been adopted widely by law schools throughout the U.S. and abroad. The third edition was published for the U.S. and Canada by Aspen and for the rest of the world by Oxford University Press. It also has been published in Russian.

This subject initially caught my attention after teaching the introductory course on ADR for seven years and realizing that we were not preparing law students directly for what they are likely to do after graduation. ADR textbooks and courses focused primarily on training neutrals during the 1980s and 1990s, not on how to represent clients in mediations. It also became apparent that the growth of mediation depended in part on educating the consumers of mediations services, especially lawyers who function as the gatekeepers. These factors convinced me to focus my research on the gatekeepers who counsel clients and represent them.

I began by first developing mediation representation teaching materials to supplement the ADR textbook that I was using.[2] There was surprisingly little written by academics, and my academic colleagues generously left wide open the mediation representation field as most of them focused on scholarship and trainings for mediators. I owe them a great depth of gratitude for choosing to focus their professional attention elsewhere.

My first bar association presentation on mediation representation occurred in January 1994 when I collaborated in designing and conducting a continuing legal education program. It was held at the annual meeting of the New York State Bar Association. I still recall meeting with the other panelists to figure out what is worth saying to practicing lawyers. Only a small group of lawyers showed up for the program.

During the next ten years of preparing the mediation representation book, colleagues offered me opportunities to further study the role of the mediation advocate. Although many of these colleagues are recognized in the acknowledgements of the first edition (*see* Part I, Ch. 2), three of them should be mentioned now. Professors Andrea Schneider and Scott Hughes asked me to chair a committee formed to develop rules for the then new ABA Mediation Representation Competition. It gave me an opportunity to work with a committee of talented academics and practitioners to formulate criteria for distinguishing good from not so good representation practices in the competition. Then, Professor Lela Love asked me to design and team-teach a new course on mediation representation at Cardozo Law School. She wanted to offer law students an alternative to the intensive trial advocacy course at her law school. This invitation gave me an opportunity to expand the three class hours of materials and exercises that I developed for the ADR course into a two-credit, 28-class hour dedicated course. These two experiences informed the development of the book.

When working on the book, I wanted to do more than prepare a "how-to book" that reflected current and better practices. As an academic,

2 At the time my book *Mediation Representation* was published, there were only two books in the U.S. on the subject-both focused on practitioners. They were published by two highly regarded practitioners and quite helpful to me. *See* Eric Galton, *Representing Clients in Mediation* (1994) and *see* Jack Cooley, *Mediation Advocacy* (2nd ed., 2002).

I wanted to develop a theory of mediation advocacy that could become a framework for understanding and performing the role of an advocate. The theory that I developed, and its rationale became the book's organizing theme. It is explained in my 2005 *Harvard Negotiation Law Review* article, "Problem-Solving Advocacy in Mediations: A Model of Client Representation" (*see* Part I, Ch. 3).

The first edition and the article presented the *Mediation Representation Formula* that morphed into the succinct Mediation Representation Triangle for the second edition. It consists of three key features (thus the triangle found on the cover of the book): 1. Need to be an effective negotiator, given that mediation is a negotiation process with the assistance of a mediator; 2. Need to understand the value added of a mediator in the negotiation room and how to enlist assistance from the mediator; and 3. Need to prepare a plan for representation throughout the six key junctures of the mediation process. As in any triangle, each side needs to be sturdy. If one side is weak, a triangle will collapse. The book considers in detail how to build a sturdy mediation representation triangle.

The book has an introductory chapter that explains the framework for mediation representation and eight additional ones with the following coverage (*see* Part I, Ch. 4).

Introduction: The Foundation for the Book

Ch. 1: Negotiating in Mediations (a full explanation of both positional and problem-solving negotiations);

Ch. 2: Familiarizing Yourself with Mediation (a primer on mediation for those not familiar with the process);

Ch. 3: Counseling Your Client About Mediation (how to assess whether mediation is suitable for your client and how to assist your client in assessing whether to use mediation);

Ch. 4: Negotiating an Agreement to Mediate (how to negotiate an agreement to mediate with the other side and how to select an appropriate mediator);

Ch. 5: Preparing Your Case for Mediation (how to prepare a plan for effective representation in mediation);

Ch. 6: Preparing Your Client for Mediation (how to prepare your client for mediation);

Ch. 7: Appearing in the Mediation Premediation Conference, Mediation Session, and Post-Session (how to participate in the mediation process with special attention on how to close any final gaps and prepare a settlement agreement); and

Ch. 8: Breaking Impasses with Alternatives to Mediation (ATM) (prepares attorneys for the possibility of the mediation not settling all the issues by considering possible next steps after the mediation); and

Appendix A: Decision Tree Plus Analysis (explains how to use decision trees for assessing whether to accept the last offer for settlement) with an additional 17 Appendixes.

For the first edition, I spent considerable time drafting a single sentence to address a key obstacle to securing the full benefits of mediation. Parties and their attorneys can view disputes narrowly as primarily about money. Out of this concern, I crafted the following sentence:

> You have little chance of discovering whether your client's dispute is about more than money if you approach the disputes as if it is only about money.[3]

This single sentence, along with an explanation, was included to persuade participants in mediation to view mediation as an opportunity to accomplish much more than settling the presenting monetary claim. Mediation offers an opportunity to do more than a typical judicial settlement conference. In 2017, I followed-up with an article written with four co-authors entitled "Are Legal Disputes Just About Money? Answers from Mediators on the Front Line." The co-authors were two U.S. mediators and two European mediators whose day jobs have been mediating for a decade or longer. In the article, each of the co-authors discussed how he or she discovered that a particular dispute is about more than money along with his or her favorite techniques for uncovering other interests and solutions for parties (*see* Part II, Ch. 5).

This Part I on mediation representation also offers a segue into Part II on Intercultural and International Mediation, as reflected in the subtitle change from the first to second edition of *Mediation Representation*, from "Advocating in a Problem-Solving Process" to "Advocating as a Problem-Solver in any Country or Culture."

The need for this title change became evident when the first edition was at the publisher. This discovery, like many in life, was by happenstance. As the *Mediation Representation* book was going through galleys, I faced a deadline to

3 *See* Harold L. Abramson, *Mediation Representation-Advocating in a Problem-Solving Process* (NITA, 1st ed. 2004), 6.

finish a new textbook on *International Conflict Resolution.* When incorporating my mediation representation materials into the international textbook, the limitations of the mediation representation framework surfaced; it was embedded in Western values. As the research progressed in collaboration with my co-authors, the pervasive Westernized assumptions became stark and personally unsettling. I needed to form a culturally neutral framework, initially for the new textbook and then more fully for the second edition of *Mediation Representation.*

During the intervening five years between the first and second editions of *Mediation Representation,* I delved into the cultural aspects of mediation representation and was afforded several opportunities to deepen my understanding. The year after the first edition was published, the ICC in Paris asked me to serve on the inaugural committee to establish its global mediation representation competition. They wanted to adapt the Rules we developed for the ABA to the needs of a global competition. I learned much helping to fashion international assessment criteria. Thanks to invitations after the initial publication of *Mediation Representation,* I also learned from conducting a considerable number of mediation representation trainings abroad. In addition, I researched and published several intercultural articles that gave attention to international mediation representation. They included a study of mediation rules around the globe that highlighted how the rules afforded opportunities and obstacles to representation (*see* Part II, Ch. 9) and an article on how to select a culturally appropriate mediator and its impact on representing clients (*see* Part II, Ch. 10).

After the culturally neutral second edition was published, I wrote a book chapter justifying and defending the claim that the "improved" mediation representation framework applies wherever you represent clients in the world (*see* Part I, Ch. 6). For a full description of the additional research and testing of materials that took place during the five intervening years, *see* Acknowledgements for Second Edition (*see* Part I, Ch. 2).

My next project in this field will be preparing the fourth edition of *Mediation Representation.*

INTRODUCTION TO PART II: INTERCULTURAL AND INTERNATIONAL MEDIATIONS

I published my first article on private international mediation in 1999. It was a short one that considered why parties in international disputes should use mediation, highlighted the infrastructure that supports the use of international mediation, and suggested what should be included in an international mediation clause.[4] I re-read the article for this book, probably the first time in more than fifteen years. Today, it seems embarrassingly simplistic. I do not think it survived the test of time! So, I did not include it in this book even though it offered an early benchmark against which to measure development of the field, and my own writings. It also included an unscientific but interesting survey of usage when I was presenting the paper in a program on international mediation in New York City. Only four out of about 100 people in the audience had ever participated in a domestic mediation and only two in an international mediation.

Even though this first article got me thinking about the subject of private international dispute resolution, I can pinpoint the moment when the subject leaped from an interesting one to a principal part of my scholarship agenda. It occurred at the annual AALS (Association of American Law Schools) conference in 2000. By that point, I had written a couple articles on the subject, was teaching the subject in my general ADR course, and the Eastern District Federal Court in New York was referring international mediation cases to me. I also was working on my first effort to canvass the field for a chapter in a practitioners' manual.[5] At that fateful AALS conference, I fortuitously sat next to Professor Ed Sherman (Tulane Law School) at the formal luncheon. As we were waiting to hear the keynote speaker, I asked him why his co-authored ADR textbook, which I have been using, did not include anything on international dispute resolution. He said it probably should and asked whether I would be interested in preparing a chapter. I promptly accepted and have been studying the subject ever since.

When conducting my initial research on private international dispute resolution, I discovered that commentators were mixing insights that applied to any mediation with insights that applied primarily to international mediation. I began inquiring what made international mediation different than domestic mediation. My study identified issues that can arise when moving from a domestic to international process. Of course, the research led me toward the large subject of cultural differences, which led toward clarifying another distinction. Cultural differences do not arise only in international

---

4 *See* Harold L. Abramson, "Time to Try Mediation of International Commercial Disputes," 4 *ILSA J. of Intl. & Comp. L* 323 (1998). (This first article was a speech reduced to writing after I presented on a panel on international commercial mediation at an international law conference sponsored by the International Law Students Association and the American Branch of the International Law Association in 1997 [NYC, November 7, 1997].)

5 *See* Harold L. Abramson, "International Mediation Basics and Representing Clients in International Mediations," in *Practitioner's Manual to International Arbitration and Mediation*, ed. Chernick, Kolkey, Rhoades (2002).

mediations: they can arise in both domestic and international processes. It is for this reason that I label this subject as "Intercultural and International Mediations."

In the introduction to the international chapter for the ADR textbook, I summarized where I thought we were in the development of international dispute resolution in 2002 when describing what the chapter would cover:

> Since the 1970s, domestic ADR has grown and evolved into a dynamic field of study and practice that has impacted on the way lawyers in the United States represent their clients. As examined in this textbook, lawyers are using new and more sophisticated methods to resolve their clients' disputes including representing their clients in mediations, minitrials, and innovative variations of arbitration. The end of the Cold War in the early 90s opened opportunities for exporting these "made in the USA" dispute resolution methods. As international markets opened up in the former Soviet Union, China, Latin America, and elsewhere, more opportunities opened up for U.S. lawyers to represent clients outside of the United States. These new opportunities have created a glaring need for lawyers to learn how to resolve disputes between parties from different countries.
>
> In this chapter, the materials explore how to adapt domestic ADR to the *special needs of international disputes.*[6] The first section on "Demystifying Cross-Cultural Dimensions" examines how cultural differences can impede international negotiations and ways to overcome the differences. The second section on "International ADR Clauses for Business Disputes" considers the ADR options for avoiding the hazards of transnational lawsuits. The section delves into the distinctive issues that arise when designing alternative private processes." (italics added).[7]

During the research for the chapter in the ADR textbook and the later international dispute resolution textbook,[8] I identified a range of issues that are

---

6 Due to limitations in space, this chapter does not examine the striking and unconventional ways that dispute resolution methods are adapted to resolve disputes for parties that are not private ones but are sovereign nations. Disputes between nations comprise a distinct field of dispute resolution with its own lessons and techniques.

7 *See* Harold L. Abramson, "International Dispute Resolution: Cross-Cultural Dimensions and Structuring Appropriate Processes," in *Processes of Dispute Resolution,* ed. Alan Rau, Edward Sherman, and Scott Peppet (3rd ed. 2002), 906.

8 *See* Abramson *supra* note 1, at chapters 4 and 5.

distinctively relevant to mediators or advocates involved with intercultural or international mediations. Participants should learn to:

1. Assess whether mediation would be a suitable forum for resolving a dispute that is intercultural or international.
2. Identify cultural differences and ways to bridge them, including identifying culturally shaped interests that need to be met and culturally shaped impediments that may be impeding settlement.
3. Work with interpreters and translators.
4. Select a suitable mediator and how to enlist assistance from a mediator with different backgrounds.
5. Convene a mediation session with parties from different countries, including possibly selecting a neutral location, reconciling time zone differences, and employing technologies like videoconferencing to lower costs due to the geographic divide among participants.
6. Fashion a culturally suitable mediation process that meets the needs of parties including the need for an acceptable mix of joint sessions and private sessions (based on openness to direct exchanges or need for intermediaries and preserving face).
7. Select suitable mediation rules with attention to rules that may provide for less familiar cultural practices.
8. Identify parties with settlement authority in hierarchical and collectivist societies.
9. Fashion adequate level of confidentiality in a cross-cultural or cross-border setting where participants are accustomed to different levels of confidentiality.
10. Develop a suitable representation plan that will be effective interculturally or cross-border.
11. Communicate effectively across cultures, including communicating between high and low context communicators.
12. Recognize how parties can negotiate differently in different communities (different conflict styles), including how offers can be presented differently, patterns for offers and counteroffers can differ, and ways to negotiate can differ (whether inclined toward problem-solving, positional, or adversarial negotiations).
13. Fashion culturally shaped resolutions and remedies including apologies.
14. Enforce settlement agreements efficiently cross-border.

15. Select a suitable back-up adjudicatory process in case a dispute does not resolve in mediation.
16. Draft international dispute resolution clauses that include multi-steps for sequencing settlement and arbitration processes and that give attention to whether the same neutral should be permitted to switch roles between mediating and arbitrating.

These issues were developed in Chapter VI of the general ADR textbook (*see* Part II, Ch. 7 A & B) and expanded substantially for the separate textbook on *International Conflict Resolution.*[9]

For the international textbook, I had primary responsibility for Part II on Private Disputes and prepared three chapters that covered the following subjects summarized in the book's table of contents:

Chapter 4: International Negotiation and Mediation in the Private Sector
A. Introduction
B. Disputes Suitable and Ripe for International Mediation
C. Distinctive Issues in International Negotiations and Mediations

Chapter 5: Drafting Dispute Resolution Clauses
A. Introduction
B. Drafting Mediation Clauses
C. Drafting Arbitration Clauses
D. Drafting Multi-Step Clauses
E. Selecting Institutional or Ad Hoc Administration of Processes

Chapter 6: Resolving Disputes Online
A. Introduction
B. Online Facilities and Processes
C. Hybrid and Exclusively Online Processes
D. Criteria for Acceptable ODR
E. Critique of ODR
F. Legal Issues

I also delved into several specific areas in six articles. They covered the following topics:

9 *Ibid.*

1. What safeguards should be adopted if international neutrals switched roles between mediating and arbitrating?
2. How do mediation rules vary around the globe?
3. What mediator credentials should be considered when selecting a mediator for a cross-cultural dispute?
4. What criteria should a mediator meet to be certified as an intercultural mediator?
5. How might mediators resolve an ethical issue that arises from a cultural conflict between the mediator and parties?
6. How should U.S. trainers modify their training materials and approach when training abroad?

Each of these articles are reprinted as chapters in this book. In this Part II Introduction, I offer a brief explanation of what prompted writing each article along with a brief description.

Early on, I became curious as to why the facially sound U.S. practice of strictly barring a neutral from switching roles (from arbitrator to mediator or the reverse) in the same case is not a universal practice. My interest was aroused after learning about contrary practices in Asia and some European countries where neutrals switching roles can be acceptable and even welcomed. This more flexible practice can offer a more efficient process for resolving disputes. So, I examined the rationale behind the strict U.S. practice. The practice is based on the preferred way for preserving the integrity of each process—by using a different neutral for each one. By using different neutrals, so the reasoning goes, then anything learned as a mediator would not contaminate the decision-making process of the separate arbitrator. Also, the arbitrator would be able to continue to arbitrate if a separatemediation fails during the arbitration because what the separate mediator learned will not contaminate the decision-making of the arbitrator.

Given what I viewed as sound reasoning, I considered how the same neutral might be able to maintain her flexibility as a settler and her impartiality as a decision-maker. In an article, I recommended that when selecting a single neutral to perform both roles, parties negotiate a set of protocols for the neutral and parties to follow. The protocols include parties agreeing that the neutral be trained as both a settler and arbitrator, be committed to preserving party self-determination when in settling role, and be barred from offering evaluations when in settling role, among other rules. The article is entitled "Protocols for International Arbitrators Who Dare to Settle Cases" (*see* Part II, Ch. 8).

As mediation rules began to surface around the globe, I thought it might be interesting to see if there are any meaningful differences among these rules. I examined seventeen sets of mediation rules from most regions to figure out whether the mediation practices reflected in local rules varied based on local cultural preferences. Although most of the rules were remarkably similar, differences could be found, and some could provide unexpected opportunities and obstacles when representing clients. I concluded that attorneys should read local rules with care in order to avoid a rare surprise in an article entitled "Mining Mediation Rules for Representation Opportunities and Obstacles" (*see* Part II, Ch. 9).

Any discussion of intercultural and international mediations should give attention to selecting a qualified mediator. In an article on selecting intercultural mediators, I highlighted two key credentials. The article distinguished between an obvious credential-whether the mediator has the training to deal with cultural differences, with a less obvious one-whether the mediator approaches the mediation in a way that fits the cultural needs of the parties.

For the more familiar first credential, the article described some of the specific skills a mediator should possess while noting that intercultural training for mediators was not widely available. When training was available, it was either part of a basic mediation training or offered as a half-day advanced training. Furthermore, at the time of the article, there were no known programs in the world for certifying intercultural mediators.

For the less familiar second credential and inquiry, attorneys should consider how the culturally preferred mediation process of each participant can coalesce to produce a distinctively productive or dysfunctional mediation process. The article presented a grid that pairs the preferred approach of the participants with the mediator's preferred approach as an aid for classifying and understanding the resulting mediation process that various combinations will likely produce.

The article concluded by considering how understanding the way a mediator will perform based on his or her cultural training and preferences can and should inform how attorneys represent their clients in the mediation. The article was initially published as a book chapter, entitled "The Culturally Suitable Mediator," and then expanded into an article entitled "Selecting Mediators and Representing Clients in Cross-Cultural Disputes" (*see* Part II, Ch. 10).

Four years after writing the selecting mediators article, I had an opportunity to help design the first ever intercultural mediation certification program. IMI (International Mediation Institute) in The Hague in 2010 asked me to chair a task force of cultural experts to design a certification program. I was the only U.S. participant.

Six of us met in Singapore for four days to finalize the draft criteria for public comments and design a two-day intercultural training program. The drafting process itself became an unplanned intercultural negotiation because of the cultural diversity of the task force members! Then IMI hosted two-day pilot programs in Paris, Brisbane, and Singapore in order to test the training materials and certification criteria before highly experienced and demanding mediators as trainees. They gave us critical and valuable feedback. After two years of drafting and testing, the Task Force presented a final report with proposed certification criteria that the IMI Board approved.

The Final Report included six criteria with Comments.

A. Knowledge. 1. Cultural Framework; 2. Self-Awareness; 3 Multi-Cultural Perspectives;
B. Skills. 4. Communication; 5. Preparation; and 6. Managing Process.

The Task Force also brainstormed and developed what we ultimately labelled "Cultural Focus Areas" (CFAs). CFAs cover six categories of behavior that can pose cultural issues in mediations. They are: 1. Relatedness and Communication Styles; 2. Mindset Toward Conflict; 3. Mediation Process; 4. Orientation Toward Exchanging Information; 5. Time Orientation; and 6. Decision-making Approaches. For the Final Report and list of Task Force members, *see* Part II, Ch. 11.

I had no plans to consider what ethical issues might arise for mediators in intercultural or international mediations until I was solicited by the editor of a new book on mediation ethics.[10] The book editor gave the other commentator, Professor Carrie Menkel-Meadow, and me the same ethically challenging hypothetical to see whether we would arrive at different results, and we did. The mediator needed to resolve a cultural conflict between herself and the parties (to be contrasted with the more familiar cultural conflict between parties across the table). The divorcing couple proposed a child custody arrangement that offended the cultural norms of the mediator. The proposal appeared to conform with the norms of the parties but would patently violate the mediator's norms. Due to the conflict, should the mediator withdraw? The article considered how a mediator might resolve the conflict in a way that would avoid the charge of cultural imperialism (your cultural practice is superior to the participants' practice).

I proposed a four-step approach. For the first three steps, the article's approach adopted steps that I have written about elsewhere—understand your

10 *See* Ellen Waldman, *Mediation Ethics: Cases and Commentaries* (1st ed. 2011).

own culture, research the other side's culture, and try to bridge any differences.[11] It is the fourth step that was new—how to assess whether to withdraw from the mediation.

For this last step, I suggested two inquiries. A mediator should first assess whether the cultural practice violated an internationally recognized norm. In the article, I illustrated one way to proceed by examining relevant international treaties as possible sources for universally adopted norms. If a universal norm can be identified and had been violated, a mediator could withdraw without charges of cultural imperialism. If no universal norm can be found, the mediator needs to confront the hard choice-whether to withdraw because the mediator can no longer be impartial or whether to proceed by striving to conduct a quality process in accordance with the mediator's code of conduct. I decided to recommend mediating the case.

The article was initially part of a book chapter in *Mediation Ethics, Cases and Commentaries* by Professor Ellen Waldman and then published as an expanded article entitled "Crossing Borders into New Ethical Territory: Ethical Challenges When Mediating Cross-Culturally" (*see* Part II, Ch. 12).

Finally, I was inspired to prepare an article on how to train in other cultures after I was asked to join a group of international scholars to observe and critique a two-day negotiation training program in Rome. Based on my observations of these experienced trainers teaching participants from diverse cultures, my personal experiences training in other countries, and cross-cultural research, I wrote an article entitled "Outward Bound to Other Cultures: Seven Guidelines for U.S. Dispute Resolution Trainers (*see* Part II, Ch. 13)." Although not primarily an article on mediation like all the prior articles in Part II, it is an article that focuses on cultural differences, a subject suitable for this Part.

In this article, I went beyond the often-repeated advice for U.S. trainers to avoid promoting intact and indiscriminately the U.S. way of doing things. As commonly advised, trainers should adapt home grown training programs for export based on an understanding of the cultural assumptions embedded in their off-the-shelf materials along with an understanding of the cultural needs of the participants abroad. The challenge is figuring out how to translate this widely cited advice into action.

I suggested seven guidelines for preparing to train abroad: 1. Acquire a Culturally Educated Lens; 2. Behalf Like a Guest; 3. Be Mindful of Cultural

---

11 *See* Harold L. Abramson, *Mediation Representation: Advocating as Problem Solver* (3rd ed. 2013), Ch. 5.20.

Assumptions and Differences; 4. Educate Participants about Training Techniques; 5. Adjust Presentation When English is not the Participants' First Language; 6. Refashion Materials Based on Purpose(s) of Training; and 7. Plan to Evaluate the Training. The article was initially published as a book chapter and then as an expanded article (*see* Part II, Ch. 13).

My next writing project was completed during the last year while working with the publisher to format this book. I published a book chapter and article that covers the UN (UNCITRAL) Initiative to prepare an international instrument to enforce cross-border mediated settlement agreements. UNCITRAL consists of sixty country delegations selected by the UN General Assembly. It makes recommendations for adoption to the General Assembly.

I have been involved with this initiative since March 2014, before it was formally presented to the UN as a project, and participated for the more than three years that it took to produce the new Singapore Mediation Convention. I represented IMI (an NGO that sets international standards for mediators based in The Hague) and IAM (an NGO that represents mediators from around the world), and assisted the U.S. Delegation (led by U.S. State Department). I also participated in many of the UNCITRAL drafting sessions and served as an "expert consultant" to UNCITRAL when I designed and moderated three mediation education programs for UN Delegates.

The book chapter and article examined the history of the initiative, the multi-party process that produced the result, and key substantive choices in the convention. I also co-chaired an international symposium on the new Convention three months after approved by the UN General Assembly. The March, 2019 symposium was sponsored by Cardozo Law School and Touro Law Center in NYC and included presentations by UN Delegates that helped draft the Convention. The symposium produced a separate reference book by presenters that offers background, research, and substantive analysis of the new Convention for States (countries) that are considering adopting it. The book, called the *Singapore Mediation Convention Reference Book*, that I edited, included an expanded version of my book chapter on the Convention (*see* Part II, Ch.14). Now that the new Convention has officially opened for signature, my next project will be supporting efforts in different states to adopt the convention.

INTRODUCTION TO PART III: NEGOTIATIONS

I ventured initially into negotiation research out of necessity. Because mediation is simply a negotiation process with the assistance of a mediator, I needed to write a negotiations chapter for the 2004 mediation representation book. I had no intention of writing anything original. The field of negotiation is populated by excellent scholars who already have done outstanding work illuminating our understanding of the negotiation process. I only needed a chapter that summarized the work of others. When preparing the negotiation chapter, which turned out to be eighty printed pages, I unexpectedly found two gaps that I thought warranted new research.

As I prepared the chapter entitled "Negotiating in Mediations" (*see* Part III, Ch. 14), I had to confront a market reality that I have been avoiding over the years. Many lawyers prefer to negotiate positionally, even though most trainers and instructors teach primarily the problem-solving approach. As I prepared the section on positional negotiations and began teaching the subject for the first time, a connection between positional and problem-solving approaches became apparent. They are not competing or alternative models, as is customarily presented. I could see for the first time how positional negotiations fit within the problem-solving process.

With this more expansive view of negotiations in mind, I realized that many negotiators unconsciously skip the creating stage of problem-solving. They jump right into the claiming stage by asserting at the outset positions—what they want.[12] Negotiators may do this out of habit, I suspect, reinforced by successes-whether when deciding where to go out for dinner with friends, bargaining for a car, or negotiating a legal settlement. By viewing negotiations as a process of both creating and claiming instead in which negotiators first expand the zone of possible agreement and then engage in the inevitable dividing up, positional negotiations naturally fits within the claiming stage. Other ways to claim include using objective standards and trading low for high value items. Rather than treating positional negotiations as an independent model, positional negotiations, in my view, can perform a useful and limited role, if needed, toward the end of the problem-solving process.[13]

I also learned during this summarizing project that the term *negotiation style* that accompanies many negotiation materials has multiple meanings, and the term is used by some interchangeably with the term *conflict style*. In my publications, I distinguish sharply between our conflict style and our negotiation

---

12 *Id.* at 21–22, *See The Manager As Negotiator: Bargaining for Cooperation and Competitive Gain* (1986), Ch. 2. (Professors Lax and Sebenius introduced the creating/claiming view of negotiations in their 1986 book.)

13 *See* Abramson *supra* note 11, at 73–84 (*see* this book, Part III, Ch. 14).

style, and divide our negotiation style into three components-good practices, tactics, and tricks.

Our *conflict style* reflects how we naturally react to conflict and can be identified by taking a simple fifteen-minute survey. In contrast, our *negotiation style* reflects the choices we make in a negotiation. And there is a lengthy list of choices that are commonly identified in various negotiation books. Each choice can be classified into one of three categories, as either a good practice (what can be effective with little or no risks, like learning interests of the other side), tactics (what negotiators do as a practice and poses some risk when discovered, like extreme first offers), and tricks (which are offensive when discovered and likely risk derailing the negotiation, like lying.) Our mix of good practices, tactics, and tricks determine our *negotiation style.*

The more we negotiate toward the good practices and tactics end of the continuum, the more problem-solving we are. The more we negotiate toward the tactics and especially tricks end of the continuum, the more adversarial we are. And studies have demonstrated that the problem-solving style tends to be more effective than the adversarial style.

This Good Practice, Tactics, and Tricks (GTT) framework was initially formulated for the Negotiation Chapter,[14] more fully developed in a separate chapter for a book on negotiations, and then expanded in an article entitled "Fashioning an Effective Style in Negotiations: Choosing Between Good Practices, Tactics and Tricks." The article was published by the *Harvard Negotiation Law Review*. For the book chapter, *see* Part III, Ch. 15.

The GTT Framework for understanding negotiation styles was applied in an in-depth study of Nelson Mandela as a negotiator during his last five years in prison. During that period, he negotiated toward liberating his country from the oppressive policies of apartheid and himself from a life time prison term. This study of one of the greatest peacemakers of the 20th century demonstrated the effectiveness of problem-solving based on good practices and a few tactics even when facing an extreme and intractable conflict. The article entitled "Nelson Mandela as Negotiator—What Can We Learn from Him?" won the award for the best professional ADR article for 2016 by the CPR Institute for Dispute Resolution (*see* Part III, Ch. 16).

My next negotiation research project also is well underway. It is based on what I learned while visiting as a full-time professor at the U.S. Air Force

---

14 *Id.* at 25–28, 43–47.

Academy this past year (2017–2018). They asked me to assist the Air Force Academy in developing an ambitious negotiation program as part of a five-year strategic plan. My contributions included helping to update the basic negotiation course, designing and teaching the first ever advanced negotiation course for the military, and developing a program to train teachers to teach the negotiation course.

During the year, I gave special attention to the distinctive negotiation challenges and needs of officers when deployed and negotiating with local military and political leaders, citizens, and allied forces. Based on these needs, I identified several topics for further research: negotiating when little time, negotiating when little trust, and negotiating when high turn-over for the negotiators (deployments are from five to twelve months). I have developed a working title for the article, although it may result in three articles: "Negotiating when Limited Trust and Time: Lessons from and for the Military."

CONCLUSION

The primary benefit of this self-indulgent book was that it forced me to pause and reflect on my writings and career. This undertaking required me to consider what contributions I have tried to make so far and to clarify my own priorities going forward. For any readers, I can only hope that you will find my contributions to be of some value in the fields of mediation representation, intercultural and international mediations, and negotiations.

Part One

MEDIATION REPRESENTATION

CHAPTER 2

Mediation Representation: Advocating as a Problem-Solver

3rd Edition

Harold I. Abramson
Professor of Law
Touro Law Center

2013

ACKNOWLEDGMENTS

Third Edition

My journey to complete this Third edition [from the 2011 Oxford edition and the 2010 second edition] was short and intense as I expanded sections, added videos, and made the book more classroom friendly. I want to acknowledge the institutions and people who helped made this possible:

Touro Law Center provided valuable summer research grants, funds for research assistance, and access to a dedicated library staff ready to do whatever was needed. The UNLV School of Law provided welcome support during my fall semester, 2012 full-time visit. The administration and faculty offered a flexible teaching schedule, ample research assistance and the type of congenial environment that encouraged my progress during the visit.

John Barkai, University of Hawaii, once again provided essential and valued assistance in selecting and formatting the large number of videos now available for student use.

My two exceptional research assistants Barbara Burke, Touro Graduate Research Fellow and Sabrina Dolson, a third year students at UNLV each supplied important contributions. Ms. Burke offered tenacious and creative research, often alerting me to little-known developments in the field that warranted attention. Ms. Dolson systematically, thoroughly, and efficiently checked, reviewed and formatted every footnote in each chapter.

The manuscript evolved from draft to book thanks to the careful and diligent work of Aspen professionals Richard Mixter, Senior Acquisitions Editor, John Devins, Senior Managing Editor, Kenny Chumbley, Production Editor, and Dave Mason, Copyeditor. They were a great team in every respect.

Finally, any acknowledgement must recognize the intellectual and personal support of Ellen Waldman, a creative thinker and wordsmith, whose own body of work inspires me to improve whatever I try to do.

Revised Oxford University Press Edition

[Note that some of the changes for the Oxford edition, like using British English and Euro examples, were removed for the Aspen edition]

My short journey between the second edition and this Oxford edition concentrated on tailoring and editing the book to meet the needs of mediation advocates outside of North America. I want to acknowledge the warm and helpful assistance from both the anonymous European peer reviewers and the European lawyers that so graciously responded to my inquiries about various ways to modify this edition. I want to specifically thank Ronnie Austin and the attorneys from Clifford Chance, Thierry Garby, Michel Kallepitis, Jeremy Lack, Alan Limbury, Karl Mackie and the staff of CEDR, Chris Newmark, Manon Schonewille, and John Sturrock.

I also want to thank Vicky Pittman at Oxford University Press who professionally, patiently, and persistently guided me during the journey that produced this edition.

Second Edition

My educational journey in mediation representation that produced the first edition in 2004, and was chronicled in that edition, has continued for another five illuminating years. Numerous people and organizations gave me extraordinary opportunities to delve broader and deeper into a field that is steadily moving toward maturity. I owe them deep gratitude for the opportunities they gave me to learn, research, test materials in a variety of settings, including cross-cultural ones, publish articles, and solidify new materials for this edition.

First, I must acknowledge the early and much appreciated encouragement from the CPR International Institute for Conflict Prevention and Resolution when it gave the first edition of this text its 2004 book award. It signaled that I was on the right track.

When the first edition was still at the publisher, I turned to a prior commitment to prepare a textbook on international dispute resolution. As the research progressed, I realized that the mediation representation framework for the first edition was embedded with Western values that needed to be highlighted. That led me to modifying the framework to form a culturally neutral one that now forms the foundation for this second edition. I benefited greatly from the feedback from my two co-authors, Professor Jacqueline Nolan-Haley at Fordham University School of Law and Pat Chew at University of Pittsburgh School of Law. The result was *International Conflict Resolution: Consensual ADR Processes* (West 2005).

In fall 2005, the ICC (International Chamber of Commerce) in Paris contacted me about helping them develop an international version of the ABA (American Bar Association) mediation representation competition for U.S. law students. I had already served as Chair of the ABA committee that developed its judging rules. When serving on the ICC planning committee, I had to consider how to adapt the ABA rules to serve the needs of the ICC's first annual global competition. That effort required me to reflect on the best international practices for mediation advocacy, practices that would form the basis for judging the advocacy of participants from around the globe.

Then the ICC gave me the opportunity to mediate and judge in every annual competition since the first one in January 2006, and as result, I was able to observe and discuss practices with coaches and teams from throughout the world. And at the second annual competition in February 2007, the student team from the National Law School in Bangalore, India, gave me the unexpected privilege of coaching them. The talented team of Parag Sayta and Vikas N. M. had progressed to the quarter finals without a coach. For the final two days of the competition, I assisted them and experienced up close their culturally shaped approach to preparing and participating in the mediations. They progressed to the final round.

Next, I began a series of projects to convert the ideas in the first edition into PowerPoint presentations and exercises for training lawyers. After teaching mediation advocacy courses and lecturing to lawyers for more than ten years, it was time to shape the materials into a discrete one-to-three-day training program for practicing lawyers.

One of my early opportunities came from Lonny Rose, the Chief Executive Officer of National Institute for Trial Advocacy (NITA), who was determined to move NITA into training mediation advocates. He asked me to design a program and teamed me up with experienced NITA trainers, including Judge Nancy Vaidik and Peter Hoffman. In April 2006, NITA invited twelve hand-picked, experienced attorneys from around the United States to participate in a pilot program. They served both as guinea pigs and critics who gave feedback after each segment of the two-day training program. Based on the feedback, the materials were modified and refined to become the basis for NITA's mediation advocacy training program.

My next exceptional opportunity came in August 2006 when Deborah Masucci, Vice President of Dispute Resolution, Litigation Management at AIG (now called Chartis) asked me and long-term friend and colleague Steve Younger to design a training program. Steve Younger is a partner at Patterson Belknap Webb & Tyler with deep experience as an advocate in mediation and as a mediator. Debbie wanted to develop a comprehensive, national mediation advocacy training program for all of AIG's in-house attorneys. She formulated a creative approach to internalize the substance and values of effective mediation advocacy. Instead of using outside trainers to train all the attorneys, she wanted consultants to design an internal program where senior in-house attorneys from around the country would train attorneys regionally. Debbie secured the critical approval of Terry Williams, Senior Vice President, Staff Counsel Executive, whose commitment ensured follow through and full participation of his staff.

Over a two-year period, Debbie, Steve, and I surveyed extensively the in-house attorneys, designed two customized pilot programs that took into account the substantial mediation experience of many of the trainees, trained twenty in-house senior attorneys in the materials and how to deliver trainings, and prepared two lengthy and comprehensive manuals for the trainers to implement intermediate and advanced mediation advocacy training programs. The in-house trainers delivered the materials regionally to over two hundred attorneys, and I was given the extraordinary opportunity to learn much not only about how to customize training programs, but also the distinctive training needs of the insurance industry. I am indebted to Debbie for giving me the opportunity to do this and to work with her and Steve.

I also had numerous other opportunities to design and refine materials in training programs and courses in the United States and abroad, along with presenting in many continuing education programs. I learned much from the inquisitive and experienced participants.

The trainings in the U.S. included ones for the New Mexico State Court System (that was piloted by two far-sighted and determined state officials, David

Levin and Celia Ludi), Federal Court in New Hampshire (piloted by the consummate professional, Dan Lynch), Federal Court in Eastern District Court of New York (piloted by two creative leaders, Judge Robert Levy and ADR administrator Jerry Lepp), Minnesota State Bar Association, the Federal Bar Council for the Second Circuit, the NYC Bar Association, and two large law firms.

I also further refined the materials abroad in one-day training programs in Geneva (piloted by the persistently creative Jeremy Lack) and the Netherlands (piloted by one of the reflective senior leaders of the field in Europe, John Bosnak), and in courses in China, Berlin, and Italy, including teaching jointly a course in Rome with one of the few other scholars in international mediation, the innovative Professor Nadja Alexander from Australia.

I also was given the rich opportunity to learn from others outside the United States when attending several invitation-only global conferences and consulting with experts, who are now friends, from China, Japan, and Turkey.

I benefitted greatly from attending the Fall 2007 Rome MEDA conference organized by Giuseppe DePalo, where he convened leaders from his European Union–funded, three-year project to promote and develop ADR programs in ten MEDA countries (Northern Africa and the Middle East). At the Second Generation Negotiation Conference in Rome in May 2008, organized by Hamline Law School (Jim Coben, Giuseppe DePalo, and Chris Honeyman), I had the unusual opportunity to observe superb trainers train and then publish an article, "Outward Bound to Other Cultures: Seven Guidelines for U.S. Dispute Resolution Trainers," published in 9 *Pepperdine Dispute Resolution Law Journal* 437 (2009) and *Rethinking Negotiation Teaching* (Editors, James Coben, Giuseppe DePalo, and Christopher Honeyman, Hamline University 2009). And then I participated in an international dialogue at the International Mediation Leadership Summit at The Hague, organized by the ABA Section on Dispute Resolution in October 2008.

Since the first edition, I had a chance to delve deeply into mediation practices of one other country in particular, China. During my three visits to China to teach, lecture, and meet with experts in dispute resolution, I benefited from lengthy get-togethers with some of the thoughtful leaders in China including Wang Hongson, Chair, Beijing Arbitration Commission and Cheng Hui, Vice Secretary General, CCPIT/CCOIC Mediation Center, Beijing, as well as an impressive young and insightful scholar, Andrew Lee at Beijing University, and a reflective practitioner, Lijun Cao, CIETAC Deputy Director of Foreign-Related Business Department (administering arbitrations), arbitrator and Guest Professor, Beijing University of Foreign Studies, Arbitration Law and Practice.

My first meeting with Lijun Cao in June 2006 turned into an extended and informative collaboration where we explored the differences between Chinese and U.S. mediation practices. After developing a list of over a dozen topics, we explored each one during ten telephone calls and one all-day meeting for a total of about twenty-four hours. We discussed practices in China, practices in the U.S., and then compared and contrasted them. We completed a full discussion and a detailed outline.

I also must acknowledge the invaluable assistance of Aaron Halegua, who seemed to know everybody involved with mediation in China. We met when he had just graduated from Brown University and was studying mediation in China with funding from a Fulbright scholarship.

I also learned much about Japan from Professor Yoshi Wada, Waseda University, Tokyo, during several meals and meetings. He is studying the emergence of Westernized style mediation in Japan and how it is being adapted.

And, I had a chance to spend time in Turkey when mediation was starting to take hold due to new Turkish laws. During my three trips to Turkey I lectured for Professor Feridun Yenisey at Bahcesehir University, Istanbul, who taught me about some of the challenges of implementing mediation programs in Turkey and spent time with Deniz Kite, a pioneer in Turkish mediation, including conducting a one-day advanced mediation training program for her.

I also want to thank several people who enticed me to write articles that helped inform the second edition.

Louis Buchman in Paris gave my name to a new European ADR publication that wanted an article relevant to developments in Europe. Because the European Union was starting to form a mediation infrastructure, I conducted a study of mediation rules around the globe. The project resulted in the article, "Mining Mediation Rules for Representation Opportunities and Obstacles," 1 *J. of Intl. Dis. Res.* 40 (Germany 2004) and 15 *Am. Rev. of Intl. Arb.* 103 (Sp. 2005).

Professor Andrea Schneider invited me along with dozens of other people to contribute to her book with Chris Honeyman, *The Negotiator's Fieldbook.* She was interested in something on the use of mediation in cross-cultural negotiations. As a result, I wrote an article about selecting mediators in cross-cultural disputes—"The Culturally Suitable Mediator" in Schneider and Honeyman, *The Negotiator's Fieldbook* (ABA 2006) and an expanded version entitled "Selecting Mediators and Representing Clients in Cross-Cultural Disputes," 7 *Cardozo J. of Confl. Resol.* 253 (2006).

Professors Ellen Waldman and Kimberlee Kovach pressured me to learn about ethical issues encountered in international mediations. ADR ethics has not been an area that I had studied in any depth, leaving that for others. Ellen convinced me to write a chapter for her upcoming book on ADR ethics, and Kim convinced me to contribute to an ethics symposium at South Texas Law School. For months, I had to read and agonize about how Westernized ethical principles might apply in cross-cultural settings. Thanks to them, I learned about distinctively international ethical issues and produced an article entitled, "Crossing Borders into New Ethical Territory: Ethical Challenges When Mediating Cross-Culturally," 49 *S. Tex. L.R.* 921 (2008) (ADR Ethics Symposium Issue).

I want to acknowledge with great appreciation IAM (International Academy of Mediators) for permitting me to post questions on its members-only online discussion group in spring 2009. I inquired about caucusing practices and sharing information in mediations. I want to especially thank the following participants for their insightful and valuable comments that helped inform my thinking: Tracy Allen, Eleanor Barr, Paul Bent, Cliff Hendler, Eric Galton, Jeff Jury, Michael Landrum, Gene Moscovitch, Bennet Picker, and David Plant.

Finally, I want to give special thanks to six individuals and good friends who gave generously their precious time and offered invaluable insights whenever I would badger them with questions and solicit feedback. They are John Barkai (University of Hawaii), John Bosnak (Netherlands), Cliff Hendler (Toronto), Jeremy Lack (Switzerland), Lela Love (Cardozo Law School, NYC, and team-teacher), and Ellen Waldman (Thomas Jefferson Law School, San Diego).

Through this persistent study and testing of ideas and approaches, the second edition emerged. I deeply appreciate all the indispensable help along the way, although I remain solely responsible for the final product.

This book would never have come to fruition without the essential and generous support from Touro Law Center, especially from Dean Larry Raful who gave me sabbatical time, summer research grants, and flexibility in course scheduling to work on this project. I also appreciated the support given by Vice Deans Gary Shaw and Louise Harmon, including Louise's severe editing of the introduction.

And this project benefited greatly from the valuable assistance of my talented research assistant of two years, Lena Davydan, who welcomed and overcame every research challenge, and Bernadette Safrath, who so thoroughly and efficiently handled every last-minute assignment as the book came together, including researching fine points, professionally and proficiently editing and formatting all the footnotes, and managing the tedious and critical process of securing copyright approvals.

I also want to specially acknowledge and thank Martha Broderick for her generous encouragement and support during the writing of this edition.

This book was brought to conclusion by the wonderful and professional staff of NITA. I am thankful for the careful, patient, and thoughtful editing of Darla Upchurch and the creative design and marketing expertise of Amy Rinehart, Anna Schmöhe, and the renowned publications guide to law professors, Jeanne Philotoff.

First Edition

This book culminates a decade of researching, developing, and testing approaches to mediation representation in a variety of demanding settings inside the classroom, in continuing legal education and training programs, as well as in mediations. These settings were filled with inquiring students, seasoned and sometimes cynical litigators, and experienced and talented mediation advocates. I owe all these anonymous teachers a deep debt of gratitude for permitting me to learn from them.

My mediation representation journey began in January 1994, when Norman Itzkoff, Cathy Cronin-Harris, Steve Younger, and I got together to design a program on mediation representation for the annual meeting of the New York State Bar Association. Planning this program with these thoughtful colleagues impelled me to prepare my first public thoughts on the subject and propelled me to focus on it in depth.

Thereafter, I began researching, interviewing experienced attorneys, and evaluating approaches to effective advocacy in mediation. I initially turned to the law students in the course I teach on dispute resolution. These students became involuntary subjects for testing concepts, ideas, and materials. As I experimented on my students, I was fortunate to be offered many opportunities in continuing legal education programs to present ideas to academics and practicing attorneys and to learn from their reactions. These programs included a workshop, sponsored by the Association of American Law Schools' 2002 conference, for law faculty on how to teach mediation representation, and two intensive half-day training programs that I was asked to design, one for the Commercial and Federal Litigation Section and Corporate Counsel Section of the NYS Bar Association in 1999 and another for the Nassau County Bar Association in 2001. I also observed numerous advocates in the legal cases that I mediated.

As I continued my research, I was helped along the way by many people whom I want to specially acknowledge and thank.

Scott Hughes and Andrea Schneider, the organizers of the ABA Mediation Representation Competition, gave me an unexpected and welcomed gift when they asked me to chair a new Mediation Representation Rules Committee. I had just finished hosting the first New York regional competition for the ABA Spring 1999 Competition. They wanted to form a committee to examine the criteria for evaluating participants in the competition and to consider whether the criteria that were being utilized needed to be revised or replaced.

They gave me the opportunity to participate in a bedazzling one-year seminar with many of the leading thinkers in the field. The committee included Beryl Blaustone, Jim Coben, Eric Galton, John Lande, Lisa Lance, Jackie Nolan-Haley, as well as Scott Hughes and Andrea Schneider. During 2000–2001, we debated and explored what were good mediation representation practices and drafted a completely new set of judging criteria based on a problem-solving approach to representation, the approach that informs this book. The new criteria have been used since 2001 in the national mediation representation competitions that continue to grow. In 2003, the competition took place in nine regions, attracting teams from almost fifty law schools throughout the United States, leading to a national final competition at the annual meeting of the ABA Section of Dispute Resolution.

Lela Love asked me to team-teach a course with her on mediation representation at Cardozo Law School. I had previously developed a substantial mediation representation segment for my ADR course at Touro. She now presented the opportunity to delve deeper into the subject by collaborating on designing a separate mediation representation course. Since January 2001, Cardozo has offered our course as an alternative to the semester break intensive trial advocacy course.

Gerald Lepp, ADR Administrator, and Magistrate Judge Robert Levy, the judge overseeing the ADR programs in the U.S. District Court, Eastern District of New York, invited me to informally counsel the court-annexed mediation program on training advocates and mediators. Their invitation offered me a rich opportunity to learn from and test approaches with an exceptionally demanding audience—New York litigators. I designed and conducted a one-day training program in 2001 for about 150 experienced litigators turned mediators on how to convert adversarial advocates in the mediation into problem-solvers. I also designed and conducted several half-day and full-day training programs for the litigators in the NYC Department of Law, a frequent participant in federal court mediations.

A number of people contributed their precious time and considerable expertise to commenting on segments of the book. I received valuable feedback on sections from James Coben, Ken Fox, Dwight Golann, Elayne Greenberg, Russell Korobkin, John Lande, Jackie Nolan-Haley, Christopher Moore, Andrea Schneider, and Barbara Swartz.

Wayne Outten, an outstanding and active mediation advocate who has thought deeply and reflectively on what constitutes good representation practices, generously reviewed and commented on a number of chapters.

It is through this rigorous and, at times, brutal screening of ideas and approaches that this book has survived, a book that develops a coherent approach to representing clients in mediation as a problem-solving process. Of course, I remain solely responsible for the final product.

This book would never have come to fruition without the essential and generous support from Touro Law Center, especially from Dean Howard Glickstein, who gave me sabbatical time, summer research grants, and flexibility in course scheduling to work on this project. I also appreciated the support given by Vice Deans Eileen Kaufman and Gary Shaw.

I benefited greatly from our all-purpose Associate Dean Ken Rosenblum, who reviewed chapters for clarity from the point of view of an attorney with no formal training and experience in mediation, and who was able to quickly locate talented law students for me whenever I needed assistance.

And finally, this project benefited from the valuable assistance of a number of particularly dedicated Touro law students, including Jonathan Kirchner, Maryam Jadali, and Jianhua Zhong, as well as Nichoel Forrett who so professionally and efficiently edited and formatted all the footnotes.

This book was brought to conclusion by the wonderful and professional staff of NITA. I am thankful for the careful, patient, and thoughtful editing of Ashley Smith and the creative design and marketing expertise of Kathy Pitts, Jeanne Philotoff, and Jude Phillips.

CHAPTER 3

Problem-Solving Advocacy in Mediations: A Model of Client Representation

10 *Harv. Neg. L.R.* 103 (Sp. 2005)*

I. WHY A DIFFERENT APPROACH TO REPRESENTATION

Recently, I was shopping for a notebook computer and encountered an unfamiliar processing chip. The salesperson explained that the Pentium Series III and 4, originally designed for a large desktop computer and modified for use in a notebook computer, proved inefficient in meeting the needs of a small, mobile device. Computer manufacturers needed a processor that was custom-designed for the needs of notebooks and so Intel built a new chip, the M Processor, from the ground up.[1] Well, that is what I tried to do in *Mediation Representation: Advocating in a Problem-Solving Process.*[2] Rather than simply tweaking the well-honed strategies and skills that work so effectively in the courtroom, I focused on building an advocacy approach from the ground up that would realize the full benefits of a problem-solving mediation process. Although much has been written about how mediators can create a problem-solving process[3] and many mediators have been trained to use a

---

* Harold Abramson, Professor of Law, Touro Law Center. I want to thank Dwight Golann, Lela Love, Ken Rosenblum, and Barbara Swartz for generously finding the time to offer valuable comments, as well as my research assistant, Joseph Wilson, for putting the footnotes in proper form.

1 *See* Tom Mainelli, "Banias: The Mobile Chip to Beat?," *PCWorld*, Oct. 15, 2002, at http://www.pcworld.com/news/article/0,aid,105957,00.asp; *see also* Kai Schmerer, "IDF: Banias Fever Breaks Out," *ZDNet UK* at http://reviews.zdnet.co.uk/ hardware/processorsmemory/0,39024015,10001951,00.htm (Sept. 16, 2002) (last visited Feb. 28, 2005).

2 *See* Harold I. Abramson, *Mediation Representation: Advocating in a Problem-Solving Process* (2004) (Recipient of 2004 Book Award of the CPR Institute for Dispute Resolution).

3 *See, e.g.*, Dwight Golann, *Mediating Legal Disputes: Effective Strategies for Lawyers and Mediators* (1996), 14–26; Christopher W. Moore, *The Mediation Process: Practical Strategies for*

problem-solving approach,[4] surprisingly little has been written on how to represent clients[5] in this burgeoning and increasingly preferred process.[6]

This article follows my personal journey of constructing a model of client representation suitable for a problem-solving mediation process. The model, labeled as the mediation representation formula, forms the foundation of *Mediation Representation*. Developing it was an incremental process that drew upon much of the excellent work done in the field of negotiation, mediation, and mediation representation.[7]

Let me start by defining a problem-solving mediation process. In such a process, the mediator's sole purpose is to assist the clients and their attorneys in resolving the dispute. The mediator knows how to structure a process that can

---

Resolving Conflict (2nd ed. 1996), 18–19, 55–56; Jay Folberg and Alison Taylor, *Mediation: A Comprehensive Guide to Resolving Conflicts without Litigation* (1984), 7–9, 38–72.

4 Even though I could not find a rigorous study of the approaches taught in mediation training programs, I came across ample anecdotal evidence that suggests that many, if not most, training programs teach mediators the interest-based or problem-solving approach. In informal surveys of mediators compiled when I have conducted advanced mediation training, for instance, I was informed that most, if not all, of the participants received basic training in some variation of problem-solving. This approach also seems to be taught in many court-connected programs, by many private trainers, and at Harvard Law School (where Professors Fisher, Sander, and Mnookin train negotiators and mediators from around the world). Also, although a significant number of mediators are trained in the transformative approach, a number of them also seem to have been trained in problem-solving.

5 My book is the first one to focus exclusively on how to be a problem-solving advocate. It develops a coherent theory and comprehensive approach to representation. Other books have ably presented an amalgam of strategies for advocates in mediation. For example, one book explains how to conduct a traditional negotiation dance of offer and counter-offers in mediation. *See* Michael P. Silver, *Mediation and Negotiation: Representing Your Clients* (2001), 121–27.

6 *See* Marc Galanter, *The Vanishing Trial: An Examination of Trials and Related Matters in Federal and State Courts* (Preliminary version Oct. 24, 2003) (prepared for the Symposium on the Vanishing Trial sponsored by the Litigation Section of the American Bar Association, San Francisco, CA, Dec. 12–14, 2003) (documenting that while the number of federal lawsuits filed has increased, the number of trials has decreased, from 11.5% in 1962 to 1.8% in 2002, with comparable trends in the state courts. One of the documented replacements for trials is mediation.); *see also* John Lande, "Getting the Faith: Why Business Lawyers and Executives Believe in Mediation," 5 *Harv. Negot. L. Rev.* 137 (2000).

7 *See generally* Abramson, *supra* note 2; Eric Galton, *Representing Clients in Mediation* (1994); Jack Cooley, *Mediation Advocacy* (2nd ed. 2002); Golann, *supra* note 3; Videotape: Representing Clients in Mediation: How Advocates Can Share a Mediator's Powers (Dwight Golann 2000) (on file with the ABA Section of Litigation); Moore, *supra* note 3; Roger Fisher, William Ury & Bruce Patton, *Getting to Yes: Negotiating Agreement without Giving In* (Penguin Books 1991) (1981) [hereinafter Fisher et al.].

provide both sides with an opportunity to fashion enduring, and when at all feasible, inventive solutions that can go beyond what a court might be willing to craft. The mediator serves as a guide by managing a structured discussion that includes gathering specific information; identifying issues, interests, and impediments; and generating, assessing, and selecting options for settlement. The mediator knows how to involve clients constructively and to use various dispute resolution techniques at propitious moments in the mediation session. The mediator poses open-ended and focused questions, reframes issues, conducts brainstorming sessions, and uses recognized strategies for defusing tensions and overcoming impasses. The mediator may use private caucuses to gain confidential information and employ suitable methods for helping participants evaluate the strengths and weaknesses of their legal cases, methods that do not involve the mediator rendering his or her assessment. If the dispute does not settle, the mediator may help the participants—the attorneys and the parties—to select a suitable alternative process, including litigation, for ultimately resolving the conflict.

There are, of course, other processes for resolving legal conflicts, a well-recognized reality that has generated much debate over what processes can be rightfully called mediation. After reading and listening to much of the thoughtful debate and observing how loosely the term is used by such diverse sources as judges, the media, and the United Nations, the final clincher in my intellectual pursuit to define mediation occurred when I encountered an oven advertisement on television. The manufacturer's salesman was presented as a "great mediator" when he offered a range that could "cook two different foods, at two different temperatures."[8] It is too late to justify a favored, circumscribed definition of mediation. Mediation is simply a negotiation conducted with the assistance of a third party. This generic definition should fit any process that can be legitimately classified as mediation.[9] Instead of

---

8 Maytag Corporation ran a national television advertisement that it called "The Great Mediator (pizza or casserole)." In the advertisement, the "Maytag Man" appears as "a great mediator" who has the answer to the question that has "aroused fierce passions for centuries: What's for dinner?" The mediator presents a new range that can "cook two different foods, at two different temperatures, for one complete meal." The advertisement ran from August 1999 to December 1999. Interview with Nicole Kaczmarek, Operations Manager, LB Works, Advertising Agency for Maytag Corporation (July 2003). The salesman was mediating using an evaluative approach in which he offered a solution that would meet the needs of both parties to eat different foods.

9 *See, e.g.*, Kimberlee K. Kovach, *Mediation: Principles and Practice* 23–25 (2nd ed. 2000); Golann, *supra* note 3, at 14–26; Moore, *supra* note 3; Folberg and Taylor, *supra* note 3, at 7–9, 38–72.

debating the definition of mediation, we should focus on defining the adjective in front of the noun. Is the mediation problem-solving, transformative, evaluative, or something else? *Mediation Representation* focuses on one particular adjective: problem-solving.

Problem-solving mediations should be distinguished from judicial settlement conferences because some mediations can resemble settlement conferences.[10] These settlement conference-type mediations, like judicial settlement conferences, can consist of the third party hearing each side's arguments, asking questions, challenging partisan points, assessing arguments and legal positions, and hinting at or urging compromised settlement terms. Such mediations, using dispute resolution nomenclature, are often a directive, evaluative process. Attorneys can prefer this sort of mediation process because they know how to represent clients in such a process, using the familiar adversarial strategies of presenting their strongest partisan arguments and criticizing the other side's case.

These adversarial strategies may be effective in settlement conference-type processes as well as in court and arbitrations where each side is trying to convince a third party to make a favorable decision or to steer the negotiations in a favorable direction. However, in problem-solving mediation, there is no third party decision maker or evaluator, only a third party assistant. The third party assistant usually is not even the primary audience.[11] The primary audience is the other side, who is surely not neutral and can often be quite hostile. In this different representational setting, the adversarial approach is less effective, if not self-defeating.

Many sophisticated and experienced litigators realize that mediation calls for a different approach, but they still muddle through the mediation sessions. They are learning on the job. Even though many attorneys prefer a

---

10 *See* Videotape: Comparing Settlement Conferences and Mediations (Abramson and Cronin-Harris, NYS Bar Association, 1999) (on file with NYS Bar Association); *see also* Carrie Menkel-Meadow, "For and Against Settlement: Uses and Abuses of the Mandatory Settlement Conference," 33 *Ucla L. Rev.* 485, 507–11 (1985). A significant difference between a directive, evaluative mediation and a judicial settlement conference is the power possessed by the third party. In mediation, the person lacks ultimate decision-making power while in a judicial settlement conference, the person may be the ultimate decision maker.

11 While the mediator may not be the primary audience, the mediator, along with the other attorney, are important secondary audiences. These secondary audiences require special attention at different points in the mediation, depending on what is happening during the mediation. For example, this article considers later how the advocate might enlist the assistance of the mediator to help break impasses, among other types of assistance. *See infra* Part V.C & D; *see also* Abramson, *supra* note 2, at ch. 5.7 (Select Your Primary Audience in the Mediation).

problem-solving approach to negotiations,[12] attorneys are still in the early stages of figuring out how to do it in mediations. Many attorneys went to law school before courses on dispute resolution were offered, and the dispute resolution courses that have emerged in law schools over the last twenty-five years have been largely limited to teaching students to be mediators, not advocates.[13] Continuing legal education programs are only beginning to focus on teaching representation skills, with many programs limited to sharing anecdotal experiences and idiosyncratic advice. *Mediation Representation* provides a comprehensive approach to representing clients in a problem-solving process, an approach that applies from an attorney's first client phone call until the mediation process is concluded.

In following my personal journey, this article first considers why I focused on the advocate in the process. It then identifies three key assumptions that underlie any model of client representation. Next, the practice of attorneys advocating adversarially is posed as the problem that the rest of the article proposes to resolve by developing a particular model of client representation for mediation.

II. EMPOWERING THE LAWYER-CONSUMER

I began thinking about mediation representation about ten years ago when asked to serve on a planning committee to design a program on the subject for the annual meeting of the New York State Bar Association.[14] I welcomed this opportunity because as a dispute resolution professor, mediator, and trainer, I had developed an uneasy awareness of the limitations on improving mediation practices by focusing on the training of mediators. Giving attention to the advocates in the process seemed like a promising prospect.

Recalling a graduate course in microeconomics, I realized that mediation policymakers, practitioners, and academics (including myself) have been focusing primarily on only one side of the marketplace equation—the supply side,

12 *See* Heumann & Hyman, "Negotiation Methods and Litigation Settlement Methods in New Jersey: 'You Can't Always Get What You Want,'" 12 *Ohio St. J. On Disp. Resol.* 253, 309 (1997) ("While sixty-one percent of the lawyers would like to *see* more problem-solving negotiation methods, about seventy-one percent of negotiations are carried out with positional methods instead.").

13 *See* Suzanne J. Schmitz, "What Should We Teach in ADR Courses: Concepts and Skills for Lawyers Representing Clients in Mediation," *Harv. Negot. L. Rev.* 6 (2001), 204.

14 The state bar association program was held in New York City in January 1994.

although for good reason. Mediation was still a relatively young profession—only about twenty to twenty-five years in the making, and much work needed to be done to ensure quality mediators. I also began to understand the limitations of what could be accomplished on the supply side. Policymakers can formulate professional standards, expand the number of hours for basic training, mandate training content, implement advanced specialized training, require mentoring, and possibly impose licensing (not something I personally endorse at this time). However, these valuable initiatives alone were unlikely to overcome the challenges posed by the nature of mediation practice. Many mediators mediate part-time and function like private settlement judges. Much of this mediation practice transpires unsupervised, behind doors locked by the confidentiality key.

Frustrated by the limitations of what can be done to improve the quality of mediation practices on the supply side, I wondered whether a valuable opportunity was being missed by failing to give sufficient attention to the other side of the equation—the consumer side. According to microeconomic theory, you can improve the quality of services in the marketplace by educating consumers to make informed decisions. With this in mind, I turned to studying mediation representation practices as well as to writing and teaching to reach one particular set of consumers:[15] lawyers who counsel clients, hire mediators, and participate in the mediation process.

If lawyer-consumers could learn more about the opportunities offered by a problem-solving process, how to select suitable mediators, and techniques of effective advocacy, they would know when to shop for a problem-solving process as well as what to look for during the mediation process. In return, mediators would realize that to get that business, they would need to hone their problem-solving skills. In addition, their behind-closed-door practices would be scrutinized by these better-educated advocates in the room, who could serve as a check on the quality of the mediation process.[16]

---

15 During the last ten years, others also turned to educating the mediation consumer. For example, the CPR Institute of Dispute Resolution, which serves a membership of 500 corporations and law firms, provides, among other services, education in ADR advocacy to lawyers and corporate clients. *See* CPR Institute of Dispute Resolution, at http://www.cpradr.org. Many bar associations currently offer education programs on mediation advocacy. *See, e.g.*, programs offered by the ABA Section on Dispute Resolution, at http://www.abanet.org/dispute/home.html (last visited Feb. 4, 2005).

16 In my advocacy training, I include a module on how the advocate can prod the mediator toward a desired process such as problem-solving when the mediator lacks either the training or the persistency to do so. The somewhat provocative title of that teaching module is: "How to Deal with Aberrant Mediators."

III. THREE ASSUMPTIONS WHEN CONSTRUCTING A MODEL OF CLIENT REPRESENTATION

I started my journey by reflecting on my experiences as a mediator and a teacher of students and mediators. After studiously observing advocates at work, hearing numerous accounts from other mediators and mediation advocates, and reading much of the relevant literature, I identified three pillars to support a model of client representation for a problem-solving process. They consisted of three succinct and widely cited propositions, which follow.

A. Problem-Solving Mediation Can Offer Dispute Resolution Opportunities That Are Unavailable in Other Dispute Resolution Forums

I will not take any space to defend this now widely accepted proposition except to recognize that mediation, when not conducted like a settlement conference, has the potential to produce creative and enduring solutions that meet the particular needs of disputing parties.[17] Any model had to be designed to realize this potential.

B. To Realize These Opportunities, Advocates Need an Approach to Client Representation Suitable for Mediation

As already suggested, the familiar adversarial approach that has proven so effective in judicial trials, as well as in judicial settlement conferences and arbitrations, does not work optimally in a problem-solving mediation. Simply adjusting and refining trial strategies would not be enough to realize the full benefits of mediation. The model had to incorporate a different representation approach, one tailored to realize the full benefits of this forum. Instead of advocating as zealous adversaries, attorneys should advocate as zealous problem-solvers.[18]

---

17 *See generally* Kovach, *supra* note 9; Golann, *supra* note 3, chs. 2 & 3; Moore, *supra* note 3; Folberg and Taylor, *supra* note 3.

18 *See* Andrea Kupfer Schneider, "Shattering Negotiation Myths: Empirical Evidence on the Effectiveness of Negotiation Style," 7 *Harv. Negot. L. Rev.* 143 (2002), 196 (in an extensive study of negotiation styles, 75 percent of true problem-solving negotiators were considered effective as compared with less than 50 percent of adversarial bargainers, a percentage that shrunk to 25 percent when examining adversarial bargainers who were unethical); Robert H. Mnookin et al., *Beyond Winning: Negotiating to Create Value in Deals and Disputes* 321–322 (2000); G. Richard Shell, *Bargaining for Advantage: Negotiation Strategies for Reasonable People* 12–14 (1999). The authors concluded that clients are usually better off when

C. Mediation is a Continuation of the Negotiation Process

Any model of client representation had to recognize that parties participating in mediation are simply continuing their negotiation in another forum. Therefore, the model needed to explicitly reveal the relationship between negotiation and mediation.

IV. THE PROBLEM: ADVERSARIAL ADVOCACY

The sort of advocacy caricatured in the negotiation session of the movie Erin Brockovich[19] has not been uncommon in mediations. Let me describe the sharp exchange of settlement offers in that negotiation. During the rest of this article, this dispute[20] will be used as a basis for demonstrating the elements of a formula suitable for representing clients in a problem-solving process.

Here is the scene and the transcript:

> The judge just dismissed each of the eighty-four motions to strike filed by the defendant and upheld the plaintiffs' causes of action in a lawsuit brought by the residents of Hinkley, who claimed that the defendant Pacific Gas and Electric [PG&E] had polluted their groundwater. The judge directed the defendant's attorneys to "tell your clients they're going to trial." As a result, the attorneys for both sides agreed to meet at the law office of the plaintiffs' attorney to discuss settling the lawsuit.
>
> SCENE: The Waiting Room.
> Ed Masry, the attorney Erin Brockovich works for, glances at the defendants' attorneys who "ooze importance" and whispers to Ms. Brockovich, "The games are about to begin." Mr. Masry recruits and dresses up two of his secretaries to look like attorneys.
>
> NEXT SCENE: The Conference Room.
> The four of them, including Ms. Brockovich, walk into the conference room and sit down. Across the

---

a lawyer adopts a problem-solving approach over an adversarial one. Other studies are cited that suggest that cooperative negotiators are more effective than competitive ones.

19 *Erin Brockovich* (Universal Studios 2000).

20 Erin Brockovich was not a lawyer in the movie; she was assisting the attorney as a sort of paralegal. Rather than dealing with the relationship between a paralegal and the attorney who must make all the critical representation decisions, I simplified the discussion in the article by focusing on Ms. Brockovich's representation choices as if she were an attorney. *Id.*

table, two attorneys representing the defendant are already seated.

The lead attorney for defendant Pacific Gas and Electric talks first and presents an opening offer:

SANCHEZ (PG&E lead attorney): ... Let's be honest here. Twenty million dollars is more money than these people have ever dreamed of.

ERIN: Oh, see, now that pisses me off. First of all—since the demur, we now have more than four hundred plaintiffs. ... and (mocking her) "let's be honest," we all know there's more out there. Now, they may not be the most sophisticated people, but they do know how to divide, and twenty million dollars isn't shit when it's split between them.

And second of all—these people don't dream about being rich. They dream about being able to watch their kids swim in a pool without worrying they'll have to have a hysterectomy at age twenty, like Rosa Diaz—a client of ours—or to have their spine deteriorate like Stan Bloom—another client of ours.

So before you come back here with another lame-ass offer, I want you to think real hard about what your spine is worth, Mr. Buda [one of PG&E's attorneys]—or what you'd expect someone to pay you for your uterus, Miss Sanchez [the other PG&E attorney]—then you take out your calculator and multiply that number by a hundred. Anything less than that is a waste of our time.

[Sanchez, throughout her speech, has been reacting in a patronizing manner—as if Erin's words were of no import. As Sanchez picks up a glass of water to sip,]

ERIN: By the way, we had the water brought in special for you folks. It came from one of Hinkley's water wells.

SANCHEZ: Stares at the water and puts it down and says: I think this meeting is over.

ED responds with: Damn right it is.

[Erin gets up and storms out first.]

This sort of intensive, adversarial posturing can damage, if not derail, a problem-solving process, whether conducted with or without a mediator. Mediation advocates who prefer a problem-solving process need a more suitable approach to client representation.

V. SOLUTION: THE MEDIATION REPRESENTATION FORMULA

Mediation Representation presents a five component mediation representation formula in which attorneys advocate by using (1) a creative problem-solving approach to achieve the two goals of (2) satisfying their client's interests and (3) overcoming any impediments to settlement. During the mediation the attorneys (4) enlist the assistance of the mediator while negotiating with the other side at (5) key junctures in the process.

The first three components of the model focus primarily on how to negotiate in the mediation.

A. Negotiation Approach: Creative Problem-Solving

Selecting the negotiation approach was easy. If an advocate views mediation as a problem-solving process, then the attorney should negotiate as a problem-solver.

A problem-solving negotiator who is creative[21] does more than just try to settle the dispute. Such a negotiator creatively searches for solutions that go beyond the traditional ones based on rights, obligations, and precedent. Rather

---

21 *See,* e.g., Mnookin et al., *supra* note 18; Fisher et al., *supra* note 7; Symposium, Conceiving the Lawyer As Creative Problem Solver, 34 *Cal. W. L. Rev*. 267 (1998); Thomas D. Barton, "Creative Problem-Solving: Purpose, Meaning, and Values," 34 *Cal. W. L. Rev*. 273 (1998); Paul Brest & Linda Hamilton Krieger, "Lawyers As Problem Solvers," 72 *Temp. L. Rev*. 811 (1999); Seamus Dunn, "Case Study: The Northern Ireland Experience—Possibilities for Cross-Fertilization Learning," 19 *Alternatives to the High Cost of Litig.*, at 153 (June 2001); Carrie Menkel-Meadow, "Aha? Is Creativity Possible In Legal Problem Solving and Teachable In Legal Education?," 6 *Harv. Negot. L. Rev*. 987 (2001); Carrie J. Menkel-Meadow, "When Winning Isn't Everything: The Lawyer As Problem Solver," 28 *Hofstra L. Rev*. 905 (2000); Carrie Menkel-Meadow, "The Lawyer As Problem Solver and Third-Party Neutral: Creativity and Non-Partisanship in Lawyering," 72 *Temp. L. Rev*. 785 (1999); Carrie Menkel-Meadow, "Toward Another View of Legal Negotiation: The Structure of Problem Solving," 31 *Ucla L. Rev*. 754 (1984); Linda Morton, "Teaching Creative Problem Solving: A Paradigmatic Approach," 34 *Cal. W. L. Rev*. 375 (1998); Janet Reno, "Lawyers As Problem-Solvers: Keynote Address to the AALS," 49 *J. Legal Educ.* 5 (1999). *See also* California Western School of Law, *Center for Creative Problem Solving* (2004), *at* http://www2.cwsl.edu/mcgill/mc_main.html (last visited Feb. 4, 2005).

than settling for win-lose outcomes, the negotiator searches for solutions that can benefit both sides.[22] To creatively problem solve, the negotiator develops a collaborative relationship with the other side and participates throughout the process in a way that is likely to result in solutions that are enduring as well as inventive. Solutions are likely to be enduring because both sides work together to fashion nuanced solutions that each side fully understands, can live with, and knows how to implement. Solutions are likely to be inventives because both sides advocate for their client's interests instead of legal positions;[23] use suitable techniques for overcoming impediments; search expansively for multiple options; and evaluate and package options imaginatively to meet the various interests of all parties.

For problem-solving advocacy to be effective, an attorney ought to engage proactively at every stage of representation, from the moment of the first client interview until the negotiation in the mediation is concluded. The attorney should be a constant problem solver. It is relatively easy to engage in simple moves such as responding to a demand with the question "why?" in order to bring the other party's interests to the surface. However, it is much more difficult to stick to this approach throughout the mediation process, especially when faced with an adversarial, positional opponent. Trust the problem-solving approach. When the other side engages in adversarial tactics—a frequent occurrence in practice—the attorney should react with problem-solving responses, responses that might even convert the other side into a problem solver.[24]

In this pitch for a problem-solving approach, I do not blindly claim that it is the only one that results in settlements. Attorneys frequently cite success stories when they use unvarnished adversarial tactics, as occurred in *Erin Brockovich*,

---

22 Instead of referring to "win-win" solutions, I suggest searching for solutions that can benefit both sides. I avoid using the more familiar, if not overused, "win-win" jargon because that jargon carries baggage that can blind people to the underlying valuable point that still retains considerable vitality. The "win-win" attitude can be sharply contrasted with the opposite one of "win-lose," neatly capturing a fundamental difference between the problem-solving and adversarial approaches. Many lawyers consider the idea that both sides can secure benefits as naïve, or not anchored in reality. However, the notion that both sides might be able to gain something in negotiations reflects an optimistic attitude that can open the mind to creative searches. The likelihood of finding such gains in negotiations is greater than in court. In negotiations, for instance, even the defendant who agrees to pay considerable damages may gain other benefits, such as no publicity, no precedent, and a continuing business relationship—benefits that are usually unavailable in court.

23 For a full discussion of how to identify clients' interests as opposed to positions, *see* Abramson, *supra* note 2, at ch. 3.2(a) and Fisher et al., *supra* note 7.

24 *See* Abramson, *supra* note 2, at ch. 1.5. R

or a hybrid of adversarial and problem-solving strategies.[25] The hybrid supporters claim that the best approach is a flexible one, a philosophy that surely is advisable in life generally as well as in legal negotiations. However, flexibility should not be confused with inconsistency. Shifting between adversarial and problem-solving tactics during the course of mediation can undercut creative problem-solving potential. A consistent adherence to problem-solving will more likely produce the best results for clients.

Finally, this pitch for problem-solving is bound to be resisted by those who fail to see any benefits for the legal cases that they typically handle. These skeptics see problem-solving opportunities for other attorneys' cases but not for their own because their cases are only about money. This common reaction reflects a misunderstanding of the opportunities offered by problem-solving.

First, whether a legal dispute is mostly about money varies from case to case.[26] An attorney has little chance of discovering whether a dispute is about more than money if the attorney approaches the dispute as if it is only about money.[27] Such a preconceived view backed by a narrowly focused adversarial strategy will likely blind the attorney to the other party's needs and inventive solutions. Both sides are more likely to discover comprehensive and creative solutions if they approach the dispute with open minds and problem-solving orientations.

Second, if the dispute or any remaining issues turn out to be predominantly about money, then at least the attorney followed a representation approach that

---

25 In the hybrid approach, attorneys switch between adversarial and problem-solving tactics, depending on how the mediation is unfolding.

26 *See* Dwight Golann, "Is Legal Mediation a Process of Repair—or Separation? An Empirical Study, and Its Implications," *Harv. Negot. L. Rev.* 7 (2002), 301–334 (in the only empirical study on the subject, the author found that "almost two-thirds of all [mediated] settlements in the survey were integrative in nature. ... The results suggest that both mediators and advocates should consider making a search for integrative outcomes an important aspect of their mediation strategy.").

At least one category of disputes is usually primarily about money. The classic personal injury dispute between strangers who will never deal with each other again can be only about money and therefore not open to creative resolutions other than a tailored payment scheme. However, even in these disputes, one side may occasionally want something more than money, such as vindication, fair treatment, etc.

27 In a recent case that I mediated, the parties arrived with extreme monetary claims on the table and a long history of failed negotiations. After more than three hours of mediation, the parties and attorneys negotiated a written apology signed by the defendant and a written introduction to future buyers signed by the plaintiff. The monetary issues were then resolved in less than a minute! The parties were apparently already on the same page for settling the money claims but were not ready to settle until some non-monetary needs were met.

may have created a hospitable environment for resolving the money issues. A hospitable environment can even be beneficial when there is no expectation of a continuing relationship between the disputing parties.

Third, the problem-solving approach can provide a framework for resolving money issues. This type of dispute can sometimes be resolved by resorting to the usual problem-solving initiatives such as the use of objective criteria.[28] If they fail, an attorney might turn to the familiar, adversarial negotiation dance of offers and counter-offers, but a version that has been tempered for a problem-solving process.[29]

In short, problem-solving provides a comprehensive and coherent structure for representation that can guide an attorney throughout the negotiation in the mediation. By sticking to this approach, the attorney will be prepared to deal with the myriad of unanticipated challenges that inevitably arise as any negotiation unfolds.

Despite these benefits, lawyers gravitate toward an adversarial approach. The reason may seem simplistic, if not superficially glib: lawyers are too preoccupied with litigating. Negotiations are so enmeshed in the litigation process that negotiations and litigation have become an integrated, single process of dispute resolution.[30] Thus, lawyers are likely to approach the negotiated settlement of a court case with a litigator's mindset,[31] one molded by an intensely adversarial legal culture and reinforced by attorney fee arrangements.

Many lawyers relish and many clients crave a fiercely combative approach to legal representation. Overly optimistic as well as insecure clients want to be protected by aggressive hired guns. They are not very receptive to reality checks and can become perturbed with lawyers who may not appear faithful to the cause when they flag legal risks and inquire about the other side's perspective and needs.

---

28 *See* Abramson, *supra* note 2, at ch. 1.3(a)(iii) on "Manage Remaining Distributive Conflicts" (considering how to use problem-solving moves to resolve easy distributive issues); *see also infra* Part V.D. 2 ("Mediators' Techniques"). For other methods, *see* Abramson, *supra* note 2, at ch. 7.2(d)(iii), and text accompanying note 52 *infra*.

29 *See* Abramson, *supra* note 2, at ch. 1.3(a)(iii) on "Manage Remaining Distributive Conflicts" (This section considers how to resolve difficult distributive issues by using tempered adversarial strategies. For example, an attorney can omit the use of traditional tricks and extreme threats, and instead emphasize principled arguments while engaging in the negotiation dance of offers and counter-offers).

30 *See id.* at 13–14.

31 *See* Mnookin et al., *supra* note 18, at 108–18, 167–72.

Legal training and experience teach lawyers to view legal disputes as zero-sum or distributive conflicts about money in which one party wins and the other one loses. The very function of courts is to declare winners and losers. Also, courts prefer awarding the winners monetary awards over such equitable relief as specific performance and inventive injunctions. Compelled by the well-established maxim that "equitable relief is not available to one who has an adequate remedy at law," courts prefer awarding damages, reserving creative equitable relief for when legal remedies prove inadequate. Before awarding most forms of non-monetary relief, counsel must convince the court that his or her client would otherwise suffer irreparable harm and that the equitable relief would be practical, convenient, and not sap judicial resources.[32]

The litigator's mindset is also molded by the only too familiar routine for pursuing litigation. First, a litigator's conception of a dispute is shaped by the way he or she converts the dispute into a legal case. When drafting a complaint or answer, the attorney sculpts and fits the dispute into recognized legal categories and then reinforces this conception of the dispute with supporting partisan arguments. The attorney next engages in various strategies to bolster the legal case because the perceived likely court outcome will impact on the settlement value of the case. In addition to using old-fashioned puffery and bluffing, the attorney typically turns to various litigation strategies. By pursuing more discovery or a motion for summary judgment, for instance, the attorney pursues the chance that more disclosure or a successful motion will strengthen the court case and its settlement value. The attorney may further press the other party to settle by resorting to litigation strategies that increase the other party's cost of staying in the litigation. By demanding voluminous discovery, for example, the attorney can purposely increase the other party's costs of not settling. As the attorneys and parties become consumed by these litigation tactics, the litigation and related negotiation become sharply adversarial.

The fee arrangements between attorneys and their clients, which can encourage unethical professional conduct, can fuel these litigation strategies. Obviously, an hourly rate arrangement can motivate less ethical attorneys to engage in adversarial strategies that prolong the litigation. It takes only one unethical attorney with the hourly rate incentive to prolong the litigation. Even though the alternative of a contingency fee arrangement may motivate early settlement (by working fewer hours, the attorney can make

32 *See* Dan Dobbs, *Law Of Remedies: Damages, Equity, Restitution*, para. 2.5 (2nd ed. 1993).

more money), it can discourage problem-solving searches for value-creating trades. A settlement that includes a new car or an apology instead of monetary damages, for instance, produces a settlement that cannot be neatly split so that the attorney receives one-third.

In short, when the litigator's mindset is adapted to legal negotiations, the approach is bound to be adversarial.[33] This adversarial approach has been long-standing, despite the finding of at least one prominent study that lawyers would prefer problem-solving strategies.[34] A study of New Jersey litigators suggested that lawyers may negotiate adversarially out of habit, a social practice that is less costly and more easily routinized than problem-solving.[35]

The negotiation in Erin Brockovich surely exemplified the classic adversarial approach. It consisted of the exchange of extreme offers and counter-offers backed by muscular language. After the defendant's attorney characterized her offer as "more money than these people have ever dreamed of," Erin Brockovich responded by scorning the defendant's offer, conveying passionately and vividly her clients' dreams, presenting an extreme and provocative counter-offer, and wrapping up her response with the unsettling water ploy that pointedly raised the health issue. The result of this series of moves was predictable, at least for that negotiation session: an impasse. However, could Ms. Brockovich have been an assertive advocate in a way that would not have sent the other side away? I will suggest how she might have advocated differently, in a way that might have transformed the negotiation into problem solving, as I explore the next four components of the representation model.

B. Goal: Advance Your Client's Interests

For the next step in constructing this model, I wanted to fashion a guiding light for the negotiation. Any light should focus client representation on one overall goal within a problem-solving framework. I sought a goal that would isolate a

33 One creative solution for changing the litigator's mindset is to change the attorney who tries to settle the case. Instead of the litigator pursuing both the litigation and the negotiations, the litigator only litigates. Any negotiations would be handled by a separate settlement counsel who is committed to a problem-solving approach. For a thoughtful development of this solution, *see* William F. Coyne, Jr., "The Case for Settlement Counsel," 14 *Ohio St. J. On Disp. Resol.* 367, 367–70 (1999). The author concluded that "the mind-set needed to do effective problem-solving is incompatible with the mind-set needed to pursue litigation whole-heartedly." *Id.* at 393.

34 *See* Heumann & Hyman, *supra* note 12.

35 *Id.* at 295–309.

key trigger for launching a problem-solving process. The obvious goal was to settle the dispute.[36]

However, settlement as a goal did not shed much light. It is the goal of most negotiations, whether the parties are adversarial or problem-solving. Also, the goal failed to shape how parties and attorneys negotiate. I needed another goal.

For the goal to be effective it had to take into account the litigator's embedded view of negotiations as a win-lose proposition; it had to be able to shift the litigator's perspective. After reflecting on a full range of techniques and moves within the self-contained problem-solving approach, one single move stood out because it could instantly shift a negotiator's perspective on a dispute from an adversarial distributive one to a problem-solving mutually beneficial one. This shift can happen when the attorney identifies and advocates his or her client's interests. More specifically, an attorney should first understand his or her client's interests, acquire an understanding of the other side's interests, and then advocate to advance his or her client's interests in a way that sufficiently addresses the other side's interests to move toward an agreement. This focus should be the primary goal in a problem-solving process, a first move that can initiate problem-solving as well as serve as a guiding light throughout the negotiation in the mediation.[37]

In *Erin Brockovich*, Ms. Brockovich could have shifted the negotiation from adversarial to problem-solving by focusing on the interests of both sides. Interests reflect parties' needs. The positions that attorneys typically advocate are solutions. In *Erin Brockovich*, the defendant offered twenty million dollars; the plaintiffs counter-offered with a hundred times the value of a spine or uterus. These monetary solutions were offered to meet each side's interests. However, there might have been other solutions. By switching the beginning of the negotiation from exchanging initial offers to exchanging information on the needs of each party, an attorney can open the door to a search for creative solutions. It is the first step in a problem-solving negotiation.

---

36 A party settles when the negotiated solution is better than the alternative to settlement known as the BATNA (Best Alternative To A Negotiated Agreement). *See* Fisher et al., *supra* note 7, at 101–11 (coining the term "BATNA"). The BATNA is your client's best option if the negotiation fails.

37 The attorney should develop a solution that meets his or her client's interests better than the solution offered by his or her client's BATNA. For a full discussion of how to identify client's interests as opposed to positions, *see* Abramson, *supra* note 2, at 98–104; Fisher et al., *supra* note 7, at 41–57.

In *Erin Brockovich,* consider what might have been the interests of each side and how identifying them would have opened the way to multiple possible solutions. The interests of the ill and scared plaintiffs became clear as the story in the movie unfolded. They wanted recognition that they had been poorly treated and lied to by the defendant; they wanted to be treated with respect and dignity; and they desperately needed health care and a safe place to live for themselves and their families. In view of these interests, solutions other than or including the payment of a lump sum might have included receiving lifetime health insurance, buying out their homes, cleaning up the contaminated groundwater, and/or a public and sincere apology.

For the defendant, PG&E, what were its underlying interests? The company might have wanted to avoid bad publicity and financial distress, if not bankruptcy. In view of these interests, other possible solutions might have included burnishing its reputation as a responsible corporate citizen by cleaning up the site, securing government help with the cleanup, or offering health insurance to the residents, which might be cheaper than paying a single lump sum payment.

There is a second reason for selecting the goal of focusing on a client's interests: to make clear what is not the primary goal of problem-solving. Problem-solving is sometimes misconstrued to mean placing a premium on getting along with the other side at the expense of a client's interests. Correcting this false perception registered high when drafting the new assessment criteria for the ABA

Mediation Representation Competition.[38] We had heard numerous competition judges criticize students' advocacy as too cooperative at the expense of their clients' needs. We resolved to send an unmistakable message to students by adding a separate and specific judging criterion entitled "Advocating Client's Interests."[39]

---

38 I served as Chair of this committee as well as host of the inaugural regional competition for the New York City area law schools. The annual competition includes about ten regional competitions with the final rounds held each year in conjunction with the annual meeting of the ABA Section on Dispute Resolution. The judging criteria are based on students performing a problem-solving lawyer role.

39 Building a relationship with the other side also is important. A separate criterion focuses on "Problem-Solving Relationship Building." However, the two criteria do not compete with each other. The Rules Committee of the Mediation Representation Competition of the ABA Section of Dispute Resolution drafted the assessment criteria during 2000–2001 that became effective for the 2001–2002 competition year. *See* American Bar Association Section of Dispute Resolution, Representation in Mediation Competition 2005: Rules and Instructions (Dec. 16, 2004), at http://www.abanet.org/dispute/rulesandinstructions2004.doc (current version of the criteria).

For these reasons, this explicit goal was added to the model: attorneys should advocate to advance their clients' interests.

C. Goal: Overcome Impediments

I also identified another primary goal, one that applies to any negotiation regardless of the objective: to overcome any impediments to settlement. This goal entailed a return to a basic premise: parties would not be in mediation unless they were facing an impediment in the negotiation; otherwise, the parties could probably settle the dispute without the assistance of a mediator. Selecting this goal was obvious. Less obvious, however, was identifying an impasse-breaking strategy that comported with a problem-solving approach.

A number of distinguished authors have devised methodologies that demystify the murky world of impasse-breaking.[40] The methodology developed by Dr. Christopher Moore,[41] for instance, relies on taking three discrete steps that can produce a tailored-made strategy for overcoming impasses. His approach is built around his critical observation that impasses can be divided into five conflict categories that he labels *relationship, data, value, interest,* and *structural.* Under his approach, you first inquire about the cause of the impasse; then you classify the cause into one of the five impasse categories; and finally, you devise a suitable intervention for overcoming the impasse.

Let me describe Moore's five impasse categories while leaving for the next section how advocates might use his classification system as a basis for enlisting assistance from the mediator.

Relationship Conflicts can arise when participants are deeply upset with each other, cling to destructive misperceptions or stereotypes of each other, or suffer from poor communication. These types of conflicts are common in disputes

40 *See* Jean R. Sternlight, "Lawyers' Representation of Clients in Mediation: Using Economics and Psychology to Structure Advocacy in a Nonadversarial Setting," 14 *Ohio St. J. On Disp. Resol.* 269, 297–331 (1999) (identifying barriers to negotiations based on economists' insights, psychologists' insights, flaws in the rationality assumption, and principal/agent conflicts); Moore, *supra* note 3 at 60–61 (identifying five causes of conflicts: data conflicts, interest conflicts, structural conflicts, relationship conflicts, and value conflicts); Golann, *supra* note 3, at 153–241 (identifying three categories of impasses—process, psychological, and merits); Frank E. A. Sander and Stephen B. Goldberg, "Fitting the Forum to the Fuss: A User-Friendly Guide to Selecting an ADR Procedure," 10 *Negot. J.* 49, 54–59 (1994) (identifying ten impediments to settlement).

41 *See* Moore, *supra* note 3, at 60–61 (presenting a Circle of Conflict in which five sources of conflicts are identified along with possible strategies for intervention).

where parties distrust each other and are occupied with hurling threats. These disabling tensions can arise between clients, between attorneys, and between an attorney and his or her client. Clearly, a bad relationship between the attorneys in *Erin Brockovich* contributed to that failed negotiation.

Data Conflicts can be caused by inadequate, inaccurate, or untrustworthy information. Alternatively, they can be caused by different views of what is relevant information or different interpretations of relevant data. Data conflicts are common in court cases where parties may hold conflicting views of what happened, what might happen in court, or what is an appropriate interpretation of decisive data such as financial statements.

A common data conflict in legal disputes arises from conflicting views of how a court will likely rule. Too many lawyers and clients fail to thoroughly and objectively analyze all the benefits, costs, and risks of pursuing a judicial remedy. This common failure leads to poor legal advice to clients, unrealistically optimistic alternatives to settlement (unrealistic BATNAs), and impasses in negotiations and mediations. Virtually all mediators have seen cases where opposing attorneys were equally optimistic about the judicial outcome. One of the attorneys was proven wrong. Inflated assessments can lead clients astray because they overestimate the benefits of returning to court, and, as a result, they may mistakenly reject what otherwise might have been acceptable settlement proposals.

A data conflict posed one of the impasses blocking settlement in *Erin Brockovich*. The sides could not agree that the town's water was polluted by the defendant, PG&E. The water ploy during the negotiation sharply raised the safety issue in a provocative, confrontational fashion.[42] Ms. Brockovich could have made the same point differently. She could have asked the other side whether they would be willing to drink this glass of water from a Hinkley well. Then she might have stated, while holding the glass of water, that she would not want to drink the water until the people at this table could resolve whether the water was safe (the data conflict). These comments would have directed the discussion to the cause of the impasse and how to garner the information each side would need to assess the safety of the water and, if unsafe, the causation. This plan would have kept both sides engaged specifically in examining ways to overcome the impediment.

---

42 Several litigators who have seen the film segment have told me that they would have sipped the water offered by Erin Brockovich. They figured that drinking so little water would have been harmless and would have thoroughly defused the tactic. This reaction reminds us how astute attorneys can neutralize clever adversarial tactics.

Interest Conflicts can arise when parties' substantive, procedural, or psychological/relationship wants conflict with each other.[43] Interest conflicts cover the classically positional conflict inherent in adversarial negotiations. They can be caused by parties wanting the same thing (such as property), wanting different amounts of the same thing (such as time), wanting different things that the other is not prepared to give (such as one party wanting a precedent that the other party opposes), or even wanting something that another is not even aware of (such as an acknowledgment or an apology). The *Erin Brockovich* negotiation presented the classic distributive conflict over money—the plaintiffs wanted more money than the defendant was willing to pay.

Structural Conflicts can be the murkiest to identify. The two most common, as well as easiest structural obstacles to spot, are impasses due to unequal bargaining power or impasses due to conflicting goals of attorneys and their clients, which are known as principalagent conflicts. Other structural conflicts can be more subtle, such as those caused by no deadline, time constraints facing one side, a missing key party, a party without sufficient settlement authority, geographical or technological limitations that impact one side disproportionately, and unequal control of resources for resolving the conflict. Because the causes of structural conflicts also frequently contribute to relationship conflicts, it can be difficult to decipher the nature of the conflict. In *Erin Brockovich,* a structural conflict that contributed to a relationship conflict between the attorneys across the table might have impeded a settlement. A large utility company that thought that it had all the power despite losing a vital motion resented being forced to defend itself against the allegations of uneducated, poor people who were represented by an under-funded and inexperienced attorney.

Value Conflicts can be the most intractable ones because they implicate a party's core personal or moral values. This narrow category can embrace matters of principle, ideology, or religion that cannot be compromised. A grassroots environmental group, for instance, may have difficulty settling with a housing developer because to do so might compromise the group's ideology of preserving all large tracts of open space.

Value conflicts can be difficult to recognize in court cases, because values can be masked by all too familiar legal categories, arguments, and remedies. When a

---

43 In a problem-solving process in which the concept of "interests" performs such a vital and pervasive role, Moore's narrow and distinctive use of "interest" conflicts can be confusing. I prefer referring to "wants" or "desire" conflicts. Parties may reach an impasse because their substantive, procedural, or psychological wants or desires are in conflict with each other.

party wants to win in court, for example, the party may be motivated by the need for a clear victory to preserve a personal value, such as personal integrity.

For the last two components of the mediation representation formula, I turned to examining the mediation process itself. This subject is mediation representation. But how does mediation fit in? The last two components cover how to enlist assistance from the mediator and how to negotiate at key junctures in the process.

D. Strategy: Enlist the Assistance of the Mediator

For this next component, I needed to consider the types of assistance that can be offered by the third party in the room, the mediator. The mediator can contribute in three general ways: by the way the mediator implements his or her orientations, uses his or her techniques, and controls the mediation stages. The particular contributions depend on the type of mediation process envisioned. In a problem-solving process in which the advocate does not scheme to manipulate or "game" the mediator, the third party can be enlisted in the various ways described in this section.

1. Mediators' Orientations

Mediators bring a mix of distinct orientations to the mediation process. They can be grouped into four discrete areas: (1) How will the mediator manage the mediation process? Will he or she be primarily problem-solving, evaluative, or transformative? (2) Will the mediator approach the problem narrowly as primarily a legal dispute or more broadly? (3) Will the mediator involve clients actively or restrictively? (4) Will the mediator use caucuses extensively, selectively, or not at all? When an advocate knows the mediator's mix, then he or she knows some of the opportunities for enlisting the mediator for assistance.

Assuming that the dispute in *Erin Brockovich* is now in mediation, Ms. Brockovich might decide that it would be helpful for her clients to personally and passionately convey their fears and suffering to the other side. It became clear after the negotiation session that the plaintiffs needed some version of a "day in court" and that the defendant did not fully understand the plaintiffs' anguish. Knowing that the mediator conducts most of the mediation in joint sessions, Ms. Brockovich would prepare her client to talk to the other side, reaffirm her preference to minimize the use of caucuses, and be prepared to object politely if the mediator prematurely moves toward a caucus.

The mediator's orientation should be especially highlighted, because it can singularly shape an attorney's representation strategy. An attorney's entire approach to interacting with and enlisting assistance from the mediator will be influenced by the mediator's process management, that is, how problem-solving, transformative, or evaluative the mediator might be.[44]

For example, realizing that the mediator will stay in a problem-solving mode gives an attorney the freedom and security to share information (including interests), brainstorm options, recognize weaknesses in his or her client's legal case, and remain open to creative solutions other than the ones in the legal papers. The attorney can feel comfortable asking the mediator for help in sorting out interests, facilitating an evaluation of the legal case, or developing multiple options. The attorney also has much freedom and security with a transformative mediator who is trained to support whatever sort of process is structured and implemented by the attorney, client, and the other side. However, the attorney cannot rely on the transformative mediator's expertise or initiatives to create or direct a process, as the transformative mediator is committed to being non-directive.

In contrast, consider the impact of mediator evaluation on advocacy. Whenever an attorney approaches me about this topic, I ask the same simple question: does knowing that the mediator might offer an evaluation influence how you would represent your client in mediation? The answer is "yes" every time.

Mediation evaluations can take a variety of forms. For instance, mediators may assess the reasonableness of settlement options, assess consequences of not settling, or recommend settlement proposals either as the mediation unfolds or as a "mediator's proposal."

Knowing that the mediator may formulate one or more of these types of evaluations can induce the attorney to approach the mediation more like an adjudicatory process than a negotiation. This mediator role can change the nature of the mediation process. Instead of viewing the mediator as a facilitator with whom the attorney can have candid conversations, the attorney is likely to view the mediator as a decision-maker who must be persuaded. Instead of formulating a negotiation strategy based on meeting parties' interests, the attorney is likely to formulate a strategy designed to convince the mediator to recommend a favorable evaluation.

---

44 *See* Abramson, *supra* note 2, at chs. 4.2(b)(i) and 5.1(e)(i).

Consider in what specific ways an attorney would circumscribe his or her representation if the attorney thought the mediator might evaluate. Would the attorney and his or her client talk less candidly if the attorney were to take into account the possibility of the mediator performing any of these other roles? Would the attorney avoid recognizing any weaknesses in his or her legal position, other than the safely obvious ones, to the mediator or the other side? Would the attorney eschew compromises, especially ones that deviate from the remedies sought in the legal case? Would the attorney hide and disguise information in order to avoid coloring unfavorably the mediator's view of the dispute? Would the attorney be likely to advance partisan legal arguments at the expense of interest-based creative option building?[45]

Affirmative answers to these questions prompt many attorneys to return to the traditional adversarial approach so familiar in the courtroom, in which the attorney withholds unfavorable information, hides any flexibility to avoid implying a lack of confidence in the legal case, and presents carefully crafted partisan arguments and positions that are designed to persuade a decision maker to act favorably.

Alternatively, an attorney might problem-solve but do so in a selective way that reduces the risk of an unfavorable assessment by the mediator. In such a constricted problem-solving approach, an attorney could still share and advocate his or her client's interests and engage in such problem-solving moves as brainstorming options and designing creative solutions, but only up to a point. The attorney will avoid sharing information or showing flexibility that may risk a less favorable evaluation from the mediator.

This strategic behavior can dilute the potential of a problem-solving process by limiting the ability of parties to uncover optimal solutions. Withholding information may hide important matters relevant to devising solutions. Hiding flexibility may cramp the search for imaginative solutions.

I have seen firsthand how attorneys and clients withhold unfavorable information and flexibility. In one instance, after three days of arbitration

---

45 *See* Jeffrey W. Stempel, "Beyond Formalism and False Dichotomies: The Need for Institutionalizing a Flexible Concept of the Mediator's Role," 24 *Fla. St. U. L. Rev.* 949, 950, 983 (1997) (passionately arguing for "flexible mediation that permits judicious use of evaluative techniques," the author still had to recognize that when the advocate knows that the case will be evaluated, the parties are "more likely to present information as advocacy and less as background for negotiation or problem-solving." In addition, "if mediation veers too far from" its facilitative assumptions, the author concluded, "it loses some of [its] creative and transformative potential.").

hearings, the parties agreed to convert the proceeding into a final-offer arbitration process in which each side would submit a final offer, and I would select one. The final offers barely resembled what each side had advocated during the hearings. While this anecdote is surely not surprising because an advocate would never be expected to reveal acceptable settlement terms during an adversarial hearing, it illustrates the point that should be as obvious as what happened in the anecdote: there is a tendency to hide flexibility in an evaluative/adjudicatory process. This point was further illustrated in a recent case where I was operating as a mediator who might evaluate. After four hours of mediating and then reaching an impasse, both sides selected the mediator's proposal scheme where I would formulate a proposal that each side would either accept or reject, without advising the other side unless both sides accepted. The party that took the most inflexible position in the mediation and tenaciously hid any hint of legal vulnerability accepted a mediator's proposal that was one-third of that side's uncompromising position in the mediation.

Consider what might have been the impact on the parties in *Erin Brockovich* if the case had gone to a mediator who might evaluate. PG&E would likely be reluctant to disclose its interest in avoiding bad publicity, because this information might be exploited by the mediator. The mediator might attach a financial value to a confidential settlement and then add the value to a recommended payment by PG&E. Disclosing that interest, however, might lead the parties to devise other beneficial solutions.

The utility company would likely be restrained when brainstorming for creative solutions, because it may want to avoid revealing too much flexibility. It may not want to imply that it would be willing to accept something qualitatively or quantitatively less than what it is seeking in court. So, even though the utility company might find it desirable to devise solutions that would avoid negative publicity, for instance, it may not want any appearance of flexibility to influence the mediator when formulating any evaluations or settlement proposals.

In view of this strategic need to hide information and flexibility, an attorney may be induced to fashion this constricted form of problem-solving advocacy, one that is based on a narrowly focused adversarial plan and presentation. Such an approach would require a sophisticated and nuanced form of advocacy in order to minimize stifling the creative problem-solving potential of the mediation process. The advocacy would consist of a blended problem-solving-adversarial strategy that could not be implemented casually because of the need to carefully identify and segregate risky information from safe information and then to artfully and persuasively disclose only the safe information. It is a strategy that would need to be actuated proficiently in the heat of the mediation, realizing that too much candor might result in a less favorable mediator assessment and too little candor might result in a less optimal negotiated result.

An attorney might be more confident pursuing a constricted problem-solving approach if the type of carefully designed safeguard in the Centre for Effective Dispute Resolution (CEDR) Mediation Rules[46] was adopted. The rules ensure that all participants approve an evaluation role at the optimum moment in the process as well as limit the type of evaluation. The rules give the mediator conditional recommendation authority:

If the Parties are unable to reach a settlement in the negotiations at the Mediation, and only if all the Parties so request *and the Mediator agrees,* the Mediator will produce for the Parties a *non-binding recommendation on terms of settlement.* This will not attempt to anticipate what a court might order but will set out what the Mediator suggests are appropriate settlement terms in all of the circumstances. (emphasis added)[47]

CEDR's Guidance Notes state that

> The intention of paragraph 12 is that the Mediator will cease to play an entirely facilitative role only if the negotiations in the Mediation are deadlocked. Giving a settlement recommendation may be perceived by a Party as undermining the Mediator's neutrality and for this reason the Mediator may not agree to this course of action.[48]

---

46 The CEDR is a major dispute resolution center based in London. *See* Centre for Effective Dispute Resolution, at http://www.cedr.co.uk (last visited Jan. 20, 2005).

47 *See* CEDR, Model Mediation Procedure and Agreement, sec. 12 (8th ed. Oct. 2002), available at http://www.cedr.co.uk/library/documents/MMPA_8thEdition.pdf (last visited Feb. 28, 2005). For a somewhat less strict approach, *see* The CPR/ CCPIT, *Mediation Procedure for Disputes Submitted to the U.S.-China Business Mediation Center,* para. 7 (2004), available at http://www.cpradr.org/pdfs/Intl_ China_Procedure04.pdf (last visited Jan. 2, 2005); Daini Tokyo Bar Ass'n, Rules of Procedure for Arbitration and Mediation, art. 25 (Advisory Opinion) (June 9, 2000), available at http://www.niben.or.jp/chusai/e_chusai/e_qanda/e_rules.htm (last visited Jan. 2, 2005).

48 *See* CEDR, *supra* note 47, Guidance Notes: The Mediation, 9–12. *See also* CPR Institute for Dispute Resolution, Mediation Procedure for Business Disputes in Europe, R.6 (1996), available at http://www.cpradr.org/formbook/pdfs/1/ medprocedures2.pdf (limiting the recommendation power to after the parties fail to reach a settlement and after parties consent to receiving the mediator's final settlement proposal).

2. Mediators' Techniques

Basic mediation training emphasizes learning and honing a set of widely used techniques, such as promoting communication through questioning and listening methods, dealing with emotional dimensions of disputes, overcoming impediments including money impasses, helping parties assess their BATNAs, and generating creative options, among other valuable skills. An advocate can solicit the mediator to use any of these techniques at propitious moments in the mediation process.

For example, an advocate might suggest to a mediator that one of the obstacles to settlement is a relationship conflict between the parties. Then the attorney might ask the mediator to assist the parties in implementing a suitable intervention. The mediator might help the parties constructively explain to each other why they are upset, assist them in clarifying their perceptions of each other, focus on other ways to improve their communications, and cultivate their problem-solving attitudes.

For a data impasse, an advocate might ask the mediator to help the parties resolve what data are important, negotiate a process for collecting reliable data, or develop common criteria that can be used to assess the data.

When a data conflict is over (the likely judicial outcome) instead of asking the mediator to give a prediction (an evaluation) a request that would likely compromise the problem-solving process[49] the attorney can ask the mediator to help each side further analyze the legal case. The attorney might ask the mediator to guide the participants in calculating the value of each client's total BATNA by using a decision-tree plus methodology.[50] A client's total BATNA can be divided into two distinct components, public and personal, and a value for each component can be separately calculated.

The *public* BATNA covers the portion that the attorney is qualified to calculate. The attorney has the expertise to predict the likely judicial outcome, the probability of success, and the likely legal fees and court costs the client will incur. Attorneys frequently make these predictions in their law practices. Based

49 *See infra* Part D.1 (suggesting that if an attorney knows that a mediator might offer his or her own evaluation of the legal merits, the attorney will likely shift from a problem-solving to an adversarial mode of advocacy in an effort to induce a favorable assessment).

50 A decision tree is a mathematical technique for estimating the value of an uncertain outcome (e.g. winning in court) by multiplying the probability of an event happening times the likely outcome if it happens (e.g., how likely to win in court). The plus component involves asking a particular set of questions that will help a client attach a value to a set of personal costs and benefits. *See* Abramson, *supra* note 2, at app. A.

on discovery, legal research, and experience information that is mostly available to both sides attorneys routinely estimate these key inputs that are used when employing decision trees for calculating the value of the public BATNA. In *Erin Brockovich*, the judge's ruling denying the defendant's motions surely gave both sides further insight into one key input, the probability of success in court. In addition, as Ms. Brockovich gathered more damaging evidence after the failed negotiations, the plaintiffs' probability of success continued to increase.

The other component, the *personal* BATNA, addresses the portion that the client is uniquely qualified to calculate. It is the component idiosyncratic to the client. For example, the client can best assess the added value of going to court to establish a judicial precedent or to be vindicated. The client can best approximate the added cost of possibly destroying a continuing relationship with the other party by going to court. The client is the expert. Only the client can quantify his or her own subjective views of these additional litigation benefits and costs. This will not be easy for the client to do. Instead of inviting the client to use a formal decision tree,[51] the attorney can take the simpler yet still demanding approach of asking him or her some probing questions. This supplement to decision trees is the plus analysis. For example, the attorney might ask the client—a plaintiff, for instance to confront and resolve how much less money he would be willing to accept to settle now and not suffer the risks of waiting out the litigation or suffer the risks of destroying a relationship in the litigation. In other words, how much money would the client be willing to sacrifice for the benefit of settling now?

Factoring in the plaintiffs' personal BATNA weighed heavily in *Erin Brockovich* when the plaintiffs began to abandon their attorneys after the attorneys recommended the use of arbitration. Only after one of their attorneys, Ed Masry, highlighted the personal costs of waiting for any money until trial (the negative personal costs of their BATNA) did the plaintiffs reluctantly accept what they viewed as the faster but less satisfactory forum of arbitration that lacked a jury and right to appeal.

The value of the client's total BATNA is simply the sum of the values of his or her public and personal BATNAs, a critical benchmark when weighing whether to settle or continue litigating.

When encountering an interests conflict, the advocate may ask the mediator to help the parties pinpoint shared or non-conflicting wants, identify

51 *Mediation Representation* does recognize that it is possible to construct a decision-tree that incorporates the probability that the litigation choice could produce personal benefits or costs. It also offers a simple example of how to do it. *See* Abramson, *supra* note 2, at 309 n.8.

objective criteria for overcoming conflicting wants, and search for increase value and productive trades. Court cases typically present conflicting substantive wants because of the nature of the litigation process in which plaintiffs' attorneys draft complaints bursting with demands and defendants' attorneys draft answers rejecting almost everything.

When the interests conflict is the classically distributive one over money, the sort of dispute that may appear unresponsive to the problem-solving methods considered in this article, the advocate might consider an approach that avoids the traditional negotiation dance of offers and counter-offers. The advocate might select a method designed to prevent the error of failing to settle due to not revealing the information that would have shown that the parties were within a settlement range. The advocate might ask the mediator to use a scheme that can provide a safe pathway for parties to move toward their bottom lines. Six such schemes are described and analyzed in *Mediation Representation*. They are: binding final-offer arbitration, a mediator's proposal, hypothetical testing, confidential disclosure of bottom lines, confidential disclosure of settlement numbers, and a safety deposit box.[52]

A structural impasse in an attorney-client conflict can arise due to the inherent structure of the relationship, a bad relationship between the attorney and client, or both. A perceptive advocate might solicit the mediator to help the other side overcome an attorney-client conflict. If it has arisen because the other attorney thinks his or her client should settle while his or her client wants to pursue the litigation, for instance, the mediator can facilitate a discussion of the different views and ways to bridge possible differences.

When an advocate recognizes that parties' personal values may be implicated in the impasse, he or she may enlist the mediator for help by suggesting the nature of the impasse. Then, the mediator might assist the parties in clarifying their core values to find out whether their values are truly at stake or truly in conflict. If in conflict, the mediator may try to help the parties work around their personal values because compromise is usually unacceptable. The mediator can help parties search for an overarching shared goal, ways to avoid defining the problem in terms of a particular value, or solutions that do not compromise the value. Or the mediator might assist parties in reaching an agreement to disagree.

Returning to *Erin Brockovich*, Ms. Brockovich, sensing a relationship conflict due to poor communications in that PG&E did not understand her clients'

---

52 *Mediation Representation* describes and assesses the strengths and drawbacks of each of these six methods. *See* Abramson, *supra* note 2, at ch. 7.2(d)(iii).

interests and perspective, might ask the mediator to help improve the communications between the parties. In making this request, the parties can benefit from the mediator's training in posing questions, active listening, and reframing what is being said.

3. Mediators' Control of the Mediation Stages

A problem-solving process follows somewhat predictable stages from beginning to end. The process stages can include the opening statement of the mediator; gathering information (opening statements of parties and attorneys, discussions in joint sessions and caucuses); identifying issues, interests, and impediments; overcoming impediments; generating options (inventing); assessing and selecting options; and concluding (agreement or impasse).[53] Knowing that a mediator exercises control over these stages gives the advocate other ways to enlist the mediator's assistance. The advocate can request that the mediator use various stages in ways that may advance a client's interests or overcome any impasses.

Frustrated that she can not secure critical data, for instance, Erin Brockovich could plan to raise this data impasse when the mediator reaches the stage of identifying impediments to settlement. Realizing that Pacific Gas & Electric is approaching the dispute as distributive, as if the dispute is only about paying a lump sum of money, Erin Brockovich could plan to invite the mediator to help the parties generate multiple options when the inventing stage is reached.

At the end of the two-credit mediation representation course at Cardozo Law School in January 2004, I asked the five experienced professional mediators who conducted the end-of-the-course mock mediations whether any of them reacted to the student-attorneys suggesting how they could be helpful in resolving the dispute. The mediators uniformly expressed both that they were surprised, because it was so rare, and how helpful it was to hear the student-attorneys' analyses and suggestions.

E. Implement Plan at Key Junctures in the Mediation Process

Finally, these four distinct components of the model had to be woven together. I had to consider how a problem-solving approach that involves the analysis of interests, impediments, and ways to enlist the mediator's assistance can be implemented by an advocate in the mediation process. The advocate needed

53 *See* Abramson, *supra* note 2, at ch. 2.3.

a representation plan that could be used throughout the mediation process.[54] However, simply saying "throughout the process" was too vague, leaving the advocate with little practical guidance. So, I perused the mediation process to isolate discrete representation junctures where an attorney should consciously implement his or her focused plan to advance interests and overcome impediments. I identified six key junctures.[55]

Three of the key junctures arise before the first mediation session, when (1) selecting a mediator, (2) preparing a pre-mediation submission, and (3) participating in a pre-mediation conference. The other three junctures arise in the mediation session when (4) presenting opening statements, (5) participating in joint sessions, and (6) participating in caucuses.

Assuming that Ms. Brockovich thinks her clients should convey personally and vividly that they have multiple interests and that the two sides are likely to reach an impasse over whether the defendant contributed to polluting the town's water (a data conflict), she might prepare a representation plan for four of the junctures as follows. When selecting the mediator (juncture one), she would choose someone who would deeply involve her clients and who would know how to handle complex scientific data. When preparing a pre-mediation submission (juncture two), she would want to explain the substantial data conflict so that the mediator would come prepared to deal with it. During the mediation session, she may want to request a caucus with the mediator (juncture six) to share any information that is especially damaging to the other side and to discuss with the mediator how to productively present this information to the other side in the joint session (juncture five).

VI. CONCLUSION

This article described the five components of the mediation representation formula as well as how the formula was derived. This model of client representa-

---

54 *See* Abramson, *supra* note 2, at ch. 5.16 (Checklist for Preparing Case and Mediation Representation Plan).

55 Junctures are not the same as "stages" in the process, in that stages identify the sequential steps in the mediation process. Nevertheless, junctures and stages can overlap.

There are other junctures in the mediation process. Attorneys should engage in problem-solving representation when (1) initially interviewing his/her client, (2) approaching the other attorney about the use of mediation, (3) preparing the case for mediation, (4) preparing his/her client, and (5) drafting a settlement agreement or developing an exit plan from an unsuccessful mediation. *See* Abramson, *supra* note 2, at 8 n.23.

tion that forms the foundation of *Mediation Representation* offers the advocate an approach to representing clients that takes full advantage of the distinctive opportunities in a problem-solving mediation process.

In *Erin Brockovich*, the plaintiffs did not use this approach, however. They used a traditional adversarial approach and achieved a settlement that was impressive, as least based on one criterion. They negotiated the largest payment ever in a direct-action lawsuit, although after a protracted period of angst and uncertainty for the plaintiffs and their attorneys. The plaintiffs were thrilled with the settlement because the payment vindicated them and seemed to offer them ample financial resources to meet their future needs. It was too late, however, for those who died or were destined to die from exposure to the contaminated water. In addition, whether this was the best solution for both sides will never be known. Parties are unlikely to know whether they achieved optimum resolutions if they approach disputes as if they are only about money.

Imagine how different the representation and the results might have been if Ms. Brockovich had identified both sides' interests and the impediments to agreement, and had enlisted help from a mediator at key junctures, searching for solutions that advanced both sides' interests. By fixating less on the size of the check and more on a tailored solution to meet both sides' interests, the result might have materialized sooner; it might have included lifetime health insurance with no deductibles, clean-up of the polluted water, the option of the utility buying residents' homes, individual lump sum payments for pain and suffering, a public and sincere apology by the utility, and more. The plaintiffs would have received what they needed while the utility might have met the plaintiffs' interests at less cost to it while beginning the process of resuscitating its debilitated reputation. This sort of crafted and possibly quicker result exemplifies the potential of mediation when attorneys advocate as problem-solvers.

This model of client representation ought to be applied by an advocate for the duration of the representation, starting as soon as the first client interview. This problem-solving role should be maintained when contacting the other side about the use of mediation as well as when preparing the case and client for the mediation session. Then, by advocating at every juncture in the ways suggested in this article, an attorney should be able to realize the full potential of a problem-solving process.

CHAPTER 4

Mediation Representation: Table of Contents and Introductory Chapter

(3rd Edition)*

---

* *Mediation Representation: Advocating as a Problem Solver*. Third Edition. Harold I. Abramson, Professor of Law, Touro Law Center, 2013. Wolters Kluwer, Law & Business.

INTRODUCTION
THE FOUNDATION OF THE BOOK

Topics in this chapter include:

1. Different Approach to Representation
2. Framework for Advocacy: The Mediation Representation Triangle
3. Answers to Essential Representation Questions
4. Coverage of the Book
5. Special Features

1. Different Approach to Representation

This text serves one goal: to provide a comprehensive approach to representing clients in mediation.[1] Although much has been written on the mediator's role

1 *See,* e.g., E. Patrick McDermott & Ruth Obar, "'What's Going On' in Mediation: An Empirical Analysis of the Influence of a Mediator's Style on Party Satisfaction and Monetary Benefit," 9 *Harv. Negot. L. Rev.* 75 (2004). (This extensive study concluded that clients do better on the basis of monetary outcome when represented in mediations. The finding is based on a U.S. nationwide study of 645 mediated EEOC cases.)

in facilitating problem-solving negotiations[2] and many mediators have been trained as problem-solvers,[3] surprisingly little attention has been paid to the role of attorneys. Attorneys can and should be zealous advocates in mediation. This text shows you how.

The problem-solving approach and style[4] presented in this book is tailored to realize the full benefits of the mediation process, a dispute resolution option that offers you access to the other side and a neutral third party, the mediator. The mediator's sole purpose is to assist the disputing clients and their attorneys to resolve the dispute.[5]

The mediation process is indisputably different from other dispute resolution processes such as arbitrations and judicial trials, where the third party makes decisions.[6] The positional strategies and techniques that have proven effective in these other forums do not work optimally in mediation. The familiar partisan strategy of presenting your strongest arguments and aggressively attacking the other side's case may be effective when each side is trying to convince a judge to make a favorable decision. But in mediation there is no third-party decision maker, only a third-party helper. The third party may not even be your primary audience.[7] The primary audience may be the other side, who surely is

---

2 *See, e.g.*, Dwight Golann, *Mediating Legal Disputes: Effective Strategies for Lawyers and Mediators* 14–26 (1996); Christopher W. Moore, *The Mediation Process: Practical Strategies for Resolving Conflict* 18–19, 58–59 (3rd ed. 2003); Jay Folberg & Alison Taylor, *Mediation: A Comprehensive Guide to Resolving Conflicts without Litigation* 7–9, 38–72 (1984).

3 Even though I could not find a rigorous study of the approaches taught in mediation training programs, I came across ample anecdotal evidence that suggests that many, if not most, training programs teach mediators the interest-based or problem-solving approach. This approach is taught in many court-connected programs, by many private trainers, and at Harvard Law School (where Professors Fisher, Sander, and Mnookin train negotiators and mediators from around the world). Of course, other approaches are taught and followed, like transformative mediation, although mediators who learn other approaches also tend to be familiar with the widely taught problem-solving approach.

4 "Approach" refers to your underlying stable structure for representation; "style" refers to the mix of techniques that you choose to use and is independent of the approach, as will be examined in Chapter 1, on negotiations.

5 For a more complete definition of mediation as well as an explanation of the process, *see* Chapter 2, "Familiarizing Yourself with Mediation."

6 For readers less familiar with the critical distinctions between mediation and arbitration, remember that arbitration is like a court where a third party adjudicates the dispute and renders a decision, although the parties usually select the third party. Mediation is a negotiation process where the parties are assisted by a third party. The mediator has no decision making power over the parties.

7 For a discussion on selecting your audience, *see* Section 5.10, "Select Your Primary Audience in Mediation."

not neutral, can often be quite hostile, and ultimately must approve any settlement. In this different representational setting, the approach commonly used in adjudicatory proceedings can be less effective if not self-defeating.

You need a different representation approach for this burgeoning and increasingly preferred[8] forum for resolving disputes. Instead of advocating as a zealous adversary, you should advocate as a zealous problem solver, a strategy that has been shown in various studies to be more effective.[9]

The prominent Schneider study of effective negotiation styles concluded:

> Only 9% of those lawyers seen as adversarial were rated as effective by their peers and only 9% of all effective lawyers were described as adversarial. Furthermore, 90% of lawyers perceived as ineffective were also adversarial. In contrast, 91% of lawyers seen as effective took a problem-solving approach to negotiation. More than half of problem-solving lawyers were seen as effective and only 4% of these problem-solving lawyers were seen as ineffective. Contrary to the popular (student) view that problem-solving behavior is risky, it would seem instead that adversarial bargaining

---

8 *See* Marc Galanter, "The Vanishing Trial: An Examination of Trials and Related Matters in Federal and State Courts," 1 *J. Empirical Legal Stud.* 459, 459 (2004) (In this study, the author preliminarily documented that while the number of federal lawsuits filed has increased, the number of trials has decreased, from 11 percent in 1962 to 1.8 percent in 2002, with comparable trends in the state courts. One of the documented replacements for trials is mediation.); John Lande, "Getting the Faith: Why Business Lawyers and Executives Believe in Mediation," 5 *Harv. Negot. L. Rev.* 137 (2000).

9 *See* Roselle L. Wissler, "Representation in Mediation: What We Know from Empirical Research" 37 *Fordham Urb. L.J.* 419, 433–434, 447, 457, 459, 470 (2010) (How clients are represented can affect the way parties assess mediation and the likelihood of settlement, with better preparation and a less adversarial approach increasing the likelihood of settlement. However, the article does point out the need for more empirical research on the "effect of how representation is carried out."); Andrea Kupfer Schneider, "Shattering Negotiation Myths: Empirical Evidence on the Effectiveness of Negotiation Style," 7 *Harv. Negot. L. Rev.* 143, 196 (2002) (In an extensive study of negotiation styles, 75 percent of true problem-solving negotiators were considered effective as compared with less than 50 percent of adversarial bargainers, a percentage that shrunk to 25 percent for adversarial bargainers who were unethical.); Robert H. Mnookin, Scott R. Peppet & Andrew S. Tulumello, *Beyond Winning: Negotiating to Create Value in Deals and Disputes,* 321–322 (2000) (Authors concluded that clients are usually better off when a lawyer adopts a problem-solving approach over an adversarial one.); G. Richard Shell, *Bargaining for Advantage: Negotiation Strategies for Reasonable People,* 12–14 (rev. ed. 2006) (Other studies are cited that suggest that cooperative negotiators are more effective than competitive ones.).

For further discussion of how style impacts negotiation effectiveness, *see* Section 1.1 on distinguishing negotiation style from approach.

represents the greater risk. A lawyer is much more likely to be viewed as effective when engaging in problem-solving behavior.[10]

Within the smaller group of effective adversarial negotiators, Schneider's study further revealed that the more adversarial the style, the less effective the negotiator becomes.[11] In short, her empirical study rejected "the myth of the effective hard bargainer"[12] while endorsing the effectiveness of the problem-solving style.

Even though many sophisticated and experienced litigators realize that mediation calls for a different plan, they still muddle through the mediation sessions guided by familiar strategies that have worked well in other forums, like arbitration and court. Many attorneys even prefer a problem solving–type method to negotiations,[13] although they may be unsure how that method translates into advocacy. Most senior attorneys have never taken a course on dispute resolution. They went to law school either before such courses were offered or before they became popular. And the alternative dispute resolution or mediation courses offered over most of the last 30 years have been largely limited to teaching students to be mediators, not advocates.[14] Although numerous continuing legal education programs are now widely available, they seem to be limited to sharing anecdotal experiences and personal advice.

But new educational opportunities are taking shape. Many more U.S. law schools have begun offering mediation advocacy courses in small classes during the last eight years;[15] law students can participate in mediation representation

---

10 Schneider, *supra* note 9, at 167.

11 *Id. at* 189–190 (When comparing the results of the 1983 Williams study with the results of her study, Schneider learned that adversarial negotiators have become more adversarial and far less effective.).

12 *Id. at* 196.

13 *See* Milton Heumann & Jonathon M. Hyman, "Negotiation Methods and Litigation Settlement Methods in New Jersey: 'You Can't Always Get What You Want'," *12 Ohio St. J. on Disp. Resol.* 253, 309 (1997) ("While 61% of the lawyers would like to see more problem-solving negotiation methods, about 71% of negotiations are carried out with positional methods instead.").

14 *See,* e.g., Suzanne J. Schmitz, "What Should We Teach in ADR Courses? Concepts and Skills for Lawyers Representing Clients in Mediation," 6 *Harv. Negot. L. Rev.* 189, 189 (2001).

15 Although no survey has been compiled, when the first edition of this text was published in 2004, only a handful of law schools were known to offer a separate course on mediation advocacy. As of 2009, more than 35 law schools offered the course based on the adoptions of the first edition, and there are other courses using other books, but it is unclear how many. These courses tend to be small classes of around 24 or less. Furthermore, separate courses

competitions, which are flourishing in the United States and globally;[16] and lawyers can enroll in one of a scattering of intensive performance-based training programs.[17] Unfortunately, practicing lawyers generally do not seem convinced of the need for formal training until they participate in a program and see firsthand what they do not know and what would be helpful to learn, as I have observed repeatedly. These training programs have not yet reached the maturity of trial practice trainings that are almost prerequisites for entering the courtroom. The value of trial practice training took years to be fully appreciated and embraced. Mediation advocacy training programs seem to be following a similarly measured path toward wide use.

In the absence of formal trainings, advocates learn on the job. It is rare that a practicing attorney will show up in U.S. mediations without some mediation experience, and those without any are likely to be embarrassed to say so. As many experienced mediators as well as advocates report, mediation practices may be reaching a point of "routine" where the process no longer feels novel and instead has become predictably scripted. I have heard full-time mediators report that they strive to keep the process fresh in order to keep the participants energized, engaged, and creative.

Even though advocates have gained considerable experience, and practices are solidifying in the United States, the skills of many attorneys seem strikingly unsophisticated, as I have heard from numerous mediators and observed in trainings. Practices do not routinely incorporate a nuanced understanding of how to select a suitable mediator, take full advantage of premediation contacts with the mediator or the other side, present effective opening statements, and

---

on mediation and ADR include segments on mediation representation, as reflected in the addition of materials to recently published mediation and ADR textbooks. Live mediation advocacy clinics also are now being offered by a number of law schools according to a 2013 survey by Alyson Carrel. *See* http://www.law.missour-i.edu/drle/adr_programs.html.

16 For a brief description of the competitions sponsored by the American Bar Association and the International Chamber of Commerce in Paris, *see* Appendix J, "Mediation Representation Competitions Judging Criteria." Also, in 2008, a national competition was launched for Canadian law schools. Since then, it has expanded to become an international competition.

17 For example, NITA launched a national mediation advocacy training program that I helped design after conducting a pilot training in 2006 for them. The ABA Section on Dispute Resolution conducts an Advanced Mediation and Advocacy Skills Training Institute, which is held each year in a different region of the United States. And the CPR International Institute for Conflict Prevention and Resolution occasionally offers a mediation and mediation advocacy training program. Some law schools, like Pepperdine, offer intensive courses to practitioners. I also have conducted training programs for law firms, courts, and bar associations locally and abroad.

optimally utilize the choice between joint sessions and caucuses. Training in mediation advocacy is needed, including training that accounts for the considerable practical experience of attorneys.

This text offers a comprehensive approach for improving your advocacy skills, an approach that applies from your first client phone call until the mediation process is concluded. During the course of your representation, you have numerous strategic choices to make, choices that are highlighted and analyzed in each chapter.

This text adopts a broad definition of problem solving that includes resolving disputes that are primarily about money—the classic distributive conflict. I feel a need to emphatically stress that it includes resolving distributive disputes for those readers who are inclined to dismiss problem solving for cases that are all about money—a point that will be more fully addressed in this section and in Chapter 1, on negotiations.

As a problem solver[18] who is creative, you do more than try to settle the dispute. You try to locate the best possible resolution for your client. You search for solutions that go beyond the traditional ones based on rights, obligations, and precedent. Rather than pressing for win-lose outcomes, you search for solutions that might benefit both sides[19] and therefore might be acceptable

18 *See,* e.g., Thomas D. Barton, "Conceiving the Lawyer as Creative Problem Solver: Introduction," 34 *Cal. W. L. Rev.* 267 (1998); Thomas D. Barton, "Creative Problem Solving: Purpose, Meaning, and Values," 34 *Cal. W. L. Rev.* 273 (1998); Paul Brest & Linda Hamilton Krieger, "Lawyers as Problem Solvers," 72 *Temp. L. Rev.* 811 (1999); Seamus Dunn, "Case Study: The Northern Ireland Experience: Possibilities for Cross- Fertilization Learning," 19 *CPR Inst. for Disp. Resol.* 153 (2001); Carrie Menkel-Meadow, "Aha? Is Creativity Possible in Legal Problem Solving and Teachable in Legal Education?," 6 *Harv. Negot. L. Rev.* 97 (2001); Carrie J. Menkel-Meadow, "When Winning Isn't Everything: The Lawyer as Problem Solver," 28 *Hofstra L. Rev.* 905 (2000); Carrie Menkel-Meadow, "The Lawyer as Problem Solver and Third-Party Neutral: Creativity and Non-Partisanship in Lawyering," 72 *Temp. L. Rev.* 785 (1999); Carrie Menkel- Meadow, "Toward Another View of Legal Negotiation: The Structure of Problem Solving," 31 *UCLA L. Rev.* 754 (1984); Linda Morton, "Teaching Creative Problem Solving: A Paradigmatic Approach," 34 *Cal. W. L. Rev.* 375 (1998); Janet Reno, "Lawyers as Problem-Solvers: Keynote Address to the AALS," 49 *J. Legal Educ.* 5 (1999); *see also Center for Creative Problem Solving,* Cal. W. Sch. L., http://www.cwsl.edu/main/default.asp?nav¼creative_problem_solving.asp&body¼creative_problem_solving/home.asp.

19 Many lawyers consider the idea that both sides can secure benefits as naive. However, the notion that both sides might be able to gain something in negotiations reflects an optimistic attitude that can open the mind to creative possibilities. The likelihood of finding such gains in negotiations is greater than in court. In negotiations, for instance, even the defendant who agrees to pay considerable damages may gain other benefits, such as no publicity, no precedent, and a continuing business relationship—benefits that are usually unavailable in court.

for settlement. You develop a collaborative relationship with the other side and the mediator, and participate throughout the process in a way that may produce solutions that are inventive as well as enduring. Inventive solutions may be uncovered because you advocate your client's interests instead of legal positions,[20] listen attentively and proactively,[21] use sophisticated techniques for overcoming impediments, create multiple options, and evaluate and package those options to meet interests of both sides. You avoid derailing the search when resolving any distributive issues by applying claiming techniques suitable for problem solving.[22] Enduring solutions, whether inventive or not, are likely because both sides work together to fashion tailored solutions that each side fully understands, can live with, and knows how to implement.

In this pitch for a problem-solving approach and style, I do not blindly claim that it is the only one that results in settlements. Attorneys frequently cite success stories, even spectacular ones, when they use hard positional tactics or a hybrid of switching between adversarial and problem-solving strategies.[23] I do claim, however, that the problem-solving method is more likely to produce consistently better results for your clients.

For problem-solving advocacy to be effective in practice, you should engage proactively in problem-solving strategies at every stage of representation. The sort of practical initiatives that are illustrated throughout this text should be used from the moment you interview your client and followed when calling the other attorney about trying out mediation, selecting the mediator, participating in premediation conferences, preparing any premediation submissions, presenting opening statements, and participating in joint sessions and caucuses.

You should avoid the hybrid method despite the claims of supporters that it is the best one due to its flexibility. You should not let the appeal of flexibility mask the inconsistency it promotes. Shifting between hard positional strategies and creative problem-solving ones during the course of mediation can

---

I refer to solutions that can benefit both sides in an effort to avoid using the more familiar and overused "win-win" jargon. That jargon carries baggage that can blind people to an underlying valuable point that still retains considerable vitality. The win-win attitude can be usefully contrasted with the win-lose attitude to capture a fundamental difference between the problem-solving and adversarial approaches.

20 For a full discussion of how to identify client's interests as opposed to positions, *see* Section 3.2(a).

21 *See* Appendix F, on cultivating information.

22 *See* Sections 1.2 and 1.3, on claiming techniques.

23 In the hybrid approach, attorneys switch between the two distinct approaches, depending on how the mediation is unfolding.

undercut the problem-solving method. For instance, a hard positional move such as a take-or-leave it bluff can thwart integrative searching moves of sharing information to uncover fresh options for settlement.

You should be a persistent problem solver. It is relatively easy to engage in simple problem-solving moves such as responding to a demand with the question "why?" in order to bring to the surface the other party's interests. But it is much more difficult to stick to this method throughout the mediation process when faced with an adversarial opponent. Trust the problem-solving approach and style. When the other side engages in adversarial tactics or tricks—a frequent occurrence in practice—you should react with responses that might convert the other side into a problem solver.[24]

You should even strive to create a problem-solving process when your mediator does not.[25] Your mediator may fail to follow this method (despite professing to) because he lacks the depth of experience or training to tenaciously maintain a consistent approach throughout the mediation process. Or your mediator may candidly disclose his practice of switching methods based on the needs of the parties—a philosophy that I have already suggested undercuts the problem-solving approach and style. Or your mediator may follow a recognized alternative method like an evaluative, transformative, or wisely directive one.[26] This book provides a framework for responding to different practices of mediators.

Finally, I should respond directly to the skeptics who think that problem solving does not work for most legal cases because they are primarily about money. Plaintiffs want only money, and defendants want only to pay the least amount possible. They see no potential to uncover creative solutions. For the skeptics, I offer a four-part response.

First, the endless debate about whether or not legal disputes are primarily about money is distracting. Whether a dispute is largely about money varies from case to case, as experience and studies have demonstrated.[27]

---

24 *See* infra Section 1.7, "Converting the Positional Negotiator into a Problem Solver."

25 You can reduce these risks by selecting the right mediator. *See infra* Sections 4.2–5.

26 *See infra* Section 5.3(b).

27 *See* Tamara Relis, "'It's Not About the Money!' A Theory on Misconceptions of Plaintiffs' Litigation Aims," 68 *U. Pitt. L. Rev.* 701 (2007). In an empirical study of medical malpractice cases, the author uncovered a stark discrepancy between what attorneys for plaintiffs and defendants think clients want—money—and what clients in fact want—such extra-legal remedies as the defendant's admitting fault, prevention of recurrences, explanations, and apology. *Id. at* 701–702. She concluded that plaintiffs' extra-legal aims "remained invisible to virtually all lawyers." *Id. at* 702. For Professor Relis's full study, *see* Tamara Relis, *Perceptions*

Second, you have little chance of discovering whether your client's dispute is about more than money if you approach the dispute as if it is only about money. Such a preconceived view backed by a narrowly focused positional strategy will likely blind you to other parties' needs and inventive solutions. You are more likely to discover creative solutions if you approach the dispute with an open mind.

Third, if the dispute or any remaining issues at the end of the day turn out to be predominantly about money, then at least you followed a representation approach that may have created a hospitable environment for dealing with the moneyed issues. A hospitable environment can be beneficial even when there is no expectation of a continuing relationship between the disputing parties.

Fourth, and most important, the problem-solving approach and style provide a framework for resolving moneyed issues. These types of disputes can sometimes be resolved by using the familiar problem-solving claiming techniques of trading benefits and applying objective standards. The framework also includes using the traditional positional dance, although a version suitable for a problem-solving process that relies on justifications and conventional tactics while avoiding tricks.[28]

These points were illustrated in a case that I mediated where the parties arrived with only monetary claims on the table, a long history of frustrating and failed negotiations, and a case that was ready for trial. After more than three hours of structuring and applying a problem-solving approach and style to the mediation, the parties and attorneys discovered that the parties had much in common as founders of successful family businesses, that the fraudulent claims arose due to a rogue employee, and that each party had unmet, nonmonetary needs. The plaintiff was upset that any reputable business person would

---

in Litigation and Mediation: Lawyers, Defendants, Plaintiffs, and Gendered Parties, ch. 2 (2009). *See also* Dwight Golann, "Is Legal Mediation a Process of Repair—or Separation? An Empirical Study, and Its Implications," 7 *Harv. Negot. L. Rev.* 301, 334 (2002) (In one of the few empirical studies on the subject, the author found that "almost two-thirds of all [mediated] settlements ... were integrative in nature. ... The results suggest that both mediators and advocates should consider making a search for integrative outcomes an important aspect of their mediation strategy.").

At least one category of disputes is usually primarily about money. The classic personal injury dispute between strangers who will never deal with each other again can be only about money and is therefore not open to creative resolutions other than a tailored payment scheme. But, even in these disputes, one side may occasionally want something more than money, such as vindication or fair treatment.

28 *See infra* Section 1.3, "Problem-Solving Approach: Key Features."

perpetrate such a fraud, and the defendant was losing business due to the claims in the litigation. With the benefit of an improved understanding of each side's perspective and the facts, they proceeded to negotiate a written apology by the defendant and a written introduction to future buyers by the plaintiff. In this collaborative environment, they then confronted the remaining monetary issue and settled it in less than a minute! They quickly and civilly exchanged a few offers and counteroffers. The parties were apparently already on the same page for settling the money claim, but could not do so until some nonmonetary needs were met.

Skeptics also frequently inquire whether this method will work if the other side has not read this book. The answer is yes, it can, as will be illustrated in each chapter. And I will go one step further. Even if the other side has read this book or any other one on problem solving and has firmly rejected the method, the representation framework still offers guidance on how to proceed. This book will show you how to represent your client in the face of an aggressive and well-honed, adversarial other side. You will learn settlement strategies for trying to convert the other side into a problem solver and coaxing the mediator to help in the conversion. In case nothing works in the mediation, you also will learn to diagnose the reasons for the impasse as well as identify alternatives to the mediation process that might work.[29]

In short, the problem-solving approach and style provide a complete and effective framework for representation that offers a pathway through the mediation process. Within the parameters of this framework, you have many choices to consider and assess for your case—choices that are highlighted throughout the text. For the experienced advocate, you also have the opportunity to reflect on and evaluate your current choices while expanding the number of options for you to choose from. By adhering to the overall method in this text, you will be prepared to thoughtfully and effectively deal with the myriad unanticipated challenges that inevitably arise as the mediation unfolds.

CRITICAL CHOICES

Problem-Solving Choices

Reflect on choices and select ones that are likely to be effective for your case.

---

29 *See infra* Chapter 8, "Alternatives to Mediation."

2. Framework for Advocacy: The Mediation Representation Triangle

The approach in this book offers mediation advocates an alternative to relying on ad hoc, intuitive strategies as the mediation process unfolds. It offers a comprehensive and coherent framework that is configured into a Mediation Representation Triangle.

The triangle provides a fitting metaphor because of the inherent interdependence of the three sides. If one side is missing or weak, the entire structure collapses. When each side is strong, the three-sided structure provides a sturdy and reliable framework.

The Mediation Representation Triangle

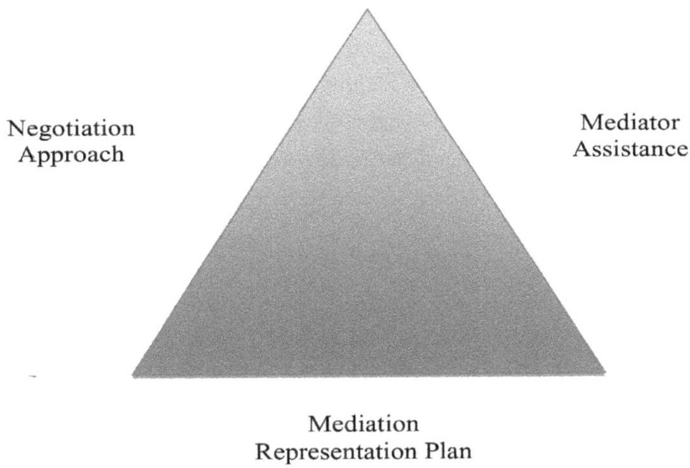

The Mediation Representation Triangle links three key features for effective representation: You need to effectively negotiate, enlist mediator assistance, and plan your representation. These three features form the three sides to a triangle and are interdependent. If you negotiate poorly, enlist the mediator ineffectually, or develop a weak representation plan, you will fashion a wobbly framework for mediation advocacy. If you do all three well, you will erect a sturdy one. You can remember these three features by remembering that you need to "negotiate with a MAP" (negotiate with mediator assistance and a Plan).

The first side of this structure focuses on your primary role as a *negotiator*. Mediation is simply the continuation of the negotiation with the assistance of a third party, as is so often remarked. So first and foremost, you need to give attention to how to negotiate effectively in the mediation. Do you want to primarily problem-solve or primarily be positional? The problem-solving negotiation method is developed in this book, and it is compared and contrasted with the more familiar positional method, a strategy popular among many U.S. trial lawyers as well as parties from bargaining cultures. The differences between the methods are reflected in the different beginnings, strategies, and likely outcomes.[30] Your choice is a vital one when you are representing clients in mediation.

The second side of this structure focuses on the second central feature of mediation advocacy—enlisting *mediator assistance.* You are in mediation. So what can the mediator contribute to resolving the dispute? As an advocate, you need a nuanced understanding of what mediators are trained to do and what they actually do in practice. Your understanding will profoundly affect how you represent your client—a point that will be accentuated throughout the book. As the mediation unfolds, you should enlist the mediator to contribute what you think would be most helpful in resolving your client's dispute.[31]

The third side forms the base for the triangle—your *mediation representation plan.* As you formulate your negotiation approach and find ways to enlist help from the mediator, you need to develop a consistent and complete plan for effective representation.[32]

Planning Triangle: Three-*I* Triangle

Your plan should further three goals, which can be configured into a planning triangle. You should advance your client's interests, overcome any impediments, and share necessary information while minimizing the risk of exploitation. These three interdependent *I*'s make up the three sides of another

30 *See infra* Chapter 1, "Negotiating in Mediations."

31 *See* Sections 2.3–8, on what mediators can contribute, and Sections 5.3–5, on the impact of the mediator's contributions on your representation.

32 *See infra* Chapter 5, "Preparing Your Case for Mediation."

triangle. These three I's shape every detail of your plan. If your plan fails to further any of these three goals, you will form a weak triangle and plan. If your plan advances all three goals intelligently, you will fashion a sturdy one to guide your representation.

The first *I*, *interests* (first side of triangle), encapsulates the primary goal of any plan—to meet your client's interests. Viewing a dispute through the lens of your client's interests can dramatically transform your view of the dispute. Because the powerful concept of interests is not always accurately understood, it will be fully developed and applied repeatedly in this book.[33] Any plan should effectively advocate your client's interests;[34] that is your bottom line.

The second *I*, *impediments* (second side), considers the reason that you are in mediation. You are likely to be in mediation because an impediment is blocking a negotiated settlement. Any plan should focus on how to negotiate with the assistance of the mediator to identify and overcome any impediments.[35]

The third *I*, *information* (base of triangle), covers what information to gather, disclose, and withhold. Sharing information can help participants understand each other's interests and the impediments as well as help uncover better solutions. But sharing poses a risk of exploitation. When the other side knows that something is important to you, for instance, they may try to extract a high price for giving you what you want. You need to resolve this notorious tension when considering what to share[36] and elicit from the other side.

Any plan should be implemented at each of six key chronological junctures in the mediation process.[37] You should advance your client's interests, overcome

---

33 *See infra* Section 3.2(a).

34 This goal of meeting interests is different from the goals in what has become known as "transformative mediation," in which mediators focus on "empowerment" of parties and parties' "recognition" of each other. *See generally* Robert A. Baruch Bush & Joseph P. Folger, *The Promise of Mediation: Responding to Conflict Through Empowerment and Recognition* (1994).

35 *See infra* Sections 3.2(b), 5.6(a).

36 *See infra* Sections 1.3(b), 5.6(a).

37 *See infra* Section 5.6(b). The term junctures is used to identify points in the process of representation when you should focus on staying in a problem-solving mode. Junctures are not the same as stages in that stages identify the sequential steps in the mediation process. Junctures and stages, however, do overlap.

Three of the six key junctures arise before the first mediation session: (1) selecting a mediator, (2) preparing premediation submissions, and (3) participating in a premediation conference. The other three junctures arise in the mediation session: (4) presenting opening statements, (5) participating in joint sessions, and (6) participating in caucuses.

The mediation representation framework also applies during other junctures in mediation representation. You should engage in problem solving to advance interests and overcome impediments, and share and gather information consistently at each juncture. You want to take thoughtful advantage of the opportunities offered at each one. The six key junctures that are fully developed in the book are as follows.

Juncture 1: Selecting a Mediator[38]

You first should assess what mediator training, orientations, and experiences would help you resolve the dispute, given the interests you want to advance and the impediments that you need to overcome. And then you should select a mediator suitable for your dispute, realizing that how the mediator approaches the mediation will shape how you represent your client during each of the remaining five junctures.

Junctures 2 and 3: Premediation Conference and Submission[39]

At each of these premediation opportunities, you want to consider how the mediator might be helpful and what information you can safely share with the other side or the mediator. Premediation conferences are usually held between the attorneys and the mediator. Premediation submissions are materials that you send to the mediator, and sometimes to the other side, before the mediation session.

Juncture 4: Opening Statements[40]

When preparing opening statements, you want to consider how to productively commence the mediation session. You have the opportunity to set the groundwork for meeting interests and overcoming impediments by revealing how you plan to negotiate and how the mediator might help.

Junctures 5 and 6: Joint Sessions and Caucuses[41]

As you plan for the mediation session, you should consider the critical choice between negotiating in a joint session with everybody in the room or in a

---

impediments in a way that takes advantage of the availability of a mediator when (1) initially interviewing your client, (2) approaching the other attorney about the use of mediation, (3) preparing your client, and (4) drafting a settlement agreement or developing an exit plan from an unsuccessful mediation.

38 *See infra* Chapter 3.

39 *See infra* Sections 5.15, 7.1.

40 *See infra* Section 5.12.

41 *See infra* Sections 2.6, 5.4, 7.2(d).

caucus with just your client and the mediator. This choice will be influenced by how best to meet your client's interests and overcome impediments, including how you think the mediator can contribute and whether you want to negotiate directly with the other side or indirectly through the mediator.

In short, to be an effective mediation advocate, you need to effectively negotiate, know how to enlist *mediator assistance,* and pull it all together in the form of a *plan* that advances your client's *interests* and overcomes any *impediments* while intelligently sharing *information* at each of the six key junctures. The first three italicized concepts—*negotiate, mediator assistance,* and *plan*—constitute the Mediation Representation Triangle; the other four italicized concepts—interests, impediments, information, and junctures—cover the key features of your representation plan. Together, they provide the foundation for this book. Be sure to focus on these seven concepts throughout this book as you proceed to Negotiate with a MAP.

3. Answers to Essential Representation Questions

The mediation representation framework in this book offers answers to the numerous and persistent strategic questions that inevitably arise when you represent clients in mediations. The answers to the following essential questions are proffered throughout the book.

- What types of cases are suitable for mediation?
- How do you approach the other attorney about using mediation without looking weak or desperate?
- What should you include in an agreement to mediate?
- What credentials and experience should you look for when selecting a mediator?
- What do you want to accomplish in a premediation conference? What information do you need to prepare for the mediation session? What should you include in a premediation submission?
- How do you prepare a mediation representation plan?
- How do you prepare your client for the mediation session?
- How do you use the mediation process to overcome any impasses and advance your client's interests?
- What information should you share with the mediator or the other side? How can you enlist the mediator to help you resolve your client's dispute?

- How do you evaluate your client's legal case using a decision tree analysis?
- How can you convert an adversarial adversary into a problem-solving one and coax your mediator?
- How do you shape creative and enduring resolutions? How do you deal with issues that are only about money? How do you learn the other side's bottom line?
- How do you conclude a mediation?

4. Coverage of the Book

This book covers negotiation techniques, the mediation process, your role at each stage of your representation, and alternative processes to mediation if the mediation is not fully successful. This third edition more fully examines how to resolve the hard, distributive aspects of disputes and expands on techniques for moving the mediation forward. It takes a fresh look at confidentiality needs in mediations and expands coverage of legal issues and judicial decisions that relate to the mediation process, as well as ethical issues that can arise during the course of your representation. It also considers various psychological influences on the bargaining process, including how these influences affect the way participants evaluate information.

Chapter 1 covers the foundational subject of how to negotiate in mediations. Realizing that mediation is simply a continuation of the negotiation process, you need to give attention to the various choices for negotiating. The same skills for preparing and participating in a negotiation apply to mediation. If you use problem-solving strategies in negotiations, you will engage in similar strategies when representing clients throughout the mediation process. The third edition places negotiations into a framework of creating and claiming, distinguishes between choosing the suitable approach and suitable style for your dispute, and further compares the narrow and familiar positional approach with an expansive view of the problem-solving approach.

If you do not already have a strong foundation in the two primary methods for negotiating, you should read this chapter with care because the methods' main points are built upon and applied throughout the text.

Chapter 2 explores the mediation process from the vantage point of an advocate. You should understand how the mediation process works, just as you need to understand how any other forum works in which you represent clients. When representing clients in court, for instance, you should know the procedures and norms of settlement conferences, court appearances, and judicial decision making. When representing a client in mediation, you should know its different stages, differences between joint sessions and caucuses, and the various approaches and techniques that mediators use to help parties resolve disputes.

Chapters 3 to 7 cover the distinctive knowledge and skills that you should possess to effectively perform four specific roles in mediation representation.

Chapter 3 covers advising your clients about the mediation option.

Chapter 4 covers negotiating an agreement to mediate with other attorneys and how to select a suitable mediator, including interviewing candidates and their references.

Chapters 5 and 6 cover preparing your case and client for the mediation session. The material focuses on how to prepare a mediation representation plan that comports with the Mediation Representation Triangle. The third edition substantially expands the coverage of confidentiality, ethics, psychological influences, and judicial decisions that shape the mediation process. It also further examines the choice to negotiate in joint sessions or through a mediator in caucuses.

Chapter 7 covers premediation conferences, the mediation session, and the postsession. The third edition expands the sections on generating movement after opening statements, proactively enlisting the mediator, and navigating legal issues when drafting agreements.

Chapter 8 prepares you for the possibility that the mediation may not result in settling all the issues. It describes a number of needs that may not be met in mediation and includes an analysis of alternative process solutions along with some guidelines on how to select the right process.

The book also includes more than 15 appendixes covering decision trees, sample agreements, attentive and proactive listening, selective mediation rules, cultural differences, and more. The book also provides access to 40 online video clips that illustrate the mediation process, exhibit particular mediator and advocacy techniques, and reenact litigated legal disputes arising out of the mediation process.

Representation in Any Culture or Country

Finally, this text provides a framework that is culturally neutral so that it should be helpful to you in representing clients in mediations between parties from different countries or between parties with different cultural upbringings within the same country.[42]

In addition, the text examines how the different upbringings of parties in a dispute can produce distinctively different interests, impasses, and communication styles that you may need to recognize and bridge. For example, the key concept of interests is examined along with how interests can vary culturally—such as in Japan, where parties can have a deep interest in apology. That awareness can help you recognize uniquely local interests that you ought to test and possibly meet. The text also includes a method for bridging any differences.

Distinctive cultural practices are highlighted throughout the text and are noted alongside U.S. practices rather than being segregated in a separate chapter, although you should find useful Appendix G-1, "Glossary of Cultural Dimensions." It informs the cultural references in the various chapters. However, the book does not provide you with an extensive catalogue of country-specific and comparative practices. There are excellent books that already do that.[43]

How to address cultural differences in a representation plan is illustrated in Section 5.20.

5. Special Features of the Text

Special features have been incorporated in the text to facilitate your use.

1. *Critical Choices boxes.*[44] You will see Critical Choices boxes inserted throughout the text. Each box signals a subject or moment in representation that is especially vital or particularly vexing and poses choices for you to consider when representing clients in mediation. At each Critical Choices box, you should pause to give additional attention to the highlighted question or topic. The inclusion of the boxes recognizes that even among those who subscribe to a problem-solving approach, there are challenging choices to weigh and make; the best answer may depend on the needs of the particular dispute and your judgment on how best to meet those needs.

---

42 *See* Harold Abramson, "Mediation Representation: Representing Clients Anywhere," *in* 2 *ADR in Business.* ch. 14 (Arnold Ingen-Housz ed., 2011) (In this chapter, I justify the claim that this representation framework works in any culture or country.).

43 *See, e.g., Arbitration and Mediation in the Southern Mediterranean Countries* (Giuseppe De Palo & Mary B. Trevor eds., 2007); *Global Trends in Mediation* (Nadja Alexander ed., 2nd ed. 2006) (comparative examination of 14 jurisdictions).

44 This is a change from the first two editions, where these boxes were labeled "Critical Juncture." I changed the label to focus on choices in order to more precisely describe the moment for the advocate—a moment of weighing and making choices.

For the choices highlighted in each of the boxes, I suggest advantages and disadvantages in the body of the text. And you are not left rudderless: I also usually make recommendations, although they are contingent on the particular details of the dispute. By making choices transparent, you can independently determine whether to adopt or adapt the recommendations in your particular case.

2. *Key concepts.* Each key concept is developed primarily in one or more sections in the text, and those sections are referenced in footnotes whenever the key concept is applied in other sections. With the text organized in this way, key concepts that are used repeatedly in the text are presented and then further developed as you progress through the different stages of client representation. In order to reduce repetition, each time a key concept becomes relevant, cross-referencing footnotes are provided. If you skipped the section where the concept was initially presented or if you need to review the concept, be sure to look for the appropriate cross-reference in the footnotes.

For example, while the need to identify your client's interests will arise many times throughout the book, the definition of interests and how to identify them are primarily discussed in Section 3.2(a), on interviewing your client about interests. Whenever the subject of interests is mentioned elsewhere in the book, the section of the book where it is primarily covered is cross-referenced in a footnote.

3. *Common dispute resolution vocabulary.* A common dispute resolution vocabulary needs to be established for this text in the face of the dearth of consensus in the dispute resolution field. Throughout the research literature, you see different labels associated with facially similar ideas,[45] which can be confusing. Negotiations can be called problem-solving, interest-based, principled, integrative, joint gain, or collaborative, for instance. Although it might be an interesting intellectual project to identify precise differences and similarities in the use of these comparable terms, it will not be done here. Key vocabulary will be defined and used consistently throughout the text. Be sure to give attention to the following terms, which are initially defined in Chapters 1 and 2 and then used throughout the text:

Problem-solving versus positional negotiations
Negotiation approach versus negotiation style (including music) Positional negotiation approach versus adversarial negotiation style Creating--claiming strategies

45 Schneider, *supra* note 9, *at* 150–152.

Interests
Attentive and proactive listening
Personal and public
BATNAs
Orientations of mediators

4. *Checklists.* At the end of most of the chapters, you will find handy checklists. Each checklist is designed to be copied and used as a portable reference tool to help you keep track of what you have done and what needs to be done for the covered subjects.

5. *Questions and online videos.* For this third edition, questions and exercises have been added to the chapter text at the end of related sections. Online videos also have been added to illustrate subjects in Chapters 1, 2, 5, and 7. You will see an icon in the right hand column to highlight the video for you to watch in connection with the question(s). The videos are from a variety of sources in order to give the reader diverse exposure to practices. These videos are available due to the generosity of the owners as acknowledged in the preface. However, because of the different sources and ages of the videos, the quality of the pictures can vary.

CHAPTER 5

Are Legal Disputes Just about Money? Answers from Mediators on the Front Line

Hal Abramson, Bennett Picker, Bill Marsh, Birgit Sambeth Glasner, and Jerry Weiss*

Alternatives 35, 9 October 2017

I. INTRODUCTION BY HAL ABRAMSON

Are most disputes in mediation just about money? That's an old and familiar question that many lawyers still seem to reply to with an emphatic "yes." Mediated cases are frequently viewed as a clash of binary claims, subject only to a sorting out of financial winners and losers. This popular vision was challenged by an American Bar Association panel of experienced commercial mediators. They explored the opportunities that they have seen for breaking out of this confining legal mold. Their years of practice have taught them that many disputes are not just about money even when money is the presenting issue.

When preparing the first edition in 2004 of my book, *Mediation Representation*, I gave attention to this persistent question when I framed a key theme as: "You have little chance of discovering whether a dispute is only about money if you approach the dispute as if it is only about money." Harold Abramson, *Mediation Representation: Advocating as a Problem-Solver*, 7 (Aspen, 3rd edition, 2013).

Whenever I lecture on the subject, I routinely get pushback from attorneys and mediators who claim that most disputes are about money. Even though the book offers multiple responses, another way to reply is to ask experienced, highly regarded commercial mediators.

---

* *See* the authors' credits in the box on page 133. A different version of this article by the authors will appear in the Cardozo Journal of Conflict Resolution.

This article is based on a panel discussion program at the annual ABA Conference on Dispute Resolution, titled "Legal Mediations Are Not Only about Money: Mediators and Advocates as Problem Solvers" (NYC; April 08, 2016). I put together the panel in my capacity as the International Academy of Mediator's Scholar-in-Residence. The contributors are all IAM Distinguished Fellows. See www.iamed.org. The panelists were co-authors Bennett Picker, of Philadelphia; Birgit Sambeth Glasner, of Geneva, and Jerry Weiss, of Cleveland. London-based Bill Marsh was asked to contribute to this article after publishing a critique of binary processes. The article offers insights from four mediators on the front line of practice—two from the United States and two from Europe. They are not part-time mediators with safe day jobs. Mediating is their day job.

Collectively, they present a mindset for mediating that affords opportunities for uncovering needs and options that go beyond the financial demands presented by the matter. Drawing on their years of experience, each contributor describes and illustrates how mediators can and must dig beneath the presenting claims to succeed in really resolving a dispute.

Each contribution was written independently, and yet the contributions offer remarkably similar critiques and observations although each person brings to bear his or her distinctive perspective.

As a group, they are sharply critical of binary processes like courts for resolving disputes. They see binary processes as ones that mask the complexity of disputes and nuanced solutions.

The mediators also emphasize the importance of preparing. They strongly endorse taking risks, being courageous, and probing deeply for the participants' interests. Each of them also identifies several of his or her favored techniques for moving beyond the mere financial exchange.

Bill Marsh focuses on the limitations and consequences of a binary process and the need to shape a better process that deals with the complexities of disputes.

Jerry Weiss zeroed in at the program on the need to do more than to get the job done. Mediators, he noted, should find the human beings that drive conflict and their resolution.

Birgit Sambeth Glasner gave attention to the need for courage and creativity to push participants out of their comfort zone to uncover more than presenting monetary issues.

Ben Picker saw mediation as about more than resolving a money dispute—it is an opportunity. He emphasized that mediators also should identify and overcome various non-monetary barriers to resolutions.

And I had the honor to moderate the program and incorporate their contributions into this article. Here are their insights.

* * *

BILL MARSH

The desire for the clarity and decisiveness that binary processes can produce can make them appealing. But, precisely because binary processes offer a win/lose, yes/no outcome—just like the courts—we need to be acutely conscious of their limitations and consequences.

The first is the swift descent into simplicity and caricature. Conflicts engender a descent into simplicity and caricature, and binary processes exacerbate that.

When I mediate, I am often struck by how those involved appear to have reduced the sheer complexity of the situation to a series of simple—and apparently certain—propositions.

Nowhere is this truer than with the history of events, with stories. However complex, multi-layered and nuanced they may have been at the time; however much "six of one and half a dozen of the other," and however much there may in fact be some shared accountability for what went on, both the conflict itself and the processes by which we address it—usually violence or litigation—often drive parties toward simplicity and caricature. By the way, if you doubt this, just look at the process of political elections!

Life is complex. Conflicts even more so. Do we not want conflict resolution processes that can handle complexity? Perhaps one of the great contributions mediators can make is to re-complexify—if that word really even exists—to re-introduce nuance.

The second downside of binary processes is that they make no space for a range of options. By definition, only two outcomes are possible. Win or lose. Sink or swim. Remain or leave. Being close (e.g., 48.1% to 51.9% in the Brexit referendum) is not enough. I realize that decisions need to be made. But they can also be deeply damaging.

A few years ago, it was my great privilege to mediate the long-running conflict in the Church of England about whether women could become bishops. (They couldn't then, they can now). Like many institutions, the Church of England has a governance system which is quite "parliamentary" in style. Because of that, the preceding decades had been marked by a "campaign" to permit women to become bishops, building up a head of steam toward a vote in the General Synod, which is the Church of England's "parliament."

Several times, the matter came up for a vote. In the usual way, votes were preceded by speeches. These speeches took the inevitable form of people speaking either for or against the motion.

Each time, a vote was then taken. Each time, it was defeated. On the final occasion before mediated talks began, the vote was extremely close, but the proposal was still defeated. The body was profoundly divided. The pain was great.

Some eighteen months of mediated talks followed. What emerged was a series of options, far removed from the binary simplicity that had gone before. The options themselves were complex, but essentially made space for differing views, to differing degrees.

Eventually the designated group involved in the talks—about forty representatives of all "sides," in total—arrived at near-unanimity on one of the options. They took that back to the General Synod and jointly proposed it as the way forward. It passed comfortably. I was very moved to be in the public gallery at the time.

Many of the speakers noted two things:

1) How the tone of the debate had radically altered from what had gone before, being now marked by a greater degree of mutual understanding and generosity of spirit, because of the extensive dialogue which had taken place; and
2) How much more appropriate it was to be voting on an option that had emerged from fulsome dialogue, and which attempted, successfully in the eyes of most, to make space for different views.

The third feature of binary processes is that they often engender decisions motivated, at least in part, by fear—the fear of losing. This is hardly surprising given the limited options of win or lose. I see this so often when I mediate. And it is important for us to recognize it, because as a mediator, I want people to make good decisions—whatever those may be. Decisions made out of fear are rarely sustainable or wise.

When I mediate, I often find myself encouraging parties—to think hard, to make difficult decisions, to have uncomfortable conversations, to consider risks, and so on. And I use the word "encourage" literally. To "en-courage"—in other words, to engender, build up, or enable a greater degree of courage. To try to ensure that wisdom, and not fear, becomes the primary motivating force in their decisions, or at least that fear is not the only one.

Persistent Question

The practice issue: What is the real purpose of this mediation?

Mediators' nagging suspicion: Money changes everything.

The best path: There is more to it than dollars. Uncover the needs and options beyond the financial demands, and the resolution, including the $$$, is more likely to emerge.

The need for courage extends beyond our role in individual disputes. The mediator's voice needs to be heard in society at large, and not just in individual disputes. We need to be "prophetic" in the best sense of that word—not as in prophesying or predicting the future, but holding up a challenge to the status quo.

True prophets in every age have done that. And it always takes courage. Perhaps we need to challenge the nature of public discourse and decision-making more. After all, there will be no shortage of it over the coming years both in private and public matters, not least on the Brexit issue.

And that task will require us first to understand the impact of binary processes—simplicity, limited options and fear—in order to be able to contribute to a discussion on a better process and results for the affected parties.

JERRY WEISS

The back and forth of the distributive bargaining model that we are accustomed to seems, to my experienced eye, outdated and contrary to the interests of durable solutions.

In two words, it is fatigued and fatiguing. Hand-to-hand combat too readily digresses in the "bargaining process" to the argument, thereby continuing the competition and all of its negative forces. What results is akin to "trial by mediation."

Add to this antiquated method the increasing velocity demanded by the market and supported by the warp-speed technology of our time, and what results is a toxic mix. These forces elevate goals of closing, expedience, money and commerce to the detriment of the real people who are integral to the dispute, and in whose control the terms, texture, quality and spirit of the resolution resides.

And yet, we neutrals can drift on in rote, almost mechanically, looking ahead to our "next game" and thereby running the risk of losing—badly losing—the human virtues of the one we are playing at the moment. Durable resolutions, where the parties and product and process are all served and where participants feel a sense of satisfaction, are often lost—and what results is sadly a sense of inadequate closure with people feeling they need a bath.

Mediation can be a punishing process that only continues to bruise the participants. The "fighters" in the contest, usually lawyers, are trained to battle and thereby run the risk of losing sight of those elements that make conflict and its resolution human.

We can do better. Much better! And it doesn't take much of a shift to affect the overall arc of a particular resolution process. We need only to be mindful of a few factors that are central to disputes and their resolution: intimacy, humanity, clarity and trust—none of which are usually found in the lexicon of commercial or other disputes and yet, all disputes and resolution processes are indeed intimate and human events with complex human interaction at their core.

Likewise, it is clear to many of us who have been doing this for a while that durable processes require good communication, where more than words and content matter, but rather where tone and non-verbal communication also are key. That said, clarity and articulation of express verbal message are too often missing, in the negotiation with disputants and their representatives often going at it without a clear idea of what is really intended by their opposing counterparts. Necessary time and discipline are often ignored because of pressures to "get it done" or worse, fear of having difficult conversations.

Concentrating on these factors can help build a foundation supporting that "meditative moment" found in the best resolution processes and practices, where the people in the room begin to feel that they might be able to break the constraints of past conflict and rely on their disputant opponents as partners.

Real peace transcends a mere signature on a piece of paper. It presents the ability to move forward in a constructive way and without the burden and deconstruction of the conflict. We can refer to this shift in mediation simply as trust and as a basis for an agreement that can endure. The day after the resolution agreement, where satisfaction comes into play, whether in terms of action or simply a sense that disputants have done something they can live with, having an adequate degree of contentment, is much more important than the agreement itself. Such action and trust—a dynamic and living human process—or at least a bridge to such thinking, are goals we should aspire to.

There are no silver bullets or simple tricks that I employ in order to draw people into a more constructive and human process. Rather, I try to concentrate on some keys, exemplify them in my behavior, and count on the fact that people will recognize their virtue and maybe, to some extent, mirror and integrate these behaviors and understandings. Here are a few suggestions:

- Running the room and establishing guidelines that expect best practices and behavior. This starts with the letter of engagement and continues to the actual meeting and encounters, where the neutral can make express statements about these expectations.
- Making clear that one expects positions and opinions to be explained. Lawyers are notorious at blurring the lines between fact and opinion and position and truth. Bringing out clear distinctions goes a long way to point out how different the theater of the lawsuit—where strangers decide—may be from necessary partnerships and virtues of mediated resolution, where the disputants take control and decide.
- Talking about partnerships and how they differ from adversaries who will never agree, and describing the disputants as partners and asking them to envision themselves as such.
- Complimenting and perhaps even rewarding courageous or noble behaviors. Even polite and professional, non-adversarial conduct may merit recognition as such behaviors support desired collaboration. This may be as minor as telling people how privileged we are to have them share the dispute in a professional and collegial manner and the opportunity for us to help them. Conversely, to have the courage to politely discourage and prevent bad behaviors either directly or privately and do so with a level tone and helpful, reflective way.
- Expressly promoting the need and desire to get the conflict resolved and the parties moving forward without the burden of past dispute. Along with this goes the promotion of open doors and clear communication including attaching articulate messages to any exchange of numbers that add meaning to those numbers. In general, we need to generate clarity during the progression of the negotiating process.
- Listening better and knowing that as neutrals who think we have the idea of where the fix lies, we really may not. Pacing the process—which often translates into slowing it—so that people can "listen" with their ears and eyes is very helpful. (I have written several blogs on listening that can be found at the IAM website at www. iamed.org/page/Blogs.)

- Having courage to say "no," politely but firmly, to people who want to avoid difficult conversations because of fear or just plain bad habits, by quietly prodding and encouraging them and complimenting them once they have successfully had them.
- Being transparent about common fears that people have about disputes and their attendant processes and sharing our own concerns about those fears with disputants in order to relate and make a human connection, instead of the fighting and denying that is too often the response to these common angsts. Reassuring people in conflict that being in a "bad place" is a common feeling and may not be so bad.
- Saying hello and goodbye together and encouraging people that such things can't hurt and just might help in setting a tone of reciprocity, decency and fairness. Along these lines, joint sessions should be encouraged so as to begin tearing down the barriers that conflict has built up. Dining together with both sides without discussing merits can also help disputing parties become partners. I have seen it happen. If they insist on working alone during that half hour or hour, then have them work at listing those elements of an agreement that are not burdened with rancor or a high degree of contest and leaving the tough issues for later. This can be a constructive exercise as it allows a start on things people can agree to and partner on, and will set a better tone for the more challenging aspects.

None of this is easy. It all requires a disciplined integration into practice over time and awareness of oneself and the totality of the room we are in—being in the moment. It also requires us to recognize that most of what we do is based on trust-building, both vis a vis the neutral and all sides of the dispute, and also and perhaps more important, among those sides.

This, of course begs the question of whether our goals should exceed merely getting it done. It's a philosophical choice, and one that I have made as I increasingly believe that it is important to give human beings the opportunity to start viewing opponents—who they have probably been vilifying and dehumanizing by virtue of what the fight does to us—as something other than the devil.

In a somewhat vulgarized brain science nomenclature, this probably translates into allowing those reactive and primitive aspects of our beings to be tamed by elevated, human and reflective virtues.

By understanding and employing these methods and by picking away at the dispute piece by piece over time, we allow ourselves to find the human beings who drive conflict and who are responsible for its enduring resolution.

BIRGIT SAMBETH GLASNER

1. What If? Let's Be Creative ...

What if you were requested to mediate an international commercial case about the sale of a chemical subsidiary of a German company to an English buyer, a publicly listed company on the London Stock Exchange?

The €59 million share and asset purchase agreement between the two European companies, and the numerous related commercial contracts, ran into large problems. They included allegations about the accuracy of financial information; misleading profit transfers; overstatement of efficiency claims; and misrepresentation of building and plant, stock shortfall, and employee grievances. It also included threats of huge interest payments and damages.

Assuming you took the case, it would be the perfect time, as a mediator, to take a step back, help the parties think outside the box, and structure an appropriate process to enable the resolution of their differences, not only on the surface, but in-depth.

2. But How?

- First, recall that a conflict is not—and almost never is—about money.
- Second, be aware that positional bargaining is not an adequate dispute resolution method. As Albert Einstein once said: "We can't solve the problems by using the same kind of thinking we used when we created them."
- Third, it needs some courage on the part of the mediator to lead the parties and their attorneys through a creative process where the discussion about money is only its very final act.
- Fourth, the first step toward success is proper preparation. As "location, location, location" is the slogan of real estate agents, "preparation, preparation, preparation" should be the slogan of any mediator for whatever topic and dispute size.

Preparing for the mediator means, of course, becoming knowledgeable about the dispute, including the interests and needs of each of the parties, the risks they are facing, and the opportunities afforded by the mediation process. A mediator needs to sincerely dig deep, listen and understand.

Moreover, preparing for the parties and their attorneys means not only investing time and energy in understanding their own interests, needs, risks and opportunities, but also those of the other side. It is also means assessing each one's Best Alternatives to a Negotiated Agreement, better known as BATNA, by means of objective criteria, such as time, costs, consequences, damages, and to make a first "reality check."

Preparing can take place with all the attorneys, and possibly with their clients, during a joint phone call when organizational issues as well as parties' expectations toward the mediation process and the mediator's role are discussed in structuring, together, an efficient and realistic process.

Subsequent private preparation meetings or calls with each of the parties will enhance the overall understandings of the mediator and the parties. Furthermore, this direct communication in a safe environment usually fosters the necessary trust toward the mediator and the mediation process, allowing creative tools and risk-taking in the process.

If, at this early stage of meetings where the focus is on preparation, it is still important to talk about money, it will finally be the time!

3. Let's Not Talk about Money Yet!

In the case study outline above, the parties and their attorneys were focused on the financial features of their dispute while fighting over accounting issues. One of the parties had requested no less than 16 legal, accounting and financial specialists to sit at the mediation table.

After thorough preparation, we met in Paris at an impressive roundtable accommodating twenty-one persons. The other party appeared at the mediation table with two counsels. At the start, I recalled the strict confidentiality of the mediation process, and we jointly fixed the time limit of our mediation day until 8:00 pm.

Immediately after the opening of the joint session and the parties' opening statements, I suggested taking the next two hours to "discuss anything but money."

If so agreed, what would the 18 other persons in the room do during this time, other than question their remuneration during that "lost" time?

Boosted by parties' trust gained during the preparation phase, I started asking some open questions to the principals on how they usually conduct their respective business and which values they have in doing so.

Astonishment—and for the attorneys in the room, even some polite and less courteous discontentment—was the response to my inquiry. I stayed this course by assisting the principals to enter into a meaningful discussion leading to a comprehensive expression of their shared values, interests, and needs around the troubled deal.

Later in the discussion, the seller stood up and said with a trembling voice: "If you are questioning the financials of the deal, it is as if I would have lied to you and I am a crook! You should know that this is intolerable to me as we have a strict code of conduct in our family business which I am very proud of." He then sat down, emotionally exhausted.

The purchaser immediately realized that it was time to reply: "I am sincerely sorry. This is not what I wanted to say and certainly not the message I wanted to convey to you, but I have some questions about the way you did your calculations and your representations. I would like to discuss those openly with you."

Trust was rehabilitated in the room. This had an immediate positive impact on the process and my role as mediator was almost over.

I spent the rest of the day facilitating this discussion, assisting the parties in structuring a new deal and organizing their tasks, responsibilities and timing for finalizing it. And the mediation concluded the same day with a settlement at 7:30 pm.

4. Some Lessons Learned

Each of us as mediators use favored techniques to uncover interests and options that go beyond presenting financial demands.

The more creative mediators dare to be, however, the more trust in the mediator and process is needed in the room for the parties. Obviously, their attorneys need to follow that path. And therefore, preparation is key.

We as mediators are hired to take risks to push parties to do what they may resist doing. Otherwise, the process is just positional bargaining with no real added value.

Attorneys may be not be at ease with a process that often pushes them out of their comfort zone, as the mediation addresses non-legal components of the dispute where attorneys can fear losing control over their clients. But lawyers play an important role in mediations, especially in coaching their clients and performing reality checks.

Good preparation with the attorneys and active engagement in the process enhances its effectiveness and gives the attorneys a sense of understanding and engages them. Good preparation also offers mediators a benefit that

Given that many mediations that initially appear to be only about the money turn out to be otherwise, what are the techniques a mediator can employ to uncover the underlying needs and opportunities for resolving disputes? they worry about losing when pushing participants—the likelihood of repeat business.

BENNETT PICKER

Regrettably, in too many mediations today, both advocates and party representatives view mediation with the same lens as they view litigation. With a one-dimensional perspective, their focus is on the summary judgment issues, the risks, the costs and the dollars.

In private meetings and caucuses, too many mediation advocates focus exclusively upon the strength of their legal positions. When we get to the negotiation stage, too many mediation advocates seem to be inspired by a line from the movie "Jerry Maguire": "Show Me the Money."

So, if it's not just about the money, what else is it about?

Of course, Mediation 101 teaches us that the process offers an opportunity to explore underlying interests and search for interest based, creative solutions—solutions unavailable in the win-lose environment of litigation.

In a recent employment case that was framed in terms of money, after an exchange between a tenured professor who had been summarily dismissed and the university provost, the university rehired the professor after concluding that it had acted prematurely, based on incomplete information.

Similarly, commercial agreements can be renegotiated, patent disputes can be resolved by pooling agreements, and outdated partnership agreements can be reformed to reflect current business realities.

While the potential for business solutions should be obvious to disputants, it is often less so to their lawyers, who need to be reminded to take a multi-dimensional view of a dispute that appears to be all about money.

Even when mediation advocates and business clients recognize the potential for business solutions to business disputes, they are far less aware of the numerous barriers to resolution that often are not about the legal issues and not even about the money.

In my experience, uncovering these hidden barriers is often the most critical work that we, as mediators, must do. While the list of possible hidden non-monetary barriers to resolution includes a host of process, psychological and merit obstacles, I have found the following to be the most prevalent.

Barriers Resulting from Relationships between Counsel and Client. Prof. Gerald R. Williams studied the negotiating behavior of more than 20 lawyers for seven years and concluded that, in rank order, the principal barrier to resolution was not a disconnect between plaintiff and defendant.

Rather, it was a disconnect between lawyer and client. Lawyers can inflate expectations made at the outset of the relationship, be unwilling to report to the client the weaknesses in a case, or fail to report the status of litigation as the litigation unfolded.

On many occasions, counsel have turned to me at the end of a mediation and said "Thank you for telling my client what I could not say" or "I told my client about the weaknesses and was told 'I thought you were my lawyer.'"

Interestingly, Prof. Williams found that counsel's interest in fees often affected the recommendation of counsel or the decision of the client. I have found this to be the case, especially when the arrangement is a contingent fee.

Emotional Barriers. Quite often, anger, frustration, resentment, guilt, jealously and so many other emotions are at the heart of a dispute. As just one example, I mediated a dispute between two brothers who owned a large, closely held business for decades. Over the years, the brother who was not in control repeatedly filed suits alleging breaches of fiduciary duties.

In mediation, I met alone with the two brothers and, after a while, the brother who filed the action said "You know, mother really liked you better." This response led to the first meaningful conversation between the two brothers in years.

With this on the table, we were able to resume negotiations and find a lasting resolution. In other mediations, I have found that apologies, when sincere, have reduced the anger of the other side and opened the door for meaningful settlement discussions.

Barriers Resulting from Disagreements between Stakeholders on One Side. Quite often, disagreements among several party representatives on one side can be the principal barrier to settlement. Each party representative may have a different priority.

In a recent dispute involving a long-term supply agreement, the general counsel was looking for a large sum of money for the plaintiff, the business manager was looking for a court decision to vindicate her decision to pull out of the agreement, and the CEO was looking for a restructured agreement, arguing that Wall Street values long-term revenue streams more highly than large sums of cash.

Again, this dispute was not about how much money the defendant would pay. Instead, much of my work focused on mediation among the representatives of one side.

Cognitive Barriers. In almost every mediation, I have observed that cognitive illusions and irrational attachments to positions distort objective evaluations and affect settlement decisions.

These barriers are usually invisible to the other side. Studies at the Program on Negotiation at Harvard Law School and at the Wharton School of the University of Pennsylvania demonstrate that advocacy bias makes it difficult for a party with an interest in the outcome or their lawyers to make a completely objective evaluation of a dispute.

Parties view their facts selectively—"selective perception"—and spend almost all of their time mining their own best arguments. Their evaluations are distorted by optimism bias, certainty bias, assimilation bias, hindsight bias, reactive devaluation and so many other errors of judgment.

Techniques to Overcome the Hidden Barriers: Given that many mediations that initially appear to be only about the money turn out to be otherwise, what are the techniques a mediator can employ to uncover the underlying needs and opportunities for resolving disputes?

While the answer would constitute a syllabus for a one-week course, I would like to offer a few big-picture approaches that I have found to be helpful in uncovering the hidden barriers and drivers of resolution.

1. *Preparation*: In addition to any possible exchanges by the parties, I invariably insist on confidential, "eyes only," submissions which go well beyond the claims and defenses and the "money." In this confidential submission, I ask counsel to address potentially hidden barriers that need to be addressed. Among these are personality issues, the need for confidentiality, links to an unrelated dispute, strategic issues, accounting and audit issues, emotional issues, need for vindication, internal company issues, and future implications.
2. *Conferencing before Mediation Session*: In almost every dispute, after I have read the submissions, I meet by phone with counsel to further explore the interests and potential barriers that may exist. Aside from the merit issues, I encourage candid responses to questions such as "can you tell me more about your client"? At times, I receive replies such as "My client is the real problem," or "I need your help," or "My client is so angry with the other side that I'm not sure we can be in the same room" or "An apology would go a long way in helping to get this matter resolved," or "Let me tell you about the other side's private agenda."

3. *Mediation Session—Ex-Parte Meetings before Joint Session*: Many years ago, I began the practice of meeting with parties before commencing a joint session. I quickly learned how powerful these meetings can be for building trust. I typically engage the decision-maker, and we talk about anything other than the dispute. We can talk about sports, opera, travel or our families. On more than one occasion, party-representatives have shown me pictures of their grandchildren. With a bond formed at the outset, I have found that parties will be far more open with me once we reach the caucus and resolution stages.
4. *Caucus Sessions—Probing for Drivers and Barriers of Resolution*: With a dose of coaching, I begin exploring with each side the potential for settlement. Regardless of the path we take in negotiations, I continue to explore whether there are psychological, relational or cognitive issues that need to be addressed. If the parties need to vent, I will listen, acknowledge and empathize. If there are relational issues—either party-to-party or within one side—I will take the time to address these issues. If the evaluations of one or both parties are distorted, I will employ various techniques to spur parties to reconsider their assessments.

I was once asked to explain mediation in one word. Without hesitation, I said "opportunity." Mediation can afford the opportunity to develop issues that otherwise would take months or years in litigation; save time and money; preserve relationships; and search for solutions not available in litigation or arbitration.

I often mention the opportunities in mediations because no one wants to lose an opportunity. In order to maximize the mediation opportunity, it is incumbent upon the mediator, in addition to addressing the legal issues, and focusing on the money, to work with the parties to address the other issues, concerns, and interests for a successful and enduring resolution.

* * *

CONCLUSION BY HAL ABRAMSON

The experiences and insights of these mediators may inspire others who are not so inclined to look beyond the financial dimension of disputes. For those mediators who tend to function like private settlement judges, the guidance suggests a pathway for doing much more. Their comments and techniques should give reticent mediators confidence to trust the mediation process and employ more daring techniques that may produce more enduring and satisfying resolutions

* * *

THE AUTHORS, IN DETAIL

Here are the contributors for this article on moving mediation parties beyond the dollars to uncover the depth of the dispute:

- Hal Abramson, a law professor at Touro Law Center, Central Islip, N.Y., writes, teaches and trains on negotiations and mediation. He has trained in 18 countries on six continents. He also works as a commercial mediator and was selected for the International Who's Who of Commercial Mediation. He won the 2016 Outstanding Professional Article award from Alternatives' publisher, the International Institute for Conflict Prevention and Resolution, for "Nelson Mandela as Negotiator: What Can We Learn from Him?" 31 *Ohio St. J. on Dispute Resolution* 1 (2016). It was his second CPR Award. For a full bio, see Tourolaw.edu/ faculty/Abramson.
- Birgit Sambeth Glasner, a partner in the Geneva office of Altenburger, is listed as the No. 1 mediator in Switzerland by Who's Who. She is a full-time mediator, the vice president of the Swiss Chamber for Commercial Mediation, a Distinguished Fellow of the International Academy of Mediators, and a member of the CPR European Advisory Board. As an International Mediator, she is accredited by the Geneva courts as well as by IMI, CEDR, the CPR Institute, SCIA and CMAP, and is listed with ICC and WIPO and as INSOL International Panel insolvency mediator. She mediates in French, German, English and sometimes Spanish.
- Bill Marsh is an international commercial mediator, based in the United Kingdom. Independently ranked as one of Europe's leading commercial mediators, he also mediates ethnic, religious and political conflicts, and advises numerous governments and other international bodies on approaches to conflict and mediation. Details at www.billmarsh.co.uk.
- Bennett G. Picker is a full-time mediator and arbitrator who is a Distinguished Fellow of the International Academy of Mediators, a member

of the CPR Institute's Panel of Distinguished Neutrals, and a member of the Master Mediator Panel of the American Arbitration Association. He is author of "Mediation Practice Guide: A Handbook for Resolving Business Disputes," published by the American Bar Association Section of Dispute Resolution.

- Jerry Weiss, founder of MediationInc (an Ohio corporation), was the first lawyer in Cleveland to dedicate his practice entirely to mediation. He mediates many high stakes, emotionally driven cases throughout the U.S. He has lectured and written extensively about conflict and people in conflict both here and abroad and he teaches aspiring lawyers the art of mediation representation and problem solving. He is a Distinguished Fellow in the International Academy of Mediators and sits on its Board of Governors.

CHAPTER 6

Mediation Representation: Representing Clients Anywhere

in *ADR in Business Practice and Issues Across Countries and Cultures*

Volume II
Edited by
Arnold Ingen-Housz
Kluwer Law International

Volume II, Chapter 14
Mediation Representation: Representing Clients Anywhere
Harold Abramson*

1. INTRODUCTION

You are bound to be skeptical of any title that claims to cover representing clients anywhere in the world. I surely would be. I reached this sweeping conclusion after much research and testing of the materials in my recently published second edition of *Mediation Representation*[1] and will justify the claim in this chapter. I will demonstrate how the framework for mediation

* The author is a full-time law professor at Touro Law Center, New York. He has published extensively on mediation representation and international mediation, mediates domestic and international commercial cases, and has taught and trained law students and lawyers on these subjects throughout the United States and Europe, as well as in India and China. This chapter is based on the author's recently published book, Harold Abramson, *Mediation Representation: Advocating as a Problem-solver in Any Country or Culture* (2nd ed., 2010).

1 Most of the footnotes in this chapter cite sections of *Mediation Representation*, the subject of this chapter, although the cited sections of the book include other citations for you to consider.

representation presented in the book reflects a universal approach that can be adapted to work within any local context with parties employing their customary practices for representation. However, I also will recommend and illustrate representation practices that may help you get the most out of mediation, practices that you ought to consider adopting if they are different than your customary ones.

My effort to develop a universal model of client representation began several weeks after I published the first edition of *Mediation Representation* in 2004. I shortly realized that the book that took ten years to research and test presented mainly a westernized approach to client representation. I became aware of these embedded cultural values when preparing an international dispute resolution textbook for which I needed to adapt the framework for use in cross-cultural disputes.[2] For the new second edition, I was determined to formulate a culturally neutral framework while refining it based on my research during the intervening five years.

Thus, the mediation representation formula in the first edition became the mediation representation triangle and the subtitle in the first edition of "Advocating in a Problem-Solving Process" became "Advocating as a Problem-Solver in Any Country or Culture." In this chapter, I present this improved and succinct framework for client representation and demonstrate that the new subtitle is not puffery. This "improved" framework can be used anywhere.

This framework is for advocates in mediations. It is tailored for resolving legal disputes in which clients are represented by attorneys. Although this chapter will be presented from the perspective of a mediation advocate, the framework also can be illuminating for mediators who have attorneys and clients in the mediation room.

However, this chapter does not explain how this framework applies in a cross-cultural or international mediation in which parties with substantially different cultural backgrounds are resolving a dispute. In this cross-cultural setting, parties may encounter unfamiliar cultural interests that may need to be met or cultural (not strategic) differences that may need to be bridged, a substantial topic that I cover elsewhere.[3] Although, I will point out where the framework applies to these cross-cultural differences as they might arise during the mediation.

---

2 *See* Nolan-Haley, Abramson and Chew, *International Conflict Resolution: Consensual ADR Processes* (2005), Ch. 4.

3 *See* Abramson, *supra* n. 1, *at* Ch. 5.20 and Appendix J.

2. THE NEED FOR A MEDIATION REPRESENTATION FRAMEWORK

Attorneys need to replace their default trial advocacy approach that works so well in court or arbitrations with a representation approach suitable for mediation. The familiar and well-honed common law adversarial or civil law inquisitorial strategies may be effective in forums where each side is trying to convince a decision maker to render a favorable decision. In mediation, however, there is no neutral third-party decision maker, only a third-party facilitator or advisor. The third party may not even be the primary audience. The primary audience may be the other side, who surely are not neutral, can often be quite hostile, and ultimately must approve any settlement. In this different representational setting, traditional approaches can be less effective if not self-defeating. Attorneys need an approach tailored for the opportunities offered by mediation.

Many sophisticated and experienced litigators realize that mediation calls for a different approach, but they can still muddle through the mediation sessions, guided by familiar strategies that have worked well in other forums. Most senior US attorneys have never taken a course on dispute resolution; they went to law school before such courses were offered or were popular. And most attorneys outside the United States, regardless of level of experience, have never taken a dispute resolution course in law school. Even today, non-US law students have few opportunities to take such courses, although the number of offerings is starting to increase. Most courses on alternative dispute resolution or mediation, wherever they are offered, are largely limited to teaching students to be mediators, not advocates.[4]

But new educational opportunities are beginning to take shape. Many US law schools during the last five years began offering mediation advocacy courses,[5] although such courses are still relatively rare outside of the United States. Law students can participate in mediation representation competitions

---

4 For a discussion of U.S. textbooks, *see* Suzanne J. Schmitz, "What Should We Teach in ADR Courses: Concepts and Skills for Lawyers Representing Clients in Mediation," 6 *Harv. Negot. L. Rev.* 189 (2001).

5 Although no survey has ever been compiled, when the first edition of this text was published in 2004, only a handful of law schools offered a separate course on mediation advocacy. As of 2009, more than thirty-five law schools offered the course according to the number of first edition adoptions, plus more offerings by other law schools that have adopted other books, but I do not know how many. Furthermore, many separate courses on mediation and ADR may be including segments on mediation representation as reflected in the addition of new sections on the subject to virtually every recent edition of a textbook.

that are flourishing in the United States, Canada and globally.[6] Numerous continuing legal education programmes on mediation representation are now widely available in the United States and are emerging elsewhere. Practicing lawyers can enroll in one of several available intensive training programmes.[7] However, lawyers do not seem convinced of the need for training until they see firsthand what they do not know and what would be helpful to learn, as I have observed repeatedly when training in the United States, Europe and China. These training programmes have not yet reached the maturity of trial practice trainings that are almost prerequisites for entering the courtroom. The value of trial practice training took years in the United States to be fully appreciated and embraced, and mediation advocacy training programmes seem to be following a similarly measured path.

In the absence of formal training, advocates learn on the job. Even though advocates are gaining considerable experience, and practices are solidifying, the skill levels seem strikingly unsophisticated, as I have observed in training and have heard from numerous mediators. The representation practices of many attorneys do not seem to reflect a nuanced understanding of how to select a suitable mediator, how to take full advantage of pre-mediation contacts with the mediator or the other side, how to present effective opening statements and how to optimally utilize the choice between joint sessions and caucuses to advance clients' interests and overcome impediments. A framework custom-designed for mediation advocacy is needed, including one that recognizes the growing practical experience of attorneys.

3. INTRODUCE A TRIANGULAR FRAMEWORK

Mediation Representation offers a comprehensive and coherent framework for client representation that applies from your first client phone call until the mediation process is concluded, and the book highlights the many choices that

---

6 For a brief description of the competitions sponsored by the American Bar Association and the International Chamber of Commerce in Paris, *see* Abramson, *supra* n. 1, *at* Appendix Q: Mediation Representation Competitions-Judging Criteria. Also, in 2008, a national competition was launched for Canadian law schools. *See* www.cnmac.org.

7 NITA has designed and launched a national mediation advocacy training programme. The ABA Section on Dispute Resolution conducts an Advanced Mediation and Advocacy Skills Training Institute that is held each year in a different region of the United States. The CPR International Institute for Conflict Prevention and Resolution occasionally offers a mediation and mediation advocacy training programme. Also, Pepperdine Law School regularly offers an intensive course to practitioners.

you should consider and weigh throughout the mediation process. It offers an alternative approach to relying on a strategy shaped by courtroom experience and ad-hoc intuition. The framework can be configured into a triangle that links three key features for effective representation (Figure 14-1): Attorneys need to know how to: (1) negotiate, (2) enlist mediator assistance and (3) plan their representation throughout the mediation process. Any plan should include how to advance a client's interests, overcome any impediments and handle gathering and sharing information.[8]

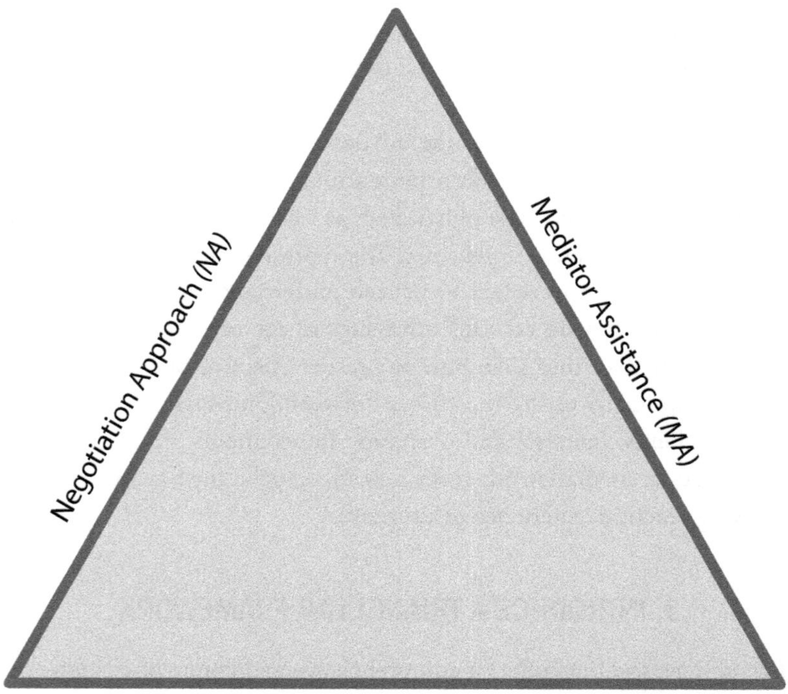

Figure 14-1. The Mediation Representation Triangle.

The triangle is a fitting metaphor because of the inherent interdependence of the three sides. If one side is missing or weak, the entire structure collapses. If you negotiate poorly, enlist the mediator ineffectually or develop a weak representation plan, you will represent your client within a wobbly framework. If

8 You can remember these three features by remembering that you need to "Negotiate with a MAP" (Negotiate with Mediator Assistance and a Plan).

you do all three well, you will erect a reliable and sturdy structure for mediation representation. In this chapter, I will examine how this triangular representational framework can be adapted to local usage and how it accommodates multiple practices, including ones that I recommend.

4. INTRODUCE LOCAL PRACTICES (CULTURAL AND STRATEGIC) INTO THE FRAMEWORK

I only dared to make the broad claim that this triangular framework can work anywhere after much study and the discovery that it was feasible to design a practical and universal approach that can incorporate local practices—whatever they might be. For this framework to be viable, you do not need to know all the cultural practices in the world and stay current as they evolve—an undertaking that is daunting if not impossible and presumably the largest obstacle to designing a universal approach. You also do not need to know all of the strategic practices around the world. Instead, you only need to know your own practices. By negotiating, enlisting mediator assistance and planning for interests, impediments and information, as you customarily do, you can intelligently and successfully represent your clients in mediation, as will be illustrated throughout the rest of this chapter.

Whether your practices are the most effective ones, however, deserve self-analysis. Are your practices a product of cultural influences or considered strategic choices? To answer this question, you should consider the differences between culture and strategy.

Culture is a collective phenomenon that is shared with others and is derived from the social environment in which we live. It reflects patterns of thinking, feeling and acting. It is learned—a key distinguishing feature. This definition can be further clarified by emphasizing what it is not. It is not universal behavior that applies to all human beings. It is not inherited—not a product of our genetic programming. We all need to eat food to survive, for example; but the food we eat can vary considerably among different cultures. We all negotiate, but how we do it also can vary across cultures. These cultural differences can reflect different approaches to meeting universal needs. Finally, cultural behavior should be distinguished from our personality, which is unique to each of us. Our personality is a product of our genetic programming, unique personal experiences and cultural upbringing.[9]

---

9 *See* Abramson, *supra* n. 1, *at* Appendix J, 449–450.

Culture shapes what are known as dimensions that can affect how parties resolve their disputes. Culture can shape the interests of parties that need to be met as well as the way parties behave during the mediation process. You can better understand your own behavior by considering the most common cultural dimensions relevant to dispute resolution and where your behavior fits along the continuum of various pairings. Common pairings include low-context to high-context communicators,[10] short-term to long-term orientations, competitive to cooperative negotiation approaches, punctuality to relaxed time orientation, individual to collective decision making, contract to relationship focus, fixed to renegotiable contracts and others.[11] In any negotiation, you may follow your familiar propensities or consider trying other ways to behave. The triangular mediation representation framework does not dictate how you should behave along these continuums.

Strategy is distinctively different from culture, although strategy can be influenced by culture. A strategic move is a choice to employ a tactic to advance your client's interests or gain an advantage over the other side. A strategic move can be influenced by culture because your preferred strategy can be based on your cultural upbringing. I remember hearing someone in China explain why Chinese people tend to make extreme first offers. "Well, that is the way we negotiate here." But strategy may not be based on cultural influences when a party varies her default practice by making a considered strategic choice for the next moment in the mediation, such as threatening to leave or raising her voice in anger. This distinction can be useful because different cultural propensities can be easier to bridge than differences based on strategic moves that are deliberately and tactically chosen.

With an awareness of cultural dimensions and strategic options, you can better understand your own choices and better assess which options might best serve your client. You may normally be a competitive negotiator as a matter of

---

10 Low-context communicators, like speakers from the United States, speak relatively more directly, with most of the meaning conveyed in the words, whereas high-context communicators, like speakers from many Asian countries, speak relatively less directly, with most of the meaning conveyed in the context, not in the explicit words.

11 If you are interested in reading more about culture and cultural differences, *See* Abramson, *supra* n. 1, *at* Appendix J. Although cultural issues are integrated throughout the book, this Appendix offers a single source reference that consists of four sub-appendixes: "Glossary of Cultural Differences" that can help you develop cultural awareness, "Guidelines for Working with Interpreters in Mediations," "Ethical Issues Facing Mediators and Attorneys in Cross-Cultural Disputes" (that offers a four-step approach for recognizing and dealing with ethical issues) and "Seven Guidelines for U.S. Trainers When Training Abroad."

practice, for instance, but upon further reflection, you may strategically elect another approach that might be more suitable for your case.

Understanding your own culturally shaped behavior along with the behavior of others can help you recognize less familiar needs of the other side or possible cultural differences between the parties that need to be bridged. Techniques for identifying culturally influenced interests and bridging differences are separate subjects that will not be covered in this chapter.[12]

As I present the key features of the triangular mediation representation frame-work, I will highlight how local practices fit within the framework as well as suggest practices that might maximize the benefits of mediation for your client.

5. NEGOTIATION

The first side of this triangular framework focuses on your primary role as a negotiator (Figure 14-2). Mediation is simply the continuation of the negotiation with the assistance of a third party, as is so often repeated. And because you will be negotiating with the other side from the beginning to the end of the mediation, an effective mediation advocate must be an effective negotiator.

You negotiate in mediation, regardless of your cultural upbringing. But the way you negotiate can be influenced by your upbringing as well as your strategy. Cultural practices can vary in striking ways. I recall when haggling in a street bazaar in China and learning the hard way that first offers are much more extreme than I was accustomed to. Rather than a dance that may lead to prices that can be 10%–30% less than initial offers, I learned that final resolutions could be more than 90% less at least when negotiating with foreigners who do not know local price values.[13] In some Mideastern, Asian and other cultures, haggling practices can include post-deal concession demands. Cultural differences are not always cross-border, as I was reminded when bidding on an apartment in New York City. Oral sales agreements are not honored while waiting for the lawyers to draft written agreements, for example, although I encountered the opposite practice when buying outside of this location.

---

12 Techniques can include researching the background of the other participants and enlisting the expertise of others at the table such as the mediator and the other side from a different culture than your own. Or, you may avoid verifying whether the differences are cultural because of the difficulties of doing so and instead focus on bridging any differences, regardless of their causes, in a way that protects your client's interests.

13 *See* Graham and Lam, "The Chinese Negotiation," *Harv. Bus. Rev.* 82, 84–90 (October 2003).

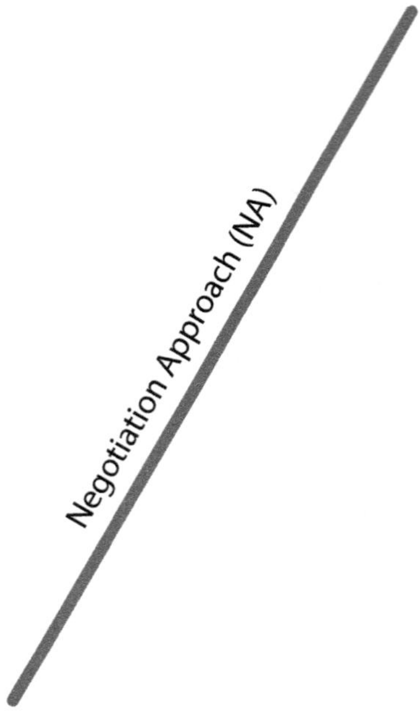

Figure 14-2. The Negotiation Approach (NA).

The triangular framework can accommodate any negotiation approach, including the two principal prototypes—positional and problem-solving.[14] Although your choice can be affected by your cultural upbringing and strategic factors, you should consider which one is the most effective for your case. You may follow your customary negotiation approach of positional negotiation to secure the largest percentage of the pie, for instance, or change for strategic reasons to problem-solving to uncover possible creative solutions.

Although you have a choice how to negotiate in mediations and the preferred approach of many lawyers can be the familiar positional approach, especially among many US trial lawyers as well as parties from bargaining cultures, I recommend a problem-solving approach to optimize the potential of the mediation process.

Let me explain the benefits of the problem-solving approach by first offering a definition for those less familiar with this approach.

As a problem-solver who is creative, you do more than try to merely settle the dispute. You search for solutions that go beyond the traditional ones based

14 *See* Abramson, *supra* n. 1, *at* Ch. 1 on "Negotiating in Mediations."

on rights, obligations, and precedent. Rather than settling for win-lose outcomes, you search for solutions that might benefit both sides.[15] You develop a collaborative relationship with the other side and the mediator, and participate throughout the process in a way that may produce solutions that are inventive as well as enduring. Inventive solutions may be uncovered because you advocate your client's interests instead of legal positions, use rational techniques for overcoming impediments, search expansively for multiple options, and evaluate and package options to meet the various interests of all parties. Enduring solutions, whether inventive or not, are likely because both sides work together to fashion tailored solutions that each side fully understands, can live with, and knows how to implement.[16]

As I advocate for problem-solving, I realize that the positional approach that can include unvarnished adversarial tactics can lead to spectacularly successful resolutions, as attorneys frequently point out. I do claim, however, that the problem-solving approach is more likely to produce better results for clients.[17]

For problem-solving advocacy to be effective in practice, you should engage proactively in problem-solving strategies at every stage of client representation, starting with your initial client interview through selection of the mediator and during the mediation session. You also should avoid a hybrid approach of both positional and problem-solving, despite the claims of supporters that it is the best one because of its flexibility. You should not let the appeal of flexibility mask the inconsistency it promotes and as a result how it can undercut the problem-solving approach. For instance, a hard positional move such as a take-or-leave it bluff can foreclose problem-solving moves of sharing information to uncover fresh options.

Skeptics think that problem-solving does not work for most legal cases because the cases are primarily about money, in which a party wants to get the most or pay the least. They see no opportunity to discover creative solutions. Consider these four responses:

---

15 Many lawyers consider the idea that both sides can secure benefits naïve. However, the notion that both sides might be able to gain something in negotiations reflects an optimistic attitude that can open the mind to creative possibilities. The likelihood of finding such gains in negotiations is greater than in court. In negotiations, for instance, even the defendant who agrees to pay considerable damages may gain other benefits, such as no publicity, no precedent and a continuing business relationship—benefits that are usually unavailable in court.

16 *See* Abramson, *supra* n. 1, *at* 4–5.

17 For a specific illustration of the potential benefits of problem-solving advocacy over the traditional positional advocacy, *see* Abramson, "Problem-Solving Advocacy in Mediation: A Model of Client Representation," 10 *Harv. Neg. L.R.* 103 (2005), 111–134.

First, the endless debate about whether or not legal disputes are primarily about money is distracting. Whether a dispute is largely about money varies from case to case as experiences and studies have demonstrated.

Second, you have little chance of discovering whether your client's dispute is about more than money if you approach the dispute as if it were only about money. Such a preconceived view backed by a narrowly focused adversarial strategy will likely blind you to other parties' needs and inventive solutions. You are more likely to discover and creative solutions if you approach the dispute with an open mind and a problem-solving orientation.

Third, if the dispute or any remaining issues at the end of the day turn out to be predominately about money, then at least you followed a representation approach that may have created a hospitable environment for dealing with the moneyed issues. A hospitable environment can even be beneficial when there is no expectation of a continuing relationship between the disputing parties.

Fourth and most importantly, the problem-solving approach provides a framework for resolving money issues. These types of disputes can sometimes be resolved by resorting to the usual problem-solving initiatives discussed throughout this book (*Mediation Representation*). If they fail, you then might turn to a positional dance, but one that has been refined to serve a problem-solving process by focusing on objective standards and justifications while avoiding tricks.

These responses were illustrated in a case that I mediated when the parties arrived with only monetary claims on the table, a long history of frustrating and failed negotiations, and their case ready to go to trial. After more than three hours of structuring and conducting a problem-solving approach to the mediation, the parties and attorneys discovered that the parties had much in common as founders of successful family businesses, that the fraudulent problem arose due to a rogue employee, and that each had unmet non-monetary needs. The plaintiff was upset that any reputable business person would perpetrate such a fraud, and the defendant was losing business due to the claims in the litigation. With the benefit of an improved understanding of each side's perspective and the facts, they proceeded to negotiate a written apology to the plaintiff and a written introduction to future buyers for the benefit of the defendant and signed by the plaintiff. In this collaborative environment, they then confronted the remaining monetary issue and settled it in less than a minute! They quickly and civilly exchanged a few offers and counteroffers. The parties were apparently already on the same page for settling the money claim but could not until some non-monetary needs were met.[18]

---

18 *See* Abramson, *supra* n. 1, *at* 6–7.

Skeptics also frequently question whether problem-solving will work if the other side does not know how to problem-solve or, worse, is familiar with the approach and has rejected it. Problem-solving offers a structure for trying to convert positional negotiators into problem-solvers by attorneys not copying the positional tactics, asking good questions and responding by focusing on interests, objective criteria and generating options.[19]

In short, problem-solving negotiations can offer an opportunity to realize much of mediation's potential.

6. MEDIATOR ASSISTANCE

The next side of this structure focuses on the second central feature of mediation advocacy-enlisting Mediator Assistance (Figure 14-3). What can the mediator contribute to resolving the dispute? What value does the mediator add? A mediator is an expert who knows how to assist parties in resolving their dispute. As an advocate, you need to understand how mediators assist in practice, and then as the mediation unfolds, you can choose how to enlist assistance from the mediator.

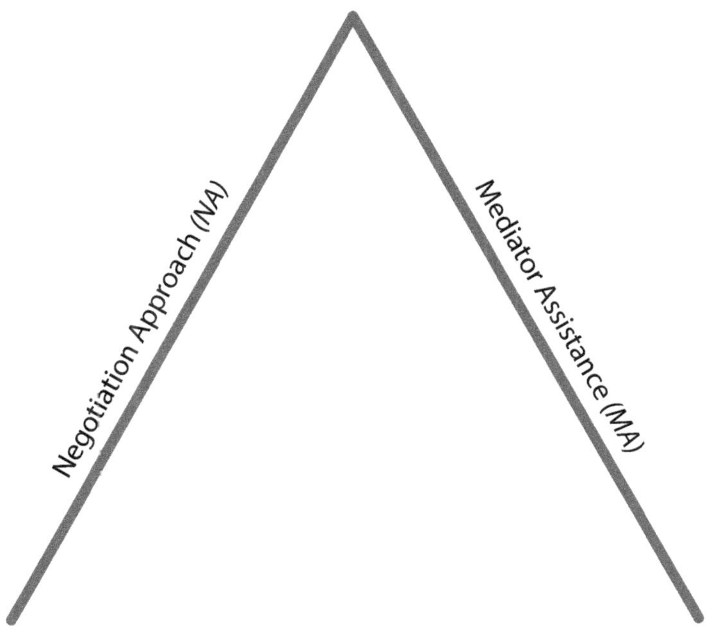

Figure 14-3. Mediator Assistance (MA).

19 *See* Abramson, *supra* n. 1, *at* Ch. 1.7.

There are three distinct ways in which mediators can be of assistance.[20] Each one is culturally neutral, although how each one gets translated into practice can be influenced by the cultural upbringing of the mediator, the cultural preferences of the attorneys and strategic considerations. The cultural upbringing of the mediator and strategic considerations can shape the mediator's default practices, the practices that the mediator automatically relies on, while strategic considerations also can cause the mediator to vary them. Even though your mediator may typically do everything in caucuses because that is what she was taught to do and she has found it to be an effective strategy, she may choose to vary that practice for strategic considerations. She may choose to switch to a joint session, for example, when it seems like it would be a productive move to bring parties together to talk directly with each other. Any of these local practices can be accommodated within the triangular representation framework.

First, a mediator brings to the mediation room his or her various approaches or orientations, which I divide into four neutral categories: (1) How will the mediator manage the process? (2) Will the mediator view the presenting problem broadly or narrowly? (3) Will the mediator use caucuses selectively, primarily or not at all? (4) Will the mediator involve clients extensively, restrictively or not at all? Practices can vary, and the practices can be a product of training and other cultural influences and driven by strategic choices by the mediator.

For example, how the mediator manages the process can vary across a continuum of practices from transformative, facilitative, evaluative, directive, wisely directive and authoritatively directive.[21] The choice can be a product of local practice. US litigators-turned-mediators tend to prefer practices in the evaluative and directive segment of the continuum, whereas British mediators, especially from London, can be more facilitative and Chinese mediators can be more inclined toward a wisely directive mediation practice. Of course, the mediator may select a different practice than his or her default one for strategic considerations, and you as an advocate can try to influence the choice of the mediator.

Caucusing practices offer another illustration of the influence of local culture. I recall training attorneys in Minnesota about how to use caucuses selectively, when an attorney informed me that they prefer mediating primarily in caucuses. I was told it was the culture in Minnesota to avoid dealing directly with each other when in conflict. When training attorneys in the Netherlands

---

20 *See ibid., at* 2.4–2.8 and 5.3–5.5.

21 *See* Abramson, *supra* n. 1, *at* Ch. 2.4.

about the benefits of selective caucusing over all caucusing, I was informed that their default practice is to mediate in joint sessions. That is how they were trained, and they had never contemplated using caucuses—until this training!

Second, mediators use various techniques to prod movement. They can use techniques to improve communications, defuse tensions, overcome impasses, generate options and for many other purposes. These needs are mostly universal, although the particular techniques to deal with them can vary across cultures, and the triangular framework does not dictate the choice. For example, the default technique for bridging any final gaps can vary. In the northeast region of the United States, many commercial mediators prefer using a mediator's proposal,[22] whereas in other regions, commercial mediators prefer offering evaluations of the legal risks to prod closure. When there is a need to improve communications, some mediators prefer facilitating discussions in joint sessions, whereas others prefer separating the parties, with the mediator carrying messages back and forth.

Third, because each mediation stage serves a different purpose, mediators can use their control of the stages to stimulate movement by steering the mediation to a suitable stage. Or, you can try to steer the mediation. The mediator might ask the parties whether they have enough information to move forward to the stage of shaping a resolution, for instance, or you may ask to move backward to the stage of clarifying and overcoming an impediment because of different interpretations of critical data. Of course, not all mediators follow the same stages. As one obvious illustration, some mediators might follow a problem-solving process in which the mediator focuses on identifying interests, generating options and assessing them, whereas others might follow a positional process in which the mediator facilitates a negotiation dance of offers and counter-offers.

How you expect your mediator to assist you will profoundly affect how you represent your client.[23] If you expect the mediator to evaluate, you will likely withhold more information and present more partisan arguments, for instance, than you would if you expect your mediator to facilitate and problem-solve.

Finally, even though this framework accommodates a range of mediator assistance practices, you should consider enlisting practices that cultivate a problem-solving process. The benefits that were highlighted when considering problem-solving negotiations can be elicited by the mediator when the mediator helps parties improve communications, understand each other's interests, over-come any impediments, search for and assess creative options

---

22 *See ibid., at* Ch. 7.2(g)(ii).

23 *See ibid., at* Ch. 5.3-5.

and bridge any final gaps without fracturing the relationship with adversarial tactics. If you think that it would be helpful for your client to communicate directly with the other side, for instance, you might ask the mediator to allow your client to participate actively in a joint session. If you are seeking a creative solution, you might ask the mediator to help the parties generate fresh ideas.

If your mediator is not oriented toward problem-solving or resists it, you can try to coax your mediator to follow a problem-solving approach. You can ask the mediator to help the parties identify their interests or work together to resolve the dispute, for example, even if the mediator does not seem to have the depth of experience to consistently problem-solve, candidly discloses his or her practice to alternative approaches or follows a recognized alternative approach such as an evaluative, transformative or wisely directive one.[24]

7. MEDIATION REPRESENTATION PLAN

The third side forms the base for the triangle—your Mediation Representation Plan (Figure 14-4). As you formulate your negotiation approach and ways to enlist help from the mediator, you should develop a consistent and complete plan for effective representation.

Any plan should further three goals that can be configured into three sides of an interdependent Planning Triangle. You should advance your client's interests, overcome any impediments and share necessary information while minimizing the risk of exploitation. These three I(s) shape every detail of your plan. If your plan fails to further any of these goals, you will form a weak triangle and therefore a weak plan for mediation advocacy. If you advance all of the goals intelligently, you will fashion an effective plan. Each of these I(s) is culturally neutral and therefore reflect planning goals for a negotiation anywhere, although the content of each one can vary across cultures.

Let's examine each of the I(s).

7.1. INTERESTS

The first I, Interests (the first side of the triangle, Figure 14-5), encapsulates the primary goal of any plan—to meet your client's interests. Interests is a term of art with particular meaning in negotiations. It focuses on the needs of the party that any resolution must meet. It is a concept that can transform parties' view of

24 *See ibid., at* Ch. 7.2(b).

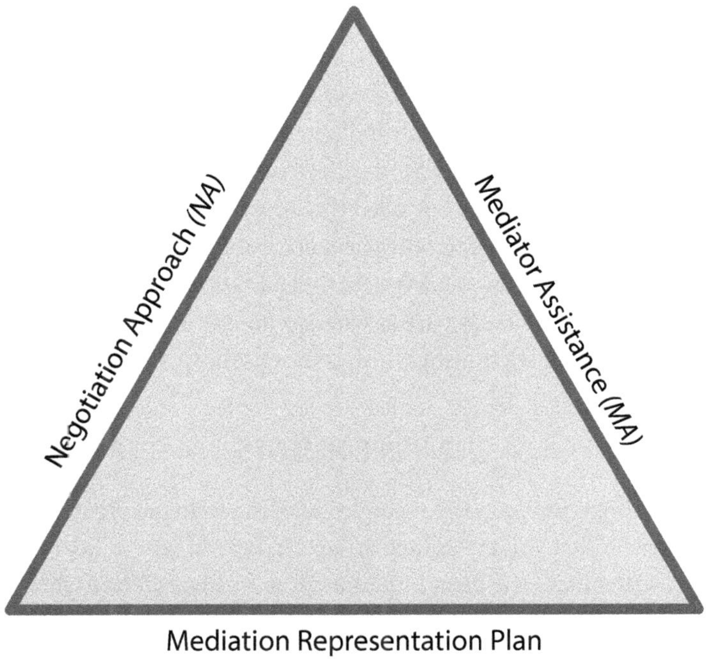

Figure 14-4. Mediation Representation Plan.

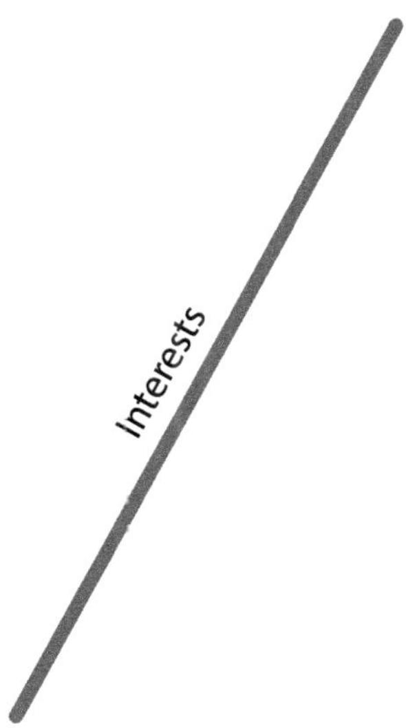

Figure 14-5. Interests.

a dispute from a distributive one with winners and losers to a dispute that might be resolved with imaginative solutions. Any plan should effectively advocate your client's interests—that is your bottom line.

The concept of interests is culturally neutral, in my view, although some have argued that it reflects narrow westernized needs.[25] However, when interests are defined broadly to include any need that must be met to settle the dispute, the term avoids limiting itself to only particular cultural needs. The term covers any need of a party. For example, Westernized parties may have a primary interest in compensation, whereas parties from some Eastern cultures may have a primary interest in the relationship, with compensation as a secondary interest.

7.2. IMPEDIMENTS

The second I, Impediments (the second side of the triangle, Figure 14-6), considers the reason that you are in mediation; an impediment may be blocking a negotiated settlement. The term impediment is a universal one when defined broadly to encompass any possible obstacle. Like with interests, impediments can be rooted in local practices, whether cultural or strategic.

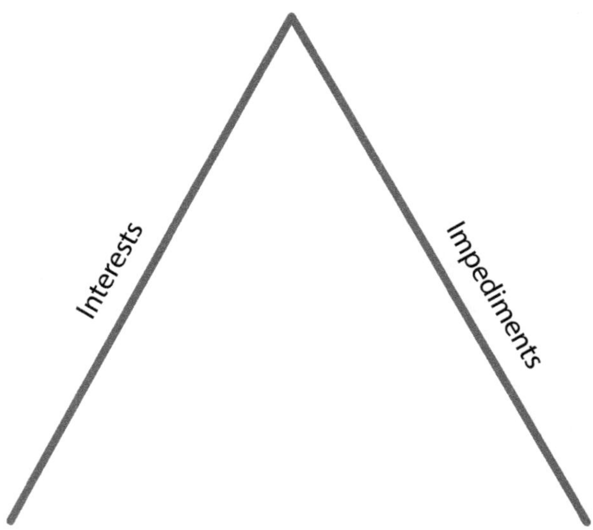

Figure 14-6. Impediments.

25 *See* Abramson, *supra* n. 1, *at* Ch. 3.2(a).

Disputes between Western parties can face impediments over the details of a contract, whereas disputes between Eastern parties may face impediments over trying to build a relationship (contract-relationship dimension), for instance. Impediments also can arise between Western and Eastern parties over a Western party's need for a detailed contract conflicting with an Eastern party's need to develop a relationship. Different styles of communicating, as anyone who has done any cross-cultural negotiations knows, can be another impediment across cultures. Westernized parties, as low-context communicators who are accustomed to talking directly and hearing direct responses such as a YES that means YES can misunderstand a high-context communicator for whom an apparent YES can mean NO in context. However, these differences also can be strategic. The interest in a relationship over a contract and an indirect Yes can be tactics by a party to avoid committing to a contract. All of these impediments can be addressed within a representation plan.

7.3. INFORMATION

The third I, Information (the base of the triangle, Figure 14-7), covers what information to gather, disclose and withhold. Sharing information can be

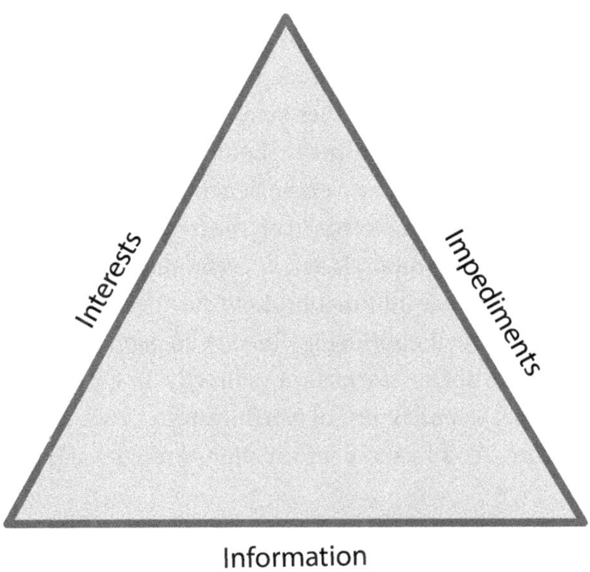

Figure 14-7. Information.

critical for helping participants understand each other's interests, identify impediments and uncover optimum solutions.

The need by parties for information is universal, regardless of locality or upbringing. However, local practices can vary regarding whether to share information, how to share information and what information to gather. As with impediments, information can be viewed and analysed through both cultural and strategic lenses.

Parties may withhold information in order to force the other side to expend resources to get the information or to avoid empowering the other side with information that the other side could use against them. A party can fear acknowledging legal weaknesses or asserting that a particular solution is important to gain in the negotiation, for instance, because the other side might exploit that information to its advantage. These withholding practices tend to be followed by US litigators who can operate under a presumption that most information should be withheld unless there is a compelling reason to disclose. In a problem-solving approach to mediation, attorneys ought to consider reversing this presumption and share information unless there is a good reason to withhold.

Once you decide to share information, you need to consider whether to share the information in a joint session or only with the mediator in a private caucus. That choice also can be influenced by culture and strategy. You may want to share information with only the mediator because you think sharing the information directly will upset the other side, may want to hear the private reactions of the mediator or may want to try convincing the mediator to become your advocate with the other side, among other possible reasons.[26] In a problem-solving process, attorneys should consider sharing information directly with the other side because of the benefits of collaborating, but exceptions can be justified, for example, based on the proprietary nature of the information or the need to test proposals before presenting them to the other side.

If a party wants to share information, how the information is conveyed can vary depending on cultural upbringing. Relative to people in the West, people from the East tend to share information indirectly. In a case study that illustrated this difference, Jeanne Brett[27] of Northwestern University found that the Japanese negotiators tend to share information through early presentation of

---

26 *See ibid., at* Ch. 5.4(b)(ii)-(iii).

27 *See* Jeanne Brett, *Negotiating Globally: How to Negotiate Deals, Resolve Disputes, and Make Decisions Across Cultural Boundaries* (HA: Jossey Bass, U.S., 2001).

proposals and counter-proposals that can be decoded by discerning any interests and priorities embedded in each proposal. If you assume that the other side will only make proposals favorable to their interests, she suggests you can infer their priorities by how their proposals and counter-proposals evolve. In contrast, the US negotiators tend to begin by asking questions and defer making proposals until after they run out of questions.

The information relevant to gather can vary based on how a party views the negotiation. A positional negotiator may see no need to learn about the other side's interests, and a problem-solving negotiator may see no value in eliciting an offer from the other side early in the information gathering stage of the negotiations, as illustrations.

Even though parties' need for information is universal, how information is handled can be shaped by various local practices that parties choose to follow. Within the favored problem-solving framework, you should consider sharing information directly with the other side unless you have a specific reason to not do so and should consider sharing and gathering information relevant to promoting a problem-solving approach.

8. KEY JUNCTURES

Any plan that addresses the three I(s) should be implemented at each of six key chronological junctures in the mediation process. The junctures cover selecting a mediator, pre-mediation contacts and the mediation session. At each juncture, you should consider how to take thoughtful and consistent advantage of any opportunities to advance interests and overcome impediments. Each juncture offers universal opportunities, but whether and how these opportunities are used can vary based on local cultural practices and strategic considerations.

The six key junctures are:

(1) Selecting a Mediator

When initiating the mediation, you may have an opportunity to select a mediator with the other side. But how and whom you select will be influenced by cultural and strategic considerations. You first should assess whether a candidate's training, orientation and experiences would help you resolve the dispute, given the interests you want to advance and the impediments. Then you should select a mediator suitable for your dispute, realizing that how the mediator approaches the mediation will affect how you will represent your client during each of the next five junctures.

In a cross-cultural mediation, you should select someone who is both culturally trained and culturally suitable.[28]

(2) & (3) Pre-Mediation Conference and Submissions

Before the first mediation session, you may want to communicate with the mediator and the other side. This option is universally available, but whether any pre-mediation contact occurs and if so, how it is done, can be influenced by local practices.

You might consider engaging the mediator and the other side in a pre-mediation conference and by submitting pre-mediation materials.[29] Pre-mediation conferences might be held between the mediator and both attorneys or separately and by phone, email or in person and can serve a range of purposes from just connecting to commencing the negotiation process. Pre-mediation submissions consist of materials sent by the parties to the mediator and sometimes the other side.

For each pre-mediation contact, you ought to consider how to advance interests and overcome impediments. You should give special attention to how the mediator might be helpful and what information you can safely share with the mediator and possibly the other side.

(4), (5) & (6) Opening Statements, Joint Sessions and Caucusing

During the mediation session, there are ample opportunities for interactions between attorneys and clients and with the mediator

(4) Opening Statements

You want to consider how to productively commence the mediation session. You have the opportunity to set the groundwork for meeting interests and overcoming impediments by revealing how you plan to negotiate (positional or problem-solving) and how the mediator might help. Practices can vary over a full range of possibilities from each side meeting separately with the mediator to both the attorney and client presenting formal opening statements to the other side and the mediator, with all sorts of variations in between, including meeting the night before over dinner or before the formal session at breakfast.

---

28 *See* Abramson, *supra* n. 1, *at* Ch. 4.2(d).

29 *See ibid., at* Ch. 5.15.

In a problem-solving process, you should consider preparing your client to present an opening statement with you to the other side as a way to set the tone and for your client to start communicating directly with the other client.[30]

(5) and (6) Joint Sessions and Caucuses

All mediations consist of joint sessions, caucuses or both. These three universal formats cover virtually all of the possibilities for conducting a mediation. Your choice and how to use each format can be influenced by cultural practices and strategic decisions, as was illustrated in the discussion of mediator assistance in which examples were cited in Minnesota of the all caucusing format and in The Netherlands of the no caucusing format.

As you plan for the mediation session, you should consider the critical choice to negotiate in a joint session with everybody in the room, in a caucus with just your client and the mediator or in another variation of caucusing such as with the mediator and only the attorneys or only the clients. Your choice can be influenced by how you think the mediator can assist and whether you want to share information with the other side or only with the mediator.

In a problem-solving negotiation, you should try to conduct most of the negotiations in joint session with extensive client involvement and limited caucusing.[31] This mix may need to be adapted to local needs for spending more or less time in joint sessions, although one anecdotal insight into evolving practices in Japan should temper any impulse to habitually adapt to current practices. A Japanese academic observer told me recently that when Western-style mediations were first introduced in Japan, many were done in caucusing because of the face-preserving needs of parties, but that joint sessions are starting to be welcomed, to his surprise.

9. CONCLUSION

As presented in this chapter, mediation advocates need to know how to negotiate within a mediation process, enlist mediator assistance and pull it all together in the form of a plan that advances client's interests and overcomes any impediments while intelligently sharing information at each of the six key junctures. By adhering to this triangular framework, advocates will be prepared

30 *See ibid., at* Ch. 5.9.
31 *See* Abramson, *supra* n. 1, *at* Ch. 5.4(a)(iii).

to thoughtfully and effectively deal with the myriad of unanticipated challenges that inevitably arise as the mediation unfolds.

Because this framework is universal and can incorporate local practices, it offers an approach to client representation that can work anywhere, as claimed in the title. This approach provides a reliable foundation for representing clients in any country or culture.

I would like to conclude with a point emphasized throughout this chapter. Even though the triangular framework can be adapted to accommodate local practices, problem-solving practices may offer advocates an opportunity to get the most out of the mediation process. If you do not already follow this approach, you might try it out.

Part Two

Intercultural and International Mediations

Ch. 7A&B	"International Dispute Resolution," in Rau, Sherman, and Peppet, *Processes of Dispute Resolution*, Chapter VI (3rd ed., 2002)
Ch. 8	"Protocols for International Arbitrators Who Dare to Settle Cases," 10 *Am. Rev. of Intl. Arb.* 1 (1999)
Ch. 9	"Mining Mediation Rules for Representation Opportunities and Obstacles," 15 *Am. Rev. of Intl. Arb.* 103 (Sp. 2005)
Ch. 10	"Selecting Mediators and Representing Clients in Cross-Cultural Disputes," 7 *Cardozo J. of Confl. Resol.* 253 (2006)
Ch. 11	*Criteria for Approving Programs to Qualify Mediators for IMI Inter-Cultural Certification* (2012)
Ch. 12	"Crossing Borders into New Ethical Territory: Ethical Challenges When Mediating Cross-Culturally," 49 *S.Tex.* *L.*R. 921 (2008) (ADR Ethics Symposium Issue)
Ch. 13	"Outward Bound to Other Cultures: Seven Guidelines for U.S. Dispute Resolution Trainers," 9 *Pepperdine Dispute Resolution Law Journal* 437 (2009)
Ch. 14	"The New Singapore Mediation Convention: The Process and Key Choices," *Sing. Ref. Bk.*, 20 *Cardozo J. Conflict Resol.* 1037 (2019)

CHAPTER 7A

International Dispute Resolution: Cross-Cultural Dimensions and Structuring Appropriate Processes*

2002

Professor Harold I. Abramson

A. DEMYSTIFYING CROSS-CULTURAL DIMENSIONS

Since the 1970s, domestic ADR has grown and evolved into a dynamic field of study and practice that has impacted on the way lawyers in the United States represent their clients. As examined in this textbook, lawyers are using new and more sophisticated methods to resolve their clients' disputes including representing their clients in mediations, minitrials, and innovative variations of arbitration. The end of the Cold War in the early 90s opened opportunities for exporting these "made in the USA" dispute resolution methods. As international markets opened up in the former Soviet Union, China, Latin America, and elsewhere, more opportunities opened up for U.S. lawyers to represent clients

---

* Chapter published in Rau, Sherman, and Peppet, *Processes of Dispute Resolution* (3rd ed. 2002).

outside of the United States. These new opportunities have created a glaring need for lawyers to learn how to resolve disputes between parties from different countries.

In this chapter, the materials explore how to adapt domestic ADR to the special needs of international disputes.[1] The first section on "Demystifying Cross-Cultural Dimensions" examines how cultural differences can impede international negotiations and ways to overcome the differences. The second section on "International ADR Clauses for Business Disputes" considers the ADR options for avoiding the hazards of transnational lawsuits. The section delves into the distinctive issues that arise when designing alternative private processes.

A. DEMYSTIFYING CROSS-CULTURAL DIMENSIONS

Cross-cultural differences among parties can hamper if not obstruct an international negotiation. Cross-cultural negotiators must know how to overcome differences by becoming cultural sensitive and learning practical strategies for bridging cultural gaps.

Most people are familiar with the concept of cross-cultural differences. We are often cited examples of cultural practices that vary from country to country, such as whether to use first names at a business meeting or take gifts to the home of a foreign host. Participants in international matters hope that their own cross-cultural faux pax do not attract the international attention and embarrassment suffered by then U.S. Ambassador to Japan, Walter Mondale, when he appeared in a kimono at a banquet in Japan. He created a stir by tucking the right side of his kimono over the left side, unintentionally using the tucking method for dressing a corpse.[2] Or with much more at risk in a delicate negotiation, then Congressman Bill Richardson unwittingly insulted Iraqi President Saddam Hussein when they met to negotiate the release of two jailed Americans. The Congressman inadvertently showed the soles of his feet to Saddam Hussein, prompting him to walk out of the room.[3]

---

1 Due to limitations in space, this chapter does not examine the striking and unconventional ways that dispute resolution methods are adapted to resolve disputes for parties that are not private ones but are sovereign nations. Disputes between nations comprise a distinct field of dispute resolution with its own lessons and techniques.

2 Nicholas D. Kristof, "Monderu-San's Last Campaign," *New York Times Magazine* (November 5, 1995)

3 Tim Weiner, "New Star Scores Home Runs for the Democrats", *New York Times* (July 18, 1995) (Fortunately, the negotiation resumed and the two Amercians were freed from a Baghdad jail.)

The challenge in dealing with cross-cultural differences is to move beyond memorizing a multitude of cultural tidbits to a deeper understanding and practical application of cross-cultural insights in the rough and tumble of complex negotiations. This does not mean negotiators must become cross-cultural experts in psychology, anthropology, or sociology, but they can learn more than cultural etiquette. Negotiators must understand that both "we" and "they" may be products of different cultures and as a result "we" may not share the same values, interests, attitudes, behavior, and linguistic styles as "they."

Even though it is very likely that the negotiators on the other side of the table view the world very differently than you do, they should always be approached with respect and with a willingness to learn. You should not try to reform the other culture at the negotiating table in hopes that they will eventually be more like yourself, for the simple reason that it will not work. On the other hand, you should not go overboard in the other direction by "going native." Most people tend to be suspicious of anyone imitating their gestures or behaviors. The soundest advice is to learn to understand and respect cultural differences while retaining one's own.[4]

1. Cross-Cultural Differences

a. What is Culture?

There is no generally accepted definition of culture. One exceptionally broad definition of culture characterizes all negotiations as "intercultural" because each person is unique. "When two individuals meet, it is an intercultural encounter since they both have different (sometimes drastically different, if not opposite) ways to perceive, discover, create reality."[5]

Professor Geert Hofstede, a Dutch social psychologist and author of renowned studies on culture, defines culture as mental programming:

> The sources of one's mental programs lie within the social environments in which one grew up and collected one's life experiences. The programming starts within the family; it continues within the neighborhood, at school, in youth groups, at the work place, and in the living community. ***
>
> A customary term for such mental software is *culture.* ***

4 Gary P. Ferraro, *The Cultural Dimension of International Business,* 143 (2nd edition, 1994)

5 Pierre Casse and Surinder Deol, *Managing Intercultural Negotiations,* xiii (1985).

> In social anthropology, "culture" is a catchword for all those patterns of thinking, feeling, and acting. ... Not only those activities supposed to refine the mind are included ..., but also the ordinary and menial things in life: greeting, eating, showing or not showing feelings, keeping a certain physical distance from others, making love, or maintaining body hygiene. ...
>
> Culture ... is always a collective phenomenon, because it is at least partly shared with people who live or lived within the same social environment, which is where it was learned. It is *the collective programming of the mind which distinguishes the members of one group or category of people from another.*
>
> Culture is learned, not inherited. It derives from one's social environment, not from one's genes. Culture should be distinguished from human nature on one side, and from an individual's personality on the other, although exactly where the borders lie between human nature and culture, and between culture and personality, is a matter of discussion among social scientists.
>
> *Human nature* is what all human beings, from the Russian professor to the Australian aborigine, have in common: it represents the universal level in one's mental software. ... However, what one does with these feelings, how one expresses fear, joy, observations, and so on, is modified by culture. ...
>
> The *personality* of an individual, on the other hand, is her/his unique personal set of mental programs which (s)he does not share with any other human being. It is based upon traits which are partly inherited with the individual's unique set of genes and partly learned. "Learned" means: modified by the influence of collective programming (culture) *as well as* unique personal experiences.[6]

Professor Gary Ferraro, an American anthropologist, further illuminates our understanding of culture by pointing out that[7] "[A]ll cultures of the world—despite many differences—face a number of common problems and share a number of common features, which we call cultural universals." Cultural

6 Geert Hofstede, *Cultures and Organizations,* 4–6 (1997).

7 Gary P. Ferraro, *The Cultural Dimension of International Business,* Ch. 2 (2nd edition, 1994); *Also, supras,* Guy Olivier Faure and Gunnar Sjostedt, *Culture and Negotiation: An Introduction in Culture and Negotiation,* 33 (Edited by Guy Olivier Faure and Jeffrey Z. Rubin, 1993).

universals include the need to develop: an economic system for producing, distributing, and consuming essential resources for living; a system for marriage, family, and raising children; a method for educating children about the life of the society; a system of preserving social order over anarchy; and a way to explain the unexplainable as through magic, religion, witchcraft, sorcery, and astrology. These universals can be met in different ways; these different ways reflect alternative cultural approaches or differences.

b. Difficulties in Identifying Cultural Behavior

It can be difficult to identify differences that are due to culture.

The other negotiator's culture cannot be simply gleaned from her nationality because her nationality is not necessarily the same as her culture. People living in the same country can follow different cultural practices. Even in the United States, with its reputation as a melting pot of immigrant cultures, many distinctive cultures flourish. The United States is more accurately a country with many cultures living together in one pot. Each culture does not merely reflect regional differences. One important work on ethnicity in the United States compiled studies of over forty American ethnic groups.[8] The studies demonstrated that the cultural values of each ethnic group is a product of multiple factors including the group's distinctive native cultural values, migration history, racist's experiences, class tensions, family life cycle stresses, and intermarriage.[9]

Difficulties in identifying cultural behavior are compounded by the likelihood that the other party is the product of more than one distinct cultural

---

8 *See Ethnicity and Family Therapy*, 1 (Eds. Monica McGoldrick, Joe Giordano, and John K. Pearce, 2nd edition, 1996). This book examines the role of ethnicity for therapists who are designing therapeutic interventions. "Ethnicity refers to a common ancestry through which individuals have evolved shared values and customs. It is deeply tied to the family, through which it is transmitted. A group's sense of commonality is transmitted over generations by the family and reinforced by the surrounding community. Ethnicity is a powerful influence in determining identity."

Although this group of articles was written for therapists, not mediators or negotiators, the readings provide valuable insights into the type of ethnocultural factors that shape the behavior of people with whom we may be negotiating. The readings give us clues about where other people as well as ourselves might be coming from. These readings are especially helpful for domestic conflicts involving parties from different ethnic groups because the readings give special attention to the factors shaping individuals who have migrated to the United States.

9 *See Ethnicity and Family Therapy*, 10–20 (Eds. Monica McGoldrick, Joe Giordano, and John K. Pearce, 2nd edition, 1996).

upbringing. The ethnic cultural experience of the other party may be further shaped by complementary and competing values of another clearly identifiable cultural experience. The other party also may be a member of a religious culture, corporate culture, international culture, and/or a professional culture of attorneys, economists, engineers, or other professionals. Each of these other cultures consists of a community with its own norms of behavior.

For instance, the other negotiator can be influenced by her professional upbringing:

> ... one should not neglect [its] complexity. ... For example, the professional culture of lawyers takes into account various elements: national differences in legal training, differences between common law and civil law traditions (the role of case law compared with the role of codified law), purely administrative experience and court experience, degree of familiarity with international law as a body of very specific rules and procedures, and relative dependence on or independence of the political authority issuing instructions. Nevertheless, despite variations within the professional culture of lawyers, who are part of different national delegations, they tend to speak a common language and are likely masters of largely identical concepts.[10]

The other negotiator may be influenced by the international culture in which she participates. The negotiator may be part of a culture that is based in the diplomatic community, business world, or a multi-country region such as the European Union. The practices of the culture are derived from the shared experience of participating and negotiating in the particular international community.

When you try to interpret another person's negotiating behavior, you may be blinded by your own cultural biases. As Jeffry Rubin and Jeswald Salacuse pointed out,[11] negotiators can operate on the mistaken assumption that:

Culture is everything. According to this view, culture has an overdetermining effect on negotiation. Armed with the stereotypes that Americans are impatient and Latins are volatile, for example, negotiators think they can function more effectively. The problem with stereotypes such as these is that,

10 Winfried Lang, *A Professional's View*, 45–46, in Culture and Negotiation (Edited by Guy Olivier Gaure and Jeffrey Z. Rubin, 1993).

11 Jeffrey Z. Rubin and Jeswald W. Salacuse, *Culture and International Negotiation: Lessons for Business,* 11 *Alternatives* 95–98 (July 1993).

even though they may contain elements of truth, the exceptions are often as or more compelling than the rule. ... Clearly, factors other than culture have an effect on what transpires in negotiation—for example, the structure of issues, the personality of the parties, and the organization of the companies involved.

They also point out that negotiators can be prisoners of their own culture:

The ways we think about culture and conflict are informed by the culture of which we are a part. American social scientists tend to think in terms of dichotomies, continua: straight lines. Would a cultural analyst from an Asian state categorize the world in similar ways, or would a circle or spiral perhaps be a more appropriate metaphor?

In short, because you view the behavior of others through your cultural biases, behavior that is the product of multiple factors, you face great difficulties when trying to identify the other side's cultural behavior.[12]

2. Cultural Conceptual Framework

A cross-cultural negotiator needs a conceptual framework in which cultural characteristics can be organized and understood. Various conceptual frameworks have been developed from studies of differences among cultures, especially differences relevant to conflict resolution. Each study considers a finite number of generic cultural characteristics, characteristics that vary in number and substance from study to study. In this section, four cross-cultural studies are considered.[13] Despite the overlap in the ideas covered, it is striking how

---

12 *See* Guy Olivier Faure, *Culture and Negotiation: An Introduction,* 5; Winfried Lang, *A Professional's View in Culture and Negotiation*; Victor A. Kremenyuk, *A Pluralistic Viewpoint,* 47–50 (Edited by Guy Olivier Faure and Jeffrey Z. Rubin, 1993)

13 For other studies, *see* Donald W. Hendon, Rebecca Angeles Hendon, and Paul Herbig, *Cross-Cultural Business Negotiations* (1996) (identified seven broad areas of cultural differences); Gary P. Ferraro, *The Cultural Dimension of International Business* (2nd edition, 1994) (identified three features of cross cultural differences and nine contrasting cultural values); David W.Augsburger, *Conflict Mediation Across Cultures* (1992) (identified nine conflict and dispute patterns); Dean Allen Foster, *Bargaining Across Borders—How to Negotiate Business Successfully Anywhere in the World,* 272–293 (1992, 1995); Terence Brake, Danielle Medina Walker, and Thomas (Tim) Walker, *Doing Business Internationally—The Guide to Cross-Cultural Success* 36–37, 44–74 (1995); David A. Victor, *International Business Communication* (1992) (developed a framework for conducting business communications across cultures); and Raymond Cohen, *Negotiating Across Cultures—Communication Obstacles in International Diplomacy,* 160–161 (1991) (makes ten recommendations for the low-context intercultural negotiator who is faced with a high-context opponent).

each study is organized to present a different view of culture that emphasizes different dimensions of culture.

In a landmark study on different cultural attitudes toward work, Geert Hofstede[14] identified **four** cultural dimensions that explain dominant value differences among cultures. First, does the culture follow low or high power distances? In a low power distance culture, people value power equalization and competence over seniority, while high power distance cultures value status, formality and hierarchy. Second, are the people in the culture risk avoiders or risk takers? Risk avoiders are uncomfortable in risky and ambiguous situations and prefer conformity and safe behavior. Risk takers (or low risk-avoiders) are more inclined toward new ideas and problem solving. Third, does the culture emphasize individualism or collectivism? In individualistic cultures, people value independence and individual needs over the needs of the community. Collectivist cultures recognize the interdependence among individuals, the paramount needs of the group, and value of cooperation. Fourth, does the culture tend toward particular gender characteristics? Societies more "masculine" value assertiveness, independence, and competitiveness, while societies more "feminine" value cooperation, nurturing, and relationships.

Glen Fisher[15] prepared a study of international negotiations for the Department of State's training programs. By applying a number of social psychological insights,[16] Fisher identified **five** considerations relevant to negotiating with persons from another culture.

First, the negotiator should collect information about how the other party views the negotiation encounter in terms of negotiating style, formalities of the setting, protocols, and who attends (title, expertise). Second, the negotiator

---

14 Geert Hofstede, *Culture's Consequences* (Abridged, 1980, 1984); *also see* Geert Hofstede, *Cultures and Organizations—Software of the Mind* (1997) and Dean Allen Foster, *Bargaining Across Borders—How to Negotiate Business Successfully Anywhere in the World,* 264–272 (1992, 1995) (shows how Hofstede's work relates to international negotiations)

15 Glen Fisher, *International Negotiation* (1980) (the author served as Dean of the Department of State's Foreign Service Institute's School of Area Studies); *also see* Glen Fisher, *Mindsets-The Role of Culture and Perception in International Relations* (2nd edition, 1997)

16 In the study for foreign service officers, Fisher first describes **four** normal features of communication and perception that interfere with effective communication across cultures. He explains how human minds, as *information processors,* are programmed differently by different cultural experiences; how the mind strives for *internal consistency* which may mean rejecting inconsistent but possibly relevant information; how we *project* our own interpretations of meanings to explain what other people mean; and the tendency to unconsciously *attribute motives* based on our own experience to explain actions of others.

needs to understand the other party's styles of decision-making—whether centralized and hierarchical and whether based on consensus or diffused among different agencies. Third, the negotiator should investigate the "national character" of the other negotiator's society. This means gathering information about the national self-image, specific values, implicit assumptions such as attitudes toward compromise or importance of defending principles, and styles of logic, reasoning, and persuasion. Fourth, the negotiator should be prepared to cope with cross-cultural "noise," background distractions unrelated to the substance of the negotiations. Common behavior of Americans may create cultural "noise" in a negotiation such as using a first name prematurely, forgetting titles, starting speeches with a joke or acting too egalitarian. Fifth, the negotiator should be cognizant of the limitations and opportunities for distortion of meanings when relying on interpreters and translators. Not all concepts or even words can be easily translated to other languages, and languages have built-in styles of reasoning that may be lost when translated.

Another valuable study[17] identified cultural values that make it more likely that the parties will achieve "win-win" solutions in negotiations. The authors found that negotiators are more likely to find joint gains if: (1) They value information sharing which is vital for identifying possibilities for trade-offs that might add value to each side. (2) They deal with information and issues polychronically instead of monochroncially. By considering many issues or tasks at once, negotiators are more likely to find integrative solutions which call for a process of trading high priority for low priority issues or connecting issues in creative ways. (3) They are oriented toward an egalitarian culture instead of a hierarchical one in which the focus on status and power may distract parties from generating joint gains. (4) They are motivated by self-interest which appears to motivate parties to persistently search for joint gains.

In the following excerpt, Jeswald Salacuse identified **ten** ways that culture impacts on negotiations:[18]

17 Jeanne M. Brett, Wendi Adair, Alain Lempereur, Tetsushi Okumura, Peter Shikhirev, Catherine Tinsley, and Anne Lytle, "Culture and Joint Gains in Negotiation," *Neg. J.* 61 79–81 (January 1998).

18 In a limited survey based on these ten ways, Professor Salacuse asked respondents to rate their negotiating style. The survey confirmed that "culture can influence the way in which persons perceive and approach certain key elements in the negotiating process." Jeswald W. Salacuse, "Ten Ways that Culture Affects Negotiating Style: Some Survey Results," *Neg. J.* 221, 237 (July 1998).

JESWALD W. SALACUSE,[19] MAKING GLOBAL DEALS 58–70 (1991) TEN WAYS CULTURE AFFECTS NEGOTIATIONS

***

Some may argue that these traits are a result of personality rather than culture. Culture certainly does not determine behavior, but it does predispose persons of a given cultural group to act in certain ways in specific situations. But rather than pursue this debate, it is enough to point out that these ten traits are common in negotiating behavior and, whether they are caused by personality or culture or both, the practical negotiator must learn to deal with them.

1. Negotiating Goal: Contract or Relationship?

An initial question is whether the two sides in a negotiation have the same goal and see the deal-making process in the same light. It is possible for businesspersons from different cultures to interpret the very purpose of their negotiation differently. For many Americans, the purpose of a business negotiation, first and foremost, is to arrive at a signed contract between the parties. Americans view a signed contract as a definitive set of rights and duties that strictly binds the two sides, an attitude succinctly summed up in the declaration that a deal is a deal.

Japanese and certain other cultural groups consider that the goal of negotiation is not a signed contract but a relationship between the two sides. Although the written contract expresses the relationship, the essence of their deal is the relationship itself. For the American, signing a contract is closing a deal; for the Japanese, signing a contract might more appropriately be called opening a relationship.

***

19 Jeswald Salacuse, a professor of international law at Tufts University and a member of Harvard's Program on Negotiation, drew upon his business experience in more than thirty countries when he identified seven barriers to successful negotiations that are common in international business deals but are not ordinarily relevant to domestic deals. Of these seven barriers, one was the impact of culture.

2. Negotiating Attitude: Win/Lose or Win/Win?

Because of culture or personality, or both, businesspersons appear to approach deal making with one of two basic attitudes: that a negotiation is either a process through which both can gain (win/win) or a process through which, of necessity, one side wins and the other loses (win/lose). As you enter negotiations, it is important to know which type of negotiator is sitting across the table from you. If one side has much greater bargaining power than the other, the weaker side has a tendency to see the negotiation as a win/lose situation: every gain for the powerful side is automatically a loss for the weaker party. As one Indian executive put it, "Negotiations between the weak and the strong are like negotiations between the lamb and the lion. Invariably, the lamb gets eaten." Win/win negotiators see deal making as a collaborative and problem-solving process; win/lose negotiators view it as confrontational.

***

3. Personal Style: Informal or Formal?

An executive's "style" at the negotiating table is usually characterized as formal or informal. References to style focus on the way a negotiator talks to others, uses titles, dresses, speaks, and interacts with other persons. A negotiator with a formal style insists on addressing the other team by their titles, avoids personal anecdotes, and refrains from questions touching on the private or family life of members of the other side. An informal style of negotiator tries to start the discussion on a first-name basis, quickly seeks to develop a personal, friendly relationship with the other team, and may take off his jacket and roll up his sleeves when deal making begins in earnest. Each culture has its own formalities, which have special meaning. They are another means of communication among the persons sharing that culture. For an American or an Australian, calling someone by his first name is an act of friendship and therefore a good thing. In other cultures, such as the French, Japanese, or Egyptian, the use of a first name at a first meeting is an act of disrespect and therefore a bad thing.

***

4. Communication: Direct or Indirect?

Methods of communication vary among cultures. Some place emphasis on direct and simple methods of communication; others rely heavily on indirect and complex methods. The latter may use circumlocutions, figurative forms of speech, facial expressions, gestures, and other kinds of body language. In a culture that values directness, such as the German, you can expect to receive a clear and definite response to questions and proposals. In cultures that rely on indirect communication, reaction to your proposal may be gained only by interpreting a series of signs, gestures, and seemingly indefinite comments. What you will not receive at a first meeting is a definite commitment or rejection.

***

5. Sensitivity to Time: High or Low?

Discussions of national negotiating styles invariably treat a particular culture's attitudes toward time. So it is said that Germans are always punctual, Mexicans are habitually late, Japanese negotiate slowly, and Americans are quick to make a deal. Commentators claim that some cultures "value" time more than others, but this may not be an accurate characterization of the situation. Rather, they value differently the amount of time devoted to and measured against the goal pursued. For Americans, the deal is a "signed contract" and "time is money," so they want to make a deal quickly. Americans therefore try to reduce formalities to a minimum and get down to business. For members of other cultures, who view the purpose of the negotiation as creating a relationship rather than simply signing a contract, there is a need to invest time in the negotiating process so that the parties can get to know one another well and determine whether they wish to embark on a long-term relationship. Aggressive attempts to shorten the negotiating time may be viewed by the other side as efforts to hide something and therefore may be a cause of distrust.

***

6. Emotionalism

Accounts of negotiating behavior of persons from other cultures almost always point to a particular group's tendency or lack thereof to act emotionally. According to the stereotype, Latin Americans show their emotions at the negotiating table, but Japanese hide their feelings. Obviously, individual personality plays a role here. There are passive Latins and hotheaded Japanese. But various cultures have different rules as to the appropriateness of displaying emotions, and these rules are usually brought to the negotiating table as well.

7. Form of Agreement: General or Specific?

Cultural factors also influence the form of agreement that parties try to make. Generally, Americans prefer very detailed contracts that attempt to anticipate all possible circumstances, no matter how unlikely. Why? Because the "deal" is the contract itself, and one must refer to the contract to determine how to handle a new situation that may arise. Other cultures, such as that of China, prefer a contract in the form of general principles rather than detailed rules. Why? Because, it is claimed, the essence of the deal is the relationship of trust that exists between the parties. If unexpected circumstances arise, the parties should look to their relationship, not the contract, to solve the problem. So in some cases, the American drive at the negotiating table to foresees all contingencies may be viewed by persons from another culture as evidence of lack of confidence in the stability of the underlying relationship.

Some persons argue that differences over the form of an agreement are caused more by unequal bargaining power between the parties than by culture. In a situation of unequal bargaining power, the stronger party always seeks a detailed agreement to "lock up the deal" in all its possible dimensions, while the weaker party prefers a general agreement to give it room to "wiggle out" of adverse circumstances that are almost bound to occur in the future. ... According to this view, it is not culture but context that determines this negotiating trait.

***

8. Building an Agreement: Bottom Up or Top Down?

Related to the form of an agreement is the question of whether negotiating a business deal is an inductive or deductive process. Does it start from agreement on general principles and proceed to specific items, or does it begin with agreement on specifics, such as price, delivery date, and product quality, the sum total of which becomes the contract? Different cultures tend to emphasize one approach over the other.

Some observers believe that the French prefer to begin with agreement on general principles, while Americans tend to seek agreement first on specifics. For Americans, negotiating a deal is basically making a whole series of compromises and tradeoffs on a long list of particulars. For the French, the essence is to agree on basic general principles that will guide and indeed determine the negotiation process afterward. The agreed-upon general principles become the framework, the skeleton, upon which the contract is built.

A further difference in negotiating style is seen in the dichotomy between the "building down" approach and the "building up" approach. In the building-down approach, the negotiator begins by presenting a maximum deal if the other side accepts all the stated conditions. In the building-up approach, one side starts by proposing a minimal deal that can be broadened and increased as the other party accepts additional conditions. According to many observers, Americans tend to favor the building-down approach, while the Japanese prefer the building-up style of negotiating a contract.

9. Team Organization: One Leader or Group Consensus?

In any international business negotiation, it is important to know how the other side is organized, who has the authority to make commitments, and how decisions are made. Culture is one important factor that affects the way executives organize themselves to negotiate a deal. One extreme is the negotiating team with a supreme leader who has complete authority to decide all matters. Americans tend to follow this approach, described as the "John Wayne style of negotiations": one person has all the authority and plunges ahead to do a job, and to do it as quickly as possible. Other cultures, notably the Japanese and the former Soviets, stress team negotiation and consensus decision making. When you negotiate with such a team, it may not be apparent who is the leader and who has the authority to commit the side. In the first type, the negotiating team is usually small; in the second, it is often large. For example, in negotiations in China on a major deal, it would not be uncommon for the Americans to arrive at the table with three persons and for the Chinese to show up with ten. Similarly, the one-leader team is usually prepared to make commitments and decisions more quickly than a negotiating team organized on the basis of consensus. ...

10. Risk Taking: High or Low?

Studies seem to support the idea that certain cultures try to avoid risk more than others. In any given deal, the willingness of one side to take "risks" in the negotiation process—to divulge information, to be open to new approaches, to tolerate uncertainties in a proposed course of action—can be affected by the personality of the negotiator and the context of the negotiation. Nonetheless, there are certain cultural traits to this effect. The Japanese, with their emphasis on requiring enormous amounts of information and on their intricate group decision-making process, tend to be risk adverse. Americans, by comparison, are risk takers. If you determine that the team on the other side of the table is risk adverse, focus your attention on proposing rules, mechanisms, and relationships that will reduce the apparent risks in the deal for them.

11. Developing Cultural Sensitivity

A cross-cultural negotiator must learn to recognize when cultural factors are contributing to a conflict and may be impeding the success of the negotiation. This cultural sensitivity cannot be acquired by simply memorizing facts about the other party's culture. In addition to the previously discussed difficulties in even identifying the other party's culture, a negotiator needs to know how to use cultural information. Gathering a large quantity of cultural information by itself does not prepare the negotiator to use the information in a particular negotiation with a particular person.

The better negotiators, the more successful global businesspeople, are not those who have memorized hundreds or thousands of do's and don'ts. Rather, they are those who have developed an international feel, a global mind-set, an empathic approach toward doing business with people from other cultures. Certainly, the better international negotiators do try to learn about the people of the country they are negotiating with. And, certainly, those more experienced with one particular country will have an advantage over those less experienced in that country. But, first and foremost, the better negotiators understand the larger process of achieving effective communication with business associates whose cultural baggage is different from their own. And they know the importance of understanding cultural differences in order to prevent such differences from undermining their negotiations.[20]

How does an attorney develop this "international feel" or "global mind-set"? In other words, how does an attorney guard against culturally-based impasses and bridge cultural gaps?

Consider this five step approach. In the first three steps, the attorney prepares for a cross-cultural negotiation by mastering a cultural conceptual framework, learning about his own cultural upbringing, and investigating the culture of the other negotiators. The next two steps provide a guide for the attorney in the negotiation sessions. The attorney should view negotiating behavior of others with an open mind and then figure out how to bridge any differences.

---

20 Dean Allen Foster, *Bargaining Across Borders*, 5 (1992).

These five steps will be elaborated through the use of a hypothetical. Consider how a U.S. attorney might react when she learns that the other party, an institutional client, will not be represented by someone with substantial settlement authority. Instead, the other side will be represented by a team of negotiators who will make decisions by consensus. Furthermore, all the team members will not be present in the negotiation sessions. Under these circumstances, the U.S. attorney is likely to suspect that the other side is acting in bad faith. The other side appears to be replacing the person with real settlement authority with an unwieldy team of negotiators. How might the attorney proceed?

The three preparatory steps are:

First, the attorney should learn a *conceptual framework* which can help her identify and understand cultural characteristics. The attorney must grasp the meaning of "cultural behavior" and how it is different from universal "human behavior." Cultural characteristics, as discussed in the previous section, have been isolated in numerous studies of culture, including studies of characteristics relevant to conflict resolution.[21]

The hypothetical implicates a cultural characteristic related to the process of decisionmaking. Does settlement authority reside with a leader or with a team that makes decisions based on consensus? This generic characteristic, as virtually all cultural characteristics, encompasses a continuum bound at each end with a value-based pole. At one extreme, societies can be found that are hierarchical in which decisions are made by leaders. At the other extreme, societies can be found that are collective in which decisions are made by consensus. The actual cultural practice is rarely one extreme or the other. The cultural practice usually falls somewhere between these two end poles of the continuum.

---

21 *See, e.g.*, Geert Hofstede, *Culture's Consequences* (Abridged, 1980, 1984); Geert Hofstede, *Cultures and Organizations—Software of the Mind* (1997) and Dean Allen Foster, *Bargaining Across Borders—How to Negotiate Business Successfully Anywhere in the World,* 264–272 (1992, 1995) (shows how Hofstede's work relates to international negotiations); Glen Fisher, *International Negotiation* (1980) (the author served as Dean of the Department of State's Foreign Service Institute's School of Area Studies); Glen Fisher, *Mindsets-The Role of Culture and Perception in International Relations* (2nd edition, 1997); Donald W. Hendon, Rebecca Angeles Hendon, and Paul Herbig, *Cross-Cultural Business Negotiations* (1996); Gary P. Ferraro, *The Cultural Dimension of International Business* (2nd edition, 1994); David W. Augsburger, *Conflict Mediation Across Cultures,* 8–10, 26–28 (1992); Dean Allen Foster, *Bargaining Across Borders—How To Negotiate Business Successfully Anywhere in the World,* 272–293 (1992, 1995); and Terence Brake, Danielle Medina Walker, and Thomas (Tim) Walker, *Doing Business Internationally—The Guide to Cross-Cultural Success,* 36–37, 44–74 (1995).

As practiced in U.S. businesses, decisionmaking is predominately hierarchical, placing the practice near the leader pole but not at the pole because input and collaboration also are valued.

Second, the attorney should fill-in this conceptual framework with a deep understanding of her *own culture or cultures.*[22] An attorney is not always cognizant of the degree to which her own behavior is universal or culturally determined. Yet, it is though this personal lens that an attorney observes and assesses the negotiating behavior of others. To reduce distortions, the attorney should learn about her own cultural upbringing in order to appreciate the extent to which her view of other people's behavior may not necessarily reflect a universal view. In the hypothetical, the U.S. attorney should be aware that her view that organizations tend to be hierarchical in which decisionmaking is centralized in "leaders" is not universal organizational behavior.

Third, the attorney should strengthen her conceptual framework with an understanding of the *culture or cultures of the other negotiator(s).* Despite the difficulties in identifying cultural behavior, the attorney should try to identify and research the culture(s) of her client, the other attorney, and the other party.[23] Furthermore, the attorney should learn as much as possible about the other negotiators as individuals, that is their personalities and ways their negotiating behavior may vary from practices of their culture(s). In the hypothetical, the research might reveal that the other side is from a society in which organizations typically make decisions based on consensus, but the research may reveal little about their individual personalities.

These first three preparatory steps are relatively easy to complete because they entail collecting mostly accessible information on cultural characteristics. The next two steps, however, are much more difficult to accomplish because they require suspending judgments and developing strategies during intense, dynamic, and fast moving negotiation sessions.

Fourth, the attorney should learn to withhold judgments about the other side and instead view key negotiating behavior with an *open mind.* This requires considerable discipline. It is too easy to for an attorney who routinely judges

22 For studies of American culture, *see* Gary Althen, *American Ways,* xiii, 4, 8, 9–10, 14, 17, 24–25, 136–137 (1988); Edward C. Stewart and Milton J. Bennett, *American Cultural Patterns-A Cross-Cultural Perspective* (1991); Alison R. Lanier (revised by Charles William Gay), *Living in the U.S.A.,* Part I (5th edition, 1996); and Dean Engel, "Passport USA" (1997), and Dean Allen Foster, *Bargaining Across Borders—How to Negotiate Business Successfully Anywhere in the World,* Chs. 3–6 (1995).

23 *See* Notes and Questions, Note 9 on Researching Culture.

negotiating behavior to prematurely judge it in a cross-cultural negotiation. In the hypothetical, the U.S. negotiator should not judge the other side's decision-making process as evidence of good or bad faith; instead she should view this key negotiating behavior as a difference that needs to be dealt with.

Fifth and finally, the attorney should search for ways to *bridge* the resulting gap. In doing so, the attorney should not assume that just because a person was brought up in a clearly identifiable culture, the person will act in accordance with its cultural norms.

Gaps might be closed by the attorney negotiating a resolution or deferring to the other side's practice. The attorney could negotiate a solution through resort to an interest-based approach, where the interests behind the practices are respected. Parties also might negotiate a compromise. In the hypothetical, instead of viewing as bad faith the other side's claim that they cannot agree to anything without a consensus, the U.S. attorney might focus on how to respect their need for consensus while still meeting her need for clients to be present with substantial settlement authority. The attorney, for example, could negotiate an arrangement in which the other side brings to the negotiation sessions all the people who must concur or at least be sure the absent people are available by telephone. Then, in the sessions, the consensus approach could be respected by giving members of the negotiating team ample time to meet privately.

As an alternative to negotiating over closure of the gap, one side may choose simply to defer to the other side's practice, especially when the other practice is not a deal-breaker or does not implicate core personal values. For instance, the U.S. attorney may defer to the other side's formal practices of carefully using titles and avoiding personal questions about family. The gap, however, can be difficult to bridge when the difference reflects engrained strategic practices, such as a conflict between a problem-solving style and haggling.

In another example applying the five steps, consider that the typical U.S. lawyer usually insists that signed business agreements cover many details and contingencies. The U.S. lawyer will likely interpret any reluctance by the other side to reduce details to writing as reluctance about the deal or a specific issue. In preparing for a cross-cultural negotiation with a Japanese lawyer, however, the U.S. lawyer should realize that his own preference for reducing everything to writing may be due to his own cultural upbringing and may not be a universal mode of behavior (step 2). The drafting of comprehensive contracts is taught in U.S. law school and reinforced in law practice. A Japanese lawyer may have been brought up differently (step 3). Instead of being concerned about the details of a written agreement, the Japanese lawyer may be more concerned about the business relationship, leaving for the written contract a general statement about the relationship and basic principles for governing the business deal.

In the negotiations, the U.S. lawyer should view the reluctance of the Japanese lawyer to put everything in writing as ambiguous behavior to be viewed with an open mind (step 4). This difference might be investigated through a conversation in which the U.S. attorney explains why he prefers detailed contracts and then inquires why the other attorney may not. If the U.S. attorney learns that the other side believes business deals are about relationships, not contracts, the U.S attorney needs to find a way to bridge this resulting gap in practices. The attorney may close the gap by respecting the reasons for the different practices. He may negotiate a compromise in which both sides seek to cultivate a relationship of trust and then enter into a contract that may cover key obligations but not every conceivable contingency (step 5.)

Notes and Questions

1. What are the common characteristics identified in the four generic studies of culture in the readings? Do each of the cultural characteristics fit the definition of culture? Are any of these characteristics influenced by other factors such as genetics and personality? If differences in negotiating behavior can be due to factors other than culture, is there any value served by focusing on differences due to culture?
2. Reflect on the key features of your negotiation approach (e.g. what information you gather before meeting, how you begin a negotiation, how you respond to the other side's initiatives, what end product you are seeking, etc.) Which of your practices are universal and which are shaped by your cultural upbringing?
3. Cultural Country Studies. When investigating the cultural practices of another country, it can be useful to read country specific studies. Here are two excerpts that describe how several cultural characteristics are practiced in two particular countries, Japan and Mexico.

a. Japan[24]

Japanese negotiators are well-known for their indirectness and vagueness of response. This arises from a fear of offending the other party out of a concern

24 For a more comprehensive cultural study of Japan, *see* Rosalie L. Tung, *Business Negotiations with the Japanese* (1984)

for maintaining harmonious relations. The tendency, therefore, is to avoid extremes and steer a middle course on the various issues.

Indirectness is partly a result of the complex nature of the Japanese company decision-making process. In large, well-established Japanese companies in which no one person wields absolute power, a definite position cannot be taken on a particular issue until a consensus has been forged. Vagueness is an avenue through which the Japanese can save face in case a reversal of a position is needed at a later time. It is not a deliberate attempt to deceive the other party. The message which the Japanese negotiating team most wants to convey will be found in its non-verbal signals. In Japan this is known as *Jiaragei* and can be described as "the process of feeling another out on an issue."

A good cross-cultural negotiator will always be responsive to the mood of the negotiation and will realize that the more important the matter being discussed, the more indirect the Japanese manner of communication will be.

***

Possibly, the most frustrating example of vagueness is found in the Japanese reluctance to say "no" to a proposal. However, there are certain expressions, consistently used, which are intended to indicate a "no" response. It is important that these be recognized because they could otherwise be misinterpreted as evasiveness or delay tactics. Standard indicators of "no" appear in the following forms:

(A) Prolonged inactivity.
(B) A discussion of deficiencies in the proposal.
(C) A suggestion that there are better alternatives.
(D) A mere failure to draw up a proposal.

Maintaining "Face"

You should make every effort to adopt a negotiating style which will respect the Japanese concern to maintain "face." Disagreement with a proposal should not be expressed in outright rejection. To do so would be construed as a failure to treat the other party with the respect that should flow from your mutual concern for the overall business relationship. You should indicate your rejection subtly by suggesting alternative proposals. Forthright statements of positions should be avoided. Although it is important to be forceful when necessary, you should generally adopt a posture that allows the other party sufficient room to change position without losing face.

Peter H. Corne, "The Complex Art of Negotiation between Cultures," *Arbitration Journal* 46 (December 1992)

b. Mexico

The difference between monochronic and polychronic societies may also be illustrated through different attitudes toward deadlines. Simply speaking, U.S. Americans have been raised believing that there is great value in planning and scheduling, quick answers, and prompt solutions. A U.S. American's day is likely to be packed with appointments and deadlines. In contrast, Mexicans believe in relaxed observation of deadlines and are likely to spend more time evaluating problems before making decisions. As a result, Mexicans often view the term "deadline" as flexible and factor it in with other priorities. For example, Mexican contracts contain an implied extension for important events. In Mexican society, interruptions are routine and delays are to be expected in both business and personal life.

***

... Mexico exemplifies an extremely high power distance culture, and the United States is recognized as a relatively low power distance culture.

Generally, high power distance countries are more comfortable with disparity of power and hierarchies in their societies. Low power distance countries, however, question the legitimacy of different levels of power and strongly attempt to de-emphasize any stratification or inequality in their societies. Accordingly, Mexico places a high value upon hierarchies and rank within the business context. Leadership is autocratic and authoritative. It is based upon the values of age, sex, connections and expedience. Subordinates rarely, question their leaders: therefore, it is important to show proper deference and respect to the senior members of a Mexican negotiating team during a mediation.

Julie Barker, "International Mediation—A Better Alternative for the Resolution of Commercial Disputes: Guidelines for a U.S. Negotiator Involved in an International Commercial Mediation with Mexicans," 19 *Loyola of LA Intl & Comp. L.J.* 32, 33–37, 39–43, 45–49 (1996).

4. Rubin and Salacuse have suggested ways for turning cultural differences into an opportunity for building a working relationship.

Too often, negotiators regard culture as an obstacle to reaching agreement. Instead, try to find ways in which culture can serve as a way to build a relationship with the other side. How can these bridging opportunity be created?

First, try to show genuine interest in the culture of the other side. Asking questions about the history and customs of the country from which the other negotiator comes is not only a sign of respect and interest, but a way of gathering valuable information that can only help you be a more effective negotiator. If you have done some reading about the culture, so that your questions and comments are knowledgeable, that will help you gain the respect of the other side.

Second, look for cultural experiences that you and the other negotiator have in common. President Anwar Sadat of Egypt, when negotiating with the Sudanese, would apparently begin by observing that his mother came from Sudan. African-Americans, in dealing with African business executives, will often stress their common cultural heritage as a way of building a bridge, and Italian-Americans often use the same approach in Italy. President Jimmy Carter used religion as a shared value system binding together Sadat, Israel's Menachem Begin, and himself at Camp David in 1978. Such appeals to common experiences, history, or values can help to remind negotiators that while they may be divided over the issues between them, they are also joined in ways that transcend the current conflict.

Third, search for a third culture that is of shared interest to both of you. For example, a Thai and an American business negotiator may discover their common love of opera in a negotiation, and that discovery may help to build a bridge between the two.

Fourth, give yourself plenty of time for what is called "pre-negotiation." The most important events in negotiation often take place *before* the parties ever come to the table. During the preliminary stages, people get to know one another, figure out what sorts of agreements will ultimately be possible and which will not, and begin developing the basis for a relationship. Follow the Japanese example: develop relationship. Among other things, this will help you learn valuable things about the people you are negotiating with. And that, in turn, will make it more likely that you will be able to get the agreement you want.

Jeffrey Z. Rubin and Jeswald W. Salacuse, "Culture and International Negotiation: Lessons for Business" 11 *Alternatives* 95, 98–99 (July, 1993)

5. You represent a client who needs a stable source of reliable computers for its large business customers. Your client asked you to negotiate the purchase of ten thousand computers over the next five years from a Japanese computer company. In telephone calls and emails, you have been trying to work out the details including the price per computer, firm delivery dates, and a liquidated damage clause to cover late deliveries. You are having difficulty getting direct answers from your Japanese counterpart who keeps telling you that everything will be fine and that your client will get what it needs. Your client is very concerned about these vague responses. To finalize the deal, your client decided to send you to Japan.

You know that your Japanese counterpart lived in Japan his whole live except for going to the United States for three years to earn his law degree at New York University. You also know that your Japanese counterpart has had little experience negotiating business deals with U.S. businesses.

Develop a cross-cultural negotiation strategy based on the five step approach. Use the information on the Japanese culture that is described in this Note and the Salacuse article on ten ways culture affects negotiations.

6. In his book, *The Mediation Process,* Christopher Moore suggested that a mediation may reach an impasse due to various causes. He points out that parties may reach an impasse because of their conflicting views of critical information (data conflicts), unequal bargaining positions (structural conflicts), or competing needs (interest conflicts). They also may be in conflict due to hostile personal relationships (relationship conflicts) or conflicting personal values (value conflicts). For each of these five sources of conflicts, Moore lists possible causes. In which of these five conflict categories might cross-cultural differences arise as a cause? See Christopher W. Moore, *The Mediation Process* 60–61(2nd edition, 1996).

7. Culture also plays an important role in mediation. For articles on the subject, see Raymond Cohen "Cultural Aspects of International Mediation" in *Resolving International Conflicts—The Theory and Practice of Mediation,* Ch. 5, 107–128 (Jacob Bercovitch, ed., 1996) (The author identifies three cross-cultural roles of mediators: the interpreter who bridges intercultural communication gap, a buffer who protects face of adversaries, and the coordinator who synchronizes dissonant negotiating conventions.); Cynthia A. Savage, "Culture and Mediation: A Red Herring" 5 *Am. U.J. Gender & Law* 269 (1996) (The author recommends that instead of approaching differences in terms of racial, ethnic, or other single identifying characteristic, negotiators should recognize differences in terms of various value orientations that also can account for individual differences and effects of multiple cultures.); Selma Myers and Barbara

Filner, Mediation Across Cultures 23 (1994) (The author identified five cultural issues that most significantly affect the mediation process: language, assumptions, expectations that others will conform to us, biases against the unfamiliar, and values in conflict.); and Paul B. Pederson and Fred E. Jandt, "Culturally Contextual Models for Creative Conflict Management" and "The Cultural Context of Mediation and Constructive Conflict Management" in *Constructive Conflict Management—Asia-Pacific Cases* 3–26, 249–275 (Fred E. Jandt and Paul B. Pederson, eds., 1996) (The authors analyze over 100 case studies of cultural components of mediations in various Asian cultures and substantive settings, including the testing of two models of constructive conflict resolution, one based on high or low context cultures and another based on separating culturally learned expectations of behavior from actual behavior.)

8. Interpreters and Translators. Cultural differences are magnified when the native language of each of the parties is different. The obvious solution of bringing in a professional interpreter or translator[25] still poses risks. Even professionals can make grave mistakes that distort communications.

Many examples of interpretation problems can be found in settings familiar to lawyers. The need for selecting qualified interpreters was conspicuously demonstrated when Secretary of State Madeleine K. Albright, who speaks fluent Czech, became frustrated with her interpreter at a news conference in Prague. She finally interrupted him with the remark "not exactly" and then served as her own interpreter.[26] Errors in translating treaties can occur, as happened when a conflict arose between two official versions of an international trade treaty, one in Spanish and the other in English. The Spanish version referred to "leyes" as a source of law which included treaties while the English version referred to "relevant statutes" which by definition did not include treaties. The conflict left unclear the authority of the adjudicatory body to rely on treaties as a source of law when resolving the dispute.[27] Even translating common dispute resolution

---

25 Interpreters translate spoken words orally from one language to another as the words are spoken to the listener(s). Translators translate contracts and other written documents into another written language. Translators have the relative luxury of more time and the opportunity to use dictionaries and other research tools.

26 R. W. Apple Jr. "Honors of a Homecoming Adorn Albright's Success," *New York Times* A3, col. 4 (July 15, 1997).

27 In the Matter of the Mexican Antidumping Investigation Into Imports of Cut-to-Length Plate Products from the United States, Binational Panel No. MEX-94-1904-02 August 30, 1995 (Chapter XIX of the North American Free Trade Agreement) (adopted Spanish language version because of ample support that treaties are an important source of law and should be used).

words into a foreign language may produce unintended meanings. For example, in Iran, the word "mediator" in Persian suggests that the person is a meddler and the word "compromise" evokes a negative meaning as in compromising one's integrity.[28]

We also have to recognize that certain ideas do not exist, or exist in very different form, in other languages. Glen Fisher observes:

> When a thought loses something in translation, that is probably the point to dig in and find out what it was that was lost, for it is precisely in those instances in which cultures do not have equivalent conceptions that the two sides in a discussion find themselves talking past each other. For example, there was no word for "democracy" when Japan was exposed to the West. Something had to be created out of three written characters to produce something like "peopleness" or populism. Usage may now make the gap smaller, but the communication problem presented is clear.
>
> Glen Fisher, *International Negotiation* 62 (1980)

In view of these risks, a negotiator should carefully select a professional interpreter or translator who is qualified for the particular negotiation. Not every bilingual person is qualified to serve in this professional capacity. These are highly skilled duties. A qualified person must possess a deep understanding of the nuances of both languages, the culture underlying both languages, the technical words and concepts relevant to the particular negotiation, and the unique demands of interpreting or translating. Because a negotiator works closely with her interpreter when interacting with the other side, the negotiator should prepare her interpreter for the substance of the negotiation and know how to skillfully work with her interpreter during the negotiation sessions.[29]

9. Researching Culture.[30] A negotiator should prepare for a cross-cultural negotiation by reading, talking to people, and visiting the other country. For example, an American preparing to negotiate a business deal in Northern China

---

28 *See* Roger Fisher and William Ury, *Getting to Yes: Negotiating Agreement without Giving In,* 34 (1981)

29 *See* Abramson, *International Mediation Basics in Practitioner's Guide to International Arbitration and Mediation,* Ch. 10.06 (Editors-Chernick, Kolkey, and Rhoades, to be published in Fall, 2001). *Also see* Ileana Dominguez-Urban, "The Messenger as the Medium of Communication: The Use of Interpreters in Mediation," *J. Disp. Resol.* 1(1997).

30 For an excellent chapter on how to research cultural information, *see* Gary P. Ferraro, *The Cultural Dimension of International Business,* Ch. 6 (2nd edition, 1994).

may derive valuable cultural information about that region from modern histories of China, cultural studies of the Chinese people, newspaper articles published in foreign and Chinese papers, articles in popular Chinese magazines, and accounts of negotiations with people from China. Chinese films and television shows also are worth watching. Additional insights can be learned from the policy choices made in Chinese laws and in the ways Chinese governmental institutions are organized. Most of this information can be found in libraries and on the internet.

The negotiator should contact people with knowledge and experience in the other culture. Insights can be collected from professionals who have business experience in Northern China. These professionals may be lawyers, accountants, bankers, or interpreters who live in the United States and have done deals in or have lived in Northern China. These professionals may be Chinese nationals, American-Chinese, or non-Chinese. The negotiator may even hire a cultural consultant who specializes in assisting others working in other cultures.

It is enormously valuable for a negotiator to spend time visiting the other culture, including learning its language. If this cannot be done before the negotiation, a negotiator should at least arrive early enough before a negotiation session in the foreign country to do some "in-country research." Spending time in the foreign culture means doing more than being a tourist. A negotiator should reach out to collect cultural information by meeting as many local people as possible, walking the streets, and visiting places where local people spend time, such as shops, markets, and parks. The negotiator also should visit museums, libraries and bookstores and read local newspapers, some of which may be published in English.

Two useful and underutilized sources of cultural data are the U.S. Department of State and local universities. A negotiator can gather information from the U.S. Department of State, especially its country desk on China and from the American Embassy or Consulate in China, especially its commercial officers in China. Contacting local universities might turn up a department specializing in the culture or region, such as a China department or a department on Asia or Pacific Rim Countries. A university department can provide access to both valuable resource materials and resident experts.

CHAPTER 7B

International Dispute Resolution: Cross-Cultural Dimensions and Structuring Appropriate Processes*

2002

Professor Harold I. Abramson

B. INTERNATIONAL ADR CLAUSES FOR BUSINESS DISPUTES

---

* Chapter published in Rau, Sherman, and Peppet, *Processes of Dispute Resolution* (3rd ed. 2002).

6. Public Dispute Resolution Systems for Commercial Disputes
   Notes and Questions

B. INTERNATIONAL ADR CLAUSES FOR BUSINESS DISPUTES[1]

From jets to jeans, turbines to telephones, oil to beans—globalization of commerce has increased exponentially in the more than fifty years since the last world wide war. During this time, businesses have expanded beyond national borders and markets into "multinational corporations" with international networks of suppliers, customers, employees, and shareholders. Domestic and multinational companies, together with state-owned enterprises, seek strategic advantages by creating joint ventures, alliances, and partnering relationships with foreign enterprises. British Air allies with American Airlines; General Motors joint ventures with Chinese state-owned enterprises; French-German-Japanese construction joint ventures build the airport and approaches in Hong Kong. ... Business arrangements are complex; potential rewards are great, but risks are also huge. The investments required to compete effectively expose businesses to all of the uncertainties inherent in any long-term interdependent relationship plus those associated with cross-cultural, transnational matters, including possible expropriation by one's partner, submission to the jurisdiction of foreign courts, and reliance on an alien legal system.

Conflict is a natural component of long-term commercial relations. It is atypical for a large scale infrastructure project, development project, or trading relationship not to produce claims, disputes and disagreements over rights, responsibilities, powers, obligations, and monetary rewards. Eric D. Green, "International Commercial Dispute Resolution: Courts, Arbitration, and Mediation—Introduction," 15 *Bost. U. Intl. L. J.* 175–176 (1997).[2]

When an international business conflict arises, private parties cannot count on access to a compulsory, binding international court system to resolve their dispute. There is none. While parties can resort to the national court system of one of the parties, cross-border litigation presents parties with a host of risks that can make the litigation process enormously expen-

---

1 The book, *Arbitration and Mediation in International Business* by Christian Buhring-Uhle, is cited frequently in this chapter. This superb 1996 book is informed by the author's empirical survey of practitioners and covers thoroughly the subject of international dispute resolution for business conflicts. Anyone deeply interested in this subject should read this significant study.

2 *Also see* C. Buhring-Uhle, *Arbitration and Mediation in International Business*, 3–17 (1996)

sive and uncertain.[3] Some of the transnational litigation risks can be reduced by parties agreeing which national court system will be used (choice of forum provision) and which law will be applied (choice of law provision). Many of these risks can be further reduced by parties designing their own private dispute resolution systems, known as alternative dispute resolution clauses or ADR clauses.

A domestic boilerplate ADR clause[4] should not be adopted wholesale for resolving an international dispute. The domestic clause should be adapted to cover the distinctive needs of resolving a dispute between parties from different countries. Some of the domestic provisions should be modified and a number of uniquely international provisions added. A few of these special provisions are recognized in boilerplate international arbitration clauses. The international clause recommended by the American Arbitration Association,[5] for instance, includes several fill-in the blank options:

> Any controversy or claim arising out of or relating to this contract shall be determined by arbitration in accordance with the International Arbitration Rules of the American Arbitration Association.
>
> The parties may wish to consider adding (a) "The number of arbitrators shall be (one or three)"; (b) "The place of arbitration shall be (city and/or country)"; or (c)"The language(s) of the arbitration shall be ___________."[6]

This section examines a number of issues that deserve special attention when negotiating and designing an international ADR clause.

---

3 *See* C. Buhring-Uhle, *Arbitration and Mediation in International Business,* 17–37 (1996); Jack J. Cole, Jr. *International Commercial Arbitration: American Principles and Practice in a Global Context,* ch. 1, Sections 1.8.1–1.8.2 (1997); and Lawrence Perlman and Steven C. Nelson, "New Approaches to the Resolution of International Commercial Disputes," 17 *Intl Lawyer* 215, 218–225 (1983).

4 Many domestic deals include short boilerplate clauses such as the one suggested by the American Arbitration Association: "Any controversy or claim arising out of or relating to this contract, or the breach thereof, shall be settled by arbitration administered by the American Arbitration Association under its Commercial Arbitration Rules, and judgment on the award rendered by the arbitrator(s) may be entered in any court having jurisdiction thereof." AAA Commercial Arbitration Rules (July 1, 1996)

5 For discussion of different arbitration rules, *see* section E.2.

6 AAA International Arbitration Rules (April 1, 1997)

1. DISTINCTIVE ISSUES WHEN MEDIATING INTERNATIONAL BUSINESS DISPUTES[7]

When going internationally with mediation, a number of distinctive issues arise. The section on cross-cultural differences considered two issues: how to bridge cultural gaps and the vital role of interpreters and translators. This section examines a number of other international issues.

a. Benefits of International Mediation

Neither domestic nor international ADR clauses routinely include a provision that obligates parties to try mediation before resorting to adjudication. This underutilitization of mediation persists despite the impressive settlement record of domestic mediations[8] and despite the fact that most international organizations have promoted the use of mediations through exhortation and publication of rules.[9] International mediations may not be widely used in part because of cross-cultural confusion and because of the difficulties and costs in convening mediation sessions. Yet, a compelling case can be made for parties first trying mediation in an international business conflict.

Walter G. Gans, "Saving Time and Money in Cross-Border Commercial Disputes,"
Dispute Resolution Journal 52–54 (January 1997)

In international agreements among parties which operate under different legal systems and in different cultural and language environs, it is all the more

7 The substance of this section was published in Abramson, "International Mediation Basics," in *Practitioner's Guide to International Arbitration and Mediation* (Editors-Chernick, Kolkey, Rhoades, to be published in Fall, 2001).

8 *See,* e.g., Jeanne M. Brett, Zoe I. Barsness, and Stephen B. Goldberg, "The Effectiveness of Mediation: An Independent Analysis of Cases Handled by Four Major Service Providers," *Neg. J* 259, 261 (July 1996) (The overall setttlement rate was 78%.) and Robert C. Meade and Philip Ferrara, Ph.D. "An Evaluation of the Alternative Dispute Resolution Program of the Commercial Division: Survey Results and Recommendations, 4–5 (July 1997) (The overall settlement rate was close to 70% for the Alternative Dispute Resolution Program of the Commercial Division of the Supreme Court, Civil Branch, New York County, New York State.)

9 ICC offered conciliation services from its beginning in 1923, UNCITRAL in 1980, and ICSID in 1965. Interestingly, before WWII, the ICC handled more conciliations than arbitrations, but the number of conciliations dropped off after WWII while the number of arbitrations increased to the point that today most ICC cases are arbitrations with only a handful of conciliations. W. Laurence Craig, William W. Park, and Jan Paulsson, *International Chamber of Commerce Arbitration,* 681–682 (2nd edition, 1990). *Also see* section D.1. on rules for mediations.

imperative to anticipate in advance differences in business philosophies, language and cultural practices, by including in the contract provisions for dispute resolution that take these differences into account.

***

Neutral forum arbitration of those disputes has certainly become the method of choice insofar as binding adjudication is concerned. But it is often far more preferable to devise procedures to resolve these disputes informally—through structured negotiations, facilitation, through mediation or other non-binding modality, all with the assistance of a mutually respected neutral—before resorting to any binding process through a third-party decision maker. There are sound reasons for requiring disputants in most cross-border transactions to go through these informal procedures *** before resorting to binding arbitration, or, in the rare case, litigation. What are some of these?

1. *Cultural differences favor inclusion of informal processes.* Most foreign companies (whether European, Latin American or Asian) do not favor, in the first instance, having their business disputes aired externally and decided for them by others. When it has become necessary to do so, it is often deemed a sign of failure on the part of the businessmen, who then tend to wash their hands of the matter, at which point it becomes strictly a legal matter to be handled by the lawyers.

Because it is so embedded in foreign culture, it is generally deemed not necessary—indeed, it often may be considered crass—to recite in a legal document informal and well-understood practices that business managers routinely use to resolve disputes. That's why ADR as we know it (apart from binding administered arbitration) was suspect in many quarters, at least in Europe and Japan. But with the sharp increase in all manner of transnational projects over the last several years, there is a greater understanding that the unwritten norms that pertain within a particular culture do not necessarily find acceptance in another. This is particularly the case insofar as that other culture is the United States. Accordingly, foreign-based companies are now much more prone to accept inclusion in the documents of even informal procedures that would be exhausted before resorting to the familiar binding adjudication.

***

2. *Businessmen should control their disputes.* There is now a view outside the U.S., which has been reinforced by the U.S. proponents of ADR, and that is finally taking hold in Europe and elsewhere, that dispute resolution should not be left exclusively to the lawyers. As mentioned, it is common practice abroad for foreign businessmen to resolve their disputes by themselves, informally, possibly with the assistance of a mutual friend or business acquaintance, but certainly not with the assistance of lawyers acting as such. If in the odd case that approach proved unsuccessful, then the matter migrated from a business disagreement to a legal dispute. At that stage, the business people bowed out and it became solely a legal matter leading to (hopefully) a so-called "correct" result: that is, one reached in a well-accepted court of law or arbitration. Expense at that point didn't really matter as long as the process was deemed to be fair or "correct."

We know that for the most part things have evolved differently in our culture. The trend here is for the business people to become active participants in dispute resolution, and for good reason. After all, such disputes typically arise out of a business transaction (legally formulated or not), or at least in a business setting. Why shouldn't those who are involved in the underlying business matter have an active stake in the resolution of the dispute emanating from it?

3. *Legal remedies are often too draconian to resolve business impasse.* Most disputes arising out of transnational transactions are business issues—what should be done if there's overcapacity? undercapacity? the need for new financing? Invocation of traditional legal remedies, as opposed to finding business solutions, is an admission that there's serious impasse and it cannot be resolved for whatever reason. Suing the other party for breach of contract or to compel dissolution or a buy-sell arrangement rarely serves the business goals as they were envisaged. Creative business solutions, on the other hand, will often resolve these problems, and the chances are better for achieving them if the respective managements recognize that dispute resolution is a management, not legal, responsibility. This can be facilitated by the lawyers who ideally would encourage management to adopt practical, cost-effective and timely solutions as opposed to proceeding immediately with costly and time-consuming adjudication. The legal advisers have the opportunity (even the duty) to counsel toward those ends, beginning at the transaction's negotiation stage, by incorporating in the contract dispute resolution processes and procedures that best facilitate a business solution. If that is not possible, then they should at least be knowledgeable and informed about modalities short of litigation that might be

invoked and, finally, an arbitration procedure that makes best sense from the client's perspective.

4. *High incidence of disputes has led to greater scrutiny of costs.* Even in civil law countries which used to believe that the "correct" result was important regardless of expense, there is now a greater consciousness of the enormous costs attendant to adjudication in courts or even arbitration tribunals. Perhaps because of the higher incidence of international disputes, scrutiny of legal (along with other) expenses has become de regueur not only by U.S. but also by foreign companies operating in the global marketplace.

5. *Traditionally high forum costs in administered arbitration.* Although arbitration of international commercial disputes has become the preferred ADR method of last resort, the attendant forum costs can be very high. Judicial fora, despite their deficiencies for international disputes, are at least made available for the most part at government expense, whereas forum costs of arbitration are borne by the parties. Even in ad hoc arbitration the fees and expenses of the arbitrators, who are likely to be experienced counsel, can be considerable. If the parties opt for institutional arbitration, there is, of course, the added cost of the administrative fee charged by the institution, which in some cases can also be a very high amount.

---

b. Convening a Mediation Session

In the optimal mediation setting, the mediator convenes in a neutral location the clients with settlement authority, along with each of their attorneys, and the mediator. All the participants work together to resolve the dispute. By meeting in the same room. everyone gets to know each other through personal, continuous and sustained interactions in both formal meetings and during breaks.[10]

This optimal meeting arrangement can be cumbersome to schedule and costly to convene for international business disputes.[11] International disputes involve parties from different countries who are usually spread out geographically and over different time zones. The participants may have no language in common, may have to communicate with each other through interpreters, and may face other cross-cultural obstacles when trying to understand each other.

---

10 For more detail, *see* Chapter 3.

11 *See* C. Buhring-Uhle, *Arbitration and Mediation in International Business,* 173–174 (1996).

In an effort to reduce these practical obstacles to convening everyone at a single location, mediators are starting to experiment with the use of new technologies for convening sessions.[12] These new technologies, when intelligently used with face-to-face sessions, can create a cost-effective, hospitable environment for international mediations.[13]

The preferred new technology is *videoconferencing*[14] because it permits participants from different locations to hear each other, to see each other, to exchange documents, and to collaborate in editing drafts. It also is the most expensive technological option due to the combination of three significant costs. First, participants must incur the cost of either buying desktop conferencing software and hardware (video camera and speakers), establishing a large screen videoconferencing facility, or renting a videoconferencing facility. Second, participants must pay the cost of a high speed, long distance transmission connection among the participants in the videoconference. Third, in less technologically advanced countries, it may take some effort to secure access to videoconferencing technology.

The cost of videoconferencing has been dropping and the quality of picture improving. Still, if the most advanced technologies are not used, the video can be choppy, the screen small, facial expressions unclear, and eye contact difficult to make due to the angle of the camera. Participants who are unfamiliar with the technology or unaccustomed to appearing in front of a camera need to become comfortable with this new means of real time interaction. These difficulties can be compounded by cultural differences and no generally accepted code of etiquette for behaving during a videoconference. Nevertheless, a videoconference in which participants use the latest technologies and prepare carefully can be an effective means of meeting.

Other technological options include teleconferencing, "chat rooms", and whiteboarding. *Teleconferencing* is easily accessible through either the telephone equipment of one of the participants or a telephone operator. The obvious limitation is that the participants can not see each other. *"Chat rooms"* through the internet provides a facility that permits all the participants to converse in writing in their own "private room." Once each of the parties has signed on, participants can communicate with each other through real time messages that all

---

12 *See* discussion of cybermediation in Chapter 3.

13 *See* Jeswald W. Salacuse, *Making Global D*eals, 19–21 (1991) (pros and cons of using technologies to facilitate negotiations of global deals).

14 *See* Evan Rosen, *Personal Videoconferencing*, 32–44 (1996).

the participants can observe simultaneously on their screens. It is even possible to caucus through side written communications. This option, by far the cheapest one, also encourages more precision in the exchanges because each participant must type his or her comments. However, participants lose the benefit of spontaneous exchanges as well as the benefit of hearing or seeing each other. A *whiteboard* on each participant's personal computer gives each participant the ability to see and edit simultaneously the same draft, an option that is similar to all the participants sitting around a table editing a draft agreement.

These technologies can be used in combination with face-to-face sessions, giving the participants a number of ways to meet during the course of a mediation. One scenario could be as follows: In the first session, everyone meets together in one location during which time the participants develop a working relationship with each other and the mediator. The participants become educated about the mediation process, parties present each of their "stories," parties' interests are explicated and understood, and issues are defined. Before adjourning, the participants develop an agenda and assignments for the next session. If they have developed a sufficient working relationship, participants may not need to meet in one location for the next session. Instead, they may be able to meet technologically. For the second session, they may meet through *teleconferencing* at which time each of the parties may report any information collected and further refine the issues. Then, they may agree to meet a third time through *videoconferencing*. By now, the parties may be ready to resolve some of the most contentious issues and even come to an agreement in principle. Next, a fourth session may be held in a *chat room* or on a *whiteboard* where the parties can exchange specific drafts in an effort to resolve some of the details, especially about some of the noncontroversial aspects of the settlement. Then, they may follow a *store and forward* approach in which detailed drafts are prepared and forwarded for comments, giving each party time to reflect and return comments. Finally, they may all convene again in one location to work out the final details and sign the settlement agreement.

c. Selecting a Mediator

Not all mediators are suitable for mediating international business disputes. Parties not only should select a mediator who is trained and experienced in the standard techniques of mediation, but also who is trained and experienced in dealing with disputes in which cross-cultural differences can contribute to the conflict and impede its resolution.

Furthermore, parties may have difficulty selecting a mediator that is viewed as neutral. Parties must be confident in the mediator's neutrality so that they will trust disclosing information and trust the mediator's initiatives. Even though professional mediators know to scrupulously maintain their neutrality, parties may still be skeptical of any mediator from the country of another party.

Fortunately, these concerns are not as weighty in mediations which is a nonbinding process then in arbitrations where the neutral possesses decisionmaking authority. Parties who do not trust the mediator can simply walk away from the mediation, an option that is not available in arbitrations in which parties must demonstrate prejudice as a basis for disqualifying an arbitrator.

International parties have several options for selecting a mediator that is viewed as neutral; each option offers different advantages:

(i) Parties may select a mediator from a neutral third country. The parties' attorneys can contact such organizations as the American Arbitration Association or Center for Public Resources to see if their rosters include mediators from the neutral country.

(ii) Parties may select co-mediators, with one mediator from the country of each party. This option offers the obvious advantage of a balanced team of mediators. But, it presents the risk of creating a mediation team of neutrals with different philosophies and styles who may have difficulty working together. Mediation is not like arbitration where the neutrals arrive from different countries with different legal and cultural upbringings but who have common training in working together in a highly structured setting for deliberation and decisionmaking. In contrast, the mediation process is much more fluid and flexible shaped by the personalities and styles of the mediators, and as result, may not proceed as smoothly with a team of mediators who are not compatible with each other. This is not to say that team mediations cannot work. There is a long history of success in the United States of using team mediations in community disputes and public policy disputes, especially environmental disputes. But, parties should be sure that they select mediators who are comfortable working with each other.

(iii) Parties may decide that the country of the mediator is not a significant factor. Realizing that the mediator has no decisionmaking power, they may be less concerned about the country of the neutral and more concerned about her credentials and experience as a mediator. Instead, they may find it convenient and less expensive to select a mediator from the country in which the mediation is being held. This approach can be attractive when the case is in a U.S. court, for instance, and all the parties (foreign and domestic) have retained local counsel. As a compromise, parties could seek out a local mediator who is a nationality of a neutral country.

d. Style of Mediator

In international mediations, U.S. attorneys should be careful to clarify the style of mediation[15] envisioned because distinctive and unusual variations of mediation can be occasionally encountered in the international business arena. Some foreign attorneys may expect a more structured and formal process than customarily practiced in U.S. domestic mediations.[16] The mediator, for instance, might investigate the facts and law and issue a written report containing her recommendations.[17] In another unfamiliar arrangement, each party in an international dispute may designate a mediator, then the mediators meet with each other to hammer out a resolution that is presented to the parties for their confirmation.[18] Because some of these approaches are not common in domestic mediations, parties should guard against surprises by inquiring specifically about the type of international mediation each party

---

15 *See* Chapter 3 on styles of domestic mediators. For articles, *see* S. Silbey & S. Merry, "Mediator Settlement Strategies," 8 *Law & Policy* 7 (1986); L. Riskin, "Understanding Mediators' Orientations, Strategies, and Techniques: A Grid for the Perplexed," 1 *Harv. Neg. L. Rev.* 7 (1996); R. Baruch Bush & J. Folger, *The Promise of Mediation: Responding to Conflict Through Empowerment and Recognition* (1994).

16 *See* L. Reif, "Conciliation as a Mechanism for the Resolution of International Economic and Business Disputes," 14 *Fordham Intl L J* 578, 582–587 (1991/92).

17 *See* L. Reif, "Conciliation as a Mechanism for the Resolution of International Economic and Business Disputes," 14 *Fordham Intl L J* 578, 585–587 (1991/92) and Tobi Dress, "International Commercial Mediation and Conciliation," 10 Loy. L. A. Intl. & Comp. L. J. 569, 574 (1988).

18 *See* William Fox, Jr., International Commercial Agreements 193 (1992) and L. Reif, "Conciliation as a Mechanism for the Resolution of International Economic and Business Disputes," 14 *Fordham Intl L J* 578, 632–633 (1991/92). A variation of a joint conciliation was developed by the AAA with a Chinese foreign trade organization in which each party appoints a conciliator and then the two conciliators jointly conciliate the dispute. Michael F. Hoellering, "World Trade to Arbitrate or Mediate—That Is The Question," 49 *Disp. Res. J.* 67, 68–69 (1994).

contemplates. This inquiry is essential in order to avoid a cross-cultural misunderstanding.

e. Confidentiality of Mediation Process

One of the great benefits of mediation, its confidentiality, can be less secure internationally than domestically[19] due to the less developed and untested laws in some countries.

f. Use of Interpreters

As already discussed in the cross-cultural section, attorneys may need to know how to select and work with interpreters when participating in an international mediation.

g. Enforcing Settlement Agreements

In cross-border disputes, attorneys should give special attention to how any resulting settlement agreement will be enforced. In domestic disputes, attorneys know that they can always fall back on the local U.S. court in the jurisdiction in which the agreement was signed to remedy any breaches. In cross-border enforcement actions, the local court option in a foreign country can be less reliable and take more time and expense. Attorneys need to retain local counsel in the breaching party's country and commence a lawsuit in a foreign jurisdiction with all the risks and uncertainties of transnational litigation. These burdens of cross-border enforcement can be less onerous, however, in a foreign country with a mature legal system where the client does regular business and already has local counsel.

In cross-border disputes, parties can more easily enforce a settlement agreement when it is the by-product of an arbitration proceeding. Rather then assuming the risks of enforcing a settlement agreement in a transnational lawsuit, parties can request an arbitral tribunal to incorporate the settlement agreement into an arbitration award. This option is explicitly authorized by both domestic and international arbitration rules.[20] The resulting "consent"

---

19 *See* Chapter 3 on confidentiality.

20 *See*, e.g., AAA Commercial Arbitration Rules, Rule 44 (July 1, 1996); AAA International Arbitration Rules, Art. 29 (1) (April 1, 1997); UNCITRAL Model Law on International Commercial Arbitration, Art. 30 (1985); UNCITRAL Arbitration Rules, Art. 34 (1) (1976); and ICC Rules of Arbitration, Art. 26 (January 1, 1998).

award may be enforceable in foreign jurisdictions under the relatively reliable procedures of the New York Convention on Recognition and Enforcement of Foreign Arbitral Awards.[21]

This method of enforcement works relatively smoothly for parties who sign a settlement agreement after the arbitration proceeding has been initiated and the arbitral tribunal formed. If no tribunal has yet been constituted, however, parties have several other options for facilitating enforcement. First, parties could add to a settlement agreement a personal jurisdiction clause. Under the clause, parties would agree to submit to the personal jurisdiction of a domestic court for the purpose of enforcing a settlement agreement. Second, parties could simply include in a settlement agreement a clause that provides that any breaches would be resolved in arbitration. This is an obvious precaution that can be too easily forgotten. The arbitration clause would give an aggrieved party access to an arbitration process that would produce an award enforceable under the New York Convention. Third, parties could initiate an arbitration proceeding for the purpose of securing a consent award. This strategy would increase the expense and time in connection with settling a dispute but may be worthwhile in order to give parties the added security offered by a consent arbitration award. However, there may be some uncertainty as to whether a consent arbitration award would be enforceable because some jurisdictions might consider this to be a sham arbitration proceeding that is "contrary to the public policy of that country."[22]

To reduce the time and costs of enforcing settlement agreements through arbitration awards, parties should consider adopting "fact-track" arbitration procedures. While these fast-track procedures were a response to the complaints about the length and expense of conventional arbitrations and have not been widely used, these new procedures can benefit parties who need a quick procedure to enforce a settlement agreement. Parties could trigger the expedited process either when the settlement agreement is signed in order to secure a "consent" award or when the settlement agreement is allegedly breached.[23]

---

21 For discussion of the New York convention, *see* Notes and Questions after subsection E. There is no international convention for the recognition and enforcement of settlements although at least one group has proposed a "Draft of a Convention for the Enforcement of Conciliation Settlements." *See* Dr. Ottoarndt Glossner, "Enforcement of Conciliation Settlements," 11 *Intl. Bus. Lawyer* 151 (1983). For discussion of NY Convention, *see* Section E, Notes and Comments.

22 New York Convention, Art. V.2.(b).

23 Expedited procedures have been adopted by several organizations. *See*, e.g., Commercial Arbitration and Mediation Center of the Americas, Arbitration Rules, Art. 39 (March 15, 1996);

Finally, parties can further reduce the costs and length of the arbitration proceeding by resorting to a non-administered arbitration process. Instead of contracting with an administering organization, parties can agree to self-administer the process by following the specially designed UNCITRAL Arbitration Rules or the Non-Administered International Arbitration Rules of the CPR Institute for Dispute Resolution.

h. Back-Up Adjudicatory Process

International mediations are not automatically backed-up by a reliable adjudicatory process. Instead of relying on the default process of transnational litigation with all of its attendant uncertainties, the attorney should add a provision that supports the settlement process with a private, binding adjudicatory process.[24] The back-up process is necessary in order to provide a means for enforcing a settlement agreement or for finally resolving the dispute.

2. INTERNATIONAL ADJUDICATORY OPTIONS

The two primary adjudicatory options for backing-up mediations are transnational litigation and arbitration. Both options have in common the designation

---

WIPO Expedited Arbitration Rules (October 1, 1994); and Stockholm Rules for Expedited Arbitrations (Arbitration Institute of the Stockholm Chamber of Commerce, July 1995). *Also see* Eva Muller, "Fast-Track Arbitration—Meeting the Demands of the Next Millennium," 15 *J. of Intl. Arb.* 5 (1998) (comparison of fast-track arbitration rules issued by seven institutions).

The new Commercial Arbitration and Mediation Center for the Americas, for instance, issued rules for expediting claims no greater than $50,000 although the procedures can be adopted for larger claims. The expedited procedures shorten an arbitration proceeding by relying on telephone notices, limiting the number of arbitrators and number of hearing days to one, shortening the procedure for selecting the arbitrator, and reducing the number of days for giving notice of hearing and for rendering an award. *See* Commercial Arbitration and Mediation Center of the Americas, Arbitration Rules, Art. 39 (March 15, 1996) (CAMCA is a Center created by major national dispute resolution organizations in Canada, United States, and Mexico for dealing with trade disputes in the free trade area created by NAFTA.)

It is even possible to expedite an arbitration proceeding under the regular rules of arbitration. This was accomplished in an ICC arbitration when the ICC along with the arbitrators, attorneys, and parties in a multi-million dollar dispute decided to make a concerted effort to expedite an arbitration proceeding. Through their determined effort, the arbitration took an unprecedented two months from initiation to issuance of the award, instead of what could have been 18–24 months. *See* Christian Buhring-Uhle, *Arbitration and Mediation in International Business,* 110–111 (1996) and articles written by participants in the ICC arbitration in "Special Section: Fast Track Arbitration," 2 *Am. Rev. Intl. Arb.* 137–162 (1991).

24 *See* Section F on combining settlement options with arbitration

of a neutral third party who will hear the case and issue a decision that will bind the parties and bring the conflict to closure. For international business disputes, the more widely used of these two options is arbitration[25] because it ameliorates a number of the risks and concerns that complicates transnational litigation.[26] Instead of parties contending with the gaps in transnational litigation law and any troublesome features of different national court systems, parties design a private, supranational dispute resolution process that operates separately from disparate national court systems. But, the private process does not operate independently; national court systems still perform an essential back-up function in case a party needs to enforce an agreement to arbitrate or an arbitration award.

In comparing transnational litigation with international arbitration, it has been suggested that international arbitration is not really an alternative to litigation but is simply a better way to litigate international business conflicts.

Christian Buhring-Uhle, *Arbitration and Mediation in International Business,*
141–143 (1996)

[I]t appears that the reasons why international commercial arbitration has become the principal means of dispute resolution in international business have more to do with the specific problems of litigating international disputes in national courts than with the desire to create a type of procedure that is fundamentally different from litigation.

The two considerations that stand out as the most significant advantages of international commercial arbitration, the *neutrality* of the forum and the *international enforceability* of the results clearly address two fundamental problems of transnational litigation: whether justified or not, players in international commerce do not seem to have confidence in the complete neutrality of national courts towards foreign litigants and therefore have a strong desire to avoid having to stand trial in the other side's "home court." This consideration

---

25 *See* W. Lawrence Craig, "Some Trends and Developments in the Laws and Practice of International Commercial Arbitration," 36 *Tex. Intl. L. J.* 1, 2 (1995).

26 *See* Chapter V B. *See also*, Gary B. Born, *International Commercial Arbitration in the United States*, 5–9 (1994) and Richard H. Kreindler, "Arbitration or Litigation? ADR Issues in Transnational Disputes," 79 *Dispute Resolution Journal* 79 (1997). (Both authors point out how the advantages of arbitration cannot be guaranteed. For example, Born notes that countries hostile toward arbitrations have enacted laws that pose obstacles to the enforcement of arbitral awards.)

is particularly important if one of the parties is a government or a state-owned entity because on the one hand governments are reluctant—and sometimes prevented by constitutional constraints—to submit to the jurisdiction of an another government and on the other hand private entities tend to abhor the prospect of confronting a sovereign in its own courts.

The participants in international commerce seem to be painfully aware of the deficiencies of the legal framework of transnational litigation and particularly the problems of enforcing judgments in a foreign jurisdiction:

> If for judgments there existed a convention similar to the New York convention, 50% of the big international commercial arbitrations would be court litigation.

A consideration that was regarded as less relevant but that is clearly connected to the enforceability aspect is the degree of *voluntary compliance* with arbitral awards which, according to the ICC is very high. Although there are no data available on *why* parties comply voluntarily, it is plausible to assume that an effective enforcement mechanism operates as a strong motivation.

The next group of advantages of international arbitration that were considered significant are, again, unrelated to any search for "alternative" methods of dispute resolution. *Confidentiality* simply means that the public—and the competitors—are excluded from the proceedings but it has no bearing on what type of procedure it is that is being conducted behind closed doors. And the objective of having the dispute decided by a "judge" with *expertise* in the subject matter and of curtailing the excesses of protracted *discovery* and lengthy *appeals* have to be understood as the desire to improve the quality and effectiveness of litigation rather than to create a different type of procedure.

Finally, the objectives which are at the heart of the quest for more informal, "alternative" methods of dispute resolution, the desire to achieve a process that is *faster, less expensive* and *more amicable,* seem to have only marginal relevance for the choice of arbitration in international commerce. This may be due either to the perception that, in international arbitration, these advantages do not materialize, or that these qualities are not among the real priorities of the participants. Both reasons seem to be—at least in part—true: more than one half of the respondents denied that arbitration is less expensive and more than one third disputed the notion that it was faster or more amicable. And only about one tenth of the respondents affirmed that speed, cost savings and amicability were "highly relevant" factors for the choice of arbitration as a method of dispute resolution. As one practitioner explained:

> ... parties are often not that concerned with costs because their main pre-occupation is with the outcome of the procedure; the advantage of arbitration is not to cut costs, it is a tailor-made procedure that emphasizes quality.

In sum, what international arbitration offers and what the participants expect is not an "alternative" to litigation but *a system of litigation that works in an international context* and avoids the pitfalls of transnational litigation in national courts. In the words of the Secretary General of the ICC Court of Arbitration:

> ... [the reasons that] people are driven to international commercial arbitration in large measure is not that they want a simpler form of justice but that they want a *forum in which to have confidence,* and this forum *is the main service the arbitral institutions have to offer ...*

These justifications for resorting to arbitration does not mean arbitrations are always preferable:

> Nonetheless, sometimes *litigation can be preferable.* Where the enforcement of judgments abroad is either unnecessary (because the defendant has sufficient assets in the jurisdiction of the court that decided the case) or where it is enhanced by international agreements such as the Brussels Convention, some of the key advantages of arbitration are obsolete. Also, in certain standard types of cases accelerated procedures like summary or documents-only proceedings may offer a more efficient form of dispute resolution. ... Another problem may be that in some jurisdictions arbitration agreements are interpreted to preclude interim measures of protection by the courts. And litigation may be the only solution where the assets of the defendant are located in a country that is not party to any relevant international agreement and generally does not enforce foreign arbitral awards. C. Buhring-Uhle, Arbitration and Mediation in International Business 88 (1996)

NOTES AND QUESTIONS

1. In the Gans article, which of his reasons for using settlement processes in international business disputes do you find most convincing? Can you think of other reasons for using settlement processes in international disputes? Why do you think mediations are not more widely used for resolving international business disputes?
2. At least three issues deserve special attention when you are considering using technologies for convening international mediations. (i) Effective Meeting Place. Do you think any of the technological ways of meeting will provide a satisfactory means of mediating? What factors should you weigh when deciding which of these suboptimal meeting options to use at a particular point in the mediation process? (ii) Access to Videoconferencing. In order to preserve the perception of neutrality, should the neutral use a separate facility even though it might be more convenient and less costly to share a facility with one of the parties? (iii} Security. Is the technology sufficiently secure for the type of information that will be discussed and exchanged?
3. In a dispute with a party from India that is pending in a New York federal court, how would you propose that the parties select a mediator that would be perceived as neutral to both sides?
4. What key provisions do you think should be included in an agreement to mediate an international dispute?
5. Do you find convincing the contention of Christian Buhring-Uhle that international arbitration is not an "alternative" to litigation but is "*a system of litigation that works in an international context*"? Can this same point be made about the use of domestic arbitration? If so, then what does it mean to describe a process as an alternative dispute resolution method?

3. INSTITUTIONAL OR AD HOC ADMINISTRATION OF PROCESSES[27]

A number of well-established and new international organizations are in the business of administering dispute resolution processes.[28] These organizations

27 *See* Chapter V B1. *Also see* C. Buhring-Uhle, *Arbitration and Mediation in International Business,* 45–51 (1996); William K. Slate II, "International Arbitration: Do Institutions Make a Difference?," 31 *Wake Forest LR* 41, 52–59 (1996).

28 *See* Chapter 4 regarding description of international arbitration institutions.

have their own professional staff, facilities, and procedural rules to govern dispute resolution processes. They are primarily in the arbitration business although they also serve mediations. The organizations can be sorted into two groups: ones that handle virtually any business dispute[29] and ones that specialize in handling certain types of disputes.[30]

The more complex the dispute resolution process and conflict, the more administrative tasks someone must handle, and the more appealing it is to use an independent organization. To set up an arbitration, for instance, someone must prepare and send notices to parties, administer the procedures for selecting arbitrators, arrange the scheduling of hearings (time, date, and place), and deal with any post-award enforcement issues. A reputable neutral institution has the know how to handle these administrative details, offers its time-tested rules, provides access to a list of professional and qualified neutrals, and insulates arbitrators from the parties. Moreover, an institution can offer expertise in determining whether an award meets legal requirements for enforcement in multiple jurisdictions. An arbitration process administered by a highly-regarded institution also gives its award additional credibility when a party seeks voluntary or legal enforcement. Due to these numerous benefits, many parties use an independent institution to administer their arbitrations.

Institutions can be especially attractive for administering an international dispute resolution process because the process can be more complex than administering a domestic one. Straightforward tasks of communications and scheduling become more complicated when parties and neutrals reside in different countries, speaking different languages. There also is a greater likelihood that parties will need professional translators, bilingual stenographic transcripts, and an understanding of different foreign legal requirements for enforcing settlement agreements, arbitral awards, or agreements to use a dispute resolution process.

All this convenience and support can be costly: a neutral institution charges substantial administrative fees and can take time to provide its services.

---

29 For example, there are the International Chamber of Commerce (ICC), American Arbitration Association (AAA), London Court of International Arbitration (LCIA), The Arbitration Institute of the Stockholm Chamber of Commerce, and the CPR Institute for Dispute Resolution.

30 For example, there are the International Center for the Settlement of Investment Disputes (ICSID), China International Economic and Trade Arbitration Commission (CIETAC), Commercial Arbitration and Mediation for the Americas (CAMCA), and World Intellectual Property Organization Arbitration Center (WIPO).

As an alternative, parties can elect to self-administer a process, known as ad hoc administration. In practice, parties can find it cumbersome and at times awkward to both self-administer a process and participate in it. But, this option can be more flexible, quicker, and cost-effective, if certain critical conditions are satisfied: if parties are cooperating, if they can efficiency negotiate the administrative details to be done, and if they can proficiently handle the administrative responsibilities.[31] However, even with ad hoc administration, parties usually find it helpful to select an "appointing authority"[32] to handle the vital stage of securing the arbitrators (selection, challenges, and replacement of arbitrators.)[33]

4. ADOPTING OR ADAPTING OFF-THE-SHELF PROCEDURAL RULES

Virtually all the dispute resolution institutions offer their own procedural rules to govern arbitrations and mediations. Some institutions offer rules that are designed for ad hoc administrations[34] such as the rules designed by the United Nations Commission on International Trade Law[35] (UNCITRAL). These

---

31 The United Nations Commission on International Trade Law (UNCITRAL), which does not serve as an administering institution, has published helpful instructions on how to organize arbitral proceedings. "UNCITRAL Notes on Organizing Arbitral Proceedings," U.N. Doc. V.96-84935.

32 A number of established institutions are willing to serve as an "appointing authority" including the ICC, AAA, CPR and Stockhom Chamber of Commerce.

33 In the standard clause proposed in the CPR's Non-Administered International Arbitration Rules & Commentary, CPR suggests that a neutral organization be "designated to perform the functions specified in Rule 6 [selection of arbitrator], Rule 7.7 (b) [challenges of arbitrators regarding independence or impartiality], Rule 7.8 [replacement of arbitrators], and Rule 7.9 [failure to act by arbitrators]." (bracketed information added.)

34 CPR also has designed rules specifically for ad hoc administration. *See* CRP's Non-Administered International Arbitration Rules & Commentary (1995).

35 UNCITRAL's arbitration rules, adopted by the General Assembly of the United Nations, are designed to be broadly acceptable in countries with different legal and economic systems, whether common law or civil law jurisdictions or capital-exporting or capital-importing nations.

UNCITRAL is not a dispute resolution institution. UNCITRAL was established by the General Assembly of the United Nations in 1966 to promote "the progressive harmonization and unification of the law of international trade" (G.A. Res. 2205, 21 U.N. GAOR, Annex 3, U.N. Doc. A/6396 and (Add. 1&2) (1966), *reprinted in* 1 *Y.B. Commn. Intl. Trade L.* 65 (1968–70), U.N. Doc. A/CN.9/SER.A/1970.)

Membership in UNCITRAL is limited to nation-states. Among its many significant contributions, it adopted Arbitration Rules in 1976 (U.N. Doc. Sales No. E.7 v. 6 (1977)), Conciliation Rules in 1980 (U.N. Doc. A/35/17 (1980)), Model Law on International

various mediation and arbitration rules can either be adopted intact or modified to meet special needs of the parties. Of course, parties can create their own rules from scratch but this option would be an expensive route to essentially re-inventing much of what has already been devised and tested by others.

a. Mediation

Almost every major international dispute resolution institution has developed and published rules for mediations. The rules generally do not contain any distinctively international provisions. They cover procedures for initiating and terminating a mediation and for appointing a mediator. They address the role of the mediator, conduct of the mediation, confidentiality of the process, and matters related to payment for mediation services.

Two of these rules deserve special attention. Because cross-cultural confusion over the role of the mediator is unlikely to be eliminated by the rules, the rules may need to be modified to clarify the style of mediation that the parties envision. Even though mediation rules generally establish the confidentiality of the process, the degree of protection can vary among the rules.[36] Deficiencies can be remedied by the parties executing a supplemental confidentiality agreement.[37]

b. Arbitration[38]

Comprehensive arbitration rules are offered by UNCITRAL and every significant dispute resolution institution. Given the abundance of choices, how do parties determine which set of rules to adopt in an arbitration clause?

Commercial Arbitration in 1985 (U.N. Doc. A/35/17 (1980)), and updated its Notes on Organizing Arbitral Proceedings in 1996 (U.N. Doc. V.96-84935).

36 *See*, e.g., ICC Rules of Optional Conciliation, Arts. 6, 10, 11 (January 1, 1988); WIPO Mediation Rules, Art. 14–17 (October 1, 1994); UNCITRAL Conciliation Rules, Art. 14 (1984); and AAA Commercial Mediation Rules, Rule 12 (January 1, 1992).

37 As noted earlier, however, an agreement cannot guarantee that the confidentiality of the process will be respected by the courts in every jurisdiction. *See* Section 1 on "Confidentiality of Mediation Process."

38 Procedural practices in international arbitrations changed significantly during the 1970s and 80s. International arbitrations developed initially as an informal process cultivated in Continental Europe, primarily in Paris under the auspices of the ICC. In the civil law tradition, international arbitrators gave considerable attention to the law while giving little attention to the development and consideration of the facts. International arbitrations were dominated by Continental academics and an exclusive "club" of gentlemen (yes, all men) engaged in business affairs.

> The nature of a contract, the type of contractual disputes likely to arise, and the sorts of interim and final remedies likely to be sought are factors which must be taken into account in selecting one of the available systems of rules. In some cases, political considerations may also play a role. For example, it has been reported that for years the People's Republic of China adamantly refused to use ICC Rules because the ICC is organized on the basis of national committees, one of which is Taiwan's. In comparing the relative advantages and disadvantages of each set of arbitral rules, the prudent lawyer must focus on the way in which each set of rules will interact with the unique components of the specific contract and the specific parties.
>
> W. Michael Reisman, W. Laurence Craig, William Park, and Jan Paulsson, *International Commercial Arbitration* 243 (1997)

Unfortunately, it is not unusual for parties to fail to examine the rules they are considering adopting. They just incorporate them wholesale into the ADR clause. The parties then hope that, if the rules must be used, any surprises in the pre-packaged rules will be small ones. In international deals, the risks of bigger surprises are bigger, increasing the importance of addressing critical questions before a conflict arises.

Parties should give special attention to a number of issues that can impact on the quality and substantive outcome of the arbitration process. Boilerplate international clauses usually recommend adding several other provisions.[39]

The ICC suggests a typical arbitration clause:

During the 1970s and 80s, procedures in international arbitrations were transformed by pressures exerted by the increased participation of Anglo-American law firms in international business deals. When the major U.S. law firms went international, they exported what they knew best; they knew how to aggressively represent their clients in adversarial proceedings. U.S. lawyers were determined to employ a U.S. style litigation strategy in the arbitrations. These pressures lead to what became known as the "judicialization" of international commercial arbitrations. *See* Yves Dezalay and Bryant G. Garth, *Dealing in Virtue—International Commercial Arbitration and the Construction of a Transnational Legal Order,* chs. 3, 4, 5 (1996). *Also see* Rau and Sherman, "Tradition and Innovation in International Arbitration Procedure," 30 *Tex. Intl. L. J.* 89 (1995).

39 *See*, e.g., ICC Rules of Arbitration (January 1, 1998), AAA International Arbitration Rules (April 1, 1997), CPR Non-Administered International Arbitration Rules & Commentary (1995), and UNCITRAL Arbitration Rules (1976).

> All disputes arising out of or in connection with the present contract shall be finally settled under the Rules of Arbitration of the International Chamber of Commerce by one or more arbitrators appointed in accordance with the said Rules.

The ICC further suggests that "[p]arties are reminded that it may be desirable for them to stipulate in the arbitration clause itself the law governing the contract, the number of arbitrators and the place and language of the arbitration."[40] If the parties omit adding these additional provisions, the parties are then electing to rely on the arbitrator(s) to impose them when needed, which may result in unpleasant surprises and undesirable results.

In the following article, the former Secretary General of the ICC Court of Arbitration discusses several key provisions that parties should consider when drafting an international arbitration clause.

Stephen R. Bond,* "How to Draft an Arbitration Clause"
J. of Intl Arb. 65 (June 1989)

So, even businessmen who wish to deal with lawyers as little as possible have a major interest in involving an attorney in the negotiation of the dispute settlement provision, unless those businessmen wish to prove, once again, the old adage that arbitration is a procedure that has too few lawyers in the beginning (when the clause is drafted) and too many in the end (when an arbitration is actually under way).

I would like to present some thoughts as to elements which should be considered in drafting and negotiating an arbitration clause.

***

[P]arties should be extremely careful not to narrow inadvertently the scope of the arbitration clause by restricting the clause simply to disputes "arising under" the contract or "related to execution or performance" of the contract.

***

40 *See* ICC Publication No. 581 which contains the new ICC Rules of Arbitration that became effective on January 1, 1998.

* The author analyzed the arbitration clauses contained in the 237 arbitration cases presented in the prior year to the ICC's Court of Arbitration.

c. The Place of Arbitration

The importance of the place of arbitration cannot be overestimated. Its legislation determines the likelihood and extent of involvement of national courts in the conduct of the arbitration (either for judicial "assistance" or "interference"), the likelihood of enforceability of the arbitral award (depending on what international conventions the *situs* State is a party to), and the extent and nature of any mandatory procedural rules that you will have to adhere to in the conduct of the arbitration. (For example, in Saudi Arabia, the arbitrators must be Muslim and male.) Such factors are of far greater importance than the touristic attractions of any particular place that sometimes appear to be the decisive factor in making this decision. ... This mention of *situs* is, after the choice of applicable law, the element most often added to the basic ICC arbitration clause. The choice of the place of arbitration may literally determine the outcome of the case. In one ICC arbitration between a Finnish corporation and an Australian corporation. London was selected as the place of arbitration in the arbitration clause. The case involved royalty payments allegedly not made and the purported cancellation of the relevant agreement in 1976. In 1982 the licensor initiated arbitration. The arbitrator found that because the arbitration was taking place in England, the statute of limitations contained in the U.K. Limitation Act had to be applied. So, even assuming that Finnish law was applicable and Finnish law had no comparable statute of limitations, the arbitrator applied the relevant U.K. 6-year statute of limitations and barred all claims arising prior to 1976, which effectively meant all claims.

***

d. Applicable Law

While the choice of the law to be applied by the arbitrators to determine the substantive issues before them is not an element necessary for the validity of an arbitration clause, it is certainly desirable for the parties to agree upon the applicable law in the arbitration clause if at all possible. Failure to do so is a significant factor in increasing the time and cost of an arbitration. Moreover, the decision of the arbitral tribunal on the matter (for it is an issue to be decided by the arbitrators, even if institutional arbitration is used) may bring an unpleasant surprise to one of the parties. Finally, where an institution is to select the chairman or sole arbitrator it is, as a practical matter, far easier to appoint the best possible person when it is known in what country's law the arbitrator should be most expert.

For these reasons, the element most often added to the contract, often directly in the arbitration clause itself, is that of the law applicable to the contract.

***

A few points should be borne in mind in deciding upon an applicable law and I will very briefly mention them.

Firstly, it is preferable that the legal system you agree upon in fact is developed in regard to the specific issues likely to arise.

Secondly, you may wish to exclude the conflict of laws principles of the chosen law, either explicitly or by specifying the "substantive law" of the particular country concerned.

Thirdly, be sure that the law you choose considers the subject matter of the contract to be arbitrable. Copyright or patent law questions, anti-trust matters, etc. are often not permitted to be resolved by arbitration, but only in the national courts.

e. Composition of the Arbitral Tribunal

The next element which should be given the most serious attention is that of the composition of the arbitral tribunal. How many arbitrators do you want? How should they be selected? Should they have any particular qualifications? No broad generalities can cover all the situations likely to arise.

***

f. Language of the Arbitration

Many parties may mistakenly believe that the language in which the contract is written will automatically be the language of any arbitration arising out of that contract. It is true that the ICC Rules, for example, state in Article 15 (3) that the arbitrator shall give "due regard ... in particular to the language of the contract" in determining the language of the arbitration. It will, however, be for the arbitral tribunal to decide the question should the parties not have agreed on it.

As can well be imagined, simultaneous interpretation at hearings and translation of all documents into two or more languages are enormously expensive and time-consuming. If it is not possible to agree on a language in the arbitration clause then it would be desirable to try to agree either that costs for interpretation and translation are shared or else borne by the party requiring the interpretation or translation.

***

CONCLUSIONS

I will not end this presentation by revealing to you the all-purpose, miraculous arbitration clause, because there is probably no single clause that is appropriate in every case. You cannot escape the need, each time you negotiate an arbitration clause, to engage in a rigorous analysis of the circumstances related to the particular transaction in order to produce an arbitration clause tailored to the situation at hand. In the long run, this work will result in immeasurable savings of time and money.

NOTES AND QUESTIONS

1. When drafting an arbitration clause, there are some other provisions that deserve special attention:

   a. Party-Appointed Arbitrators
   In international arbitrations, parties ardently favor tripartite tribunals in which each party appoints an arbitrator and then either the party-appointed arbitrators or an appointing institution selects the chair of the tribunal. This preference for party-appointed arbitrators is surprising because it appears to violate the principles of neutrality and independence that form the foundation of judicial justice.[41] Yet, parties commonly select this procedure because:

   > In arbitration, parties accept virtually non-appealable finality of the arbitrators' decision largely in exchange for the ability to participate in the selection of their tribunal rather than accept an anonymous, governmentally chosen decision maker—a judge—whose rulings may be less predictable but generally are subject to appellate review. … Party-appointed arbitrators also may be expected to play a role in selecting the third arbitrator, bringing their judgment and experience to bear on this important task.

   James H. Carter "Living with the Party-Appointed Arbitrator: Judicial Confusion, Ethical Codes and Practical Advice," 3 *Am. Rev.* 153 (1992)

41 Alan Scott Rau, "Integrity in Private Judging," 38 *S. Tex. L. Rev.* 485, 497–514 (1997).

> At least one of the persons who will decide the case will listen carefully—even sympathetically—to the presentation, and if the arbitrator is well chosen, will study the documents with care. That fact alone is likely to spur the other arbitrators to study the documents as well, whether or not they would have done so in any case. Thus the presence of a well chosen party-appointed arbitrator goes a long way toward promising (if not assuring) a fair hearing and a considered decision.
>
> [I]n an international case a party-appointed arbitrator serves as a translator. I do not mean just of language. ... I mean rather the translation of legal culture, and not infrequently of the law itself, when matters that are self-evident to lawyers from one country are puzzling to lawyers from another.
>
> Andreas F. Lowenfeld "The Party-Appointed Arbitrator in International Controversies: Some Reflections" 30 *Tex. Intl L.J.* 59, 65 (1995)

Must a party select an arbitrator one who is independent and impartial?[42] Party-appointed arbitrators in international arbitrations strive for greater neutrality[43] than observed in domestic arbitrations.[44] The

---

42 *See* Chapter V D on party-appointed representatives and international commercial arbitrations.

43 *See* ICC Rules of Arbitration, Arts. 7 (1) and 11 (1) (January 1, 1998); International Bar Association Ethics for International Arbitrators, Rule 5 (1987) (restricts communications between arbitrators and parties); UNCITRAL Arbitration Rules, Art. 10 (1) (1976) (challenges to arbitrator's impartiality and independence); James H. Carter, "Rights & Obligations of the Arbitrator," 52 *Disp. Res. J.* 56 (1997); and Stephen Bond, "The Selection of ICC Arbitrators and the Requirement of Independence," 4 *Arb. Intl* 300 (1980) (examines the ICC rules and practices on appointment of independent arbitrators).

In the new AAA International Arbitration Rules, Article 7 states that "[n]o party or anyone acting on its behalf shall have any ex parte communication relating to the case with any arbitrator, or with any candidate for appointment as party-appointed arbitrator except to advise the candidate of the general nature of the controversy and of the anticipated proceedings and to discuss the candidate's qualifications, availability or independence in relation to the parties, or to discuss the suitability of candidates for selection as a third arbitrator where the parties or party-designated arbitrators are to participate in that selection. No party or anyone acting on its behalf shall have any ex parte communication relating to the case with any candidate for presiding arbitrator." AAA International Arbitration Rules, Arts. 7 (April 1, 1997) (amendments to the 1993 International Arbitration Rules).

44 In domestic arbitrations, party-appointed arbitrators are sometimes described as non-neutral arbitrators or partisan arbitrators who may not observe the same rules of ethical conduct as neutral arbitrators. In the 1977 Code of Ethics for Arbitrators in Commercial

expected degree of neutrality guides parties in how they relate to their party-appointed arbitrator. Should parties be permitted to interview candidates? What can parties discuss during an interview? What ex parte contacts, if any, can parties have with their party-appointed arbitrator during the arbitration proceeding?

b. Interim Relief

The availability of interim relief by a court in aid of arbitration—in the form, for example, of an attachment or a temporary injunction—is often quite unclear. This is discussed in Chapter V at p. xxxx. It is important, therefore, for parties to investigate relevant arbitration rules and national laws to determine whether they can secure interim relief in court or from the arbitration panel pending the issuance of the arbitration award.

c. Currency of Awards[45]

Parties may want to resolve in what currency any awards or settlement will be paid. If the choice is among currencies that are freely convertible in international markets, parties should resolve which party will assume the foreign exchange risk. Foreign parties should determine whether the local law where the arbitration is taking place requires the foreign party to accept payments in the local currency which could be a problem if the local currency is not freely convertible. The party then must figure out whether the local government permits exchanging local currency for hard currency.

d. Waiver of Sovereign Immunity[46]

If one of the parties is a governmental entity such as a state owned automobile manufacturer, the other party should determine whether the governmental entity has waived its immunity from lawsuits. Many countries have adopted laws that waive sovereign immunity for "commercial acts." To be safe, the non-governmental party should negotiate a waiver of sovereign immunity that would be included in the dispute resolution clause of the business contract.

Disputes, Canon VII identifies which ethical obligations a "nonneutral arbitrator" should observe and which obligations are not applicable. For instance, in contrast with neutral arbitrators, nonneutral party-appointed arbitrators "may be predisposed toward the party who appointed them." *See Code of Ethics for Arbitrators in Commercial Disputes,* Canon VII (ABA and AAA, 1977)

45 Jeswald W. Salacuse, *Making Global Deals,* Ch. 7 (1991)

46 *See* Chapter VB1 where the use of the ICSID is considered for the Paris Disneyland contract between Disney Productions and the French Government.

2. An attorney's position on a provision may be shaped as much by her cultural upbringing and professional experience as by her strategic views of what best serves the interests of her client.

a. Discovery

Different philosophies about discovery can shape each party's views of appropriate discovery for arbitrations. U.S. lawyers are taught in law school and in practice to engage in thorough pre-hearing discovery. Many civil law lawyers view the U.S. style of discovery as excessive and oppressive, especially the broad and liberal view of what is discoverable and the wide use of depositions. Civil lawyers are brought up to rely on restricted discovery, limited to production of relevant, critical documents. It is in this environment of competing upbringings that parties try to negotiate a compromise discovery provision with which everyone can be comfortable. In practice, discovery in arbitrations reflect a philosophy closer to civil law than common law norms.[47]

b. Punitive Damages

Parties from different parts of the United States and the World follow different views on whether arbitrators should have the power to award punitive damages. Even if parties agree to adopt rules that make it clear that the tribunal has the authority, the award still may not be enforced by a local court that views the payment of punitive damages as a violation of local public policy.

c. Awarding Costs of Arbitration

Parties may enter negotiations with a cultural preference for either the English or American Rule for determining who will pay attorney fees and other costs of the arbitration. The American rule of each party paying her own costs regardless of outcome is not the practice everywhere.[48] Many civil law jurisdictions follow the English rule of the loser paying. Parties should be aware of these competing national practices when negotiating over which practice they want arbitrators to apply.

3. International arbitration has been widely embraced due in great part to the vital opportunity to enforce domestic arbitral awards in foreign courts. In

47 Jack J. Coe, Jr., *International Commercial Arbitration: American Principles and Practice in a Global Context,* 242–244 (1997).

48 *See* Dan B. Dobbs, *Dobbs Law of Remedies,* Section 3.10 (Vol. 1, 2nd edition, 1993) (description of American rule including comparison with English rule).

what is probably the most important treaty in the field of international dispute resolution—the New York Convention,[49] the signatory countries gave up some of their sacred sovereignty by agreeing to enforce arbitration awards issued by foreign arbitration tribunals. Over a hundred nations have ratified the New York Convention.

The key features of the New York Convention can be found in its first five articles. Article I establishes the general obligation of a state to recognize and enforce foreign arbitral awards. The Article also gives each state the option to limit this obligation to awards made in the territory of another contracting state (reciprocity reservation) and to disputes that are commercial under its own national law (commercial reservation). The United States has adopted both of these reservations. Article II limits enforcement of *agreements to arbitrate* to agreements that are (1) in writing and (2) that a local court does not find to be " null and void, inoperative or incapable of being performed." When these two conditions are met, the local court will refer the parties to arbitration. Article III imposes a national treatment-type obligation; a contracting state shall not impose "substantially more onerous conditions" on enforcement of foreign awards than enforcement of domestic awards. Article IV establishes the only conditions that must be satisfied by a party who seeks *enforcement of an arbitration award*. The conditions deal with authentication and certification of the award. Article V(1) sets forth grounds for refusing recognition and enforcement of a foreign award, grounds that can be asserted by a party against whom enforcement is sought. In addition to grounds familiar in domestic arbitration laws (e.g., procedural defects and lack of arbitrability), a court can refuse recognition when the foreign award had been set aside in the foreign country. Article V(2) sets forth grounds for a local court to act on its own motion to refuse recognition and enforcement. The two grounds include are when the subject matter is "not capable of settlement by arbitration under the law" of the local country and when recognition and enforcement "would be contrary to the public policy" of the local country.

At the recent celebration of the fortieth anniversary of the New York Convention, scholars and practitioners from around the world convened for the day at the United Nations to consider what the treaty has accomplished and what

49 1958 Convention on Recognition and Enforcement of Foreign Arbitral Awards, 21 U.S.T.2517, 330 U.N.T.S.38, T.I.A.S. No. 6997 (1959) (known as the New York Convention). *See* Appendix G.

should be done to improve the treaty.[50] Everyone seemed to agree that the New York Convention has been a great success. Participants still suggested several areas for improvement. Procedures for local enforcement should be more uniform among different states.[51] Article II(2) provision on only enforcing arbitration agreements in writing should recognize the validity of agreements created by modern means of contract formation.[52] A supplementary convention should be adopted to provide for foreign enforcement of provisional and conservatory relief.[53] Finally, a local court should not be barred from enforcing a foreign award because a foreign court nullified the award, especially when the reasons may be considered internationally intolerable.[54] Participants thought that these improvements could be implemented through adoption of a supplementary treaty or more likely through enlightened domestic law or judicial interpretations.

4. Draft a three step dispute resolution clause in which the international parties agree to first try negotiating a settlement, then to try mediation, and finally to resolve any remaining issues in binding arbitration.

5. COMBINING SETTLEMENT PROCESSES WITH ARBITRATION

In this subsection, two very different dispute resolution designs are considered. Each design incorporates a process sequence that combines arbitration with settlement processes. The term settlement processes encompasses any initiative to settle a case ranging from full-fledged mediations by independent mediators to arbitrators simply encouraging parties to settle.

---

50 *New York Convention Day*—June 10, 1998 A/CN.9/1998/INF.1 (UN, 20 May 1998).

51 Robert Briner, "Philosophy and Objectives of the Convention," in *New York Convention Day*, June 10, 1998 A/CN.9/1998/INF.1 pp. 2–3 (UN, 20 May 1998).

52 Neil Kaplan, "New Developments on Written Form," in *New York Convention Day*, June 10, 1998 A/CN.9/1998/INF.1 pp. 5–6 (UN, 20 May 1998).

53 V. V. Veeder, "Provisional and Conservatory Measures," in *New York Convention Day*, June 10, 1998 A/CN.9/1998/INF.1 p. 8 (UN, 20 May 1998).

54 Jan Paulsson, "Awards Set Aside at Place of Arbitration," in *New York Convention Day*, June 10, 1998 A/CN.9/1998/INF.1 p. 10 (UN, 20 May 1998). For a contrary view, *see* William W. Park, "Duty and Discretion in International Arbitration," 93 *Am. J. Intl. L.* 805, 814 (1999): "Deference to good faith annulments often furthers the very same interests as enforcement of the arbitration agreement and award, holding the parties to their bargain. Just as an agreement to arbitrate in London means driving to hearings on the left side of the road, so it means that proceedings are subject to the English Arbitration Act."

a. Set-Arb-Set-Arb

Private, inventive process designs are needed more in disputes between parties from different countries than in disputes that are domestic. At least when parties fail to plan for domestic disputes, parties can fall back on their own familiar and stable public court systems. Parties may not always find their domestic systems inviting but they are more manageable than the international default process of transnational litigation with its additional risks and unfamiliarity. When parties wait until an international dispute arises to design the dispute resolution process, parties face the unwieldy obstacles of again convening attorneys and possibly their clients when relationships are strained and when they are separated by large distances, time zones, culture and language. Therefore, international parties who want to avoid the public default process should try early to design a private process.

In the following excerpt, Christian Buhring-Uhle builds on the familiar two step med-arb option[55] by recommending a more dynamic process design in which parties shift back and forth between consensus-based and adjudicatory processes until the dispute is resolved. This process sequencing can be called: Set-Arb-Set-Arb.

Christian Buhring-Uhle, *Arbitration and Mediation in International Business,*
389–391 (1996)

[T]he guiding principle for dispute resolution process design should be to maximize the consensual element in any solution and to have third-party decisionmaking available but to limit it to the indispensable minimum.

3. BASIC ELEMENTS OF THE SYSTEM

[T]he two main elements of the proposed system for dispute resolution process design are *interest-based negotiations* and a *rights-based adjudication* procedure as a *back-up* in case no agreement is reached.[55]

The best way to achieve consensus is through negotiation. Since interests are the yardstick for commercial dispute resolution the *negotiations* should

55 A Med-Arb clause establishes a two step sequence in which parties agree to first use mediation and then if it is unsuccessful, they agree to resolve the dispute in arbitration. *See* Chapter V.E.3 and, James T. Peter, "Med-Arb in International Arbitration," 8 *The Am. Rev. of Intl. Arb.* 83 (1997).

The system proposed here is inspired by Ury, Brett & Goldberg, *Getting Disputes Resolved* (1989) but tries to take the model suggested there one step further and to adapt it to the particularity of international commercial disputes.

be primarily *interest-based.* There are a number of ADR techniques, most notably mediation, that can improve the effectiveness of negotiation. They should therefore be considered when structuring the negotiation element of the system.

Previous chapters have shown that arbitration is the most effective *back-up* available in international commercial disputes. Litigation, however, is also a rights-based adjudication procedure and has to be considered as an option in specific contexts where arbitration is not available or where international agreements such as the Brussels Convention have improved the legal framework for transnational litigation.

There are two intermediate steps between these two principal elements: *rights-based negotiation* as a filter to adjudication and *loop-backs* as a way to revert to interest-based negotiation.

Rights-based negotiations are an important *filter* to adjudication. Rather than incurring the costs of going through an adjudication procedure the parties try to anticipate its result in negotiations. These negotiations typically take the form of an exchange of legal arguments and a confrontation of conflicting predictions about the outcome of the back-up procedure. This form of "bargaining in the shadow of the law" characterizes conventional settlement negotiations. It can be enhanced through certain forms of predictive ADR, most notably mini-trials and related mediation structures. In practice, interest-based and rights-based negotiation are blended into one procedure which in the shadow of an impending adjudication is dominated by rights-based negotiation. However, it is important to make this distinction, mentally and through the structure of the process, in order not to loose sight of the ultimate goal of dispute resolution process design—a consensual solution that reconciles the interests of the parties on the highest possible level. Both interest-based and rights-based negotiations can be brought to their maximum effectiveness through the assistance of a mediator but in mediation, too, it is important to distinguish problem-solving and predictive techniques in order to accomplish the two objectives of realizing the interests of the parties and having their rights respected.

A *loop back is* a structure that permits the participants of a rights-based adjudication procedure to revert to interest-based negotiation, always in line with the guiding principle to maximize consensus and to minimize third-party decisionmaking. Examples for loop backs are mediation windows in arbitration and post-award-settlements which through negotiation try to improve the result of adjudication.

HOW MEDIATION WINDOWS WORK

... [S]ettlement facilitation during an on-going arbitration in the form of low-intensity mediation efforts by the tribunal itself are a common feature of the practice of international arbitration. By contrast, a full-scale mediation as a separate procedure in the "shadow" of an on-going arbitration, and with the participation of high-level executives from the parties, is less usual though not entirely uncommon. It can be conducted by the tribunal or by a separate mediator. Such a "mediation window" does not necessarily disrupt the arbitration since there are long periods during any arbitration where no hearings are conducted and the participants simply prepare for the next step in the proceedings. Setting aside a few days for a mediation attempt—the maximum duration will be of one or two weeks—is therefore possible without causing a noticeable disruption. Christian Buhring-Uhle, *Arbitration and Mediation in International Business*, 371 (1996).

B. ARB-SET-ARB

This subsection considers the opportunities for third party assistance in settling a dispute after the parties have activated the international arbitration clause and the arbitrators have been selected. This process sequencing can be called Arb-Set-Arb.

This sequencing of dispute resolution methods is already familiar to litigators. Pursuant to parties' agreement or a court order, their court case is channeled into a separate mediation process. If the case does not settle in mediation, the case is returned to court for final resolution. This process sequence is also available in international arbitrations for parties who elect to channel the case into mediation and if unsuccessful, to return the case to arbitration.

As an alternative to referring the case to a separate mediator, the arbitrators could try to settle the dispute. This can be a practical option that takes advantage of the infrequent presence of all the international participants for the arbitration and that avoids delays due to the time it would take to select a mediator and reconvene all the participants for the mediation. This is a very controversial process design because of the inherent difficulties posed by one neutral trying to serve two very different processes. Much has been written about the risks to the integrity of each process.[56] As a result, international arbitrators rarely assist in settlement efforts.[57]

---

56 *See* Chapter V.E.3 on "Med-Arb" and Abramson, *"Protocols for International Arbitrators Who Dare to Settle Cases,"* 10 *Am. Rev. of Intl. Arb*. 1, 3–5 (1999).

57 Christian Buhring-Uhle, *Arbitration and Mediation in International Business,* 188–192, 193–196, 211 (1996). (Attorneys appear more receptive to settlement initiatives by arbitrators than the actual practice of international arbitrators!)

International arbitrators have been known, however, to occasionally resort to settlement techniques that range from mild to intensive interventions.[58] Arbitrators may (1) suggest that parties try to negotiate a settlement of the case, (2) actively participate in settlement negotiations (at parties' request), (3) propose a settlement formula (at parties' request), (4) meet with parties separately to discuss settlement options (with parties' consent), (5) hint at possible outcome of the arbitration, and (6) render a "case evaluation" (at parties' request). The more intensive the intervention, the more controversial its use.

The next article suggest how international arbitrators may safely try to settle cases by following safeguards that are designed to preserve the impartiality of the neutrals while giving them some settlement flexibility.

Harold Abramson, "Protocols for International Arbitrators Who Dare to Settle Cases,"

10 *Am. Rev. of Intl. Arb.* 1–2, 7–15 (1999)

[The author emphasizes that the protocols are designed to create a small opening through which arbitrators can try to settle cases. This excerpt lists the twelve protocols and includes explanations for three of them.]

Ideally, I think international arbitrators should stay out of the direct settlement business. I favor the optimal arrangement in which the neutral who tries settling a case is different from the neutral who decides the case.* This arrangement preserves the impartiality of the neutral as decisionmaker while giving the neutral as settler the maximum flexibility to do her job well.

But as a pragmatist, I worry about lost opportunities for settlement in international arbitrations. It is extremely cumbersome to convene all the parties and attorneys. The first opportunity to meet face-to-face may be the first day of the arbitration hearings (or the night before in a foreign city while recovering from jet-lag). This may be their first real opportunity to discuss settling the case. In this paper, I consider whether these settlement discussion can be facilitated by the arbitrators.

---

58 Christian Buhring-Uhle, *Arbitration and Mediation in International Business*, 188–192 (1996).

* In international arbitrations, parties may engage a "shadow mediator" who attends the arbitration hearings and confers with parties and attorneys at promising moments during the arbitration proceeding such as at the beginning or end of each hearing day. *See* James J. Myers, "10 Techniques for Managing Arbitration Hearings," 51 *Dis. Resol. J.* 28 (January/ March, 1996). In the CPR Non-Administered Arbitration Rules, Rule 17 explicitly authorizes the arbitration panel "to permit the Mediator to attend conferences and hearings held in connection with the arbitration." CPR Non-Administered Arbitration Rules and Commentary, Rule 17 (1994).

***

In this section, I suggest a series of protocols that parties and their neutral(s) should follow. These protocols may work best when settlement initiatives are restricted to quasi-mediations. In some limited situations, adopting these protocols may make it feasible for arbitrators to engage in real mediations.

(1) *Neutral is Trained in Both Processes*
(2) *Neutral Consents to Serve Both Roles*
(3) *Neutral as Settler Will Respect Principle of Party Self-Determination*
(4) *Clients with Settlement Authority Should Be Present*
(5) *Documents and Statements in Settlement Process are Confidential*
(6) *Neutral as Settler Will Not Evaluate Merits, Evidence or Reasonableness of Positions*

Any evaluation by the neutral as settler poses a significant risk of compromising the neutral's impartiality if she resumes the role of arbitrator. The arbitrator who offers an evaluation during the settlement process may appear to have prejudged the case when the arbitration proceeding resumes. When the neutral returns to arbitrating, the neutral also may discover that the evaluation done in the settlement process may contaminate her view of the record in the arbitration proceeding. This protocol barring evaluations directs the neutral as settler to resist slipping prematurely into an adjudicatory mindset. ...

This restriction should not be interpreted to bar a mediator or quasi-mediator from helping the parties evaluate the case. The settler can still ask even-handed questions about the quality of evidence, credibility of witnesses, clarity of law, and likelihood of success in the arbitration proceeding. The settler can introduce to the parties the use of decision tree analysis to help the parties asses alternatives to settlement. ...

(7) NEUTRAL WILL NOT CAUCUS, UNLESS PARTIES AGREE TO EXCEPTION

Arbitrators turned settlers increase the risk of compromising their appearance of impartiality when they hold private meetings. The excluded party may become concerned that the neutral played one party against the other during settlement efforts. The excluded party also may become suspicious that the other party corrupted the neutral's view of the case under circumstances where the excluded party could not challenge the information. Presumably for these reasons, international practitioners have judged caucuses as the least appropriate technique for arbitrator-turned-mediator.

Barring caucuses means barring the use of a tool that many quasi-mediators and mediators consider vital for settlement efforts to be successful. Many settlers believe that private meetings create a unique and safe opportunity for neutrals to help parties vent and release anger, clarify positions and interests, and assess the acceptability of alternative settlement options. ...

(8) PARTIES AGREE TO RECONFIGURE ARBITRATION PANEL TO SUIT SETTLEMENT PROCESS

Arbitrators can take many different pathways toward helping parties settle a case. Each pathway offers different ways for preserving the impartiality of the neutral as arbitrator while opening opportunities for settlement. Many of these pathways are built around the flexibility offered by the usual international tribunal of three arbitrators. Five configurations are considered here although other permutations can be imagined. [This excerpt describes one option.]

[W]hen a typical panel of a neutral chair with two party-appointed arbitrators is constituted, the two party-appointed arbitrators could work together as a settlement team without the participation of the chair. This arrangement would preserve the neutrality of the chair who would not be tarnished by settlement efforts.

The settlement team could serve as quasi-mediators or even full-fledged mediators. They might function like a panel in a minitrial, hearing the parties' claims and helping them settle the dispute. The settlement team of party-appointed arbitrators may even be permitted by the parties to use caucuses because the third arbitrator, the chair, remains in reserve, insulated from the settlement process (Protocol 7). The settlement team should caucus only as a team which means each party-appointed arbitrator should avoid any *ex parte* contacts with the appointing party.

If settlement efforts are unsuccessful, the chair could serve as a sole arbitrator. This option, however, may be resisted by many international attorneys who prefer their party-appointed arbitrators to participate in the deliberations. In the alternative, all three arbitrators could hear the case. The impartiality of the panel may survive because any partiality by the party-appointed arbitrators would off-set each other, leaving the chair with the neutral and decisive role in the deliberations.

(9) *Arbitrator Will Not Be Influenced by Information Revealed in Settlement Process*
(10) *Parties Agree Not to Challenge Arbitrator or Award Based on Combined Roles*
(11) *Settlement Initiatives Should Not Unduly Delay the Arbitration Proceeding*
(12) *Parties Consent to Combined Processes*

NOTES AND QUESTIONS

1. What is the difference between the use of "mediation windows" in an international arbitration and a referral to mediation in a domestic court proceeding? Draft a dispute resolution clause that implements the Set-Arb-Set-Arb Process.
2. Do the protocols establish sufficient safeguards to protect the impartiality of arbitrators who try to settle cases? Do the protocols that bar evaluations and caucusing disable arbitrators from engaging in meaningful efforts to settle? Are there other configurations of tripartite tribunals that can serve the twin goals of maintaining the impartiality of the arbitrators and giving them sufficient flexibility to engage in effective settlement efforts?
3. Is it easier to justify the same person serving as settler and arbitrator in domestic or international arbitrations? Who is in a better position to help parties design dispute resolution processes—mediators or arbitrators? Why is it generally acceptable for judges, but not arbitrators, to try to settle their own cases?

6. PUBLIC DISPUTE RESOLUTION SYSTEMS FOR COMMERCIAL DISPUTES

Various countries around the world have formed regional and international institutions and processes for resolving business-related disputes.[59] The disputes, however, are not business disputes that arise out of private business deals. The disputes arise under commercial treaties that establish rules of fair business behavior in the global marketplace. These commercial treaties

59 *See* Schneider, "Getting Along: The Evolution of Dispute Resolution Regimes in International Trade Organizations," 20 *Mich. J. of Intl. L.* 697 (1999).

between governments regulate many types of governmental and business policies. These treaties deal with such issues as tariffs on imports, technical standards that might create non-tariff barriers to trade, and pirating of intellectual property rights. They also prohibit governments from unfairly subsidizing exports and prohibit businesses from dumping goods at less than their costs in foreign markets. Furthermore, the treaties try to facilitate doing business in the global marketplace by establishing mechanisms for coordinating and harmonizing various business policies and technical standards of different countries.

These commercial treaties create public systems of dispute resolution for disputes that arise under them. These public systems operate separately and independently from the private justice systems established by businesses in their dispute resolution clauses. Like private systems, public systems must include several key features in order to be credible dispute resolution processes. In evaluating these public processes, consider these questions: Is the decisionmaker neutral? Does the hearing give parties a reasonable opportunity to be heard? Is the decision of the adjudicatory body transparent? Did the signatory countries agree to be bound by the decision? Are the remedies meaningful? And, is there an effective mechanism for enforcing the decision? Two other questions deserve special attention by attorneys representing private clients: What *type of disputes* falls within the jurisdiction of the adjudicatory process? And, can a *private party* either initiate or participate in the public dispute resolution process? Each of these adjudicatory features can be conceived in different ways as demonstrated in the following brief descriptions of the dispute resolution processes administered by the World Trade Organization and under the North American Free Trade Agreement.

1. World Trade Organization[60] (WTO)

The new WTO,[61] the successor to GATT, administers a unified dispute resolution process through its *Dispute Settlement Body* (DSB) which is composed of

60 Final Act Embodying the Results of the Uruguay Round of Multinational Trade Negotiations, Annex 2: Understanding on Rules and Procedures Governing the Settlement of Disputes, Apr. 15, 1994, app. 1, in *The Results of the Uruguay Round of Multilateral Trade Negotiations*, 33 I.L.M. 1226, 1224; *See* Gabrielle Marceau, "NAFTA and WTO Dispute Settlement Rules—A Thematic Comparison," 31 *J. of World Trade* 26, 53–72 (1997); *Also see* Ernst-Ulrich Petersmann, *The GATT/WTO Dispute Resolution System: International Law, International Organizations and Dispute Resolution* (1997).

61 The treaty has been ratified by over one hundred countries.

all the members of the WTO. The DSB handles disputes that may arise under a number of covered treaties.[62]

Under WTO's strict timetables, governmental parties first try to resolve any disputes through a process of informal *consultation.* If unsuccessful, the complaining country can request the DSB to convene a *panel* of three to five governmental or non-governmental individuals. The panel hears the dispute and issues a written report. The report is automatically adopted by the DSB unless rejected by consensus of the DSB's members or a party appeals the report to the *Appellate Body.* Review by the Appellate Body is limited to issues of law covered in the report and legal interpretations made by the panel. A decision of the Appellate Body is automatically adopted by the DSB, unless rejected unanimously by its members.

The terms of the report are enforced in three steps. First, the losing party must *conform* with the terms of the report within a "reasonable period of time." Second, if the losing party fails to conform, the complaining party can ask the losing party to *negotiate* mutually acceptable compensation. Third, if the parties cannot agree upon terms of compensation, the complaining party can request the DSB for authorization to *retaliate.* Retaliation does not include punitive actions; it usually consists of the complaining party suspending equivalent concessions or obligations made to the violating party. Claims of excessive retaliation are subject to review in arbitrations.

2. NAFTA[63] (North American Free Trade Agreement)

NAFTA creates a free trade area in North America consisting of Canada, United States, and Mexico. In contrast with WTO procedures, NAFTA does not offer a unified dispute resolution process. Instead, NAFTA establishes primarily two very different processes for handling disputes under the treaty. Each process is quite elaborate and intricate. This description provides only an overview of each process.

Chapter 19 of NAFTA[64] creates a binding dispute resolution process for challenging governmentally imposed antidumping and countervailing

---

62 The better known treaties include the General Agreement on Tariffs and Trade (GATT 1994–goods), General Agreement on Trade in Services (GATS), and Trade-Related Intellectual Property Agreement (TRIPS.)

63 North American Free Trade Agreement, Dec. 17, 1992, 32 I.L.M. 289.

64 NAFTA, Chapter 19. *Also see* Leon E. Trakman, *Dispute Settlement Under The NAFTA: Manual and Source Book,* Ch. 4 (1997); In the Matter of the Mexican Antidumping Investigation into Imports of Cut-to-Length Plate Products from the United States, Panel No. MEX-94-1904-02 (August 30, 1995).

duties.[65] This process can be initiated by private parties. This process stands out as unusual because each country surrendered some domestic sovereignty to binding review by an international adjudicatory body. The process works as follows: When a local agency decides to impose an antidumping or countervailing duty on imports, the complaining foreign party can circumvent local court review by appealing the final agency decision to a NAFTA binational panel. The binational panel consists of two panelists from each country and a fifth panelist selected by agreement of the parties. The binational panel does not apply international law; it reviews the agency decision based on domestic law and in accordance with the domestic standard of review. The panel's decision on the validity of the duty is binding on the parties.

There is a limited opportunity to appeal the panel's decision to a three member Extraordinary Challenge Committee (ECC). This right to appeal can only be exercised by a NAFTA party (country, not private party.) The grounds for a challenge are limited to issues that may threaten the integrity of the binational review process such as whether a panel member is guilty of gross misconduct. Parties are barred from appealing a panel's decision to a local court.

Chapter 20 of NAFTA establishes a non-binding process for handling most other types of disputes under the treaty.[66] This process can only be initiated by governments at the federal level. Private parties are relegated to trying to convince their own government to initiate the dispute resolution process. The process consist of three stages: First, governments *consult* with each other to try to resolve the conflict. Second, the conflict can be referred to the *Free Trade Commission (FTC)*, the central institution of NAFTA which is comprised of cabinet-level representatives of each NAFTA country. The FTC can employ a variety of ADR methods in an effort to secure a negotiated resolution of the dispute. However, the FTC cannot arbitrate the dispute. Third, the dispute can be referred to a *five member panel* which will issue a report that is not binding on the parties. If the parties still do not resolve the conflict, the successful complainant can suspend equivalent NAFTA benefits to the nonconforming NAFTA party. This unilateral retaliation can be reviewed by a panel to determine whether the retaliation is "manifestly excessive."

---

65 Antidumping duties are imposed on imported goods to offset the below cost prices charged by an importing business. Countervailing duties are imposed on imported goods to offset foreign governmental subsidies that are used to reduce the price of the imported goods.

66 NAFTA, Chapter 20. *Also see* Leon E. Trakman, *Dispute Settlement Under The NAFTA: Manual and Source Book*, Ch. 1 (1997).

NOTES AND QUESTIONS

1. Other regional treaties create public dispute resolution mechanisms for handling cross-border disputes. An important and well developed system has been established by the European Union(EU) for disputes among members of its custom union. The EU Court of Justice and Court of First Instance resolve disputes relating to the interpretation and implementation of various EU treaties. The cases can be brought by private parties, member states or an EU agency. The Court can hear cases directly or take cases referred by local courts.[67]
2. The emergence of these public dispute resolution processes may some day impact on the continued use of private international arbitration. Consider this tantalizing possibility for the future use of a public international dispute resolution processes:

> We now ask if the construction of large regional markets—the European Community, NAFTA—or detailed mechanisms for regulating international commerce—the World Trade Organization under GATT—could also disrupt the landscape and introduce new stakes and even an "international new deal." The restructuring of the international market of disputes would build on emerging institutions such as the European Court of Justice, NAFTA, GATT, and even revived and transformed antitrust regulations. These institutions and approaches offer new opportunities for business. Even if it is not at first apparent, these institutions compete with the International Chamber of Commerce and private arbitrations. At the same time, new approaches and institutions may facilitate the recompositon of this field of practice closer to the pole of the state. ...
>
> If this line of development continues, the field of transnational business justice will be more closely connected to states and to supranational, state like entities than it was in the period when the ICC gained its eminence. Major business conflicts would be fought

67 The ANDEAN Common Market of several South American countries also has established a Court of Justice for resolving regional disputes. Furthermore, it has been recommended that the free trade area of ASEAN (Association of Southeast Asian Nations), known as AFTA, adopt a dispute settlement mechanism for resolving trade disputes. *See* Jeffrey A. Kaplan, "ASEAN's Rubicon: A Dispute Settlement Mechanism for AFTA," 14 *UCLA Pac. Basin L. J.* 147 (1996).

on terrain closer to the states—with the states implicated in the contests and the contestants. We cannot say at this point whether this development will take place, and whether, if so, the world constituted around the ICC and its networks will assume a secondary position.

Yves Dezalay and Bryant G. Garth, *Dealing in Virtue—International Commercial Arbitration and the Construction of a Transnational Legal Order,* 312, 315 (1996)

3. What additions to the dispute resolution processes of the WTO or NAFTA would be necessary before either of the processes would be acceptable to private business parties? Are these changes likely to be acceptable to the signatory countries such as the United States?

CHAPTER 8

Protocols for International Arbitrators Who Dare to Settle Cases

1999

Harold I. Abramson*

I. INTRODUCTION

The best time to settle an international business dispute can be after the international arbitration proceeding has been commenced. Just like in court litigation, parties may be ready to settle only after the adjudicatory process has begun and even has progressed. In court, judges commonly open the door to settlement; they hold settlement conferences and even actively participate in settlement negotiations. But arbitrators rarely open the door to settlement; when they do, they risk losing their jobs.[1] So, what can international arbitrators safely do? What dare they do?[2]

---

* Professor of Law, Touro Law Center; LL.M. Harvard Law School, 1984; M. P. A., Harvard School of Government, 1983; J. D., Syracuse University, 1974; B.B.A., University of Michigan, 1971. The author teaches courses on dispute resolution and international business and serves as a mediator and arbitrator in business and public policy disputes. Drafts of this paper were presented in programs sponsored by the Dispute Resolution Committee of the International Law and Practice Section of the NYS Bar Association (October, 1998) and the Section of Dispute Resolution of the ABA (May, 1999). The author thanks his research assistant, Michael Hack, for his tenacious and timely pursuit of numerous research assignments.

1 Because I only consider settlement efforts attempted after the formal arbitration has been commenced, I do not use the more common term "med-arb" which usually envisions a mediation process followed by an arbitration process. Instead, I consider a different sequencing of processes which might be called "arb-settlement-arb." For a background article on "med-arb" *see* Barry C. Bartel, Comment, "Med-Arb As a Distinct Method of Dispute Resolution: History, Analysis, and Potential," 27 *Williamette L. Rev.* 661 (1991); James T. Peter, "Med-Arb in International Arbitration," 8 *Am Rev. Intl Arb.* 83 (1997).

2 This paper does not consider whether domestic arbitrators should try to settle cases. Different considerations apply to domestic arbitrations, considerations that were not examined

International arbitrators can safely encourage parties to settle. They can suggest that parties consider settling or trying mediation with another neutral of their choice. When taking these initiatives, arbitrators stay out of direct participation in settlement negotiations.

Arbitrators also might dare to participate directly in settlement efforts.[3] This initiative is controversial and fraught with risks. This initiative should not be tolerated as an occasional move done on the sly. Instead, when and how arbitrators participate in settlement efforts should be openly studied and debated.[4]

Ideally, I think international arbitrators should stay out of the direct settlement business. I favor the optimal arrangement in which the neutral who tries settling a case is different from the neutral who decides the case.[5] This arrangement preserves the impartiality of the neutral as decisionmaker while giving the neutral as settler the maximum flexibility to do her job well.

But as a pragmatist, I worry about lost opportunities for settlement in international arbitrations. In many international disputes, it can be extremely cumbersome to convene all the parties and attorneys. The first opportunity for

---

in this paper. For instance, the justifications for domestic arbitrators settling cases may be weaker because it can be easier to bring in a separate neutral in domestic arbitrations where the participants do not typically face significant cross-cultural and vast geographical obstacles to convening a meeting. Nevertheless, I encourage the testing of these ideas and proposals in domestic arbitrations.

3 In this paper, the terms "settlement efforts" and "settlement initiatives" are used to cover a broad range of options, including mediation.

4 There are remarkably few articles on how international arbitrators should go about trying to settle cases. *See, e.g.*, David Plant, "Mediation in International Commercial Arbitration-Some Practical Aspects," 4 *Ilsa J. Intl. and Comp. L.* 329 (1998) and Kenji Tashiro, "Conciliation or Mediation during the Arbitral Process: A Japanese View," 12(2) *J. Intl. Arb.* 119 (1995). Instead, most authors consider only the threshold question of whether arbitrators should settle cases and then point out that it is done in other countries in Western Europe and Asia. *See* next section on "Can One Neutral Serve Two Processes?."

5 In international arbitrations, parties may engage a "shadow mediator" who attends the arbitration hearings and confers with parties and attorneys at promising moments during the proceeding such as at the beginning or end of each hearing day. *See* James J. Myers, "10 Techniques for Managing Arbitration Hearings," *Disp. Resol.* Jan. /Mar. 1996, AT 28. Rule 17 of the CPR Non-Administered Arbitration Rules (1994) explicitly authorizes the arbitration panel "to permit the mediator to attend conferences and hearings held in connection with the arbitration."

Selecting a mediator at the beginning of the arbitration proceeding may eliminate any temptations for arbitrators to settle. But, parties must invest foresight, time and effort to mutually select a mediator and to invest the additional expense of retaining a fourth neutral. Parties can find it difficult to make these investments when they are occupied with preparing for and participating in an arbitration proceeding.

the participants to meet face-to-face may not arrive until the first day of the arbitration hearings (or the night before in a foreign city while recovering from jet-lag). This first opportunity to meet may be the first real opportunity for participants to discuss settling the case. In this paper, I consider whether these settlement discussions can be facilitated by the arbitrators. This may be feasible when done under strict safeguards. When participants agree to follow carefully crafted protocols, this suboptimal arrangement may be capable of preserving the impartiality of arbitrators while offering limited opportunities for efficient, cost-effective, and fair settlement of disputes.

In this paper, I explore the dilemma presented when one neutral tries to both arbitrate and settle a case, consider the range of settlement initiatives available for arbitrators who try to settle, and then recommend protocols that arbitrators should adopt if they dare to try to settle cases.

II. CAN ONE NEUTRAL SERVE TWO PROCESSES?

Practitioners and scholars have debated extensively whether one neutral can serve as both arbitrator and settler in the same case.[6] The benefits are self-evident. Arbitrators who settle cases can save parties time and money. Savings accrue because the case settles rather than continue in the arbitration proceeding. Furthermore, the case settles without adjourning the arbitration to select a mediator who must then be educated about the dispute at a rescheduled session. These savings are magnified in international arbitrations where

6 For articles that consider pros and cons of the same neutral serving as arbitrator and mediator, *see*, for example, Barry C. Bartel, Comment, "Med-Arb As a Distinct Method of Dispute Resolution: History, Analysis, and Potential," 27 *Williamette L. Rev.* 661 (1991); James T. Peter, "Med-Arb in International Arbitration," 8 *Am. Rev. Intl. Arb.* 83 (1997); Nels E. Nelson and A. N. M. Meshquat Uddin, "Arbitrators as Mediators," *Lab. L. J.* April 1995, at 205; Kenji Tashiro, "Conciliation or Mediation during the Arbitral Process: A Japanese View," 12(2) *J. Intl. Arb.* 119 (1995); V. Fischer-Zernin and A. Junker, "Arbitration and Mediation: Synthesis or Antithesis?," 5(1) *J. Intl. Arb.* 21, 24–25, 35–37, 39–40 (1988); Stephen J. Burton, "Combining Conciliation with Arbitration of International Commerce Disputes," 18 *Hastings Intl. and Comp. L. Rev.* 637, 652–57 (1995); Michael F. Hoellering, "Mediation and Arbitration: A Growing Interaction," 52 *Disp. Resol. J.* 23 (1997) (reaffirms "conventional wisdom that arbitration and mediation operate best when employed as separate processes"); M. Scott Donahey, "Seeking Harmony; Is the Asian Concept of the Conciliator/ Arbitrator Applicable in the West?," 50 *Disp. Resol. J.* 74 (April 1995); Lon Fuller, "Collective Bargaining and the Arbitrator," *Wis. L. R.* 3, 23–24 (1963) and Lon L. Fuller, "Collective Bargaining and the Arbitrator," 1962 *Proc. of the 15th Ann. Mtg. of the Nat'l Acad. of Arb.* 8, 29–30, 33 (1962) (Classic objections to one neutral serving two roles).

communications and scheduling of sessions are more difficult among neutrals, parties and attorneys who are from different countries. It is for these reasons that when everybody is already convened in one location for the arbitration proceeding, parties can find the option of the arbitrator settling a case to be extremely attractive.

The primary risk is that one neutral may not be able to perform effectively the two distinctively different roles of arbitrator and settler in the same case.[7] In order to preserve the integrity of each process, the neutral must simultaneously maintain her *impartiality* as arbitrator and her *flexibility* as settler.[8]

The neutral must figure out how to preserve her impartiality when trying to settle a case. Settlers, for instance, may solicit confidential information for purposes of settlement, hold *ex parte* meetings (caucuses), engage in "reality testing," and even assess merits of claims (evaluations). These initiatives may benefit the settlement process but may expose the arbitration process to legal attack. A party may challenge the arbitrator or the award on the grounds that the arbitrator was influenced by information learned during settlement efforts. A party also may claim that the arbitrator prejudged the case during settlement efforts when she offered an evaluation of the merits of the case. A party might even complain that the arbitrator retaliated against the party in the arbitration proceeding for not heeding her advice during settlement discussions. Therefore, arbitrators face the daunting risk of engaging in settlement initiatives that may disqualify them as arbitrators. In trying to reduce this risk, arbitrators may feel compelled to limit their use of some basic techniques that might otherwise make settlement efforts effective.[9]

7 *See* Lon L. Fuller, 1962 Proc. *supra* note 6, at 8, 29–30, 33. (Fuller made his now widely-cited observations that a neutral may confuse the two distinctive roles of mediator and arbitrator each of which call for different purposes and moralities, with mediation focused on settlement and arbitration focused on decisions according to the law.)

8 *See* Christian Bühring-Uhle, *Arbitration and Mediation in International Business*, 203, 204 (1996). The author distinguishes *impartiality*, which "refers to the absence of pre-disposition with respect to the merits of the dispute" from *independence* which refers to being "capable of making their own judgment without being impaired by some type of dependence or obligation to a party."

9 Christian Bühring-Uhle succinctly elaborated on this point:

> In mediation, the quest for an efficient solution that creates value for the parties makes it necessary to explore the real interest underlying the parties' legal positions. Hence, the neutral may have to obtain confidential information from the parties regarding points on which, as an arbitrator, he is not supposed to base his decision. Another important element of effective mediation is "reality-testing"-the mediator has to confront and question the parties' positions on the merits in order to narrow the difference between them and to deflate exaggerated

Other problems arise when the same neutral serves two processes. For settlement efforts to be successful, parties must talk candidly with the neutral. Parties may be reluctant to talk candidly for strategic reasons when they realize that the neutral may later serve as the arbitrator. Moreover, when the arbitrator tries to convert an on-going arbitration into a formal mediation, the arbitrator-turned-mediator may short-circuit the mediation process. This alternative pathway into mediation may require the neutral to omit some valuable steps in the mediation process that are designed to orient parties toward settlement such as the preparation of a mediation briefing paper and opening statements of mediator, attorneys and clients.

In the area of international dispute resolution, this familiar debate follows different cultural paths to practices that can vary among different regions of the world. In many Asian countries[10] and in several Western European countries,[11] arbitrators and parties are more receptive than U.S. participants to arbitrators settling cases. For instance, "the most complete integration of the role of the arbitrator and conciliator is in the Chinese model, where the arbitrator may become a conciliator, then become an arbitrator again at any stage of the proceedings."[12]

---

demands. Both reality-testing and the exploration of the parties' real interests work best when the mediator meets the parties separately, and generally in order for mediation to be effective the neutral has to build an intensely personal relationship with the parties.

By contrast, the task of adjudicating a dispute requires a high level of detachment and emotional distance from the parties and their interests and positions. The integrity of the adjudicative process is imperiled when the arbitrator obtains information that he must disregard when deciding the dispute; and his impartially is threatened when he expresses his views on the merits before having seen all the evidence and legal arguments.

As a consequence, the arbitrator will tend to be rather cautious in expressing his views and eliciting sensitive information. This, in turn, reduces the effectiveness of his mediation attempts. Bühring-Uhle, *supra* note 8, at 366.

10 *See* M. Scott Donahey, *supra* note 6, at 74, 76; Tashiro, *supra* note 6, at 119; and Huang Yanming, "Mediation in the Settlement of Business Disputes: Two Typical Examples of Cases Settled by Mediation at the CIETAC's Shenzhen Commission," 8(4) *J. Intl. Arb.* 23 (1991).

11 *See*, e.g., V. Fischer-Zernin and A. Junker, *supra* note 6, at 30, 34–35 (1988). ("The prevailing opinion [in most continental Western European countries] is that a separation between arbitration and mediation is unnecessarily duplicative. ..." In Austria, Germany, the Netherlands and Sweden, arbitrators attempt to settle their cases.)

12 M. Scott Donahey, *supra* note 6, at 74, 76. When CIETAC (China) recently updated its arbitration rules, it tried to govern the longstanding practice of Chinese arbitrators conciliating disputes during the arbitration proceeding. Among the changes, arbitrators can only conciliate with the consent of both parties, and any information learned during conciliation cannot be used in the arbitration proceeding. *See* Michael J. Moser, "China's New International Arbitration Rules," 11 (3) *J. Intl. Arb.* 5, 11–12 (1994).

In a survey of U.S. and German practitioners,[13] German respondents reported that they "often" encountered arbitrators participating in settlement negotiations while U.S. participants reported that they "very rarely" saw arbitrators do this.[14] When asked about the propriety of arbitrators participating in negotiations, 92% of German respondents thought it was appropriate, while 71% of U.S. respondents rejected this role for arbitrators.[15] Thus, different cultural experiences may shape participants' attitudes toward one neutral serving two processes.[16]

III. RANGE OF SETTLEMENT INITIATIVES: FROM QUASI-MEDIATIONS TO REAL MEDIATIONS

Arbitrators may engage in a range of settlement initiatives,[17] such as

(1) suggesting that parties try to negotiate a settlement of the case;
(2) actively participating in settlement negotiations (at parties' request);
(3) proposing a settlement formula (at parties' request);
(4) meeting with parties separately to discuss settlement options (with parties' consent);
(5) hinting at the possible outcome of the arbitration; and
(6) rendering a "case evaluation" (at parties' request). Arbitrators are more likely to resort to mild interventions such as suggesting to parties that they try to settle the case than more intensive interventions such as "case evaluations."18 The more intensive the intervention, the more controversial its use.

Because some of these techniques are commonly used by mediators, these settlement efforts may appear to be a mediation process. Participants may think

13 Bühring-Uhle, *supra* note 8, at 189–96.
14 *Id.* at 191.
15 *Id.* at 193–94.
16 These different attitudes may be converging as parties are exposed to different cultural practices, leading to U.S. lawyers becoming more acquainted with Asian practices of conciliation and Asian lawyers becoming familiar with the more adversarial U.S. model of arbitration. *See, e.g.*, Alan Scott Rau and Edward F. Sherman, "Tradition and Innovation in International Arbitration Procedure," 30 *Tex. Intl. L. J.* 89, 105–109 (1995). In a survey, attorneys appeared more receptive to settlement initiatives by arbitrators than the actual practice of international arbitrators. *See* Bühring-Uhle, *supra* note 8, at 188–92, 193–96, 211.
17 Bühring-Uhle, *supra* note 8, at 189. (The author surveyed practitioners about the use of these six settlement techniques.)
18 Bühring-Uhle, *supra* note 8, at 188–92.

that they are experiencing mediation. But, usually, they are not experiencing the real thing.

Real mediation[19] for the type of disputes that arise in international arbitrations is a structured negotiation conducted by a specially trained expert, a mediator. The mediation process is a separate and self-contained process that has a beginning, middle and end. The mediator guides parties and their attorneys through each distinct stage of the process.

Each stage and each step by the mediator has a purpose, starting with the mediator's usual request for each party to prepare a mediation briefing paper. Preparing the briefing paper orients parties toward the goals of the mediation, goals that typically involve resolving any relationship or substantive problems.[20] At the mediation session, the mediator normally starts with an opening statement that reinforces the goals of the mediation. The mediator then manages a structured discussion in which the mediator employs various techniques that are designed to encourage client involvement, explore clients' interests, and create a collaborative environment for settling the dispute.

The mediator guides the participants by employing a mix of highly refined techniques. The mediator poses open-ended and focused questions, re-frames issues, conducts brainstorming sessions, and uses strategies to defuse tensions and overcome impasses. The mediator may use private caucuses to gain confidential information and use various methods for helping participants to evaluate the strengths and weaknesses of the case. If the case does not settle, the mediator may help the participants design alternative pathways out of the conflict.

This real mediation is not typically done by arbitrators. Typical settlement efforts by arbitrators should be more accurately described as something other than mediation. The process may be more akin to a judicial settlement conference in which the trial judge or a different settlement judge may employ various techniques to promote settlement.[21] Because some of

---

19 *See generally* Dwight Golann, *Mediating Legal Disputes—Effective Strategies for Lawyers and Mediators*, Chs. 2 and 3 (1996); Christopher W. Moore, *The Mediation Process—Practical Strategies for Resolving Conflict*, 63–68 (2nd ed., 1996); Jay Folger and Allison Taylor, *Mediation—A Comprehensive Guide to Resolving Disputes without Litigation* 7(1984); and Fischer-Zernin and A. Junker, *supra* note 6, at 25–26.

20 Compare these goals with the goals in "transformative mediation" in which mediators focus on the goals of "empowerment" and "recognition". *See* Robert A. Baruch Bush and Joseph P. Folger, *The Promise of Mediation—Responding to Conflict through Empowerment and Recognition* (1994).

21 There is a vast literature on the role of judges in the settlement of cases. Many of the authors evaluated specific settlement techniques of judges. In a recently published *Judges'*

the settlement techniques may be used by mediators, the process might be called quasi-mediation.[22]

Labeling typical settlement efforts as quasi-mediation should flag the fact that the settlement initiatives are not real mediation. A separate label also makes clear that arbitrators may take two different pathways toward settlement: arbitrators can mediate or quasi-mediate. This division also alerts us to the reality that settlement initiatives are not monolithic but instead consist of a collection of techniques, some of which may be acceptable and some inappropriate for arbitrators who try to settle cases.

IV. PROTOCOLS FOR ARBITRATORS SETTLING CASES

Parties and neutral(s) should adopt protocols that will reduce the inherent risks that arise when one neutral serves two processes.[23] Any protocols must manage the tension between the need to preserve the impartiality of the arbitrator and the need to give the neutral sufficient flexibility to conduct effective mediations or quasi-mediations. This tension erupts when the neutral as mediator contemplates caucusing with one party or providing an evaluation of the case. Does the use of these two settlement techniques by a neutral inherently compromise the appearance of impartiality of the neutral when she resumes arbitrating? The tension also surfaces when the neutral as mediator learns information during settlement efforts that should be disregarded by the neutral in the arbitration proceeding. Is it possible for the neutral to erect a mental wall that strictly separates information, insights, and views developed during settlement efforts from the record of evidence developed in the arbitration proceeding?

Guide, the authors analyzed a large number of techniques, deeming which are "acceptable" and which are "inappropriate" for judges to use in settlement conferences. For example, they concluded that it is acceptable for judges who will not decide the case to "evaluate a litigant's case with the litigant in a separate caucus "but that judges who will decide the case should be "more circumspect." In contrast, they concluded, it is inappropriate for a judge to "require the litigant to explain to the judge why the litigant won't accept the settlement." *See* Jona Goldschmidt and Lisa Milord, *"Judicial Settlement Ethics," Judges' Guide* 42 (American Judicature Society and State Justice Institute, 1996). This same study offers an excellent bibliography. (*See Annotated Bibliography of Judicial Settlement Literature, in id.* at 92–104.)

22 *See* Bühring-Uhle, *supra* note 8, at 201 (referring to "low-intensity" forms of mediation).

23 *See, e.g.*, Plant, *supra* note 4, at 329 and Tashiro, *supra* note 6, at 129–32.

The antagonism against the same neutral serving as both mediator and arbitrator in the same case is reflected in the clear prohibition found in most arbitration and mediation rules.[24] But most rules authorize an exception: they permit parties to waive this prohibition. For this waiver to be meaningful, the consent must be informed and uncoerced. Informed consent can be achieved through a discussion of the protocols described below. The protocols elaborate on a number of issues that participants should consider before giving consent. Uncoerced consent is more likely when a party first suggests that the participants try settling than when an arbitrator makes the suggestion. An arbitrator's suggestion may be interpreted as an order that if not followed will alienate the arbitrator.

Nevertheless, arbitrators can try to broach the topic tactfully and creatively.[25] For example, they might sincerely advise the parties that they routinely and

---

24 *See,* e.g., ICC Pre-Arbitral Referee Procedure prohibits a referee from serving as an arbitrator in the same case, unless the parties agree otherwise. ICC Pre-Arbitral Referee Procedure, Rule 2.3 (effective January 1, 1990). The ICC Rules of Optional Conciliation bar a conciliator from serving in any related judicial or arbitration proceeding unless the parties agree otherwise. ICC Rules of Optional Conciliation, Art.10 (effective January 1, 1988). The Mediation Rules of the World Intellectual Property Organization (WIPO) also prohibit mediators from acting in any other capacity in any pending or future proceedings unless authorized by the parties. WIPO Mediation Rules, Art. 20 (effective October 1, 1995). The widely used Arbitration Rules of the China International Economic and Trade Arbitration Commission explicitly authorize the arbitration tribunal to conciliate cases during the arbitration proceeding if the parties consent. The rules maintain a separation between the two processes by barring the use of information developed in the mediation from use in subsequent arbitration or judicial proceedings. CIETAC Arbitration Rules, Arts. 46–51 (effective March 17, 1994). The UNCITRAL Conciliation Rules and the Non-Administered International Arbitration Rules of the CPR Institute for Dispute Resolution also specifically prohibit a mediator from serving as an arbitrator in the same case unless the parties agree to modify the rules. UNCITRAL Conciliation Rules, Arts. 1, 19 (1980) and CPR Institute for Dispute Resolution Non-Administered International Arbitration Rules 1.1, 18.2 (1995). Surprisingly, the AAA International Arbitration Rules and AAA Mediation Rules do not consider the med-arb issue. The AAA Domestic Arbitration Rules, however, specifically prohibit an arbitrator from serving as a mediator, unless the parties agree otherwise. AAA Commercial Arbitration Rules, Rule 10 (effective on July 1, 1996).

25 In a recent domestic arbitration, while walking with the attorneys from the waiting room to the hearing room for a pre-arbitration conference, I casually asked the attorneys whether they had settled the case while waiting for me. They both responded that they could settle the case, but the clients could not. I responded glibly that this sounded like a case for mediation. Both attorneys greeted this off-the-cuff remark enthusiastically, drilled me about how mediation works, and agreed to use mediation. Incidentally, I advised them that if the mediation failed, I would not serve as the arbitrator! I did not think that this domestic case with local parties and attorneys justified the use of this suboptimal arrangement.

non-judgmentally ask whether any parties are interested in trying to settle the case.

The following protocols may work best when settlement initiatives are restricted to quasi-mediations. In some limited situations, adopting these protocols may make it feasible for arbitrators to engage in real mediations.

(1) Neutral is Trained in Both Processes

The neutral who serves as both settler and arbitrator should be trained in the ethics, norms, and techniques of each process. The neutral must strive to maintain the integrity of each separate process, and this is no easy task. Only an exceptionally qualified neutral is likely to succeed.

(2) Neutral Consents to Serve Both Roles

The neutral should carefully consider whether to assume both process roles. The neutral should first assess whether she has the expertise to perform both roles (Protocol 1). The neutral also should ascertain whether the mandate to preserve her impartiality as an arbitrator prevents her from serving effectively as a settler. Finally, the neutral should make an independent assessment as to whether the particular case is ripe for settlement.

(3) Neutral as Settler Will Respect Principle of Party Self-Determination

When trying to settle a case, the neutral should respect the right of each party to enter into a voluntary, uncoerced agreement. Each party should be free to determine whether or not to settle. This principle of party self-determination is adopted in the mediator's code of conduct.[26] This principle can be easily violated in an arrangement in which the settler also has the power to decide the case. This arrangement may create a coercive atmosphere for settlement.[27]

---

26 *See* Standards of Conduct for Mediators, Articles I and VI (adopted by American Arbitration Association, Society for Professionals in Dispute Resolution, and American Bar Association Section on Dispute Resolution, 1994).

27 In a detailed study of settlement techniques by judges, the authors drew a sharp distinction between initiatives by trial judges, the judges who will decide the case, and settlement judges, the judges who will only try to settle the case. They concluded that trial judges should be "more circumspect" when using certain more aggressive techniques. "This is because the judge's authority over the trial makes it more likely that his or her actions will be perceived as coercive, as demonstrating a premature judgment on the case, or as bias toward or against a litigant." Goldschmidt and Milford, *supra* note 21, at 7.

As a result, the neutral as settler must be especially careful to avoid any initiatives that may be viewed as coercive in order to preserve the principle of party self-determination.

(4) Clients with Settlement Authority Will Be Present[28]

Settlement efforts are usually more successful when the settlement process includes active participation by not only attorneys but also their clients-the people with the personal knowledge of the dispute, personal interest in the outcome, and settlement authority. Real mediations in the United States succeed in part because of the unique opportunity for attorneys and clients to meet with their counterparts in a non-adversarial and confidential setting.[29] However, the familiar division of roles between attorneys and clients in the U.S. is not necessarily followed in civil-law jurisdictions. In other countries, clients may perform less active roles and their attorneys may possess greater settlement authority and personal knowledge of the clients' situation, especially in business matters.

Therefore, this protocol may need to be modified to accommodate different cultural practices while ensuring that the people with broad settlement authority and personal knowledge participate in settlement efforts.

(5) Documents and Statements in Settlement Process are Confidential

Parties and neutral(s) should execute a confidentiality agreement that prohibits introducing in the arbitration proceeding any information disclosed or developed in the settlement process and that is otherwise not independently discoverable. Executing confidentiality agreements has become standard practice in mediations because of the belief that confidentiality promotes candor and risk-taking in settlement discussions.[30] It is obviously impossible to secure complete confidentiality when the settler will also serve as arbitrator. Nevertheless, this protocol should contribute to erecting a wall between settlement and arbitration.

---

28 In federal court, a judge has the authority to order a party or its representative to attend a settlement conference with the judge. *See* FED. R. CIV. P. 16(C).

29 *See* Golann, *supra* note 19, at Sec. 5.1.3.

30 *See* Golann, *supra* note 19 at Secs. 13.0, 13.1 (1996) and Nancy H. Rogers and Craig A. Mcewen, *Mediation—Law, Policy, Practice*, Secs. 9.01, 9.02, 9.23 (1994, Supp. 1995).

(6) Neutral as Settler Will Not Evaluate Merits, Evidence or Reasonableness of Positions[31]

Any evaluation by the neutral as settler poses a significant risk of compromising the neutral's impartiality if she resumes the role of arbitrator. The arbitrator who offers an evaluation during the settlement process may appear to have prejudged the case when the arbitration proceeding resumes. When the neutral returns to arbitrating, the neutral also may discover that her evaluation may have contaminated her view of the record in the arbitration proceeding. This protocol barring evaluations directs the neutral as settler to resist slipping prematurely into an adjudicatory mindset. This prohibition should reinforce the wall that separates the settlement process from the arbitration process.

This restriction should not be interpreted to bar a mediator or quasi-mediator from helping the parties evaluate their case. The settler can still ask even-handed questions about the quality of evidence, credibility of witnesses, clarity of law, and likelihood of success in the arbitration proceeding. The settler can introduce the use of decision tree analysis to help the parties assess alternatives to settlement.[32] The settler can even encourage the parties to bring in a jointly-selected expert to evaluate decisive aspects of the case, such as conflicting evidence or conflicting interpretations of law.

This protocol, followed by mediators who subscribe to a facilitative style of mediation,[33] eliminates a tool for settlers who use their personal evaluations as a technique to break impasses and prod settlements. Even though I strongly recommend against the use of evaluations, I realize that some participants may still want to take the risk and seek evaluations from arbitrators-turned-settlers. In these circumstances, participants should limit evaluations to matters not likely to be adjudicated in the arbitration, such as

31 In an extensive but some what dated survey of lawyers, the lawyers strongly preferred judges to evaluate cases but preferred that the evaluations be done by judges who would not ultimately decide the case. *See* Wayne D. Brazil, *Effective Approaches to Settlement: A Handbook for Lawyers and Judges* 391, 392, 403–407, 418–24 (1988). (Almost 1900 lawyers were surveyed in 1983–1984 for an ABA study.)

32 *See, e.g.*, Marjorie Corman Aaron and David P. Hoffer, "Decision Analysis as a Method of Evaluating the Trial Alternative," *in Mediating Legal Disputes*, ch. 11 (Dwight Golann ed., 1996) (In decision tree analysis, parties identify adjudicatory paths for resolution, estimate probability of success along each branch of the path, and approximates the likely substantive outcome, if a party makes it to the end of the adjudicatory path.)

33 For an explanation of different styles of mediation, *see* Leonard L. Riskin, "Understanding Mediators' Orientations, Strategies, and Techniques: A Grid for the Perplexed," 1 *Harv. Neg. L. Rev.* 7 (1996).

future-oriented issues or compromised-based solutions that do not clearly reflect who has the stronger case.

(7) Neutral Will Not Caucus, Unless Parties Agree to Exception

When to use caucuses and how best to use them are debated among mediators. Some mediators even advocate avoiding caucuses altogether because the private meetings between the neutral and one side may interfere with the opportunity for parties to work with each other to resolve their own problems.[34]

Arbitrators turned settlers increase the risk of compromising their appearance of impartiality when they hold private meetings.[35] The excluded party may become concerned that the neutral played one party against the other during settlement efforts. The excluded party also may become suspicious that the other party corrupted the neutral's view of the case under circumstances where the excluded party could not challenge the information. Presumably for these reasons, international practitioners have judged caucuses as the least appropriate technique for the arbitrator-turned-mediator.[36]

Barring caucuses means eliminating a tool that many quasi-mediators and mediators consider vital for settlement efforts to be successful. Many settlers believe that private meetings create a unique and safe opportunity for neutrals to help parties vent and release anger, clarify positions and interests, and assess the acceptability of alternative settlement options.[37] In private confidential sessions, parties may be more inclined to engage in reality testing with the settler and openly recognize weaknesses of their own case as well as strengths of the other side. The private meetings also can create an environment in which parties may feel secure to reveal their real interests to the neutral, who can then use this information to help parties explore mutually acceptable solutions.

After weighing the risks and benefits of using caucuses, parties might still want the settler to use caucuses. Parties may decide to permit the use of

---

34 *See* Golann, *supra* note 19, at Sec. 3.2 (detailed discussion of goals, techniques, and common mistakes in caucuses).

35 *See* IBA Ethics for International Arbitrators, Section 8, Involvement in Settlement Proposals ("... the arbitral tribunal should point out to the parties that it is undesirable that any arbitrator should discuss settlement terms with a party in the absence of the other parties since this will normally have the result that any arbitrator involved in such discussions will become disqualified from any future participation in the arbitration").

36 Bühring-Uhle, *supra* note 8, at 206, 207.

37 *Id.* at 206–208 and Golann, *supra* note 19, at Sec. 3.2 (detailed discussion of goals, techniques, and common mistakes in caucuses).

caucuses generally or restrict their use to less risky settings. Caucuses are less risky when the settlement effort is focused on forward-looking solutions such as a continuing business relations hip instead of backward-looking issues of the type that typically arise in the arbitration.

The reasons for the foregoing distinction are relatively straightforward. If the settlement discussions can be separated in time or subject matter from the issues in the arbitration, the arbitrator is much less likely to be infected from the settlement discussions with off-the-record information or impress ions that may affect the arbitrator's view of the merits of the issues being arbitrated on the record. Concomitantly, the larger the overlap between the subject of the settlement discussions and the issues being arbitrated, the greater the likelihood of the arbitrator's being affected by what the arbitrator sees or hears in the settlement discussions.[38]

Caucuses also are less risky when parties re-configure three-person panels to accommodate the settlement process. These options are considered in Protocol 8.

(8) Parties Agree to Reconfigure Arbitration Panel to Suit Settlement Process

Arbitrators can take many different pathways toward helping parties settle a case.[39] Each pathway offers different ways for preserving the impartiality of the neutral as arbitrator while opening opportunities for settlement. Many of these pathways are built around the flexibility offered by the usual international tribunal of three arbitrators. Five configurations are considered here, although other permutations can be imagined.

First, when a typical panel of a neutral chair with two party-appointed arbitrators is constituted, the two party-appointed arbitrators could work together as a settlement team without the participation of the chair. This arrangement would preserve the neutrality of the chair who would not be tarnished by settlement efforts.

The settlement team could serve as quasi-mediators or even full-fledged mediators. They might function like a panel in a minitrial, hearing the parties' claims and helping them settle the dispute. The settlement team of party-appointed arbitrators may even be permitted by the parties to use caucuses

38 Plant, *supra* note 4 at 331.

39 *See* Bühring-Uhle, *supra* note 8, at 196–201.

because the third arbitrator, the chair, remains in reserve, insulated from the settlement process (Protocol 7). The settlement team should caucus only as a team which means each party-appointed arbitrator should avoid any *ex parte* contacts with the appointing party.[40]

If settlement efforts are unsuccessful, the chair could serve as a sole arbitrator. This option, however, may be resisted by many international attorneys, who prefer their party-appointed arbitrators to participate in the deliberations.[41] In the alternative, all three arbitrators could hear the case. The impartiality of the panel may survive because any partiality by the party-appointed arbitrators would offset each other, leaving the chair with the neutral and decisive role in the deliberations.

Second, the typical panel of a neutral chair with two party-appointed arbitrators could be reconfigured so that the chair serves as the settler,[42] preserving the relative impartiality of the party-appointed arbitrators. The neutral chair may serve as a quasi-mediator or full-fledged mediator. The neutral chair should still be prohibited from using caucuses and evaluations in order to protect the impartiality of the chair who performs such a vital role on the arbitration panel. If the case does not settle, the three-person panel would hear the case but only the two party-appointed arbitrators would issue an award. With this arrangement, there is a significant risk of a tie between the two party-appointed arbitrators. Any tie could be broken by the chair, although the chair's neutrality may be suspect despite the prohibition on her use of caucuses and evaluations. When deciding whether to adopt this configuration, parties should consider whether this procedure for breaking a tie is adequate.

---

40 In contrast, it is not uncommon for party-appointed arbitrators in China (CIETAC) to conciliate through *ex parte* meetings with the appointing party. *See* Bühring-Uhle, *supra* note 8, at 198–200.

41 *See*, e.g., Andreas F. Lowenfeld, "The Party-Appointed Arbitrator in International Controversies: Some Reflections," 30 *Tex. Intl. L. J.* 59, 65 (1995) and James H. Carter, "Living with the Party-Appointed Arbitrator: Judicial Confusion, Ethical Codes and Practical Advice," 3 *Am. Rev. Intl. Arb.* 153 (1992).

42 In the Commentary for CPR Non-Administered Arbitration Rules, it is suggested that a non-party-appointed arbitrator may be a candidate to serve as a mediator even though this is not as a rule a preferable option.

The members of the tribunal will be thoroughly familiar with the case, and an arbitrator not appointed by either party may well be able to serve as mediator. However, the parties may hesitate to confide in an arbitrator, and an arbitrator would be inhibited in making settlement proposals or giving advice to the parties. CPR Non-Administered Arbitration Rules and Commentary Rule 17. Settlement and Mediation 28–29 (1994).

Third, when three neutral arbitrators are selected, one could serve as a settler while the other two function only as arbitrators. This arrangement would preserve the impartiality of two arbitrators. The arbitrator-turned-settler could serve as a quasi-mediator or even as a full-fledged mediator, employing a wide range of mediation techniques including using caucuses. But the neutral should avoid any evaluations, because she might still serve on the arbitration panel (Protocol 6). If the case does not settle, the remaining two arbitrators would issue the award. If the two arbitrators reach an impasse, then the third arbitrator-turned-settler would be available to break the tie. Again, parties will want to consider whether this tie-breaking procedure is adequate.

Fourth, three arbitrators, whether all neutral or with two party-appointed ones, could serve as a settlement team. This arrangement poses a significant risk of the impartiality of the arbitrators being compromised as settlement efforts are tried. Under these circumstances, the arbitrators should limit themselves to serving as quasi-mediators who employ relatively safe initiatives such as encouraging the participants to try settling the case on their own, requesting parties with settlement authority to be present, helping participants define legal and factual issues in dispute, or suggesting at a propitious moment that the parties "split the difference." If the issues in the settlement process are limited to forward-looking ones, the settlement team might try a broader range of settlement initiatives.

A fifth pathway may be possible in the rare case when a single international arbitrator is selected. This pathway should be a narrow one. A sole arbitrator should be limited to the role of a quasi-mediator who employs only a few selected and safe initiatives. This restriction is necessary because of the inherent difficulty in preserving the appearance of impartiality of a single arbitrator who tries to settle a case.

(9) Arbitrator Will Not Be Influenced by Information Revealed in Settlement Process

The neutral must erect a mental wall to guard against information learned in the settlement process from contaminating her understanding of the record in the arbitration proceeding. The neutral as arbitrator should not be influenced by off-the-record information and insights gleaned from settlement efforts.[43] This

43 For example, neutrals need to guard against any personal reactions to contacts with witnesses or a decision of a party not to settle.

fundamental tenet can be too easily violated when a neutral is in the throes of an actual case. The neutral as arbitrator must tenaciously strive to make any decisions based on the arbitration record in order to preserve the integrity of the arbitration process.[44]

(10) Parties Agree Not to Challenge Arbitrator or Award Based on Combined Roles

When an arbitrator has tried to settle a case, his impartiality as an arbitrator and the fairness of the arbitration process can be easily challenged by a dissatisfied party. A party who is willing to consent to the combined roles should waive any later objections related solely to the arbitrator trying to settle the case.[45] Any challenges should be restricted to cases in which a party can make a clear showing that the arbitrator prejudged the case or improperly considered information learned in the settlement process.

(11) Settlement Initiatives Will Not Unduly Delay the Arbitration Proceeding

Parties who are anxious to conclude a dispute frequently resist settlement efforts out of concern that the efforts might delay the arbitration proceeding. They are concerned that settlement efforts might extend the arbitration proceeding due to time lost trying to settle or worse yet time lost due to repeating the arbitration selection process because disqualified arbitrators must be replaced. To guard against unduly prolonging the arbitration proceeding, parties could agree to continue the arbitration proceeding in parallel with settlement efforts, or parties could negotiate a short timetable for suspending the arbitration proceeding. To guard against disqualification of the settling arbitrators, parties and neutrals should strictly follow the other protocols.

---

44 A Hong Kong ordinance establishes an unusual procedure for reducing this risk by requiring the arbitrator to disclose confidential information learned while conciliating that "he considers is material to the arbitration proceedings." Hong Kong Arbitration Ordinance, Ch. 341, 2B (3) (1996).

45 *See* Bühring-Uhle, *supra* note 8, at 208–211; Linda C. Reif, "Conciliation as a Mechanism for the Resolution of International Economic and Business Disputes," 14 *Fordham Intl. L. J.* 578, 620–22 (1990/1991) (describes procedures in British Columbia and Hong Kong that restrict objections to a conciliator resuming the role of arbitrator); *see also*, JAMS/Endispute Comprehensive Arbitration Rules and Procedures, Rule 27(b) (January, 1997) (Parties must confirm in writing that they will not try to disqualify arbitrator(s) who assist in settlement efforts).

(12) Parties Consent to Combined Processes[46]

The parties serve as the ultimate safeguard of the arbitration process. No settlement initiatives by arbitrators should be tried unless the parties consent. This is a vital and indispensable requirement. In order to increase the likelihood of parties making an informed decision, parties should be given a copy of these protocols and a disclosure statement on the advantages and risks of the neutral serving two processes. Parties and neutral(s) may even develop their own set of protocols and then sign an agreement to abide by them.

V. ADOPTING THE PROTOCOLS

The protocols can be regrouped into two basic categories: The first group of three consists of typical practices followed in real mediations. The remaining nine protocols relate to issues that arise from combining two processes with one neutral.

The first group of three protocols should be easy for participants to adopt because the protocols incorporate sound and widely accepted practices that are followed in most mediations: Settlers should respect the principle of party self-determination (Protocol 3). Clients with settlement authority should participate in any settlement process (Protocol 4).[47] And, participants should agree to maintain the confidentiality of documents and statements generated in the settlement process (Protocol 5).

The remaining protocols deal with distinctive issues that arise when arbitrators try to settle cases. Six of these protocols should be *relatively* noncontroversial and *relatively* straightforward to discuss and adopt. The neutral should be trained in both processes (Protocol 1). The neutral should consent to serving both roles (Protocol 2). The arbitrator should not be influenced by information revealed in the settlement process (Protocol 9). Parties should agree not to challenge the arbitrator or the award based on the arbitrator trying to settle the case (Protocol 10). Parties should guard against unduly delaying the arbitration proceeding (Protocol 11). And, parties should consent to participate in the combined processes (Protocol 12).

---

46 *See, e.g.*, Code of Ethics for Arbitrations in Commercial Disputes, Canon IV. H. (1977) (Code states that arbitrators can suggest that parties try to settle a case but arbitrators should not participate in settlement discussions unless requested by all the parties.). *See supra* note 24 (selection of international rules on requiring parties consent).

47 As noted in the earlier discussion of this protocol, this protocol may need to be modified to accommodate different cultural practices.

Three of these protocols will require considerable attention and negotiations. Two of them are bound to be particularly controversial: the prohibitions on evaluations (Protocol 6) and caucusing (Protocol 7). These prohibitions will be controversial because many participants want the insights gained from credible evaluations and desire the settlement opportunities created in private caucuses. But these benefits must be weighed against the risks that arise when the settler also decides the case. It is safer to prohibit the use of these techniques by arbitrators. If participants still prefer that the techniques be used, the participants should consent only after they have been made fully aware of the risks.

Finally, the protocol for reconfiguring the arbitration panel needs to be thought through. It serves as the centerpiece of the settlement process (Protocol 8). Each possible configuration should be carefully assessed by the participants who should consider which configuration is most likely to preserve the impartiality of the arbitration tribunal while opening the door to the type of settlement initiatives that they want used.

These protocols can be customized to suit the particular preferences of the participants. For instance, they may want to modify the protocols to accommodate different and even competing cultural practices. The protocols include several choices for participants. Participants need to select an optimal configuration for the arbitration panel (Protocol 8). They need to resolve whether to permit caucuses (Protocol 7). They also may decide to modify the protocols by permitting evaluations (Protocol 6) or settlement efforts in the absence of clients (Protocol 4). At a minimum, a discussion of the protocols should generate a focused and illuminating exchange in which the participants can design protocols that are suitable to their circumstances.

VI. CONCLUSION

A colleague recently commented that he had served on an international arbitration panel that violated almost every one of these protocols and the panel still successfully settled the case! This possibility does not surprise me. Arbitrators can surely breach these protocols and still successfully settle cases. But my colleague also speculated what would have happened if the case had not settled; he suspected that parties would have objected to the panel resuming the arbitration.

These protocols provide a roadmap for navigating around the risks posed by arbitrators trying to settle cases. Settlement efforts inherently pose the risk that either the arbitrators will be disqualified or will act so cautiously as to undermine the effectiveness of settlement efforts. The protocols cannot guarantee the safety of the trip. But, they should provide arbitrators and parties a safer route for settling cases. These protocols should not be adopted wholesale as rigid rules. Instead, they should be the starting point for negotiating the details of protocols that will safeguard the arbitration process and create a narrow settlement opening.

CHAPTER 9

Mining Mediation Rules for Representation Opportunities and Obstacles*

2005

Harold I. Abramson**

Buried in mediation rules can be found a few surprises, some desirable and some not. The rules, usually few in number and quite compact, can contain unexpected opportunities and pitfalls when developing a mediation representation plan.[1] This article considers several distinctive issues[2] that can arise when applying mediation rules to international mediations.

---

* A version of this article was published in 1 *J. Intl. Disp. Resol.* 40 (Germany, 2004). This article is based on a study of seventeen sets of mediation rules that were issued by the United Nations and dispute resolution organizations in Europe, the United States, Egypt, Hong Kong, and China. Next year, an expanded version of this article will be published that will analyze over fifty mediation rules from every region of the globe.

** The author, a professor at Touro Law Center in Huntington, New York, publishes, teaches and trains in the areas of domestic and international mediation, methods for resolving disputes, and representing clients in mediations. In addition to teaching courses on dispute resolution, he teaches domestic and international sales, international business and trade, and remedies. His email address is hala@tourolaw.edu.

1 For a full examination of how to represent clients in mediations, including how to prepare a mediation representation plan, *see* Harold Abramson, *Mediation Representation: Advocating in a Problem-Solving Process* (2004).

2 For a fuller discussion of a number of distinctive issues that can arise in international mediations, *see* Harold Abramson, *International Dispute Resolution, in* Alan Rau et al., *Processes of Dispute Resolution,* 929–938 (3rd ed. 2002) and Harold Abramson, "International Mediation Basics," in *Practitioner's Handbook on International Arbitration and Mediation,* Ch.II.1 (Rufus Rhoades et al., eds. 2002).

I. SELECTING A NEUTRAL MEDIATOR

How do you select a mediator in a cross-border dispute whom both sides view as neutral? Parties must be confident in the mediator's neutrality so that they will trust disclosing information and trust the mediator's initiatives. Even though professional mediators know to maintain scrupulously their neutrality, parties may still be skeptical of any mediator from the country of another party.

Mediation rules occasionally include a default mediator selection process designed for parties from different countries.

The *mediator from a third country* approach is used in the UNCITRAL Model Law. It suggests that the person recommending a mediator "shall take into account the advisability of appointing a conciliator of a nationality other than the nationalities of the parties."[3]

The *one from each country* approach is taken in a Chinese rule where each party appoints a mediator and the two mediators jointly conciliate the case.[4] If you elect the co-mediation solution, rules can provide different approaches to selecting the mediators. The Chinese and a German rule adopt the international arbitration model of party-appointed third parties; each party appoints a conciliator.[5] But the UNCITRAL Model Law, while preferring this approach in earlier drafts and characterizing it as the "prevailing view,"[6] in its Draft Guide, ultimately rejected this approach in favor of requiring parties to "endeavour to reach agreement on ... conciliators" unless they agreed on a different procedure.[7]

A third approach, implicit in rules that are silent on selecting international mediators, is to select a *qualified mediator in the location of the mediation*. Realizing that the mediator has no decision-making power, a party may not be too concerned about the country of the mediator as long as the mediator has excellent credentials and experience.

---

3 United Nations Commission on International Trade Law (UNCITRAL) Model Law on International Commercial Conciliation, Art. 5(4) (2002) [hereinafter the Model Law], *available at* http://www.uncitral.org/english/texts/arbitration/ml-conc-e.pdf.

4 China Council for the Promotion of International Trade (CCPIT) and China Chamber of International Commerce (CCOIC), Conciliation Rules, Arts. 9(3), 12 (2000), *available at* www.cmac.org.cn/BCC/a19.html (last visited on January 28, 2005).

5 German Institution of Arbitration, DIS Mediation/Conciliation Rules, Sec. 7(2), (January 1, 2002), *available at* www.dis-arb.de (last visited on January 28, 2005).

6 United Nations Commission on International Trade Law (UNCITRAL), Draft Guide to Enactment and Use of the UNICTRAL Model Law on International Commercial Conciliation, 35th Sess. at para. 46, U.N. Doc. A/CN .9/514 (May 27, 2002), [hereinafter the Draft Guide].

7 The Model Law, *supra* note 3, Art. 5(2).

Ultimately, you will have to come to terms with what selection process will give you confidence in the mediator. Fortunately, these concerns are not as weighty in mediations as in arbitrations. In mediations, you have the safeguard of simply walking away from the mediation if you lose trust in the mediator, while in arbitrations, you must demonstrate prejudice as a basis for disqualifying the neutral.

II. CHOOSING ROLES FOR THE MEDIATOR

There is no more important decision in mediation representation than choosing the roles of your mediator. You want to be sure that you select a mediator who will employ the mix of approaches and techniques that you think are warranted. Hidden in the flexible language of mediation rules can be found particular and sometimes unexpected mediator roles that can impact the way you represent your client.

In international mediations, you should carefully clarify the roles of the mediator because unusual variations of mediation can occasionally be encountered. In one atypical arrangement, the mediator might investigate the facts and law and issue a written report containing her recommendations.[8] In another uncommon arrangement, each party may designate a mediator and then the mediators meet with each other to hammer out a resolution that is presented to the parties for their confirmation.[9] You should guard against surprises by specifically discussing the roles of the mediator that each side contemplates. This inquiry is essential in order to avoid cross-cultural misunderstandings.

This vital discussion of mediator roles is not left to chance by the Oslo Chamber of Commerce Rules: "The Mediator, in cooperation with the parties, shall see to it that an Agreement is made"[10] that covers this subject. This prophylactic measure is a particularly appealing one because it can ensure that the parties face essential design questions and formulate a suitable process before

---

8 *See* Linda C. Reif, "Conciliation as a Mechanism for the Resolution of International Economic and Business Disputes," 14 *Fordham Intl. L. J.* 578, 585–87 (1991/92) and Tobi Dress, "International Commercial Mediation and Conciliation," 10 *Loy. L. A. Intl. and Comp. L. J.* 569, 574 (1988).

9 *See* William Fox, Jr., *International Commercial Agreements,* 193 (1992) and Reif, *supra* note 8 at 632–33.

10 Oslo Chamber of Commerce, Rules of the Arbitration And Dispute Resolution Institute of the Oslo Chamber Of Commerce, Art. 34 (2003), *available at* www.Chamber.no/tekster.cfm?artid=53.

the first mediation session. The more typical approach, however, gives parties the option of negotiating the roles. And, if they do nothing, the default process in the rules would control. The default rules usually give the mediator broad authority to do what is "appropriate" along with some other particular powers such as caucusing (meeting privately with one side).

One mediator power that can potentially overshadow the entire mediation process is the power to recommend settlements. This mediator power, which can occasionally be found in rules, has the potential to singularly pigeonhole and shape your entire mediation representation strategy.[11] Realizing that the mediator may formulate settlement proposals, you may be induced to approach the mediation more like a judicial process than a negotiation. Instead of viewing the mediator as a facilitator, you may view the mediator as a decision maker. Instead of formulating a negotiation strategy based on meeting parties' interests, you may be impelled to formulate a strategy designed to persuade the mediator to recommend favorable settlement proposals.

The new UNCITRAL Model Law, for instance, gives the mediator the power to "make proposals for settlement," "at any stage of the conciliation proceedings."[12] This provision is especially surprising because the Model Law also makes clear that the mediator cannot act as an arbitrator without approval of the parties,[13] stating reasons, in the Draft Guide, that apply equally to barring mediators from making proposals.

The UNCITRAL's Draft Guide to Enactment recognized the dilemma for the advocate when a mediator might subsequently act as an arbitrator by pointing out that "[a] party may be reluctant to strive actively for a settlement ... if it has to take into account the possibility that if the conciliation is not successful, the conciliator might be appointed as an arbitrator ..."[14] The same underlying point applies when the conciliator might formulate proposals. Permit me to indulge in editing the Guide: "A party may be reluctant to *participate candidly* ~~strive actively for a settlement~~ ... if it has to take into account the possibility

---

11 For a more a more in-depth analysis of the impact that mediator evaluation can have on advocacy, *see* Harold Abramson, "Problem-Solving Advocacy in Mediations: A Model of Client Representation," 10 *Harv. Neg. L. R.* (2005) (forthcoming). (The article considers how to implement a "constricted problem-solving" approach to advocacy when the mediator may engage in evaluation.)

12 Model Law, *supra* note 3, Art. 6(4). Similar authority is given the mediator by the AAA International Mediation Rules. *See* American Arbitration Association, Commercial Arbitration Rules and Mediation Procedures, Rule M-10 (July 1, 2003), *available at* www.adr.org.

13 The Model Law, *supra* note 3, Art. 12.

14 Draft Guide, *supra* note 6 at para. 70.

that if the conciliation is not successful, the conciliator might *formulate a settlement proposal based on what was learned during the conciliation* ~~be appointed as an arbitrator~~ ..." (edits in italics)

The risk of the recommendation power overshadowing the mediation can be reduced by the type of carefully crafted approach adopted in the CEDR Mediation Rules. The Rules give the mediator *conditional* recommendation authority:

> If the Parties are unable to reach a settlement in the negotiations at the Mediation, and only if all the Parties so request and the Mediator agrees, the Mediator will produce for the Parties a non-binding recommendation on terms of settlement. This will not attempt to anticipate what a court might order but will set out what the Mediator suggests are appropriate settlement terms in all of the circumstances.[15] CEDR's *Guidance Notes* state that "[t]he intention of paragraph 12 is that the Mediator will cease to play an entirely facilitative role only if the negotiations in the Mediation are deadlocked. Giving a settlement recommendation may be perceived by a Party as undermining the Mediator's neutrality and for this reason the Mediator may not agree to this course of action."[16]

Another mediation rule that is quite common bars a mediator from switching to the role of arbitrator unless both parties specifically authorize the mediator to switch roles. The temptation to ask the mediator to switch roles to resolve conclusively the dispute can be considerable when the parties have reached an impasse after spending a day or more together mediating the dispute. This temptation can be especially powerful when fueled by the cultural practices of one side. For instance, consider the Conciliation Rules of the China Council for the Promotion of International Trade ("CCPIT") and the China Chamber of International Commerce ("CCOIC"). The specific wording of Rule 21 starkly reveals the attitude of the Rules: "If conciliation fails, the conciliator(s) may be appointed by one of the parties as arbitrator(s) in the subsequent arbitration

15 Centre for Effective Dispute Resolution (CEDR) Model Mediation Procedure and Agreement, para. 12 (2002), *available at* www.cedr.co.uk/library/documents/ MMPA.8thedition.pdf.

16 CEDR Guidance Notes for Model Mediation Procedure and Agreement, The Mediation 9–12 (October 2002). *Also see* CPR Mediation Procedure for Business Disputes in Europe, Rule 6 (1996) (limits the recommendation power to after the parties fail to reach a settlement and after parties consent to receive a mediator's final settlement proposal).

proceedings, *unless such appointment is opposed by the other party* (emphasis added)."[17] The Introduction to the China International Economic and Trade Arbitration Commission ("CIETAC") Website, in commenting favorably on combining arbitration and conciliation, points out,

> Many years of practice has [sic] indicated that the combination of arbitration with conciliation can make good use of the advantages of both arbitration and conciliation, so as to settle disputes more efficiently and turn hostility into friendship. It may also save parties expenses and help to maintain the friendly relations and cooperation between them. This practice in Chinese arbitration has received worldwide attention and approval.[18]

The convenient benefits and compromising risks posed by the same neutral serving two roles are widely known.[19] If you elect this scheme, you should consider adopting a number of protocols for minimizing its risks, protocols that are designed to preserve the integrity and effectiveness of each dispute resolution process.[20]

III. ENSURING CONFIDENTIALITY OF THE MEDIATION PROCESS

Confidentiality, one of the great benefits of mediation, can be less secure internationally than you might be accustomed to at home due to the less developed and untested laws in some countries. Even though virtually every set of mediation rules provides confidentiality, the scope of protection can vary from set to set, although you should be aware of an incipient effort to promote uniformity in mediation rules.[21] You ought to assess carefully whether the rules that you

17 *See* CCPIT and CCOIC RULES, *supra* note 4.

18 Introduction, Section XV. Combination of Arbitration and Conciliation, *available at* www.cietac.org.

19 *See* Harold Abramson, "Protocols for International Arbitrators Who Dare to Settle Cases," 10 *Am. Rev. Intl. Arb.* 1, 3–4 (1999).

20 *See id.* at 7–15 (The twelve suggested protocols, designed for when an arbitrator mediates, need some modifications for when the mediator arbitrates).

21 The Model Law on International Commercial Conciliation, adopted by UNCITRAL and recommended by the United Nations General Assembly in 2002, is designed to promote uniformity in mediation law among nations. The Uniform Mediation Act, approved by the National Conference of Commissioners on Uniform State Laws in August 2001 and amended in August 2003 to coordinate with the UNCITRAL Model Law, is being considered for adoption by a number of states in the United States.

are considering provide sufficient protection and will be enforced in relevant jurisdictions.

IV. ENFORCING SETTLEMENT AGREEMENTS

In cross-border disputes, you need to give extra attention to how any resulting settlement agreement will be enforced. In domestic disputes, you can rely on your local court system for enforcement. However, pursuing cross-border enforcement in the local court of a foreign country can take more time and expense and sometimes can be less reliable.

An intelligent and efficacious solution is offered by the Stockholm Chamber of Commerce Rules. Parties can agree to appoint the mediator as an arbitrator and "request him to confirm the settlement agreement in an arbitral award."[22] The resulting "consent" award can then be enforced in numerous other jurisdictions under the relatively reliable procedures of the New York Convention on the Recognition and Enforcement of Foreign Arbitral Awards.[23]

V. CONCLUSION

I was surprised to discover surprises in these mundane and essential mediation rules. They can open up opportunities and present obstacles when one is representing clients in international mediations. Do not leave home without studying them.

22 Rules of the Mediation Institute of the Stockholm Chamber of Commerce, Art. 12 (April 1, 1999), *available at* www.sccinstitute.com.

23 1958 Convention on the Recognition and Enforcement of Foreign Arbitral Awards, 21 U.S.T. 2517, 330 U.N.T.S. 38, T.I.A.S. No. 6997 (1959).

CHAPTER 10

Selecting Mediators and Representing Clients in Cross-Cultural Disputes*

2006

Harold Abramson[1]

I. INTRODUCTION

Even an adept negotiator can be baffled by cultural differences.[2] When a negotiation reaches an impasse because of an unfamiliar cultural interest or a miscommunication between the parties due to different styles of communicating, negotiating, or decision-making, the negotiator might find it helpful to enlist assistance from a culturally-trained and culturally-appropriate mediator. This article considers how such a third party can help you, as a negotiator, bridge cultural differences. It considers when to seek aid from a mediator, what the credentials of the mediator ought to be, and the impact of the mediator's approach on the way you represent your client.

---

* This article is based on the author's chapter, "The Culturally Suitable Mediator" in *The Negotiator's Fieldbook*, Schneider and Honeyman, eds. (2006).

1 Harold Abramson, Professor of Law at Touro College School of Law, has taught dispute resolution courses at Cardozo since 2000 and has published extensively in the areas of mediation representation and international mediation. Professor Abramson's domestic and international practice includes mediating, facilitating, and arbitrating business, organizational, and public policy disputes. He has mediated intellectual property disputes as well as disputes involving employment, service, licensing, purchase, distribution, and international business contracts. His international mediations have involved parties from Belgium, China, Columbia, Egypt, Guinea, India, Israel, Hong Kong, Russia, South Korea, and Venezuela.

2 These differences can arise in disputes between parties from different countries as well as between parties within the same country when the parties come from different regions or from different religious, ethnic, or professional groups.

II. WHEN TO ENLIST A MEDIATOR?

In a cross-cultural negotiation, a party may need a process that can address cultural differences. Parties brought up in dissimilar cultures might require a process that helps them recognize and bridge their different upbringings. They may need a process with a mediator who can help them overcome such cultural gaps as when an Asian or South American party may be more interested in the relationship than the U.S. party who may be more interested in a detailed contract, or when the U.S. party wants extensive discovery while the civil law party sees no need for it. They also may benefit from a mediator who deeply involves the parties, the ones with the greatest knowledge of the dispute, when the negotiation seems to be failing because the cultural practice of one side replaces the principal with her lawyer. By turning to mediation, parties can create a forum in which barriers that parties may not be able to overcome on their own can be addressed.

I recently observed how attorneys can perceptively engage in cross-cultural analysis when they enlisted assistance from me as a mediator in a pre-mediation conference. The attorneys informed me that they thought negotiations had failed so far not because they were not on the same page, but because one of the parties from a small Western African country could not negotiate with someone whom he thought had acted so unethically. The party said that where he is from, you do not deal with someone like the other party. He would rather take a chance in court and lose, a significant risk according to his own attorney, than settle with someone who acted so unethically. The attorneys indicated that they needed a mediator that could help the parties overcome this impasse.

III. WHAT CREDENTIALS SHOULD THE MEDIATOR POSSESS?

When dealing with cross-cultural disputes, you need a mediator whose training and experience goes beyond the familiar basic credentials. The standard checklist should be expanded to include two additional questions that are culturally-related: is the mediator trained to deal with cultural differences? And a second less obvious question, does the mediator approach mediation in a way that fits the cultural needs of the parties? The next sections consider these two questions.

A. Is the Mediator Trained to Deal with Cultural Differences?

A mediator should be trained and experienced in helping parties recognize culturally-shaped interests and overcome culturally-based impasses.

i. Culturally-Shaped Interests

The primary purpose in a negotiation, like in any dispute resolution process, is to advance and meet your client's interests, whatever they might be. Some commentators have critiqued such an interests inquiry as a narrow cultural one, shaped by western cultural individualism. This simplistic view fails to take into account other culturally-driven goals such as interdependence and relatedness.[3] A broader view of parties' interests, however, can better capture the full range of a client's cultural needs, framing each party's cultural upbringing the content of his or her interests.

Spotting cultural interests can be difficult to do because they can be buried when positions are presented. A dispute that appears to be primarily about money, for instance, might be mostly about protecting a principle, saving face, preserving relationships, or promoting particular community norms and collectivist interests. Although these interests are not unfamiliar in the U.S. culture, these interests can be deeply compelling ones for parties from some non-U.S. cultures.[4]

In collectivist societies, such as in China and Japan, parties can have an interest in preserving face, an ingrained personal value that involves being treated with respect and dignity, maintaining positive relationships, and preserving an honorable reputation and social standing in the community. "Face-saving" according to Fisher and Ury, however, "carries a derogatory flavor [in the English language]. People say, 'We are doing that just to let them save face,' implying that a little pretense has been created to allow someone to go along without feeling badly. The tone implies ridicule. ... This is a grave misunderstanding of the role and importance of face-saving. Face-saving reflects a person's need to reconcile the stand he takes in a negotiation or an agreement with his principles and with his past words and deeds."[5]

Parties also can have an interest in a solution appropriate for the community. In a study of mediation in an Islamic country, the author found:

> The settlement must be an appropriate outcome for the community as a whole as well as for the actual disputants. The group's interests guide the process. This is consistent with collectivist culture generally where

---

3 *Compare* Amr Abdalla, "Principles of Islamic Interpersonal Conflict Intervention: A Search within Islam and Western Literature," 15 *Journal of Law and Relations* 151, 161–62, 165, 176 (2000–2001); Roger Fisher et al., *Getting to Yes*, 41, 48 (2nd ed., 1991).

4 *See* Jeanne M. Brett, *Negotiating Globally: How to Negotiate Deals, Resolve Disputes, and Make Decisions across Cultural Boundaries*, 8–9 (2001). *See also* Fisher et al., *supra* note 4.

5 *See* Fisher et al., *supra* note 4.

> communal and societal interests will preside over individual party interests. It enables this form of mediation to serve an educative role by articulating the social norms and providing acceptable behaviours and solutions for the disputants and for the community as a whole. In this way it differs from western mediations where confidentiality and privacy constraints, for the benefit of the individuals involved, limit a wider instructive role.[6]

Finally, consider this international mediation where a culturally shaped interest was not being met.[7] In a dispute between two businessmen from Latin America and a U.S.-based multinational company, the lawyer from the U.S. company could not fathom why the Latin American businessmen wanted an apology from the U.S company for its apparent negligence in losing a valuable commodity. It was not until the U.S. lawyers realized that the two businessmen had spent on legal fees and travel almost as much money as they were seeking in court that the U.S. lawyer understood that an interest other than money needed to be met.

When these sorts of culturally shaped interests might arise in a dispute, you may want to select a culturally-trained mediator who can assist parties in recognizing these less familiar and yet essential needs.

ii. Culturally-Shaped Impasses

Disputing parties can encounter impediments due to their different cultural upbringings that can foster conflicting wants and approaches to the negotiation. Any study of culture reveals numerous examples of behavior common in one culture that could be misinterpreted by someone brought up in another culture. These misunderstandings of behavior may result in or produce an impasse. When these cultural differences result in an impasse in a negotiation, you might turn to a culturally-trained mediator to help generate movement.

An appropriately trained mediator can help you recognize and overcome culturally-based impasses. The mediator can help you classify an impasse as well as develop a suitable intervention. The mediator might use the following five steps.[8]

---

6 *See* Black, "Alternative Dispute Resolution in Brunei Darussalam: The Blending of Imported and Traditional Processes," 13 *Bond LR* at p. 26 (Dec. 2001) or http://www.bond.edu.au/law/blr/vol13-2/black.doc.

7 This dispute was mediated by the author.

8 Harold Abramson, "International Dispute Resolution: Cross-Cultural Dimensions and Structuring Appropriate Processes," in Alan Rau et al., *Processes of Dispute Resolution,* 918–21 (3rd ed., 2002).

During the first three steps, the mediator prepares for the cross-cultural negotiation by mastering a cultural conceptual framework, learning about her own cultural upbringing, and investigating the culture of the other negotiators. The next two steps provide a guide for the mediator as the mediation progresses. The mediator approaches the negotiating behavior of others with an open mind and then helps parties bridge any differences.

These five steps can be illustrated through the use of a hypothetical. Consider how a U.S. attorney might react when he learns that the other party, an institutional client from Japan, will not be represented by someone with substantial settlement authority. Instead, the other side will be represented by a team of negotiators who will make decisions by consensus. Furthermore, all the team members cannot be present in the negotiation session. Under these circumstances, the U.S. attorney is likely to suspect that the other side is acting in bad faith. The other side appears to be replacing the person with real settlement authority with an unwieldy team of negotiators. How might the mediator proceed?

First, the mediator comes to the mediation with a *conceptual framework* that can help her identify and understand cultural characteristics. The mediator must be able to grasp the meaning of "cultural behavior" and how it is different from universal "human behavior." Cultural characteristics have been isolated in numerous studies of culture, including studies relevant to conflict resolution.[9]

The hypothetical implicates a cultural characteristic related to the process of decision-making for each side. This generic characteristic, like virtually all cultural characteristics, encompasses a continuum bound at each end with a value-based pole. At one extreme, societies can be found that are hierarchical, with decisions made by leaders. At the other extreme, societies can be found that are collective, with decisions made by consensus. The actual cultural practice is rarely one extreme or the other; it usually falls somewhere between these two end poles of the continuum. Second, the mediator fills in this conceptual framework with a deep understanding of her *own culture or cultures.*[10] A skilled mediator must be cognizant of the degree to which her

---

9 *See,* e.g., Geert Hofstede, *Culture's Consequences* (abridged 1980, 1984); Geert Hofstede, *Cultures and Organizations: Software of the Mind* (1997); Dean Allen Foster, *Bargaining across Borders: How to Negotiate Business Successfully Anywhere in the World,* 264–72 (1992, 1995) (showing how Hofstede's work relates to international negotiations).

10 For studies of American culture, *see,* e.g., Gary Althen, *American Ways,* xiii, 4, 8, 9–10, 14, 17, 24–25, 136–37 (1998); Edward C. Stewart and Milton J. Bennett, *American Cultural Patterns: A Cross-Cultural Perspective* (1991).

own behavior is universal or culturally determined, because it is through this personal lens that the mediator observes and assesses the negotiating behavior of others. To reduce distortions, the mediator must learn about her own cultural upbringing in order to appreciate the extent to which her view of other people's behavior may not necessarily reflect a universal view. In the hypothetical, a U.S. mediator should be aware that her possible view that organizations tend to be hierarchical, where decision-making is centralized in "leaders," is not universal organizational behavior. Third, the mediator strengthens her conceptual framework with an understanding of the *culture or cultures of the negotiator(s)*. The mediator should try to identify and research the culture(s) of the clients as well as the attorneys that will be participating in the mediation. In doing so, the mediator should not assume that just because a person was brought up in a clearly identifiable culture, the person will act in accordance with its cultural norms. Furthermore, the mediator should learn as much as possible about the negotiators as individuals, that is, learn about their personalities and ways their negotiating behavior may vary from practices of their culture(s). In the hypothetical, the research might reveal that one side is from a society in which organizations typically make decisions based on consensus, but the research may reveal little about their individual personalities.[11]

These first three preparatory steps are relatively easy to complete because they entail collecting mostly accessible information on cultural characteristics. The next two steps, however, are much more difficult to accomplish because they require the mediator to suspend judgment and develop strategies during an intense, dynamic and fast moving mediation session.

Fourth, the mediator withholds judgments about the parties' negotiating behavior by viewing key behavior with an *open mind*. This mental process requires considerable discipline. It is too easy for a person who routinely judges negotiating behavior to prematurely judge it in a cross-cultural negotiation. In the hypothetical, the mediator should not view one side's collective decision-making process as evidence of good or bad faith; instead she should view this key negotiating behavior as a difference that needs to be addressed.

---

11 *See* Loretta Kelly's description of an Aboriginal Australian representative whose behavior was sharply at variance with those he supposedly represented. Loretta Kelly, *Indigenous Experiences in Negotiation*, Ch. 35, in *The Negotiator's Fieldbook*, ed. Schneider and Honeyman (2006).

Fifth and finally, the mediator searches for ways to *bridge* any resulting gap by helping the parties identify the nature of the impasse and by facilitating an intervention. The mediator might facilitate an interest-based negotiation, a compromise, or a decision to defer to one side's practice. In the process of doing so, the parties are likely to learn whether the gap reflects a cultural difference that can be bridged or a strategic ploy (which also could be cultural) that may impede or derail the negotiation.

In the hypothetical, the parties appear to have different views of who must be present in the mediation session. The U.S. party expects the other side to bring a single person with settlement authority, and the other side expects multiple people to sign off and they all cannot be present.

The mediator could facilitate a negotiated solution by resorting to an interest-based approach, where the interests behind the different practices are explicated and respected. In the hypothetical, instead of viewing the Japanese party's claim that it cannot agree to anything without a consensus as bad faith, the mediator might focus on how to respect the Japanese party's need for consensus while still meeting the U.S. party's need for the presence of clients with substantial settlement authority. The parties, for example, could negotiate an arrangement in which the Japanese party brings to the negotiation session all the people who must concur, or at least makes sure the absent people are available by telephone. Then, in the session, the Japanese consensus approach could be respected by giving members of its negotiating team ample time to meet privately.

This calibrated approach can smoke out whether the gap is based on a bridgeable cultural difference or a strategic ploy. It might reveal, for instance, an ingrained strategic practice such as haggling that includes a last minute demand by a senior person that is purposely not at the table.

Sometimes, a gap might be bridged by one side simply deferring to the other side's practice, especially when the other practice is not a deal-breaker or does not implicate core personal values. For instance, a U.S. attorney may defer to the other side's formal practices of carefully using titles and avoiding personal questions about family.

In another example, consider how a mediator might handle an impasse that can arise when a U.S. lawyer insists that signed business agreements cover many details and contingencies and the Japanese lawyer displays little interest in reducing details to writing. The U.S. lawyer will likely interpret this disinterest as reluctance about the deal or a specific issue. In preparing for a cross-cultural mediation, a U.S. mediator will realize that his own preference for reducing everything to writing may be due to his own cultural up-bringing and may not be a universal mode of behavior (step 2). The drafting of comprehensive contracts is taught in U.S. law schools and reinforced in law practice. A Japanese lawyer may have been brought up differently (step 3). Instead of being concerned about the details of a written agreement, the Japanese lawyer may be more concerned about the business relationship, leaving for the written contract a general statement about the relationship and basic principles for governing the business deal.

In the negotiations, the mediator would view the reluctance of the Japanese lawyer to put everything in writing as ambiguous behavior to be viewed with an open mind (step 4). These different approaches might be investigated by the mediator asking why the U.S. attorney prefers detailed contracts and why the Japanese attorney may not. As each side learns more about the other side's practice, the mediator can focus on ways to bridge this gap. The two sides may close the gap by respecting the reasons for the different practices. They may negotiate a compromise in which both sides seek to cultivate a relationship of trust and then enter into a contract that may cover key obligations but not every conceivable contingency (step 5).

B. Does the Mediator's Approach Fit the Cultural Needs of the Parties?[12]

Asking whether a mediator's approach fits the cultural needs of the parties can be an unfamiliar but necessary inquiry in order to formulate an effective cross-cultural process. You may want to inquire what sort of third party assistance the parties and the other attorney are accustomed to as this can influence the sort of mediator that they will respond to. This familiar problem-solving approach may run counter to their experiences, and a result, not be readily acceptable. You may need to select a mediator whose approach comports with the other participants' cultural upbringings in order to create an efficacious process.

This mediator selection method, in which cultural preferences drive the choices, is different from the method I have suggested for selecting U.S. mediators in a non-cross-cultural context.[13] In that context, parties should select a

12 Substantial portions of this section are excerpted and edited from Nolan-Haley, Abramson, and Chew, *International Conflict Resolution: Consensual ADR Processes*, 123–37 (2005).

13 *See* Harold Abramson, *Mediation Representation: Advocating in a Problem-Solving Process*, 133–45 (2004).

mediator that will use an approach that will meet the parties' needs for resolving the dispute. It is a choice driven by an analysis of the advantages and drawbacks of various mediator approaches in view of the parties' needs, including possible cultural considerations.

The culturally-driven selection method suggested here, however, may be only a intermediary method during this transitional period toward globalization of mediation practices. I recently saw evidence of the changes taking place when participating in a U.S.-Chinese Retreat of dispute resolvers hosted by the CPR Institute.[14] One of the Chinese participants noted that when Chinese companies negotiate with each other and use a mediator, they prefer a more directive approach to mediation (the common Chinese practice), however, when Chinese companies use a mediator with non-Chinese businesses, (i.e. international disputes), they use a facilitative approach (a new mediation approach in China). As the practices across the globe expand to encompass a broader range of mediator approaches, the emphasis in the mediator selection discussion is likely to shift away from cultural analysis and toward analysis of the various approaches.

Before suggesting a culturally nuanced way to classify mediator approaches, the term "mediation" needs some clarification and definition. There has been much debate over what processes can be legitimately called mediation. It seems to me that it is just too late to convincingly defend a favored, circumscribed mediation definition. I prefer a broad, generic definition that has the flexibility of accommodating the diversity of approaches to third party assistance found around the globe: Mediation is simply a negotiation conducted with the assistance of a third party. Instead of focusing on the noun of mediation, I prefer focusing on the adjective in front of the noun. Is the mediation facilitative, evaluative, directive, transformative, some mix, or something else? Various adjectives are highlighted in the classification system in this article.

i. U.S. Problem-Solving and Self-Determination Approach

U.S. practices reflect a culturally shaped view of mediation, a view that is vividly conveyed in the highly regarded original Model Standards of Conduct for

14 The CPR Institute (International Institute for Conflict Prevention and Resolution) conducted this invitation-only one-and-half day retreat at the Mohonk Mountain House in October, 2005.

Mediators.[15] Its definition of mediation, found in the Preface, reveals much about the problem solving role envisioned in the United States.

> Mediation is a process in which an impartial third party—a mediator—facilitates the resolution of a dispute by promoting voluntary agreement (or "*self determination*") by the parties to the dispute. A Mediator *facilitates communications, promotes understanding, focuses the parties on their interests,* and *seeks creative problem solving* to *enable the parties to reach their own agreement.* These standards give meaning to this definition of mediation. [Italics added].[16]

This definition, however, has been modified in the recent changes to the Model Standards to reflect a momentous broadening of the term mediation to encompass different "styles." The revised definition provides that: "Mediation is a process in which an impartial third party facilitates communication and negotiation and promotes voluntary decision making by the parties to the dispute."[17] According to the Reporter's Notes[18] "It [the new definition of mediation] is not designed to exclude any mediation style or approach *consistent with* Standard I's commitment to support and respect the parties' decision-making roles in the process." [Italics added].[19] Therefore, this ostensibly broader definition has a firm limit. It only welcomes those styles of mediation that comport with the Westernized fundamental principle of party self-determination.

This fundamental policy of party self-determination reflects a distinctively U.S. cultural value that is not given the same sacred regard in more directive practices found in some other areas of the globe, as described below under evaluatively directive and wisely directive mediations.

Although the Model Standards' particular vision of the mediator's role reflect the dominate approach to training mediators in the United States and a widely practiced approach, it is not the exclusive one used. No culture can claim

---

15 The Model Standards were prepared and approved by three leading organizations in the United States dispute resolution field: American Arbitration Association, the Litigation and Dispute Resolution Sections of the American Bar Association, and the Society of Professionals in Dispute Resolution (1992–1994). For a discussion of the Model Standards by the chair of the drafting committee, *see* Feerick, "Toward Uniform Standards of Conduct for Mediators," 38 *S. Tex. L. R.* 455 (1997). A comprehensive review and revision of the Model Standards was adopted by the three sponsoring organizations in 2005. See http://moritzlaw.osu.edu/programs/adr/ (last visited Aug. 2006).

16 *Id.*

17 *Id,* at Preamble (Sept. 2005).

18 *Id* at 7, in Reporter's Notes (Apt. 10, 2005).

19 *Id.*

a single, monolithic mediation approach, and the United States is no exception. Two other widely used approaches are transformative and evaluative mediation.

ii. Transformative Mediation

A transformative mediator engages in a mediation practice based on communication and relational theory. Instead of promoting the goal of settlement for the parties, the transformative mediator allows the parties to determine their own direction and supports the parties' own opportunities for perspective-taking, deliberation, and decision-making. The mediator focuses on the parties' interactions and supports their shifts from destructive and alienating interactions to more constructive and open interactions (referred to as empowerment and recognition shifts). In this model, parties are likely to be able to make positive changes in their interactions with each other and, consequently, find acceptable resolution for themselves, where such terms genuinely exist.[20]

iii. Evaluative Mediation

Mediation becomes evaluative when the mediator gives recommendations such as offering his or her views of the strengths and weaknesses of the legal case, assessing the reasonableness of particular settlement options, or proposing what might be a reasonable settlement. Mediator power to give recommendations can be found domestically in the recently adopted AAA International Dispute Resolution Procedures,[21] in foreign domestic laws such as the Indian Arbitration and Conciliation Act of 1996,[22] and in the United Nation's new Model Law on International Commercial Conciliation of the United Nations Commission on International Trade Law.[23]

---

20 *See* Abramson, *supra* note 9, at 71–72; *also see* Robert A. Baruch Bush and Joseph P. Folger, *The Promise of Mediation: Responding to Conflict through Empowerment and Recognition* (1994). For an extensive resource list, *see* Institute for the Study of Conflict Transformation, Inc. *at* http:// www.transformativemediation.org (last visited Mar. 14, 2006).

21 *See* Rule M-10 Authority of the Mediator, American Arbitration Association, International Dispute Resolution Procedures (Including Mediation and Arbitration Rules), Amended and Effective July 1, 2003.

22 The Indian Arbitration and Conciliation Act of 1996, Article 67(4), adopted verbatim the Article 7(4) of the UNCITRAL 1980 Conciliation Rules.

23 United Nations General Assembly, Resolution 57/18 Model Law on International Commercial Conciliation of the United Nations Commission on International Trade Law, Article 6(4), (Jan. 24, 2003). The UNCITRAL Model Law incorporated the power to make proposals for settlement found in the UNCITRAL Conciliation Rules, Article 7 (4) (Report of the UNCITRAL on the Work of it's Thirteenth Session, GAOR, Thirty-fifth Session, Supplement, No. 17, UN Document No. A/35/17 (1980)).

The adjective *evaluative* only refers to the power to offer an evaluation, not the power to persuade or pressure the parties to accept the evaluation. However, the mere expression of an evaluation can influence parties, that is assert a mildly directive influence, without the mediator doing anything more than offering the evaluation. Thus, an evaluation is inherently directive and therefore risks diluting the principle of party self-determination. When the mediator goes the next step and assertively persuades and pressures, the mediation moves pass mere evaluation toward more directive forms of mediation.

iv. Evaluatively Directive Mediation

When the mediator evaluates and then pushes his or her evaluation, the mediator shifts toward an evaluatively directive form of mediation, an approach that poses a clear threat to party self-determination. This form of mediation is practiced in the U.S. when mediators implement their evaluative power by either gently encouraging or by assertively pressing parties to move toward or adopt their evaluations.

In Continental Europe, the mediator's expected, if not preferred, role can be influenced by his or her civil law upbringing. In a study that compares mediation practices in Australia, a common law jurisdiction, with Germany, a civil law jurisdiction, Nadja Alexander noted that in Germany: "Like the government legal centres offering conciliation services, most of the dispute resolution processes associated with these conciliation centres [chambers of commerce] do not follow an interest-based mediation model.

There are many mediators within the U.S. and around the globe that are known to be evaluatively directive, although the particular practices can vary across a continuum of less to more directive. The more directive a practice becomes, the greater the threat to party self-determination.

v. Wisely Directive and Authoritatively Directive Mediations

In some cultures, disputing parties are accustomed to relying on a "wise" third party as a source of the "right" answers who will assertively if not aggressively direct them toward a solution. A wisely directive mediator investigates the dispute, evaluates it, and formulates and promotes solutions based on the wisdom for which he or she was selected. That wisdom could be informed by local cultural norms, religious values, or the mediator's age, legal knowledge, or leadership or authoritative position. Parties expect to receive answers and are receptive to, if not desirous of, adopting them. There seems to be little regard to protecting party self-determination. Therefore, while the role of the wise third party may be to "mediate," the third party effectively functions as a quasi-adjudicator imposing a resolution on the parties. Wisely directive mediators can be found in some Islamic, Islamic/Arabic, and Chinese cultures, among other places.[24]

In Lebanese cultures, George Irani, noted that:

> ... as in Arab culture in general, the mediator is perceived as someone having all the answers and solutions. He therefore has a great deal of power and responsibility. As one participant put it: 'If [the third party] does not provide the answers, he or she is not really respected or considered to be legitimate.[25]

In Egypt, John Murray observed the assertive role of third parties in his study of three public disputes and his own experiences living and teaching in Cairo:

> ***[I]t is acceptable, indeed expected, that the third party will also apply pressure to help bring about agreement. This is why the resources and status of the third party are so valuable. Third-party pressure is welcomed even by those who feel its sting. ...[26]

In a study of traditional rural mediation in Brunei Darussalam, a country with a strong Islamic influence, Ann Black documented these mediator credentials and behavior:

---

24 *See* George Irani, "Islamic Medication Techniques for Middle East Conflicts," 3 *Middle Eastern Review of International Affairs* 4 (June 1999); John Murray, "The Cairo Stories: Some Reflections on Conflict Resolution in Egypt," 13 *Negotiation Journal* 39, 53–54 (1997); Ann Black, "Alternative Dispute Resolution in Brunei Darussalam: The Blending of Imported and Traditional Processes," 13 *Bond Law Review* 16, 26 (Dec. 2001), *available at* http://www.bond.edu.au/law/blr/vol13-2/black.doc; Salah Al-Hejailan, "Mediation as a Means for Amicable Settlement Disputes in Arab Countries," presented to WIPO Conference on Mediation, Geneva, Switzerland (Mar. 29, 1996), *available at* http://arbiter.wipo.int/events/conferences/1996/hejailan.html; Eric Glassman, "The Function of Mediation in China: Examining the Impact of Regulations Governing the People's Mediation Committees," 10 *UCLA Pacific Basin Law Journal* 460 (1992); Michael T. Colatrella, Jr., "Court-Performed Mediation in the People's Republic of China: A Proposed Model to Improve the United States District Courts' Mediation Programs," 15 *Ohio State Journal on Dispute Resolution* 391, 404–08 (2000); Robert Perkovich, "A Comparative Analysis of Community Mediation in the United States and the People's Republic of China," 10 *Temple International and Comparative Law Journal* 313 (1996).

25 *See* George Irani, "Islamic Mediation Techniques for Middle East Conflicts," 3 *Mid. E. Rev. of Intl. Aff.* 4 (June 1999).

26 *See* Murray, "The Cairo Stories: Some Reflections on Conflict Resolution in Egypt," *Neg. J.* 39, 53–54 (January 1997).

> Equally important is for the mediator to have good knowledge of the rules to apply and to employ these to determine what is the right or fair outcome, and then to direct and guide the parties towards a similar solution. An ability to persuade, even to coerce parties by moral imperatives, to a settlement, is an attribute.[27]

In the chart below, Ms. Black highlighted differences between traditional mediation in a collectivist society of the sort she studied in Borneo and the western form of mediation found in individualistic societies.[28]

She also observed how this traditional mediator's role, in which the wise third party promotes particular outcomes, can diminish when people leave the intimacy of their villages that are bound by social and kinship ties for more anonymous living in urban areas.

Table 1 Comparison of Features of Western and Traditional Mediation

Western/Independent Mediation [individualist culture]	**Traditional/Iban Mediation [collectivist culture]**
Goal of mediation is for parties to reach an agreement that ends the dispute to their mutual satisfaction. ***	Goal of mediation is to end the dispute between parties so that harmony can return to the longhouse community. ***
Mediators should not have social ties, or be related to, the disputants. Accreditation has objective basis—such as courses, professional qualifications, recognition by authoritative bodies. ***	Mediators are connected to the disputants through social relationships or kinship ties. Accreditation has subjective basis—trust and respect of that community. There is no training, other than community enculturation. ***
Mediations occur in private settings—an office/ room neutral for the parties. ***	Mediations typically occur in a public setting—*raui* of the longhouse. ***
Mediators should be impartial, objective and even-handed. Criticism of disputants' behaviour or character is unacceptable. Parties direct the outcome—mediator should not persuade or coerce.	Mediators should be fair, kind, loving and subjectively appraise options. Criticism is acceptable where this is relevant to the dispute. Moral persuasion and coercion can be justified in the interests of the longhouse community.

27 *See* Black, "Alternative Dispute Resolution in Brunei Darussalam: The Blending of Imported and Traditional Processes," 13 *Bond LR* at p. 26 (Dec. 2001) or http://www.bond.edu.au/law/blr/vol13-2/black.doc (last visited Aug. 2006).

28 *See id.* at 21.

Although most of the mediation case studies that illustrate the work of a wisely directive mediator have been in community disputes, the practice also has been described in the mediation of commercial disputes. When considering the role of the mediator in resolving private commercial disputes (such as intellectual property disputes) in the Arab world, the Chairman of the Higher Board of Euro-Arab Arbitration System and a lawyer in Saudi Arabia, Salah Al-Hejailan, gave this wisely directive characterization of the mediator's role:

The mediator is normally a person of a prestigious social standing who is known for his thorough knowledge, honesty and impartiality. Seniority and respect for elders are particularly resonant in the Arab World. Such a person enjoys the respect of the disputants who *invariably feel satisfied with any award he may deem appropriate* [italics added].[29]

Even though these historic wisely directive practices have been confirmed in my recent travels to Turkey and China to discuss mediation practices as well as in numerous meetings with visiting Chinese, Egyptian, Japanese, Indian attorneys, and other visiting foreign attorneys, these discussions also hinted at a transformation that may be taking place. When discussing the nature of wisely directive practices, the respect for these third parties seem to be diminishing although not necessarily the clout. Wisely directive mediation may be in the process of being supplanted with a form of mediation that I call "authoritatively directive." Although these two sorts of mediators function similarly-as quasi-adjudicators, their sources of clout are different. While the wise mediator's source of influence may be his or her recognized wisdom, the authoritative mediator's source may be his or her position of official authority, especially in countries with authoritative governments or collectivism as a pervasive cultural value.[30]

vi. Distinguishing Wisely Directive Mediation from Other Settlement Processes[31]

The dominant function of the wisely directive mediator is similar to the function of an *evaluative mediator* in which the third person assesses the merits of

29 *See* Salah Al-Hejailan, "Mediation as a Means for Amicable Settlement of Disputes in Arab Countries," presented to WIPO Conference on Mediation, Geneva, Switzerland (March 29, 1996) at http://arbiter.wipo.int/events/conferences/1996/hejailan.html (last visited Aug. 2006).

30 The authoritative mediator may be one appointed by the government to serve as a Judge to settle cases or as a mediator.

31 This section is based on Abramson's analysis in Nolan-Haley, Abramson, and Chew, *International Conflict Resolution: Consensual ADR Process*, 136–137 (2005).

the dispute or solutions, the *judge* in a *judicial settlement conference* in which the third person hints at what she might do in court or urges a particular settlement, and an *arbitrator* in *nonbinding arbitration* where the third person issues a decision on the merits. In all these processes, the third party offers evaluations.

It is important to note that parties' responses to the evaluations in the U.S. differ from the responses to the wisely directive evaluation in other countries. An evaluation from a U.S. mediator can provide valuable input, however, parties are relatively free to reject the recommendation and resist any pressure if the mediator is also directive, with little consequence to the parties. An evaluation as well as any pressure from a settlement judge can be riskier to repel especially if the parties want to avoid alienating the judge that might decide the case. Nevertheless, parties are not shy about resisting pressure when they must to protect their interests-a proud trait for those brought up in an individualistic society. In addition, a nonbinding decision from an arbitrator can influence parties without the parties being pressured by the third party, who will not be further involved in resolving the dispute.

In contrast, a wise third party's evaluation and pressure is received quite differently in other cultures. Based on history and experience in a collectivist society as suggested in the various case studies, disputing parties in other cultures expect the wisely directive mediator to steer them toward the right solution that they are then receptive to adopting. Why else would they go to a third party for help, they would wonder? In short, they expect the third party to dress like a mediator but act like a wise quasi-arbitrator.

Although wisely directive mediation may no longer be embraced intact by either mediators or parties in modern societies, its influence can still be felt in the mediation preferences of some cultures around the globe, including the possibility of it shaping an emerging authoritative form of directive mediation.

As should be apparent from these descriptions of wisely directive or authoritatively directive practices, they offer forms of mediation that seem to give the least regard to preserving party self-determination.

This section on various adjectives suggests a continuum of cultural influences and practices around the globe. Any generalizations are risky, especially because no country has a monolithic approach. Nevertheless, these generalizations, based on likely cultural propensities, can at least sensitize attorneys to the range of possible adjectives to look for. A tentative continuum might be constructed with Chinese and Islamic cultures being the most directive, Civil Law cultures less, followed by the U.S. and Australian cultures, with English practices being the most elicitive along with transformative mediation in the

U.S. It remains to be seen whether this continuum[32] will withstand the ongoing study of global mediation practices. This next section considers how a participant's preference point on the elicitive-directive continuum shapes the resulting mediation process.

vii. Preferences Grid: Mediation Processes Based on Coalescing Preferences

As Professor Leonard Riskin has emphasized, it takes two to create a mediation process. It is not formulated by the mediator alone or the parties/attorneys alone. Each participant can influence the shape of the resulting mediation process.[33] Rather than focusing on influence here, however, I will consider how the cultural preference of each participant, when coalesced in the mediation, produces a distinctive mediation process. Instead of mapping each participant's ability to influence the final resulting process, this grid maps each participant's preference.

The preferences grid consists of two axes. The horizontal one maps the mediator's dominant approach to the mediation. It incorporates Riskin's elicitive-directive continuum, a continuum that reflects a range of mediators' approaches found around the globe. Mediators can be highly elicitive, facilitative, predominately facilitative, facilitative-directive, and varying degrees of directiveness. Riskin carefully defines directiveness broadly to include evaluations and assertive mediator behavior.[34]

The vertical axis maps the cultural preference of the parties/attorneys for third party assistance in resolving disputes.[35] It focuses on their preferred

---

32 Although this analysis concentrates on one prominent feature of mediation, the elicitive-directive continuum along with the corollary party self-determination continuum, a more nuanced analysis of the adjectives would consider other culturally distinguishing features. Mediation processes can be further differentiated based on the degree of impartiality of the mediator and the degree of influence the mediator has over the parties, whether the mediator focuses primarily on process or on process and content, the importance of confidentiality, and whether mediator training is required, among other distinguishing features.

33 *See* Leonard Riskin, "Decision-making in Mediation: The New Old Grid and the New New Grid System," 79 *Notre Dame Law Review* 1, 37–46 (2003).

34 *See id.*

35 The vertical axis reflects the parties'/attorneys' composite preference for a mediator although the preference of each attorney and each client may differ, especially in a cross-cultural mediation. A separate preference axis could be mapped for each participant. The vertical axis in the grid reflects the result negotiated by the participants among themselves regarding the sort of mediator that they want to select. Presumably, it is a result that fits the cultural needs of the parties.

relationship with the mediator. The axis maps a continuum of party/attorney preferences that ranges from preferring elicitive to directive mediators. You would expect parties/attorneys brought up in an individualistic society to lean toward preferring a more elicitive approach and to be less deferential to a mediator's directiveness while a side brought up in a more collectivist society is more likely to prefer a more directive mediator.[36]

Parties/Attorneys' Preference
Prefer Elicitive Approach

Mediator's Approach
Elicitive

<table>
<tr><td rowspan="2">A
Problem-Solving</td><td>F
Dysfunctional</td></tr>
<tr><td>B
Evaluative</td></tr>
<tr><td></td><td>E
Evaluatively Directive</td></tr>
<tr><td>D
Dysfunctional</td><td>C
Wisely Directive</td></tr>
</table>

Prefer Directive Approach

This second axis firmly demonstrates how it takes two to tango—to create the mediation process. A mediator who is directive, even aggressively so, for instance, does not necessarily result in the parties/attorneys being deferential to the mediator's procedural moves or substantive direction. As the second axis clarifies, the parties/attorneys must be willing partners—that is, be receptive to a more directive approach for the resulting process actually to *be* directive.

The preferences grid illustrates the importance of the mediator and parties/attorneys sharing compatible preferences in order for the mediation process to function, and shows how these preferences shape the resulting process. Consider several combinations:

If the mediator is extremely elicitive and the parties/attorneys prefer an extremely elicitive approach, then the result can be a classically problem-solving mediation that preserves party self-determination. See point A.

If the mediator is modestly directive and the parties/attorneys prefer a modestly elicitive approach, the result can be a classically evaluative mediation where the mediator offers evaluations and the parties/attorneys give some weight to them. See point B.

---

36 *But see* Christopher Honeyman et al., "Skill is Not Enough: Seeking Connectedness and Authority in Mediation," 20 *Negotiation Journal* 489 (2004) (comparing U.S. practices with community mediations in China and Australia).

If the mediator is extremely directive and the parties/attorneys prefer an extremely directive approach, the result can be a wisely directive mediation. See point C.

If the mediator is extremely elicitive and the parties/attorneys prefer an extremely directive approach, the mediation process may become dysfunctional. The parties/attorneys are likely to become quite frustrated because they are not getting the mediation service that they prefer. See point D.

Within these prototypical results, many gradations may be encountered. For example, if the mediator is evaluative and considerably directive and the parties/attorneys prefer a considerably directive approach, the result is likely to be an evaluatively directive mediation process. See point E. If the mediator is evaluatively directive and the parties/attorneys prefer primarily an elicitive approach, the mediation process also may become dysfunctional because the parties/attorneys are likely to become frustrated with the process. See point F.

In the spirit of Riskin's caveats in his article about his "New New Grid System," this grid hopefully promotes understanding and discussion while avoiding being so complicated that it becomes confusing and unmanageable.[37] The tension between formulating a nuanced grid and one that is easily accessible is inherent in this undertaking. I also prefer to err in favor of simplicity in order to present succinctly the encounter between distinctively cultural approaches of mediators and the preferences of parties/attorneys. The resulting grid, however, should not be blindly followed as a confident predictor of the resulting mediation process. Its value is in offering a framework for discerning and selecting the type of mediator who might formulate the sort of mediation process that may be effective with your client and the other side.

IV. IMPACT OF MEDIATOR'S APPROACH ON CLIENT REPRESENTATION

After you select a mediator who is culturally trained and suitable, you need to figure out how to effectively represent your client before that sort of mediator. Knowing that the mediator is *culturally trained* does not radically impact your approach to representation; it only expands the possibilities of what can be achieved in the mediation. The mediator can assist you in clarifying any culturally-related interests of the parties and overcoming any culturally-related impasses. Selecting a *culturally suitable* mediator, however, can singularly shape

37 *See* Riskin, *supra* note 35, at 50–53.

your entire representation strategy. Your whole approach to enlisting assistance from the mediator can be shaped by your understanding of how the mediator will approach the process; in other words, your approach will be fashioned by the "adjective."[38]

If you select a problem solving mediator (one that will stay in that mode), you, as the attorney, can advocate as a problem solver.[39] You have the freedom and security to share information including interests, to brainstorm options, to recognize weaknesses in your client's legal case, and to be open to creative solutions that go beyond the ones in the legal papers. You can feel secure[40] asking the mediator for help—whether to sort out interests, facilitate evaluating the legal case, or develop multiple options. You also have much freedom and security with a transformative mediator, who is trained to support whatever sort of process is structured and implemented by you, your client, and the other side, although you cannot rely on the mediator's expertise or initiatives to create or direct a process, as the transformative mediator is committed to being non-directive.

In contrast, consider the impact of selecting an evaluative (non-directive) mediator on your approach to advocacy. Mediator evaluations can take a variety of forms, including the mediator assessing the reasonableness of various settlement options, assessing the consequences of not settling, or recommending settlement proposals either as the mediation unfolds or as a "mediator's proposal." Knowing that the mediator may formulate one or more of these types of evaluations can induce you to approach the mediation more like an adjudicatory process than a negotiation. Instead of formulating a negotiation strategy based on candid conversations with the mediator and meeting parties' interests, you are apt to return to the traditional adversarial approach, so familiar in the courtroom, in which you withhold unfavorable information, hide any flexibility to avoid implying a lack of confidence in the legal case, and present carefully crafted partisan arguments and positions that are designed to persuade a decision-maker to act favorably.

---

38 The following analysis of how the adjective can shape your representation strategy is taken from Harold Abramson, "Problem-Solving Advocacy in Mediations: A Model of Client Representation," 10 *Harvard Negotiation Law Review* 103, 124–28 (2005). *Also see* Nolan-Haley, Abramson and Chew, *International Conflict Resolution: Consensual ADR Processes*, Ch. 4 (2005).

39 For a full discussion on how to advocate as a problem solver, *see* Abramson, *supra* note 9.

40 *But see* the section on mediation's structural biases in Christopher Honeyman, "Understanding Mediators," Ch. 67 in *The Negotiator's Fieldbook*, ed. Scjmeoder and Honeyman, (2006).

Alternatively, you might problem solve, but in a selective way that reduces the risk of an unfavorable assessment by the mediator. In such a constricted problem solving approach, you still share and advocate your client's interests and engage in problem solving moves such as brainstorming options and designing creative solutions, but only up to a point. You will avoid sharing information or showing flexibility that may risk a less favorable evaluation from the mediator. This carefully calibrated strategic plan can dilute the potential of a problem solving process by limiting the ability of parties to uncover optimal solutions. Withholding information may bury valuable data and insights relevant to devising solutions. Hiding flexibility may cramp the opportunity to search for, and devise, creative solutions. But, in return, you can secure an evaluation that might spur parties toward settlement.

As a mediator's approach moves further toward the end of the directive continuum, your problem solving approach will become more constricted until it morphs into a traditional adversarial strategy. When the mediator's approach becomes highly directive, or wisely directive, you are likely to view the mediator as a decision-maker and will advocate accordingly.

Finally, this discussion implies that a mediator will stay within the selected approach throughout the mediation process. But Riskin reminded us that mediation is not a static process. Some, if not many, mediators purposely vary their roles as the mediation progresses by facilitating at one point, evaluating at the point that seems useful, being directive when necessary at another point, and returning to facilitating when it seems appropriate—a practice that they espouse as necessary for resolving disputes.[41] Unfortunately, Riskin omitted assessing the impact of this mediator practice on how attorneys represent their clients. When the mediator freely switches roles, you are likely to abandon a nuanced representation approach and adopt the safest mode of client representation, an adversarial one, because it is likely to provide the best protection against an unfavorable evaluation.

V. CONCLUSION

This article suggests when you might want to bring in a mediator to help parties resolve a cross-cultural dispute. When you decide to do so, you

41 *See* Riskin, *supra* note 35, at 13–17, 17–21, 28–29 (noting further how each role can either foster or impair party self-determination).

should consider enlisting a third party who is both culturally-trained and culturally-suitable for the dispute. After selecting the mediator, you need to contemplate how to effectively represent your client in the process. There is no one all-purpose strategy that will maximize the opportunities before every sort of mediator. The optimum advocacy approach depends on the sort of mediator selected.

CHAPTER 11

Criteria for Approving Programs to Qualify Mediators for IMI Inter-Cultural Certification

2012
International Mediation Institute
www.IMImediation.org

IMI set up a Task Force[1] in April 2010 to develop criteria for inter-cultural mediator training and IMI Certification. The Task Force's goals were to develop criteria that are succinct, flexible, and feasible to implement by trainers and QAPs (Qualifying Assessment Programs).

These Criteria are the result of the Task Force's work, which was part-funded by the General Electric Foundation. It involved, during 2011, online public consultation and pilot programs in Paris, Brisbane and Singapore, with participants from across the globe who provided active and direct input into this initiative, for which IMI is very grateful.

Training, professional and provider organizations wishing to offer IMI Inter-Cultural Certification are invited to submit their applications to become Inter-Cultural Qualifying Assessment Programs (ICQAPs) to the Chair of the IMI Independent Standards Commission (ISC)[2]. Once approved, ICQAPs will be displayed at: http://imimediation.org/find-an-icqap. This link will enable mediators seeking this certification to easily find approved ICQAPs offering training programs.

---

1 Chair, Professor Hal Abramson (U.S.), Touro Law Center, New York; Co-Chair, Joanna Kalowski (Australia), Mediator and Trainer; Gigi de Groot (The Netherlands/Sweden), Manager Director, itim international (Professor Hofstede's consulting org.); Jeremy Lack (Switzerland), Mediator and Trainer; Professor Joel Lee (Singapore), National University of Singapore; Professor Ian Macduff (Singapore/New Zealand/Malaysia), Singapore Management University; Hannah Tumpel (France/Germany), Manager, ADR Centre, ICC (Paris).

2 ISC.Chair@IMImediation.org

These Criteria will be regularly reviewed by the ISC and may be modified in the future.

All comments and suggestions are welcomed. Please send all comments and suggestions to icqaq@imimediation.org.

CRITERIA SUMMARY

IMI Inter-Cultural Certification is available to any experienced mediator who is qualified by an Inter-Cultural Qualifying Assessment Program (ICQAP) that has been approved by the IMI Independent Standards Commission (ISC). ISC will approve any ICQAP that meets the following criteria:

- I. GENERAL REQUIREMENTS
  - A. Methodology
  - B. Transparency
  - C. Integrity
  - D. Diversity
- II. SUBSTANTIVE CRITERIA
  - A. Knowledge
    - i. Cultural Framework(s)
    - ii. Self-Awareness
    - iii. Multi-Cultural Perspectives
  - B. Skills
    - i. Communication
    - ii. Preparation
    - iii. Managing Process
- Appendix 1: Cultural Focus Areas (CFAs)

These Criteria are described in more detail below:

I. GENERAL REQUIREMENTS

Any ICQAP must meet the following general criteria in order to be able to qualify mediators for IMI Inter-Cultural Certification:

A. Methodology

All ICQAPs must implement a performance-based assessment methodology for assessing whether each candidate's performance meets each of the Substantive Criteria in Section II below.

Comment*: The assessments may be based on written material, role-play or live action evaluations, other suitable method, or any combination, and may include videotaped and online assessments such as web dramas, self-assessments, interviews, peer reviews, user feedback and other in-practice skill evaluations.*

B. Transparency

The benchmarks and criteria applied by an ICQAP must be published and be openly accessible on the organization's website.

Comment: *Details of all approved programs will be listed on the IMI web portal www.IMImediation.org and will include a direct link to each credentialing organization's website for that program.*

C. Integrity

Each Assessor must have substantial experience of evaluating the performance of mediators and in working in inter-cultural situations. At least one of the Assessors on each Program must be independent of the ICQAP training faculty for Inter-cultural Certification.

D. Diversity

The ICQAP must be accessible on an equal basis to experienced mediators regardless of their professional affiliations, gender, race, ethnicity, age, religion, sexual orientation or other personal characterization. This should be clearly stated on each ICQAP's website.

II. SUBSTANTIVE CRITERIA

Any training program that offers IMI Inter-Cultural Certification must meet these minimum substantive criteria when teaching mediators the following inter-cultural elements:

A. Knowledge.

1. Cultural Framework(s): Ability to apply at least one recognized cultural theory for identifying Cultural Focus Areas relevant to facilitating inter-cultural mediations (*see* Appendix 1). The theory and approach shall include an appreciation of similarities and differences among cultures.

Comments:

(a) Any selected framework should provide suggestions as to how to use culture and possible Cultural Focus Areas derived from the framework, while avoiding stereotyping when setting up and participating in mediations.

Although there are many recognized and respected theories, the goal is not to learn comparative theories about culture or to master a particular theory. The goal is to be able to apply a selected theory or theories about culture in such a way as to help mediators consider appropriate issues when setting up and facilitating an inter-cultural mediation.

(b) Understanding culturally shaped norms and expectations can help explain parties' different perspectives and possible impasses that these perspectives may create. However, it is important to avoid considering culture as an overly inclusive concept to try to explain all behaviours that individuals may manifest, which may not always be group-related but also can be linked to individual considerations (e.g., age, gender, residence, etc.). Mediators should strive to apply their understanding of culture as a tool to foresee possible patterns of behaviour while considering mediation as a social process that can help people from different cultures to communicate optimally with one another.

(c) Any discussion of culture in the context of mediation needs to consider how the concepts of "parties", "participants", "conflict", "resolution", "mediation", "conciliation" and "process" can have different meanings in different cultures.

2. Self-Awareness: Ability to recognise one's own cultural influences and their possible effect on the mediation.

Comments:

(a) Mediators should be conscious of their own culturally influenced practices including how culture may form lenses through which mediators can view and interpret the behaviour of others.

(b) Mediators should consider how their culturally shaped preferences or behaviour might be viewed and interpreted by participants.

(c) Mediators should learn to recognize signs of their own surprise, discomfort, or cognitive dissonances when facing cultural differences, and develop adaptive strategies for re-establishing balance, coping with cultural ambiguities, and managing unfamiliar or contrary practices.

Comments:

(a) Mediators should be sensitive to the participants' possible perceptions of the behaviour of the mediator and the behaviour of other participants, and sensitive to participants' preferences in handling procedural issues or substantive topics.

(b) Mediators should not react negatively when faced with different ways of doing things, unless the behaviour violates the mediator's fundamental personal values.

(c) When working with multiple cultural perspectives, mediators should learn to deal with possible uncertainty, ambiguous information or circumstances, unintentional mistakes (e.g. cultural malapropisms), and possible unconscious biases or behavioural scripts of participants.

(d) Mediators should consider the best styles and processes for dealing with issues related to multiple perspectives, including whether to address different perspectives in caucuses or joint sessions or directly or indirectly with the participants, as well as how to generate procedural options that all participants can work with.

(e) When managing multiple cultural perspectives, mediators should consider how and whether to co-mediate with neutrals from other cultures or involve interpreters as cultural consultants when preparing for and participating in mediations.

B. Skills

4. Communication: Ability to adjust one's own communication style to the styles of participants from other cultures, and to help participants communicate optimally with each other, including establishing suitable processes to facilitate communications.

Comments:

(a) Mediators should be able to employ suitable inter-cultural communication skills when interacting with participants as well as with co-mediators from other cultures. For example, under one theory, selecting the suitable communication style for mediators may involve identifying a point on the direct-indirect communication continuum relevant to a participant, a point that can be influenced by a number of other cultural parameters such as the power distance index and relationship orientation of the participant.

(b) Mediators need to check for compatible communication styles among the participants and consider whether, how and when to assist participants in communicating in the event of possibly incompatible communication styles.

(c) Mediators should be able to assist participants in understanding how information may be conveyed in different ways across cultures.

(d) Mediators may need to help participants adjust the way they communicate with each other based on such parameters as the participants' comfort in displaying emotion, their ability to empathize or understand others' perspectives, their comfort with face-to-face discussion of sensitive topics, and their preference to pursue delicate matters through indirection (e.g., to avoid "loss of face"). Mediators may need to be prepared to help the participants render explicit what may have been implicit in their behaviour, or to state less explicitly what a participant may prefer to learn implicitly. Mediators also might help the participants generate a new set of behavioural norms for the purposes of the mediation.

(e) Mediators need to learn to assess if, when, and how to use caucuses with participants to facilitate communications.

5. Preparation: Ability to prepare for a mediation by identifying possible cultural patterns and preferences (e.g., identifying specific Cultural Focus Areas for each mediation) and designing appropriate processes and possible interventions.

Comments:

(a) Mediators should learn to prepare for inter-cultural mediations by researching and anticipating possible culture affects and by figuring out what process may work best for the participants based on any Cultural Focus Areas that the mediator may have identified. When preparing for a mediation, mediators should consider holding preliminary interviews with the participants, designing culturally appropriate procedural rules for behaviour and interaction, and formulating interventions to help parties recognize and address any culturally-influenced communications, interests, or impediments.

(b) The aim of this preparation should be to construct hypotheses for how to proceed initially given what a mediator may know about the participants, their representatives and their wider constituencies, and plan how to test and adapt these hypotheses as the mediation progresses. It should be remembered that preparation only gives rise to hypotheses, and mediators should not assume that their hypotheses can be relied on.

(c) When identifying interests, mediators should consider the possibility that there may be wider interests at stake than only those of the participants at the table. Those interests may include the interests of other constituencies or stakeholders (e.g., family members, elders, communities, tribunals, affiliates, and regional, national or political groups or entities). This analysis also should consider whether there may be impediments due to the participants' different sense of status or different needs for procedural certainty, autonomy, fairness, or relatedness.

(d) Mediators should be flexible and open to re-assessing and modifying their procedural preferences and styles of intervention, as illustrated by the following examples:

i. Whether to convene a pre-mediation meeting with each party, certain parties only, or their representatives.
ii. Whether to request prior written submissions and the type of submissions that may be helpful.
iii. Where the mediation should take place, who should attend, and what food, dietary needs, external resources, social activities or welcoming rituals should be considered.
iv. Whether to work with the parties to design a procedure to meet any needs for mutual respect, autonomy, affiliation, certainty, or procedural fairness, in which statuses and roles are relevant (e.g. dress code, seating arrangements, and forms of address).
v. Whether to help participants avoid cultural norms that may be deemed politically or culturally incorrect by others, as well as avoid being manipulated by cultural norms.
vi. How participants or their representatives should communicate optimally with one another prior to and during the mediation, including whether to specify the role of the mediator (e.g., as non-evaluative or evaluative), the need for co-mediators or interpreters, who may speak and write, the order of any initial presentations, possible deadlines, the length of mediation sessions, and how time should be allocated.
vii. How proposals might be presented (e.g., in some cultures, parties may not be comfortable presenting options, may not be familiar with brainstorming processes, may not understand what is expected of them, and may not want to present because may appear weak, unfocused, lose face, or lose the respect of other participants or stakeholders).
viii. Whether, when and how to provide for evaluative feedback.

6. Managing the Process. Ability to detect whether, when and how cultural considerations (e.g., any Cultural Focus Areas) may be impacting on the mediation process as the mediation progresses including abilities to adapt the process accordingly and design appropriate interventions, that also encompass any settlement and compliance phases.

Comments:

(a) Although managing the process is important in all mediations, this responsibility requires special attention in inter-cultural mediations where signposts of progress and impediments may be less evident. Also, suitable interventions may be different.

(b) Due to cultural considerations, mediators may need to become more or less directive or facilitative at times on procedural issues, depending on the mutual needs or requests of the participants.
(c) Even though the mediator and the participants may feel they are advancing well, each individual may think they are heading in a direction whose outcome may be culturally influenced and different. In order to provide a check and elicit the range of different understandings, mediators should be able to assess the extent to which participants' expectations are aligned, can be reconciled, and can be respected.
(d) Mediators may need to help participants set parameters for a final work product or action items, so that the participants can feel they have reached satisfactory closure.
(e) Conflicts underlying a mediation are seldom ended by only an oral agreement, nor are they always ended when there has been a signed agreement. In inter-cultural disputes, mediators should be aware of additional procedural or ceremonial steps that may be necessary to enable participants to feel that they can bring closure to the conflict.

APPENDIX 1: CULTURAL FOCUS AREAS[3]

Examples Relevant to Mediating Intercultural Disputes

Introduction

The IMI Inter-Cultural Task Force identified six Cultural Focus Areas that mediators may want to consider when mediating inter-culturally. Each of these behavioural categories is offered as examples that may be relevant when preparing for mediation, interacting with participants, and bridging differences. Under each CFA, several specific illustrations are included.[4]

The Task Force does not view this list of CFAs as comprehensive, and therefore encourages the ICQAPs to consider these CFAs, adapt them, and develop other ones based on the theory(ies) of culture or method(s) of

3 The term "Cultural Focus Areas" was formulated to label the areas that culture can impact on mediating intercultural disputes. Appendix 1 offers examples of six possible Cultural Focus Areas along with illustrations of each area. Each ICQAP should identify Cultural Focus Areas that apply to the types of mediation the trainees practice.

4 After much discussion, a separate CFA was not given to "relationships" because that cultural category is so pervasive that it could not be easily segregated to stand alone. The category relates to several other CFAs, as noted in the illustrations.

mediation they teach. As more experience is gained with the CFAs, these six CFAs may be refined and new examples added.

Cultural Focus Areas (CFAs)

1. **Relatedness and Communication Styles**
   Illustrations: Formal-Informal Direct-
   Indirect Emotional: High-
   Low Emotional
   Expressiveness Physical-
   Non-physical
   Verbal, Para-verbal and Non-verbal
   Personal-Impersonal Sequential-
   Circular Reasoning
2. **Mindset Toward Conflict**
   Illustrations: Negotiation Attitude (how participants may prefer to negotiate) Attitudes to conflict: Positive-Negative
   Risk taking: High-Low
   Relationship-Building-Task Orientation
3. **Mediation Process**
   Illustrations: Expectations about:
   Roles of Mediator and Participants
   Predictability of Process
   Need for an agenda
   Social protocols
   Separate or identifiable phases during the process
   Fairness
   Goals or Outcomes
4. **Orientation Toward Exchanging Information**
   Illustrations: Transparent-Non-transparent
   Legal or other norms or social conventions Broad-Narrow
   Non specific-Contextual Fact related -Non fact related
5. **Time Orientation**
   Illustrations: Polychronic-Monochromic
   Long-Term/Short-Term Orientation Past-Present-Future
   Deadlines, Deliverables, Punctuality
   Duration and Frequency
   (of joint and/or separate meetings)

Expected timelines for reaching outcomes
Time Pressure-No Time Pressure

6. **Decision-making Approaches**

Illustrations: Individualist, Majority-led or Collectivist
Relationship oriented-Outcome-oriented
Participant driven-Constituency driven
Compromising-Non compromising
Norms based-Subjective interests based
Mediator as norms-generator, norms-educator or norms-advocator
Problem solving-Outcome generating
Structured-Unstructured
General-Specific Forms of Agreement (oral, written, behavioural)
Inductive-Deductive Reasoning
Measurable-Non measurable

CHAPTER 12

Crossing Borders into New Ethical Territory: Ethical Challenges When Mediating Cross-Culturally

2008
49 *S. Tex. L. Rev.* 921
Harold Abramson*

---

* Professor of Law, Touro Law Center. The author teaches, researches, and publishes in the areas of domestic and international mediations and mediation representation. He also mediates private domestic and international commercial disputes. He wants to thank Cliff Hendler, Jackie Nolan-Haley, and Nancy Welsh for their helpful comments on the draft article. He also thanks his research assistant, Yelena Davydan, for diligently and tenaciously pursuing numerous and challenging research assignments and for preparing thoughtful and timely responses. A shorter version of this article will be published in a book tentatively entitled, Practical Ethics for Mediators (Ellen Waldman ed., Jossey-Bass, forthcoming 2008).

I. INTRODUCTION

No mediator wants to be charged with cultural imperialism when mediating private international disputes. And yet, mediators run this risk whenever the mediator resists doing what the parties want done. This cultural challenge is different than what mediators customarily encounter. Instead of the gap arising between the parties, the gap is between the mediator and the parties. In this article, I will consider how a mediator might ethically bridge mediator-parties gaps while generally avoiding the harsh charge of cultural imperialism. Through a hypothetical in which a mediator's values clash with the values of the parties, I will develop a four step approach for international mediators.

I found myself investigating this subject thanks to the persuasive powers of Ellen Waldman who convinced me to prepare a commentary on a difficult hypothetical dilemma for her upcoming book on mediation ethics. She assured me that it would be a fascinating exercise and would not take too long. Well, she was right about it being fascinating. But, it has been a lengthy and tumultuous undertaking. In this article, I will describe the ups and downs of the journey, summarize the approach that emerged from the trip, and then apply the approach to some familiar cultural conflicts between mediators and participants.

II. THE CHALLENGE FOR THE MEDIATOR: A CROSS-CULTURAL DISPUTE

This dispute is a distressing one with an acute cultural overlay. And, despite the obvious unfairness to one party, at least from a Westernized point-of-view, it was not an easy dilemma to resolve. Here is the dispute and the challenge for the mediator:

A Muslim woman asked her Imam at her Mosque for advice on obtaining a divorce from her husband. As part of the process of counseling, the Imam met with both spouses and advised them about the principles of Islamic law that they should follow in dissolving their marriage contract or nikkah. Both spouses want to resolve their conflicts Islamically and in accordance with Quranic principles.

Their Imam advised them that a husband can ask for and obtain a divorce for any reason (talaq). However, he is obliged to support his children until they reach the age of majority and provide for the wife's needs for a "waiting period" of seclusion, if the wife remains in the husband's home to observe the waiting period (the iddath, which lasts three menstrual cycles to check that the wife is not pregnant). In addition he is obliged to pay his wife the amount stipulated in the marriage contract (the mahr) that she must receive if the marriage ends. The marriage contract provided for $40,000.

A wife cannot receive a divorce without her husband's consent. If she initiates the divorce, she forfeits her right to the mahr although the obligation of the husband to support his children continues until each child reaches eighteen years old.

The Wife is pressing for divorce and the Husband is resisting giving consent. The Wife, who has little means to support herself, is deeply unhappy in the relationship, especially since her Husband took a second wife, which he is entitled to do Islamically. The Imam advised them that the husband cannot force his wife to continue with him and should not unreasonably withhold his consent—but that giving consent would release him from any obligation to pay his wife the mahr.

The Wife, who is distraught and humiliated, says that she wants permission for an Islamic divorce from her Husband in order to move on with her life. The Husband says that he will not grant her request unless she forfeits her mahr and any other financial support for herself and agrees to give up custody of each child at puberty. The Husband insists that he wants custody of their six-year-old son when he turns seven years old. He wants custody of their thirteen-year-old daughter when she turns fifteen years old. When reaching the stated age, the Husband told the Wife that the child would be taken into the care of the Husband's female relatives.

At the mediation, the Wife capitulates and says she will waive all rights to financial support and agree to his requests regarding the transfer of custody at the given ages so long as the Husband grants her request for a divorce. Having extracted these concessions, the Husband seems pacified. The Wife and Husband are heading toward this agreement. Such an agreement would be broadly supportable under Islamic law principles and within the norms of the Iranian community in which the parties live.[1] What should a western mediator do?

---

1 This hypothetical stems from a forthcoming book by Ellen Waldman; in the book there is a second disturbing feature not analyzed here. The Wife seems to be a victim of psychological abuse, at least when viewed through a mediator's Western lens. *Practical Ethics for Mediators* (Ellen Waldman ed., Jossey-Bass, forthcoming 2008). However, after researching the techniques that mediators use to screen for abuse as well as ancient and modern Islamic marriage practices, I realized that analyzing this additional cultural issue would lengthen considerably the paper without further illuminating the methodology.

For the mediator, this is a cross-cultural conflict with a twist.[2] Instead of the cultural conflict arising between the parties, the conflict arises between the mediator and the parties. It is in this peculiar context that this hypothetical presents one overarching and challenging feature: The parties agree to a Rule that when applied by these parties results in a mediated agreement that is unfair based on the Mediator's westernized values and may even violate western domestic law.

Consider the way the Husband's power over granting a divorce was being used to extort a one-sided agreement, at least from a westernized point-of-view. A western Mediator would likely view such an agreement as grossly unfair where the unemployed Mother waives needed financial support and relinquishes rights to her children in return for the Husband consenting to the divorce. Under westernized common law and statutory laws, such a one-sided agreement also is likely to be invalid and unenforceable due to the unclean hands of the withholding Husband and the duress suffered by the Mother who wants the divorce.[3]

This culturally shaped family mediation starkly raises an old issue in new packaging: Should a mediator withdraw when the mediator encounters a rule, practice, or emerging agreement that the mediator thinks is unfair? In this dispute, the new packaging entails an objectionable foreign cultural rule and its impact on the resulting mediated agreement. Without this cultural overlay shaping the parties' behavior and resulting agreement, I suspect that many

---

2 Let me orient this discussion by placing it into the broader context of bridging cultural differences in mediations. Mediators more typically face cultural conflicts between the disputing parties or their representatives, and they employ various approaches to help participants bridge any cultural gaps. *See,* e.g., Harold I. Abramson, *Mediation Representation: Advocating in a Problem-Solving Process,* 173–81 (2004) (Five Steps: Develop Cultural Framework, Understand Own Culture, Learn Other Culture, Be Open Minded, and Bridge Gap). In this article, the five steps are reduced to three (Know Own Culture, Learn Other Culture, and Bridge Gap) with a new fourth step added on (Assessing Whether to Withdraw). In contrast with a mediation that fails due to an impasse between the parties and the parties terminating the mediation, the conflict here is between the mediator and the parties and the mediator is weighing whether to withdraw.

3 *See* Lisa Zornberg, "Beyond the Constitution: Is the New York Get Legislation Good Law?," 15 *Pace L. Rev.* 703, 726–27 (1995) (describing New York cases that held agreements void when the husband withheld permission for a Jewish divorce (withheld giving a get) in order to extort unduly favorable terms); *see generally* Nancy A. Welsh, "The Thinning Vision of Self-Determination in Court-Connected Mediation: The Inevitable Price of Institutionalization?," 6 *Harv. Negot. L. Rev.* 1, 59–78 (2001) (summarizing legal approaches for overturning settlement agreements).

western mediators would withdraw from the mediation, as will be explored later.[4] With the cultural overlay, however, it is less clear what a mediator might do. In analyzing what a mediator might do, I will suggest a four-step approach for proceeding ethically and for avoiding the charge of cultural imperialism.

III. BRIDGING CULTURAL CONFLICTS BETWEEN MEDIATOR AND PARTIES: A METHODOLOGY

Cross-cultural mediators live under the constant threat of cultural imperialism charges. Mediators do not want to be guilty of parochial ignorance and arrogance when objecting to what might be a cultural practice. Mediators want to avoid claiming that they are right and the parties wrong. In order to reduce this risk, cross-cultural mediators should approach mediations with a healthy respect for cultural pluralism and a clear understanding of the other cultural practice. This sequence of four initiatives is designed to guide mediators along this pathway.

First, a cross-cultural mediator should understand his or her own cultural practices.

Second, the mediator should research the other cultural practice to be sure that the mediator understands its terms and its rationale.

Third, the mediator should try to bridge any cultural gap between the mediator and parties by posing questions to the parties to be sure that the parties are making informed and voluntary decisions free of coercion.

Fourth, if the mediator cannot bridge the gap and finds the practice to be fundamentally abhorrent, then, as a last resort, the mediator should consider withdrawing if the mediator concludes that the practice violates an internationally recognized norm or compromises the mediator's impartiality or the mediation process.

A. Understand Own Culture

A mediator inescapably views a dispute through his or her culturally shaped lens, whether conscious of it or not. And, a mediator must be self-aware of this perspective in order to distinguish universal behavior and other cultural behavior from the mediator's own cultural views when reading a dispute. Developing self-awareness requires doing some research. I have found it helpful to read

4 *See infra* Part III.A.

articles and books that describe cultural categories like forms of communicating in different cultures and describe American culture for foreigners (and it is especially fascinating to read how others view your own culture). When it comes to mediator ethics in the United States, the Model Standards of Conduct for Mediators[5] provide the primary cultural lens through which mediators see their disputes. So, I began this journey by re-acquainting myself with the Model Standards and especially the values that they reflect.

These ethical standards emerged from a long-standing and heated debate over whether a mediator ought to be responsible for the resulting agreement.[6] During the early development of the modern field of mediation, Larry Susskind argued for broad responsibility, at least for environmental disputes. He thought that the mediator among other goals "ought to accept responsibility for ensuring ... (2) that agreements are as fair and stable as possible, and (3) that agreements reached ... set constructive precedents."[7] However, Susskind realized it may be "difficult to retain the appearance of neutrality and the trust of the active parties."[8] In the same journal, Josh Stulberg replied that compromising the commitment to neutrality compromises the principled basis for the mediation service. The guiding principle of neutrality clarifies what parties can expect from a mediator and gives parties confidence to share sensitive information and to trust mediator advice. He then highlighted some of the daunting challenges faced by a mediator who tries to implement Susskind's activist vision for an environmental mediator.[9]

This fundamental debate was resolved formally when the Model Standards of Conduct for Mediators in the United States vested mediators with the responsibility of ensuring a fair process, not a fair result, under the assumption that a fair process will result in a fair result from the point-of-view of the parties.[10] The Model Standards implements this vision by establishing as the primary

5 *Model Standards of Conduct for Mediators* (2005).

6 *See* Lawrence Susskind, "Environmental Mediation and the Accountability Problem," 6 *Vt. L. Rev.* 1, 4–6 (1981).

7 *Id.* at 18 (emphasis added).

8 *Id.* at 47.

9 *See* Joseph B. Stulberg, "The Theory and Practice of Mediation: A Reply to Professor Susskind," 6 *Vt. L. Rev.* 85, 86–88, 110–16 (1981).

10 However, the underlying debate over whether mediators should assume more than process responsibility has persisted. *See generally* James R. Coben, "Gollum, Meet Sméagol: A Schizophrenic Rumination on Mediator Values Beyond Self-Determination and Neutrality," 5 *Cardozo J. Conflict Resol.* 65, 66, 78–84 (2004) (providing an excellent summary of the debate, relevant literature, and open questions).

obligation of mediators to tenaciously preserve party self-determination as to process and outcome.[11] The Model Standards define self-determination as "the act of coming to a voluntary, uncoerced decision in which each party makes free and informed choices as to process and outcome."[12] In support of this obligation, the Standards further oblige mediators to conduct an impartial[13] and quality process that includes promoting procedural fairness and party competency.[14] In short, as long as mediators follow these ethical standards, the parties can arrive at whatever result that they choose to adopt.

These principles reflect the values of the mediation culture in the United States.[15] These principles give mediators a rationale for avoiding becoming entangled in judging the fairness of the result. However, these principles of party self-determination, impartiality, and quality process still offer much for mediators to ponder and evaluate, as this hypothetical illustrates.

In view of these principles and without the cultural overlay, the mediator might withdraw from the mediation. The one-sided agreement is unlikely to be viewed as an agreement that the wife entered into voluntarily, consistent with the principle of party self-determination.[16] The agreement is so problematic that it would likely be held invalid and unenforceable because of the unequal bargaining relationship.[17] This westernized view of the emerging agreement may also poison the mediator's view of the Husband, and as a result, compromise the mediator's ability to maintain his or her impartiality.[18] Further, the combination of these two possibilities may make it difficult for the mediator

---

11 Standard I provides that "A mediator shall conduct a mediation based on the principle of party self-determination." Model Standards of Conduct for Mediators Standard I (2005).

12 *Id.* Professor Coben expanded this brief definition of self-determination based on a number of practice principles that were summarized by Professor Nancy Welsh as follows:

> [T]he parties are at the center of the mediation process; the parties are the principal actors and creators within the process; the parties actively and directly participate in the communication and negotiation; the parties choose and control the substantive norms to guide their decision-making; the parties create the options for settlement; and the parties control whether or not to settle.

Coben, *supra* note 10, at 71.

13 *Model Standards of Conduct for Mediators* Standard II.

14 *Id.* Standard VI.

15 *But see infra* Part IV (comparing American principles with the principles found in the codes of ethics in other countries).

16 *Model Standards of Conduct for Mediators* Standard I.

17 *See id.* Standard I, VI (discussing some of the reasons why the one-sided agreement would likely be held invalid and unenforceable).

18 *Id.* Standard II.

to meet his or her obligation to conduct a quality process.[19] In the face of these types of problems, the Model Standards instruct the mediator to "take appropriate steps including, if necessary, postponing, withdrawing from or terminating the mediation."[20]

Frequently, nonmediators object to the Model Rule's focus on process. They are concerned about the mediation process giving its imprimatur to an unfair outcome. Are there any circumstances, I am often asked, when a mediator might worry about substantive fairness of an outcome? It turns out that for family cases like this one a different approach is encouraged. The Model Standards of Practice for Family and Divorce Mediation adopted by the ABA[21] require a mediator to "consider suspending or terminating the mediation" when the mediator "reasonably believes" the agreement to be "unconscionable" or when parties are using the mediation to "further illegal conduct" or to "gain an unfair advantage."[22]

Therefore, both of these model ethical codes provide ample justifications for a mediator to withdraw. But, in a dispute laden with non-westernized practices and behavior, the mediator should take additional steps before deciding whether to withdraw. The mediator needs to research the other culture and try to bridge any cultural gaps, if the mediator wants to avoid the charge of cultural imperialism.

B. Research Other Culture

A mediator cannot help bridge a cultural gap without learning and understanding the cultural practices of the parties. Researching culture is not easy to do, as anyone who has tried knows only too well.

In the face of sometimes difficult to find materials that may reveal amorphous, as well as conflicting, information, the mediator needs to become acquainted with the terms of a practice as well as its rationale. Learning about someone else's culture can be a treacherous inquiry because the mediator is trying to understand a practice that not only might be contrary to his or her own, but also abhorrent—based on the mediator's cultural upbringing. This inquiry is vital if the mediator wants to avoid the charges of ethnocentrism and cultural imperialism. The inquiry can be an uncomfortable, if not repulsive,

19 *Id.* Standard VI.

20 *Id.*

21 *Model Standards of Practice for Family and Divorce Mediation* (2001).

22 *Id.* Standard XI.

one however, because the mediator must be open to the possibility that what appears, in abstract, to be an offensive practice, may turn out to be tolerable when understood in context.[23]

For example, it may feel offensive to be open to investigating a practice of arranged marriages involving payment, a practice apparently condemned in the United Nations Report of the Committee on the Elimination of Discrimination against Women,[24] but you might find it helpful to learn a justification for the payment practice as explained by one commentator: "The payment of mahr (dower), which involves payment or preferment, is a central feature of the marriage contract in Islam and, as a measure intended to safeguard [a woman's] economic position after marriage, [the mahr is offered to the bride]."[25]

It also may feel repugnant to be open to investigating a practice that gives men a right to a greater share of property, a practice also apparently condemned in the Convention on the Elimination of All Forms of Discrimination against Women.[26] But you might find it helpful to learn how it is justified, as the same commentator explained that in Islam, men have financial obligations to others that are not shared with women so men need a disproportionate amount of assets to meet those other obligations.

Of course, neither of these explanations provides the final word. These explanations offer leads that can give the mediator a line of challenging research to pursue.

For the hypothetical, a mediator would need to learn the cultural explanation for a practice that confers on the Husband the exclusive power over approving a divorce and therefore the potential to extract a one-sided divorce settlement.

---

23 *See generally* Bharathi Anandhi Venkatraman, "*Comment,* Islamic States and the United Nations Convention on the Elimination of All Forms of Discrimination against Women: Are the Shari'a and the Convention Compatible?," 44 *Am. U. L. Rev.* 1949, 2000–3, 2006–7 (1995) (discussing attempts to understand cultural bias in light of the Women's Convention).

24 Comm. on the Elimination of Discrimination against Women, Report of the Committee on the Elimination of Discrimination against Women, para. 44 (2006). This Report was prepared to guide interpretations of the Convention on the Elimination of All Forms of Discrimination against Women. *Id.* para. 247.

25 Venkatraman, *supra* note 23, at 2001 (first alteration in original) (citations and internal quotation marks omitted).

26 Convention on the Elimination of All Forms of Discrimination against Women, art. 16(h), Dec. 18, 1979, 1249 U.N.T.S. 13 (entered in to force Sept. 13, 1981) [hereinafter CEDAW].

Although my preliminary research uncovered some insights, more research is needed in the actual case.[27] The Egyptian government explained that:

> [W]omen are accorded rights equivalent to those of their spouses so as to ensure a just balance between them. This is out of respect for the sacrosanct nature of the firm religious beliefs which govern marital relations in Egypt and which may not be called in question and in view of the fact that one of the most important bases of these relations is an equivalency of rights and duties so as to ensure complementary which guarantees true equality between the spouses. The provisions of the Sharia lay down that the husband shall pay bridal money to the wife and maintain her fully and shall also make a payment to her upon divorce, whereas the wife retains full rights over her property and is not obliged to spend anything on her keep. The Sharia therefore restricts the wife's rights to divorce by making it contingent on a judge's ruling, whereas no such restriction is laid down in the case of the husband.[28]

C. Bridge Any Cultural Gap

With some understanding of the cultural context of the practice, the mediator should next proceed with a sophisticated party self-determination inquiry. As a threshold matter, I assume that the parties have legal counsel. I also assume that the parties were encouraged to seek counsel from a trusted family member or friend so that each party has the benefit of a support system that each party trusts.

The mediator might give the Wife and Husband an opportunity to express their reactions to the Rule and to consider its rationale, benefits, and drawbacks. Then, the mediator might follow-up with clarifying and reality-testing questions. This is not a simple inquiry, giving rise to the old adage that it can be easier to describe what to do than to actually do it. But, it is an essential

---

27 For example, an academic researcher learned that because the Husband pays a marriage gift called the mahr to the bride as well as maintenance, including food, clothing, and shelter, for the duration of the marriage and for a period of time after any divorce, the wife cannot divorce the husband without the husband's permission. *See* Judith Romney Wegner, "The Status of Women in Jewish and Islamic Marriage and Divorce Law," 5 *Harv. Women's L. J.* 1, 20–23 (1982).

28 CEDAW, *supra* note 26, Egypt's Reservations to art. 16, available at http://www2.ohchr.org/english/bodies/ratification/8.htm. Article 16 addresses equality of men and women in matters relating to marriage, family relations, and dissolution of marriage. *Id.*

inquiry if mediators want to seriously pursue party-self-determination. One of two basic scenarios might emerge for the mediator to pursue: the Wife accepts the Rule or the Wife objects to it.

Under the first scenario, if the Wife understands and accepts the Rule despite the disadvantageous trade-offs that it can produce when dissolving the marriage, at least she is making an informed choice to follow the Rule and live with its consequences. Formal consent under these circumstances, however, should not end the inquiry as succinctly emphasized by one insightful commentator on culture and international human rights. She explained that the most difficult situation is when

> those who do it and those who endure it offer no objection. ... But this surely does not mean that nothing may be done. First, there is an abiding suspicion that things are not what they seem in such examples. Are they really just as happy? Does the fact that they have no other way of life open to them make a difference? In short, a good deal more information is needed about the conditions those persons face and the sources of our knowledge about those conditions. Second, intervention comes in degrees, not wholesale. ... [Look for ways to] increase their range of choice. ... It is one thing to embrace a way of life when none other is available, an entirely different one to cling to it when alternatives present themselves.[29]

The mediator can test consent by tempting the Wife with options. It turns out that the Wife has an alternative if the mediation is taking place in New York State. There is a state law designed to diminish the ability of a husband to extort an unduly favorable settlement under a religious rule that gives the power to divorce to the husband.[30] The mediator might inquire whether the parties or attorneys are aware of the applicable law. (How a mediator might delicately initiate this inquiry is beyond the scope of this article.) Through their attorneys, the parties would learn that New York law authorizes a court to consider whether the Husband exploited a barrier to remarriage when the

---

29 Kory Sorrell, "Cultural Pluralism and International Rights," 10 *Tulsa J. Comp. and Intl. L.* 369, 408–9 (2003).

30 N. Y. Dom. Rel. Law, para. 253 (McKinney 1999). Although the law was designed to address the exploitive withholding of the get by husbands in Jewish divorces, the legislation was drafted neutrally so that it would apply in a similar situation in other religions. *Id.* Even though this law is constitutionally suspect and controversial, it seems to have been effective in reducing the unequal bargaining positions of the parties. Zornberg, *supra* note 3, at 756–62.

court determines the distribution of marital property and appropriate maintenance.[31] Therefore, the Wife would have an option for ameliorating the influence of the Rule and a choice to make. She could agree to the onerous terms, or to turn to or threaten to turn to the secular courts to reduce her unequal bargaining power.

This may not seem like a real choice for someone who wants to preserve her standing in her own religious community. But it gives the Wife an opportunity to choose which value is more important to her—preserving her standing in her community or improving the terms of divorce.

I found this part of the journey to be unsettling because how easy it can be to justify a self-determination result: The parties knowingly selected the rule and chose to follow it. Despite the alternative offered by secular courts, the Wife would probably pursue the religious divorce. The substantive result may be unfair by westernized standards, but not necessarily unfair based on the values adopted by the Wife.

I was unexpectedly aided in my journey by a visit to my office by a bright, articulate, reflective, and extremely distraught female law student. She wanted to talk about her separation and divorce. Her arranged marriage was a disaster; after less than a year, she had moved out the day before. As a practicing Muslim woman born in the U.S. who is determined to live within the customs and practices of her religion, she was deeply upset. To proceed with the divorce would make it difficult to remarry within her Muslim community and to continue with the marriage would make her life painfully miserable—a reality that even her parents recognized. As she told me her choice, I was starkly reminded about our limited role as mediators who persevere to honor the principle of party self-determination. All mediators can do is conduct a process where the parties can make an informed choice, regardless of how personally painful the choice may be to one of the parties and how unfair the result may seem to the mediator.

Under the second scenario, if the Wife, a dedicated member of her religious community, objects to the Rule and its consequences, then the conflicting values between the mediator and one of the parties disappear. The mediator can no longer be accused of imposing his or her values on the parties when those values are being asserted by one of the parties. The cultural values now coincide between the mediator and the Wife, giving the mediator a shield from the charge of cultural imperialism,[32] although not

31 N. Y. Dom. Rel. Law, para. 236B(5)(h) (McKinney Supp. 2008).

32 *See* Sorrell, *supra* note 29, at 412–13.

from the charge of partiality.[33] The mediator no longer needs to bridge a cultural conflict between the mediator and the parties. The mediator can now return to the familiar territory of trying to bridge a gap between the parties.

D. Assess Whether to Withdraw

Even in the face of the parties' consent or apparent consent, the mediator may still find the practice so personally abhorrent that the mediator may want to withdraw. But, how can a mediator withdraw and avoid the charge of cultural imperialism?

1. Assess Whether Cultural Practice Violates Internationally Recognized Norms

I next pursued the grand inquiry in cultural studies—the search for universal norms, against which the mediator could judge the practice. How to identify these norms is the subject of numerous articles, books, and much debate.[34] Rather than exploring the challenges and highly contested nuances of agreeing on universal norms, I attempted a shortcut, although one with its own hazards, by researching ratified international treaties as a source of norms. Recalling that ratification means approval in accordance with a country's domestic political process, a ratified treaty arguably reflects the values of the ratifying country, shared values of the ratifying countries, or universal values if widely adopted. Then, if the practice, in this case the Rule, violates an international treaty ratified by the parties' country or countries with similar cultures, the mediator could defend against the charge of imperialism by withdrawing, not on the basis of a violation of his or her own cultural norms, but based on the violation of an independently recognized norm.

With this promising approach in mind, I started researching international treaties, reading articles on international human rights, and consulting with human rights professors. I quickly learned about two international treaties with surprisingly relevant and specific provisions.

First, I read the Universal Declaration of Human Rights that was adopted by the United Nations General Assembly and learned that even Iran among

33 *See infra* Part III. D. 2 (considering how to handle threats to impartiality).

34 *See* Sorrell, *supra* note 29, at 370–71; Guyora Binder, "*Comment,* Cultural Relativism and Cultural Imperialism in Human Rights Law," 5 *Buff. Hum. Rts. L. Rev.* 211, 211 (1999).

other Muslim countries voted for it.[35] And it gets even better because Article 16 (1) is right on point. It provides that, "[t]hey [men and women] are entitled to equal rights as to marriage, during marriage and at its dissolution."[36] But, then this pathway turned bumpy. The Universal Declaration turns out not to be a treaty ratified by member nations. It is more of an enabling legislation.[37] Fortunately, it led to an impressive treaty on point.

In the Convention on the Elimination of All Forms of Discrimination against Women, Article 16 provides that the "States Parties shall take all appropriate measures to eliminate discrimination against women in all matters relating to marriage and family relations and in particular shall ensure, on a basis of equality of men and women: ... (c) The same rights and responsibilities during marriage and at its dissolution."[38] This treaty was ratified by one hundred and eighty-five countries.[39] Now, that is an impressive level of agreement—except, unfortunately, Iran did not ratify the treaty nor did the United States![40] Not ready to give up, I next checked to see if any countries in Iran's neighborhood had ratified the treaty and discovered that many did, including Egypt, Iraq, Jordon, Lebanon, Saudi Arabia, and Syria.[41] New hope! But then I noticed these small footnotes called reservations and quickly secured copies of each footnote. Each of these countries either generally or specifically opted out of Article 16(c). The reservations opted out, for example, when the terms violated "norms of Islamic Law" (Saudi Arabia)[42] or were "incompatible with the provisions of the Islamic Shariah" (Syria).[43]

This promising pathway failed. It did not reveal universal norms, but instead, revealed unambiguously the lack of universal agreement for the principle of equality in the dissolution of marriage. This inquiry failed to discover a principled source of internationally recognized standards that could be the basis for withdrawing from the mediation.

---

35 United Nations Dep't of Pub. Info., The Universal Declaration of Human Rights: DPI Press Kit, Dec. 1997, U.N. Doc. DPI/1937/A, available at http://www.unhchr.ch/udhr/miscinfo/carta.htm.

36 Universal Declaration of Human Rights, G.A. Res. 217A, art. 16, U.N. GAOR, 3rd Sess., 1st plen. mtg., U.N. Doc. A/810 (Dec. 10, 1948) (emphasis added).

37 *See* Nausheen Hassan, "*Note,* U.S. Involvement in the Sanctions Against Iraq: A Potential Basis for a Legal Claim by Iraqi Women?," 11 *S. Cal. Rev. L. and Women's Stud.* 189, 211 (2001).

38 CEDAW, *supra* note 26, art. 16(c).

39 *See* Office of the United Nations High Commissioner for Human Rights, http://www2.ohchr.org/english/bodies/ratification/8.htm (last updated Feb. 15, 2008).

40 *Id.*

41 *Id.*

42 CEDAW, *supra* note 26, Saudi Arabia's Reservations to art. 16(c).

43 *Id.* Syria's Reservations to art. 16(c).

2. Assess Whether Still Impartial or Conducting a Quality Process

At last, I reached the final step in this journey. If the Rule does not violate a universal standard, is there any other principled basis for withdrawing? A mediator might withdraw under Standard II of the United States Model Code if the mediator could no longer be impartial because the mediation is being conducted under a Rule that violates the mediator's personal values.[44] Threats to impartiality arise anytime the mediator becomes conscious of something unfair in the mediation that is impacting on one of the parties.[45] This is familiar territory for mediators, and mediators know to withdraw when the mediator thinks he or she can no longer be evenhanded. The mediator also might withdraw under Standard VI if the mediator feels that this unfair Rule compromises the quality of the mediation process.[46] Of course, if the mediator's decision to withdraw is based on his or her own cultural value, the decision would expose the mediator to the ultimate charge of cultural imperialism—the charge that the mediator is claiming that "my cultural value is better than your cultural value." However, the mediator would reach this result as a last resort after respectfully and diligently researching the other cultural practice and confronting fully his or her own value to determine whether the implicated value is so fundamental that the mediator could not mediate a case in which it is violated.

Despite these concerns, I suspect that many westernized mediators would not withdraw. Instead, they would likely rely on the common refrain that "it is the parties' process"—as I and others have often declared—"so we should defer to their choice." Nevertheless, in this particular case, I would likely withdraw, so I thought.

Withdrawal was the direction I was going until my research assistant innocently asked what would happen next. "Would what would happen after withdrawal be better than the mediator continuing," she inquired. Yes. She queried what their BATNA[47] would be if the negotiation in the mediation was prematurely halted.

---

44 *Model Standards of Conduct for Mediators* Standard II (2005).

45 *See id.*

46 *Id.* Standard VI.

47 BATNA (best alternative to a negotiated agreement) is a term coined in the widely-used book, *Getting to Yes. See generally* Roger Fisher and William Ury, *Getting to Yes: Negotiating Agreement Without Giving In*, 97–106 (Bruce Patton ed., 2nd ed., Penguin Books 1991) (1981) (focusing on what happens when the parties leave the negotiating table).

To work through her inquiry, I ventured down two different pathways. I first wondered whether the BATNA would provide a fair (or at least a fairer) process. If it would, a decision to withdraw would seem easy to make. The parties would be relegated to a better process, and the Wife would have the opportunity to possibly improve her situation.

The second pathway entailed the opposite inquiry—whether the BATNA would not likely lead to a better process. If it would not, a decision to withdraw would negatively impact on the disadvantaged party. If the mediator withdraws, the wife would lose access to help by a third party with expertise in dispute resolution, a third party who might be culturally sensitive to this unequal power dynamic, and who might be able to help the parents negotiate further details within the parameters of the agreement. A mediator who continues with the mediation might be able to help the parties negotiate valuable details that might benefit the children including addressing such issues as visitation by the non-custodial parent and education plans for the children.

This was the most difficult decision moment for me. After trying to research the wife's BATNA[48] and much cogitating, I thought I still would withdraw if faced with this dilemma. I would not want the mediation process (or me) to be associated with such an unfair mediated result. I would want to avoid conferring the imprimatur of mediation on a process and result that violated such a core value of fairness—even when my definition of fairness was shaped by distinctively westernized values. This is what I had concluded in two presentations of the paper and in what I thought was my final draft. Thanks to challenges by colleagues and friends, however, I discovered that I was so determined to withdraw that I had become blinded to the significant benefits of continuing for the parties. I am now inclined to continue to mediate.[49] If both parties want

48 I realized that I needed more information before I could research the parties' BATNAs. It would have been helpful to know the name of the parties' local community and the Mosque of the Mullah because I learned that Islamic religious dispute resolution is not yet well developed in the United States. It seems that the current processes rely heavily on private conciliation and decision making by local Mullahs and Imams of each Mosque, although a more formal private arbitration process, shaped by diverse religious and secular views, is emerging, especially in Canada. *See* Caryn Litt Wolfe, "*Note*, Faith-Based Arbitration: Friend or Foe? An Evaluation of Religious Arbitration Systems and Their Interaction with Secular Courts," 75 *Fordham L. Rev.* 427, 440, 464–65 (2006); Nicholas Pengelley, "Faith-Based Arbitration in Ontario," 9 *Vindobona J. Intl. Com. L. and Arb.* 111, 114–15 (2005); Abdul Wahid Sheikh Osman, "Islamic Arbitration Courts in America and Canada?," *Hiiraan Online*, Dec. 21, 2005, http://www.hiiraan.com/op/eng/2005/dec/Prof_Abdulwahid211205.htm.

49 One non-ADR colleague, Fabio Arcila, with a deep commitment to human rights asked: "Is there ever an occasion when the culture is so foreign to you that you will not be able

to continue with me and the mediation, I think I should try to mediate the best agreement which the parties are willing to enter into so long as the agreement is not illegal.

When conferring with others, I was repeatedly asked why these parties would hire a western, non-Muslim mediator. I suspect many parties would not. They would probably prefer a Muslim mediator, and they would have many choices these days. The next section considers less extreme and more likely cultural conflicts that may arise in the routine practice of private international mediation.

IV. APPLYING THE METHODOLOGY TO ORDINARY CROSS-CULTURAL DISPUTES

A conflict between a core cultural value of a mediator and the culture of the participants is surely rare, but less fundamental conflicts can more frequently arise. This section will illustrate how the approach outlined in this article can help a mediator in more ordinary commercial cases avoid the charge of cultural imperialism.

Conflicts may arise in a variety of ways. Here are several examples. A conflict may arise when parties request a western mediator to switch roles to arbitrate, and the mediator is reluctant to do so. A conflict may also arise when a western mediator prefers a detailed settlement agreement and the parties are ready to settle based on general principles. And a conflict may arise when a western mediator does not hear a clear agreement on each term (low context communicator), and the parties think that they have reached an agreement (high context communicators).

Let us examine how two of these examples may arise in a routine international dispute and how each one might be resolved.

Example 1: What should a western mediator do when both Chinese-American parties request that the mediator switch roles to arbitrate the dispute? This request raises a widely-recognized cultural difference between the attitude of the West and China toward a neutral switching role.

---

to achieve sufficient cultural competence and therefore should decline the appointment?" Interview with Fabio Arcila. Clearly, the standard practice of mediators is to decline appointments when lacking competence. This inquiry raised the prospect that some cultures may be so foreign that even diligent research will be insufficient. That is an interesting possibility for further study. (This exchange took place on January 30, 2008. Fabio Arcila is a law professor at Touro Law Center.)

Step 1. Understand Your Own Culture

U.S. mediators are reluctant to switch roles to arbitrate because each role is so different with each one calling for vastly different responsibilities and approaches. Mediators and parties are especially concerned that the mediator's neutrality when switching to arbitrate may be compromised or appear compromised due to what happened during the mediation. The mediator may have learned information that should not be used when arbitrating or may appear to have prejudged some issues during the mediation.[50] Nevertheless, U.S. mediation rules and the Model Standards of Conduct of Mediators permit neutrals to switch roles—but only if the parties consent.[51]

Western concerns about neutrals switching roles can be gleaned from the detailed requirements that must be satisfied before switching roles. The U.S. Model Standards require the mediator to secure consent, to inform parties of the implications of the change in role, and to understand the different duties and responsibilities of the additional role.[52]

Step 2. Research Other Culture

Even though the current code of conduct for mediators in China also requires the consent of the parties,[53] the underlying attitude toward switching roles is markedly favorable, as can be discerned from the prior code of conduct for mediators in China, Chinese mediation rules, the China International Economic and Trade Arbitration Commission's (CIETAC) webpage, and CIETAC's arbitration rules.

The 1992 China Council for the Promotion of International Trade (CCPIT) Ethical Code for Conciliators did not even regulate conciliators switching roles to arbitrate; it only barred conciliators from acting as "arbitration agents of either party in subsequent arbitration proceedings."[54] The 1992 CCPIT Rules of Conciliation, however, did address the issue and did

---

50 Harold I. Abramson, "Protocols for International Arbitrators Who Dare to Settle Cases," 10 *Am. Rev. Intl. Arb.* 1, 3–4, 7 (1999).

51 *Model Standards of Conduct for Mediators* Standard VI (2005).

52 "A mediator shall not undertake an additional dispute resolution role in the same matter without the consent of the parties. Before providing such service, a mediator shall inform the parties of the implications of the change in process and obtain their consent to the change. A mediator who undertakes such role assumes different duties and responsibilities that may be governed by other standards." *Id.* Standard VI.A.8.

53 *See* CCPIT/CCOIC Code of Conduct for Mediators, art. 9 (2005) (P.R.C.) ("A mediator shall not act as an arbitrator in the subsequent arbitration proceeding for the same dispute dealt with in the mediation procedures, unless otherwise agreed by the parties.").

54 *See* CCPIT/CCOIC Ethical Code for Conciliators, para. 12 (1992) (P.R.C.).

so favorably by approving conciliators arbitrating, unless "opposed by the parties."[55]

Several years ago, the introduction to CIETAC's website commented favorably on the practice of arbitrators mediating by pointing out that:

> Many years of practice has indicated that the combination of arbitration and conciliation can make good use of the advantages of both arbitration and conciliation, so as to settle disputes more efficiently and turn hostility into friendship. It also may save parties expenses and help to maintain the friendly relations and cooperation between them. This practice in Chinese arbitration has received world wide attention and approval.[56]

Today, even though the Introduction still reflects a favorable attitude toward combining processes, it now highlights that the practice is consensual:

> The CIETAC arbitration is marked by its unique combination of arbitration with conciliation, an advantageous mixture of the merits of both, which not only resolves disputes, but also renews positive business and personal relations between the parties.
>
> This combination is possible during the arbitration proceedings with the parties' consent. Also, the arbitrators may, at any time during the proceedings, play the role of conciliators in an attempt to resolve the dispute. Either party may end the combination at any time if it thinks it is no longer necessary or will be fruitless.[57]

The current Arbitration Rules of CIETAC also construct a supportive pathway for combining conciliation and arbitration.[58]

---

55 "If conciliation fails, the conciliator(s) may be appointed by one of the parties as arbitrator(s) in the subsequent arbitration proceedings, unless such appointment is opposed by the other party." CCPIT Rules of Conciliation, art. 21 (2000) (P.R.C.).

56 *See* Jacqueline M. Nolan-Haley, Harold I. Abramson and Pat K. Chew, *International Conflict Resolution: Consensual ADR Processes,* 139 (2005) (emphasis added). Unfortunately, the author (me), did not note the year that this language was on the CIETAC webpage. This quote was found on the website around 2004. The introduction has since been modified.

57 *See* CIETAC, Introduction, www.cietac.org.cn/english/introduction/intro_1.htm (last visited on Apr. 16, 2008).

58 Article 40, Combination of Conciliation with Arbitration, states:

> 2. Where both parties have the desire for conciliation or one party so desires and the other party agrees when approached by the arbitral tribunal, the arbitral tribunal may conciliate the case during the course of the arbitration proceedings.

This favorable Chinese attitude toward combining roles has been confirmed in my conversations with CIETAC arbitrators and mediators. They seem mystified by the western preference to keep the roles of mediators and arbitrators separate when the goal is to settle disputes.

Step 3. Bridge Any Cultural Gap

This gap might be bridged by the mediator pursuing a line of inquiry with the parties that helps them make an informed choice to authorize the mediator to switch roles to arbitrate.

The mediator should pose such questions as:[59] Do the parties feel confident that the mediator has had adequate training and experience to switch roles to arbitrate?; Do the parties feel secure that the confidentiality agreement will bar admitting information in the arbitration that was generated in the mediation?; Do the parties think that the mediator as arbitrator might be influenced by information learned during the mediation?; Did the mediator offer any evaluations that may convey the appearance of prejudging an important issue in the arbitration or may contaminate the arbitrator's view of an issue that may be decided in the arbitration?; and Did the mediator's use of caucuses (such as the ex-parte sharing of information by one party that could not be responded to by other party) compromise the appearance of neutrality when arbitrating?

Step 4. Assess Whether to Withdraw

Even if the parties' consent to the mediator switching roles, the mediator can still consider whether to decline the request. Unfortunately, there are no internationally recognized standards to guide the mediator. One possible source might have been the UNCITRAL Model Law on International Commercial Conciliation. Although approved by the UN General Assembly, the Model Law

---

3. The arbitral tribunal may conciliate the case in the manner it considers appropriate. ...
7. Where conciliation fails, the arbitral tribunal shall proceed with the arbitration and render an arbitral award.
8. Where conciliation fails, any opinion, view or statement and any proposal or proposition expressing acceptance or opposition by either party or by the arbitral tribunal in the process of conciliation shall not be invoked as grounds for any claim, defense or counterclaim in the subsequent arbitration proceedings, judicial proceedings or any other proceedings.

CIETAC Arbitration Rules, art. 40 (2005) (P.R.C.), available at http://www.cietac.org.cn/english/rules/rules.htm.

59 For a fuller discussion of these types of questions, *see* Abramson, *supra* note 50, at 7–17. Even though the article examines protocols for an arbitrator who might mediate, the list of protocols can be adapted to the reverse situation-when a mediator might arbitrate.

has not been widely adopted.[60] The Guide to its Enactment and Use states that the Model Law is "essentially neutral"[61] on the subject of conciliators arbitrating, but an examination of the Model Law connotes otherwise. The structure of the Model Law conveys an unfavorable attitude by providing for a default rule that bars the practice unless overruled by an agreement of the parties.[62]

With no internationally recognized source for guidance, a mediator still might decline to arbitrate based on familiar disqualification considerations such as whether he or she may not appear impartial when arbitrating in view of what happened during the mediation.[63] The mediator also might decline because he or she may not feel qualified to arbitrate. Otherwise, if the parties so consent, the mediator presumably would agree to arbitrate.

Example 2: What should a U.S. mediator do when both Asian parties are ready to sign an unsettlingly vague agreement?

Step 1. Understand Own Culture
The mediator must first become aware of his or her cultural upbringing in which the mediator as a lawyer was taught to draft detailed contracts that anticipate most contingencies.

Step 2. Research Other Culture
The mediator learns that the parties are from a culture in which business deals and settlement agreements are built on relationships, not detailed contracts. If something goes wrong, the parties do not think about breach but instead think about how to fix the problem.

Step 3. Bridge Any Cultural Gap
A conflict can arise because the mediator may become concerned that such a relationship-based settlement agreement may fall apart at the implementation stage due to vague obligations or unclear consequences. The mediator can bridge this gap by asking questions that help the parties make an informed

---

60 UNCITRAL Model Law on Intl. Commercial Conciliation (2002), available at http://www.uncitral.org/uncitral/en/uncitral_ texts/arbitration/2002Model_conciliation_status.html.

61 United Nations Comm'n on Intl. Trade Law, Guide to Enactment and Use of the UNCITRAL Model Law on International Commercial Conciliation, art. 12 cmt. (2002), available at http:// www.uncitral.org/pdf/english/texts/arbitration/ml-conc/ml-conc-e.pdf.

62 "Unless otherwise agreed by the parties, the conciliator shall not act as an arbitrator in respect of a dispute that was or is the subject of the conciliation proceedings or in respect of another dispute that has arisen from the same contract or legal relationship or any related contract or legal relationship." *Id.* art. 12.

63 *Model Standards of Conduct for Mediators* Standard II (2005).

choice to enter into a vague agreement. Rather than measuring the adequacy of the agreement against what a U.S. attorney would do, the mediator would assess the agreement's adequacy based on what both parties are willing to sign.

Step 4. Assess Whether to Withdraw

The practice of relationship-based agreements does not appear to violate any internationally recognized standards, and presumably these conflicting values between the mediator and the parties do not compromise the mediator's impartiality. Nevertheless, if the mediator thinks that the parties have not reached a sufficiently clear agreement even after completing the Step 3 bridging the gap inquiry, the mediator might consider withdrawing on the grounds that the mediator believes that the participants' conduct jeopardizes the quality of the mediation.[64] At this juncture, the mediator would be withdrawing based on his or her cultural view of what constitutes an adequate agreement, and in doing so, would be making an informed choice to be culturally imperialistic.

V. CONCLUSION

When crossing borders, mediators are crossing into new ethical territory. Ethical issues can arise due to differences in culture between the mediator and the parties. In order to navigate this new territory, mediators need to be aware of their own culturally shaped behavior and perspective and be open-minded and nonjudgmental when proactively learning about other ways of behaving. And, mediators should diligently search for ways to bridge any gaps between the mediator and the parties before confronting the difficult possibility of withdrawing. By conscientiously following the four steps outlined in this article, mediators should be able to avoid the charge of cultural imperialism, except when the mediator decides to be imperialistic.

---

64 *Id.* Standard VI.

CHAPTER 13

Outward Bound to Other Cultures: Seven Guidelines for U.S. Dispute Resolution Trainers

2009

Harold Abramson*

I. INTRODUCTION

"Would you like to go to Delhi to train people in negotiations?" the email message inquires. "Are you kidding?" you think to yourself. "Of course, I would get to do in an exotic location what I enjoy doing at home helping others to resolve conflicts. And I also would meet fascinating people and tour an intriguing city and country with a local host." "YES," you reply after working out the logistical details. Now as you begin to pack your off-the-shelf training materials, you start to wonder how you should adapt your training for this foreign location. You do not want to be accused of cultural imperialism or insensitivity. This article will explore what to do before getting on the airplane, from the point-of-view of a U.S. trainer.

So, what do we need to do? We need to adapt our off-the-shelf training materials to account for cultural differences. Wow, now that is not a particularly

---

* Harold Abramson, Professor of Law at Touro Law Center, has taught dispute resolution courses for over twenty years, written extensively in the areas of mediation representation and international mediation, mediated numerous domestic and international cases with parties from more than a dozen countries, and taught or trained throughout the U.S. and in China, Germany, Holland, Hungary, India, Italy, Russia, and Switzerland. He wants to recognize the valuable comments on earlier drafts by John Barkai (Hawaii), Julia Gold (Seattle), Louise Harmon (Touro), Andrew Lee (Beijing), and Mario Patera (Vienna). He also wants to thank his research assistant, Benjamin Noren, for his diligent work. This article also was published as a chapter in *Rethinking Negotiation Teaching: Innovations for Context and Culture* (C. Honeyman, J. Cohen, and G. De Palo eds., DRI Press 2009).

surprising or insightful answer. We already know that. We routinely say so. We also routinely criticize training programs for failing to do so. We criticize traveling trainers as cultural imperialists, promoting the U.S. way of doing things without any meaningful effort to respect or account for cultural differences. To avoid these charges, we need to meticulously adapt our materials and presentations for export. And we need to do this based on understanding the cultural assumptions embedded in our off the shelf programs and the cultural upbringings of the participants.

This article was inspired by the opportunity to observe a two-day negotiation training program[1] put together by Hamline University School of Law in Rome. It was called "Developing 'Second Generation' Global Negotiation Education." The trainers conducted a high level program for around thirty sophisticated professionals. And over forty scholars observed the training and then spent another two days discussing what was observed. Based on that experience as an observer and my own experience teaching and training abroad, along with additional research, I have identified seven guidelines for U.S. trainers. These guidelines should help trainers reduce any cultural mishaps, prepare for the inevitable surprises, and ultimately deliver an effective program in other cultures.

II. GUIDELINES FOR TRAINING ABROAD

1. Acquire a Culturally Educated Lens

We all wear culturally shaped lenses through which we observe and judge behavior around us. When someone is unwilling to make a commitment in writing, or does not bring all the people with settlement authority, or just shows up late, we are likely to interpret these behaviors negatively, based on our experiences at home. But in other cultures, these behaviors may not be negative; they may just reflect different practices. Before we, as U.S. trainers, go abroad, we need to acquire a new prescription. We need to be able to discern which behaviors of ours are culturally shaped, as well as the range of cultural behaviors that may be exhibited where we are training.

Many excellent books and articles provide conceptual models of culture, and they further illustrate particular cultural practices including practices that

1 The program was held in May, 2008. The subjects that were superbly presented would be familiar to any experienced trainer. The program covered positional and interest-based negotiations, communication skills, impasse-breaking, and ethics with the bonus of a culture and gender module.

can impact how people negotiate.[2] These materials have taught us about a multitude of behavior continuums that can be found across cultures.[3]

We need to be acquainted with them. Well-known continuums include high to low context communicators,[4] individualism to collectivism,[5] universalism to particularism,[6] high to low power distances,[7] long-term to short-term orientations,[8] and high to low uncertainty avoiders.[9] Unless we arrive fitted with an educated lens through which we can recognize our own cultural behaviors as well as others, we may be misunderstood by local participants, and miss or misinterpret their contributions and comments.

For example, during a debriefing of a negotiation exercise in Argentina, an uneducated trainer may misinterpret comments by participants in a commercial dispute when the participants explain that they spent most of their time on small talk and getting to know each other. Thinking that the participants failed to meet the disputing parties' interest in a new contract, a perfectly reasonable interpretation in Westernized terms, a trainer might suggest ways the parties could have moved in that direction within the time constraints of the exercise. In so doing, the trainer would have failed to inquire about the possibility that culturally, the participants had less interest in the terms of any new contract and more interest in the relationship (that the parties may operate closer to the relationship pole on a contract-to relationship continuum).

Unfortunately, we cannot simply read books to learn about the participants' cultural practices because the practices of each participant can be a product of multiple cultural experiences, and those experiences are not frozen

---

2 *See* John Barkai, "Cultural Dimension Interests, the Dance of Negotiation, and Weather Forecasting: A Perspective on Cross-Cultural Negotiation and Dispute Resolution," 8 *Pepp. Disp. Resol. L. J.* 403 (2008), B.C. Gob, "Typical Errors of Westerners," in *The Negotiator's Fieldbook*, 293 (Andrea Kupfer Schneider and Christopher Honeyman eds., 2006), Geert Hofstede, *Culture's Consequences: International Differences in Work-Related Values* (1980), Michelle Lebaron and Venashri Pillay, *Conflict across Cultures: A Unique Experience of Bridging Differences* (2006), Michelle Lebaron, *Bridging Cultural Conflicts: A New Approach for a Changing World* (2003), Jeswald W. Salacuse, *Making Global Deals: What Every Executive Should Know about Negotiating Abroad* (1991).

3 *See, e.g.*, Barkai, *supra* note 2, Goh, *supra* note 2, Hofstede, *supra* note 2, Lebaron and Pillay, *supra* note 2, Lebaron, *supra* note 2, Salacuse, *supra* note 2.

4 *See, e.g.*, Lebaron and Pillay, *supra* note 2, at 32–36.

5 *See id.*

6 *See id.* at 39.

7 *See id.* at 33, 45–48.

8 *See, e.g.*, Hofstede, *supra* note 2, at 359.

9 *See id.* at 161.

in time-they can evolve based on life's experiences and external influences. All we can do is observe participants' behavior with a sensitive vision.

When we are fitted with this educated lens, we can identify the embedded cultural assumptions in our own off-the-shelf training as well as more accurately understand what is happening in the training as it unfolds. But we are not yet ready to get on the plane. We need to modify our training materials and presentations.

2. Behave Like a Guest: Be Flexible, Open-Minded, and Elicitive

As any experienced trainer knows-when we train, we vigorously multi task, and we may do that for seven to ten uninterrupted hours in a single day, as we try to make the time together fun, engaging, and educational.[10] And when we go abroad, we must add another task: to behave like a guest-as an outsider in the room-who is flexible, open-minded, and elicitive.

As guests, we should be flexible and therefore prepared for the unexpected. Our success does not depend on avoiding all cultural blunders. Our success depends on how well we deal with inevitable surprises. If we inadvertently cause someone to lose face, for instance, find a way for the person to regain face-quickly. If we mistakenly pair people of different ranks in a hierarchical society, correct it. We need to be prepared to adjust the training as it unfolds.

As guests, we should not get carried away with our "expertise." We arrive as experts, but only from where we come from. We are outsiders to the culture where we are training. When it comes to local cultural practices, the experts are our hosts and participants. We can learn from them. We should be open-minded, which includes being non-judgmental and respectful of differences as we learn about their culture(s).[11] And, we need to be more than inquisitive. We should elicit a continuous stream of input as we formulate our programs and deliver them.[12] Before we leave, we can ask our hosts about local practices by conferring with them or employing a formal survey. At the training, we can

10 When training, we are not just presenting lectures. We are lecturing, organizing, and administering exercises, using multiple technologies (power points, DVDs, flip charts, and sometimes more), facilitating fragile discussions, and most importantly, doing what is necessary to maintain the energy of the participants for a long day (by constantly fine tuning the pace and schedule including the timing of feeding breaks).

11 *See* Harold Abramson, *Mediation Representation-Advocating in a Problem-Solving Process,* 175–180 (2004).

12 Morgan Brigg, "Mediation, Power, and Cultural Difference," 20 *Conflict Resol. Q.* 287, 30 I (2003).

give genuine attention to getting to know the participants, especially in relationship-based cultures, in an effort to draw the participants out and learn from them.

For example, recently I needed to learn about the nature of the relationship between attorneys and clients in Switzerland for a mediation representation training program in Geneva. We know that the relationship can vary in different regions of the world. In the U.S., clients tend to rely heavily on their attorneys, with their attorneys taking the lead. But, in some European countries, especially civil law ones, business clients can assume a more prominent role. Before the Geneva training, I asked my host to educate me about attorney-client relationships and then began the relevant training segment by pointing out that how responsibilities between attorneys and clients are shared is a choice. I then elicited from the participants what the local practices were and used their responses to explore other types of arrangements when representing clients in mediations.

We should be flexible, open-minded, and elicitive about local practices throughout our trainings.[13] In short, we should be the consummate guest.

3. Be Mindful of Cultural Assumptions and Differences, and Adapt Training

We need to be cognizant of how our own cultural values may be reflected in our training materials and presentations in order to effectively deliver our trainings.[14] Otherwise, participants may misunderstand us, or worse, privately dismiss what we are presenting because they may think "it does not work in our culture." We cannot necessarily rely on participants to raise cultural differences, because they may be too polite. So, we need to edit our training materials and revise our presentations to acknowledge our practices, and incorporate differing practices of the trainees.

a. Getting to Yes Concepts

Because *Getting to Yes* concepts form the foundation of most, if not all, U.S. based negotiation and mediation trainings, we should acknowledge and discuss the cultural critique of the concepts when training abroad. The main critique characterizes "interests" and "separating the people from the problem" as

13 *Id.* at 300.
14 *Id.* at 301.

Western values, although I think that much (but not all) of this critique is based on misunderstandings.[15]

The critique views interests narrowly as a Western concept that reflects social norms of individualistic, independent, and autonomous values of parties.[16] In contrast, Islamic values, for instance, focus on needs that go beyond narrow Western interests and reflect social norms of interdependence and community involvement, even in interpersonal matters.[17] The separating the people from the problem principle also has been critiqued as one that runs counter to the values of some other cultures. It has been suggested that relationship issues can be as significant as any substantive issue, especially in cultures based on interdependence and relatedness among community members.[18] While these narrow characterizations of interests and the separation of people from the problem principle can be encountered in the West, a close reading of *Getting to Yes* reveals a broad definition of interests, one that can include relationship needs. Fisher and Ury explained in what is now a widely-cited quote that: "Interests motivate people; they are the silent movers behind the hubbub of positions. Your position is something you have decided upon. Your interests are what caused you to so decide."[19] Fisher and Ury highlighted how broad interests can be when they emphasized that: "The most powerful interests are basic human needs. In searching for the basic interests behind a declared position, look particularly for those bedrock concerns which motivate all people ... Basic human needs include: security,

15 Amr Abdalla, "Principles of Islamic Interpersonal Conflict Intervention: A Search within Islam and Western Literature," 15 *J. L. and Religion* 151, 160–61 (2000–2001).

16 *See id.* at 162.

17 *See id.*

18 *See id.* at 165. Niko Besnier suggests that in some cultures, you cannot separate the people from the problem because the human emotional dimension and problem are culturally "intricately interwoven." Niko Besnier, "Language and Affect," 19 *Annual Rev. of Anthropology* 419,431 (1990). Also, cultural protocols can impede the ability of parties to articulate interests in a mediation session. Morgan Brigg, "Mediation, Power, and Cultural Difference," 20 *Conflict Resol. Q.* 287, 296 (Spring 2003).

19 Roger Fisher and William Ury, *Getting to Yes,* 41–48 (Bruce Patton ed., Penguin Books 1991) (1983). Even though Menkel-Meadow contends that we should recognize "needs" as something that goes beyond the rational that underlies interests, her definition of needs that "include such intangibles as respect, dignity, care, sympathy, empathy, apology, and recognition" sound like the ones covered by the broad definition of interests offered by Fisher and Ury. Symposium, "Correspondences and Contradictions in International and Domestic Conflict Resolution: Lessons from General Theory and Varied Contexts," 2003 *J. of Disp. Resol.* 319, 343 (2003). *See also* Fisher and Ury, *supra* note 19, at 48.

economic well being, a sense of belonging, recognition, [and] control over one's life."[20]

And Fisher and Ury did not ignore or subordinate concerns about a party's interest in relationships. They recognized that it can be a more important interest than a party's substantive interests, and they made this point in their chapter entitled "Separate the PEOPLE from the Problem."[21]

As a result of this analysis and my own experience, I have come to believe that the term "interests," as broadly construed, is culturally neutral, while the content can be culturally shaped. Success stories of Western trainers in non-Western societies support this distinction and should help us feel secure presenting this powerful *Getting to Yes* concept abroad.[22] But, we should not ignore the stories of caution.[23] We should remain open to new cultural understandings as we learn more about conflict resolution in non-Western societies, including continuing testing the distinction between neutral interest and cultural content.

We also ought to test the cultural acceptability of other *Getting to Yes* concepts like "inventing options" and "objective criteria." Professor John Barkai has raised the possibility that inventing options can be uncomfortable in a high uncertainty avoidance culture, and selecting what is objective can be influenced by cultural values.[24]

As a guest presenting the *Getting to Yes* concepts, we can elicit, examine, and incorporate insights from the participants. Let me illustrate one possible approach. We could commence discussions by offering a broad conception of interests, and then inquire what might be the interests of each side in a particular problem. We could assertively involve the participants in identi-

20 *See* Fisher and Ury, *supra* note 19, at 48.

21 *See id.* at 17–39. Len Riskin, in his classic article on the orientations of mediators, also broadly defines interests to encompass the "relatedness and community" mentioned by Abdalla when he suggests that third parties can approach parties' needs over a continuum of four levels from a narrow perspective of a legal dispute to the broad perspective of community interests. *See* Leonard L. Riskin, "Understanding Mediators' Orientations, Strategies, and Techniques: A Grid for the Perplexed," *Harv. Negot. L. Rev.* 7, 18–22 (1996), and Abdalla, *supra* note 15, at 175.

22 Wallace Warfield, "Response to Carrie Menkel-Meadow's "Correspondences and Contradictions in International and Domestic Conflict Resolution: Lessons from General Theory and Varied Contexts," *J. of Disp. Resol.* 417–26 (2003) (Warfield successfully taught interest-based negotiation in Rwanda).

23 *See* Brigg, *supra* note 12, at 296–97 (concerned that the local cultural context impeded the ability of Aboriginal Australian people to articulate interests in a mediation session).

24 *See* Barkai, *supra* note 2, at 445.

fying possible interests including ones unfamiliar to us based on their own personal values, and then use those answers to sort out whether they are articulating interests or positions-familiar teaching territory for any experienced trainer.

b. Cultural Variations in the Negotiation Dance

We should recognize that the negotiation dance can vary in other cultures. As Adair and Brett hypothesized and showed in their empirical study:

> We predict that like dancers from different cultures, negotiators from different cultures will share a holistic view of the negotiation process that will lead them through similar cooperative and competitive stages. Like dancers from different cultures, we also expect negotiators from different cultures to enact different behavioral sequences at the bargaining table, leading to difficulty in synchronization and inefficient deals.[25]

Therefore, we should incorporate in our exercises, including the debriefings, a discussion of the variations in the negotiation dance because the trainees may dance differently than we do. Here are three illustrations.

i. The Haggle

The familiar haggle can vary in other cultures. I became personally familiar with how different it can be when haggling for purchases in China; my students were getting much better results than me. I was negotiating based on the norms I was familiar with. It turns out that not only were opening offers and the concession process different, so was the nature of the interaction. Chinese negotiators generally pad offers more than Westerners, are more enamored with the back-and-forth process, and favor compromises that result from the ritualistic haggle.[26]

---

25 Wendi L. Adair and Jeanne M. Brett, "The Negotiation Dance: Time, Culture, and Behavioral Sequences in Negotiation," 16 *Organizational Science* 1, 35 (2005), *available at* http://watarts.uwaterloo.ca/-wladair/papers/Org%20Sci%202005%20negotiation%20dance.pdf. "[A]lthough the functional stages of a normative negotiation model may be universal (or etic), we expect some of the behavioral content of stages to be culture-specific (or ernie)." *Id.* at 37. *See also* Barkai, *supra* note 2, at 403.

26 John L. Graham and N. Mark Lam, "The Chinese Negotiation," *Harv. Bus. Rev.*, Oct. 2003, at 1, 3, *available at* http://cumba.net/hbr/negotiation.pdf.

ii. High-Low Context Communicators/Negotiators

As a likely low-context communicator and trainer from the U.S., we may need to consider how high-context communicators may handle differently the scope and ways of sharing information during the negotiations.[27] These differences in communicating can produce different dance steps.[28] In their empirical study, Adair and Brett found that high context communicators were skilled in both direct and indirect forms of communication, and used more diverse, strategic moves than low-context negotiators who rely on relatively more direct means of conveying information.[29] In contrast, low-context negotiators showed less ability to communicate in, or understand, high-context communications.[30]

iii. Different Speeds Through Stages of Negotiations

The speed for progressing through the stages of negotiations can vary culturally. Task-oriented Western negotiators can move quickly through the information exchange stage to the longer stage of exchanging and testing proposals.[31] In contrast, relationship-oriented negotiators, such as from many Asian and Latin American countries, can move slowly through the information-exchange stage until sufficient, mutual trust is established, and then move more quickly through the stage of exchanging proposals and bargaining.[32]

c. Common Terms with Different Meanings

We should be alert how some terms we frequently use in our trainings may have different meanings in other cultures. Because these terms may be understood differently than we intended, we risk confusing the trainees. Here are a few illustrations. The prior section showed how the common characterization of negotiation as a dance can imply practices that can vary across cultures. Other terms that convey meanings that may vary culturally include: attorney-client

---

27 *See* Adair and Brett, *supra* note 25, at 48.

28 *See id.* at 37–38.

29 *See id.* at 46.

30 *Id.* In this study, there is some positive news for those of us who are low-context communicators training in high-context societies. The study implicitly suggests that participants who are high-context communicators are better able to understand and communicate with us than if the situation was reversed, and we were high-context communicators trying to train low-context communicators. *Id.* at 46–48.

31 G. Richard Shell, *Bargaining for Advantage: Negotiation Strategies for Reasonable People,* 119 (Viking Penguin ed., 1999).

32 *Id.* at 119–20.

relationships, mediation, apologies, parties, preserving face, and the ubiquitous inquiry, why.

The familiar understanding of the "attorney-client relationship" in the U.S., in which the attorney is a central advisor, can vary in other cultures where the attorney may perform a more limited role. The nature of the relationship can shape how the attorney participates in the negotiation or mediation process.

The commonly used word "mediation" envisions a process that can vary in different cultures and even within the same culture. In the U.S., for instance, there are at least three distinctively different visions of mediation (transformative, facilitative, evaluative), and many Asian countries lean toward a version of mediation that has been called wisely directive.[33] In Europe-a Western culture, Jeremy Lack, a lawyer and mediator in Switzerland and astute observer of European practices, suggests that there are four different conceptions of mediation practiced.[34] He has identified the U.K. efficiency approach, the French philosophical approach, the Dutch pragmatic approach, and the Ostro-Germanic perfection approach.[35]

While an apology in the U.S. may be viewed as an admission of liability and as a result is rarely offered, in some other places an apology can be an essential and expected offering, unrelated to making an admission.

While the party to a dispute in the U.S. is usually the person directly involved with the dispute, although family members may sometimes provide psychological support or input, the party in some other cultures can be the family of the person directly involved with the dispute. The family can be the de facto party. Family members can be part of a tightly knit unit, and the dispute may be viewed as involving the whole family.[36] Family members may want to be present, with the head of the family playing a leading role.

Preserving face in the U.S. has been described as reflecting "... a person's need to reconcile the stand he takes in a negotiation ... with his principles and with his past words and deeds."[37] This U.S. view is narrower than in some other

33 Harold I. Abramson, *Mediation Representation: Advocating in a Problem-Solving Process*, 70–72 (National Institute for Trial Advocacy 2004).

34 *See generally* Jeremy Lack, *ABA International Mediation Leadership Summit: A Swiss Perception of Different Models of Mediation around the World*, Hague 2008, http://www.abanet.org/dispute/hague/Jeremy%20Lack%20–%20ABA%20Mediation%20Surnrnit%20(The%20Hague%2031.10.2008)%20–%20short%20version.pdf.

35 *See generally id.*

36 *See generally* Geert Hofstede, Culture's Consequences, 225–30 (2nd ed. 2001).

37 *See* Fisher and Ury, *supra* note 19, at 28.

cultural views, which is apparent whenever I read this definition to students and lawyers from Asian cultural backgrounds and hear their surprise and their much deeper and broader view of the need to preserve face.[38]

The essential why inquiry for uncovering underlying interests can be offensive in other cultures as I was startled to learn when recently training Dutch lawyers in the Netherlands. After I praised this simple and powerful inquiry profusely, I was politely informed that mediators are taught not to ask why because the question suggests a touch of criticism and could be experienced as too probing and not neutral. I was advised to begin such an inquiry with "what"-as in, "What is the reason for you wanting that result?"

d. Familiar Body Language and Behavior with Different Meanings

We should be conscious of how body language and behavior familiar to us can have different meanings in different cultures. In the Rome training, for instance, I heard one participant suggest the following self-test to assess whether you were really listening: 1) Are you letting the speaker speak without interrupting? and 2) Are you making appropriate eye contact?

This advice may be sound when listening in the United States; however, it is imbued with Western cultural values. We know, for instance, that in some other cultures eye contact is considered immodest and to be avoided.[39] Also, speaking without being interrupted is not the norm everywhere, as President Jimmy Carter stumbled on during the Camp David mediation. In his daily diary, President Carter commented that: "With one exception of interrupting other speakers, Begin was the epitome of propriety and good manners."[40] Afterwards,

---

38 *See* Graham and Lam, *supra* note 26, at 9:

> In Chinese business culture, a person's reputation and social standing rest on saving face. If Westerners cause the Chinese embarrassment or loss of composure, even unintentionally, it can be disastrous for business negotiations. The Chinese notion of saving face is closely associated with American concepts of dignity and prestige. Mianzi defines a person's place in his social network; it is the most important measure of social worth ... [W]hen those negotiating with the Chinese break promises or display anger, frustration, or aggression at the negotiation table, it results in a mutual loss of face. In the West, sometimes a mock tantrum is used as a negotiating tactic, but in China it invariably backfires one way or another. Causing the Chinese business partner who brought you to the table to lose mianzi is no mere faux pas; it's a disaster.

39 *See* Andrew Sagartz, "Resolution of International Commercial Disputers: Surmounting Barriers of Culture Without Going to Court," 13 *Ohio St. J. on Disp. Resol.* 675, 687 (1998). "[E]ye contact can be revealing. Japanese usually avoid eye contact because they consider staring impolite." *Id.*

40 Jimmy Carter, *Keeping Faith: Memoirs of a President,* 344 (Bantam Books 1982).

he said he finally understood Begin's behavior when he "visited the Israeli Knesset and tried to speak above the hubbub."[41] Carter realized where Begin got his training and negotiation habits.[42]

e. Culturally Influenced Reframing

When we teach reframing, a powerful technique for shifting the attitude or orientation of the parties, we should point out that what we select to reframe and how we do it can reflect our own cultural vision of productive or unproductive behavior in the negotiation.[43]

Consider reframing "interests" and "separating the people from the problem."[44] When we reframe to cull out a party's interests, we may be projecting what we think are the interests.[45] Our particular wording may be based on our views of what we think would be important to us in our own culture.[46] When we reframe to remove toxic words, we may be reframing to reduce the charged emotional language, under the assumption that a less charged negotiation will help.[47] When we reframe to be empathetic, we may be reframing in a way that we think will demonstrate our understanding of how the other side feels, in an effort to defuse hard feelings.[48] These types of reframings, to remove toxic words and to be empathetic, may be motivated by an effort to separate the person from what is perceived to be a separate substantive problem.[49] But, do these reframings comport with the cultural needs of the recipients? Are such phrases even the right ones to reframe? Some humility here will be appreciated by the participants, and as always, we should elicit their reactions and suggestions.[50]

f. Hypotheticals that Resonate with Participants

We should edit our hypotheticals to resonate with local participants. I discovered the importance of modifying hypotheticals when I taught my

---

41 *See id.*

42 *See id.*

43 *See* Brigg, *supra* note 12, at 295–97.

44 *See* Fisher and Ury, *supra* note 19, at 17–39.

45 *See* Brigg, *supra* note 12, at 297.

46 *See id.* at 295.

47 *See id.* at 295–96.

48 *See id.* at 295–97.

49 *See id.* at 295–96.

50 *See id.* at 297–98.

first course abroad in Moscow, a year after the break-up of the Soviet Union. I embarrassed myself by using examples that had no meaning to the students. I mistakenly gave a hypothetical about comparative shopping for cars at a time when there was only one supplier of automobiles. I then used what I thought was a humorous intellectual property case involving Johnny Carson and a toilet bowl company using the slogan "Heeere's Johnny!" in its advertisements. The students had never heard of Johnny Carson.

John Barkai, an experienced trainer, tells the story of how he tried to be culturally sensitive when training in Micronesia by revising one of his favorite exercises, the Ugli Orange. He substituted a coconut for the orange that the disputing parties wanted. He focused the integrative lesson on one party wanting the coconut milk and another person the coconut meat-but was later told that the same coconut can rarely serve both needs in Micronesia.

Here is one brief illustration of how we might revise a hypothetical. A U.S. off-the-shelf problem is likely to be based on the practice of the contract as the deal-that is what American lawyers learned in law school and is reinforced in law practice. However, that cultural assumption may be jarring in some foreign locations, such as in Asia and Latin America, where deals are based more on relationships, although that is changing. We can modify the problem to emphasize the importance of the relationship over the contract details. And when in doubt about local practice, we can also inquire during the debriefing about local propensities and then incorporate local insights accordingly.

We can reduce the risk of cultural blunders by re-reading all our hypotheticals for cultural appropriateness and, when possible, by asking our hosts to review them. We want to avoid facts and situations that are so obviously foreign or inaccurate to the participants that they become distracted or, even worse, alienated. The payoff for editing out blunders can be enormous.

g. Studies or Readings Relevant to Location

We should be aware of the source and cultural focus of the studies or articles that we cite or assign to support our learning points. If they are written by Western authors for Western audiences about Western practices, and we are now training in a non-Western country, we should acknowledge the sources as distinctly Western. In addition, we should try to find studies relevant to the location. It is not always easy to find them, but trainees appreciate it when we can cite Western authors discussing non-Western practices, or even better, non-Western authors discussing non-Western practices.

4. Educate Participants about Training Techniques

We may need to prepare the participants for our use of active learning methods,[51] the centerpiece of any U.S. training program, because these methods can be unwelcomed and intimidating to participants not familiar with these pedagogies.

I recall my first experience using an interactive learning method abroad when teaching a law course in Moscow in 1993. Employing the Socratic method, I expected students to be prepared for class and called on them, my practice for years at home. The result was a daily decline in attendance. After the third day, a student apologized for the dwindling attendance and explained that Russian students do not come prepared for class and are not accustomed to being called on. They first hear the lecture and then read the materials afterwards. They did not like the Socratic approach.

Similar resistance was encountered when a major U.S. sponsor of commercial mediation used role-playing exercises in its first training program in Beijing in 2004. Shortly after the program began, several participants requested that the role-playing exercises be discontinued. It seemed that some of the most senior participants did not feel comfortable performing with colleagues and less senior people. At the host's request, the trainer conducted the rest of the program through illustrated lectures.

Even though these active learning methods are becoming progressively more familiar to participants abroad, we may not want to use these techniques intact. We may want to adjust them to fit local cultural conditions.

When the trainer returned to Beijing in 2005, for instance, he was able to use role-playing after learning that the younger Chinese participants, many of whom had studied in the West, did not object to the role-playing and some were intrigued by it. He then successfully conducted the training with younger Chinese participants and several Americans.

I have facilitated the use of role-plays by "training" students on how to participate. In China, for instance, I met with the Chinese students the day before a negotiation exercise with U.S. law students. We met for over an hour to review the role-plays and how to participate. For each of the three years that I did this, the Chinese students diligently prepared for and enthusiastically participated in the exercises. Of course, less ambitious trainings are feasible.

---

51 U.S. trainers thrive on using a mix of training techniques that include National Institute for Trial Advocacy's (NITA) learning-by-doing methods such as: role-play exercises, small group collaborations, fishbowl exercises, public and private self-critiques, and interactive discussions; all while minimizing the number and length of lectures.

The use of self-criticism may also need some adapting, depending on the local cultural practices. One experienced U.S. academic trainer made these illuminating comparative comments about his experiences: Because U.S. students lacked experience in self-criticism, he needed to coach them on how to reflect on both positive and negative experiences. For Mexican males who were reluctant to engage in public self-criticism presumably because of concerns for preserving face-he asked participants to prepare private self-reflective memos for him. For Japanese students who had considerable experience in self-criticism and could comfortably and naturally comment on what they did wrong, he found that they had difficulty sharing any positive comments. They did not want to be viewed as boasting, so during the debriefing he gave disproportionately more attention to commenting on the positive.[52]

Instructor feedback, a prized part of good training programs, may need to be further refined in cultures where criticism by an authoritative figure can be devastating, as in Japan.[53] We may need to give even more attention than usual to delivering carefully crafted negative feedback, and we might try to supplement our comments with feedback from the other participants, who may offer more culturally credible reactions.

But, not all active learning techniques are unfamiliar to people abroad. Some of the techniques could be especially suitable in particular cultures. For instance, collaborating in small groups may be congruent with some foreign local values, and even more so than in the United States.[54] In those cultural settings, we may want to create more teamwork-based exercises, especially at the beginning of the training, before we move toward less familiar forms of active learning.

The lessons from these experiences are clear-do not surprise participants with unfamiliar active learning methods. Educate and prepare them. Warn them in advance that we will be using these methods, take time to explain how to participate in the exercises, including role modeling the techniques before using them,[55] and start with methods that may be more congruent with the

52 Michael F. Fowler, "Culture and Negotiation: The Pedagogical Dispute Regarding Cross-Cultural Simulations," 9–10 (Feb. 1, 2009) (unpublished article, on file with International Studies Perspectives).

53 *Id.* at 10.

54 *Id.* at 9.

55 Professor Lela Love at Cardozo Law School likes to model techniques with her co-trainer. By modeling a simulated role or self-criticism, for instance, the participants not only see how to use the technique but also might be more comfortable doing it when copying someone else's behavior.

local culture. Also, be sensitive to our guest status, our authoritative role, any local face-saving values, and hierarchical concerns in hierarchical societies. Even with all this preparation and sensitivity, we may still encounter some resistance. Therefore, we ought to progress slowly, look for any hesitancy, and most importantly, be flexible. We may need to adjust our techniques, exercises, and schedule even in the midst of the training.

5. Adjust Presentation When English is Not the Participants' First Language

Even when trainees say that they can participate in English, their English may not be as fluent as that of the trainees at home. In the Rome program, for instance, some of the Italian participants complained that a few of the presenters talked too quickly. We as trainers need to adjust, and it is not easy to change a lifetime habit of presenting.

First, try to not only talk slower (not louder!), but also to cover less and give more attention to simplifying key points. I was surprised at the Rome program when I could not keep up. I thought that most of the speakers covered too much material even for me, a specialist who was familiar with most of the substance-only the delivery was different. This consumer experience has since caused me to reduce my coverage when training abroad.

Second, be aggressively conscious of the use of vernacular and unfamiliar metaphors. Remember, for instance, that baseball is a uniquely American sport when you are about to say, "That was a home run point," or that the Cadillac is better known as a car when you are about to say that, "This is a Cadillac version of the training," or that "No name calling" does not mean to not use each other's names, as a Japanese trainee recently thought.[56] Obviously, we need to be self-conscious, but do not panic if one of these dual-meaning references slips out. Just correct it by gracefully translating the point like, "Yes, this is a premium program."

Third, use visual aids to supplement lectures and exercises. We commonly use visual aids at home in an effort to reach different learning styles of the participants. Visual aids can be essential supplements when trying to reach participants whose first language is not English.

Fourth, permit participants to use their first language when it can enhance the learning without diluting the effectiveness of the overall training

---

56 Professor John Barkai reported this experience when training Japanese attorneys and businesspeople in November, 2008. *See* Barkai, *supra* note 2, at 403.

program.[57] Using their first language can reduce educational losses that may result from participants learning in a non-native language. Participants can practice translating key points into their own language, and use their own language when participating in simulations and small group collaborations and discussions. By practicing in their native language, they will more likely internalize the lessons and use what they learned. However, participants speaking in their first language can reduce our understanding of what is happening in the exercises and therefore reduce our opportunities to teach. In order to restore some capacity to teach during the exercises, we can walk around with an interpreter who can summarize what is being said in each group or ask participants to switch to English, the language of the program, when we come by to listen.

Fifth, give them take-home points. Many trainers already use end-of training exercises to help the participants solidify what they learned. We may brainstorm with the participants a final list of key lessons or ask each person to report the one or two new lessons that will be used. When English is not their first language, this type of exercise can be essential for bringing together key concluding points. You might even solicit what they think will work or not work in their own cultures. However, this type of exercise can be quite humbling for us when the take-home points the trainees register are different than the ones we thought we were conveying.

And sixth, when in serious doubt about the participants' English language facility, use interpreters. Simultaneous interpreters are usually preferred although more expensive than consecutive ones, because we can cover more materials and do so more coherently when we do not have to pause repeatedly to wait for the interpretation. When relying on headsets for the simultaneous interpretation, we should have a back-up plan with consecutive interpreters on call in case the headsets fail to work-an annoying and sometimes damaging disruption to the training. If we use consecutive interpreters, there are advantages that may not always be obvious. The slower pace can give the participants an opportunity to improve their English by hearing the English followed by the interpretation as well as give us more time to observe whether the participants seem to be processing what is being taught.

We should know the particular art of effectively using interpreters,[58] including preparing interpreters by giving them samples of the materials we will

---

57 These suggestions are offered by Professor John Barkai who has done considerable training in Japan, China, and several Pacific Ocean Islands. *See generally* Barkai, *supra* note 2.

58 For sample guidelines, *see* Harold Abramson, *Mediation: Guidelines for Working with Interpreters in Mediations* (2008), *available at* http://www.tourolaw.edu/facultybios/med interpreter.pdf.

be using. By doing so, the interpreters can become familiar with the vocabulary of the training and can research and identify appropriate words to fit less familiar U.S. or Western concepts. As we know already, words like "BATNA", "compromise," and "mediation" do not have counterparts in all languages. I recall my own awkward occasion when I failed to prepare the interpreters adequately. As I was lecturing to a group of judges in Hungary about the multi-door courthouse concept, the judges broke into loud laughter. When I asked the audience what was so funny, I learned that the simultaneous interpreter translated the concept as the disputant peeping through the key holes of each door for the right process. It created the image of a peeping Tom, which connected with some peculiar local humor. Therefore, remember to prepare the interpreters.

6. Refashion Materials and Presentation Based on Purpose(s) of Training

The illustrations in this paper assume that the purpose of the training is to teach negotiation skills for domestic use in a foreign country (exporting domestic negotiation training). However, this is not the only purpose of a negotiation training program. At the Rome conference, I heard people passionately assert that in today's globalized world, in which many countries have become melting pots of multiple cultures, we need to know how to negotiate cross-culturally within our own countries. This assertion illustrates a second purpose of training-to teach negotiation skills to parties who negotiate cross-culturally (cross-cultural negotiation training). The purpose we choose will shape the role of culture in our trainings.

This paper has explored what needs to be done when exporting domestic training. We should identify the cultural assumptions embedded in our standard training program and then adapt the materials by flagging those assumptions and incorporating new ones relevant to the participants. In addition to the illustrations already offered, consider how we might adapt teaching impasse breaking strategies. Rather than relying primarily on our off-the-shelf examples, we might solicit the participants for examples of likely impediments in a hypothetical case. When conducting advanced mediation training in Istanbul, I asked the participants to spend time over lunch identifying impediments that they thought might be encountered in their culture. After lunch, I used the examples as a basis for discussing impasse-breaking strategies.

When training to negotiate cross-culturally, we shift our focus. Instead of adapting domestic materials for use in another culture, our training focuses on cultural differences that might arise between the parties, and how to bridge them. Even though the raw material on culture is similar, how we use the material is distinctively different. If we are training participants to negotiate cross-culturally, we examine strategies for identifying cross cultural impasses, impasses that can arise due to the different cultural backgrounds of the parties. There are numerous opportunities for behavior that is common in one culture to be misinterpreted by someone raised in another culture. Consider the potential for misunderstandings and impasse when low-context communicators, such as U.S. parties who talk directly, negotiate with high-context communicators, as in China where "no" is likely to be conveyed without actually saying "no."[59]

We can refashion our trainings to accomplish both purposes in the same program because much of the training material overlaps and can be complementary. However, such dual purpose training is a lot to accomplish in a one or two day program and possibly too much. If we try, we need to carefully design a program with deliberate compromises and be clear with the participants regarding our dual purposes.

7. Plan to Evaluate the Training Program

We should plan in advance to evaluate our training programs-many of us routinely do this now. When training in another culture, we should additionally evaluate whether the program was culturally responsive and effective in the specific foreign location with the specific mix of participants. We should evaluate what worked well, what did not, and what can be done to improve the training. If possible, we should design and distribute an evaluation form for the participants to fill out either after each segment or at the end of each day. Also, we should plan to spend time afterwards reflecting on the training with any co-trainer, the hosts, and some participants. This evaluation process can help our hosts assess the benefits of the program-and help us prepare for that next invitation to train abroad.

III. CONCLUSION

These seven guidelines call for considerably more preparation than when training at home. By following them, we will be ready to pack our materials and get on the plane. We will be ready to train and to transform the inevitable cultural surprises into learning opportunities. Have a great trip!

---

59 *See generally* Graham and Lam, *supra* note 26.

CHAPTER 14

The New Singapore Mediation Convention: The Process and Key Choices*

Hal Abramson**

This article presents the backstory of the New Singapore Mediation Convention, which is really two stories: one on the multi-party negotiation process that produced the Convention and one on the substantive choices in the Convention. The two stories also illustrate the relationship between a well-designed process and result.

---

* This article is based on a book chapter written by the author and published in *Mediation in International Commercial and Investment Disputes* (Catharine Titi & Katia Fach-Gomez eds., Oxford Univ. Press 2019).

You will notice that the word "enforcement" is not used in the title of this article, in this article (with a couple exceptions), or in the title of the Convention. The Convention is formally entitled "United Nations Convention on International Settlement Agreements Resulting from Mediation" and will be known as the "Singapore Convention on Mediation." For more information, see U.N. Comm'n on Int'l Trade Law, Report of the U.N. Comm'n on Int'l Trade Law, Fifty-first session, U.N. Doc. A/73/17, annex I (2018) [hereinafter Singapore Convention].

Common law attorneys will likely be surprised by this language choice even though the Convention fashions a process for "enforcing" cross-border mediated settlement agreements. Civil law lawyers also are likely to be surprised that the familiar phrase "recognition" is omitted in the Convention and replaced by a functional definition in the Convention. The background on this language choice is explained under Section III where the five-point compromise called "The Compromise" is described.

** Professor of Law, Touro Law Center, New York. Served as a delegate for International Mediation Institute (IMI) and International Academy of Mediators (IAM) at the UNCITRAL Working Group II drafting meetings on the Singapore Mediation Convention. He has written extensively on mediation and negotiations and serves as a commercial mediator. For biography, see www.tourolaw.edu/faculty/abramson. The author wants to recognize the valuable comments on earlier drafts by Corinne Montineri and Tim Schnabel. The author also wants to thank Cardozo Law School research assistant, Nicholas Gliagias, for diligent work checking and formatting footnotes.

The most important milestone of this story occurred on February 9, 2018 when Working Group II of the United Nations Commission on International Trade Law ("UNCITRAL") finished almost three years of drafting the Convention. On that day, Working Group II recommended a draft convention that would facilitate cross-border compliance with settlement agreements that result from qualifying mediations. The purpose of the Convention would be to offer a simpler and more expeditious alternative for enforcing mediated settlement agreements than expensive and uncertain breach of contract litigation. In December 2018, the United Nations General Assembly formally adopted the Singapore Mediation Convention.

What is UNCITRAL?

For those less familiar with UNCITRAL, you might find helpful this brief description before reading anything else. UNCITRAL was established by the UN General Assembly to help harmonize and modernize the law of international trade and commercial law. UNCITRAL's sixty state members are elected by the General Assembly and selected to ensure representation by geographic regions and principal economic and legal systems. As an organ of the General Assembly, UNCITRAL follows the General Assembly's rules of procedures for its sessions and working groups. UNCITRAL determines its work program based on proposals received from States or organizations. It sets its own agenda, reviews the work of its various working groups to which the Commission assigns projects, and prepares reports, models laws, and conventions for the UN.

This mediation settlement initiative was assigned by the Commission to Working Group II, which formerly focused on "Arbitration," then was expanded to cover "Arbitration and Conciliation," and currently is named "Dispute Settlement." Any recommendations from Working Group II are sent to UNCITRAL for its adoption, and any proposed conventions, as occurred in this case, are first sent to UNCITRAL and then to the General Assembly for consideration and adoption.[1]

This article focuses primarily on the deliberations of Working Group II when drafting the mediation settlement convention.

---

1 UNCITRAL, A Guide to UNCITRAL: Basic Facts About the United Nations Commission on International Trade Law 6, para. 48 (2013).

My Vantage Point

At the outset, I should explain my vantage point. I present these two stories from the perspective of an active "observer," not as a member of a country delegation. I represented two NGOs (non-governmental organizations) with observer status, International Mediation Institute ("IMI") and International Academy of Mediators ("IAM"),[2] attended most of the drafting meetings over the three-year process, and participated in multiple discussions. I also served as an "expert consultant." In that capacity, I organized and moderated three mediation education programs for delegates and the public under the auspice of UNCITRAL.[3] Finally, I also bring the perspective of an arbitrator, mediator, and full-time academic in the field of dispute resolution for over 25 years and author of multiple publications on negotiations, mediation, and international conflict resolution.

I feel a need to explain the writing style that includes a disproportionate use of pronouns and passive voice over my preference for active voice and acknowledging the contributions of others. The writing style respects the norms of the UNCITRAL deliberative process where reports are written with pronouns, in passive tense, and with few references to individuals or organizations in order to promote candid discussions.[4] Even though the public documents omit names, I will mention some key players and unreported exchanges thanks to the permission that I was given. Nevertheless, many of the heroes in these stories are sadly omitted although they are known to people who participated in the drafting process.

With these writing guidelines in mind, I will discuss the negotiation process and some of the illuminating stories on how key provisions came together.

---

2 IMI is an international organization that develops global standards for mediators, advocates, and others in dispute resolution. *See About IMI*, IMI, imimediation.org (last visited Aug. 10, 2019). IAM is an organization of peer-selected top commercial mediators from around the world. *See* "About the IAM," IAM, iamed.org (last visited Aug. 10, 2019).

3 *See* Part II.C (The three programs are briefly described in note 10).

4 When preparing this article, I was advised that I could safely discuss any information that is publicly available, but asked not to refer to any discussions that were not expected to be public. Consultations and informal discussions during breaks are productive in part because participants can speak freely without public attribution and need to anticipate reactions of constituencies as they are working through problems.

I. INITIATING THE MEDIATED SETTLEMENT PROJECT

This Project officially started on Friday, March 21, 2014 at 3:54 p.m., at least for me, when I received an email from a Tim Schnabel with the U.S. Department of State. He introduced himself as the U.S. representative to UNCITRAL's Arbitration and Conciliation Working Group. His office, he indicated, was considering proposing a project on the enforcement of mediated settlement agreements. He was interested in my thoughts on whether such a project would be desirable to pursue. In our telephone call, he mentioned that the project idea was initially raised at a State Department's advisory committee meeting by Professor Stacie Strong.[5] I learned that Mr. Schnabel was systematically reaching out to various people to figure out whether the enforcement project was worth proposing to UNCITRAL.

After several months of consulting with various interest groups and experts, Tim Schnabel prepared a proposal for future work to UNCITRAL for its July 2014 Session. The proposal, formally submitted on behalf of the U.S., was referred by UNCITRAL to Working Group II for evaluation.[6]

At the Working Group II Session in New York in February 2015, the Delegates along with NGOs and other observer groups engaged in a thorough review of the U.S. proposal. The week-long session was conducted by Michael Schneider, the Swiss Delegate who served as a diligent and disciplined Chair. I sat in the room in awe as a first-time observer. The Chair tightly managed the substantive discussions among more than a hundred people representing 91 States and organizations. I was especially impressed by his skill in summarizing what he heard to be sure he understood each point and his incisive follow-up questions. He usually posed one or two probing questions to test the depth of understanding of the speaker and to delve deeper, although I was less enamored with his technique when I was in the hot seat.

5 The idea for the convention was generated at a public meeting of the Department of State's Advisory Committee on Private International Law in February 2014. At that meeting, Professor S.I. Strong of the University of Missouri Law School presented her article comparing the legal environment surrounding international commercial arbitration with the legal environment surrounding international commercial mediation and suggested creating a new convention in the area of international mediated settlements. *See* S.I. Strong, "Beyond International Commercial Arbitration? The Promise of International Commercial Mediation," 45 *Wash. U. J. L. & Pol'y* 11 (2014).

6 U.N. Comm'n on Int'l Trade Law, Note by the Secretariat, *Planned and Possible Future Work—Part III, Proposal by the Government of the United States of America: Future Work for Working Group II*, U.N. Doc. A/CN.9/822 (June 2, 2014).

Mr. Schneider seemed skeptical about the wisdom of this project as he engaged with speakers from topic to topic. For those of us favoring the project, the meeting was a cliff hanger. I recall us trying to guess whether the Chair was inclined toward or against the project by the questions he asked, his tone, and his body language—variables that those of us in the dispute resolution field think we are pretty good at reading. During the breaks, we shared our guesses and tried to read the tea leaves, rarely confident about each of our predictions. We were acutely aware of how the meeting would end: Depending on how the Chair reads the group, he would declare a consensus to proceed or not. We were pleased that the week ended with a recommendation that the project be adopted by the Commission.

You can gain an understanding of the thoroughness and range of discussion by reviewing the detailed Working Group II report after the session. It neatly divides the discussion into General Remarks, Legal and Practical Questions, Feasibility and Possible Form of Future Work, and Recommendation to the Commission.[7] Working Group II concluded that:

> After discussion, the Working Group agreed to suggest to the Commission that it be given a mandate to work on the topic of enforcement of settlement agreements, to identify the relevant issues and develop possible solutions, including the preparation of a convention, model provisions or guidance texts. Considering that differing views were expressed as to the form and content, as well as the feasibility, of any particular instrument, it was also agreed to suggest that a mandate on the topic be broad enough to take into account the various approaches and concerns. (See the Recommendation to the Commission after February Working Group II Session at U.N. Doc. A/CN.9/832, IV. D. Paragraph 59 (February 11, 2015)).

II. PROCESS STORY: WORKING GROUP II'S MULTI-PARTY NEGOTIATIONS

Before exploring the next section on the substantive choices in the Convention, you might find informative this brief description of the underlying multiparty process that produced the result. It was well-designed, in my view, to fully engage participants in a robust deliberative process.

---

7 Report of Working Group II (Arbitration and Conciliation) on the work of its sixty-second session (New York, 2–6 February 2015), U.N. Doc. A/CN.9/832, paras. 57–59 (Feb. 11, 2015).

Working Group II selected as Chair of this project, Natalie Morris-Sharma, a member of the Singapore delegation. Under her watchful and skillful supervision, she chaired this almost three-year deliberative process, in collaboration with the expert assistance of UNCITRAL's Secretary to Working Group II, Corinne Montineri. Ms. Morris-Sharma proved to be an impressive Chair due to her thoughtful use of "consultations" discussed below and active listening skills. I was astonished to learn afterwards that she had no formal mediation or facilitation training. She was a natural. She summarized comments succinctly, checked-in with speakers to verify that she accurately understood what she heard, and proficiently used open and closed questions to promote sharing and clarifying information among participants. She also effectively used instinctive humor that helped lubricate the serious deliberations. For example, when the discussions were moving too quickly at one point, she triggered collective laughter when apologizing for her hyperactivity while proclaiming that she had not even drank her first cup of coffee that day.

The Working Group met twice a year for one- to two-week sessions to deliberate issue-by-issue and draft section-by-section with input from the EU Commission and various NGOs in the room.

The consensus-building process featured six methods that were each employed to produce a productive process. I thought it illustrated best practices for managing a large multi-party negotiation.

A. Whole Group Meetings

Working Group II members primarily met together to deliberate in a General Assembly-style room. The Chair guided the discussions for each session by following an agenda and the numbered paragraphs in a report that was published in advance of each session. She piloted the Working Group with an attentive ear for any emerging consensus, opportune moments to break for a "consultation," and differences that may warrant deferring a topic for later discussion.

The room set-up placed the State Delegations in the front half at their delegation tables while the NGOs, regional representatives, and international organizations sat at their tables in the second half of the room. Each seat included an electronic or plastic placard that displayed the name of the country or organization along with headsets to connect with one of five simultaneous translators. Behind each seat were other chairs with headsets to accommodate other members of a delegation or organization. Some of the State Delegations included two to six members so that the number of people in the front of the room could sometimes reach a hundred, and the number of NGOs and regional representatives could add another fifty to seventy-five participants.

The procedure for contributing was simple. Anyone wishing to speak could press a speaker button in NYC or turn the plastic placard upright in Vienna and wait to be called by the Chair. In NYC, where there was no screen that listed speakers waiting for their turn, a speaker did not know how many speakers were in the queue. In Vienna, speakers could gauge when they would be called by seeing the number of placards upright. Speakers were by and large savvy in diplomatic language, respectful, substantive, and worked at maintaining the deliberative thread by referring to prior presenters' remarks. This approach left me feeling that speakers were mostly listening to each other and not just giving speeches.

B. Consultations

The Chair strategically adjourned meetings for a "consultation" when she thought that no consensus was emerging on a significant issue and informal discussions might help. She would frame the issue and invite delegates to meet for thirty or more minutes in small groups to develop proposals for the full group. These consultations, that were used several times for each session, would lead to small group meetings, mini-negotiations, and draft proposals. The Chair would move around the floor listening unobtrusively to small group discussions and gently offer prompts to help keep the consultations on track. The method was exceptionally effective in resolving some of the most contentious issues. I think the consultations succeeded in part because key participants approached these opportunities with a mindset to learn from each other and reconcile differences.

C. Educational Programs for the Delegates and Public

Mediation programs were conducted to educate delegates and the public about issues relevant to key stages of the drafting process. UNCITRAL hosted or co-sponsored three mediation education programs that were organized at the initiative of experts in mediation. I was asked to organize each of the three programs that were each scheduled to coincide with a concurrent Working Group II session.[8] Like other UNCITRAL educational programs, the goal was to help

8 After the first Working Group Session in Vienna in September 2015, the Executive Director of IMI, Irena Vanenkova, offered to put together a mediation education program for delegates who might be interested in gaining more background on mediation to help inform their contributions. UNCITRAL responded positively to the offer. IMI asked me to put together

inform the ongoing deliberative process. These programs appeared valuable because most of the state delegates were more expert on arbitration than mediation. I leave to others who attended to judge the programs' benefits.

D. Contributions by NGOs and EU

UNCITRAL encourages NGOs to attend, participate, and contribute to working group meetings. UNCITRAL values the experience and expertise of NGOs because they reflect the audience that will ultimately use the texts. When this new mediation project was announced, many mediation-related groups registered with UNCITRAL for observer status and sent representatives to the meetings. The format at the sessions made it easy for NGOs to contribute. They had full access to documents, were assigned seats with microphones and headsets, and could offer remarks during the formal meetings and freely talk with State delegates on the floor during breaks and consultations. NGO representatives participated in formal and informal ways as issues emerged. I will cite several examples in this section as illustrations although there were numerous other significant interactions.

---

a program and recruited Professor Janet Martinez at Stanford Law School to participate. We designed the first program for the second working group session on February 2, 2016 at the U.N. in NYC. It compared mediation with the more familiar arbitration process.

After the NYC meeting, there was a sense that another program might be helpful. The second educational program was held during the next session at the U.N. in Vienna on September 21, 2016. That program was well-timed personally because I went to Vienna on the way to my son's wedding in Cyprus the following week! The program was hosted by the Vienna International Arbitral Center and co-sponsored with IMI and IAM. It included the following panelists: Eileen Carroll, QC (Mediator, Co-founder, CEDR, London), Birgit Sambeth Glasner (Mediator, Geneva), Michel Kallipetis (Mediator, London), Allan Stitt (Mediator, Member of Canadian Delegation, Toronto), Josephine Wan-Wen Hadikusumo (Senior Counsel, Asia, Texas Instruments, Singapore), Norris Yang (Mediator, Former Chair of Hong Kong Mediation Council, Hong Kong). I moderated the program that was entitled an opportunity to ask questions of mediators and users.

After the Vienna meeting, some felt that one more program might be useful. The third program was held at the next session at the U.N. in NYC on February 8, 2017. It was hosted by JAMS, and co-sponsored by IMI and IAM. The panel included: Michel Kallipetis (Mediator, London), Louise Otis (Mediator, retired justice of the Quebec Court of Appeals, President of the Administrative Tribunal of OECD, Montreal), Dr. Karl Mackie (Mediator, President, Co-founder, CEDR, London), Pedro Ribeiro (MCIArb, Arbitrator and Mediator, Vice President of CAMARB—Câmara de Arbitragem Empresarial, Brazil), Roland Schroeder (General Electric Global Litigation Counsel, United States), and Allan Stitt (Mediator, Member of Canadian Delegation, Toronto). Similar to the previous program, I moderated it, and we invited participants to ask questions of mediators and users.

An early issue was whether a mediation settlement instrument was even needed when Working Group II was assessing whether to recommend proceeding with the mediation project. At the first session in February 2015, Professor S.I. Strong of the University of Missouri Law School, representing the American Society of International Law, helped bolster the case for the initiative when she presented an empirical study she conducted as evidence of the need for the instrument.[9]

A second original supporting study was conducted by the Institute for Dispute Resolution at New Jersey City University. It was undertaken for IMI and presented at the September 2016 Vienna Session. The study found that the majority of users and stakeholders in the survey and at the Global Pound Conference believed that a global mechanism to enforce mediation settlements would improve commercial dispute resolution in international business transactions.[10]

Another issue that got my personal attention was whether the enforcement instrument should apply to only monetary terms in a settlement. At the first Working Group II meeting in February 2015, several delegations and at least one NGO representative asserted that any instrument should be limited because of the practical difficulties of enforcing non-monetary terms. This suggestion was alarming, in my view. If an international treaty restricted enforcement to only monetary terms, parties may view mediation primarily for resolving this narrow class of disputes. This view would foreclose the full

---

9 The delegates were provided with a preliminary report that was subsequently published as a law review article. S.I. Strong, "Realizing Rationality: An Empirical Assessment of International Commercial Mediation," 73 *Wash. & Lee L. Rev.* 1973 (2016). *See also* S.I. Strong, "Use and Perception of International Commercial Mediation and Conciliation: A Preliminary Report on Issues Relating to the Proposed UNCITRAL Convention on International Commercial Mediation and Conciliation" (University of Missouri School of Law Legal Studies, Research Paper No. 2014–28). Preliminary findings from the study had previously been reviewed by the UNCITRAL Secretariat and the United States and were referenced in documents circulated prior to the February 2015 meeting. *See* UNCITRAL, Note by the Secretariat, *Settlement of commercial disputes: enforceability of settlement agreements resulting from international commercial conciliation/mediation*, U.N. Doc. A/CN.9/WG.II/WP.187, at 6 n.16 (Nov. 27, 2014). *See also* Comments Received From States, Settlement of Commercial Disputes: Enforceability of Settlement Agreements Resulting From International Commercial Conciliation/Mediation—Revision of the UNCITRAL Notes on Organizing Arbitral Proceedings, U.N. Doc. A/CN.9/WG.II/WP.188, at 6 n.7 (Dec. 23, 2014).

10 *Sing. Ref. Bk.*, David S. Weiss & Michael R. Griffith, "Report on Empirical Study of Business Users Regarding International Mediation and Enforcement Mechanisms," 20 *Cardozo J. Conflict Resol.* 1133 (2019).

benefits of mediation for uncovering other terms that may better meet parties' interests. After researching whether enforcement was so limited for enforcing arbitration awards under the New York Convention (United Nations Convention on the Recognition and Enforcement of Foreign Arbitral Awards, New York, 10 June 1958), I presented to the working group the NY Convention precedent and its successful experience with a broader instrument and the substantive and policy reasons favoring that approach. Fortunately, a broader view was ultimately adopted by Working Group II, and the final convention covers compliance with all settlement terms.[11]

Mediation-related NGOs especially rallied at the Vienna meetings in September 2016 when several difficult questions converged for discussion: Would the convention apply to private parties on an opt-in or opt-out basis? Should an enforceable agreement be certified as one that was the product of a private mediation, and if so, how would it be certified? And, would a defense to enforcement include certain types of misbehavior by the mediator, and if so, how narrow would the defense be framed? These questions fell clearly within the bailiwick of the mediation-related NGOs, and their representatives offered much formal and informal input into various proposals. These questions were ultimately resolved as part of the break-through "compromise" discussed in the next section.[12]

As these several examples illustrate, NGOs contributed in various ways during the drafting process. They were welcomed by many State delegations, in my experience. However, like any multi-party process, it is difficult to assess the impact of most individual contributions. Nevertheless, I think NGOs can safely claim that their participation enriched the discussion and understanding of a number of key issues.

In addition to various NGOs participating, the European Union ("EU"), as a regional economic integration organization represented by the European Commission, participated actively throughout the three years. EU member states made up more than 25 percent of the delegates on the floor at any meeting.[13] They were ably represented by Norel Rosner, Legislative Officer, who

11 One delegation, in an effort to find a solution that may appeal to all sides, proposed that the convention cover non-monetary features with the option for a State to file a reservation to exclude enforcement of long-term or complex obligations.

12 *See* Section III.

13 UNCITRAL membership of 60 States included 13 members from the EU (21.6%). For the Working Group II meetings, attendance varied. For the February 2017 Session in NY, for example, 12 out of the 41 members in attendance were members of the EU (29%) plus 9

contributed much to the whole group meetings, during consultations, and in informal discussions.

E. The Travaux Preparatoires (Official Record of the Negotiation)

The *travaux preparatoires,* known as travaux, reports, and secretariat notes, were prepared before each session and at the end of each meeting day. These various documents aided the deliberations as they unfolded by creating a record so that participants could track where they have been and where they were going.

These documents standout for two reasons. First, they offered a detailed contemporaneous record of what transpired (issues that were considered and what was discussed). Second, there were no personal names, countries or NGOs associated with the remarks and exchanges. The entire written record was anonymous in order to promote candid exchanges and reduce the need to grandstand for constituencies back home.

Corrinne Montineri, as the secretary of UNCITRAL Working Group II, performed the herculean task of preparing the numerous lengthy documents that aided the working group's deliberations. Ms. Montineri, with help from her colleague, Jae Sung Lee, prepared before each upcoming session a provisional agenda, a Report of Working Group II that covered what happened at the prior session, and a Note by the Secretariat as background and guide for the session. Then Ms. Montineri with her colleague prepared daily "draft" reports of what transpired each day and distributed them before the next day of meetings. At the end of each day, she would return to her office to meticulously prepare the draft report for the next day while the delegates and other representatives took a break for the evening to socialize and meet informally before returning for another workday.

These *travaux preparatoires* are posted on the UNCITRAL website, making them a widely available source for clarifying and interpreting the final model law and convention. You will see many references to these sources in this article.

---

more EU countries as observers. UNCITRAL, Report of Working Group II (Dispute Settlement) on the work of its sixty-sixth session (New York, February 6–10, 2017), U.N. Doc. A/CN.9/901 (Feb. 16, 2017). In the last meeting in February 2018, when the final draft was adopted, 12 out of the 33 members in attendance were members of the EU (36%) plus 4 more countries as observers. *See* UNCITRAL, Report of Working Group II (Dispute Settlement) on the work of its sixty-eighth session (New York, February 5–9, 2018), U.N. Doc. A/CN.9/934 (Feb. 19, 2018).

F. Voting

Decisions were made by consensus. No formal voting took place as a general rule, so I was surprised to learn at my first meeting. The Chair, Ms. Morris-Sharma, had the responsibility of recognizing when the working group reached a consensus. She used various techniques to test for one. For example, she would declare "that not hearing any more comments or disagreements she will move on." That comment would ferret out further concerns if there were any. Or, she would invite other comments with the remark that "if there are no more, she will declare a consensus." These types of prompts helped surface an emerging consensus or an occasion for consultation or deferring an issue. This form of decision making imposed a heavy responsibility on the Chair to listen attentively, astutely read the group, and proactively build consensus.[14]

These six methods to engage participants were used throughout the week-long sessions over the almost three years of deliberations.

III. SUBSTANTIVE STORY: KEY ISSUES AND HOW RESOLVED

This section explains key provisions of the Convention including the five-point compromise that likely will be of interest to mediation-savvy readers and states that are contemplating adopting the Convention. For states that might not be ready to ratify the Convention, the working group prepared, as an alternative, an amendment to the Model Law on International Commercial Conciliation. The Model Law will not be discussed.

A. Article 1. Scope of Application

Article 1 frames the narrow scope of the Convention.

Article 1.1 limits its application to disputes that are international, presumably to little surprise, and includes a definition of international that focuses on the place of a party's business, where a "substantial part of the obligations under the agreement is performed," or where the subject matter is "mostly closely connected."

Article 1.2 and 1.3 further limits the scope by specifying what disputes and settlement agreements are *not* covered, with limits that will surprise and disappoint some.

---

14 UNCITRAL, *supra* note 1, at 6, para. 14.

Article 1.2 states that the Convention does not apply to settlement agreements that arise out of consumer transactions or relate to family, inheritance, and employment law.

Article 1.3 tries to avoid overlap with other enforcement regimes that might apply to mediated settlement agreements. Some delegations wanted to avoid duplicating regimes such as the Hague Conference instrument, while others were fine with states providing multiple avenues for relief under different instruments. They were less concerned with overlap and more concerned about avoiding gaps by other instruments imposing ceilings, not floors.

The Working Group ultimately decided to restrict the scope so that the Convention would not apply to settlement agreements that have been approved by a court or concluded in the course of a court proceeding and would be enforceable as a State court judgment. Also, it would not apply to settlement agreements enforceable as an arbitral award.

B. Article 2. Definitions

Article 2.3 offers a definitions section with a surprise that I suspect will be embraced by much of the contemporary mediation world. It replaced the word "conciliation" with the word "mediation." After UNCITRAL has used the word "conciliation" in the Conciliation Rules (1980) and in the Model Law on International Conciliation (2002), Working Group II made this long overdue word change. It then labeled the Convention as "United Nations Convention on International Settlement Agreements Resulting from *Mediation* (italics added)."

The Working Group offered the following explanation:

> ... the Commission decided to use the term 'mediation' instead in an effort to adapt to the actual and practical use of the terms and with the expectation that this change will facilitate the promotion and heighten the visibility of the instruments. This change in terminology does not have any substantive or conceptual implications.[15]

Although some might object because they think there is a worthwhile distinction to maintain between mediation as a more facilitative process and

15 U.N. Comm'n on Int'l Trade Law, Note by the Secretariat, *Settlement of Commercial Disputes, International Commercial Mediation: Draft Convention on International Settlement Agreements Resulting from Mediation*, U.N. Doc. A/CN.9/942, at II.B(1) (Mar. 2, 2018).

conciliation as a more evaluative process, I would expect most of the mediation audience will welcome this change in terminology.

C. Article 4. Requirements for Reliance on Settlement Agreements

Parties must supply evidence of a "settlement agreement that resulted from mediation." This unexpected proof requirement was subject to considerable discussion and reflects what the drafting group characterized as a "balance between, on the one hand, the formalities that are required to ascertain that a settlement agreement result from mediation and, on the other hand, the need for the draft convention to preserve the flexible nature of the mediation process."[16] It is in this spirit that this proof requirement should be interpreted.

This requirement was born out of the fear that the Convention might be used for illegitimate purposes. Some delegates wanted to be sure that the treaty would not be used for an illegal scheme like money laundering or for mediations that are not genuine in the view of some delegates such as when a couple of friends in a dispute meet in a pub. It is for these reasons that the Convention not only requires that the agreement be signed by the parties but also that there is "evidence that the settlement agreement resulted from mediation" by one of four ways: the mediator's signature on the settlement agreement, the mediator's signature on a separate document indicating a mediation was carried out, an attestation by an administering institution, or "any other evidence acceptable to the competent authority."[17]

D. Article 5. Grounds for Refusing to Grant Relief

Article 5 on defenses posed the risk of crippling the Convention by establishing facially sound grounds for refusing relief that could be abused. Some delegates argued that preserving defenses was vital for protecting parties with a valid reason for not complying with a settlement agreement. At the policy level, they offered a persuasive argument. But if all or most possible defenses were preserved, the Convention would fail to serve its primary purpose of expediting compliance. This Article was subject to multiple rounds of discussion at different meetings including a gallant effort in the final session to regroup and refine the grounds to avoid overlap. As this last effort unfolded, I was hoping it would lead to changes that would reduce the risk of misuse. The failure to gain consensus was due to the "need to accommodate the concerns of different

16 U.N. Doc. A/CN.9/942, *supra* note 15, at II.B(7).

17 *Id.* at II.A, art. 4.1(a) & (b).

domestic legal systems"[18] and left disconcerting space for abuse, in my view.

Preserving several limited defenses made sense like the opportunity to present proof that the party "was under some incapacity" or that the settlement agreement was not binding, was subsequently modified, or has been performed. Other defenses, however, leave space to ferment trouble by defendants who want to avoid compliance.

Two troublesome defenses stand out. One is the defense that an agreement is "null and void, inoperative or incapable of being performed under the law to which the parties have validly subjected it. . . ."[19] Another is the defense that the obligations in the agreement are "not clear or comprehensible."[20] By asserting these defenses, defendants may be able to transform this new expedited process into a more protracted and expensive one similar to the one before the Convention. Courts should construe narrowly these defenses[21] and others in view of the purpose of the Convention.

E. "The Compromise"

As the deliberations progressed from semi-annual meeting to semi-annual meeting, Working Group II resolved the easier issues while deferring the harder ones. Among those favoring a Convention, we feared that when deliberations reached the remaining more controversial and complex issues, the resolutions risked gutting the instrument. The fears were palpable in the hallways. Several worrisome questions occupied me: Would the Convention include a large hole for a stream of legal claims based on mediator misconduct that would be difficult to prove and would prolong the compliance process? Would the benefits be limited to only parties that elect to opt-in to the Convention? If so, only diligent parties who overcome the status quo bias will likely elect an enforcement process that is supposed to be the better one. Would the entire enterprise for a convention be derailed by the argument that formulating global standards is premature for what some viewed as an incipient field?

18 *Id.* at II.B, para. 8.

19 *Id.* at II.A, art. 5(1)(b)(i).

20 *Id.* at II.A, art. 5(1)(c)(ii).

21 For the "null and void," etc. defense, Working Group II specifically states that it intends a narrow interpretation based on adopting language from the New York Convention. *See* U.N. Comm'n on Int'l Trade Law, Note by the Secretariat, *Settlement of Commercial Disputes, International Commercial Conciliation: Preparation of an Instrument on Enforcement of International Commercial Settlement Agreements Resulting from Conciliation*, U.N. Doc. A/CN.9/WG.II/WP.202, para. 43 (July 14, 2017).

These sort of questions among others moved different sides toward a "compromise proposal." The compromise was the result of numerous discussions among delegates, NGO representatives, and the EU in full working group meetings, consultations, informal gatherings, hallways, and over meals. The five elements of the compromise were initially "cobbled" together by about a dozen delegates during lunch on Tuesday, February 7, 2017 and presented after lunch to the full Working Group. The timing left the remaining three days of the session to flesh out the details. And then a snow blizzard on Thursday closed down the island of Manhattan, including the UN for the day. This lost day turned into an opportunity. Instead of enjoying the freshly fallen snow in Central Park, a number of delegates and NGOs met at a private law office near the UN. They worked together to overcome some final hurdles and solidify details that could be presented to the full Working Group.[22] The five-point "compromise," which it became known as, created a pathway for resolving the remaining most contentious issues.

1. Opt-out Provision (Convention, Article 8.1(a) & (b))

Should the Convention apply automatically with an opt-out provision? Those favoring opt-out argued that the instrument should apply automatically like the New York Convention applies to enforcement of arbitral awards. This approach also would be consistent with the objective of the instrument to make it easier to secure compliance with settlement agreements. Others argued for party autonomy. Parties should opt-in only after they understood how the Convention operates and made an informed choice to do so.

This party autonomy argument appealed to several mediation experts, so I learned when preparing for the Vienna expert panel program in September 2016. During the evening before the program as the panelists were conferring, some panelists expressed concern that an opt-out provision ran counter to the principle of party self-determination that forms the foundation for the mediation process. Parties should make an informed choice to use the Convention, so they argued as some state delegates did during the meetings. I was stunned by the resistance because the benefits of an opt-out provision seemed so obvious. Instead of the after-dinner meeting offering a congenial opportunity to get acquainted over drinks and prepare for the next day, it turned into an intense and lively discussion. We met late into the night as we explored the

22 U.N. Doc. A/CN.9/901, *supra* note 13, paras. 51–93.

pros and cons of opt-in and opt-out and the foundational principle of party self-determination.

By the end of the evening, I struggled to succinctly frame the issue as: Would the new instrument offer a better default process for enforcement than the one now in place without the instrument? If so, that process should apply subject an opt-out provision. If not, I suggested that we should not be supporting the new instrument. When we reconvened our planning meeting over lunch the next day, the panel unanimously favored the opt-out approach. It became apparent to all of us that opt-out favored the default process, and this enterprise was aiming to fashion a better process for enforcing mediated settlement agreements.

Ultimately, the Drafting Group adopted the policy of automatically applying the Convention with an opt-out option for a party to the settlement agreement.[23] Even though the Convention omits explicitly authorizing private opt-outs, the understanding is that parties to a settlement agreement can agree to exclude the application of the Convention, and the clause will be upheld under Article 5.1(d) as a defense based on complying with the settlement terms.[24]

However, Article 8.1(b) authorizes a State party to the Convention to opt-out of the Convention's automatic application in a declaration. If a State opts-out, private parties can still opt-in to the Convention by private agreement (such as in the settlement agreement or the agreement to mediate).

2. Grounds for Refusing to Grant Relief Based on Mediator Behavior (Convention, Article 5.1(e) & (f))

Some delegates wanted to include a defense to enforcement based on bad mediator behavior. They saw a need to protect parties against unfair treatment by a mediator or failure of a mediator to disclose information that calls into question his or her impartiality. Initial concerns related to the impact of a mediator's non-compliance with professional conduct standards or domestic law.

---

23 Art. 8 distinguishes between "parties to the convention," which are Contracting States, and "parties to the settlement agreement," which are private parties. For further explanation, see U.N. Doc. A/CN.9/942, *supra* note 15, at II.B(3).

24 U.N. Doc. A/CN.9/934, *supra* note 13, para. 78; U.N. Comm'n on Int'l Trade Law, Report of the U.N. Comm'n on Int'l Trade Law, Fifty-first session (25 June–13 July 2018), U.N. Doc. A/73/17, at III C.2., para. 68 (2018); U.N. Comm'n on Int'l Trade Law, Report of the U.N. Comm'n on Int'l Trade Law, Fifty-first session (25 June–13 July 2018), U.N. Doc. A/73/17, at III B.1., paras. 37–40 (2018).

For people in the mediation field, this defense roused fears of abuse by parties who are looking for an excuse to get out of an agreement. Although it is rare that these mediator misbehaviors occur and have an impact, the claims are theoretically possible, and some delegates thought should be guarded against. For many in the mediation field as advocates or mediators, these claims are familiar ones that can be asserted by a party trying to avoid a commitment. These claims also can be used by a party to protract the compliance process and make it costlier as leverage for re-negotiating a settlement.

When discussing these concerns at the February 2016 New York session, it was considered how mediation is different than arbitration. It was recognized that parties voluntarily use mediation, a mediator lacked authority to impose a settlement, any resulting agreement is voluntarily entered into, and parties are free to withdraw from the process at any time. At the end of the discussions, delegates were encouraged to consider before the next meetings in Vienna whether these mediator misconduct risks might be covered by other defenses like the public policy defense in the instrument and to review the practical and judicial experiences in their jurisdictions.[25]

At the following Vienna session in September 2016, a drafting process began with the goal of protecting against these risks of mediator misbehavior while limiting the opportunity for abuse and leverage to renegotiate settlements. One of the early drafts that stimulated an energetic drafting process stated:

> Draft provision 8 (Grounds for refusing [recognition] and enforcement) (key language in italics)[26]
> (1) [Recognition and] enforcement may be refused … if that party furnishes … proof that:
> (e) *The conciliator failed to maintain fair treatment of the parties, or did not disclose circumstances likely to give rise to justifiable doubts as to its impartiality or independence.*

25 UNCITRAL, Report of Working Group II (Arbitration and Conciliation) on the work of its sixty-fourth session (New York, February 1–5, 2016), U.N. Doc. A/CN.9/867, paras. 170–75 (Feb. 10, 2016).

26 U.N. Comm'n on Int'l Trade Law, Note by the Secretariat, *Settlement of Commercial Disputes, International Commercial Conciliation: Preparation of an Instrument on Enforcement of International Commercial Settlement Agreements Resulting from Conciliation*, U.N. Doc. A/CN.9WG.II/WP.198, at II.D, para. 35 (June 30, 2016). The final draft became art. 5 in the Convention.

After much discussion of divergent views, exchange of multiple drafts, and parsing of language that included active participatiopan by NGOs, the emerging view was that serious mediator misconduct could probably be covered by other defenses in the instrument. The delegates that wanted additional protections emphasized the significant role of the mediator and the need to retain a defense even if it is difficult to prove a party has been treated unfairly. Unlike arbitration, it was asserted by those favoring a protective provision, there was no means to challenge the mediation process or the conduct of the conciliator.

As delegates searched for a proposal that met everyone's concerns, it was suggested that the scope of challengeable behavior be limited to when it has a "direct impact on the settlement agreement," to "exceptional circumstances," or when the conduct has a "material impact" or "undue influence." It also was suggested that subparagraph (e) above be divided into two separate subparagraphs: one on fair treatment and the other on disclosure.[27]

The final version approved by Working Group II adopted the two subparagraphs approach and retained narrow defenses that addressed the underlying goal of protecting parties from a badly behaving mediator while fashioning language that reduced the risk of parties exploiting defenses to evade commitments. The final language of Article 5, with italics to highlight safeguards against abuse, are:[28]

> Section 1(e) There was a *serious* breach by the mediator of standards applicable to the mediator or the mediation *without which breach that party would not have entered into the settlement agreement*; or
> (f) There was a failure by the mediator to disclose to the parties circumstances that raise *justifiable* doubts as to the mediator's impartiality or independence and such *failure to disclose has a material impact or undue influence on a party without which failure that party would not have entered into the settlement agreement.*

---

27 *See* U.N.G.A., Daily Minutes, U.N. Doc. A/CN.9/WG.II/LXV/CRP.1/Add.4, paras. 5–11 (Sept. 16, 2016) (Draft report, addendum, distributed day after discussions); U.N.G.A., Daily Minutes, U.N. Doc. A/CN.9/WG.II/LXV/CRP.1/Add.7, paras. 15–18 (para. 18 refers to compromise solution) (Sept. 21, 2016) (distributed day after discussions).

28 For a more complete analysis of this section on mediator misbehavior, including the hurdles to proving the defense, see Sing. Ref. Bk., Michel Kallipetis, "Singapore Convention Defences Based on Mediator's Misconduct: Articles 5.1(e) & (f)," 20 *Cardozo J. Conflict Resol.* 1197 (2019).

3. Avoid Overlap with Other Enforcement Regimes (Convention, Article 1.3)

Another issue was whether the compliance mechanism in the Convention should avoid overlap with other compliance regimes. As discussed under Article 1.3 on Scope of Application above, the Working Group decided to try to minimize overlap by not applying the Convention to settlement agreements enforceable as a court judgment or arbitration awards.[29]

4. Defining "Recognition and Enforcement" (Convention, Article 3)

Another issue was whether to use the language "recognition and enforcement" of settlement agreements in the Convention, a phrase that figures prominently and frequently in the New York Convention on arbitral awards including in its title.[30] Because part of the phrase, "recognition," has a different meaning in civil law jurisdictions than in common law jurisdictions, delegates wanted to draft a convention that would reduce the risk of confusion. It was not easy at the meetings for me as a common law trained lawyer to understand the explanations and reconcile the different interpretations. The solution fashioned by the delegates was to omit the term "recognition" and design a separate article, that became the short and significant Article 3.

Article 3 separated the two concepts. Article 3.1 covers "enforcement" by giving each party to the Convention the right to enforce a settlement agreement in accordance with the Convention.[31] Article 3.2 covers "recognition" without using the term. Instead, the "recognition" concept is replaced with a functional definition that uses other words to address key aspects of recognition such as the ability to assert a mediated settlement as a complete defense if another party tries to raise the underlying settled claims.

Other articles in the Convention do not repeat Article 3's meticulously negotiated and somewhat convoluted language. Instead, the other articles use the blanket term "relief" when referring collectively to the concept of "enforcement" in Article 3.1 and the functional "recognition" description in Article 3.2.[32]

---

29 *See* Singapore Convention art. 1.3(a) & (b).

30 United Nations Convention on the Recognition and Enforcement of Foreign Arbitral Awards, June 10, 1958, 21 U.S.T. 2517, 330 U.N.T.S. 3, arts. I–VII.

31 The term "enforcement" shows up in a few other places but for other purposes. *See* Singapore Convention arts. 1(3)(a)(ii) & (b), art. 12(4).

32 *See* the use of the term "relief" in Singapore Convention arts. 4, 5, 6, & 12.

For a full understanding of this two-paragraph, complex provision, read *Recognition by Any Other Name: Article 3 of the Singapore Convention on Mediation* by Timothy Schnabel in the *Singapore Mediation Convention Reference Book.*[33] In the article, Tim Schnabel emphasizes the central importance of this Article to the entire Convention when he points out that: "Yet only Article 3 imposes affirmative obligations on Parties to the Convention. All other articles merely play supporting roles, such as placing boundaries on the Convention's application, setting forth procedural rules or exceptions, and providing the mechanics for the Convention to operate as a treaty. In other words, all the other articles are used to determine whether and how the Article 3 obligations apply, but only Article 3 itself imposes substantive duties on states that join the Convention." Those duties are to enforce a settlement agreement in accordance with the terms of the Convention.

5. Two Options for States: Convention or Model Law

Central to the five-point compromise was the dual instruments proposal. It resolved a distributive choice that was blocking progress: Would there be a convention or model law? The proposal avoided a choice that would have produced a winner and loser. It offered something to both sides. For those states that opposed a convention because they wanted more time to gain experience with mediation and compliance issues, they could adopt the model text in their domestic law and join the convention later. For those states that favored a convention because they are ready for its benefits, they could ratify it under the dual instruments resolution. The General Assembly, it also was suggested, should not express any preference between the two options.[34]

The Working Group formulated this formal resolution to encapsulate its goals for adoption by the Commission and for the General Assembly:

> Recalling that the decision of the Commission to concurrently prepare a convention on international settlement agreements resulting from mediation and an amendment to the UNCITRAL Model Law on International Commercial Conciliation was intended to accommodate the different levels of experience with mediation in different jurisdictions, and

33 *See Sing. Ref. Bk.*, Timothy Schnabel, "Recognition by Any Other Name: Article 3 of the Singapore Convention on Mediation," 20 *Cardozo J. Conflict Resol.* 1181 (2019).

34 U.N. Doc. A/CN.9/901, *supra* note 13, paras. 89–93; U.N. Doc. A/CN.9/942, *supra* note 15, at II.B Annotations, para. 12.

to provide States with consistent standards on cross-border enforcement of international settlement agreements resulting from mediation, without creating any expectation that interested States may adopt either instrument. See A/CN.9/942, II.B Annotations, Paragraph 12 (2 March 2018).

After the five-point compromise was reached, the delegates wrapped up the drafting process by addressing some standard and not particularly controversial provisions, although one routine provision provoked an entertaining exchange with substantive implications. It was proposed in the draft provision that the Convention become effective six months after the third state ratifies it. During the discussions, a delegate suggested that the Convention should not be effective until ten states ratify it, followed by other delegates suggesting other numbers ranging from three and ten ratifying states. The Chair, using her instinctive humor to make a point, remarked that this is starting to sound like a bingo game or haggling at a bazaar. She then asked delegates to support any proposed number with a rationale. In a very short time, the discussion returned to the original number of three ratifying states and reached a consensus.[35]

This last discussion highlighted another feature of the Convention mentioned by a delegate that is worth noting as a final point. The Convention is not a bilateral treaty. It is not limited to compliance with settlements "from" a State that is also a party. This means that settlements are subject to the Convention in any country that is a Party even if the person or entity suing is not from a country that ratified the Convention.

IV. CONCLUSION—WHAT HAPPENED NEXT?

The recommendations of Working Group II were adopted by UNCITRAL on June 25, 2018. On that warm day at the UN in NYC, delegates and representatives sang a celebratory song composed for the occasion.[36] It was entitled "Good Memories" and was sung to the melody of *Home on the Range*. It also paid tribute to Tim Schnabel's leadership for moving this initiative

35 U.N. Doc. A/CN.9/942, *supra* note 15, at II, art. 14.

36 The song was composed by three UNCITRAL members who are too modest to be publicly recognized for their authorship of this original composition for the 51st Commission of UNCITRAL—New York—25 June 2018.

forward and to Singapore for offering to host opening the Convention for signature.

> Oh give me a forum
> Where mediation is at home
> Where debate and amendments flow free
> Where seldom is heard, a discouraging word
> And results are here for us to see
>
> *Ohhhhh forum to engage, where each of us wrote a page, where Tim took the lead and we followed with speed—mediation convention hurray*
>
> When the work first begun
> And the quorum was found
> With the New York Convention as guide
> We all shared our views
> And now we share the news
> The Singapore convention is live *ohhhh forum to engage …* .

At the June 25th Commission meeting, the Commission adopted by consensus the following decision and recommendation for the General Assembly:[37]

> *The United Nations Commission on International Trade Law,*
>
> *Recalling* its mandate under General Assembly resolution 2205 (XXI) of 17 December 1966 to further the progressive harmonization and unification of the law of international trade and in that respect to bear in mind the interests of all peoples, in particular those of developing countries, in the extensive development of international trade,
>
> *Recognizing* the value of mediation as a method of amicably settling disputes arising in the context of international commercial relations,
>
> *Recalling* General Assembly resolution 57/18 of 19 November 2002 noting the adoption of the UNCITRAL Model Law on International Commercial Conciliation and expressing the conviction that the Model Law, together with the UNCITRAL Conciliation Rules recommended

37 U.N. Doc. A/73/17, *supra* note 24, at III C.2, para. 68.

by the General Assembly in its resolution 35/52 of 4 December 1980, contributes significantly to the establishment of a harmonized legal framework for the fair and efficient settlement of disputes arising in international commercial relations,

Convinced that the adoption of a convention on international settlement agreements resulting from mediation that is acceptable to States with different legal, social, and economic systems would complement the existing legal framework on international mediation and contribute to the development of harmonious international economic relations,

Recalling that the decision of the Commission to concurrently prepare a convention on international settlement agreements resulting from mediation and an amendment to the UNCITRAL Model Law on International Commercial Conciliation was intended to accommodate the different levels of experience with mediation in different jurisdictions, and to provide States with consistent standards on cross-border enforcement of international settlement agreements resulting from mediation, without creating any expectation that interested States may adopt either instrument,[38]

Noting that the preparation of the draft convention on international settlement agreements resulting from mediation was the subject of due deliberation in the Commission and that the draft convention benefited from consultations with Governments and interested intergovernmental and international non-governmental organizations,

Having considered the draft convention at its fifty-first session, in 2018,

Drawing attention to the fact that the text of the draft convention was circulated for comment before the fifty-first session of the Commission to all Governments invited to attend the meetings of the Commission and the Working Group as members and observers,

Considering that the draft convention has received sufficient consideration and has reached the level of maturity for it to be generally acceptable to States:

38 U.N. GAOR, 72nd Sess., supplement no. 17, U.N. Doc. A/72/17, paras. 238 & 239 (2017). *See also* U.N. Doc. A/CN.9/901, *supra* note 13, para. 93.

1. *Submits* to the General Assembly the draft convention on international settlement agreements resulting from mediation, as it appears in annex I to the report of the United Nations Commission on International Trade Law on the work of its fifty-first session;
2. *Recommends* that the General Assembly, taking into account the extensive consideration given to the draft convention by the Commission and its Working Group II (Dispute Settlement), consider the draft convention with a view to (a) adopting, at its seventy-third session, on the basis of the draft convention approved by the Commission, a United Nations Convention on International Settlement Agreements Resulting from Mediation; (b) authorizing a signing ceremony to be held as soon as practicable in 2019 in Singapore, upon which the Convention would be open for signature; and (c) recommending that the Convention be known as the "Singapore Convention on Mediation";
3. *Requests* the Secretary-General to publish the Convention, upon adoption, including electronically and in the six official languages of the United Nations, and to disseminate it broadly to Governments and other interested bodies.

The General Assembly approved the Convention and the title as the Singapore Convention on Mediation on December 20, 2018.

The last step started on August 7, 2019 when the Convention opened for signature in Singapore and 46 countries signed it.[39] The opening ceremony launched the final stage of "ratification, acceptance, approval, or accession" by the states.[40] The Convention becomes effective six months after the third state proceeds from signing to adopting the Convention. Each state has its own requirements for ratification.

39 *See* Singapore Convention art. 11. The official list of signatories that will be updated in perpetuity can be found on the UNCITRAL website by searching for "Singapore Convention on Mediation." *See Status: United Nations Convention on International Settlement Agreements Resulting from Mediation*, UNCITRAL, https://uncitral.un.org/en/texts/mediation/conventions/international_settlement_agreements/status (last visited Sept. 10, 2019).

40 *See* Singapore Convention art. 14.

I hope that this article will help inform discussions and choices as states study the Convention, assess its benefits, and decide whether to adopt it. I also hope that this article will be of value after the Convention becomes effective for when parties are implementing and interpreting the Convention.

Part Three

Negotiations

Ch. 15 *Mediation Representation*, Ch. 1, "Negotiating in Mediations," 3rd Edition (Aspen Coursebook, Wolter-Kluwer, 2013)

Ch. 16 "Fashioning an Effective Negotiation Style: Choosing Between Good Practices, Tactics and Tricks," in *The Negotiator's Desk Reference* (Andrea K. Schneider and Christopher Honeyman, eds., DRI Press/Mitchell Hamline School of Law and NDR Books LLC, 2017) (Expanded version of article published in 23 *Harv. Neg L.R.* 319 (2018))

Ch. 17 "Nelson Mandela as Negotiator—What Can We Learn from Him?," 31 *Ohio State Journal of Dispute Resolution* 19 (2016)

CHAPTER 15

Mediation Representation

3rd Edition
2013
Harold I. Abramson
Wolters Kluwer, Law & Business

Chapter 1
"Negotiating in Mediations"

"What is needed are more problem solvers who care, not just about winning, but about really solving the problems."
Carrie J. Menkel-Meadow[1]

Topics in this chapter include:

1. Effective Negotiation Approach and Style for Mediation Advocacy
Questions

2. Positional Approach and Style
Questions

3. Problem-Solving Approach and Style
Questions

4. Negotiation Stages as a Roadmap

5. Stages of the Positional Approach (Roadmap)

6. Stages of the Problem-Solving Approach (Roadmap)

7. Converting the Positional Negotiator into a Problem Solver
Questions

8. Checklists: Positional and Problem-Solving Negotiations

---

1 Carrie J. Menkel-Meadow, "When Winning Isn't Everything: The Lawyer as Problem Solver," 28 *Hofstra L. Rev.* 905, 923 (2000). *Also see* Carrie J Menkel-Meadow, "Toward Another View of Legal Negotiation: The Structure of Problem Solving," 21 *UCLA L. Rev.* 754 (1984); and Robert Mnookin, Scott Peppet and Andrew Tulumello, *Beyond Winning—Negotiating to Create Value in Deals and Disputes* (2000).

1. EFFECTIVE NEGOTIATION APPROACH AND STYLE FOR MEDIATION ADVOCACY

If you know how to negotiate effectively, you possess the foundation for advocating effectively in mediation. Remember the often-cited axiom "The mediation process is simply a negotiation process with the assistance of a third party"—a proposition captured by the Mediation Representation Triangle. The first side of the triangle represents your negotiation approach.

The negotiations examined in this book involve the settlement of legal cases that are in court or moving toward court. Any litigator knows that negotiations are an integral part of the litigation process. Before initiating a court case, litigators typically try to negotiate a settlement. After initiating the court case, both sides customarily try again. After some discovery, the sides are likely to try again, and to keep trying right up to the doorsteps of the courthouse. (*See* chart.)

Negotiations are so enmeshed in the litigation process that colorful descriptions of the intimate relationship between negotiations and adjudication have been coined. One thoughtful observer conjured up the illuminating image of "bargaining in the shadow of the law."[2] Another astute observer suggested that instead of being viewed as separate processes, litigation and negotiation should be viewed as a single process of disputing, called "litigotiation." He defined litigotiation as "the strategic pursuit of a settlement through mobilizing the court process."[3]

Negotiations as Part of the Litigation Process
1. Negotiate
2. Serve Complaint/Answer
3. Negotiate
4. Preliminary Discovery and Motions
5. Negotiate
6. More Discovery and Motions
7. Negotiate
8. Trial
9. Negotiate
10. Appeal
11. Negotiate

2 *See* Robert H. Mnookin & Lewis Kornhauser, "Bargaining in the Shadow of the Law: The Case of Divorce," 88 *Yale L. J.* 950 (1979).

3 Marc Galanter, "Worlds of Deals: Using Negotiation to Teach about Legal Process," 34 *J. Legal Educ.* 268, 268 (1984).

In these legal negotiations, attorneys frequently try to demonstrate that they are likely to win in court and then use this predicted outcome as the reference point for forming settlement proposals and compromises. So it is not surprising that attorneys involved in litigation negotiate like litigators by asserting the positions they take in court in the negotiation. But to realize the full potential of mediation, attorneys should consider negotiating differently. Instead of negotiating positionally, they should negotiate as problem solvers.[4]

Negotiation Approach as Process of Creating and Claiming

A negotiation can be defined simply as a process where disputing parties create and claim value. Parties may initially try to create value that can be divided between them, a process popularly known to the point of clichè as "expanding the pie." After employing various creating strategies or choosing not to try, parties employ strategies for claiming the value.[5] Strategies for creating and claiming value are conventionally divided into two negotiation approaches: positional, also known as competitive or adversarial, and problem-solving, also known as interest-based, principled, or possibly cooperative.

The positional approach, explored in detail in this chapter, is the customary claiming strategy, where you view the dispute as distributive in that you claim something, usually money, at the expense of the other party. This chapter also considers claiming strategies where your gain is not necessarily at the expense of the other side, such as when an employee trades receiving a good job reference and help finding a new position for getting laid off so that the employer can retrench. Both parties can gain without significant cost to the giving side, especially when compared to what the giving party gains.

Under the problem-solving approach, also examined in detail in this chapter, the dispute is viewed as potentially integrative, and parties engage in both creating and claiming strategies. In addition to considering various

---

4 *See* Andrea Kupfer Schneider, "Shattering Negotiation Myths: Empirical Evidence on the Effectiveness of Negotiation Style," 7 *Harv. Negot. L. Rev.* 143, 196 (2002). (In an extensive study of negotiation styles, 75 percent of true problem-solving negotiators were considered effective as compared with less than 50 percent of adversarial bargainers, a percentage that shrunk to 25 percent when limited to adversarial bargainers who are unethical.)

5 *See* David A. Lax & James K. Sebenius, *The Manager as Negotiator,* ch. 2 (1986); *also see generally* Charles B. Craver, "The Inherent Tension Between Value Creation and Value Claiming During Bargaining Interactions," 12 *Cardozo J. Conflict Resol.* 1 (2010); Keith G. Allred, "Distinguishing Best and Strategic Practices: A Framework for Managing the Dilemma Between Creating and Claiming Value," 16 *Negotiation J.* 387 (2000).

creating and claiming strategies, this chapter considers the potential tension between the two, and ways to avoid or manage it. This tension, known as the negotiator's dilemma, arises when a strategy for creating may be exploited by the other side when it comes time to claim. If you want to share information to find new value, such as sharing that you want to continue to work with an employer, for instance, the other sidemay use the information against you when claiming value, by expecting you to make greater financial sacrifices to stay with the employer.[6]

Any competent negotiator should know both negotiation approaches, the distinctive structure and stages of each, the choices to be made within each one, and how to incorporate the positional approach into a comprehensive problem-solving approach. This comprehensive approach along with the accompanying critical choices are illustrated throughout this text.

Distinguish Negotiation Approach from Style

Negotiation *approaches* need to be clearly distinguished from negotiation *styles*. Styles encompass a mix of descriptors that are labeled as traits, strategies, and goals in a highly regarded study by Professor Andrea Schneider.[7] In the study, the descriptors fell within two clusters of adjectives—one cluster associated with a problem-solving style and the other with an adversarial style. A negotiator who is rational, ethical, and interested in other clients' needs, and who wants to maximize a fair settlement, for example, is engaged in problem solving, while a stubborn and argumentative negotiator who makes unrealistically extreme opening demands is engaged in a style at the opposite, adversarial end. These clusters of descriptors do not constitute a negotiation approach; they describe a style.

Designating the descriptors as adjectives, Schneider's study found that the top six problem-solving traits and skills are ethical, experienced, personable, rational, trustworthy, and self-controlled; the top six adversarial traits and skills are stubborn, headstrong, arrogant, assertive, irritating, and argumentative.[8] The top four problem-solving bipolar pairings of negotiation strategies are no derogatory personal references, interest in other client's needs, courteous, and no offensive tactics; and the top three adversarial bipolar clusters are disinterest

---

6 Lax and Sebenius, *supra* note 5, at 38–41.

7 *See generally* Schneider, *supra* note 4.

8 *Id.* at 210.

in clients' needs, extreme opening demand, and an unrealistic initial position.[9] The top three problem-solving goals are ethical conduct, maximizing settlement, and fair settlement; while the top adversarial goals are maximizing settlement, outdoing the other, and profitable fee.[10]

In an article appearing ten years after her study on effectiveness of negotiation style, Professor Schneider unpacked style by identifying the underlying distinctive skills and choices available to negotiators.[11] This text agrees with her focus on style as a distinctive set of skills to be learned and goes further by elaborating style over a continuum of practices from problem-solving to adversarial. Professor Schneider identified five skill sets—assertiveness, empathy, flexibility, social intuition, and ethicality—all of which are relevant to locating a negotiator's style on the continuum. The less ethical a negotiator is, the more adversarial he is likely to be, and the more empathetic he is, the more problem-solving the style is likely to be, for instance.

Distinguishing style from approach is critical for illuminating each self-contained negotiation approach, with its own distinctive stages and skills.[12] For the positional approach, negotiators need to learn how to formulate first offers and how to engage in effective negotiation dances, for instance. For the problem-solving approach, negotiators need to learn how to structure a process for uncovering creative solutions and then productively claiming. These skills relate to the approach, not the style.

Style matters because your style, regardless of approach, can affect your effectiveness.[13] Studies show that negotiators who follow problem-solving behaviors engage in a negotiation style that makes them more effective as a group than negotiators who follow an adversarial one. And a negotiator who practices a cautious approach to problem solving is not adopting a worthy compromise, because you are likely to be significantly less effective than a committed problem solver.[14]

---

9 *Id.* at 211.

10 *Id.* at 212.

11 *See* Andrea Kupfer Schneider, "Teaching a New Negotiation Skills Paradigm," 39 *Wash. U. J. L. and Pol'y* 13, 19–36 (2012).

12 However, Professor Schneider rejects this approach-style distinction, characterizing it as confusing. *Id.* at 20.

13 *See* Nancy A. Welsh, "The Reputational Advantages of Demonstrating Trustworthiness: Using the Reputation Index with Law Students," 28 *Negotiation J.* 117, 130 (2012) (citing Donald G. Gifford, *Legal Negotiation: Theory and Practice,* 21 (2nd ed. 2007)).

14 Schneider, *supra* note 4, at 148 (stating that negotiators who were cautious in their problem solving were perceived to be significantly less effective than "true" problem-solving peers).

Professor Craver, a leading scholar on legal negotiations, summed up his more than three decades of work in his article "What Makes a Great Legal Negotiator?"[15] Making points consistent with a problem-solving style, he concluded that great negotiators select the most effective negotiation style, thoroughly prepare,[16] establish a rapport with the other side and a positive negotiation environment, communicate effectively and persuasively,[17] and finally are patient and persevere.

And if you do adopt an adversarial approach, labeled as positional in this text,[18] you will be more effective if you maintain a problem-solving style, such as engaging in good listening and rational discussion even though your underlying approach may entail exchanging positions and trying to gain an outcome at the expense of the other side. You have choices along a problem-solving–adversarial continuum of practices, or what will be called the negotiation music, and the closer you engage in practices (style) at the problem-solving end of the continuum, the more effective you are likely to be as a positional negotiator.

If you elect to engage in a style that is closer to the adversarial end within a positional approach, the choices within that style can make a difference, with an ethical adversarial style being relatively more effective than an unethical one, for instance.[19]

You also need to be able to spot the difference between approach and style during the heat of a negotiation in order to avoid being lured by a negotiator who may appear to be problem solving when in fact she is positional. A problem-solving style that disguises an underlying positional approach may induce you to engage in unsuitable or risky problem-solving moves of generating

---

"[A]pproximately 25% of the negotiators in the new cautious problem-solving group are effective, whereas 75% of the true problem-solvers are described as effective." *Id.* at 175.

15 *See generally* Charles B. Craver, "What Makes a Great Legal Negotiator?," 56 *Loy. L. Rev.* 337 (2010).

16 *See id.*

17 *See* Appendix F, on cultivating information.

18 I prefer to call the approach positional because its central feature entails exchanging positions, as will be highlighted later in this chapter.

19 Schneider, *supra* note 4, at 184 ("Seventy-five percent of the unethical adversarial group is considered ineffective. Only two attorneys out of the seventy-seven attorneys in this group, 2.5%, were considered effective. In comparison, the ethical adversarial bargainer is more likely to be average if not effective. Forty percent of ethical adversarials were ineffective, 44% were average and 16% were effective. These are still clearly lower ratios for effective and average behavior than the problem-solving negotiator and even the cautious problem-solving negotiator. On the other hand, they are notably better than the unethical adversarial bargainer is.").

options or sharing information while the other side is engaging in a negotiation of exchanging positions. When the other side emphasizes the problem-solving music of justifications, for instance, you may be distracted from discerning the underlying negotiation structure and therefore from fashioning an effective response to a positional negotiator.[20]

In this text, I crystallize style by characterizing it as the music that accompanies the negotiation, map the music along a continuum of practices from problem-solving to adversarial, and then divide the music into three types: good practices, tactics, and tricks. This scheme is used to clarify the choices facing negotiators as they fashion their preferred negotiation style.

Embedded in each type of music is information that can be found in words, tone, and body language. And information fuels negotiation. The Introduction, on the Mediation Representation Triangle, highlighted the role of strategic sharing and hiding of information in negotiations and the tension between sharing information to uncover fresh possibilities for settlement and withholding information to prevent exploitation. This music is performed independent of the selected negotiation approach and is designed to influence, persuade, or pressure the other side to make concessions—in other words, to claim value.[21]

Good Practices, Including Justifications

You should routinely play this music because good practices can usually generate benefits for your clients, subject to some limitations, identified below, that can be imposed by the other side.

Several good practices are briefly identified here and will be elaborated when each topic naturally arises during the course of the text.

- Present rational justifications; this includes doing research on your BATNA, client's interests, and impediments.[22]
- Engage in rapport building.[23]
- Listen actively and empathetically.[24]

---

20 *See* Craver, *supra* note 5, at 5–7.

21 For a catalogue of negotiating tactics and tricks, *see* Charles B. Craver, *Effective Legal Negotiation and Settlement,* ch. 10 (7th ed. 2012).

22 *See infra* Chapter 5.

23 *See infra* Appendix F, "Cultivating Communications—Attentive and Proactive Listening."

24 *See id.*

- Ask suitably framed questions.[25]
- Manage the emotional dimensions of the dispute.[26]
- Apply social skills and awareness.
- Act ethically and maintain a reputation for trustworthiness and fairness.[27]
- Advocate for interests.[28]
- Overcome impediments constructively (using decision trees, for example).[29]

When you move from negotiation to mediation, you should use good practices as a problem solver when you:

- Prepare a mediation representation plan.[30]
- Enlist mediator assistance.[31]
- Use opportunities offered by joint sessions and caucuses.[32]

Following are several illustrations of good practices. You may justify a claim based on rational and principled explanations—what I suggest as the best of the good practices. You may cultivate a hospitable environment for settlement by establishing rapport with the other side through small talk, finding connections unrelated to the dispute, and creating comfortable surroundings for meeting. You might promote information exchange by listening attentively and actively to the other side, including by reacting empathetically, acknowledging emotional pain, and asking well-framed open and closed questions. And you can lubricate the negotiations by creating trust and acting ethically, including keeping your word and not misrepresenting critical information.

Limitations on Good Practices

You should not employ good practices blindly. When a particular practice has become ineffective or possibly harmful, you should stop playing that music.

---

25 *See id.*
26 *See* Section 1.3(a)(ii).
27 *See infra* Section 5.17.
28 *See infra* Section 3(a).
29 *See infra* Section 3.1(b) and Appendix A.
30 *See infra* Chapter 5.
31 *See infra* Sections 5.3 to 5.5.
32 *See infra* Section 5.4.

For example, using justifications can cultivate a rational, reciprocal discussion, but if your effort is failing and, worse yet, you think the other side is using the pretense of a rational discussion to delay the negotiations, you probably should suspend the music. If you think the other side is requesting information that they are not really interested in, or is requesting additional time to get information that should be readily available, for instance, they may be using your practice of promoting a full, rational discussion against you to delay resolving the dispute.

If your efforts to build rapport are being rejected or your well-framed questions are being dodged, you also probably should suspend those efforts until negotiations are more hospitable.

However, some practices, like ethical behavior, should be unconditional. Regardless of the ethicality of the other side's behavior, for example, you will probably come out ahead for your client in the long run by establishing a reputation as an ethical negotiator.

Tactics

Tactics are generally accepted conventions in negotiations. Tactics are not considered to be Good Practices and are not encouraged, although there are acceptable ones that also may be necessary in some negotiation contexts. They also are so commonly used that parties expect to encounter them.

There are numerous tactics that can be considered to be generally accepted and practiced ones, although there is no agreement on all the acceptable tactics. The ABA Professional Model Code Rule 4.1, Comment 2 recognizes negotiation conventions in its exemption of several negotiation practices from the bar against false statements of material fact. It treats as puffery, and not as a code violation, for example, misrepresentations of the bottom line in negotiations.[33]

Many tactics can be difficult to decipher, because the moves also can be done in good faith. Your statement about your bottom line might be a sincere effort to convince the other party that this is as far as you can go or it may be designed to mislead the other side. And a threat to leave can be a sincere act of frustration or a pretense to scare the other side into making a concession. An opening offer can be a sincere statement or a preliminary gambit. If tactics were easy to recognize, they would be ineffective. Once the other side knows your

33 Model Rules of Prof'l Conduct R. 4.1 cmt. 2 (1983). For further discussion, *see* Section 5.17, ABA Model Rules etc.

demand is intentionally inflated to anchor their thinking, for example, they can identify the tactic and avoid being manipulated by it. Once discovered, a tactic is defeated and can undermine progress in the negotiation.

While making inflated offers and trying to anchor the other party are fairly standard and uneventful practices, even when discovered, other tactics, like aggressively belittling the other side, although not unusual, introduce a more adversarial tone to the negotiation. Alternatively, despite being a conventional tactic, efforts to build rapport, when seen as insincere, may undermine the other side's trust in you.

Tricks

Tricks are ploys that are inherently adversarial and can be subtly or blatantly aggressive. They are controversial practices that can be considered dirty or unethical. And they are, by definition, not generally accepted practices. They are used for the same reasons that tactics are used—to influence, persuade, and pressure the other side to make concessions.

An example of a trick is engaging in a "good guy/bad guy" strategy—that is, setting up a good guy to psychologically exert pressure to settle by apologizing and protecting the other side from the hostile treatment of the "bad" teammate. More illustrations of tricks are offered in the section on the positional negotiation approach.

As with tactics, there is no broad consensus regarding what techniques constitute tricks. Furthermore, the boundary between tricks and tactics can be murky although the core difference is not: Tactics are more acceptable than tricks.

Tricks, like tactics, can be difficult to recognize, because the move could be good-faith behavior. A demand for something that is declared important might be genuine or might be a false demand. A no-authority claim may reflect that the bargaining has unexpectedly reached a limit in terms of authority or that the other side purposely arrived with authority that it knew would be limited.

As with tactics, if tricks were easy to recognize, they would be ineffective. Once the other side thinks you are engaging in a "good guy/bad guy" routine, for example, they can identify the trick, not be manipulated by it, and lose trust in you by becoming suspicious and expecting other tricks. When any trick is discovered, you may become trusted less, and you might hurt, if not destroy, the negotiation because the other side now knows that you are capable of engaging in tricks, which, by definition, are not generally acceptable.

Morphing of Practices

Many practices that are considered to be good ones can morph into adversarial ones—tactics or tricks, depending on how you choose to perform them.

For example, you may engage in problem solving by active listening and reframing empathetically, a tactic by purposely showing little interest in learning from the other side, or a trick by reframing to show disrespect for the other side in order to put them on the defensive. You may problem solve by candidly replying to questions, employ a tactic by delaying answering, or resort to a trick by responding with lies. You may try overcoming an impasse with a good practice like identifying the missing data and developing a plan to gather the information, with a tactic by making it difficult and expensive for the other side to get the information, or with a trick by destroying key documents.

It is obvious that you as a negotiator have choices to make. You need to decide what sort of negotiating style you want to adopt, recalling the studies showing that the more adversarial you become, the more you risk being less effective, and that the more problem-solving your style, the more effective you can be.

This chapter fully explains each negotiation approach and offers a roadmap to guide you through the stages of each approach. It concludes with strategies for converting a primarily positional negotiator into a problem-solving one. At the end, you will find a handy checklist that you can use when planning your negotiation.

Hypothetical

Throughout this chapter, the following employment dispute will be used to demonstrate the two approaches to negotiations.

Stephen Saleson founded, owns, and runs a small company in Buffalo called Shirts for You. The company sells several major-brand-name shirts to retail outlets and is staffed by two support people and one other salesperson, Philip Upton. When Stephen hired Philip several years ago, Philip signed an employment contract in which he agreed that if he left his position, he would not compete against Shirts for You within the city of Buffalo for three years.

During the first year of employment, Stephen spent considerable time teaching Philip the secrets of good salesmanship. Under Stephen's tutelage, Philip quickly learned the job and did superlative work solidifying and maintaining the existing customer base in Buffalo. Unfortunately, the personal relationship between Philip and Stephen soured during their third year together. Philip felt that Stephen was stifling Philip's professional development by preventing him from developing new customers. Stephen reserved those opportunities for himself. So, even though Philip continued to admire Stephen's sales skills and welcomed his mentoring, he quit the sales position and went into his own business, selling a different brand of shirt. Because Philip had become such an excellent salesman, he was able to secure a group of retail customers in Buffalo that Stephen had never solicited for sales.

Stephen, who is upset that his protégé abandoned him, sued Philip for breach of the employment contract not to compete and is seeking an injunction and damages in the amount of $100,000 for lost sales. Philip responded by claiming that he is not violating the non-compete clause because he is selling a different brand of shirt to a different group of retail customers in Buffalo.

Questions

1. Do you find the distinction between negotiation approach and style useful in clarifying your choices as a negotiator? Please explain.
2. How would you classify each of the following strategies (a good practice, tactic, or trick). Please explain. Do any of these strategies not fit one of these three types of music? If not, can you identify any other types of music?
   a. A negotiator shows up late purposely in order to demonstrate limited interest in negotiating a resolution.
   b. At the beginning of the negotiation, a negotiator presents a take-it-or-leave-it offer with a full explanation of why the offer is fair and how it takes into account the other side's needs.
   c. Your offer is summarily dismissed. It is characterized as shockingly inadequate and is coupled with a request for a more reasonable offer.
   d. The other side summarily rejects your offer and storms out of the negotiation.
   e. The other side summarily rejects your offer for convincingly irrational and bizarre reasons.
   f. The other side makes a retreating offer: If you do not accept it by a specified date, they will withdraw the offer and return to preparing for trial.
   g. After both sides have reached a settlement agreement, the other side calls the next day to apologize and explains with great embarrassment that the principal will accept the agreement only if your side makes one last concession.

2. POSITIONAL APPROACH AND STYLE

This section examines in detail the key features of the positional approach to negotiations—the conventional approach to claiming value at the expense of the other party. Claiming strategies that are not at the expense of the other party will be considered under the problem-solving approach.[34]

By parsing the familiar positional approach, you will have the opportunity to reflect on and improve your own practices as well as better understand the differences and benefits offered by the problem-solving approach. In this edition, the positional approach is stripped down to its essential features as primarily a claiming strategy. This austere representation of the positional approach is later integrated into the problem-solving approach and style, and it is enhanced by incorporating it into a broader approach, where the positional approach is presented as one of several possible claiming strategies.

When reduced to its essential features,[35] this approach begins with each negotiator gathering the information she needs before engaging in the classic claiming dance strategy of starting with firm, extreme, and opposite positions and then making calibrated concessions until the negotiators are close enough to either split the difference or adopt one of the last offers on the table. Each party prepares by establishing the parameters of the negotiation dance, which usually includes forming an aspirational goal, a bottom line, an opening offer strategy, and a concession plan with music along the continuum from problem-solving to adversarial techniques.

This section uses the label positional rather than adversarial or hard bargaining because the central feature of this negotiation approach is a sequence of positions exchanged between parties. Adversarial, hard bargaining, and similar labels more accurately reflect the style of the negotiator, not the structure of the negotiation, as emphasized in the introduction to this chapter.

As a positional attorney, you should consider the orientation that you bring to a negotiation process restricted primarily to claiming. This orientation influences how you prepare for and participate in the negotiation.

View Dispute as a Distributive Problem or a Zero-Sum Game

See the dispute as primarily distributive, a contest over who gets the targeted resource.

---

34 *See infra* Section 1.3(c).

35 *See, e.g.*, Gary Goodpaster, *A Primer on Competitive Bargaining*, 1996 J. Disp. Resol. 325.

View Strategy as Win-Lose
Try to win at the expense of the other party.

View Resources as Fixed (Fixed Pie)
See the dispute as one only about a set amount of money or a single asset, like a building.

Compete for Larger Piece of the Pie
Compete to win the largest piece of the fixed pie. Stephen sees a sales pie of $100,000 that Philip stole from him. The negotiation is over how to split the $100,000 pie, and Stephen, of course, wants the whole pie.

View Dispute as Involving Only One Issue, So No Opportunity for Trades
In the employment contract dispute, Stephen views the dispute as being about money: How will he recover the money he lost because of the customers "stolen" by Philip? Stephen either wins by recovering money for lost sales or loses by getting nothing or only a nominal recovery.

View Problem Narrowly
The dispute is framed narrowly: Did Philip breach the employment contract? The parties do not look for multiple issues or opportunities for mutually beneficial trades.

Advocate for Client's Position
View your role as an advocate for your client's position, not his interests. Stephen expects his attorney to forcefully advocate his position that he should be paid $100,000.

Maintain Disinterest in Other Side's Case
Don't try to understand the other side's case when consumed by an adversarial mindset. In this environment, Stephen has difficulty seeing any merit in Philip's view that he is not competing just because he is selling a different brand of shirt to different customers.

This section considers how positional attorneys with these orientations prepare for the negotiations and what strategies they are likely to employ at the negotiation table. For a summary of the features and style, see the "Positional Approach and Style" in accompanying table. Be sure to note that the defining features of the approach are in bold, while the defining styles are in italics.

Positional Approach and Style

a. **Preparation**
- i. **Gather Information**
  - **Establish Two Key Financial Parameters**
  - **Establish Aspirational Goal, Based on Legal Rights**
  - **Establish Bottom Line (total BATNA)**
- ii. **Develop Plan**
  - **Formulate First Offer Strategy**
  - **Prepare Opening Offer**
  - **Plan Concession Dance**
- iii. **Develop Questions**

b. **Strategies and Stages at the Table**
- i. **Exchange Information**
  - *Ask questions*
- ii. **Bargaining**
  - **Implement First Offer Strategy**
  - **Engage in Concession Dance of Offers and Counteroffers, Driven by Reciprocity Norms**
  - **Play Music**
    - *Good Practices*
    - *Tactics*
    - *Tricks*

c. **Closure**
- *Deadline*
- *Finish Final Bargaining*
- *Secure Commitment*

a. Preparation

In preparing for the negotiation, you have homework to do that includes formulating the parameters for your negotiation dance. You need to establish your aspirational goal and your bottom line as well as develop a strategy for presenting an opening offer and engaging in the highly stylized negotiation dance.

i. Gather Information

Establish Two Key Financial Parameters

You need to establish the financial range for the negotiation dance. Any settlement should fall within two key parameters: your client's aspirational goal and his bottom line.

Establish Aspirational Goal, Based on Legal Rights

Your client's aspirational goal sets the high or low end of what he wants out of the negotiation. It is the most he can achieve. His aspirational goal should be optimistic, but not indefensibly unrealistic. The selected goal is affected by the strength of his legal rights and the likely judicial remedies. It is formed in the shadow of the law. A thoughtful, realistically high goal is critical to your success in the negotiation, because it reduces the risk of your becoming anchored by the other side's first offer or your client's bottom line. You might too easily adjust your goal based on what the other side does or what your client minimally wants at the expense of a better possible result for your client. Negotiators who set realistically high aspirational goals tend to achieve better outcomes.

Because Stephen has not done any discovery, he may not have the necessary data for calculating lost sales. But based on some sense of what might have been lost and an optimistic judicial result, he will likely establish an aspirational goal that is less than the $100,000 demanded in the court papers. The goal will likely be less because he probably demanded an excessive amount in order to protect himself from understating the damages before discovery as well as to get the other side's attention.

Establish Bottom Line (Total BATNA)

Your client's bottom line sets the minimum amount that he needs to settle. The bottom line forms a tripwire that when crossed would trigger him to leave the negotiation table. The bottom line, also known as the reservation value, is derived from your client's BATNA—the best alternative to a negotiated agreement.[36]

The bottom line is the value that the settlement offer must meet or improve upon for your client to accept. A plaintiff's bottom line is the minimum benefit

36 BATNA (best alternative to a negotiated agreement) is a term coined by Roger Fisher and William Ury. Fisher et al., *Getting to Yes: Negotiating Agreement without Giving In*, 102 (3rd ed. 2011). It refers to the best option that is available to the party if he leaves the negotiating table. *See also* Russell Korobkin, *Negotiation Theory and Strategy*, 27–46 (2nd ed. 2009).

that the party must secure to settle. A defendant's bottom line is the maximum cost that the party is willing to incur to settle. Although the bottom line is related to the BATNA, the BATNA offers a different perspective on the negotiation. Instead of focusing on what you need at the negotiation table to settle, the BATNA focuses on what you will receive or lose after leaving the table. While the bottom line and BATNA are different concepts, their values are usually the same when a client accounts for both the public and personal costs and benefits of the BATNA.[37]

For example, the BATNA of going to court can be calculated by using a decision tree analysis[38] that factors in the risk of winning and that of losing when you are computing the monetary benefit and cost of litigating. But calculating the public BATNA fails to explicitly factor in such personal costs of litigating as inconvenience, aggravation, and uncertainty or such personal benefits as creating precedent or feeling vindicated. You need to approximate a value for these personal costs and benefits and then add or deduct it from the value of your public BATNA. The total produces the net benefit or cost of exercising your BATNA, a calculation that becomes the bottom line that must be beat at the negotiation table.

You also should gather information on the other party's bottom line.

You need this information so that you know how far you can push before the other side will leave the table. Obviously, obtaining this information can be difficult. You will usually be forced to rely on an educated guess.

Following is an illustration of how to use decision tree analysis to calculate the total BATNAs for the plaintiff and the defendant.

Stephen, as the plaintiff, needs to develop a list of possible alternatives to settlement. Stephen could do nothing, could complain to Philip's new customers about Philip, could solicit Philip's new customers, or could sue Philip for

---

37 *See* Korobkin, *supra* note 36, at 33–38 (describing five factors that can affect the reservation value: differences in ability to satisfy preferences, differences in riskiness of the options, differences in transaction costs associated with the alternatives, differences in the timing of the transactions, and differences in effects on future opportunities); *see also infra* Appendix A.

38 For a full explanation of the use of decision trees for calculating the value of the BATNA, including an explanation of what an expected value is and the differences between a public BATNA and a personal one, *see* Appendix A. Attorneys can assess the court alternative through the use of decision tree analysis, a process that involves estimating the probability of key events and the likely outcome for each event. *See generally* Marjorie Corman Aaron & David P. Hoffer, "Decision Analysis as a Method of Evaluating the Trial Alternative," in *Mediating Legal Disputes: Effective Strategies for Lawyers and Mediators*, 307–334 (Dwight Golann ed., 1996).

breach of his employment contract not to compete. Of these options, Stephen might decide that his most attractive alternative to settlement is going to court, the public BATNA.

Stephen's attorney would research the strengths and weaknesses of the court case, predict the likelihood of winning and the likely court outcome, and then prepare a decision tree analysis to arrive at the expected value of going to court (the public BATNA). His attorney may predict a 60 percent chance of a favorable jury verdict[39] in the amount of $80,000. After deducting his estimated attorney fees and other litigation costs of $20,000, the attorney estimates a net benefit of $60,000. By multiplying his net benefit of $60,000 by the 60 percent chance of winning, Stephen would arrive at a positive value of $36,000.

Next, Stephen needs to incorporate the risk of losing. If Stephen loses, he would still have to pay his attorney fees and other litigation costs of $20,000. By multiplying the $20,000 by his 40 percent chance of losing,

Stephen would calculate a negative value of $8,000. Finally, by subtracting the negative value of $8,000 from the $36,000 positive value, Steven would arrive at the expected value of his public BATNA in the amount of $28,000.

Stephen's public BATNA value needs to be adjusted for a number of personal benefits and costs in order for Stephen to arrive at his bottom line in the negotiations. Stephen's personal costs might include time preparing for the case, the emotional angst of being consumed by litigation, and living with the 40 percent chance of losing. Stephen must make a rough subjective estimate of what he is willing to give up to avoid suffering these costs. He may decide that he is willing to sacrifice up to $10,000. By deducting the $10,000 from the value of his public BATNA of $28,000, Stephen arrives at a total BATNA of $18,000.

Thus, if Stephen cannot secure at least $18,000 at the negotiation table, a settlement that would result in his avoiding the personal costs of litigating, he should leave the table for a chance of securing the positive value of his public BATNA, the likely litigated net outcome of $28,000.

Philip also needs to identify and assess his alternatives to settlement and calculate his total BATNA. Philip, as the defendant, does not have many options once the suit is under way. Philip can do nothing and risk a default judgment.

39 Stephen faces a risk of losing the court case because it is not clear whether Philip has breached the covenant not to compete as Philip is selling a different brand of shirts to a different group of customers in Buffalo.

Philip could ask his former customers, the ones still serviced by Stephen, to lobby Stephen to drop the lawsuit. Or Philip could defend by trying to win the jury trial. Of these options, Philip might decide that his most attractive alternative to settlement is defending himself in court, his public BATNA.

Philip's attorney would research the strengths and weaknesses of the court case and then predict the chances of winning and the likely court outcome.[40] His attorney may predict that if a jury holds Philip liable, he would likely be liable for $80,000. Philip's attorney also might predict that attorney fees and other litigation costs would be $20,000, for a total loss of $100,000. Then, by multiplying the $100,000 by his attorney's predicted 40 percent chance of losing, Philip would calculate a negative value of $40,000.

Next, Philip needs to calculate the value of winning. If Philip wins, he would still have to pay his attorney fees and other litigation costs of $20,000. By multiplying the $20,000 by his 60 percent chance of winning, Philip would calculate a negative value of $12,000. Finally, by adding together the negative $12,000 from winning and the negative $40,000 from losing, Philip would arrive at the expected value of his public BATNA in the amount of $52,000.

Now Philip needs to adjust his BATNA to account for the personal costs and benefits of going to court in order to arrive at his bottom line in the negotiations. Philip may incur the costs of spending time preparing for the case and suffering the emotional stress of litigation. But these costs may be exceeded by two possible benefits of litigating. Philip may welcome the 60 percent chance of winning and paying nothing, a risk-taking propensity common among defendants as a group and he may want to try to exonerate himself in court so that he can freely pursue his lucrative business in Buffalo. Philip may estimate that the personal benefits of his BATNA are worth roughly $10,000 more than the personal costs.[41] Philip would deduct this positive $10,000 benefit from the negative public BATNA of $52,000 to arrive at a fully analyzed BATNA, a

---

40 Stephen faces a risk of losing the court case because it is not clear whether Philip has breached the covenant not to compete when Philip is selling a different brand of shirts to a different group of customers in Buffalo.

41 It is not unusual for repeat defendants to attach a positive value to litigating for the purpose of scaring off future potential plaintiffs. This personal benefit can be incorporated into the reservation value by the defendant's estimating the positive value of litigating to send a message and then deducting that amount from any expected loss.
If the defendant estimates the expected loss to be $40,000 and the benefit to be $10,000, then the defendant's fully analyzed BATNA or reservation value would be $30,000. The defendant would be willing to pay no more than $30,000. Otherwise, the defendant would turn to his public BATNA of an expected average loss of $40,000.

reservation value of negative $42,000. Thus, if settlement possibilities involve Philip paying more than $42,000, Philip should leave the table to litigate in court, where he may pay nothing but his attorney fees and risk losing, on the average, $52,000.

In short, Stephen's bottom line is $18,000; Philip's is $42,000.

ii. Develop Plan

CRITICAL CHOICES

Develop a plan for an opening offer strategy and dance.

Formulate First Offer Strategy

You need to decide on a first offer strategy. Should you put the first offer on the table or induce the other side to present the first offer? Many articles have been written about this early strategic moment in a negotiation, because the first offer can have an impact on how the rest of the negotiation unfolds, including what the other side will do next, as well as frame the bargaining range.[42]

Before considering the pros and cons of you versus the other side presenting the first offer, you should consider two critical factors that affect the first offer strategy: the anchoring phenomenon of offers and the likely ZOPA (zone of possible agreement).[43]

First, when engaging in any negotiation, you should be aware of how an offer can anchor the recipient's view of what is possible in the negotiation. When you are the recipient, be aware of how the other side's offer can anchor your view. Their offer can influence your estimate of what the case is worth and cause you to unconsciously adjust your expectations toward their offer.

You should guard against being victimized by this anchoring phenomenon. You can be easily manipulated by it if you do not actively resist its impact. The other side's offer should not be a substitute for your independent assessment of your BATNA and what can possibly be achieved in the negotiation. However, you should consider how you might use the anchoring phenomenon proactively to influence the other side. By justifying your offer, you might be able to anchor their thinking about what is possible. Anchoring can be powerful and subtle, so be aware of its influence.

---

42 *See generally* Craver, *supra* note 21, para. 6.02.

43 *See id,* para. 6.02(4).

Second, the negotiation is ultimately over dividing the ZOPA (zone of possible agreement). The ZOPA is the overlap between the bottom lines of the two parties. If Stephen's bottom line is $18,000 (the minimum he wants from the settlement) and Philip's bottom line is $42,000 (the maximum amount he is willing to pay), the ZOPA is the difference of $24,000.

Zone of Possible Agreement (ZOPA)	
$24,000 (ZOPA)	
P-Stephen	*D-Philip*
$18,000	*$42,000*
Bottom Line	*Bottom Line*

Each person would like to secure as much of the ZOPA as possible. Plaintiff Stephen would want to receive up to $42,000 (his bottom line plus ZOPA, or $18,000 þ $24,000), which is also Defendant Philip's bottom line, and Philip would like to pay no more than $18,000 (his bottom line minus ZOPA, or $42,000 $24,000), which is also Stephen's bottom line. Of course, each side is unlikely to know the precise ZOPA because each side is unlikely to know with confidence the other side's bottom line.

The amount of the ZOPA you will strive for depends on your aspirational goal. If Stephen's aspirational goal is to receive $90,000, he will try to secure the whole ZOPA, although he may not realize that is what he is doing. (His aspirational goal is greater than Philip's bottom line to pay no more than $42,000.)

Zone of Possible Agreement (ZOPA)		
P-Stephen's Aspirational Goal: $90,000		
$24,000 (ZOPA)		
P-Stephen		*D-Philip*
$18,000		*$90,000*
Bottom Line	*$42,000*	*Aspirational Goal*
	Bottom Line	

If Philip's aspirational goal is to pay as little as $20,000, he will try to secure up to $22,000 out of the $24,000 ZOPA (Philip's bottom line minus Philip's aspirational goal, or $42,000 $20,000). If successful, Philip would pay Stephen $20,000 and secure $22,000 of the ZOPA, while Stephen would receive $2,000 of the ZOPA or $2,000 more than his bottom line (Philip's aspirational goal minus Stephen's bottom line, or $20,000 $18,000).

Zone of Possible Agreement (ZOPA)		
	P-Philip's Aspirational Goal: $20,000	
	$24,000 (ZOPA)	
P-Stephen	*D-Philip*	*D-Philip*
$18,000	*$20,000*	*$42,000*
Bottom Line	*Aspirational*	*Bottom Line*

First Offer by Other Side In view of the difficulties of learning the ZOPA, you might want to enlist the other party to present the first offer in order to benefit from the other party's errors. They might open with a more generous offer than you anticipated because their offer overestimates the strength of your case (overestimates your bottom line) or reflects weaknesses in their own case that you did not know about (reveals favorable range of their bottom line). You also may want to avoid making your own error by presenting an unnecessarily generous offer that overestimates the strength of their case.[44]

Philip will be relieved that Stephen's first offer is only $100,000 if Philip had made several hundred thousand dollars and feels he would be vulnerable in court. He will benefit from Stephen's underestimation of damages. He also has learned the upper amount of Stephen's bargaining range. Stephen will be happy if Philip makes a first offer of $20,000, because it would be more than Stephen's bottom line of $18,000. Philip would have overestimated Stephen's bottom line and as a result would have given away $2,000 of the ZOPA before Stephen made his first offer.

You also might want the other side to make the first offer so that you can establish an advantageous midpoint between their offer and your counteroffer. This tactic is known as "bracketing." Realizing that the midpoint can be a natural settlement number, you can control the midpoint with your counteroffer. Philip would like to steer the midpoint close to his aspirational goal and Stephen's bottom line. If Stephen surmises that Philip's bottom line is around $40,000, he would like to counter Philip's $20,000 initial offer with $70,000, which would create a midpoint above the $40,000. And then his next counteroffer would establish a midpoint of $40,000. Any additional counteroffers would hover around the $40,000 midpoint.

With the other side making the first offer, followed by your counteroffer, you also can benefit from the reciprocity norm discussed in connection with bargain-

44 *See* Harry T. Edwards & James J. White, *The Lawyer as a Negotiator,* 115–116 (1977).

ing and the concession dance. This norm can put pressure on the other side to make the next offer, the first real concession after you have exchanged initial offers.

Thus, it appears that whoever makes the first offer risks doing less well in the negotiation.

First Offer by You Nevertheless, you might want to make the first offer when you are prepared and the other side is not. Your first offer can anchor the other party's view of the settlement range and move his counteroffer toward your offer. Your first offer might even influence his view of his bottom line.[45] Because you are prepared and fairly confident of other side's bottom line, you can make the first offer with little risk of giving away part of the ZOPA.

Your first offer also can preempt the other side from presenting an extreme and wholly unacceptable first offer. By making a first offer of $80,000, less than the $100,000 in the complaint, for example, Philip may discourage Stephen from starting with an unacceptable offer of zero. In this way, your offer might encourage the other side to present a more reasonable counteroffer.

Prepare Opening Offer

In a positional negotiation, you usually prepare a first offer or counteroffer that will create a range for settlement discussions.[46] You set your initial offer higher than your aspirational goal, with an eye on an advantageous midpoint between the two sides' initial offers. You need to create space for the dance of offer, counteroffer, and concessions. If your offer is too extreme, however, it can chase the other side away. Stephen purposely asks for the upper limit of $100,000 in order to leave room for the inevitable concessions and compromises. Then, if Philip responds with zero or a nominal $5,000, Stephen can counteroffer with an amount that is still above or near his aspirational goal. He wants to create a margin to work with.

When formulating your first offer, you might be guided by two challenging questions: What would be a reasonable number for the other side to begin with? (This helps put you in a realistic mode.) What would be a reasonable number for you to start with?[47]

---

45 *See* Lax & Sebenius, *supra* note 5, at 132–134; Howard Raiffa, *The Art and Science of Negotiation*, 127–128 (1982).

46 For an analysis of whether the first offer should be moderate or extreme, *see generally* Russell Korobkin and Chris Guthrie, "Opening Offers and Out-of-Court Settlement: A Little Moderation May Not Go a Long Way," 10 *Ohio St. J. on Disp. Resol.* 1 (1994).

47 These two questions are posed by Andy Little in J. Anderson Little, *Making Money Talk: How to Mediate Insured Claims and Other Monetary Disputes*, 79 (2007).

You should keep in mind that the amount of the first offer conveys information. The first offer locks in the outer range of the settlement. When Stephen puts on the table an offer of $100,000, he forecloses any chance of getting more.[48] The offer also anchors the other side's view of the settlement value. Philip may not know his outside exposure until Stephen presents his $100,000 offer, which anchors Philip's thinking about the range of settlement.

A realistic first offer reveals that the offeror has prepared for and is serious about settling the dispute. A too extreme offer suggests that the offeror has not done his homework or may have made some faulty assumptions. A too extreme offer also could mean that the offeror has adopted a highly competitive strategy, which may provoke the other side to respond in kind or abandon the negotiations.

Plan Concession Dance[49]

You need to develop a plan for your dance, one that is not based primarily on reacting to the other side's next move. You should develop a two-part independent concession plan, with the first part centered on reaching your aspirational goal and the second centered on moving toward your bottom line. If you encounter an insurmountable impasse with the first plan, then you shift to the second one.

Any dance should be choreographed based on the well-recognized norm of reciprocity—of taking turns. You should diligently alternate steps with your counterpart to protect yourself from being trapped into bargaining against yourself (making the next concession after making the last concession). If the other side resists, be patient and do not capitulate. You can point out that it is their turn, and that it would be unfair to expect you to bargain against yourself.

The financial amount of each concession should be calculated with an eye on the midpoint that you want to steer the other side toward, whether toward your aspirational goal or near your bottom line. When bracketing, you should leave a reserve near your bottom line for a final, closing concession. If Stephen's bottom line is $20,000, he should bracket around a midpoint of $22,000 so that he has a reserve of $2,000 if necessary to close a final gap.

---

48 However, this upper range could be exceeded if during the negotiations it becomes evident that a court might award damages greater than the $100,000.

49 This subsection and the related ones on bargaining and closure draw heavily on Craver, *supra* note 21, para. 6.02(1)–(2), para. 7.02, para. 8.02; Little, *supra* note 47, at 76–82; and G. Richard Shell, *Bargaining for Advantage,* 166–174 (2nd ed. 2006).

The size of each concession should be based on the message that you want to convey. Unfortunately, there are no reliable rules of interpretation to ensure that your signals will be accurately understood. You should try to be clear as you accommodate two competing considerations: If your concession is too big too early, you may appear anxious to settle and will give the other side leverage against you. If it is too small too early, you may appear stubborn and not serious about settling. You might start with a relatively significant concession to signal that you are ready to settle, and then move to progressively smaller concessions to signal that you are reaching the end of the dance. You should maintain a steady and transparent course in order to keep your signals clear, although you ought to adjust your plan based on verifiable new information.

For a multi-issue negotiation, you should consider making big moves on less important issues and small moves on more important ones. You might be guided by the mutual concession principle: "If you agree to give us A, we will agree to give you B."

You also need to plan the number of rounds, realizing that the largest number of concessions occur toward the end of the negotiation. You want to reserve most of the rounds for the progressively smaller concessions that occur during the hard bargaining at the end.

Regardless of your concession pattern, you ought to dance slowly. You should be patient and be careful not to concede too quickly. The sooner you concede, the greater the risk that the concession will appear unimportant. This concession devaluation may cause you to lose the opportunity to elicit a reciprocal concession out of the other side. You also should not accept their initial offer or concession too quickly. The quicker you are to accept, the greater the risk that the other side will experience "buyer's remorse." Your quick acceptance may leave them feeling that their concession may be a bad deal for them, and they might try to find a way out of the commitment.

You can help keep your signals clear and promote reasoned discussion by supporting each concession with a rationale. Your rationale will usually be related to the likely court outcome or will have some other principled basis, including the citing of new information learned during the negotiation. Your justifications also can reduce the likelihood of the other side reactively devaluating the significance of your concession.[50] When conceding with an explanation such as "We are adding $20,000 to the offer to account for your legal

50 Reactive devaluation occurs when the other side discounts your concession by assuming that if you are conceding, the concession must not be significant for you.

fees so that your client will have enough net recovery to cover her documented medical bills," you are justifying the new concession as well as modeling a reason-based negotiation discourse. However, you might cease offering rationales as you move toward the final rounds to signal that you are reaching your bottom line and pressing for closure.

iii. Develop Questions

When gathering information and formulating an opening offer strategy and concession dance plan, you may encounter information gaps. You can try to fill them at the beginning of the negotiation session by preparing gap-filling questions. For instance, Stephen might try to learn about Philip's bottom line by posing some indirect questions about Philip's developing business to get a sense of his financial needs and how anxious he is to settle the case.

b. Strategies and Stages at the Table

After exchanging information with the other side, you implement your opening offer strategy and dance plan. The opening offer induces a negotiation dance of counteroffers, concessions, and compromises. Positions are supported by the strategic use of information packaged in the form of justifications (good practices), tactics, and tricks.

i. Exchange Information

The beginning of any negotiation commences with exchanging information.[51]

Ask Questions

Before bargaining, you should ask the questions you prepared. You should avoid distracting speeches and surprises when your goal is to learn information. Studies have shown that, at least in the United States, skilled negotiators ask more questions, and they clarify answers and summarize what they hear more than average negotiators. Of course, asking good questions does not ensure that you will get reliable answers; you still need to assess whether the answers are accurate or designed to mislead.

---

51 These three aspects of gathering information are identified and developed in Shell, *supra* note 49, at 138–155.

ii. Bargaining

Implement First Offer Strategy

You typically begin bargaining by orchestrating the first offer. Depending on your strategy, you try to induce the other side to present the first offer, or you do so yourself. As already discussed, the first offer is likely to be extreme in order to establish an ample bargaining range.

Engage in the Concession Dance of Offers and Counteroffers, Driven by Reciprocity Norms

Next you implement your planned concession dance for dividing up the ZOPA. The dance follows the routine of initial extreme offers and swirling rounds of calibrated concessions and compromises. Rather than being driven primarily by the other side's last offer, you should try to steer the dance first toward your aspirational goal and then, if necessary, toward your bottom line.

The dance can be propelled by norms of reciprocity that permeate our daily living, including the negotiation process of exchanging positions. When someone does something for us, we customarily feel compelled to reciprocate. This social practice enriches our lives and promotes cooperation, including moving forward the dance of concessions. When you make an offer that is viewed as an authentic concession, the other side can feel compelled to reciprocate with a concession in the form of a counteroffer, and so the concession dance proceeds. If you are seen as unreasonably violating this norm, you risk alienating the other side and closing down the negotiation process.

This natural process of exchange can be accompanied by music that can invigorate the dance. The music can range from good practices of justifications to manipulative moves of acceptable tactics and questionable tricks, as will be illustrated in the next section.

Play Music

This dance of offers and counteroffers is performed to the musical styles of good practices, tactics, and tricks, as described in the introduction to this chapter. Each type of music is embedded with information that you should knowingly convey as well as try to interpret accurately when conveyed by others.

Before we expand on the three types of music, keep in mind how the music can vary in a positional negotiation along the problem-solving– adversarial continuum. A problem-solving style may consist of you presenting a position based on principled justifications, with only limited use of tactics like an inflated offer or a threat to leave the room. Stephen, for example, might ask for $80,000 in damages based on the projected lost sales due to Philip's having recruited ten identifiable customers. At the other extreme—the adversarial extreme—you may aggressively use a range of tactics and tricks. Stephen might belligerently demand the $100,000 today without justifying the level of damages and threaten to go to court tomorrow to ruin Philip's reputation as a reputable salesperson.

Some attorneys favor and successfully use contentious adversarial strategies for extracting concessions, although these strategies pose hazards. The more adversarial the negotiation becomes, the greater the risk that you will reach an impasse or that value will be left on the table. Impasses can occur when the adversarial moves cut off communications, including reasoned discussion, and alienate the other side. Value can remain untapped because the adversarial tactics and tricks can preoccupy parties and blind them to creative opportunities. While Stephen is occupied with strategically pressuring Philip, for instance, he may push Philip away from the negotiation table and miss the opportunity to work with him again.

Following are some illustrations of how the different types of music described in the introduction to this chapter can influence, persuade, or pressure the other side to make concessions.[52]

Good Practices, Including Justifications

The music of good practices can be the most effective negotiation style, as already elaborated in detail.[53] For example, you may try to persuade the other side by justifying a claim based on rational and principled explanations while helping the other side preserve their credibility and save face because justifications can give them a rationale for making a concession. Stephen might argue that Philip is liable because the non-compete clause clearly bars competing within the city of Buffalo. By justifying his demand for damages based on his interpretation of the key clause, Stephen is giving Philip a rationale to make a concession if he is persuaded by the interpretation.

Justifications also can provide a reasoned basis for maintaining your position. For example, you may point out that new information learned during the

---

52 For a catalogue of negotiating tactics and tricks, *see generally* Craver, *supra* note 21, ch. 10. For a full discussion of the norms of reciprocity examined in this chapter, *see* Jennifer K. Robbennolt and Jean R. Sternlight, *Psychology of Lawyers: Understanding the Human Factors in Negotiation, Litigation, and Decision Making*, 127–128, 281–285 (2012).

53 *See infra* Section 1.1.

negotiation should convince the other side of the merits of your position. Furthermore, the use of justifications can be an effective way to steer a positional negotiation toward a reasoned discussion, as parties shift from exchanging positions to exchanging explanations.

When making a concession in the negotiation dance, you may want to justify it by educating the other side about its value. You are likely to value your concession as a loss more than the beneficiary values it as a gain because "losses loom larger than gains," as emphasized by Professors Robbennolt and Sternlight. Losses are magnified because parties do not like give up something (known as the endowment effect) and parties place more value on losing the safety of the known than on the possibility of gain from risking the unknown (labeled the status quo bias). Because of this difference in the way a giver and receiver value the same concession, you may want to explain its significance by bringing the other side'sreasoned attention to it. If you drop your demand from $1,000,000 to $800,000, for instance, you might want to highlight the significance of the concession by citing relevant reference points—for example, that it is a 20 percent drop, that it is a much larger concession than the other side has made, or that you made it because your client prefers to pay the other side to settle the case over incurring the same costs to prove she is right in court.

Recall the limitations of these good practices, however. When you encounter a party that is clearly unresponsive and may be using your good practices against you, for example, they may be exploiting your practice of justifications as a delaying tactic.

Tactics

Tactics have already been defined as generally accepted conventions in negotiations designed to influence, persuade, and pressure. There are numerous possible tactics, and although not everyone will agree on the list, these illustrations can be safely classified as common tactics that sometimes can be essential to use in a positional negotiation.

- Making inflated or deflated opening offers to create room for making concessions
- Making inflated or deflated proposals to anchor the other side's thinking to an upper or lower range
- Puffing about your bottom line by using various techniques such as conveying misleading clues and shading information to influence the other side's perception of your bottom line

- Disclosing or withholding selective information to strengthen the appearance of your own legal case (BATNA)
- Formulating a concession plan to convey information (for example, signaling movement toward your bottom line by making your concessions progressively smaller)
- Making partisan arguments and belittling the other side's arguments, including presenting "evidence" to undermine the other side's case or proposals
- Making selective threats to leave the negotiation
- Exploiting the reciprocity norm with a tactic to induce a concession

You might psychologically manipulate the other side with an initially extreme anchor that is likely to be rejected, followed quickly by a reduction that feels less onerous, as if you are making a concession. Then the other side may be spurred to make a reciprocal concession. Depending on the way you do it, this strategy may be a tactic, as illustrated here, or as a trick, as illustrated in the next section.

I recall experiencing this psychological pressure to make a concession when I was told that the construction of a new cabinet in my home did not include the cost of the stone top, when I thought it did, and that the top would cost an additional $3,000. Before I had a chance to react to this startling increase in the cost of the project, I was told the contractor would split the additional cost with me due to the misunderstanding, and that the contractor would rebid the top. Then the cost dropped to $1,500 and my additional cost became $750. I of course accepted the proposal and then realized that these exchanges went from me not paying anything more to feeling relieved it was only $750 more. What happened? While I do not think he intentionally manipulated me, I was manipulated by the "concession" presentation. I felt a need to say yes because the contractor seemed reasonable and the increase was only 25 percent of the initial estimated increase—what a deal.

In court cases, you can manipulate others by including a high demand in the pleadings and making a lower first offer in the negotiations. If the pleading sets forth a claim for a million dollars and your first offer is $750,000, for example, the other side is likely to experience your move as a substantial concession, even though they may have thought the amount in the pleading was a preposterous number. Or the other side may offer to pay nothing and then, after some discussion, bid against themselves by offering to pay something that is more than nominal. This low anchor with a concession to pay more may prompt you to reciprocate with a concession.

Stephen, who is demanding $100,000, might make a first offer of $90,000. This concession, when measured against his initial demand, may spur a counteroffer from Philip.

Stephen also may adopt a different tactic of withholding disclosure of his interest in working with Philip in the future to protect himself from being exploited. Instead of seeing this disclosure as an opportunity to uncover a better solution, Stephen fears that Philip might use this information to secure a reduction in the damage claim in return for working with him again.

As already highlighted, tactics pose risks. Once discovered, they can hurt the negotiation.

Tricks

Tricks, as already discussed, are inherently adversarial and controversial and can be considered dirty or unethical. Because they are less acceptable to the other side than tactics, tricks, when discovered, not only defeat them but also can undermine if not destroy the bargaining process.

Here are several examples of possible tricks, although some negotiators might consider a few of them to be tactics:

- *Limited settlement authority*: You claim you cannot settle because your client lacks sufficient settlement authority, which may force the other side to either concede within the range of your settlement authority or renegotiate later with a person with sufficient settlement authority. This trick might breach a local rule that requires you to appear with requisite settlement authority unless you can demonstrate that the level of authority is sufficient for the amount in dispute or it reflects what you saw as the value of the case.
- *Lying about a fact*: An example is misrepresenting in a breach-of-contract dispute that you have offers for buying the product that the defendant did not timely deliver. Such a misrepresentation would violate Rule 4.1 of the ABA Professional Code of Conduct, on truth telling.
- *Irrevocable commitment*: You make a commitment that cannot be changed so that the other side must either concede or not settle.
- *Misleading through intentional ambiguities*: You make somewhat vague statements that give you wiggle room to get out of an apparent commitment.
- *Exploit the reciprocity norm with a trick*: You set up a sham to manipulate the other side into making a concession. For instance, you might make several

demands, including a false one, and then concede the false demand. Your false concession may spur the other side to make a concession.

If you choose a style of positional negotiations toward the adversarial end of the continuum of practices, you are apt to ratchet up the tactics, and especially the tricks, while minimizing any justifications in an effort to extract a final favorable concession. You may exploit tricks such as pressing false demands and appearing with limited settlement authority. And you may make aggressive threats about dragging the other side through lengthy and expensive court proceedings. You may deviously disclose partisan information to pressure the other side into making key concessions. You may hide vital information for fear that disclosure will result in the sacrificing of advantages at trial or to exploitation by the other side in the negotiations.[54] Also, you might persist with your position until the other side capitulates or walks away. Is this the sort of music that will provide the best result for your client?

How you package good practices with tactics and especially tricks will determine how problem solving or adversarial you will be. The packaging adopted by the other side signals their propensity toward a problem solving or adversarial style.

CRITICAL CHOICES

What music do you want to play when negotiating (where on the problem-solving–adversarial style continuum do you want to practice)?

A. Justifications
B. Tactics
C. Tricks

Recommendations: You should try to maintain a problem solving style of good practices and tactics in order to increase your negotiation effectiveness.

c. Closure

i. Deadline

As will be more fully considered under problem-solving negotiations, you may need to establish a deadline to accelerate closure to the negotiation—to alert the participants that it is time to make their last, best efforts to resolve the dispute.

54 *See* Menkel-Meadow (1984), *supra* note 1, at 780–782 (Professor Menkel-Meadow points out that fear of disclosure may be displaced in this era of discovery and that disclosure of preferences in negotiations is not the same thing as disclosing "evidence.").

ii. Finish Final Bargaining

As the bargaining session rushes toward closure, you and the other side can be under heavy pressure to compromise, including pressure to make a last minute concession and split any remaining difference. The music at the end can get intense, with parties threatening to leave. Be careful. Keep firmly in mind your dance plan and bottom line.

During these intense final moments, you should patiently maintain the reciprocal concession pattern, even if the other side tries to pressure you to bargain against yourself. You should justify the significance of any concessions until you reach this final round while appealing calmly and firmly to the other side that it is their turn to make a meaningful concession. Keep count of the offers and counteroffers to guard against the other side asking to split the difference when it is their turn to make a concession. If you split prematurely, the split may favor the other side.[55] Also, you should measure each concession against your bottom line tripwire so that you do not unknowingly cross it and get stuck with a deal you cannot live with.

As the negotiation moved toward closure, Stephen and Philip confined themselves to the problem narrowly framed by Stephen's legal claim of damages for breach of the non-compete covenant. They limited themselves to rounds of concessions over money damages with an eye on the familiar formula of splitting the difference between the last two offers. After Stephen initially offered $100,000 and Philip countered with $5,000 to get rid of the nuisance claim, Stephen made a counteroffer of $90,000, and the concession dance continued until Stephen asked for $40,000 and Philip offered $20,000. As the day rushed toward the end and both threatened to leave, they progressed to $35,000 and $25,000, then $32,500 and $27,500, and finally they split the difference and settled for $30,000.

iii. Secure Commitment

If your negotiation is successful, you will need to secure a commitment for the participants to implement the key terms of the agreement. You should design a commitment device that comports with the risk of noncompliance; options

55 For example, if you ask for 30 and they counteroffer with 10, the split is 20. If you ask for 30, they counteroffer with 10, you counteroffer with 20, and they ask to split, the split is 15—a more favorable result to the other side than if they made the same number of offers as you did. If they made a second counteroffer of 15, so that each side would make two offers each, the split would be 17.50.

can range from social rituals to formal contracts to risk-free mechanisms, as further discussed under problem-solving negotiations.

If your negotiation is not yet successful, you should secure a commitment on what to do next. Options can range from agreeing to meet again to selecting another process for resolving the dispute.

d. Limitations

Negotiating along the positional path can be effective for distributive disputes, but this approach has several inherent limitations that were recognized in this section and will now be summarized. You should keep them in mind when negotiating this way.

i. Limits Creative Opportunities

If you prematurely view a dispute as distributive, you may foreclose your ability to see solutions other than moneyed ones. When you view the dispute as distributive, you do not leave space for discovering creative solutions because the moneyed offer and counteroffer establish the upper and lower ranges of settlement possibilities, leaving parties to negotiate along that continuum. The first offer and counteroffer also anchor parties' thinking about what is possible.

ii. Drains Creative Energy

You spend much of your creative energy planning and executing first offer strategies as well as planning the music rather than using that energy to investigate creative resolutions.

iii. Pressure to Split Differences

Once the dance of offers and counteroffers is under way, there is pressure on you and the other side to split any difference. Knowing this, parties present proposals with a strategic eye on the midpoint.

iv. Stresses Relationships

Positional negotiations can stress the relationship between you and your client, because the first offer can become a reference point for success or failure in the negotiation. Your client can forget that the initial offer was only an opening gambit, and can get upset when the final settlement proposal is far from the beginning points of the negotiation dance.

v. Generates Risk of Impasse

When you are engaged in a dance of offers and counteroffers, along with the use of tactics and especially tricks, the risk of impasse can be high, even though you and the other side may not be far apart. You may not know you are close, because both sides are occupied with the strategic dance.

e. Lawyers Favor the Positional Negotiation Approach

Why do many lawyers adopt a positional approach to negotiations? The simple and glib answer is that lawyers are preoccupied with litigating. As suggested in this chapter's introduction, negotiations are so enmeshed in the litigation process that negotiations and litigation have become an integrated, single process of dispute resolution. Thus, lawyers are likely to approach the negotiated settlement of a court case with a litigator's mindset.[56] This mindset is molded by a win-lose legal culture and reinforced by attorney fee arrangements and client preferences.

Legal training and experience teach lawyers to view legal disputes as zero-sum or distributive conflicts about money, in which one party wins and the other one loses. The very function of courts is to declare winners and losers. Judicial relief is usually limited to the defendant winning by paying nothing or losing by paying something. Based on the well-established maxim that "equitable relief is not available to one who has an adequate remedy at law," courts prefer awarding legal remedies, primarily damages. Before a court will award more creative relief, such as specific performance or inventive and tailored injunctions, a party must demonstrate that she would suffer irreparable harm and that the nature of the equitable relief would be practical and convenient, and would not sap judicial resources.[57] Otherwise, a court will limit relief to a monetary award.

The litigator's mindset is also shaped by the only too familiar routine for pursuing litigation. First, a litigator's conception of the dispute is shaped by the way he converts the dispute into a legal case. When drafting a complaint or answer, the attorney sculpts the dispute and fits it into recognized legal

---

56 Mnookin, *supra* note 1, at 108–118, 167–172.

57 Dan B. Dobbs, *Dobbs Law of Remedies,* para. 2.5 (2nd ed. 1993).

categories and then reinforces this conception of the dispute with supporting partisan arguments. The attorney then engages in various strategies to bolster the legal case because the perceived likely court outcome will impact the settlement value of the case. In addition to using old fashioned puffery and bluffing, the attorney typically turns to various litigation strategies. By pursuing more discovery and a motion for summary judgment, for instance, the attorney pursues the chance that more disclosure or a successful motion will strengthen the court case and its settlement value. The attorney may further press the other party to settle by resorting to litigation strategies that increase the other party's cost of staying in the litigation. By demanding voluminous discovery, for example, the attorney can increase the other party's costs of not settling. As the attorneys and parties become consumed by these litigation tactics, the litigation and accompanying positional negotiation strategy can quickly become sharply adversarial.

These litigation strategies can be fueled by the fee arrangements between attorneys and their clients, arrangements that can encourage questionable professional conduct. Obviously, an hourly rate arrangement can motivate attorneys to engage in strategies that prolong the litigation. And it takes only one attorney with an hourly rate incentive to prolong the litigation. Even though the alternative of a contingency fee arrangement can encourage early settlement (by settling early, the attorney can make more), it can discourage problem-solving searches for value-creating trades. A settlement that includes a new car or an apology, for instance, produces a settlement that cannot be neatly split into three shares, one of which goes to the attorney.

These litigation strategies are unconstrained by any incentive for a party to disclose weaknesses in his own court case. Neither party wants to be the first to blink. Each party wants to avoid any appearance of self-doubt that might empower the other party to intensify the litigation until the blinking party capitulates.

And then there are the expectations of clients. Many clients crave a fiercely combative approach to legal representation after watching lawyers in action in movies, television shows, and the news. Overly optimistic clients want to be protected by aggressive hired guns. They can resist reality checks and become uneasy with lawyers who may not appear faithful to the cause when they flag legal risks and inquire about the other side's perspective and needs.

In short, when the litigator's mindset is adapted to legal negotiations, his approach is bound to be positional, leaning toward an adversarial style.[58] This

58 One creative solution for changing the litigator's mindset is to change the attorney who tries to settle the case. Instead of pursuing both the litigation and the negotiations, the litigator only

approach to negotiations has been long-standing, despite studies showing that negotiators can be more effective as problem solvers[59] and that lawyers prefer problem-solving strategies.[60] The study of New Jersey litigators suggests that lawyers may negotiate adversarially out of habitual social practice and that such a style is less costly and more easily routinized than problem solving.[61]

Questions

1. Prepare to participate in a negotiation exercise in which the dispute is primarily distributive. Use a positional approach with a negotiation style that leans toward problem-solving or adversarial, depending on what your instructor requires. Try to achieve the best result possible for your client.
2. Suppose you know your dispute is primarily distributive, and you have a legally weak case. How would you approach the dance of concessions, and what music would you play? What are the risks of your strategy?

Assume that you are representing a defendant doctor who used an inadequately tested medical procedure for relieving back pain. The doctor was sued by a single patient for damages (medical bills and pain and suffering) for $5 million. The patient has no interests other than securing compensation.

Although the doctor was confident that the procedure would have had greater success, he now realizes that for a not insignificant number of patients, conditions were made worst by the procedure despite a number of wildly successful outcomes. The patients were never advised of the experimental nature of the procedure and were instead told that the procedure has been quite successful in relieving back pain, which is true. The doctor is worried that many other potential plaintiffs may appear, and he wants you to settle this case as quickly as possible. You realize that the pain and suffering is significant, and

---

litigates. Any negotiations would be handled by a separate settlement counsel who is committed to a problem-solving approach. For a thoughtful development of this solution, *see generally* William F. Coyne, Jr., "The Case for Settlement Counsel," 14 *Ohio St. J. on Disp. Resol.* 367 (1999). The author concluded that "the mind-set needed to do effective problem solving is incompatible with the mindset needed to pursue litigation whole-heartedly." *Id.* at 393.

59 *See generally* Schneider, *supra* note 4.

60 Milton Heumann and Jonathan M. Hyman, "Negotiation Methods and Litigation Settlement Methods in New Jersey: 'You Can't Always Get What You Want'," 12 *Ohio St. J. on Disp. Resol.* 253, 309 (1997). "While 61% of the lawyers would like to see more problem-solving negotiation methods, about 71% of negotiations are carried out with positional methods instead." *Id.*

61 *Id.* at 295–309.

based on prior jury verdicts, you conclude that your client should not pay more than $4 million so long as the settlement includes a confidentiality clause. You aspire to settle for $2 million.

3. *Helping the client evaluate the legal case and calculate the bottom line*
   a. Why is understanding a client's BATNA (best alternative to a negotiated agreement) vital in legal negotiations?
   b. Assessing rigorously your client's total BATNA can be difficult, and calls for vital judgments by you as the attorney and by your client. Estimate the value of Ms. Earnest's total BATNA in the hypothetical found in Section 5.19. Ms. Earnest claims she was discriminated against and wants $50,000 in damages. Assume that Ms. Earnest does not want to return to work with Cutting Edge Computers and, as the facts indicate, is anxious to settle because she needs the money for a down payment on her new home. After researching the facts and the law, you as her attorney estimate that she has (a) a 60 percent chance of winning (b) $50,000 at trial and that (c) the attorney fee and other costs would be about $10,000 (in real life, you would have to make these three difficult judgments). Cutting Edge has offered to settle the case by paying $16,000. Should Ms. Earnest accept the offer? Use the methodology explained in Appendix A, on decision tree plus analysis.
      i. Calculate Ms. Earnest's public BATNA.
      ii. Calculate Ms. Earnest's minimum personal BATNA amount that would justify accepting the settlement offer. What questions might you pose to Ms. Earnest to help her estimate her personal BATNA?
      iii. Should Ms. Earnest accept the $16,000 settlement offer?
   c. Explain the total BATNA calculation in plain language to your client, Ms. Earnest. Be sure to give specific attention to the significance of the expected value calculation.
   d. See Online Video at 1.2 (Mumbai) to observe one way a decision tree is used by a mediator to educate a party about her BATNA as the party figures out her next offer.

3. PROBLEM-SOLVING APPROACH AND STYLE

This section first examines in detail the key features and strategies of the problem-solving approach, highlighting within each feature the problem solving style of good practices. The key features are converted later in the chapter into problem-solving stages that serve as a handy roadmap to engaging in problem-solving negotiations.[62]

Let's start with a succinct description of the problem-solving approach that captures key features introduced at the beginning of this chapter. The problem-solving approach is designed to create and claim, with negotiators choosing a style along a continuum of practices from problem-solving to adversarial. These practices can be classified as good practices, tactics, and tricks, as already considered, although selecting the right label is less important than developing an understanding of how practices fall along a continuum of good, accepted, and controversial ones. The problem-solving approach incorporates the positional approach as one strategy to consider during the claiming stage.

The starting point and structure of the problem-solving approach are starkly different from those of positional negotiations that focus primarily on claiming. Instead of executing opening offer strategies, negotiators begin by gathering information about each other's interests and BATNAs (alternatives to settlement). Instead of engaging in the ritualistic negotiation dance of exchanging positions, problem solvers create value by brainstorming options and then claim value by trading benefits, using objective standards, and bargaining positionally in order to meet their interests and achieve a result better than their BATNAs.

This section first describes the distinctive problem solver orientations that shape how the negotiator prepares for and participates in the negotiation session.

View Problem Broadly to Encompass Underlying Interests and Needs

Central to the problem-solving enterprise is the lens through which the negotiator views the dispute. By viewing the dispute broadly, you search beyond the issues specifically raised in the court case. You do not feel confined to resolving the legally defined dispute.

View as Shared Problem

You do not approach the other side as an arch adversary, but as a working partner trying to resolve a shared problem.

View Dispute as an Integrative Opportunity, Not a Distributive Problem

You do not view the dispute as a limited distributive problem over how to divide a fixed resource. By uncovering the underlying interests and needs of

62 *See infra* Section 1.6.

both sides, you search for opportunities to increase resources (create value) and discover possible solutions.

View Dispute as Search for "Win-Win" and Pareto Optimal Solutions

You are looking for ways both sides can gain or ways one side can gain without making the other side worse off. You are looking for the often-cited "win-win"[63] and Pareto optimal solutions.[64]

In the example Stephen does not view the dispute as a narrow breach-of-contract claim but instead views it more broadly as the breakdown in the employment relationship between him as teacher and Philip as protégé. He approaches the breakdown as a shared problem that he and Philip could work together to resolve in a way in which both might gain something or in which the harm to one side might be minimized.

Think Creatively Outside the Legal Box

Through the problem-solving lens you search for solutions outside the box of legal rights, obligations, precedent, and traditional remedies. By not viewing the dispute as limited to dividing up a fixed resource, you look for solutions that are more inventive than simply paying money from one person to another.

Claiming Without Early Opening Offer Strategy

In a problem-solving process, you do not prepare an opening offer strategy to launch the claiming process. Instead, you focus on developing proposals

---

63 In case you missed the explanation of the "win-win" terminology in the Introduction, I repeat it here. I think the overused "win-win" terminology still retains utility because of the contrast that it makes with the opposite view of "win-lose." These contrasting attitudes neatly capture the fundamental differences between problem-solving and positional approaches. However, for many lawyers, the idea that both sides can win something seems naive and not anchored in reality.

That lawyers should consider that the idea that both sides might be able to gain something in negotiations reflects an optimistic attitude that can open the mind to creative searches. Moreover, the possibilities of a gain in negotiations are greater than in court. In negotiations, even the defendant who has to pay considerable damages may gain other benefits, such as no publicity, no precedent, and maybe even a continuing business relationship.

64 Pareto optimal solutions are reached by parties making a series of Pareto superior moves until they reach the point where there are no more improvements that can make one party better off without making the other party worse off. A Pareto superior move is simply when an improvement for one party does not make the other party worse off. *See* Raiffa, *supra* note 45, at 139.

through a discussion of each other's interests and then claiming based on trading, objective standards, and positional bargaining.[65]

Promote Effective Communications and Exchange of Information

You are committed to opening up communications between the parties. In contrast to a positional negotiator, you appreciate the benefits of judiciously exchanging accurate information about key issues, interests, BATNAs, potential resources and value, and options for settlement.

Value Relationship

In contrast with positional negotiations, especially the more adversarial style where relationships can be subject to great stress and even destroyed, you approach the relationship with respect and with an eye toward improving it, even if there is no prospect for a continuing relationship.

Be Open to Other Side's Views and Interests

You are interested in learning about the other side's perspective, needs, and priorities. As discussed below under "Preparation," this information is valuable in developing a solution that meets the interests of both sides, a solution that is more likely to be adopted by both sides.

Approach Search for Solutions with an Open Mind

You do not enter the negotiations with a preconceived view of the right solution. Instead, you approach the negotiations with an open mind, ready to learn about the other party's interests and to engage in a process of generating monetary and nonmonetary options and searching for opportunities to trade value and use objective standards. Stephen would not enter the negotiations convinced that the right solution is for Philip to pay him $100,000. Even though Stephen would arrive with an understanding of his alternative to settlement as a tripwire, he would approach the initial negotiations as an opportunity to learn more about Philip's interests and to engage in a process of generating options for resolution.

This section considers how problem-solving attorneys with these orientations prepare for the negotiations and what strategies they are likely to employ at the negotiation table. For a summary of the features and style, see the accompanying table "Problem-Solving Approach and Style." Be sure to note that the

65 *See* Fisher et al., *supra* note 36, at 173–174.

defining features of the approach are in bold while the defining styles of good practices are in italics under each feature. Even though the good practices style will be illustrated, you should be aware that a style of tactics and tricks, toward the more adversarial end of the continuum, offers other choices, although they are discouraged in this text.

Problem-Solving Approach and Style

- a. **Preparation**
  - i. **Gather Information Identify Interests Identify Issues**
    - *Identify Impediments*
    - *Assess Bottom Line (Total BATNA)—Primary Bargaining Power*
    - *Assess Leverage—Other Power*
    - *Stimulate Client to Create and Claim*
  - ii. **Plan for Emotions as an Obstacle and Opportunity**
    - *Check Your Own and Others' Emotional Temperatures Form an Emergency Plan*
    - *Proactively Cultivate Positive Emotions*
  - iii. **Plan Questions and Judicious Sharing of Information**
    - *Develop Questions*
    - *Plan to Share Information Judiciously*
- b. **Strategies and Stages at the Table**
  - i. **Exchange information**
    - *Establish Rapport and Open Communications*
    - *Ask Questions*
    - *Share Information Judiciously*
  - ii. **Advocate for Client's Interests**
  - iii. **Overcome Any Impediments**
  - iv. **Create Options**
  - v. **Claim**
    - *Trading Benefits*
    - *Comport with Objective Criteria*
    - *Positional Bargaining*
- c. **Closure**
  - i. *Establish Deadlines*
  - ii. *Finish Final Bargaining*
  - iii. *Secure Commitment*

a. Preparation

i. Gather Information

Identify Interests

"Interests motivate people; they are the silent movers behind the hubbub of positions. Your position is something you have decided upon. Your interests are what caused you to so decide."[66]

> **CRITICAL CHOICES**
>
> *Identify Interests*
>
> You should give attention to the essential question that forms the foundation of a problem-solving negotiation: What are the interests of your client?

You should advocate zealously for your client's interests in the negotiation, as both an essential feature of the problem-solving process and a good practice in any negotiation process. Your success will be measured by whether your client's primary interests are met better in the negotiation than they would have been by your client's BATNA. This is the ultimate measure of your effectiveness as a negotiator. You want to avoid the situation where you fail to identify and advocate for your client's interests because you are blinded by your focusing on the solution you want to achieve.

To uncover your client's interests, you must search behind your client's demands (positions) by posing the simple and penetrating question of "why." By bringing to the surface the underlying interests of your client and surmising the interests of the other party, you avoid a contest over competing positions, a contest that usually produces a narrow legal solution. Discovering interests is much harder than it appears. Techniques to do so when interviewing clients are examined in detail in Section 3.2.

Stephen's attorney would not advocate Stephen's legal position that he be paid $100,000 in damages. Getting $100,000 is not Stephen's ultimate goal. His goal is to meet his interests. When asked why he wants the money, he may answer that he wants compensation for stolen business opportunities and recognition for providing Philip good training and mentoring. These answers suggest that Stephen's interests are in making money and in being recognized

66 *Id.* at 43.

for how he helped Philip. The damages claim is only one way (or position) for satisfying these interests.

Stephen's interests might be met in other ways, including rehiring his successful protégé, developing a partnership, getting verbal recognition to supplement any monetary recognition, and other possibilities. Stephen will have to figure out which of the options will best meet his interests and be acceptable to Philip.

Identify Issues

Out of the massive collection of facts, you should develop a list of tentative issues for resolution. Issues are the subjects that you will negotiate over. They usually can be framed as questions. For example, what is the risk of the defendant being held liable? What are the damages? What opportunities might there be for a continuing relationship? For the Shirts for You dispute, you might propose the following as an issue: Are there any options for Stephen and Philip to work together in the future? Another way to frame the issue might be: Are there any ways that Philip might be helpful to Stephen in the future?

Identify Impediments

You need to identify any impediments that might be hampering a resolution and develop a plan to overcome them. Identifying impediments is a key feature of problem solving, and how you overcome them offers choices including good practice options. A good practice methodology is fully explained in Chapter 3, on counseling your client, where impediments are classified into five categories—relationship, data, interests, structural, and value—and strategies for each category are considered, with additional strategies provided in Chapter 5, on developing a mediation representation plan.

If Stephen thinks Philip stole some customers, it may be necessary to review audited customer lists to find out whether there are any overlapping customers. And if there are some, further examination may need to focus on whether similar or different brands were sold to each customer. Until this data conflict is resolved, Stephen may feel he does not have sufficient information to move forward in the negotiation.

Assess Bottom Line (total BATNA)—Primary Bargaining Power

You can justify asking something more for your client by demonstrating that if you do not get what you are asking for, you will leave the negotiation to get something better. That something better is her BATNA—the best alternative to a negotiated agreement—and is a key source of bargaining power.

You should diligently research your client's total BATNA as a good practice. For attorneys representing clients in court cases, the BATNA will typically, but not always,[67] be the outcome in court plus the client's personal costs and benefits of litigating. When your client knows her BATNA, your client can enter the negotiations knowing her bottom line, against which she can evaluate whether to accept or reject any emerging settlement packages.

Her BATNA serves as a tripwire for marking when to leave the negotiation. For a full discussion of how to calculate your client's total BATNA, see the subsection on establishing your bottom line in Section 1.2 and Appendix A, on decision trees.

You also should surmise the other party's BATNA in order to learn when the other party is likely to leave the table. His alternative may be different from your BATNA. This information provides you with an essential reference point for understanding the minimum that you can achieve in the negotiations. You cannot expect the other party to agree to something less attractive than his alternative to a negotiated agreement. However, if you think the other party has an unrealistically optimistic view of his BATNA, you need to plan to educate the other party.

Neither Stephen nor Philip can be confident about winning in court. Stephen risks losing the court case because it is not clear whether Philip has breached his covenant to not compete when Philip sells a different brand of shirts to a different group of customers in Buffalo. Philip risks losing because Philip is competing in the same market as Stephen—selling shirts to retail outlets in Buffalo. These dual uncertain BATNAs should motivate both parties to settle the dispute.

Assess Leverage—Other Power

You also can justify getting more for your client by identifying and exerting any other leverage you have in the negotiation. Richard Shell, in his book *Bargaining for Advantage,* helpfully divides leverage into three types—positive, negative, and normative.[68]

---

67 For example, sometimes the most attractive alternative to settling a court case might be filing for bankruptcy, doing nothing, or publicizing the dispute. In one case that I mediated, the defendant spent most of the mediation session trying to convince the plaintiff that if he did not accept the defendant's offer, the defendant would be forced to file for bankruptcy and the plaintiff would get nothing.

68 Shell, *supra* note 49, at 101–105.

You have positive leverage when you have something the other person wants or cannot do without. You gain leverage over the other side and justify getting something when you discover a way to meet the other side's interests such that this agreement would be better than no agreement (a second translation of BATNA—better alternative to no agreement). Philip can assert positive leverage by offering Stephen access to new customers if Philip is allowed to return to work with him.

You have leverage that is negative when you can make the other side worse off. In legal negotiations, your BATNA of going to court may impose negative consequences on the other side. If they fail to offer you a better settlement than your BATNA, you can go to court and inflict on the other side a court-imposed consequence that would presumably be worse than settling. The stronger your legal case, the more negative leverage you can assert against the other side. Parties also can assert negative leverage by their power to prolong the litigation and, as a result, impose legal expenses on the other side.[69] Stephen, who is threatening a lawsuit, has negative leverage over Philip, and the stronger his case, the more power he has to extract settlement benefits from Philip. By Stephen suing to enjoin Philip from competing, for instance, Stephen may motivate Philip to settle rather than risk a court's preventing him from soliciting particular customers.

You have normative leverage when you can appeal to principles, such as consistency, reciprocity, ethics, morality, or fairness, that the other side subscribes to. These appeals can influence people who abide by any of these normative principles, especially when the other side has a continuing relationship with your side. Philip can gain leverage by appealing to the principle of reciprocity when he offers to bring Stephen some new customers. This reciprocity appeal puts pressure on Stephen to find a way to offer a benefit to Philip.

Stimulate Client to Create and Claim

> **CRITICAL CHOICES**
>
> *Stimulate Your Client to Create and Claim*
>
> Your client can be a vital source of inventive ideas, including undiscovered value and tailored solutions.

---

69 In the United States, because each party usually pays her own legal costs, the party who wants to prolong the litigation can increase the costs incurred by the other side. In England and most civil law countries, where the loser pays all the legal costs, the party with the stronger case can impose her legal costs on the other side if the other side does not settle.

You should prod your client to think broadly, creatively, and outside the traditional legal box for value (resources) that might form the basis for inventive and tailored solutions—solutions that meet the needs of both parties. While the positional negotiator focuses primarily on options within the legal box of rights and remedies, a problem-solving one searches more expansively for options.

In preparing for the negotiation, you should try to stimulate your client's creative juices. Your client can be a vital source of original and inventive ideas and of information that only she may know about and can live with. At this juncture, your goal is not to formulate firm proposals; it is too soon. You want the proposals to emerge from the negotiation.

When asked to think more broadly about his dispute, Stephen may begin to imagine other ways to make money than recovering damages for lost sales. He might be able to make more money than he could recover in court by working together again with Philip. Options for working together could be explored at the negotiation table.

You also should prompt your client to begin identifying objective criteria that might be the basis for claiming options and dividing the zone of possible agreement.

Objective criteria[70] can provide a fair basis for claiming during the fashioning of solutions. They comprise neutral standards that can be either substantive or procedural and can be used as a basis for decision making (claiming) between the parties. Objective criteria can be derived from practice, custom, precedent, scientific findings, mathematical and econometric models, expert opinion, and any other autonomous source. The criteria must be independent and cannot be influenced by any of the parties at the table. They also must be legitimate and practical to use. Examples of substantive standards include calculating the value of a home based on the average price of four-bedroom houses in a particular neighborhood, and calculating salary increases based on the cost-of-living index of the U.S. Department of Commerce. Examples of procedural standards include the formula for splitting the difference or taking turns and the procedure for asking an expert to make a decision.

Stephen and Philip might agree to select a new sales commission rate for Philip based on the average rate for salespeople in the Buffalo area with more than ten years of experience.[71] This rate might be acceptable to both parties because it would be derived from independent sources, making it an objective criterion.

---

70 For a full discussion of objective criteria, *see* Fisher et al., *supra* note 36, at 82–95.

71 This proposal assumes that there are no antitrust risks in compiling this information.

When you initiate a discussion of sources for value and objective criteria, you begin to probe for possible solutions, although you will defer fully generating and assessing options until the mediation session, as explored in subsections iv and v.

ii. Plan for Emotions as an Obstacle and Opportunity

Emotional reactions by you, your client, or the other side can impede the resolution of the dispute. You already know that from experience. You need a plan for dealing constructively with this predictable reality.

Negative emotions can impact negotiations in damaging ways. When a party is controlled by his emotions, his ability to think clearly and creatively can be clouded. Emotions can distort what he sees and hears and can control his behavior. And emotions can escalate the dispute by fueling the emotions of the other side and generating a relationship conflict that can impede moving forward.[72]

You should develop a plan to prevent negative emotions from hijacking the negotiations and a plan to harness the positive ones to facilitate the negotiations. This discussion of emotions is from the excellent book *Beyond Reason: Using Emotions as You Negotiate*, by Roger Fisher and Daniel Shapiro (2005). They propose a three-part plan consisting of, first, checking the emotional temperature in the room; second, formulating an emergency plan to deal with negative emotions as they arise; and third, proactively cultivating positive emotions.

Part 1: Check Your Own and Others' Emotional Temperatures

You should frequently check the emotional temperature in the room. As a benchmark, you might monitor for three levels of temperature: normal—that is, manageable; risky—when emotions are simmering and approaching a dangerous level; and out of control—when emotions move past the boiling point, and things are said that should not be said.

It is easier to check your behavior than that of others, because you know yourself better and are more likely to recognize when your behavior does not "feel" normal. It is harder to take the emotional temperature of others, but your first clue may be when they start acting out of the ordinary. I recall a negotiation where the other attorney was impressively even-tempered after hours of a

---

72 Relationship conflicts as an impediment are examined in Section 3.2(b), on interviewing your client, and in Section 5.6(a), on developing a mediation representation plan.

highly charged negotiation, and then he began telling a story about problems with a summer home he was buying. He turned red in anger and referred to the seller in uncharacteristically profane terms. It became apparent that the negotiation was taking an emotional toll on him. His temperature was increasing to the risky level.

Part 2: Form an Emergency Plan

You should have a plan in place to manage your own emotions and the emotions of your client. Fisher and Shapiro suggest a three-part emergency plan: first, know how to sooth yourself and others; second, learn to recognize triggers of strong emotions; and third, before you react emotionally, formulate a purpose.[73]

A. Soothe Yourself and Others: Cool Down the Temperature

You should become aware of what techniques help to calm your emotions. They might include taking a break, counting backward from ten, changing the subject or negotiation environment, thinking about a positive BATNA, letting upsetting comments fly by you, and assessing whether an issue really is important to you.

You can try to calm the emotions of others by adapting the techniques that calm you along with other techniques, such as expressing your understanding of their underlying concerns or diplomatically trying to change the negotiator by inviting other parties to the table. You should avoid rewarding their negative emotions with a gain in the negotiations.

B. Identify Triggers of Strong Emotions

Consider what behaviors can trigger your emotions and the emotions of others. Emotions can distract and divert you until you understand the message that they are conveying. To help us understand the underlying causes, Fisher and Shapiro identify five core concerns that, when impinged, can cause negative emotions. These concerns dig deep into our core as human beings, and the triggers may vary culturally.[74] Their book devotes considerable attention to explaining these five core concerns. Impinged ones can generate relationship conflicts that can impede the resolution of a dispute.

73 Roger Fisher and Daniel Shapiro, *Beyond Reason: Using Emotions as You Negotiate,* 149–163 (2005).

74 *Id.* at 25–140.

This subsection summarizes the core concerns and illustrates how they can be the source of negative emotions and relationship conflict. In the next subsection, you will see illustrations of how to overcome this impediment.

Appreciation: Feeling Unappreciated

Are the upset person's thoughts, feelings, and actions being devalued? Stephen feels unappreciated because Philip does not seem to value the special professional relationship they had.

Affiliation: Feeling Unaffiliated

Is the upset person being treated as an adversary and feeling isolated and disconnected? Philip is upset that his mentor has sued him. Instead of feeling affiliated, he now feels alienated because his mentor is treating him as an adversary.

Autonomy: Impinged On

Is the upset person's freedom to make decisions being impinged upon? Does the person feel that he was not consulted before others decided? Stephen may be upset that Philip invaded his sales territory without his permission, in violation of the agreement not to compete. He is disturbed that his protégé failed to consult him.

Status: Feeling Denigrated

Is the upset person's standing treated as inferior to that of others? Does the person feel demeaned? Does the person feel that his particular status is not acknowledged? Stephen may be upset that after he mentored Philip like a son, Philip is demeaning that relationship by setting up a business to compete with him.

Role: Feeling Unfulfilled

Are the upset person's current role and activities not personally fulfilling? Is the role trivialized and restricted? Philip may still be upset about how his work with Stephen became unfulfilling because Stephen stifled Philip's growth.

C. Formulate a Purpose Before Reacting Emotionally

If you are going to express your anger, do so for a purpose. And then express your anger in a way that serves your purpose. Here are three constructive purposes suggested by Fisher and Shapiro.[75]

You may need to vent—to feel the release of expressing your emotions. You should focus on understanding, not blaming, and dig for core concerns in order to understand the reasons for your emotions. As you vent, you risk

75 *Id.* at 156–163.

creating a litany of justifications that can further entrench your point of view. You might consider venting to a third party, like a mediator, who is not unconditionally biased in your favor and can moderate self-justifications and your perspective.

You as the attorney also can be an effective third-party listener for your client.

You may want to educate the other side about how upset you are about their behavior. They may not appreciate the emotional impact of what they did. You might want to express your emotions in order to influence the other side. For example, you can communicate the importance of an interest by expressing it intensely.

Part 3: Proactively Cultivate Positive Emotions

The third part of the plan is to promote positive emotions. The more positive the emotions, the more likely the parties will be to cooperate, be creative, and find ways to meet each other's substantive interests. The more proactive you are, the less likely you are to impinge a core concern and trigger a relationship conflict that might impede moving forward.

You can stimulate positive emotions by focusing on the five core concerns.

Express Appreciation

You should appreciate others by understanding their points of view; finding merit in what they think, feel, and do; and communicating your understanding. Philip can stimulate positive feelings by expressing authentically how much he appreciates Stephen's invaluable mentoring.

Build Affiliation

You should try to build connections as a colleague or confidante rather than letting the other negotiator feel alone and disconnected. Stephen can generate positive feelings by offering to rebuild his connection with Philip—to build an affiliation by, for example, resuming socializing. In two contentious cases, I recall the parties agreeing to get together for dinner as the attorneys were drafting the settlement agreement.

Respect Autonomy

You should recognize that most people want the freedom to affect or make decisions. You should respect their freedom to decide important matters and "always consult before deciding" (ACBD), according to Fisher and Shapiro.[76] Philip can induce positive feelings by consulting Stephen, as his former mentor, about his plans to sell a different brand of shirts in Buffalo. He may solicit his advice and possibly his acquiescence.

Acknowledge Status

You should acknowledge everyone's particular status rather than compete with others over who has higher status. You should give full recognition where it is deserved. No one likes to feel demeaned. Philip can cultivate positive feelings by recognizing what a valuable mentor Stephen has been and hopefully will continue to be. He might further acknowledge that Stephen has been like a father to him.

Choose a Fulfilling Role

You should help people work together and expand their activities to make their roles fulfilling and meaningful so that they feel they can make a difference. Stephen can engender positive feelings by apologizing for how he might have stifled Philip's growth and by helping him develop a more fulfilling professional role. He might give Philip some leads, for example.

Thus, this three-part plan should prepare you to identify and productively handle the inevitable emotional dimensions of the dispute.

iii. Plan Questions and Judicious Sharing of Information

Develop Questions

As you gather as much information as you can on your own, you are bound to encounter some information gaps. You should prepare gap-filling questions to pose at the beginning of the negotiation. You may need to ask about the other side's interests, possible impediments, issues that need to be resolved, and alternatives to settlement.

For example, although you may have surmised what you believe to be the interests of the other side, a potent source of positive leverage in the negotiation, you may want to try to clarify or confirm their interests. You may have a good sense of the impediments, but may want to verify them at the negotiation—but be careful. If you probe too deeply, you might solidify a vague obstacle.

---

76 *Id.* at 84.

Plan to Share Information Judiciously

The most vexing question during problem solving is: What information should you disclose? Disclosure offers benefits and poses risks because of the clash of two essential goals in negotiations.[77] To maximize the creation of joint value, you should disclose full and accurate information about interests, priorities, issues, impediments, and potential resources (value). But to maximize your client's benefits—in other words, to claim the largest possible share of the pie—you may need to strategically conceal and misrepresent interests, priorities, and resources. You do not want the information disclosed during creating to disadvantage you when claiming value.

For example, if Philip disliked working by himself and wants to work again with Stephen, he should disclose that interest when trying to create value. By sharing that information, the parties would know to focus on creating options that include rehiring Philip in some capacity. But Philip may fear that Stephen would exploit this information by trying to extract a concession, such as a lower sales commission until Philip pays him back the lost sales. Philip also would lose leverage for gaining a higher commission to reflect his professional growth since going out on his own.

Because of these risks of exploitation or lost leverage, attorneys may play it safe by withholding information. This instinctive reaction should be resisted and tested against the following three challenging questions.

CRITICAL CHOICES

What Information to Disclose and How:
The Creating/Claiming Dilemma

1. What information should you disclose to create value?
2. Is there a risk that disclosing the information may hurt you when claiming?
3. How can you disclose the information in a way that minimizes the risk of exploitation or lost leverage?[1]

The first two questions can be merged with the third one and serve as your primary inquiry: How can you disclose the information that needs to be shared in a way that minimizes the risk of exploitation or lost leverage? Philip can indicate that he might consider returning if the terms were sufficiently attractive. This

77 *See* Barriers to Conflict Resolution 8 (Kenneth Arrow et al. eds., 1995).

conditional answer puts his interest on the table for discussion while reducing his exposure to exploitation. And Philip can try to leverage favorable rehiring terms by pointing out his impressive sales record when he was on his own. In short, it is not about withholding information. It is about disclosing information judiciously.

b. Strategies and Stages at the Table

i. Exchange Information for Specific Purposes

Establish Rapport and Open Communications

As a problem-solving negotiator with a problem-solving style, you approach the other side respectfully and cordially, formulate carefully framed questions, and use passive and active listening techniques.[78] You present points in a way that is likely to be heard by the other side. Instead of posturing and making contentious positional arguments, you present points with reasoned explanations.

You can facilitate the exchange of information by cultivating a positive relationship with the other side. For instance, you might inquire about common experiences unrelated to the negotiation, but you should not overdo it by coming across as inauthentic. You are trying to develop a working relationship and rapport.

Instead of Stephen and Philip approaching each other as arch enemies, they approach each other as parties who want to meet, talk, and communicate with each other (actually understand each other's perspective). Rather than Philip attacking Stephen for interfering with Philip's professional growth, Philip explains that he left because he was running out of opportunities to grow. As a young salesperson, he wanted new and challenging professional opportunities. This reasoned explanation leaves the door open for Stephen to pick up where Philip left off and explore how working again at Shirts for You might be an attractive professional opportunity for Philip.

As part of establishing rapport, you should manage the emotional climate of the negotiation. You should avoid impinging any of the five core concerns that can trigger emotional reactions in yourself and others. And, based on your plan, you should take your emotional temperature plus that your client and that of the other side, and constructively channel your own negative emotions.

---

78 These techniques, commonly used by mediators, are discussed in Section 2.7(b), "Promoting Communications," and in Appendix F, "Cultivating Information—Attentive and Proactive Listening."

Thereafter, you can proactively cultivate positive emotions in an effort to open communications and avoid emotional impediments.

Ask Questions

You should ask the questions you prepared about interests, impediments, issues, and BATNAs. You should avoid distracting speeches and surprises when your goal is to learn information. Instead, you should ask open questions and use your other effective listening skills.[79] Skilled negotiators, at least in the United States, ask more questions, and clarify and summarize answers more than average negotiators.

Share Information Judiciously

You should find a judicious way to share information about your client's interests, priorities, and resources (value). You also should share information about your view of impediments, any leverage, and issues to be resolved.

But do not be stupid. Share the information in a way that reduces the risk of the other side exploiting any disclosures against you, as discussed in Section 1.3.a.iii. For example, your priority may be to continue as the exclusive seller of a product in your geographic area. You may conditionally express your priority in a breach of contract dispute against the product manufacturer of by saying something like: "I value continuing the exclusive relationship but only if the total settlement package makes it worthwhile to continue to invest and cultivate the market for the product."

You also should acquaint the other side with any leverage—positive, negative, or normative—you may have, but be careful; be diplomatic so that your effort to educate the other side does not backfire and come across as a threat. Threatened people can get upset and escalate the dispute. You might say, "In this negotiation, I think my client might be able to meet some of your needs" (positive leverage). "And my client prefers to resolve this today even though he has other options that he can turn to if we are not successful" (negative leverage to deprive them of a settlement).

If Stephen has an affidavit from one of Philip's new customers that suggests he improperly solicited the customer, Stephen may want to show this information to Philip so that he can better understand his risk of liability. But Stephen should be careful not to come across as threatening him, because a threat can inflame the other side and derail the negotiation.

---

79 *See infra* Appendix F, "Cultivating Information—Attentive and Proactive Listening."

As already emphasized in the section on preparation, and as will be again in the next section, on advocating interests, the interests of the parties form the starting point in problem-solving negotiations. These include not only the interests behind the legal positions, but also the interests that go beyond those raised in the legal case. Now is the occasion for you to be sure that your client's interests are understood by the other party. Now is the occasion for you and your client to clarify to the extent possible your understanding of the other party's interests. With these understandings, the parties can more intelligently develop viable proposals.

Because each party's BATNA (the alternative of returning to court) casts a strong shadow over the negotiations, you usually allocate some time to discuss how attractive it is for each side to return to court. Remember that the more attractive a litigated outcome is, the less motivated the party will be to find a resolution at the table. Therefore, parties need to understand each other's BATNA. But any evaluation during the negotiations should be done gingerly, to guard against the parties' stumbling into an intense debate that escalates out of control and back into court.

By discussing their BATNAs, Stephen and Philip both may realize (at least privately) that they are facing uncertain results in court, and therefore more attractive options in settlement. Both of them might acknowledge that neither side can be confident of winning in court.

After sharing facts, learning about each other's interests and BATNAs, and identifying any impediments, you are ready to advocate for your client's interests, and both sides may be ready to formulate the issues to be resolved in the negotiations, including the impediments.

ii. Advocate for Client's Interests

Throughout a problem-solving negotiation, you should fashion every move to advance your client's interests, because meeting your client's interests is the ultimate measure of success. You advocate for interests based on needs, not a particular solution. Stephen wants to make money; he does not necessarily want the $100,000 in damages for Philip's stealing his business.

iii. Overcome Any Impediments

As the negotiation unfolds, you might get stuck or hampered by an impediment that you had anticipated or have just discovered. For example, you might encounter different views of critical facts (data conflict), a deeply fractured relationship (relationship conflict), or one of the other impasses (interest, structural, or value conflict). In a problem-solving negotiation, you may need to overcome any impediments before you can move forward, and you may employ a good practice to overcome it, as in this illustration.

Stephen may not be able to negotiate with Philip until he explains why he left to start his own business. Stephen may still be upset about the abrupt way his protégé abandoned their relationship. Philip may have impinged Stephen's core concern to be appreciated for what he did. Philip may help Stephen overcome this relationship conflict by expressing his sincere appreciation for all that Stephen did to help Philip launch his career. Once Stephen learns that Philip left because of his need to build his career, Stephen may be able to move forward in the negotiation.

You do not necessarily have to completely overcome all impediments, however. You may only need to clarify them to make progress. You may be reluctant to bargain without knowing more about the claim from the other side (data conflict), but realize that you may not be able to get all the information you want at this time. So you may get what you think is essential and then try to resolve the dispute with incomplete information.

iv. Create Options

Now is the time to get creative—to perhaps uncover options in addition to paying monetary sums. Everything you have done so far in the negotiation has prepared you for this adventure in discovery—unearthing value. Everything that you have learned as a litigator can quash your appetite to take this trip. Your litigator's mindset of viewing disputes as distributive and being only about money can blind you to the possibility of other solutions.

At this creative stage, you have the opportunity to increase value by exploring whether other options might benefit the parties and better meet their interests. This stage does not require much time. I want to emphasize that: It does not require much time. And when successful, it can shift you from impasse to resolution as well as upgrading your settlement from meager or sufficient to favorable, with a few savory terms that might have been unavailable in court.

Our legal training limits our perspective of what is possible. We see constraining causes of actions and conventional legal remedies—a perspective essential for success in the courtroom and one that allows efficient clarity about likely solutions. But we need to search beyond the familiar—a challenge in all areas of our lives, not just in our lives as lawyers.

I have mediated cases that were racing toward conventional judicial solutions until the mediation uncovered better possibilities. In a narrow suit to enjoin copyright infringement and recover damages, the resolution led toward the plaintiff's retaining the defendant as a consultant to help further improve the software at issue. In a suit involving startling business fraud and extensive damages, the defendant drafted a letter of apology for the behavior of a rogue employee, and the plaintiff drafted a letter recommending others to use the defendant's services. In a horrific wrongful death action, the defendant considered setting up a medical research fellowship to honor the accomplishments of the deceased wife. As these new ideas emerged and were refined, the contentious damage claims became easier to resolve. And, yes, money was still paid in all three cases.

You need techniques that can jostle the brain and prod you and the other side to search outside the familiar legal framework that brought you to the negotiation. It is not easy, as I have frequently experienced and observed. But the rewards can be enriching and gratifying for your client as well as for yourself.

Let me summarize a few techniques for creating that can help.[80]

The way you frame the question can open the mind to fresh solutions. When framing the question as "How much money does Philip owe Stephen?" you limit the possible solutions to a monetary range. But if you frame the question as "What are the options for resolving the dispute between Stephen and Philip?" you invite a broader range of possible solutions.

Your choice of a key word, such as a noun or adjective, can suggest the relevant range of solutions. "Should Steven and Philip form a partnership?" "Should Steve and Philip form a business relationship?" The word *partnership* limits the nature of the relationship, while the label *business relationship* invites more possibilities.

You also might ask participants to look at solutions from different perspectives: "Let's first consider options as if there will be no future relationship between Stephen and Philip. Then let's consider options that might involve a future relationship." Each focus can trigger new ideas without distracting the parties with other possible inquiries. The answers to the two separate questions can present a richer picture of possibilities.

---

80 *See generally* Jennifer Gerarda Brown, "Creativity and Problem-Solving," 87 *Marq. L. Rev.* 697 (2004); Janet Weinstein and Linda Morton, "Stuck in a Rut: The Role of Creative Thinking in Problem Solving and Legal Education," 9 *Clinical L. Rev.* 835 (2003); Carrie Menkel-Meadow, "Aha? Is Creativity Possible in Legal Problem Solving and Teachable in Legal Education?," 6 *Harv. Negot. L. Rev.* 97 (2001).

You might try role reversals to help instill a fresh perspective and understanding of each other's interests: "What do you think are the needs of my client?" This new perspective can provoke new possible solutions. "What would be some bad ideas?" This counterintuitive perspective for clarifying what cannot work can reveal insights into what might work.

You might use humor or some other positive technique to clear the mind and shift the mood in the room. Humor can be powerful at the right moment. As the mediator in a business partnership breakup where the two hostile parties wanted to separate and start their own businesses, I suggested, with a smile, that one option might be to share the same factory space at different hours. This idea was patently absurd given the highly charged accusations. They reacted with shared laughter. Then I asked whether they had any other ideas. This humorous moment seemed to prime them to generate more realistic options. However, humor can be disastrous if it offends. Be careful.

You also can clear your mind and others' by taking breaks, changing topics, or finding a pleasant common ground for conversation unrelated to the dispute.

This next subsection describes a common and more elaborate technique—brainstorming, where you separate the process of generating new ideas from the process of evaluating them so that the critique of ideas does not stifle the effort to generate them.

Brainstorming

Brainstorming provides a mechanism for generating a list of inchoate and uncensored ideas. The parties can feel secure suggesting ideas under the protection of two basic rules: (1) *No evaluation.* By refraining from evaluating ideas as they are voiced, you and the other side can generate ideas without any self-critique filtering or anticipating the critique of others. (2) *No ownership.* Given the freedom to suggest incomplete and unpolished ideas, the parties can test alternatives, including ones that may turn out to be disadvantageous, without endorsing them or needing to defend them.

While brainstorming for fresh ideas, you or the other side might discover relevant objective criteria and possibilities for trading before reaching the claiming stage, as well as possible inventive solutions—the subject of the next section.

Through brainstorming, Stephen and Philip may develop a list of options for working together in the future that might add value. The uncensored list might include merging businesses, rehiring Philip, Philip buying Stephen's business and retaining Stephen as a consultant, no future business relationship, and so on. The list might allude to objective criteria like commission rate practices if Philip is rehired or standard terms if a merger is contemplated.

v. Claim

Next you reach the claiming stage, and the character of the exchange changes markedly. Your focus shifts from freely generating incomplete options to evaluating and selecting the ones that could become part of the settlement. At this juncture, parties become narrowly focused on what they may get out of the negotiation.

You and the other side might preliminarily refine the options, which might be loosely formulated, consisting of overlapping, vague, and incoherent ideas. You might clarify and combine the options into a list of specific and discrete ones, and then select the most attractive candidates to assess.

You and your client may need to translate any emerging options into terms that can be meaningfully compared with your client's bottom line. In contrast with positional negotiations, in which the likely settlement is usually monetary, the result from a problem-solving approach and style may include difficult-to-quantify, nonmonetary features. You may want to try converting them into monetary equivalents so that they can be compared for the purpose of determining whether an emerging settlement is equal to or better than the client's bottom line.

For example, Philip may have difficulty comparing his bottom line of paying no more than $42,000[81] with a two-part proposal in which he would pay

---

81 In Section 1.2.b.i, Philip's reservation value of $42,000 was calculated as follows: His attorney predicted a 40 percent chance of a jury verdict holding Philip liable for $80,000 plus litigation costs of $20,000, for a negative value of $40,000. If Philip wins, he would still have to pay his attorney fees and other litigation costs of $20,000. By multiplying the $20,000 by his 60 percent chance of winning, Philip calculated a negative value of $12,000 and then added it to the negative $40,000, for a public BATNA in the amount of $52,000.

Next Philip adjusted his public BATNA value to account for a number of private costs and benefits in order to arrive at his bottom line. By going to court, Philip faced the private costs of spending time preparing for the case and suffering the emotional stress of litigation. But these costs were offset by two possible private benefits of litigating. Philip welcomed the 60 percent chance of winning and paying nothing, and he wanted to try to exonerate himself in court so he could freely pursue his lucrative business in Buffalo. Philip estimated that the private benefits of his BATNA are worth roughly $10,000 more than the private costs. Therefore, Philip's public BATNA value was decreased by $10,000, to produce a fully analyzed BATNA or reservation value of $42,000. Thus, if settlement possibilities involve Philip paying more than $42,000, Philip would leave the table to litigate, where he would be at risk of paying $52,000 and of facing the various private costs and benefits.

$45,000 and be freed from the non-compete clause to develop his business in Buffalo. Philip needs to translate the nonmonetary feature into a rough monetary equivalent so that the settlement proposal can be meaningfully compared with his bottom line.

Philip must confront the difficult question of what it is worth to him to secure a negotiated release today. The value of the release if secured in the litigation was already incorporated in his bottom line when Philip estimated the net personal benefits of $10,000 of litigating, including the release he would secure if he wins in court. But the emerging settlement proposal offers an unexpected, not easily quantifiable equivalent benefit—a negotiated release that would free him now to pursue his business in Buffalo.

Getting this release today is worth something to Philip. He should try to estimate its worth. If it is worth more than $3,000—the difference between his bottom line of $42,000 and the $45,000 settlement offer—Philip should accept the offer. If Philip estimates the release to be worth $5,000, for instance, the settlement offer will cost him only $40,000 plus an additional $5,000 for the release today, for a total of $45,000. The $40,000 cost is less than his bottom line of $42,000. By accepting the offer, Philip avoids the risk of losing $52,000 and the release in court.[82]

Techniques for Claiming

As the claiming opportunities crystallize, you need to figure out how to divide and distribute any zone of possible agreement. If you and possibly the other

82 In subsection 1.2(b)(i), Philip's reservation value of $42,000 was calculated as follows: His attorney predicted a 40 percent chance of a jury verdict holding Philip liable for $80,000 plus litigation costs of $20,000 for a negative of $40,000. If Philip wins, he would still have to pay his attorney fees and other litigation costs of $20,000. By multiplying the $20,000 by his 60 percent chance of winning, Philip calculated a negative value of $12,000 and then added it to the negative $40,000 for a public BATNA in the amount of $52,000.

Next, he adjusted Philip's public BATNA value to account for a number of private costs and benefits in order to arrive at his bottom line. By going to court, Philip faced the private costs of spending time preparing for the case and suffering the emotional stress of litigation. But these costs were offset by two possible private benefits of litigating. Philip welcomed the 60 percent chance of winning and paying nothing, and he wanted to try to exonerate himself in court so he could freely pursue his lucrative business in Buffalo. Philip estimated that the private benefits of his BATNA are worth roughly $10,000 more than the private costs. Therefore, Philip's public BATNA value was decreased by $10,000 to produce a fully analyzed BATNA or reservation value of $42,000. Thus, if settlement possibilities involve Philip paying more than $42,000, Philip would leave the table to litigate, where he would be at risk of paying $52,000 and at risk of experiencing the various private costs and benefits.

side followed a problem-solving style up to this point, you should have created a hospitable environment for claiming, even though parties may be facially at odds with each other and resolution possibilities seem fragile.

Even if you jointly generated various settlement options, this method does not preclude the need for one party to speak first—to put forward a "first offer." At this advanced point in the negotiations, any offers should flow from what has transpired. When you present your first offer based on any of these claiming techniques, be sure to show how your claim is rooted in the negotiation discussions. Instead of claiming options based on the exercise of brute power (negative leverage), you and the other side should assess and select options based on specific rational and principled justifications.

The advantages of parties articulating specific reasons that justify are many.

> In the process of considering possibilities, the problem solver articulates reasons why a particular solution is acceptable or unacceptable, rather than simply rejecting an offer or making a concession. Articulating reasons during the negotiation facilitates agreement in a number of ways. First, it establishes standards for judging whether a particular solution is sensible and should be accepted. If the reason is focused on the parties' underlying needs, the negotiator can consider whether the proposal is satisfactory to the parties. She need not be concerned with such conventional evaluation as "Is this the most I can get?" or its counterpart, "Is this the least I can get away with?" Second, principled proposals focus attention on solving the problem by meeting the parties' needs rather than winning an argument. Furthermore, continuously focusing justification on the parties' needs may cause negotiators to see still other solutions, rather than simply to respond with arguments about particular offers. The use of principled proposals can decrease the likelihood that unjustified and unnecessary concessions will be made simply to move toward agreement. Finally, the use of principled proposals causes the parties to share information about their preferences that they might otherwise be reluctant to reveal.[83]

This music of justifications should accompany the use of the three primary claiming techniques and emerge naturally because each technique offers a rational basis for claiming; however, when you reach the third technique of positional bargaining, you may need to add the music of tactics.

---

83 Menkel-Meadow (1984), *supra* note 1, at 825.

CRITICAL CHOICES

Claiming Stage

The most challenging point in a negotiation arises when parties must face the claiming stage. At this moment, it may appear that any resolution will benefit one party at the expense of the other.

You should claim options that meet your client's interests and are better than your client's BATNA.

Claiming can be accomplished by using these three primary techniques:

1. Trading benefits
2. Comporting with objective standards
3. Positional bargaining

You should consider making claims only for options that meet two threshold criteria. Any options should sufficiently meet your client's interests and should be better than your client's total BATNA. Otherwise, the option is not worth pursuing.

Trading Benefits

You present a strong justification for adopting an option when you can point out that the option furthers the interests of both parties or furthers the interest of one party while not making the other party worse off or at least minimizing harm to the other party. When the other side's interests are in making money or enhancing their reputation or continuing to work with the same employer, for instance, any option that furthers these interests will be appealing to them and offers you a persuasive justification.

You may see an opportunity to meet the interests of both sides by claiming something of value to you by giving up something of less value to you than to them. Stated differently, you might trade something of relatively low value (give up) for something of relatively high value (claim). This trading entails both sides claiming something in their interests but something different for each side. This formula may help both sides avoid a stark distributive conflict by folding propositions into a set of trades and then trading the distributive conflict away.

This trading can be fueled by the power of reciprocity, as examined in the previous section on positional negotiations.

If Stephen and Philip are trying to negotiate the amount of damages for lost sales—a classically distributive negotiation—Stephen might offer to give up part of his damages claim in return for Philip's working again at Shirts for You. Stephen essentially agrees to trade taking less money for securing a great salesman—both of which meet his interests. Philip may like this trade because he pays less and gets his old job back, presumably with more favorable terms now that he has a proven sales record and his own business contacts—benefits that meet Philip's interests.

You can uncover sources of value for trading by tapping common interests, exploiting economies of scale, and taking advantage of differences between the parties. This process of creating value also can reveal how each side might claim its share through trading,[84] as the examples that follow illustrate.

Common Interests That Do Not Conflict

When parties have common interests, they may find ways to work together to secure joint benefits. Stephen and Philip may have a common interest in a continuing relationship that will produce more money for both of them. Instead of competing with each other, they may approach their common interests as an opportunity to work together selling shirts.

Economies of Scale

Parties can work together to create value. By sharing costs, they can gain economies of scale and lower their overall costs. Both Stephen and Philip need a back office to support their sales effort. By joining together, Stephen and Philip could save money by maintaining one shared back office. They could share the fixed costs of rent, office equipment, and one support person.

Differences between parties can be a source of value for enlarging the pie and for trading that can benefit the parties.

Different Interests That Do Not Conflict

One party can bring value to the table that can satisfy the interests of the other party without hurting his own interests. At no cost to himself, Philip may be able to satisfy Stephen's interest in being recognized for providing good training and mentoring. In addition to thanking him, Philip may express his appreciation by referring to Stephen sales prospects for brand-name shirts that Philip does not stock. Then norms for reciprocity might induce Stephen to refer sales prospects for shirts that Stephen does not stock.

Different Resources to Trade

Each party may have something different to contribute. By trading, the parties can increase value at the table. Stephen has business relationships with many

84 *See* Mnookin, *supra* note 1, at 12–17, 25–27; Fisher et al., *supra* note 36, at 72–77.

retail outlets and several major-brand-name shirts. Philip now has business relationships with a number of new retail outlets and makers of a different brand of shirts. The parties can trade by each giving the other the opportunity to sell his brand name(s) in the other's retail outlets.

Different Relative Valuations

Each party may value the same contribution differently. The contributing party can give something that cost him little but provides a large benefit to the receiving party. At little cost, Stephen may be able to provide Philip a better opportunity to grow professionally than if Philip worked alone. Stephen could provide Philip access to new customers, support staff, and his experience and wisdom. This access would cost Stephen very little but could be worth a lot to Philip.

Different Forecasts

Each party may predict a different future. These differences can be the basis for constructing a resolution. Although Stephen is impressed by Philip's salesmanship, he thinks Philip needs more experience. Stephen is not as optimistic as Philip about his ability to recruit new retail customers over the next couple years. Therefore, when Philip asks for 10 percent ownership interest in Shirts for You because he predicts he will increase the number of retail outlets by 10 percent, Stephen may suggest tying increased ownership to Philip's reaching the 10 percent increase in number of retail outlets. In this way they are constructing a resolution that takes account of each party's different forecast. This resolution gives Philip what he wants, 10 percent ownership interest. If his forecast is correct, he will secure the ownership interest quickly; if Stephen's forecast is correct, he will secure the interest much later.

Different Risk Preferences

Even if the parties have identical forecasts, they may tolerate the risk of being wrong differently. Different risk preferences open the door for trading: The risk-averse party can pay money or other things of value to the more risk-tolerant party to assume the risk. Stephen and Philip project the same 10 percent increase in new retail outlets that Philip will enlist for Shirts for You. In view of these similar forecasts, Philip wants an increase in ownership interest of 2 percent for each 2 percent increase in retail outlets. Stephen does not want to give Philip any ownership interest until he reaches the 10 percent goal. Stephen is less willing to assume the risk of Philip's not reaching the goal than is Philip. Stephen may be willing to pay Philip to assume the risk that Philip may not reach his 10 percent goal. Philip will not receive any ownership interest until he achieves the 10 percent increase in the number of retail outlets for the company. When he reaches the 10 percent, Stephen will give him a 2 percent bonus, for a total of a 12 percent ownership interest.

Different Time Preferences

Each party may value the timing of events differently. One party may need something today; the other party may prefer something later or have more flexibility. The party that needs something today may be willing to pay the other party money or other value to get it today. Philip may need money today because he is getting married and plans to buy a new house. Therefore, he may be willing to accept a lower sales commission in exchange for advances on his commission.

Here is an illustration of trading benefits through a positional negotiation.

Establish Bargaining Range

Your aspirational goals and bottom lines are determined by your priorities for each issue. You and your client need to decide what is important. Is it more important to get early payment (need for cash) or to have a guarantor to secure the payment (security in payment)? Is it more important to stop the defendant from using the trademark immediately (eliminate confusion in the marketplace) or to be compensated by the defendant for the infringement immediately (need for money)? Is securing the job promotion with the same employer more important than receiving the lump sum compensation?

Formulate First Offer Strategy

Next you formulate an opening offer strategy. You want to guard against giving away part of the ZOPA (zone of possible agreement) for the reasons examined under positional negotiations.

For example, if you offer to give the other side 12 months to pay you $10,000 when they wanted only 6 months, you will have given away 6 extra months to get the compensation. Or you may ask the other side to stop using the trademark today and offer in return to waive any claim for damages when they were willing to pay you some damages. You need a first offer plan to reduce the risk of giving away part of the ZOPA.

First Offer by Other Side

By inducing the other person to make the first offer, you might benefit from the other side's error in understanding what is important to you and avoid giving away part of the ZOPA. The other side might give you more than you would have asked for. The other side might offer you more time to make the payment than you needed. Or, in an employment discrimination case, the other side—

the employer—might offer to pay more if your client—the employee—agrees to keep the settlement terms confidential. And your client was planning to agree to confidentiality without an additional payment.

By the other side going first, you also might learn what is important to them. If you do not know whether the other side wants confidentiality, you might prefer that they make the first offer to see if confidentiality is important to them. By your not first proposing confidentiality, you reduce the risk of being exploited by their exacting a concession for something they wanted anyhow.

You also might want to influence the midpoint of a critical part of the trade. If your client is willing to agree to confidentiality for compensation, you might want to go second so that your counteroffer has a chance of influencing the midpoint of the compensation.

But, as discussed in the section on positional negotiations, do not be manipulated by letting the other side's offer anchor your thinking about what is possible. Their offer cannot be a substitute for your independent assessment of what is important to your client. Anchoring can be a powerful phenomenon, and you must guard against being trapped by it.

First Offer by You

However, you might want to anchor the other side's view of what is possible to settle for as you move toward closure. You may want to try to set a final favorable settlement zone. Your anchoring proposal may cause the other side to unconsciously adjust their expectations.

For example, you might want to be the first one to make an offer to pay damages with the condition that you have two years to make payments in order to anchor the other side to a lengthy installment plan. And then if the other side counters with no installment plan, you can try to negotiate toward a mid-range that you can live with.

Your reasonable first offer also can discourage the other side from anchoring any counterproposals that are too disadvantageously extreme. Especially at this late stage in the negotiation, when both sides are trying to bring closure, the other side will likely not want to alienate you with a patently extreme response, especially after you anchored with a reasonable range.

Prepare Opening Offer

In a multi-issue final negotiation where there is an opportunity for trading, you might start by presenting an opening offer based on lower-priority trade-offs. And then be guided by the mutual concession principle: "If you agree to give us A, we then will agree to give you B." You should start with the lower-priority trade-offs, because any trade-off proposal implicitly signals what is important to you and therefore risks the other side trying to lever a larger concession from you.

Plan Concession Dance

You should develop an independent concession plan that does not depend on what the other side does. Your plan should be driven by your priorities on the remaining issues. As trust and momentum grow, you can present higher-priority trades. Also, by making big moves on less important issues and small moves on the more important ones, you give yourself a margin on the more important issues as you move through the dance. As always, try to follow the principle of reciprocity, in which you alternate making proposals, and do not concede too quickly.

Opening Offers Exchanged and Dance with Music

After the first offers are exchanged, you move forward with your planned concession dance. Based on the usual strategy, you initially offer less important trading proposals to test the other side's reactions. After you achieve the first trade, you may progress toward your higher-priority ones. This is a tricky process, because your proposals can signal what is important to you. This rapidly executed final dance is performed to the familiar music of justifications, with a few tactics and no tricks used within a problem-solving approach.

Comport with Objective Criteria[85]

You may justify options based on how they comport with objective standards, such as how a monetary settlement proposal might reflect the strengths and weaknesses of the legal case or how a pay increase reflects the increases in the cost-of-living index during the last five years. You are likely to uncover objective standards, if you are on the lookout for them.

You probably have experience using the most common and unimaginative objective standard, splitting the difference between the last two offers.[86] This method is simple, easy, and quick to implement, and does not require any elaborate justification. It appears even-handed and fair. It is a fairly customary practice at the end of a negotiation.

But be careful. First, be sure that the midpoint is a fair one. If you have been presenting reasonable offers while the other side has been more aggressive, the midpoint will reward the other side for their aggressive stance at your

---

85 Objective criteria are independent reference points that neither party can control. *See infra* Section 1.3(a).

86 A familiar procedural solution is the overused, last-resort formula of splitting the difference between the last two offers. For a fuller discussion of options, *see* Russell Korobkin, "A Positive Theory of Legal Negotiation," 88 *Geo. L. J.* 1789, 1821–1829 (2000).

expense. Try to offset any skewed offers by the other side before agreeing to split the difference. Second, be clear that you are selecting the midpoint after each side has made a similar number of concessions, as already discussed. If you have made three concessions and the other side has made only two, the split may advantage the other side. And third, do not split too early, because to do so may lead to a premature settlement—one made before you had a chance to uncover other mutually beneficial resolutions.

You should search for other more discerning objective criteria. For example, in a discrimination case in which the employer agrees to reinstate an employee, the employer and employee may still need to calculate the amount of back pay for the years of discrimination. This last issue presents a distributive conflict, because every dollar increase in back pay will result in a gain for the employee at the expense of the employer. Instead of positional bargaining, they could negotiate the details of a neutral formula based on the average salary increases of employees in the particular job category during the relevant years. This is an objective formula because neither party can manipulate the results.[87]

In view of their common interests in making money, Stephen and Philip may select the option of joining forces and working together. They may resolve the distributive issue of how to share profits by adopting the objective and facially fair standard of splitting profits based on the percentage of business each person brings to the partnership each year.

In legal disputes, you might be able to rely on the arguably objective standard of the public BATNA—what might happen in court if the case does not settle. You can justify an option by showing how it is better than the BATNA of either side.

The BATNA is arguably objective, because neither party can control the legal outcome; it is based on the facts and law although each side can influence it due to the quality of its investigation and advocacy. Therefore it is not purely independent. Also, it can be highly contested. Nevertheless, the public BATNA can be a helpful, relatively objective standard against which to assess the attractiveness of settlement options.

Positional Bargaining

Not all distributive conflicts can be neatly resolved based on trading or conforming to objective standards. When you cannot reach such a resolution, you

87 There might be some areas of discretion in the compilation of the historic salary data; however, any different views can be isolated, narrowed, and resolved by using neutral or positional techniques.

have reached the most intractable moment in any negotiation—the purely distributive conflict. Do you now turn to the classical positional approach? Yes, as a last resort.

As you will recall from the extensive discussion in the section on positional negotiations, you need to formulate a plan in which you identify your aspirational goal and bottom line and develop a first offer strategy and concession dance that steers the other side in the direction you want things to go. Then you need to implement your first offer strategy and the dance with the music of good practices—mostly justifications and probably some tactics. As you negotiate over splitting up the ZOPA, you should be conscious of the way the reciprocity norms can propel the exchange of offers and can influence and manipulate the way parties value the concessions being exchanged. Also, you should keep an eye on your midpoints between offers and counteroffers, and guard against being affected by the other side's anchoring your view.

After Philip recognizes that a court will likely hold him liable for violating the non-compete clause, both sides need to calculate the amount of profits lost by Stephen. He claims he lost around $100,000. Both parties realize how difficult it will be to arrive at an objectively established amount and do not want to expend large fees on retaining experts.

Instead of belligerently threatening protracted and expensive litigation, Philip initiates the following exchange:

PHILIP: I think we are stuck over how much I should pay you. You seem to agree that it would be too expensive to retain outside experts to estimate what you would have sold if I had not started selling shirts in Buffalo. We have already tried to calculate lost sales from each of our sales records. What do you think of us exchanging realistic offers for settlement that are based on those sales records?

STEPHEN: Sounds good to me. Let's use each of our audited sales records for the last 12 months.

PHILIP: Okay. Let me take a fresh look at those audited records and present an offer. [*He takes time to study the sales records.*]
Instead of me starting with the traditional and unproductive offer of paying nothing or only a nominal amount, I offer to pay you $10,000. This amount is based on the assumption that the most that you lost was 10 percent of what I sold because you did not have the time to cultivate a significant number of new customers while maintaining your existing customer base. [*Philip is testing the good faith of Stephen by seeing how he reacts to his rationale.*]

STEPHEN: I want to thank you for a serious offer, although I think it is inadequate. I undoubtedly lost more than $10,000 in sales due to your breach of the non-compete clause. I expended considerable time trying to solicit new customers. I spent about 25 percent of my time on the road contacting new prospects and was specifically told by at least three prospects that they were not interested because they were being served by you. After reviewing your audited sales records, I learned that I had solicited six of your customers, to whom you sold a net total of $75,000 worth of shirts. Let's see if we can settle this for $75,000, the amount of profits that would have otherwise gone to me.

Thus, the positional negotiation dance of offers and counteroffers is launched, accompanied by the music of justifications.

Finally, here is an illustration of how to use the combination of these three claiming techniques as you try to move the negotiation toward the final stage of closure.

Plaintiff, a clothing store, is suing for breach of contract for the delivery of defective computers and is seeking damages of $50,000 due to lost orders and harm to their reputation resulting from upset customers who did not receive purchased items. Plaintiff no longer wants an exclusive contract with the defendant, and defendant does not want to lose an important customer. Defendant, who has two years remaining on the exclusive contract, recognizes that some of the computers did malfunction and is concerned about harm to its own reputation. For this dispute, parties might claim as follows.

Trading Benefits

To meet each of their interests in protecting their reputations, the parties may trade signed confidentiality agreements so that more third parties do not learn about the problems that plagued the two companies.

The parties might meet the interests of Plaintiff in flexibility and damages and the interests of Defendant in maintaining a business relationship and reducing financial liability by trading benefits that each can offer the other. Plaintiff may offer a continuing, non-exclusive relationship and waive any direct payment for harm to its reputation. In return, defendant may offer to waive the two remaining years of exclusivity and continue to sell computers to Plaintiff on a non-exclusive basis, if the computers are from an approved manufacturer and priced 10 percent less than any other bids for the next two years,

Comporting with Objective Criteria

Both parties might resort to objective criteria for resolving the amount of lost sales by soliciting an expert to present a non-binding estimate of possible losses to the Plaintiff.

Positional Bargaining

Based on the non-binding expert report, parties may engage in a positional dance of offers and counteroffers to arrive at a sales loss amount.

c. Closure[88]

At some point in the negotiation process, you need to bring closure by either settling or exiting. It is crunch time. You should consider options for advancing closure; different ways to engage in any final bargaining; and what commitments to secure before leaving the session.

i. Establish Deadlines

If the negotiation lingers, seems prolonged by meaningless delays, or is rapidly going nowhere, you may want to move the negotiation forward by establishing a deadline. There is nothing like a deadline to get people's attention—to convince parties that it is time to make any last best efforts. If a settlement is not reached by the deadline, the settlement opportunity will be lost. This technique capitalizes on the scarcity effect and loss aversion of parties. You need to get the timing right, however, because deadlines can backfire if parties feel too rushed.

You should identify a deadline that is credible and not unreasonable.

The most effective deadlines are imposed by events or people that the parties do not control. Judges can create meaningful deadlines when they direct parties to settle by a specified day or return to court. A judge might even suspend deciding a dispositive motion until after a settlement deadline. Also potentially effective are legal deadlines such as a statute of limitations or a due date for a quarterly financial report that covers the financial contingency of the litigation.

There are a number of other ways for you to create a deadline, but these other options risk alienating the other side, who may feel you are manipulating them with an artificial deadline that they may view as a tactic or trick.

---

88 Parts of this section are based on Shell, *supra* note 49, at 178–182, 191–194.

You may need to convince the other side that these deadlines are reasonable and that you are acting in good faith; you may have another appointment that day, a plane to catch, vacation plans, a court date in another case, or some other obligation. You also can offer a disappearing proposal—one that if not accepted by a particular date will be permanently withdrawn. You may need to convince the other side that you have a credible reason for withdrawing the offer—for example, the offered position needs to be filled or the funds supporting the payment will be expended on another project if your offer is not accepted.

Another risky but potentially effective deadline can be created if you threaten to walk out if no further movement occurs or if you walk out spontaneously so that if you return, the message will be that you returned for one last round. These theatrical tactics or tricks when done convincingly can be effective in persuading the other side of the importance of the issue, but they also can produce resentment and impasse.

ii. Finish Final Bargaining

Now it is time to wrap up and resolve any remaining issues. You will have exhausted your search for solutions but may not have entirely resolved all the issues despite using the various claiming techniques. You may be encountering resistance to finishing the bargaining. It is time to bring closure to the final issues that are blocking you and your client from going home.

As the bargaining of any final distributive issues rushes toward conclusion, you and the other side can be under heavy pressure to compromise, including pressure to make a last-minute concession and split any remaining difference. As was described in the context of positional negotiations, the music at the end can get intense. Do not get distracted. Keep any eye on your dance plan and bottom line. As the negotiating is accelerating toward closure, however, you should pause and proceed deliberately and thoughtfully.

If the final issues are distributive during this closing period, you should patiently maintain the reciprocal concession pattern, even if the other side pressures you to bargain against yourself. You should justify the significance of any concession made so far while announcing calmly and firmly to the other side that it is their turn to make a meaningful concession. Also, you should continuously measure each concession against your bottom line tripwire so that you do not unknowingly cross it and get stuck with a deal that you regret.

iii. Secure Commitment

Successful Negotiation

If the negotiation is successful, you need more than an agreement. You should secure a level of commitment that corresponds with the risk of nonperformance of the other side. As the risk increases, the more secured any commitment should be, as reflected in these three progressively more exacting options.[89]

For the lowest risks, you might rely on a social ritual like a handshake when the parties trust each other and have a long-term relationship, or you may opt for a public announcement like a press conference that would make noncompliance a public embarrassment. The nature of these rituals varies across cultures from a simple handshake or bow to elaborate meals or social events. These devices are designed to link the personal reputations of the parties to compliance.

In legal disputes, you will usually need to do more, especially in the United States and Europe. You will want parties to enter into an enforceable signed agreement—whether one with key terms to be subsequently incorporated into a fully executed agreement, or a fully executed agreement if you have the ability to finish it before people leave the session. The noncomplying party then can be sued for breach and held accountable in court.

When you think there is a high probability of nonperformance, you may want to design a method that further limits if not eliminates any risk of noncompliance. For example, you might insist on a guarantor in case of non-payment or require simultaneous exchanges like executing a release upon receipt of the certified check.

These options are certainly not the only ones. But they illuminate the possibilities for custom-designing commitments in accordance with the perceived risks of noncompliance.

Negotiation Not Yet Successful

If the negotiation is not successful, you may still want a commitment—concerning what to do next. It might be as simple as agreeing to a time to meet again or agreeing to a time to talk about whether to meet again. Or you might agree on another process for resolving the dispute, such as a third-party evaluation or arbitration.[90] You never know what ideas might emerge from "a what to do next" discussion. Just try to have it before you leave the session.

---

89 For a further discussion, *see* Shell, *supra* note 49, at 191–194.

90 For a full discussion of alternative process options, *see* Chapter 8.

Questions

1. Prepare to participate in a negotiation exercise in which you engage in a problem-solving approach with a negotiation style that leans toward problem-solving or adversarial, depending on what your instructor tells you to do. Try to achieve the best result possible for your client.
2. Prepare to participate in a negotiation exercise in which the dispute is primarily distributive, and in which you will engage in the problem-solving approach. Try to achieve the best result possible for your client.
3. These problems give you an opportunity to practice the proactive listening skills covered in Appendix F. For each "summary statement," practice summarizing the statement. For each "reframe statement with follow-up questions," practice reframing the statement to remove toxic words, then reframing empathetically, and then reframing perspective. Also, for each statement, practice framing suitable open and closed follow-up questions.
   a. *Context*: A husband and wife are seeking a divorce. You, your client, the other attorney, and her client are meeting to negotiate a settlement.

      Summarize statement: Husband says to you, the opposing attorney representing the wife, "We have two children, a daughter in fifth grade and a son in third grade. We need to resolve who will have custody of our children, and the details of a schedule for visitation. We both want custody of our two children."

      Reframe statement with follow-up questions: Husband says to you, the opposing attorney representing the wife, "She is a horrible parent. She is always yelling at our children, spending more time punishing them than parenting them."

      Reframe statement with follow-up questions: Your client, the wife, says, "He is trying to destroy my relationship with my children by telling them that I am a terrible parent who does not love them."
   b. *Context*: An independent contractor is suing the company that hired him for failing to pay for the services he rendered to the company. You, your client, the other attorney, and his client are meeting to negotiate a settlement.

      Summarize statement: The independent contractor says to you, the opposing attorney, "We did everything possible to secure the government's approval for the project. It is not our fault that the agency failed to approve the project. We want to be paid for our services."

      Reframe statement with followup questions: Your client, the company representative, says, "We are upset that the inept contractor did an incompetent job and failed to secure the government license for the project, and yet still expects to be paid for its shoddy work."

Reframe statement with followup questions: The other client, the independent contractor, says to you, "Your client, the company, is an irresponsible deadbeat for not paying its obligations."

c. *Context*: The staff of the state banking department has convened a meeting of interest groups to draft new disclosure rules for loan agreements. The banking department is considering what provisions in loan agreements should be conspicuously disclosed (i.e., in large and bold print). You are mediating a negotiation that includes the banking department and various interest groups.

The state banking department, a representative of the banks, and a representative of the consumer groups engage in the following exchanges.

Summarize statement: A staff member of the state banking department remarks, "We are thinking of proposing rules that require the conspicuous disclosure of arbitration clauses." The representative of the consumer groups responds by endorsing the proposal: "Customers should be aware that they are waiving their right to go to court when they sign a loan agreement that contains an arbitration clause." The representative of the banks objects: "There are already too many provisions that must be conspicuously disclosed. As contracts get longer, it is less likely that any of the provisions will stand out."

Reframe statement with followup questions: The representative of the banks says, "Consumer groups have no clue what bank customers want."

Reframe statement with followup questions: The consumer group representative says, "The banks' representatives want to trick consumers into giving up their right to go to court."

d. *Context*: Caucus with Defendant MedPro who terminated exclusive distributor of medical device in India because it claims that Mumbai's sales in India are too low. Mumbai claims it expended $500,000 to develop the market in India. *See* Online Video at 1.3 (Mumbai).

   i. Do you think this reframing of Mumbai's damages claim makes it easier for the defendant to pay money?

   ii. If you were representing Mumbai, could you have re-framed the damages claim into a claim for reimbursement of expenses when negotiating directly in joint session? What was the advantage, if any, of relying on the mediator in a private meeting with MedPro to reframe the damages?

   iii. At what stage is the mediation?

4. *Dealing productively with emotions*[91]
   a. Exercise before class on emotions. Identify one conflict in your personal life, from your professional life (work or law school), or reported in the media, and identify whether any unaddressed core concerns might be fueling the conflict and what might be done to address those concerns. Prepare a written description of no more than one page.
   b. Analyze recent movie. What core concerns of a person might have been impinged in a recent movie that you saw? Refer to specific scenes and exchanges in the movie. How might those concerns have been addressed by the person doing the impinging?
   c. Analyze prior class problem. Consider one of the assigned class problems and identify whether any core concerns of one of the parties have been impinged by the other side, and what the other side might have done to address those impinged core concerns.
   d. Exercise after class on emotions. Apply what you learned. Proactively stimulate positive emotions by addressing a core concern of another person and report on the results. Prepare a written description of no more than one page.

4. NEGOTIATION STAGES AS A ROADMAP

If you find linear schemes a useful way to map routes, you may find it helpful to view negotiations as consisting of a number of predictable stages. (*See* tables for positional and problem-solving negotiations in Sections 1.5 and 1.6.) Each stage serves a different purpose, and as your purposes change, so does the stage. The stages map a pathway toward settlement, with each stage providing a signpost to guide you. By understanding negotiation as a route with a destination, you acquire a diagnostic tool that can help you figure out where the negotiation is and where it still needs to go.

Are both parties ready to move forward to the next stage? If one party is still at the information gathering stage, for instance, then that party is not ready to go to the next stage, identifying issues and interests or impediments.

Are both parties at the same stage of the negotiation? If one party is trying to deal with impediments while the other party is trying to bargain, then the parties are at different stages. The party working on impediments is not ready to bargain.

---

91 *See generally* Daniel Shapiro, "Teaching Students How to Use Emotions as They Negotiate," 22 *Negotiation J.* 105 (2006). (These exercises are based on this article.)

Is one party regressing? If both parties have moved forward to creating and one party starts to ask questions, then that party has regressed to the information gathering stage. That party needs more time to gather information before the party can return to the creating stage.

Do both parties need to regress? As issues are being identified, for instance, some issues might seem unclear and confusing. The parties may need to return to the stage of gathering information to develop the information they need to clarify the issues.

Negotiation is a dynamic process. Even though this description of the stages projects a linear approach, negotiations are not so neat and compartmentalized in practice. Negotiations naturally move forward and backward, sometimes called cycling, among the stages. Negotiators can even be at several stages at the same time. Negotiators can engage simultaneously in gathering information, identifying issues, and overcoming impediments, for instance.

The next two sections provide roadmaps—first for the austere, positional approach for claiming and then for the problem-solving approach that incorporates positional negotiations as part of the claiming stage. Both roadmaps are derived from the prior discussions of the key features of each negotiation approach. These stages summarize succinctly each step of the particular approach, without suggesting a suitable negotiating style. You still need to select a style, which can range from problem-solving to adversarial. Once you decide which negotiation approach you want to take, you can use the relevant stand alone roadmap to help illuminate the way.

5. STAGES OF THE POSITIONAL APPROACH (ROADMAP)

Stages of Positional Approach

a. *Stage 1: Preparation*
   i. *Gather Information*
   ii. *Develop plan*
   iii. *Develop questions*
b. *Stage 2: Exchange Information for Specific Purpose*
c. *Stage 3: Bargaining: Implement First Offer Strategy*
d. *Stage 4: Bargaining: Engage in Concession Dance with Music*
e. *Stage 5: Closure*
   i. *Deadline*
   ii. *Bargain final time*
   iii. *Secure commitment*
   iv. *Implement*

a. Stage 1: Preparation[92]

i. Gather Information

You gather necessary information, including investigating the facts, law, and BATNAs, and begin to identify issues. You also help your client establish the two critical parameters for the negotiation: her aspirational goal and bottom line.

ii. Develop Plan

You formulate a first offer strategy, opening offer, and a concession dance, and consider the negotiation music you want to play.

iii. Develop Questions

You develop the questions that you want to ask at the beginning of the negotiation.

b. Stage 2: Exchange Information for Specific Purposes

You pose questions that are designed to enlist any specific information that you need before launching the bargaining process. You also may need to reply to questions.

c. Stage 3: Bargaining: Implement First Offer Strategy[93]

You implement your first offer strategy by presenting your opening offer with an eye on your aspirational goal, bottom line, and where you want to steer the negotiation.

d. Stage 4: Bargaining: Engage in Concession Dance with Music[94]

You engage in your concession dance of offers, counteroffers, and compromises performed to your selected music of good practices, tactics, and tricks. This central and critical bargaining process over dividing up any zone of possible agreement is examined in detail in the section on the key features of positional negotiations.

---

92 For full discussion, *see* Section 1.2(a).

93 For full discussion, *see* Section 1.2(a–b).

94 For full discussion, *see* Section 1.2(a–b).

e. Stage 5: Closure[95]

This stage is similar to the closure stage for problem solving and is included in both sections for the convenience of the reader.

i. Deadline

You may need to establish a deadline to advance the negotiation toward closure—to alert the participants that it is time to make their last best effort to resolve the dispute. The options and considerations were examined under "Positional Approach and Style."

ii. Bargain Final Time

As the negotiation rushes to closure, you may engage in intense, final positional bargaining.

iii. Secure Commitment

If your negotiation is successful, you secure a commitment for the participants to implement the key terms of the agreement. You should design a commitment device that fits the risk of noncompliance; options can range from social rituals to formal contracts to risk-free mechanisms.

If your negotiation is not yet successful, you secure a commitment on what to do next; options can range from agreeing to meet again to selecting another process for resolving the dispute, such as mediation or arbitration.

iv. Implement

After an agreement is signed, your work still may not be quite finished. Depending on the details and intricacy of the agreement, you may need to execute or monitor its implementation. Post-agreement tasks may be as straightforward as paying a lump sum, or more involved, such as exchanging goods for services over several years.

---

95 For full discussion, *see* chapter 1.2(c) and chapter 1.3(c).

6. STAGES OF THE PROBLEM-SOLVING APPROACH (ROADMAP)

Stages of the Problem-Solving Approach
a. *Stage 1:* Prepare
i. Gather Information (interests, issues, impediments, bottom line, leverage, client views)
ii. Plan for emotions
iii. Plan questions and judicious sharing of information
b. *Stage 2:* Rhetoric
c. *Stage 3:* Cultivate Relationship and Negotiate Negotiation Process
d. *Stage 4:* Exchange Information for Specific Purposes
e. *Stage 5:* Identify Issues, Interests, BATNAs, and Impediments
f. *Stage 6:* Formulate Agenda
g. *Stage 7:* Overcome Impediments
h. *Stage 8:* Create Options
i. *Stage 9:* Claim
j. *Stage 10:* Closure
i. Establish deadline
ii. Bargain final time
iii. Secure commitment
iv. Implement

a. Stage 1: Preparation[96]

You gather information, including investigating the facts, law, and your client's BATNA, and begin to identify both side's interests as well as the issues, impediments, and leverage. You also prod your client to begin identifying sources of value, inventive solutions, and possibilities for trading and objective standards. And you develop a plan for dealing with the inevitable emotional dimensions of the dispute, the questions you want to ask, and the judicious sharing of information.

b. Stage 2: Rhetoric

If the other side has adversarial propensities, they are likely to discharge a lot of noisy rhetoric. Rhetoric can take the form of extreme posturing about demands and may include threats. The posturing may be designed to anchor

96 For full discussion, *see* Section 1.3(a).

your thinking of what is possible in the negotiations. It may take place in the media, at pre-negotiation meetings, and during the negotiation session. Within the rhetoric can be found relevant information for the negotiation.

c. Stage 3: Cultivate Relationship and Negotiate Negotiation Process[97]

While keeping any rhetoric in perspective, you should try cultivating a working relationship. This is not so easy to do when faced with adversarial tactics and tricks, but you should try, because negotiators with a less combative relationship can work together more effectively. This early relationship building can help lubricate the negotiation process.

As you cultivate a working relationship, you also may need to negotiate how participants are going to negotiate. This stage is essential if the other party has put down the positional gauntlet. Instead of responding in kind or trying to unilaterally impose a problem-solving approach, you might invite a discussion about the process. You can ask problem-solving questions that engage the other side in considering ways to negotiate:

Are you interested in trying an alternative to my counter offering and the two of us haggling until we are at the point where we can split the difference? What do you think of us discussing our clients' interests—that is, what they would like out of these negotiations as a starting point?

Even though you and the other side might try to quickly determine the sort of negotiation process that participants want to follow, relapses are likely to occur as the negotiations proceed. When evaluating options, for example, the other party may instinctively push positionally for a particular option instead of testing it against interests or objective standards. You may need to sporadically revisit how participants are negotiating.[98]

d. Stage 4: Exchange Information for Specific Purposes[99]

At this early stage, you should try to establish a rapport, begin managing the emotional climate, and start exchanging information.

You, your client, or the other side may need to vent frustrations or anger before negotiating productively. Each party may need to tell his story about what happened. Only after being heard might each party be able to move

---

97 *See* Mnookin, *supra* note 1, 62–63, 121–125, 207–211.

98 *See* Section 1.7, on how to transform adversarial negotiations into problem-solving ones.

99 For full discussion, *see* Section 1.3(b).

forward. Venting and being heard have considerable value all by themselves. But when participants vent and tell their stories, valuable information is shared.

Additionally, each side poses questions designed to elicit specific information about interests, value, impediments, issues, and leverage, including BATNAs. You also may want to share information about these subjects.

e. Stage 5: Identify Issues, Interests, BATNAs, and Impediments

Based on the garnered information, you and the other side formulate the issues for resolution, learn about each other's interests and BATNAs, and isolate any impediments to settlement.

f. Stage 6: Formulate Agenda

In complex cases, you and the other side may need to negotiate the order in which issues and impediments will be considered. Should parties progress from the easiest to the most difficult issues or the reverse? Should parties progress from the most important issues to the least important or the reverse?

g. Stage 7: Overcome Impediments[100]

You negotiate with the aim of overcoming any impediments that are blocking forward movement. If a conflict over access to vital data is blocking the negotiations, for instance, then you would negotiate a process for providing equal access to the data.

h. Stage 8: Create Options[101]

In the search for inventive possibilities, you can try techniques that are designed to prod and stimulate out-of-the-legal-box options for each issue. One popular approach entails inventing ideas and separately evaluating them, and then generating options by brainstorming and using other techniques, as explained under "Problem-Solving Approach."

---

100 *See* Section 5.6(a), on dealing with impediments to settlements.

101 For full discussion, *see* Section 1.3(b).

i. Stage 9: Claim[102]

As explained earlier, parties next assess and justify options that meet their interests and are better than their BATNS by trading benefits; comporting with objective criteria, and resorting to the positional bargaining dance and music—the three primary claiming techniques. In this claiming stage, parties identify and formulate possible resolutions as they move toward the final stage of closure.

j. Stage 10: Closure[103]

This stage is similar to the closure stage for positional negotiations and is included in both sections for the convenience of the reader.

i. Establish Deadlines

You may need to establish a credible deadline to advance toward closure of the negotiation—in order to alert the participants that it is time to make their last, best effort to resolve the dispute.

ii. Bargain Final Time

You wrap up bargaining and resolve any final issues that are impeding closure. For these remaining intractable conflicts, you may need to bargain intensely and positionally.

iii. Secure Commitment

If your negotiation is successful, you need to secure a commitment for the participants to implement the key terms of the agreement. You should design a commitment device that comports with the risk of noncompliance; options can range from social rituals to formal contracts to risk-free mechanisms.

If your negotiation is not yet successful, you should secure a commitment regarding what to do next; options can range from agreeing to meet again to selecting another process for resolving the dispute, such as arbitration.

---

102 For full discussion, *see* Section 1.3(b).

103 For full discussion, *see* Section 1.3(c).

iv. Implement

After an agreement is signed and you have secured a commitment, your work still may not be done. Depending on the details and intricacy of the agreement, you may need to execute a full agreement or monitor its implementation. Post-agreement tasks may be as straightforward as paying a lump sum, or more complex, such as the exchanging of goods for services over several years.

7. CONVERTING THE ADVERSARIAL NEGOTIATOR INTO A PROBLEM SOLVER

[OMITTED]

8. CHECKLISTS: POSITIONAL AND PROBLEM-SOLVING NEGOTIATIONS

[OMITTED]

CHAPTER 16

Fashioning an Effective Negotiation Style: Choosing between Good Practices, Tactics and Tricks

2017

Hal Abramson*

Oscar Wilde once wrote that, "In matters of grave importance, style, not sincerity, is the vital thing" (Wilde 1899: Act III.19). In negotiations, both count and are, in fact, interrelated. Style in negotiations combines strategies with sincerity and stagecraft. This chapter offers guidance for fashioning an effective style.

Because our *negotiation* style—the subject of this chapter—can be influenced by our personal *conflict* style—a subject widely examined in negotiation literature and trainings—the distinction between the two should be clarified to avoid confusion. *Conflict* style describes who we are; *negotiation* style describes who we want to be when negotiating.

Conflict style reflects instinctive responses; it describes how we each individually respond to conflict. We might be more comfortable avoiding conflicts or compromising, for instance, than being competitive. *Conflict* style is a product of our personal experiences, family, culture, genetics, and personality.[1] It describes our default reactions to conflict. *Negotiation* style is different. It reflects

---

* Author thanks Professor Waldman for her comments on the draft and his research assistant, A Shamel Manuel, for formatting the footnotes.

1 As more fully explained by Professor Shell, "These inclinations [labels "conflicts styles" as "personal bargaining styles"] can come from many sources—childhood, family, early professional experiences, mentors, ethical systems or beliefs, and so on. And your inclinations can change over time as your knowledge of negotiation grows and you gain more confidence in a wide range of skills. But I genuinely believe that most of us have a set of core personality traits that make radical changes in our basic negotiation preferences difficult." (Shell 2006: 12)

conscious, deliberate choices among alternative strategies. It is the result of choices we make among good practices, tactics, and tricks (GTT), although our choices can be influenced by our personal *conflict* style.

This chapter focuses on *negotiation* style by examining good practices, tactics, and tricks, and the effectiveness of each one, including how bargaining power can affect the choices we make in negotiations. It then considers how our style for handling conflict needs to be understood and considered when forging an effective negotiation style.

1. NEGOTIATION STYLE

Should you say what you really want out of a negotiation? Should you be nice or nasty? Should you exaggerate? Should you hide unfavorable information? Should you ever lie when negotiating? These questions and others hover over us as we negotiate. Long lists of choices in negotiations have been compiled and described in numerous books and articles on negotiation techniques [Craver, *Distributive Techniques*]. The choices we make determine our *negotiation* style. This section provides a framework for classifying each choice into one of three categories-good practices, tactics, and tricks, and in so doing affords a method for analyzing the benefits and risks of diverse techniques. Assessing each choice is more important than correctly classifying it. This classification scheme is designed to facilitate thoughtful choices.

a. Good Practices, including Justifications

Good practices (Abramson 2013) can be unconditionally used and will likely produce the best negotiated results. They include asserting your interests rather than your positions, advancing rational and principled justifications to persuade the other side, and engaging in reasonable information exchanges. They include acting ethically and fairly. They also include building rapport, relationships, and trust, and using effective communication techniques such as summarizing, paraphrasing, framing, and questioning. They can include using objective standards and searching for creative options. These sorts of negotiation practices can be routinely performed because they pose no inherent risk of harm other than in the limited circumstances suggested at the end of this section.

The opposite of a good practice is not automatically a bad one, however. If you do not advocate for your client's interests or build rapport, for example, you are not necessarily engaging in a bad practice. The use of justifications may be a good practice, but to not present them may be a tactic as discussed in the next section—and not necessarily a bad one.

Here are several illustrations of good practices at work.

You may justify a claim based on rational explanations and objective standards—what I might suggest as the best of the good practices. The use of justifications can be an effective way to steer a positional negotiation toward a reasoned discussion. You may cultivate a hospitable environment for settlement by establishing rapport with the other side through small talk, finding connections unrelated to the dispute, and creating comfortable surroundings for meeting. You might promote an information exchange by listening attentively and actively to the other side, including reacting empathetically, acknowledging emotional pain, and asking open and close questions. And, you might create trust that can lubricate the negotiations by acting ethically, including not misrepresenting critical information.

Good Practices Subverted by Other Side

You should not employ good practices blindly, however. During the heat of a negotiation, you need to spot when your good practice is being used against you. You want to avoid being lured by a negotiator who may appear to be engaging in good practices to exploit your good practices. For example, you might present justifications to cultivate a rational, reciprocal discussion, but if your effort is failing because you think the other side is using the pretense of a rational discussion to delay the negotiations, you should consider suspending the good practice. If you think the other side is requesting information that they are not really interested in, or are requesting additional time to get information that should be readily available, the other side might be engaging in a trick. They may be using the appearance of problem-solving to prolong the negotiation and make it more expensive for your client. Figuring out whether a good practice is being used against you can be difficult to do. You need to test the practice and guard against your making a "fundamental attribution error" (*see,* e.g., Korobkin and Guthrie 2004).

Nevertheless, I might dare suggest that some good practices, such as ethical behavior or rapport building, should be *unconditional*. Regardless of the other side's behavior, you are likely to come out ahead for clients by establishing a reputation as an ethical and approachable negotiator [Tinsley et al, *Reputations*].

In short, good practices are primarily safe ones. However, when crossing over to tactics or tricks in the next two sections, you are selecting practices with inherent risks that you should ponder and appraise.

b. Tactics

Tactics are moves that negotiators conventionally use, not because they are good practices but because they reflect customary ones. Tactics are so widely used that parties expect to encounter them. Making extreme first offers to create room for concessions, exaggerating arguments, and denigrating the other side's arguments are popular examples. These practices are generally accepted ones that can offer tactical benefits if they are done convincingly. Because they are viewed as generally accepted practices, if discovered they do not severely undermine relationships or the negotiation process, as can happen with tricks.

There are numerous generally accepted tactics that negotiators use routinely. The ABA Professional Model Code Rule 4.1, Comment 2 recognizes negotiation conventions when it exempted several practices from the bar against false statements of material fact. It treats the misrepresentation of a bottom line as puffery, not as a code violation, for example (ABA Model Rules2016; Abramson 2013).

Although not everyone may agree which moves are tactics, some common ones can be confidently identified. Here are a few more examples:

- Making inflated or deflated proposals to anchor the other side's thinking to an upper or lower range.
- Exaggerating a bottom line (puffery) by using various techniques such as conveying misleading clues and shading information to influence the other side's perception of your bottom line.
- Disclosing or withholding selective information to strengthen the appearance of a legal case, the BATNA (Best Alternative to a Negotiated Agreement) (Fisher, Ury, and Patton 1991).
- Threatening to leave the negotiation when the person does not plan to leave.
- Making a false demand for something unimportant, and then giving it up in return for something important.
- Exploiting the reciprocity norm (variation of a false demand) by making an unimportant concession to manipulate the other side into

making a concession. A negotiator might make several demands, including a false one, and then concede the false demand. The false concession may spur the other side to make a concession.

Many tactics can be difficult to decipher because the moves also can be done in good faith and therefore be a good practice. The negotiator's declaration that this is her bottom line might be a sincere effort to convince the other side that is as far as she can go, or the statement might be designed to mislead the other side to extract a concession. A negotiator's threat to leave can be a sincere act of frustration or a pretense to pressure the other side into making a concession. If it were easy to recognize tactics, tactics would be ineffective. Once aware of a tactic, the object of the tactic usually can avoid being manipulated by it. When the object of the tactic believes that the demand is intentionally inflated to anchor his view of the settlement value, for example, he can try to neutralize the effect by independently assessing the claim (as negotiators ought to routinely do anyhow.)[2]

Tactics Pose Risks

The degree of risk posed by a tactic depends on the particular tactic, of course. Presenting modestly inflated initial offers and trying to anchor others are standard moves with limited risks of harm. When uncovered, an inflated offer may be viewed as expected or simply as irritating. Other tactics can pose a higher risk of harm. For example, aggressively belittling the other side or walking out of a negotiation and later returning may not be uncommon tactics, the moves set a more adversarial tone and pose a higher risk of corroding trust, impairing the relationship, and hindering progress.

c. Tricks

Tricks are not good practices or conventionally accepted ones. They are innately adversarial; they can be unethical, repugnant, and highly risky. When

2 In court cases, others can try to manipulate you by anchoring you with a high demand in the pleadings and making a lower first offer in the negotiations. If the pleading sets forth a claim for a million dollars and the first offer is $750,000, for example, you may experience their move as a substantial concession even though you may have thought the amount in the pleading was a preposterous number. Or, the other side may offer to pay nothing, and then after some discussion, bid against themselves by offering to pay something that is more than nominal. This low anchor with a concession to pay more may prompt you to reciprocate with a concession.

done convincingly and undiscovered, they can produce positive and sometimes spectacular results. Unlike tactics, tricks, if discovered, can severely damage if not destroy the relationship with the other side, as well as the immediate negotiation. Tricks used by negotiators can include lying about material facts, employing such games as good guy-bad guy roles, and arriving purposely without sufficient settlement authority.

In order to figure out whether your move will be perceived as a tactic or trick, you should assess the move before employing it. I have found that it is more difficult to figure out which moves are tricks than tactics although the core difference is clear: tricks are not acceptable; tactics can be. Whether the move will be viewed as a trick may depend on life experiences and sensibilities of the other side. Some people may view insufficient settlement authority as a tactic; others might see it as a trick, especially if the other side thinks you cannot be trusted, for instance.

One way for you to gauge whether a move is a tactic or trick is to ask yourself two questions: How would you react if you were the target of your move? How do you think the other side will react if they discovered what you had done? When gauging whether a move is a trick, you should keep in mind that studies have documented how the same move is likely to be viewed more negatively by the recipient than by the author. Because of this distortion risk, you might also pose the two questions to a nearby friend or even better, a person with different sensibilities in order reach a more reliable classification. If the move is perceived by you and others as one that would severely hurt or derail the negotiations if discovered, it is probably a trick.

Here are several examples of possible tricks:

- Lie about a Material Fact—when seeking damages for lost profits in a breach of contract dispute involving non-delivery of goods, a plaintiff might misrepresent that she had offers for the re-sale of the goods that the defendant did not timely deliver. Such a misrepresentation would violate Rule 4.1 of the ABA Professional Code of Conduct on truth telling [Hinshaw, *Ethics*].
- Insufficient Settlement Authority—a lawyer claims he cannot accept the offer because it is more than his client has authority to accept and pay. The client came purposely with insufficient settlement authority in order to pressure the other side to concede within an unreasonable settlement range. This trick might breach a local rule that requires the negotiator to appear with settlement authority, unless he can demonstrate

that the level of authority was sufficient for the amount in dispute or it reflected what he saw as the value of the case.

- Irrevocable Commitments—a party makes a unilateral commitment that effectively removes an issue from the negotiation. A franchisor in a termination dispute, for example, might replace a franchisee while the dispute is unresolved so that the franchisee can no longer negotiate over retaining an exclusive arrangement as part of the resolution.
- Misleading through Intentional Ambiguities—a negotiator makes purposefully vague statements that give him wiggle room to get out of an apparent commitment.
- Good Guy/Bad Guy Strategy—a negotiator sets up a team whereby one member performs the role of the good guy to psychologically assert pressure to settle by apologizing and protecting the other side from the hostile treatment of the other team member, who performs the role of the bad guy.

Tricks also can be difficult to decipher, like tactics, because, in a different context, the same move could be categorized as a good practice or a tactic. An irrevocable commitment can be necessary (good practice) or strategic (tactic or trick) to limit the scope of possible resolution. A "no authority" claim may be due to the other side unexpectedly reaching an authority limit (good practice) or due to purposely arriving with limited (tactic) or severely limited (trick) authority. The negotiator's apparent conviction can make it easy to conceal tricks, just as it can be used to conceal tactics. As with tactics, if it were easy to recognize tricks, they would be ineffective and would lose their power to manipulate.

Tricks Pose Risks

Tricks, like tactics, pose risks, although the discovery of tricks is much more consequential. When a negotiator's trick is uncovered, it can severely undermine the other side's trust in the negotiator and poison the relationship. The other side learns to suspect whatever the negotiator does and to be vigilant. Tricks also can induce the victim to try undoing the deal and find ways to retaliate.

The more adversarial the negotiation becomes due to the use of tricks, the greater the risk of impasse because the adversarial moves can cut off communications, obstruct a reasoned discussion, and alienate the other side. Adversarial tactics and tricks also can leave value on the table because they can focus the parties on protective moves and revenge rather than on problem-solving and probing for inventive solutions.

Tricks with Power

Not all discovered tricks, however, impede a negotiation, even though the use of tricks can make the duplicitous negotiator untrustworthy. The target of the trick still may need to deal with the untrustworthy other side. Even if the other negotiator plays the good guy/bad guy ploy or lies about a material fact in violation of professional conduct rules, the target still may want the employment opportunity or to purchase the land parcel, for example. Or she cannot afford to wait to get a better outcome at trial, or has a weak legal case if she goes to trial.

The relatively greater bargaining power of the deceitful negotiator may allow him to use a trick with impunity. Because of this power advantage, the negotiator may be tempted to operate at the tactics and tricks end of the continuum, especially if he does not care about his reputation and the relationship. Negotiators, however, ought to take a long view and resist claiming easy advantages. They should weigh the costs and possible time-limited gains if the adversarial strategies trigger retaliatory actions by the other side. The negotiator also should consider the empirical evidence on the effectiveness of good practices described in the next section on optimum negotiator styles.

In concluding this section on Negotiation Style, you should be aware of how good practices can be converted into tactics and tricks, depending on how they are performed. For example, a negotiator may engage in active listening and reframing *empathetically* as a good practice, although he can purposely *show little interest* in listening as a tactic, or listen *disrespectfully* to the other side in order to put them on the defensive, as a trick. A negotiator may candidly reply to questions as a good practice, or she might use the other side's good practice of gathering information as an opportunity to delay answering, as a tactic, or respond to questions with lies, as a trick. A negotiator may try overcoming an impasse with a good practice of identifying missing data and formulating a plan to gather the information, or respond to this good practice with a tactic, by making it difficult and expensive for the other side to get the information, or with a trick, by destroying key documents. Even a hard bargaining move like a "take or leave it" proposal or an exploding offer (that expires in a short time period) can vary depending on how it is done. The move could be a good practice if it can be justified. It could be a tactic if supported by a threat to leave. It could be a trick if it is being used to hide information about a possible defense.

Finally, even though this chapter focuses on developing an effective style, these categories also offer a method for discerning the other side's style. Whether the other side is engaging in a good practice, tactic, or trick can guide you in how to respond effectively. If the other side engages in a good practice like focusing on interests or presenting justifications, you should feel confident responding similarly, for example. But if the other side engages in a tactic like a threat to leave or trick like withholding information, you should tailor your response to their move. You might ignore the threat (as just noise) or seek judicial intervention to compel disclosure (to send the message "I will not tolerate tricks"), for example. These brief illustrations provide only a glimpse of how the other side's style can inform your responses. How to respond to each category of moves is beyond the scope of this chapter.[3]

2. OPTIMUM NEGOTIATION STYLE

Negotiation style matters because your style affects your effectiveness. In Andrea Schneider's landmark study on negotiation styles, she "... found that problem-solving behavior is perceived as highly effective" (Schneider 2002: 148). The more problem-solving the style is, the more effective the negotiator is perceived to be. And a cautious approach to problem-solving is likely to be viewed as significantly less effective than a full-fledged problem-solver (Schneider 2002: 148, 175). The statistics were stark: "Only 9% of those lawyers seen as adversarial were rated as effective by their peers ... Furthermore, 90% of lawyers perceived as ineffective were also adversarial. In contrast, 91% of lawyers seen as effective took a problem-solving approach to negotiation" (Schneider 2002: 167).

The study described the style of problem-solving and adversarial negotiators by using descriptors that fit the good practices, tactics, and tricks distinctions.

---

3 Craver identifies 28 negotiation techniques and possible responses. Each technique can be classified in one of the three categories (Craver, *Distributive Techniques*, in this volume.)

Problem-Solving Style

In Schneider's description, problem-solvers conform to good practices. Problem-solvers are ethical, trustworthy, interested in the other side (fair-minded, communicative, perceptive, helpful), flexible, and prepared (rational, realistic). They also are assertive while remaining ethical, understand their clients very well, and represent clients zealously and within bounds of the law. They do not use particular tactics and tricks; they "d[o] not make unfair representations, use haranguing or offensive tactics, make threats, or advance unwanted claims" (Schneider 2002: 165). Their highest goals are to conduct themselves ethically, maximize settlement, achieve a fair settlement, and meet both sides' interests (Schneider 2002: 163–166).[4]

Adversarial Style

In contrast, her descriptions of adversarial negotiators align with tricks and adversarial tactics, although some of the adversarial behavior was non-strategic. In other words, not all adversarial behavior is negotiation behavior. Some adversarial behavior, like being arrogant and egotistical, may be a product of the personality of the person or conflict style as discussed in the final section.

In the study, adversarial negotiators were "inflexible (stubborn, assertive, demanding, firm, tough, forceful) and self-centered. ..." They liked to "fight (irritating, argumentative, quarrelsome, hostile) and the method of fighting is suspect (suspicious, manipulative, evasive)". They were described as not concerned with other side ("not interested in my client's needs ...") and as classically adversarial in that they were "rigid, aggressive, and starting off high (made extreme opening demand and unrealistic initial position.)". The only completely positive adjectives were that they were "confident" and "experienced." Their highest goals were to maximize settlement, outdo the other side and earn a profitable fee (Schneider 2002: 163–6).

---

4 For further discussion of the key practices of problem-solvers, *see* Menkel-Meadow, "Toward Another View of Legal Negotiation: The Structure of Problem-Solving," 31 *UCLA L. Rev.* 754 (1984) (offers an early and enduring description of a problem-solver negotiator) and Charles B. Craver, "What Makes a Great Legal Negotiator?" 56 *Loy. L. Rev.* 337 (2010) (Author summed up his more than three decades of scholarship and teaching negotiations by identifying what he thinks makes a great negotiator. Consistent with a problem-solving style, he concluded that great negotiators thoroughly prepare, establish rapport with the other side and a positive negotiation environment, communicate effectively and persuasively, and finally are patient and persevere.)

Relative Effectiveness of Adversarial Style

Some adversarial negotiators can be viewed as relatively more effective than other adversarial negotiators even when they are "egotistical, arrogant, irritating and quarrelsome ... as long as you are not additionally annoying by complaining or being overly hostile" (Schneider 2002: 177). Relatively effective adversarial negotiators also were perceived as acting in the best interests of their clients, representing their clients zealously and within bounds of the law, and as both intelligent and active (Schneider 2002: 177–78).

The "ineffective adversarial bargainer is perceived as engaging in all sorts of tactics that his effective peers do not" (Schneider 2002: 178). Less effective adversarial negotiators start with extreme opening demands and unrealistic initial positions and are uninterested in the other attorney. They take a rigid position, refuse to move, and use such strategies as take it or leave it offers. They see negotiations as producing winners and losers. They are "perceived as unreasonable and to have inaccurately estimated the value of the case" (Schneider 2002: 178).

The study also found that ethical adversarial negotiators are more effective than unethical ones (Schneider 2002: 176–184). The statistical results were unambiguous: "Seventy-five percent of the unethical adversarial group is considered ineffective. Only ... 2.5% were considered effective. In comparison ... [f]orty percent of ethical adversarials were ineffective, 44% were average and 16% were effective" (Schneider 2002: 184). Although these ethical effectiveness percentages are much lower than for problem-solving negotiators, they are still "notably better than the unethical adversarial bargainer" (Schneider 2002: 184).[5]

The lesson for the adversarial lawyer is clear when selecting among good practices, tactics, and tricks. If the adversarial lawyer incorporates some key good practices like active listening, rational discussions, and especially ethical practices, he will be perceived as a more effective adversarial negotiator.

Schneider compared her results with the landmark study done earlier by Gerald Williams and his colleagues (Williams 1983) and came to a sobering observation relevant to negotiators inclined toward the tactics and tricks end of the continuum: "[A]dversarial negotiators have gotten more extreme

5 For a description of behaviors associated with unethical adversarial negotiators and not ethical ones, *see* Table. They are perceived as rigid, arrogant, unreasonable, and insincere. They make extreme first offers and inflict needless harm (Schneider 2002: 182).

over the past 25 years, they also have become both nastier and less effective" (Schneider 2000).[6]

Schneider concluded her study with: "When lawyers are able to maximize their problem-solving skills balancing assertiveness and empathy, they are more effective on behalf of their clients. They are able to enlarge the pie through creativity and flexibility. They are able to understand the other side with listening and perceptiveness. They argue well for their clients with confidence, poise, and zealous representation. In short, these lawyers set the standard to which other lawyers and law students should aspire" (Schneider 2002: 197).

Let me conclude this section by briefly illustrating how negotiation choices can vary along a problem-solving to adversarial continuum. With a problem-solving negotiation style, you might present an offer based on a rational justification, with only limited use of tactics like inflating the offer. You might ask for $80,000 in damages based on the projected lost sales due to the delivery of defective products even though you might be willing to settle for $70,000. By citing projected lost sales, you have provided a rationale for your offer. If you move toward the adversarial end of tactics and tricks, you might belligerently demand $100,000 today without justifying the level of damages, backed up with a threat to file a suit in court with the aim of bankrupting the other side and embarrassing them publicly.

In any negotiation, you ought to select a mix of techniques that you think will yield the most effective style, realizing that a problem-solving one has been shown to be usually more effective than an adversarial one.

3. NEGOTIATION STYLE INFLUENCED BY CONFLICT STYLES

As highlighted at the beginning of this chapter, your *negotiation style* that determines your effectiveness can be influenced by your personal *conflict style.* So, you need to be aware of and adjust for your default conflict style when shaping your negotiation style.

Several excellent self-assessment instruments have been designed to identify a person's *conflict* style. These instruments are widely used when training and teaching negotiation skills in order to help negotiators understand how they

6 Changes in effectiveness of adversarial bargainer between the two studies are striking. Adversarial negotiators were 25% effective in the Williams study and 9% effective in the Schneider study. They were 33% ineffective in the Williams study and 53% ineffective in the Schneider study (Schneider 2002: 148, 189).

naturally deal with conflict as well as how others might deal with conflict. Each instrument poses questions that require the respondent to choose between two behaviors or rate on a scale how the person would react to a particular situation. The respondent is usually given a context for answering the questions like a legal negotiation or a personal family conflict, because the answers can vary based on context. Each choice or question tries to avoid messaging socially desirable behavior. Each choice is equally desirable or each question is facially neutral. The respondent does not know how each answer relates to one of the conflict style labels. This careful framing of the survey instrument makes it difficult for the respondent to manipulate the result to reflect how he sees himself or how he wants to be seen.

The inquiries and conflict style labels can vary among the assessment instruments, although the label definitions are similar among the instruments. The most popular instruments used in the dispute resolution field are the *Kraybill Conflict Style Inventory*, the Thomas-Kilmann Instrument, and the more recent DYNAD conflict styles test, which is designed to align the test more closely to modern views of negotiation (Shell 2006; Kraybill 2011; Schneider and Brown 2013).

The widely used TKI labels classify conflicts styles into five categories (Schneider and Brown 2013):

Collaborating[7]

Collaborators are both highly assertive and highly empathetic. They advocate for their interests while building relationships across the table, including inviting various views and learning about the needs of others. Collaborators can relish challenging problems and the process of negotiating. They can be creative and try to shape the so called win-win solutions. Collaborating is the closest conflict style to one of the two primary negotiation styles, problem-solving. This style receives much praise in the negotiation literature and instruction. The drawbacks of this conflict style include taking a lot of time and becoming overly focused on process and problem analysis that can exhaust others. Collaborators can transform simple problems into more interesting complex ones. To others, they can appear stubborn and unreasonable, and especially irritating to people who prefer closure.

7 Kraybill uses the label of "cooperating." (Kraybill 2011: 11)

Competing[8]

Competitors are highly assertive, with low empathy and concern for relationships. They make strong, partisan arguments, are firm, like to take charge, and have little interest in input from others. The competitive negotiator also enjoys negotiating, and when doing so, wants to win. The competitive conflict style is closest to the other primary negotiation style, known as adversarial. This style can be hard on relationships, undermine trust across the table, and hurt future dealings.

Compromising

Compromisers are moderately assertive and moderately empathetic. They primarily focus on making the deal, which can be done by meeting halfway. Splitting the difference is a desirable resolution, and they favor objective standards when possible. They can be cooperative and act quickly and fairly. When overused, the style can result in mediocre, unprincipled and suboptimal resolutions where no one is really happy. Compromisers can move too quickly, ask too few questions, and adopt the first fair standard rather than the best one. They also can patch over the problem while leaving unaddressed the underlying symptoms and causes.

Accommodating[9]

Accommodators are highly empathetic with a priority on developing and preserving relationships, while at the low end of assertiveness. They are agreeable, "reasonable," and want to placate the other side, at least in the short run. They are flexible, easy to work with, and have good relationship-building skills that can include being sensitive to the emotional needs and body and verbal signals of others. They can convince themselves that the conflict is no big deal. Their orientation is "I lose/you win." When overused, the style can frustrate others who want to collaborate and jointly problem-solve. For the accommodator, the style risks causing personal resentment, depression, stunted growth, and dependency on others. The accommodator can be highly vulnerable to competitors.

Avoiding

Avoiders are both the least assertive and least empathetic. Avoiders, as you would expect, defer and dodge conflicts; they are conflict averse. They give little attention to relationships by withdrawing or delaying responses and suppressing personal

8 Kraybill uses the label of "directing." (Kraybill 2011: 11)
9 Kraybill uses the label of "harmonizing." (Kraybill 2011: 11)

emotions. They can employ a range of conflict-reducing methods like applying clear rules and resorting to formal decision-making authority over negotiating. They also can avoid face-to-face negotiations by relying on emails, memos, and intermediaries. Avoiders can appear to others as tactful and diplomatic and can help dysfunctional groups function better. When overused, however, an avoiding style can let conflicts fester and contribute to a bottleneck, because the avoider evades necessary interpersonal interactions. For the avoider, benefits can include freedom from entanglement in trivial issues or insignificant relationships while maintaining stability and status quo. But there are personal costs. Avoiders can sporadically explode due to pent-up anger, stagnate, and experience diminished energy. Avoiding can lead to no relationship or the slow death of one. And the avoider can miss out on opportunities that otherwise might be available if he would just ask.

By understanding your *conflict* style, you can be attentive to its influence on your *negotiation* style so that you can avoid your conflict style leading you toward sub-optimal results.

If you know that compromising is your *conflict* style, for example, you can use that insight to guide you in selecting a suitable mix of particular good practices and tactics. You might compensate for your conflict style's inclination to prematurely split the difference by deliberately slowing down the negotiation pace and selecting the best objective standards instead of the first facially fair one.

If you tend to avoid conflicts or accommodate to preserve relationships, you might compensate for your conflict style by conscientiously advocating your client's best interests, a good negotiation practice, instead of settling for what might be comfortable to do.

Awareness of various *conflict* styles also can help you recognize conflict styles of others that can affect how you ought to adjust your *negotiation* style. For example, if you think the other person has a compromising style, you ought to act reasonably and fairly, and with a degree of efficiency—all values that compromisers subscribe to, when trying to influence and persuade the other person. You may need to highlight how your proposals recognized that you must give up something based on the principle of reciprocity and why a particular proposal seems fair to both parties.

If the other person has a take-charge, competitive conflict style, you might use good active listening skills including suitable questions to lead the person toward the issues you want to discuss, while reducing the risk of a contest over who is directing the negotiation. If the other side insists that his issue gets addressed first, for example, you might agree to that and ask when your concerns will be considered.

If the other side has an avoiding conflict style, you may need to move slowly to give the person time and space to deal with the issues in the negotiation. You also might educate the other side about the interests of your client in a way that gets the attention of an avoiding person. Of course if the other person is avoiding an issue as a tactic to wear you down as a competitive move, then you would adopt a different response. You might file a motion to dismiss if tenable in order to create a deadline, for example.

In summary, neither your conflict style nor their conflict style should monopolize the negotiations. Instead, you should consider which conflict styles are at play when selecting the good practices and tactics that shape your style of *negotiation*.

CONCLUSION

As a negotiator, you have choices to make. The tripartite schema of good practices, tactics and tricks provides a method for assessing and selecting problem-solving and adversarial techniques for fashioning an effective *negotiation* style.

REFERENCES

American Bar Association. 2016. *Model Rules of Professional Conduct R. 4.1: Truthfulness in Statements to Others*. Chicago: Center for Professional Responsibility, ABA.

Abramson, H. I. 2013. *Mediation Representation: Advocating as a Problem-Solver.* New York: Wolters Kluwer Law & Business. 25–26, 44–45, 66–67, 146–165, 319–326, 461–472, and 493–502.

Craver, C. B. 2010. "What Makes a Great Legal Negotiator?." *Loyola Law Review* 56: 101–125.

Fisher, R., W. Ury, and B. Patton. 1991. *Getting to Yes: Negotiating Agreement without Giving In*. New York: Penguin Books.

Kraybill, R. 2005. *Style Matters: The Kraybill Conflict Style Inventory*. Silver Spring, Maryland: Riverhouse ePress.

Korobkin, R. and C. Guthrie. 2004. "Heuristics and Biases at the Bargaining Table." *Marquette Law Review* 87: 795–808.

Menkel-Meadow, C. 1984. "Toward Another View of Legal Negotiation: The Structure of Problem-Solving." *UCLA Law Review* 31: 754–842.

Schneider, A. K. 2000. "Perception, Reputation and Reality: An Empirical Study of Negotiation Skills." *Dispute Resolution Magazine* 6 (4): 24–28.

Schneider, A. K. 2002. "Shattering Negotiation Myths: Empirical Evidence on the Effectiveness of Negotiation Style." *Harvard Negotiation Law Review* 7:143–233.

Schneider, A. K. and J. G. Brown. 2013. "Negotiation Barometry: A Dynamic Measure of Conflict Management Style." *Ohio State Journal on Dispute Resolution* 28 (3): 557–580.

Shell, G. R. 2006. *Bargaining for Advantage: Negotiation Strategies for Reasonable People.* New York: Penguin Group.

Wilde, O. 1899. *The Importance of Being Earnest: A Trivial Comedy for Serious People*. London: Chiswick Press.

Williams, G. R. 1983. *Legal Negotiation and Settlement*. Minnesota: West Publishing Company.

CHAPTER 17

Nelson Mandela as Negotiator: What Can We Learn from Him?

2016

Hal Abramson*

---

* Professor of Law, Touro Law Center, New York, *see* www.tourolaw.edu/faculty/abramson. He wants to recognize the valuable comments on earlier drafts by Judge Richard Goldstone and John Brand from South Africa. He also wants to thank Avi Waldman for her editing suggestions and two Touro law students for their superb contributions, Matthew Ingber for his research assistance and Amanda Spinner for her research assistance and for verifying and putting footnotes in proper form.

PREFACE

This article considers how the greatest negotiator of the twentieth century, Nelson Mandela, approached negotiating the unbanning of the African National Congress (ANC), the dismantling of apartheid, and his own freedom after twenty-seven years of imprisonment. He employed classically good negotiation practices in the face of intense and violent opposition while confined in prison for life. If he could be successful, why cannot lawyers succeed when facing less daunting disputes?

This article focuses on the period starting in 1985, when Mandela refused an offer to be released if he would condemn violence, until 1990, when President de Klerk gave his historic unbanning speech, Mandela was freed, and he gave his first speech as a free man.

I. INTRODUCTION

Several hours after we landed in Johannesburg, we heard the news that flashed around the globe. Nelson Mandela had passed away. With that announcement on December 6, 2013, we became accidental eyewitnesses to history and participants in ten extraordinary days of mourning, remembrance, and for-learning.[1] On the day of Mandela's burial, we went to the Apartheid Museum in Johannesburg where his exceptional life was vividly presented. The exhibit explored Mandela's life through six overarching themes: character, comrade, leader, prisoner, negotiator, and statesman. The negotiation theme caught my attention. In this article, I examine Mandela as a negotiator from 1985, when he refused an offer to release him from prison if he would denounce violence, until his release in 1990 to see what we can learn from the greatest negotiator of the twentieth century.[2]

Nelson Mandela's story is one of legendary proportions. After a lifetime as a freedom fighter, twenty-seven years in prison, and only four years after his release, he became South Africa's first democratically elected President at the age of seventy-four years old.[3] While he was known internationally as Nelson

---

1 Harold I. Abramson, *Accidental Witness to History: My Trip to South Africa*, Scholarly Works Paper, DIGITAL COMMONS @ TOURO LAW CENTER (2014), 593. http://digitalcommons.tourolaw.edu/cgi/viewcontent.cgi?article=1678& context=scholarlyworks.

2 *See* Robert Mnookin, *Bargaining with the Devil: When to Negotiate, When to Fight* (2010), 134–35 (conferring this title).

3 Nelson Mandela, *Long Walk to Freedom: The Autobiography of Nelson Mandela* (1995), 620–21.

Mandela, he was known locally as Tata, meaning the father, and Madiba, his clan name.[4]

Nelson Mandela faced the most challenging dispute for any negotiator a distributive one. And not just one. He faced several: he was either in or out of prison; he either renounced the armed struggle or not; his organization, the African National Congress (ANC), was banned or not; and majority rule was adopted or not. The resolution of each of these issues would result in a winner and loser, and he was determined to win each one. He also faced an agonizing conflict of interest. He endured numerous temptations to compromise the interests of his country to achieve his personal freedom. As I probed how Mandela handled these distributive challenges, his distinctive negotiation approach emerged.

To begin unpacking Mandela's approach, I examine his first speech as a free man.[5] He gave this historic speech at Cape Town City Hall to a worldwide audience. City Hall also was the location of the first memorial service that I attended. We listened to eyewitness recollections of that day, February 11, 1990, when Mandela was seen and spoke in public for the first time since he was incarcerated at Robben Island at the robust age of forty-six.[6] The last published picture of Mandela was seen in 1962 at the age of around forty-four.[7] He reappeared on the balcony of City Hall at the age of seventy-one.[8]

When viewed through a negotiation lens, the speech is revealing.[9] His remarks succinctly captured the arc of apartheid history, from its oppressive

---

4 Names, *Nelson Mandela Found.*, https://www.nelsonmandela.org/content/page/names (last visited Apr. 10, 2016).

5 Padraig O Malley, "Remarks by Nelson Mandela in Cape Town on February 11, 1990 After his Release from Victor Verster," *Nelson Mandela Found.*, https://www.nelsonmandela.org/omalley/index.php/site/q/03lv03445/04lv04015/05lv04154/06lv04191.htm (last visited Apr. 10, 2016).

6 Mandela was born on July, 18, 1918. In his autobiography, he noted that when he was being taken on local trips, no one recognized him because his last published picture of him was taken in 1962. *See* Mandela, *supra* note 3, at 533.

7 *Id.*

8 *Id.*

9 The speech received decidedly mixed reviews. *See* Patti Waldmeir, *Anatomy of A Miracle: The End of Apartheid and the Birth of the New South Africa* (1997), 157 (Patti Waldmeir, the journalist and author who was present at the speech, said it was written by a committee deeply suspicious of de Klerk that had penned a speech from hell, a speech without warmth, vision, humanity; a speech for the warpath. ... Mandela was a disappointment). *See* Martin Meredith, *Nelson Mandela: A Biography* (1997), 405–6 (concluding, It was a speech which raised doubts about the quality of Mandela's leadership. ... To whites, the speech seemed needlessly militant. To many blacks, it seemed ambiguous ... [was he calling

beginnings to his aspirations for the future, while unveiling in his words his approach to negotiating freedom for his country and himself. For anyone steeped in South African history, the underlying events are well known.[10] The events and speech are assessed in this article against good negotiation practices.[11]

II. THE POWER OF THE BATNA (BEST ALTERNATIVE TO A NEGOTIATED AGREEMENT)

The first sentence that caught my attention called for the continuation of the armed struggle: Our resort to the armed struggle in 1960 with the formation of the military wing of the ANC ... was a purely defensive action.

... The factors which necessitated the armed struggle still exist today. We have no option but to continue.[12]

This declaration surprised and perplexed me. He made it on the day of his release and a week after President de Klerk met all of the ANC's pre-conditions for negotiations in his monumental Parliamentary speech, known as the unbanning speech.[13] Violence as a strategy is spurned by professional dispute resolvers, so to hear it advocated by one of the great peacemakers of our

---

for arms or negotiations?]); Tom Lodge, *Mandela: A Critical Life* (2006), 168 (noting that Margaret Thatcher ... expressed dismay at the old ritual phrases. ... de Klerk felt that for once, Mandela completely failed to rise to the occasion. Lodge concluded that this collectively scripted statement was not written for them. It was written to reassure Mandela's South African constituency); Anthony Sampson, Mandela: The Authorized Biography (2000), 403 (noting that he had to show his solidarity with the ANC because of the fears generated by the secret talks. He needed to reaffirm the use of the tools that gave him leverage-sanctions and the armed struggle. In Mandela's authorized biography, Anthony Sampson said that any disappointment with the speech betrayed ignorance about Mandela's relationship with the ANC, and his true political importance. ...).

10 *See generally* Mandela, *supra* note 3 (Mandela's life has been thoroughly studied by many observers and historians, including Mandela in his thoughtful autobiography). *See also* Lodge, *supra* note 9; Meredith, *supra* note 9; Waldmeir, *supra* note 9; Sampson, *supra* note 9; Mnookin, *supra* note 2, at 106–36; Allister Sparks, *Tomorrow Is Another Country* (1995); F. W. De Klerk, *The Last Trek A New Beginning: The Autobiography* (1998).

11 *See generally* Harold I. Abramson, *Mediation Representation: Advocating as a Problem-Solver* (3rd ed. 2013) (discussing good practices. Chapter 1 compares the two widely used negotiation approaches, positional and problem-solving and suggests how to integrate the two into a unified approach. The chapter summarizes various negotiation practices including the good ones along with numerous cites from key literature in the negotiation field.).

12 O Malley, *supra* note 5.

13 Organisations Unbanned, *Nelson Mandela Found.* (Jan. 1, 2015), https://www.nelsonmandela.org/news/entry/organisations-unbanned.

time was jarring. His view contrasts starkly with the other two great peacemakers, Mahatma Gandhi and Martin Luther King Jr., who were admired for their abiding commitment to civil disobedience.

Nelson Mandela endorsed the use of violence early in his life as a freedom fighter. But why, in what form, and for how long?

Mandela understood one of the basic tenets of negotiations: your negotiating power is fueled by the strength of your alternative to settlement, known as the BATNA (Best Alternative to a Negotiated Agreement).[14] He realized that parties will negotiate when the outcome at the table will be better than the outcome away from the table. The ANC wanted to negotiate. The status quo away from the table was horrific continuation of the personally and economically oppressive and violent apartheid policies. They had a weak BATNA. The Nationalist Government did not want to negotiate. They preferred the status quo away from the table. It meant that the white minority would maintain control with all of its benefits over the majority of the population. They had an appealing BATNA.

Mandela and the ANC needed to change the Government's alternative to a negotiated solution. He endorsed an armed struggle in order to induce the Government to come to the table. Mandela recognized that, [W]e could not defeat the Government on the battlefield, but could make governing difficult for them.[15]

Mandela did not begin his freedom-fighting career wedded to armed resistance. When helping to organize the first mass demonstrations against the new apartheid laws in 1952, Mandela adopted a nonviolent approach as a tactic that fit the conditions.[16] He arrived at this pragmatic conclusion in a committee discussion that considered whether a policy of nonviolence was an ethical and morally superior principle that should be unconditionally followed.[17] Mandela rejected the Gandhiam principle in a meeting that included Manilal Gandhi, Mahatma's son.[18] Advocating for a nonviolent campaign similar to his father's in India, Gandhi endorsed a commitment to key

---

14 Roger Fisher and William Ury, *Getting to Yes: Negotiating Agreement without Giving In* (Bruce Patton ed., 2011), 99–108. *See* Mnookin, *supra* note 2, at 29–30.

15 Mandela, *supra* note 3, at 520 (explaining this strategy in 1985 when he was visited in prison by Samuel Dash, a professor of law at Georgetown University and former counsel to the U.S. Senate Watergate Committee).

16 *See id.* at 127–28.

17 *Id.*

18 *Id.*

Satyagraha (truth-firmness) principles of nonviolence.[19] Mandela, however, saw nonviolence in the Gandhian model not as an inviolable principle but as a tactic to be used as the situation demanded … for [as] long as it was effective.[20]

Mandela took the lead in meticulously training supervisors and organizing the nonviolent demonstrations. During the six months of demonstrations, the organizers were proud that there was not a single act of violence by any of the resisters due to their exemplary discipline.[21]

In the following year, Mandela crossed the line in his rhetoric. He publically endorsed violent resistance in a rabble-rousing speech to a large crowd with a pronounced police presence.[22] Mandela said,

> [T]hat the time for passive resistance had ended, that nonviolence was a useless strategy and could never overturn a white minority regime bent on retaining its power at any cost. … [V]iolence was the only weapon that would destroy apartheid and we must be prepared, in the near future, to use that weapon.[23]

The ANC's National Executive Committee reacted swiftly to this unilateral pronouncement and severely reprimanded Mandela for departing dangerously from accepted ANC policy.

At the time of his remarks, he had begun to analyze the struggle differently:

> The ambition of the ANC was to wage a mass struggle, to engage … in a campaign so large and powerful that it might overcome the status quo of white oppression. But the Nationalist government was making any legal expression of dissent or protest impossible. I saw that they would ruthlessly suppress any legitimate protest. … A police state did not seem far away.[24]

He distinguished South African conditions from conditions in India:

> Gandhi had been dealing with a foreign power that ultimately was more realistic and farsighted. … Nonviolent passive resistance is effective so long as your opposition adheres to the same rules as you do. But if

---

19 *Id.*
20 *Id.* at 128.
21 *Id.* at 123, 127–28, 138–39.
22 *Id.* at 157–58.
23 *Id.* at 157.
24 *Id.*

> peaceful protest is met with violence, its efficacy is at an end. ... [T]here is no moral goodness in using an ineffective weapon.[25]

During his later years in prison, in 1985, Mandela explained how the conditions under which Martin Luther King and he struggled were totally different too.[26] The United States was a democracy with constitutional guarantees of equal rights that protected nonviolent protest ...; South Africa was a police state with a constitution that enshrined inequity and an army that responded to nonviolence with force.[27]

The nonviolence policy was maintained by Mandela and the ANC until the deadly 1960 Sharpeville Massacre of black protestors.[28] In response, the ANC formed a military wing, Umkhonto we Sizwe (which is Zulu for Spear of the Nation and was known as MK), and Mandela became its co-founder and head.[29] In its manifesto, MK declared:

> We shall not submit and we have no choice but to hit back by all means within our power in defence of our people, our future, and our freedom. The government has interpreted the peacefulness of the movement as weakness; the people's non-violent policies have been taken as a green light for government violence. ... Umkhonto we Sizwe will be at the front line of the people's defense. It will be the fighting arm of the people against the government and its policies of race oppression.[30]

In Mandela's often cited speech at the Rivonia Trial where he was sentenced to life in prison, Mandela admitted to the use of violence and justified its use:

---

25 *Id.* at 158, 166. *See* Norman G. Finkelstein, *What Ghandi Says: About Nonviolence, Resistance, and Courage* (2012), 32–45 (concluding from Gandhi's writings that while Gandhi's commitment to nonviolence was primary, it was not unconditional. Gandhi recognized exceptions based on the need for courage and self-defense. The author also identified contradictions in his writings.).

26 *See id.*

27 Mandela, *supra* note 3, at 520–21, 568, 574.

28 *See id.* at 271–74.

29 *See id.* at 280.

30 Padraig O Malley, "Manifesto of Umnkhonto We Sizwe," *Nelson Mandela Found.*, https://www.nelsonmandela.org/omalley/index.php/site/q/03lv02424/04lv02730/05lv02918/06lv02950.htm (last visited Apr. 10, 2016). *See* Mandela, *supra* note 3, at 274.

> I do not, however, deny that I planned sabotage. I did not plan it in a spirit of recklessness nor because I have any love of violence. I planned it as a result of a calm and sober assessment of the political situation that had arisen after many years of tyranny, exploitation, and oppression of my people by whites.[31]

In planning MK's activities, the High Command identified four levels of violence,[32] and started with sabotage because it would cause the least harm to human life. MK initially targeted, with handmade bombs, electric power plants and government offices in several cities. If sabotage did not produce the desired results, MK would move to the next stages of guerrilla warfare and terrorism.[33]

Nevertheless, Mandela believed that ultimately apartheid would not be defeated by an armed struggle; he understood its limits. It would be defeated by negotiation. The ANC lacked the military power to remove the Nationalist Party from governing. It could only make the country ungovernable, and nonviolence and passive resistance alone had achieved little.[34] Mandela hated violence but was not a pacifist. ... He understood the power of violence and used it strategically to force the government to negotiate.[35]

Mandela could not single-handedly shape a negative BATNA for the Government. He could not do much personally because he was incarcerated shortly after the Sharpeville Massacre. The negative BATNA had to be forged on multiple fronts by numerous anti-apartheid leaders and sympathizers. Much action took place in the streets and courtrooms of South Africa and in legislative bodies and the United Nations outside of South Africa. Each action has been given a name in the history of the anti-apartheid movement and encapsulates a consequential chapter of the Long Walk to Freedom.[36] They collectively formed a negative BATNA for the Government. Several of the chapters and

---

31 Mandela, *supra* note 3, at 364.

32 *See id.* at 271–74, 282–86, 364–65, 520 (explaining sabotage, guerrilla warfare, terrorism, and open revolution).

33 *See id.*; Mnookin, *supra* note 2, at 117–18.

34 Mandela, *supra* note 3, at 364–65, 520–21.

35 Mnookin, *supra* note 2, at 135. *See Mandela: Character, Comrade, Leader, Prisoner, Negotiator, Statesman*, Apartheid Museum, http://www.apartheidmuseum.org/sites/default/files/files/downloads/theme5.pdf (last visited Apr. 10, 2016) (emphasizing that "Bringing the apartheid regime to the negotiating table was Mandela's guiding objective. He always made it very clear that he regarded armed struggle as a tactic ...").

36 *See generally* Mandela, *supra* note 3.

key leaders are mentioned here and further described in Appendix A on the Negative BATNA for the Nationalist Government:

1960	The Sharpeville Massacre brought global attention to the conditions under apartheid when the police killed sixty-nine protestors within two minutes most of whom were shot in the back as they were fleeing. These shootings changed the landscape for fighting apartheid as both the intensity of protests and the responses by the Nationalist Government escalated in full view of the world.[37]
1961	Umkhonto we Sizwe (Spear of the Nation) (MK), a military wing of the ANC, was organized in the wake of the Sharpeville Massacre.[38]
1962–1964	The Rivonia Trial brought further international attention to the oppressive apartheid conditions. The Nationalist Government charged Mandela and other ANC leaders with sabotage, violent revolution, and conspiracy with others. The Trial engendered much international condemnation including from the United Nations Security Council.[39]
1969–1977	The Black Consciousness Movement (BCM), marked by the formation of the South African Student Organization in 1969 and co-founded by activist Steve Biko, transformed student discontent into a political force and shifted attention from the ANC priority on non-racialism to black pride and black self-reliance. The BCM spurred a new era of activism in the face of aggressive clamping down by the Nationalist Government, culminating in Biko's brutal September 1977 death in police custody.[40]
1976	The Soweto Student Uprising triggered violent protests and mass resistance to apartheid throughout South Africa. The uprising erupted in June 1976 when high school students protested against introduction of Afrikaans as the medium of instruction.[41]

37 *Id.* at 236–39. *See infra* App. A.

38 *See infra* App. A.

39 Mandela, *supra* note 3, at 360–78.

40 *See infra* App. A.

41 *Id.*

1985	Mandela rejected President Botha's offer to be released if he would denounce violence.[42]
1983–1990	The United Democratic Front (UDF), a coalition of organizations, led much of the internal resistance while the ANC was banned. The UDF, in an effort to render the country ungovernable, mobilized people and organizations across the country. More than 600 organizations joined, including labor, political, youth, women s, religious, civic, and student and teacher organizations. The Government believed that the UDF was created by the ANC, although the UDF was ultimately viewed as independent.
1960–1990	International sanctions and economic and political isolation, dating back to the Sharpeville Massacre, escalated as each chapter unfolded.[43]

In addition to these events, numerous anti-apartheid leaders and sympathizers acted boldly while putting their professional and personal lives at risk, with some paying the ultimate price for their actions. Each name is renowned in the anti-apartheid movement. They collectively contributed greatly to shaping the negative BATNA that Mandela understood was essential for persuading the Nationalist Government to come to the table. Only a few of the many courageous leaders are mentioned here, although many more made profound contributions,[44] including some under the public radar.[45]

---

42 *Id.*

43 *Id.*

44 For example, Judge Goldstone whom I met when researching this article was a sitting judge under apartheid laws and did what he could to interpret the laws to temper its harshness and undermine its effects within the parameters of his judicial role. He later became a confidant to Nelson Mandela after his release. Their friendship grew from Goldstone's activities as the Chairman of the Standing Commission of Inquiry Regarding the Prevention of Public Violence and Intimidation. The Commission made public evidence that senior members of the South African Army and Police were involved with attempts to abort the negotiation process.

45 Hundreds of people did what they could within their personal corner of the apartheid world including participating in peaceful or violent protests, aiding someone in flight, signing petitions, or representing victims. For example, our host, John Brand, did what he could as a young associate with a century-old South African law firm, Bowman Gilfillan. He was part of a small group of lawyers that represented hundreds of defendants in the Soweto Uprising and worked with George Bizos, Mandela's personal attorney, and black anti-apartheid leader Shun Chetty, in addition to practicing other professionally-risky legal work for an attorney at

- Chief Albert Luthuli was the early President of the ANC and received the 1960 Nobel Peace Prize.[46]
- Oliver Tambo helped revive the ANC in the early 1940s and lead the ANC while in exile, while Nelson Mandela was in prison.[47]
- Walter Sisulu, active with the ANC, helped lead the Defiance Campaign and transform the ANC into a mass-based militant national organization.[48]
- Stephen Biko, co-founder of the Black Consciousness Movement (BCM), did much to generate black pride and protests, as described above, and his brutal death made him an international martyr in opposing apartheid.[49]
- Winnie Mandela, Nelson's wife, was an energetic, colorful, and controversial force in the anti-apartheid movement, especially when her husband was in prison.[50]
- George Bizos was a human rights lawyer who served as Nelson Mandela's personal attorney throughout much of his life.[51]
- Albie (Albert) Sachs was a human rights lawyer who participated in the Defiance Campaign, the drafting of the Freedom Charter, and defended people charged under apartheid's racist laws.[52]

These people, among many others, made governing difficult and the status quo unbearable for the Nationalist Government. The increasingly negative BATNA spurred the Nationalist Government to reluctantly and intermittently come to the bargaining table to talk with Mandela during his last five years in prison.

In the Cape Town speech, Mandela tied the negative BATNA to the negotiations when he said: We express the hope that a climate conducive to a negotiated settlement will be created soon so that there may no longer be the need for the

---

a white-shoe law firm. In 2006, John Brand successfully petitioned the High Court of South Africa to posthumously reinstate Shun Chetty after Chetty had to flee the country in 1978 for his personal safety and was then disbarred for trumped up charges that included abandoning clients.

46 *See infra* App. A.

47 *Id.*

48 *Id.*

49 *Id.*

50 *Id.*

51 *Id.*

52 *Id.*

armed struggle.[53] After formally sanctioning an armed struggle for almost thirty years, Mandela endorsed suspending it six months after his release in 1990.[54]

III. NEGOTIATION STYLE OF NELSON MANDELA

Mandela's negotiation strategies can be classified based on three types of negotiation practices: good practices, tactics, and tricks.[55]

Good practices will likely produce the best negotiated results.[56] They include asserting interests rather than positions, acting ethically and fairly, and building rapport, relationships, and trust on your side of the table and across the table.[57] They also include relying on rational and principled justifications, engaging in suitable information exchanges, and using effective communication techniques such as summarizing, paraphrasing, framing, and questioning.[58]

Tactics are conventionally used, not because they are good practices, but because they reflect customary practices.[59] Making extreme first offers to create room for concessions, exaggerating arguments, and denigrating the other side's arguments are examples, along with threatening to leave the negotiation.[60] These practices are generally accepted ones that can offer tactical benefits if they are executed convincingly. Because they are viewed as generally accepted

53 O Malley, *supra* note 5. The term armed struggle is associated with the ANC efforts, although there was a broader level of violence taking place that was not directed by the ANC. In the rhetoric of violence, the same term had different meanings for different audiences. In the Cape Town speech, Mandela likely used the term because it resonated with his key constituency on that day the ANC and its sympathizers. For the Nationalist Government and many whites, they heard that Mandela was not denouncing violence, whether generated by the ANC or any other sources.

54 In August 1990, Mandela endorsed suspending the violent struggle as a concession to demonstrate good faith, improve the climate for negotiations, and secure target dates for meeting particular demands of the ANC. Mandela, *supra* note 3, at 586. To garner support on his side of the table, he supported suspending, not terminating it. *Id.* De Klerk, in his autobiography, viewed this concession differently. He thought that the ANC made a common commitment towards the resolution of the existing climate of violence ... and to a peaceful process of negotiations, during their first negotiations in May 1990, as expressed in the Groote Schuur Minute. De Klerk, *supra* note 10, at 182.

55 Abramson, *supra* note 11, at 22–29, 43–47.

56 *Id.* at 25–26, 43–44.

57 Professor Mnookin refers to negotiating as a two-level game where a party is negotiating with people behind the table and across the table. Mnookin, *supra* note 2, at 133–34.

58 *See* Abramson, *supra* note 11, at App. F.

59 *Id.* at 25–27, 45–47.

60 *Id.* at 35–37.

practices, if discovered, they do not severely undermine relationships or the negotiation process, as can happen with tricks.

Tricks are neither good practices nor conventionally accepted ones.[61] Tricks are unethical and highly risky. When executed convincingly, they can be effective. If discovered, they can severely undermine, if not destroy, the relationship with the target and the negotiation process. Tricks can include lying about material facts, employing such games as good guy/bad guy roles, and arriving purposely without sufficient settlement authority.[62]

There is no agreed upon list of tactics or tricks. Although most people can probably agree which moves can be labeled as tactics, people agree less on which moves are tricks. The move needs to be assessed. The answer can depend on the context of its use and the experience of the target. Some people may view insufficient settlement authority as a tactic; others might see it as a trick, as I do, for instance. If the target views the move as a trick, it can affect whether and how the matter can be settled.

The strategies selected by a negotiator define his particular style over a continuum of good practices, tactics, and tricks. Studies have shown that the more negotiators engage in practices toward the good practices and tactics end of the continuum, the more effective the negotiator can be.[63]

A. Good Practices

Mandela, in his Cape Town remarks and during the secret negotiations, employed several strategies and moves that were good practices.

1. Advocating Interests

Mandela uncompromisingly advocated his primary interests in the liberation of South African blacks in the face of potent temptations to sacrifice them to meet his interest in personal liberation. An interest of a party, as defined in the negotiation literature,[64] focuses on a party's needs instead of particular solutions that can be contested by the other side. By focusing on interests, parties are more likely to uncover multiple solutions of which some might be acceptable or tolerable to the other side. Mandela advocated his primary interests while priming the other side with possible solutions that he would prefer.

---

61 *Id.* at 27–28, 46–47.

62 *Id.* at 38.

63 *Id.* at 2–3.

64 Fisher and Ury, *supra* note 14, at ch. 3.

In his Cape Town speech, he firmly set out the primary interests. He spoke about the need for a democratic, nonracial, and unitary South Africa.[65] He called for an end to white monopoly on political power and a fundamental restructuring of our political and economic systems to ensure that the inequalities of apartheid are addressed and our society thoroughly democratized, including universal suffrage.[66] He also repeated the interests articulated in his speech at the 1964 Rivonia trial where he expressed how he cherished the idea of a democratic and free society where people live together in harmony and with equal opportunities.[67]

He relentlessly advocated for replacing apartheid with a democracy for almost fifty years even as obstacles relentlessly mounted. His primary goal of establishing a democracy has a long history dating back to his formative years as a freedom fighter in 1943–1944.[68] He advanced this interest in: the 1955 Freedom Charter,[69] the 1961 Manifesto establishing the military arm of ANC,[70] his famous I am prepared to die remarks at the 1964 Rivonia Trial,[71] and his remarks read by his daughter when he rejected Botha's conditional release offer in 1985.[72]

---

65 O Malley, *supra* note 5.

66 *Id.*

67 Nelson Mandela's Statement from the Dock at the Opening of the Defense Case in the Rivonia Trial, *African Nat L Cong.*, http://www.anc.org.za/show.php?id=3430 (last visited Apr. 10, 2016).

68 In 1944, Mandela helped form a Youth League for the ANC, with a manifesto that focused on overthrowing white supremacy and establishing a truly democratic form of government. Mandela, *supra* note 3, at 98–100.

69 The Freedom Charter was prepared by a committee of the National Action Council (a coalition of diverse organizations) and reviewed by ANC's National Executive Council in 1955. *Id.* at 170–76. It was scheduled to be presented and subject to vote by the Congress of the People at a convention of around 3,000 delegates. *Id.* The meeting attended by Mandela was disbanded by a brigade of police before a formal vote. *Id.* The Freedom Charter nevertheless lived on as an enduring political statement. *Id.* The Freedom Charter provided that the people shall govern and set out multiple requirements for a democratic South Africa including that any rights ought to be the same regardless of race, colour, or sex. *Id.*

70 The 1961 Manifesto of Umkhonto we Sizwe (MK), which Mandela helped to draft, stated that they were working for the winning of liberty, democracy and full national rights and equality for all the people of this country. O Malley, *supra* note 30.

71 At the end of his four-hour presentation justifying why he joined the freedom struggle, Mandela gave his famous remarks that he quoted in his 1990 Cape Town speech: he cherished the ideal of a democratic and free society in which all persons will live together in harmony and with equal opportunities. ... But if needs be, it is an ideal for which I am prepared to die. O Malley, *supra* note 5. *See* Mandela, *supra* note 67.

72 Pete Brook, "Mandela's 1985 Refusal of Release from Prison," *Prison Photography* (Dec. 5, 2013), http://prisonphotography.org/2013/12/05/mandelas-1985-refusal-of-release-from-prison/.

He encountered one of his greatest temptations to compromise his primary interest in 1985 when President Botha offered Mandela an opportunity to be released from prison after twenty-one years. Botha imposed only one condition: Mandela had to publicly reject violence as a political weapon.[73]

This offer was made three years after Mandela was upgraded from Robben Island, where he had slept for eighteen years on a floor mat in a tiny cell, to Pollsmoor Prison that Mandela described as a five-star hotel when compared to Robben Island.[74] At Pollsmoor, Mandela and three of his comrades were given the top floor with regular beds, much improved food, and considerable freedom of movement. They were given access to a fairly wide range of newspapers and magazines, including for the first time foreign sources like Time Magazine and The Guardian. Mandela had his first physical contact in twenty-one years with Winnie and his family, an especially moving and indelible moment.[75] The authorities apparently wanted to remind Mandela how life out of prison could be and what he was missing as they tested negotiating with him.

Mandela rejected the conditional offer of release in a speech read by his daughter, Zindzi, at a public rally of supporters.[76] Mandela explained how this offer was not an offer to be freed, and in doing so, he highlighted his primary interest. He focused on what the offer would not give him when he left the prison. His organization would still be banned. He could be arrested on a pass offense. His wife would still be banished in Brandfort. He would need to ask permission to live in an urban area. His own South African citizenship would not be respected. This offer was not one to free him, he emphasized.

In confronting his conflicting interests, he prioritized freedom for everyone else over his personal freedom:

> I cherish my own freedom dearly, but I care even more for your freedom. Too many have died since I went to prison. Too many have suffered for the love of freedom. I owe it to their widows, to their orphans, to their mothers and to their fathers who have grieved and wept for them. Not only I have suffered during these long, lonely, wasted years. I am not less life-loving than you are. But I cannot sell my birthright, nor am I prepared to sell the birthright of the people to be free. I am in prison as the representative of

---

73 *See* Mandela, *supra* note 3, at 521.

74 Mandela, *supra* note 3, at 513–18.

75 *Id.* at 517.

76 *Id.* at 522–23.

> the people and of your organisation, the African National Congress, which was banned.[77]

Even though this conditional offer was unambiguously rejected by Mandela,[78] it was accepted by a number of other prisoners serving long jail terms for sabotage.

The Nationalist Government continuously tempted Mandela to compromise the nation's interests to meet his personal interests, as recounted by George Bizos, his lifelong friend and personal lawyer. Bizos was one of the few people that had regular contact with Mandela when in prison. In an interview with Bizos after Mandela's release, the questioner noted that Mandela, in the 80s, was submitted to what one might describe as a series of temptations, and one of them was the temptation of his freedom in exchange for abandoning the armed struggle.[79] George Bizos responded with:

> ... Yes. I think that the apartheid government believed its own propaganda almost right to the end, and it's the reason why they lost out. They believed that they could bribe Mandela in the manner in which they had bribed the bantustan leaders. What they were saying to him, These exiles are led by the nose by the communists and by the Soviet Union. The people of South Africa would reject that. You have an existence independent of this organization. You come with us, and we will settle the matter, get some authority and we will give some sort of qualified rights to the majority of the people, and all will go well. They didn't know Mandela ... This is why I think they gave him special facilities, at Pollsmoor and at Victor Verster prisons, and this is why they allowed him almost to run an office in the

---

77 *Id.*

78 The backstory of this offer includes a vigorous effort by Kobe Coetsee, Botha's Minister of Justice, to persuade Botha to not make it. He was convinced Mandela would never accept it, and the rejection would make it difficult to fashion another way out without looking weak. He thought asking Mandela to renounce the armed struggle would be asking him to renounce his past, and given what Coetsee had learned about Mandela, he would not do this. Coetsee also considered the offer one-sided. The ANC would get nothing by sacrificing its strongest bargaining chip for Mandela's freedom. Coetsee wanted Botha to avoid offering Mandela a negative proposal to renounce violence and instead offer a positive one by asking Mandela to commit to a future peaceful process. *See* Sparks, *supra* note 10, at 49–51.

79 Interview by John Carlin with George Bizos, "The Long Walk of Nelson Mandela," *PBS*, http://www.pbs.org/wgbh/pages/frontline/shows/mandela/interviews/bizos.html (last visited Apr. 10, 2016).

> late 80s, where the warder and his son did the cooking, served the meal, the wine and gave him a telephone. That the house was locked but not to prevent Mandela from going out, but preventing people from coming in. And they thought that he would not have [been] able to resist this special treatment. ... They still believed that they would be able to drive a wedge between Mandela and the others.[80]

In short, Nelson Mandela, as any skilled negotiator, understood his interests, knew his priorities, and advocated for them.

2. Understanding Other's Side Interests

Mandela also had the remarkable capacity to understand the other side's interests, convince them he did, and find ways to meet their interests. By definition, a negotiation can succeed only if the other side agrees to the outcome. It is easy to be blinded to the other side's interests when occupied with advancing your own. This blind spot may not be fatal when trying to persuade a neutral third party judge, but it can be in a negotiation where the other side's consent is required.

Throughout the secret prison negotiations, as described in Appendix B, Mandela reassured the other side that he and the ANC wanted and needed the white minority to be part of the country's future. During the prison meetings, Mandela made a point that is often quoted when he stressed that, [T]he majority would need the minority. We do not want to drive you to the sea.[81] In his letter to President Botha in anticipation of their first meeting, Mandela highlighted the interests of both sides that must be met when he recognized the need to address white South Africa's concerns about the impact of majority rule on them.[82] In his first meeting with President de Klerk, there was much discussion of ways to address each other's interests, including Mandela indicating why the Government's group rights proposal did not meet the Government's interests.[83] In response, President de Klerk said, You know, ... my aim is not different than yours. Your memo to P. W. Botha said the ANC and the Government should work together to deal with white fears of black domination. ...[84] In describing his first press conference the day after he was freed, Mandela said:

---

80 *Id.*

81 Mandela, *supra* note 3, at 539.

82 *Id.* at 547.

83 *Id.* at 555–56.

84 *Id.* at 555.

> [I] wanted to impress on the reporters the critical role of whites in any new dispensation. ... We did not want to destroy the country before we freed it, and to drive the whites away would devastate the nation. I said that there was a middle ground between white fears and black hopes ... Whites are fellow South Africans, I said, and we want them to feel safe and to know that we appreciate the contribution that they have made toward the development of this country. Any man or woman who abandons apartheid will be embraced in our struggle for a democratic, nonracial South Africa. ...[85]

Mandela worked diligently to find ways to meet the interests of the white minority while not compromising his side's interests. His efforts to meet their interests was facilitated by the relationships cultivated along his path toward freedom and statesman as described in the next section.

3. Building Relationships and Forward Thinking

Mandela built rapport and relationships with a clear eye on the future without becoming mired in past grievances and need for revenge. Mandela cultivated connections across the table even with the most hostile and resistant parties who were most threatened by his democratic agenda.[86] His natural ability to do this is legendary. His instinct to do so contributed greatly to his success in helping negotiate a democratic future for South Africa.

Many of us marvel at Mandela's ability to treat his oppressors with respect and negotiate directly with them. In mediation parlance, he negotiated in joint sessions, a format subject to much debate.[87] A significant number of attorneys and mediators prefer keeping parties separate because they think parties in conflict are too angry with each other to work productively in the same room. And, Mandela had good reason to be angry. He had been sentenced to life in prison, confined for eighteen years in a tiny cell on Robben Island where he lived in unbearably harsh conditions, separated from his wife, children, and friends for twenty-seven years, and more. Mandela's ability to move past all that and focus on the future was essential to his success.[88] Focusing on the future can be

85 *Id.* at 568–69.

86 Mnookin, *supra* note 2, at 135–36.

87 *See* Abramson, *supra* note 11, at ch. 5.4.

88 During the ten days of mourning, we heard testimonials at the various memorial services that if Mandela could move forward given what he suffered under apartheid, so could they. I was much affected by an exchange with the nineteen-year-old son of a long-time friend in

necessary for resolving many sorts of disputes, as any experienced negotiator and mediator know.

How could Mandela negotiate directly with his oppressors?
Mandela's view of the enemy helped him work with individuals who had engaged in horrific and immoral deeds or were part of system that did so. He viewed the enemy as the system that turned everyone against each other, and it was that system that he hated. He concluded that, [T]he liberation struggle was not a battle against any one group or colour, but a fight against a system of repression.[89] I wanted South Africa to see that I loved even my enemies while I hated the system that turned us against one another.[90]

He also believed in the humanity of people. He thought that, [N]o one is born hating another person because of the colour of his skin. ... People must learn to hate, and if they can learn to hate, they can be taught to love ...[91]

a. Reaching out to Both Sides of the Table

In his Cape Town remarks, he reached out to build relationships with people on his side of the table as well as across the table.[92] Mandela had a large number of people on both sides to attend to and he did.

In his first speech as a free man, he had to reestablish the confidence of the people on his side of the table.[93] Mandela had to secure credibility with the ANC leadership and the larger body politic including blacks, coloreds, Indians, and sympathetic whites.[94] He had to demonstrate that the twenty-seven years

---

South Africa. He identified himself as a member of the born free generation. Reflecting on Mandela's sacrifices, this young man was in awe that Mandela spent more years in prisons than he had yet spent on this earth and was still able to move forward.

89 Mandela, *supra* note 3, at 620.

90 *Id.* at 568.

91 Waldmeir, *supra* note 9, at 88.

92 Professor Mnookin noted that it takes great skill for a negotiator to manage the tension between what is going on across the table with your adversary and what is happening behind the table among your constituents. Mnookin, *supra* note 2, at 133–34 (emphasis added). Behind the table, any negotiator may need to work with a client, spouse, supervisor, members of a board of directors, a constituency, the public, and so on.

93 Mandela, *supra* note 3, at 566–67.

94 Colored or Coloured is a term used in South Africa to identify people of mixed races. The label is not inherently derogatory as when used outside of South Africa. *See, e.g.*, Eusebius McKaiser, "Not White Enough, Not Black Enough," *N. Y. Times: Latitude Blog* (Feb. 15, 2012, 8:38 AM), http://latitude.blogs.nytimes.com/2012/02/15/in-south-africa-after-apartheid-colored-community-is-the-big-loser/?_r=0.

in prison did not break him that he did not sell out. He thanked a long list of specific people and groups and unqualifiedly reaffirmed his membership and agreement with the objectives, strategies, and tactics of the ANC.

He also reached across the table and praised President de Klerk, who headed the government responsible for his decades of confinement. Mandela said:

Mr. [d]e Klerk has gone further than any other Nationalist president in taking real steps to normalise the situation. ... It must be added that Mr. de Klerk himself is a man of integrity who is acutely aware of the dangers of a public figure not honouring his undertakings.[95]

When praising de Klerk, Mandela put at risk his fragile relationship with people on his side of the table. Yet, he chose to elevate de Klerk as a credible negotiating partner and send a reassuring message to the fearful white minority, whose support he would need.[96]

b. Meeting with the Presidents

In prison, Mandela asked to meet with President Botha and later President de Klerk. Mandela's recollections of those meetings remind us of the benefit of meeting directly with the other side. Personal interactions can open up opportunities for relationship building that may facilitate future hard bargaining.

Mandela recalled how tense he felt about meeting with Mr. Botha. He was known as the Great Crocodile, and Mandela had heard many accounts of Botha's ferocious temper.[97] Mandela resolved that if Botha acted in that finger-wagging fashion with him, Mandela would stand up and adjourn the meeting (an unusual option for a prisoner).[98] After the meeting, Mandela said, "[H]e completely disarmed me. He was unfailingly courteous, deferential, and friendly."[99]

At the end of his first meeting with de Klerk, Mandela concluded, "I was able to write to our people ... that Mr. de Klerk seemed to represent a true

95 O Malley, *supra* note 5.

96 Unfortunately, President de Klerk thought Mandela did not succeed across the table because he called for continuing the armed struggle and sanctions. In his autobiography, de Klerk thought that, [h]is message, which [had] evidently been drafted by hardline ideologues within the ANC alliance, brought us little comfort or reason to share in the general rejoicing. For once, Mandela failed completely to rise to the occasion. De Klerk, *supra* note 10, at 169–70.

97 Mandela, *supra* note 3, at 549.

98 *Id.* at 550.

99 *Id.* at 549–50.

departure from the National Party politicians of the past. Mr. de Klerk ... was a man we could do business with."[100] For seven years after his release, he had to negotiate with de Klerk as President and then as his Deputy President.

c. Secret Negotiations in Prison

Unbeknownst to the rest of the world, Mandela negotiated with the Nationalist Government while in prison. A special committee was formed that included Mandela and four senior and powerful representatives of the Government. They held the power to improve or degrade the quality of Mandela's prison life as well as to release him.

The secret committee, that met forty-seven times beginning in 1987,[101] included:[102]

1. Kobie Coetsee, who was the Minister of Justice and served as Chair. He extended the first olive branch from the Government to Mandela in 1985 when he made a surprise visit to Mandela in the hospital. Before the committee convened, he spent time getting a sense of Mandela by reading internal reports and meeting with people who knew him well including George Bizos, Mandela's personal attorney, and Winnie Mandela. In early 1986, he escorted Mandela during the eminent persons visits where he observed Mandela greet and interact with several dignitaries from abroad and concluded that he could be the man.[103]
2. General Willemse, who was the Commissioner of Prisoners.
3. Fanie van der Merwe, who was the Director General of the Prisons Department.
4. Dr. Niel Barnard, who was head of the National Intelligence Service (NIS), the agency that collected intelligence on the activities of ANC and sympathizers. To the ANC, he was viewed as evil incarnate.[104] He also was a key member of the inner circle known as the State Security Council and protégé of President P. W. Botha. Mandela was most disturbed by Barnard's participation but decided not to object because Mandela did not want to alienate Botha.

---

100 *Id.* at 556.

101 Mnookin, *supra* note 2, at 122.

102 The information concerning the secret committee can be found in Mandela, *supra* note 3, at 533–34.

103 SPARKS, *supra* note 10, at 15–20, 28–36.

104 Mnookin, *supra* note 2, at 123.

In these meetings, they discussed key issues familiar to everyone, although each person's view had been shaped by his partisan bias.[105] What made these discussions new was that Mandela and the other side could discuss these issues directly with each other. As Mandela observed, when he began the meetings he realized that, "[T]hey were the victims of so much propaganda that it was necessary to straighten them out about certain facts. ... I spent some time in the beginning sketching out the history of the ANC and then explaining our positions on the primary issues that divided [both sides]."[106]

Three of the Government representatives significantly contributed to the ultimate transition to majority rule. Kobie Coetsee engaged in increasingly important roles in facilitating Mandela's release, supporting his role as leader of the ANC, and advising Presidents Botha and de Klerk on how to work positively with Mandela. After Mandela's release, Coetsee became one of the key negotiators for the Nationalist Government and was elected President of the Senate in the post-apartheid legislature.[107] Dr. Niel Barnard progressively became more deeply involved in preparing Mandela for his release including facilitating the meeting with Botha. He also helped fashion a post-apartheid South Africa.[108] Barnard continued as head of NIS from 1979–1992, and then became Director General of Department of Constitutional Development. Fanie van der Merwe became an early and passionate convert to majority rule and De Klerk's chief constitutional advisor.[109]

Mandela's facility to use these opportunities and others to forge relationships with people across the table helped build support for and trust in Mandela to lead South Africa into a post-apartheid world. Professor Mnookin concluded that,

> Mandela was a negotiator to whom one could make concessions and yet maintain one's self-respect. Mandela worked hard to establish and maintain a personal, human connection with Afrikaner leaders whose life experiences and attitudes were radically different from his own. ... Waldmeir [in her book on the negotiations] concludes. ... They learned to trust him with their fate.[110]

105 *See infra* App. B (providing a detailed negotiation analysis of these meetings).

106 Mandela, *supra* note 3, at 537.

107 *See* Waldmeir, *supra* note 9, at 100–2.

108 *See id.*

109 *Id.*

110 Mnookin, *supra* note 2, at 136. *See also* Waldmeir, *supra* note 9, at 102.

4. Listening

We know that one of the greatest challenges for lawyers who are occupied with advocating is to also listen, although any student of negotiations knows how vital listening skills are.[111] President de Klerk recognized Mandela's skills after the first day of post-release negotiations. He concluded, "My first impressions of Nelson Mandela were confirmed during this extended meeting. He was a good listener. …"[112]

5. Apologizing

This negotiation study uncovered an apology three months after Mandela's release when the formal post-apartheid negotiations were commencing. Even though this study is limited until the day of his release, this post-release event is mentioned because of how frequently the value of apologies is dismissed. This example illustrates the benefits.

Mandela recorded that President de Klerk suggested that the system of separate development had been conceived as a benign idea, but had not worked in practice. For that, he said, he was sorry, and hoped the negotiations would make amends.[113]

The benefits of sincere apologies in negotiation and mediations have been the subject of multiple studies. They have focused on how to deliver an effective apology, including assessing the impact of full and partial apologies.[114]

In a full apology, the apologizer accepts complete and unconditional responsibility for what the person did. In a partial apology, the apologizer limits his responsibility by justifying what he did.[115]

De Klerk offered an apology with an explanation, which makes it a partial one. He did not take full responsibility for what happened; he apologized for an idea that did not work out as planned. A partial apology poses risks and can be worse than no apology when responsibility for what happened is clear or the injury is severe. It risks exacerbating the conflict because the recipient can resent the failure of the apologizer to take full responsibility.

---

111 *See* Abramson, *supra* note 11, at App. F.

112 De Klerk, *supra* note 10, at 181.

113 Mandela, *supra* note 3, at 579.

114 *See* Abramson, *supra* note 11, at 396–401 (providing a summary of the literature on apologies).

115 *See id.*

Given Mandela's view that the Nationalist Government was responsible for substantial harm, the Government's partial apology could have provoked an antagonistic beginning for the meetings. However, Mandela reacted positively at the time, It was not an apology for apartheid, but it went further than any other National Party leader ever had.[116]

This risky partial apology might have been well received by Mandela because he understood the historical significance of the statement and could focus on the future. It was the first formal acknowledgment by the Nationalist Government that apartheid was ill conceived, and it was offered at the beginning of the formal negotiations, which presented an opportunity to fulfill any commitment to make amends.[117]

---

116 Mandela, *supra* note 3, at 579. President de Klerk never did apologize for the idea of apartheid, only for how it was implemented. South African journalist Allister Sparks, in his book on the negotiation process, indicated that, De Klerk still will not apologize for apartheid, which he dismisses as simply a political mistake that had to be rectified. It began, he insists, as an honourable vision of justice one that would allow separate development for white South Africans and the various black tribal groups. Only when it proved to be unworkable did it become unjust, he says, and when we realized that we changed it. *Id.* at 91–92.

117 At the time of this apology, it was probably unlikely a full apology would be offered because of the political risks to de Klerk's governing party that relied on conservative white voters who were resisting change. Also, a full apology might have undermined the party's legitimacy to stay in power and provided a basis for the victims to seek reparations that the financially-strapped government could not afford. Christopher Wren, "The World; South Africa and Apartheid: No Apologies," *N. Y. Times* (Feb. 24, 1991), http://www.nytimes.com/1991/02/24/weekinreview/the-world-south-africa-and-apartheid-no-apologies.html. Several years later, when former President de Klerk submitted his official submission to the Truth and Reconciliation Commission, he put the apartheid policies of the Nationalist Party in a historical context and concluded with another partial apology: I and many other leading figures, have already publicly apologized for the pain and suffering caused by former policies of the National Party. ... I reiterate those apologies today. Padraig O Malley, "Submission to the Truth and Reconciliation Commission by Mr. F. W. de Klerk, Leader of the National Party," *Nelson Mandela Found.*, https://www.nelsonmandela.org/omalley/index.php/site/q/03lv02167/04lv02264/05lv02303/06lv02331/07lv02332.htm (last visited Apr. 10, 2016). In a 2012 CNN interview (twenty-two years after Mandela's release), de Klerk gave another partial apology when he said, I have made the most profound apology in front of the Truth Commission and on other occasions about the injustices wrought by apartheid. He also stated, What I haven't apologized for is the original concept of seeking to bring justice to all South Africans through the concept of nation states (essentially creating two states, one black and one white). But in South Africa it failed. And by the end of the 70 s, we had to realize, and accept and admit to ourselves that it had failed. Lucky Gold, "De Klerk: No Animosity with Mandela," *CNN Amanpour Blog* (May 10, 2012, 9:13 PM), http://amanpour.blogs.cnn.com/2012/05/10/de-klerk-no-animosity-with-mandela/. When asked if apartheid failed because it was unworkable or morally repugnant, he offered three reasons why apartheid turned out to be unworkable. He did not condemn a policy of apartheid as morally repugnant. *Id.*

These various examples of good practices by Mandela in this section are outstanding illustrations of an effective negotiation style. In the next two sections, I consider whether Mandela used tactics and tricks.

B. Misrepresentation Good—Practice, Tactic, or Trick?

In his Cape Town speech, Mandela misrepresented to the people on his side of the table that:

> Today, I wish to report to you that my talks with the Government have been aimed at normalizing the political situation in the country. We have not as yet begun discussing the basic demands of the struggle. I wish to stress that I myself had at no time entered into negotiations about the future of our country, except to insist on a meeting between the ANC and the Government.[118]

Based on Mandela's own description of what transpired in those prison meetings, it is evident that he discussed the basic demands of the struggle and "entered into negotiations about the future of [the] country."[119] He participated in multiple meetings, including ones with Presidents Botha and de Klerk where he discussed in detail the four basic issues dividing the ANC and Government.[120]

He might have been able to contend technically that he never entered into negotiations because he never agreed to anything or endorsed any compromises. However, I doubt these lawyerly distinctions would have been persuasive to the public.

Furthermore, when Mandela initially reached out to the Government and agreed to meet with the special government committee while in prison, he avoided telling his colleagues in prison what he had already done when inquiring whether he should initiate negotiations. Mandela said, I chose to tell no one of what I was about to do.[121] Mnookin euphemistically described Mandela as "shading the truth" and as resolving "the quandary in the usual way, with partial (and misleading) disclosures to his ANC prison mates."[122]

---

118 O Malley, *supra* note 5 (emphasis added).

119 *Id.*

120 *See infra* App. B.

121 Mandela, *supra* note 3, at 526.

122 Mnookin, *supra* note 2, at 122–23.

Two weeks after his speech, Mandela met with the ANC leadership and candidly disclosed for the first time the nature of the secret talks with the Government. In Mandela's own words: "I described the demands I had made, and the progress that had been achieved."[123] When making these disclosures, Mandela knew he had to prove he had not sold out the ANC while in prison. ANC members had heard reports of Mandela's private conversations with the Government, were aware of his prison upgrades, and were concerned that Mandela had been out of touch with what was happening on the ground since 1964. This disclosure was a critical one for Mandela as a negotiator who wanted to establish the trust of the people on his side of the table after being absent for so long. Apparently he was successful. At the meeting, they elected him deputy president of the ANC.[124]

Was this misrepresentation a negotiation trick? Misrepresentations are typically a hallmark of a trick, with high risks of harm if discovered. Even though he made a false statement, I do not think this negotiating behavior was a trick. Mandela unilaterally concluded that the misstatement could be justified because the secret meetings were for the benefit of the ANC and its members. He said that,

> I knew my colleagues ... would condemn my proposal [to meet with government representatives], and that would kill my initiative even before it was born. There are times when a leader must move out ahead of his flock, go off in a new direction, confident that he is leading his people the right way.[125]

If the negotiating behavior can be justified, can it be classified as a good practice? I do not think so because it risked undermining trust in Mandela and the negotiation process he had been participating in. The misrepresentation revealed that Mandela was capable of being deceitful when he thought it could be justified. A good practice is to reliably tell the truth. Good practices like effective listening, being ethical, advocating for interests, and so forth rarely need to be justified to others.

Was this misstatement a tactic that could be viewed as generally accepted behavior with moderate risks if discovered? Misrepresentations that are

---

123 Mandela, *supra* note 3, at 571–72.

124 *Id.*

125 *Id.* at 526. *See id.* at 525–26, 534–36.

generally accepted conventions in negotiations are exempted under the Model Rules of Professional Conduct of the American Bar Association, for instance. The Rules treat as non-material misrepresentations estimates of price or value placed on the subject of a transaction and a party's intentions as to an acceptable settlement of a claim.[126] Mandela's particular misstatement would not qualify for an ABA-type exemption, of course.

This misrepresentation was a misstatement of objective fact that could be considered material. Material misrepresentations are typically viewed as tricks. A material fact is one that the listener will likely attach importance to and influence the listener's choice or decision.[127] Mandela had reason to believe that his supporters would regard this statement as important when determining their choice to support him at the Cape Town celebration of his release. The misstatement reassured people on Mandela's side of the table that he did not make any concessions in private negotiations on behalf of the freedom struggle.

If he had made an accurate representation that the secret negotiations were substantive and that he made no concessions, the statement might have generated suspicions that Mandela was not being honest without knowing more. They might have wondered whether he had discussed the issues most important to them or made concessions that were inadequately vetted. A brief, accurate representation might have risked hurting the liberation struggle on Mandela's first day of freedom when confidence in his leadership was so vital for moving toward.

One way for a negotiator to test whether his move is a tactic or trick is to inquire how he would react if someone made the misrepresentation to him. Presumably Mandela considered this perspective when choosing to make this misstatement and deferring disclosure until he had an opportunity to explain the benefits to the ANC leadership. By the ANC leadership reaffirming their confidence in him when electing him to a leadership position, the ANC apparently

---

126 Model Rules of Prof L Conduct, r. 4.1 cmt. at 2 (AM. BAR ASS N 1983).

127 A statement is material for the purposes of Rule 4.1(a) if it could have influenced the hearer. Annot. Model Rules of Prof L Conduct, 385 (AM. BAR ASS N 2007). Information is also considered material if it would or could have influenced the decision-making process significantly. *In re* Merkel, 138 P.3d 847, 850 (Or. 2006). The Restatement (Second) of Torts, para. 538 provides that a matter is material if a reasonable man would attach importance to ... [it] in determining his choice of action, or the speaker knows ... that the recipient [party] regards ... the matter as important in determining his choice of action. Restatement (Second) of Torts, para. 538 (1977).

viewed the material misrepresentation as acceptable or tolerable and therefore as a tactic.

C. "Prepared to Die Good"—Practice or Tactic?

Mandela's concluding remarks at the Rivonia Trial illustrated the difference between good practices and tactics. Mandela gave his often-cited "I am prepared to die" remarks when he and the other defendants were being tried for treason.[128] Mandela was not only facing the death sentence, he was convinced it would be imposed.[129] At the end of his four-hour presentation justifying why he joined the struggle, he gave his famous remarks that he also quoted in his Cape Town speech.

His concluding remarks were:

> During my lifetime I have dedicated myself to this struggle of the African people. I have fought against white domination, and I have fought against black domination. I have cherished the ideal of a democratic and free society in which all persons will live together in harmony and with equal opportunities. It is an ideal for which I hope to live for and to achieve. But, if needs be, it is an ideal for which I am prepared to die.[130]

In the 1964 Rivonia Trial, the claim was probably a good practice. He wanted to convince people that he was so committed to achieving democratic ideals that he was prepared to be a martyr. In any negotiations, a party not only should clearly express his priorities; a party needs to convince the other side that the priorities are his real ones in order to be taken seriously.

When Mandela repeated the quote on the day of his prison release, the same claim was probably a tactic. He wanted to persuade others that he was as committed to his goals that day as he was more than twenty-seven years earlier.

---

128 Mandela, *supra* note 3, at 368.

129 *Id.*

130 Mandela, *supra* note 67. Mandela's attorney, George Bizos, was concerned that the statement might invite the death sentence and objected to it. They arrived at a compromise where Mandela agreed to add the phrase if needs be. Interview by John Carlin with George Bizos, *supra* note 79. He convinced Mandela to add these additional words at the last minute in order to moderate his language. *See* Rebecca Lowe, "Friend, Client, Confidant: George Bizos on 65 years of friendship with Nelson Mandela," *Int L Bar Ass N* (Dec. 12, 2013), http://www.ibanet.org/Article/Detail.aspx?ArticleUid=515d7b65-e271-4d56-82af-743491dd2ba0.

This time, the claim was probably puffery a conventional practice of exaggerating claims to make a point. I doubt that Mandela or anyone believed Mandela wanted to be a martyr at this juncture. He employed a rhetorical phrase to demonstrate that he was still dedicated to the cause of democracy.

D. Win-Win Resolution?

President de Klerk stunned the country and the world on February 2, 1990, when he gave his momentous unbanning speech.[131] He announced at the opening session of Parliament that the Government would meet key preconditions for negotiations set by Mandela and the ANC. President de Klerk unilaterally rescinded the ban against ANC and other organizations, released political prisoners, and made other moves designed to "normalise the political process."[132] He laid the groundwork for a new constitution under which every person "will enjoy equal rights, treatment and opportunity in every sphere of endeavor—constitutional, social, and economic."[133] He announced that, "The agenda is open. ... Among other things, those aims include a new, democratic constitution; universal franchise; no domination; equality before an independent judiciary; the protection of minorities as well as of individual rights. ..."[134]

He gave particular attention to stopping the violence as a key feature of the Government's negative BATNA. He stated that he was moving "away from measures which have been seized upon as a justification for confrontation and violence."[135] "Our country and all its people have been embroiled in conflict, tension and violent struggle for decades. It is time to break out of the cycle of violence and break through to peace and reconciliation."[136] He went on to say that, "Without conceding that violence has ever been justified ... [t]he justification for violence which was always advanced, no longer exists. ... [T]here is no longer any reasonable excuse for the continuation of violence."[137] He also addressed sanctions, another key component of the Government's negative BATNA, when he called on "the international community to re-evaluate its

131 Organisations Unbanned, *supra* note 13.

132 Padraig O Malley, "F. W. de Klerk's Speech at the Opening of Parliament 2 February 1990," *Nelson Mandela Found.*, http://www.nelsonmandela.org/omalley/ index.php/site/q/03lv 02039/04lv02103/05lv02104/06lv02105.htm (last visited Apr. 10, 2016).

133 *Id.*

134 *Id.*

135 *Id.*

136 *Id.*

137 *Id.*

position and to adopt a positive attitude towards the dynamic evolution which is taking place in South Africa."[138]

And he made the announcement that everyone was waiting for but on terms not anticipated. He declared that, "I wish to put it plainly that the Government has taken a firm decision to release Mr. Mandela unconditionally."[139]

Analysis of Resolution

Mandela achieved an impressive negotiated outcome when you consider that Mandela prevailed on each distributive issue: he was unconditionally released without renouncing violence, the ANC and other organizations were unbanned, and de Klerk announced an agenda for forming a post-apartheid government. Mandela did not make a single concession in the secret negotiations.

Mandela reached this result in the face of temptations to compromise and make concessions. Mandela's appetite for liberty was strategically whetted beginning in 1982 when he was transferred out of Robben Island. He was exposed to snippets of life outside of prison including an improving standard of living, road trips, physical contact with family members, and social and professional interactions with friends and colleagues. He nevertheless negotiated with an unwavering eye on his primary interest the liberation of his country over his personal liberation.

Is this a case study where only one side's interests were met? Did Mandela win?[140] Did de Klerk capitulate and the Nationalist Government receive nothing? It might appear so. Mandela did have a strong bargaining position by 1990 because he had become an internationally revered leader in prison while the Nationalist Government had an unbearable BATNA.

A closer examination of the results suggests that this outcome met significant interests of the Government (and the white minority it represented).

First, the resolution opened the door toward political and economic stability including the Government rejoining regional and global communities of public and economic affairs. The country had become ungovernable, and apartheid policies had made South Africa an international pariah. A dramatic

---

138 *Id.*

139 *See id.* One week later, de Klerk met with Mandela to inform him that he would be released the next day unconditionally. Mandela walked out of prison with Winnie by his side and went to Cape Town City Hall to give his first speech as a free man. Mandela, *supra* note 3, at 557–58.

140 Sampson, *supra* note 9, at 396. Sampson concluded that after the unbanning Mandela had won. *Id.*

move of liberalization would likely win necessary diplomatic support from conservative administrations in London and Washington, D.C.

President de Klerk opened the door by making two essential commitments: the unsurprising decision to release Mandela and the sensational commitment to dismantle apartheid and move toward a new form of democratic government.

While de Klerk's commitment to release Mandela was specific and unconditional, his commitment to dismantling apartheid was only in principle. He did not commit to any details, which he left open for later negotiations.

He laid out the government's lofty and broad guidelines for the future while emphasizing that he was refraining from discussing the merits of numerous political questions that would soon be debated and subject to multilateral negotiations. He put on the agenda an analysis of various models of democratic constitutions without committing to a particular model. He put on the agenda the issue of non-domination and the need to protect individual and minority rights code terms for protecting the white minority. He put on the open agenda an aim for universal franchise, a more ambiguous term than majority rule demanded by Mandela. Universal franchise is associated with a right to vote regardless of race and gender, although the term left unclear what the vote would be for and whether white and black voters would be treated as equals.

At the time of the speech, de Klerk privately planned to share power with blacks, subject to an effective white veto, not to hand it over.[141] After the speech, he persisted in trying to fashion a power-sharing scheme based on groups rights in the new Constitution. He had no intention of negotiating the National Party out of power.[142]

In his autobiography, de Klerk made clear what he wanted to achieve with the announcement:

> We had prepared a comprehensive media strategy to ensure the speech received maximum favourable publicity. ... We had succeeded in catching the media, the political opposition and the world completely by surprise. ... We had achieved our objective of convincing our friends and foes alike that the National Party had made a paradigm shift. ... Within the scope

141 Waldmeir, *supra* note 9, at 149. *See id.* at 111–13, 149–51. The majority rule proposal was subject to considerable debate, compromise, and trading for other benefits for the white minority before it was ultimately adopted in the new South African Constitution. *Id.*

142 Lodge, *supra* note 9, at 169. In the weeks after Mandela's release, de Klerk proposed a bicameral legislature designed to ensure the minority Nationalist Party significant power in the new government. *Id.*

> of eight days [the date of the speech and the later announcement that Mandela would be released the next day], we had succeeded in dramatically changing global perceptions of South Africa.[143]

Second, the announcement gave the Government what it perceived as the moral high ground by calling to halt the violence including removing any excuses for engaging in violence. You will recall that Mandela had rejected earlier calls for suspending the armed struggle.

Third, the announcement gave the Government a negotiating partner, Nelson Mandela. The Nationalist Government needed a black leader that it could work with and who might be able to lead the black majority while decreasing the likelihood of a civil war. As far back as 1981 when Kobie Coetsee became Minister of Justice, an internal background report he requested described Mandela as a "practical and pragmatic thinker" with "capacity for integrated and creative thought" who "maintains outstanding personal relations ... and always behaves in a friendly and respectful way towards figures of authority."[144] It concluded that: "There exists no doubt that Mandela commands all the qualities to be the Number One black leader in South Africa."[145] This assessment was corroborated by the relationships and trust that Mandela developed with members of the secret committee during the forty-seven meetings. The accounts of those meetings showed how Mandela "tried to establish a 'personal link' with each member of the committee."[146] The accounts also revealed that the Government representatives learned much about how Mandela approached key substantive issues that divided them including his understanding of the need to engage the white minority in any post-apartheid South Africa. After de Klerk's first meeting with Mandela, de Klerk noted that he "took his [Mandela's] measure while he spoke. I think we both reached more or less the same conclusion: that it would be possible for us to do business with each other."[147]

The Government helped prepare Mandela for this daunting leadership role by acclimating and educating Mandela about the world he would be re-joining when the Government upgraded his prison facilities, gave him access to mass media and people, and took him on field trips.

---

143 De Klerk, *supra* note 10, at 158.

144 Sampson, *supra* note 9, at 295.

145 *Id.*

146 Mnookin, *supra* note 2, at 123–25. *See* Waldmeir, *supra* note 9, at 101–2 (describing the positive relationship Mandela developed with the conservative head of security, Barnard, who Mandela did not want to be part of the secret committee because of Barnard's role in monitoring the activities of the ANC).

147 De Klerk, *supra* note 10, at 158.

The appropriate choice of Mandela has not only been proven by history, it has been validated by Mandela's own description of the importance of his relationship with de Klerk. When commenting on receiving jointly the 1993 Nobel Peace Prize, he said, "To make peace with an enemy one must work with that enemy, and that enemy becomes one's partner."[148] Mandela confessed to friends, "My worst nightmare is that I wake up one night and that de Klerk isn't there. I need him. Whether I like him or not is irrelevant, I need him."[149]

This deal like any negotiated resolution met the interests of both sides sufficiently for it to be done, although without a formal signing of an agreement. As illustrated throughout this article, Mandela achieved this result by relying primarily on good negotiation practices.

Postscript: 1990–1994

This study focused on Mandela as the chief negotiator when in prison although many other people were also participating in the negotiations on Mandela's side of the table. After Mandela's release and the negotiations became public, arduous and agonizing negotiations still laid ahead. The next stage began as more people came to both sides of the table and the parties moved from broad principles to the details of how a post-apartheid democratic government would be fashioned and function. The bitter and complex negotiations proceeded in a brutal environment of violent and deadly conflicts between whites and blacks as well as between different black political factions. The negotiations took place across the table as well as behind the table with deep divisions of how to proceed among whites and among blacks. It ended after the elections on May 2, 1994, when Mr. de Klerk made his concession speech and May 10, when Nelson Mandela was sworn in as the new, democratically elected President of South Africa, with de Klerk as his Deputy President.[150]

IV. CONCLUSION

Nelson Mandela illustrated the use of good negotiation practices in this exceptional negotiation from 1985–1990 over the decision to dismantle apartheid and free him. So what did Mandela teach us new about how to negotiate? Nothing. He did what any good negotiator should do.

---

148 Mandela, *supra* note 3, at 612.

149 Mnookin, *supra* note 2, at 136. *See* Waldmeir, *supra* note 9, at 231.

150 Mandela, *supra* note 3, at Part 11; Sparks, *supra* note 10, at chs. 10–15; De Klerk, *supra* note 10, at chs. 16–35; Mnookin, *supra* note 2, at 127–33.

Mandela followed a textbook approach, although it is unlikely that he read any of the classics in negotiation like *Getting to Yes*. Mandela uncompromisingly advocated interests, convincingly addressed the other side's interests, helped shape an unattractive alternative to negotiations for the Nationalist Government, and consistently engaged in good negotiation practices with some tactics. And, the negotiation produced a result that significantly met both sides' interests when he was released.

Mandela and de Klerk, for their negotiation achievements including after 1990, were awarded the Nobel Peace Prize for their work for the peaceful termination of the apartheid regime, and for laying the foundations for a new democratic South Africa.[151]

At the main international memorial service for Mandela, President Obama delivered a stirring speech that highlighted practices of Mandela's that are commonly associated with good negotiating.[152] Obama said that Mandela

> taught us the power of action, but ... also ... ideas; the importance of reason and arguments; the need to study not only those you agree with, but those who don t. ... Mandela understood the ties that bind the human spirit. There is a word in South Africa Ubuntu a word that captures [his] greatest gift: his recognition that we are all bound together. ...[153]

Professor Robert Mnookin when labeling Mandela as the "greatest negotiator of the twentieth century" concluded that, "Mandela understood that the goal of negotiation is to persuade your adversaries. He ultimately achieved through negotiation an outcome that could never have been accomplished solely through violence or resistance. Moreover, he did this without making any concessions with respect to his core political beliefs."[154]

---

151 Mandela, *supra* note 3, at 611–12. The award surprised Mandela, who thought he would be disqualified for embracing armed struggle for over thirty years, starting with the founding of Umkhonto we Sizwe (MK). *Id.*

152 President Obama spoke at the main international memorial service in the First National Bank Stadium in Johannesburg. We were in Cape Town giving a training program and gathered with others to watch the televised ceremony celebrating Mandela's inspiring life, while looking out the window at Robben Island where Mandela spent eighteen of those years confined to a tiny cell.

153 President Barack Obama, "Remarks at the Memorial Service for Former South African President Nelson Mandela" (Dec. 10, 2013), White House Office of the Press Secretary, https://www.whitehouse.gov/the-press-office/2013/12/10/remarks-president-obama-memorial-service-former-south-african-president-.

154 Mnookin, *supra* note 2, at 135.

Can we learn anything from Nelson Mandela as a negotiator? Yes. His negotiation story offers compelling evidence for anyone who is not persuaded that these negotiation practices are effective. If Mandela could use these techniques successfully when facing the complex, heated, and intractable distributive conflicts in South Africa, lawyers and people in conflict should confidently use them when resolving routine disputes.[155]

155 Abramson, *supra* note 11, at 5–6. These techniques are part of a problem-solving approach to negotiations. In problem-solving, negotiators advocate for interests over positions, look for solutions that go beyond traditional ones based on rights, obligations, and precedent, and engage in a range of good practices over tricks including resolving distributive features using non-adversarial (without tricks) techniques suitable for problem-solving.

APPENDIX A: NEGATIVE BATNA FOR THE NATIONALIST GOVERNMENT

These events and people helped induce the Government to come to the negotiating table by making no agreement unattractive and unacceptable. They did much to shape the Government's negative BATNA (Best Alternative to a Negotiated Agreement).

Events

1960 Sharpeville Massacre brought global attention to the conditions under apartheid when the police killed sixty-nine protestors within two minutes most of whom were shot in the back as they were fleeing and wounded another four hundred people. Several thousand protestors, as part of a massive anti-pass campaign, had showed up at a local police station without their passes and a riot broke out. After the Sharpeville Massacre, the ANC organized a nationwide protest strike that included the public burning of passbooks by Mandela and many leaders. The government declared a state of emergency, suspended habeas corpus and banned the ANC. The landscape for fighting apartheid changed in one day as both the intensity of protests and the responses by the Nationalist Government escalated in full view of the world.[156]

1961 Umkhonto we Sizwe (Spear of the Nation) (MK), a military wing of the ANC was organized in the wake of the Sharpeville Massacre to engage in armed struggle and endured for the next thirty years. Mandela's early leadership in MK contributed to his life imprisonment conviction. He continued to endorse the work of MK until almost six months after his release.[157]

1962–1964 The Rivonia Trial brought further international attention to the oppressive apartheid conditions. The Nationalist Government charged Mandela and other ANC leaders with sabotage, violent revolution, and conspiracy with others, including foreign states. Mandela, convinced that he and the

156 Mandela, *supra* note 3, at 236–39.

157 *Id.* at 585–86.

other defendants would be sentenced to death, decided not to defend himself. He chose to use the trial as a platform to publicize the cause for freedom. Mandela waived his right to present direct testimony and appeal any conviction. Instead, he read a carefully prepared four-hour statement from the dock. He surprised the prosecution by admitting key charges and spending most of his time justifying the actions by MK and ANC and why he shifted from nonviolent to violent approaches. The Trial engendered much international condemnation including by the United Nations Security Council.[158]

1969–1977 Black Consciousness Movement (BCM) marked by the formation of the South African Student Organization in 1969 and co-founded by activist Steve Biko, transformed student discontent into a political force and shifted attention from the ANC priority on non-racialism to black pride, black self-reliance, black psychological liberation, and black leaders.

Through a movement based on black power, blacks actively opposed the apartheid government during the 1970s. The Movement spurred a new era of activism in the face of aggressive clamping down by the Nationalist Government, culminating in Biko's brutal September 1977 death in police custody. His death attracted international attention and unleashed new protests within and outside of South Africa.[159]

1976 Soweto Student Uprising triggered violent protests and mass resistance to apartheid throughout South Africa. The uprising erupted in June 1976 when high school students protested against introduction of Afrikaans as the medium of instruction. This language of the governing white minority was viewed as the language of the oppressor. Resistance was brewing aided

158 *Id.* at 360–78.

159 "Black Consciousness Movement," *South African History Online*, http://www.sahistory.org.za/20th-century-south-africa/black-consciousness-movement (last visited Apr. 10, 2016). *See* "Black Consciousness Movement," *South Africa: Overcoming Apartheid, Building Democracy*, http://overcomingapartheid.msu.edu/multimedia.php?id=65-259-11 (last visited Apr. 10, 2016).

by the Black Consciousness Movement along with other developments. The violence on the first day spread quickly and casualties mounted for the rest of the year. The Uprising provoked an international outcry that was fueled by the now iconic photograph of the dying 12-year-old Hector Pieterson being carried by a distressed fellow student. The Government's forceful repression of protests exposed the Government's disintegrating ability to govern.[160]

1985 Mandela Rejected President Botha's Offer to be released if Mandela would denounce violence. Botha made this conditional offer to Mandela after twenty-one years of confinement, as violence reigned in South Africa, pressure mounted abroad, and the country became barely governable. Botha presented the proposal in Parliament and tried to put the onus of violence on Mandela as well as his fate when Botha said that it is no longer the South Africa government which now stands in the way of Mr. Mandela's freedom. It is he himself.[161] This offer was the sixth conditional offer for his release in ten years.

Mandela's daughter, Zindzi, read Mandela's reply at a public rally. It was the first time Mandela's words were legally heard in more than twenty years. Mandela not only refused to reject violence, he unambiguously justified the benefits of an armed struggle by the ANC, explaining that other forms of resistance were unavailable. He then shifted the onus of violence to Botha when he called on him to renounce violence and dismantle apartheid.

1983–1990 *United Democratic Front (UDF)*, a coalition of organizations, did much to make South Africa ungovernable while the ANC was banned.[162] The UDF was formed in response to President

160 "The Jone 16 Soweto Youth Uprising," *South African History Online*, http://www.sahistory.org.za/topic/june-16-soweto-youth-uprising (last visited Apr. 10, 2016). *See* "Soweto Student Uprising," *South Africa: Overcoming Apartheid, Building Democracy*, http://overcomingapartheid.msu.edu/sidebar.php?id=65-258-3 (last visited Apr. 10, 2016).

161 Mandela, *supra* note 3, at 521.

162 "Origins of the United Democratic Front," *South African History Archive*, http://www.saha.org.za/udf/origins.htm (last visited Apr. 10, 2016).

Botha's initiative to form a tricameral parliament, in which coloureds, Indians, and whites would vote separately for racially segregated houses of parliament.[163]

The majority of Africans would be put into Bantustans or independent homelands, where they would be allowed to vote only for a national government in that Bantustan.[164] The UDF mobilized people and organizations across the country and called for the creation of a united, non-racial, non-sexist, and democratic South Africa.[165]

More than 600 organizations from across South Africa, including labor, political, youth, women, religious, civic, and student and teacher organizations,[166] joined the UDF's movement to oppose the apartheid government and its policies.[167] The National Executive Committee stated, the strength of the UDF lies in the democratic nature of its composition. ... These organizations represent people of all colours and creeds from all strata of South African society.[168] The UDF organized consumer boycotts and stay-aways, a one million signature campaign to oppose the new proposed form of government, and created local structures which played key roles in the political education and mobilization of the masses, among other things.[169]

---

163 "Against Botha's Deal," *South African History Archive*, http://www.saha.org.za/udf/bothas_deal.htm (last visited Apr. 10, 2016).

164 *Id.*

165 "Black Consciousness Movement," *supra* note 159.

166 Zac Yacoob, "List of Organisations Which Support and Are Affiliates of the Regional United Democratic Front," *African Nat L Cong.*, http://www.anc.org.za/show.php?id=3802 (last visited Apr. 10, 2016).

167 Padraig O Malley, "United Democratic Front (UDF)," *Nelson Mandela Found.*, https://www.nelsonmandela.org/omalley/index.php/site/q/03lv02424/04lv02730/05lv03188/06lv03222.htm (last visited Apr. 10, 2016).

168 National Executive Committee of the United Democratic Front, Statement of the UDF National Executive Committee on the National Launching of the UDF, *African Nat L Cong.*, http://www.anc.org.za/show.php?id=3795&t=United%20Democratic%20Front (last visited Apr. 10, 2016).

169 O Malley, *supra* note 5. *See Consumer Boycotts*, SOUTH AFRICAN HISTORY ARCHIVE, http://www.saha.org.za/udf/consumer_boycotts.htm (last visited Apr. 10, 2016).

The Government believed that the ANC created the UDF[170] and therefore restricted it, including subjecting the organization to the state of emergency and its members to arrests. However, UDF ultimately was not viewed as a creation of or controlled by the ANC.[171] From the outset it was clear that the UDF preferred to be the heir, rather than a clone, of the ANC.[172]

1960–1990 International Sanctions and Economic and Political Isolation, dating back to the Sharpeville Massacre, escalated as each momentous chapter unfolded. The negative impact of the sanctions was evident when in early discussions after Mandela's release, de Klerk asked Mandela to mute the call for the continuation of international sanctions. Mandela thought that in our view sanctions remained the best lever to force him to do more. I explained to Mr. de Klerk that we could not tell our supporters to relax sanctions until he completely dismantled apartheid and a transitional government was in place.[173]

The United Nation's General Assembly and the Security Council adopted a succession of resolutions that condemned apartheid and progressively isolated South Africa. The first Security Council resolution, in 1960, denounced the actions of the South Africa government in the wake of the Sharpeville Massacre and called for abandonment of apartheid and racial discrimination. Several years later, the General Assembly and the Security Council, with Great Britain, U.S., France, and Brazil abstaining, urged South Africa to end the Rivonia Trial and grant amnesty to the defendants. Over twenty-nine years, resolutions called for arms embargo, oil embargos, suspending cultural, educational, sporting, and other exchanges, voiding South Africa's racist constitution, and negotiating to

170 Raymond Suttner, "Legacies and Meanings of the United Democratic Front (UDF) Period for Contemporary South Africa," in *From National Liberation to Democratic Renaissance In Southern Africa* (Cheryl Hendricks & Lwazi Lushaba eds., 2005), 59–81.

171 O Malley, *supra* note 5.

172 Suttner, *supra* note 170.

173 Mandela, *supra* note 3, at 582.

end apartheid, with the last resolution adopted two months before Mandela's release.[174]

Through a string of resolutions and decisions by the General Assembly, the UN also effectively removed South Africa from UN membership from 1970, when it would not approve the credentials of the South African delegation, until June 1994, when it formally approved them.[175]

Anti-apartheid boycott and disinvestment campaigns took hold in the United States in the 1970s and 1980s as well as in the United Kingdom and other nations. The U.S. campaigns induced U.S. campuses, cities, and states to disinvest in companies doing business in South Africa. In 1986, the U.S. federal government joined the boycotts when Congress overrode President Reagan's veto and banned new investment and bank loans in South African businesses, barred a range of imports, imposed embargos on particular exports like oil and munitions, and cancelled landing rights.[176]

---

174 "The United Nations: Partner in the Struggle against Apartheid," Nelson Mandela International Day, http://www.un.org/en/events/mandeladay/apartheid.shtml (last visited Apr. 10, 2016). *See* Douglas Linder, *Behind the Scenes: International Pressure on South Africa to Not Execute Nelson Mandela and Other Rivonia Defendants,* http://law2.umkc.edu/faculty/projects/ftrials/mandela/behindscenes.html (last visited Apr. 10, 2016).

175 The General Assembly in 1970 did not approve the credentials of South Africa's representatives; in 1973, it declared that the South African regime had no right to represent its people; in 1974, it would not accept the credentials of the representatives of South Africa, even though the Security Council failed to recommend expelling South Africa from the UN due to the vetoes by France, United Kingdom, and the United States. The President of the Assembly interpreted refusing credentials as tantamount to barring the delegation from participating, and his ruling was upheld by the General Assembly; and in 1974, it recommended that the South African regime be totally excluded from participation in all international organizations under the auspices of the UN. *See* "United Nations and Apartheid Timeline 1946–1994," *South African History Online,* http://www.sahistory.org.za/topic/united-nations-and-apartheid-timeline-1946–1994 (last visited Apr. 10, 2016).

176 *"A Struggle From the Ground Up: The Anti-Apartheid Movement in South Africa," Tavaana,* https://tavaana.org/en/content/struggle-ground-anti-apartheid-movement-south-africa (last visited Apr. 10, 2016); Arianna Lissoni, "The Anti-Apartheid Movement, Britain and South Africa: Anti-Apartheid Protest vs Real Politik," *African Nat L Cong.,* http://www.anc.org.za/show.php?id=5695 (last visited Apr. 10, 2016); "The Anti-Apartheid Movement of the 1960s," *Forward to Freedom,* http://aamarchives.org/history/1960s/79-history/124-the-anti-apartheid-movement-in-the-1960s.html# (last visited Apr. 10, 2016).

People

In addition to these significant events, as pointed out in the text of this article, numerous anti-apartheid leaders and sympathizers acted boldly and at great personal risk to inflict a negative BATNA. Only a few of the courageous leaders are mentioned here, although many more made profound contributions including people below the public radar screen.

Chief Albert Luthuli became President of the ANC in 1952 and moved the organization into a more activist role as the Defiance Campaign spread. He was awarded the 1960 Nobel Peace Prize for his role in the nonviolent struggle against apartheid. He was the first African and also the first person from outside Europe to be awarded the prize.[177]

Oliver Tambo helped revive the ANC in the early 1940s and opened a law practice with Nelson Mandela. When banned, he became a Mission in Exile and a central ANC leader. He actively built support for the ANC's cause in Africa, United Kingdom, Russia, China, the U.S., and with political and business leaders around the world. He led the ANC in exile while Nelson Mandela was in prison.[178]

Walter Sisulu, active with ANC early, helped lead the Defiance Campaign and transform the ANC into a mass-based militant national organization. He worked with Nelson Mandela and others to form MK and became part of its High Command as political commissar when Mandela became its Commander in Chief. Along with Mandela, he was sentenced to life in prison in the Rivonia Trial and sent to Robben Island. He became part of the underground political leadership at Robben Island, known at the High Organ.[179]

Stephen Biko, co-founder of the Black Consciousness Movement (BCM), did much to generate black pride and protests as described above under the Events section and his brutal death made him an international martyr in opposing apartheid.[180]

177 "Chief Albert John Luthuli," *South African History Online,* http://www.sahistory.org.za/people/chief-albert-john-luthuli (last visited Apr. 10, 2016).

178 "Oliver Reginald Tambo," *South African History Online,* http://www.sahistory.org.za/people/oliver-reginald-tambo (last visited Apr. 10, 2016).

179 "Walter Ulyate Sisulu," *South African History Online,* http://www.sahistory.org.za/people/walter-ulyate-sisulu (last visited Apr. 10, 2016)

180 "Stephen Bantu Biko," *South African History Online,* http://www.sahistory.org.za/people/stephen-bantu-biko (last visited Apr. 10, 2016).

Winnie Mandela, Nelson's wife, was an energetic force in the anti-apartheid movement, especially when her husband was in prison. During President Botha's regime, her opposition earned her the title of the Mother of the Nation. For her activities, she was tortured, harassed, banned, separated from her children, held in solitary confinement for eighteen months, and exiled to a remote area of South Africa. She also was controversial among sympathisers. She endorsed the practice of necklacing (burning people alive using tires and petrol) and was charged with ordering her body guards, known as Mandela United Football club, to kidnap and murder suspected police informers including 14-year-old Stompie Seipei, the most notorious case.[181]

George Bizos, a human rights lawyer served as Nelson Mandela's personal attorney throughout much of his life. He co-represented Mandela in the Rivonia Trial. As his attorney, he was one of the few people who could visit Mandela when in prison and as a result was a vital link between Mandela and the outside world.[182]

Albie (Albert) Sachs, human rights lawyer who participated in the Defiance Campaign, helped draft the Freedom Charter, and defended people charged under apartheid racist laws. He worked closely with Oliver Tambo. He was banned, subject to solitary confinement without trial, and went into exile in 1966. In 1988, when a car bomb was planted by South African police, he lost an arm and sight in one eye. He was one of the chief architects of the post-apartheid constitution and was appointed by Mandela to serve on the newly established Constitutional Court.[183]

181 "Winnie Madikizela-Mandela," *South African History Online,* http://www.sahistory.org.za/people/winnie-madikizela-mandela (last visited Apr. 10, 2016).

182 "George Bizos," *South African History Online,* http://www.sahistory.org.za/people/george-bizos (last visited Apr. 10, 2016). *See generally* George Bizos, *Odyssey to Freedom: A Memoir by the World-Renowned Human Rights Advocate, Friend and Lawyer to Nelson Mandela* (2009).

183 "Judge Albert Louis Albie Sachs," *South African History Online,* http://www.sahistory.org.za/people/judge-albert-louis-albie-sachs (last visited Apr. 10, 2016).

APPENDIX B: THE SECRET PRISON NEGOTIATIONS

Nelson Mandela's represented in his remarks at Cape Town when he was released that:

> Today, I wish to report to you that my talks with the government have been aimed at normalizing the political situation in the country. We have *not as yet begun discussing the basic demands of the struggle.* I wish to stress that *I myself had at no time entered into negotiations about the future of our country,* except to insist on a meeting between the ANC and the Government.[184]

The Secret Negotiations

As concluded in the text, Mandela's statement misrepresented that he had not entered into negotiations with the Government while in prison. This conclusion is supported by the description of the secret negotiations in this Appendix.

During the early 1980s, the Government began sending feelers to release Nelson Mandela if he would meet particular conditions including denouncing violence. The Government seemed to be testing Mandela in order to learn what he was willing to trade for his freedom. The feeler that morphed into the secret prison negotiations was extended by Kobie Coetsee, the Minister of Justice, in 1985.[185]

Coetsee briefly visited Nelson Mandela in a Cape Town hospital when he was hospitalized for a routine surgical medical procedure for an enlarged prostate. Coetsee's visit was unexpected and amazed Mandela because Coetsee had not responded to Mandela's prior written efforts to set up talks between the ANC and the Government. The cordial and informal exchange in the hospital was viewed as a signal by Mandela. He thought that, "The government, in its slow and tentative way, was reckoning that they had to come to some accommodation with the ANC. Coetsee's visit was an olive branch."[186]

---

184 Padraig O Malley, "Remarks by Nelson Mandela in Cape Town on February 11, 1990 after His Release from Victor Verster," *Nelson Mandela Found.*, https://www.nelsonmandela.org/omalley/index.php/site/q/03lv03445/04lv04015/05lv041 54/06lv04191.htm (last visited Apr. 10, 2016) (emphasis added).

185 Mandela, *supra* note 3, at 523–31. Mandela described this visit and what he did soon afterwards to try to initiate discussions with the Government.

186 *Id.* at 524. This pivotal visit has an interesting backstory. For Mandela, it was a total surprise, but for Coetsee, the visit was the result of two fortuitous circumstances that Mandela appar-

When Mandela was discharged from the hospital, officials did not return him to the shared facilities with his three comrades in Pollsmoor prison. Instead, he was moved into a ground floor section in the prison, with three rooms and a separate toilet for his exclusive use. For the first time since being incarcerated, he was isolated, and by prison standards, living in "palatial" conditions. He realized that these new circumstances gave him the freedom to try initiating discussions with the Government, and he could do so confidentially.

Mandela recognized that both the ANC and the Government had imposed firm preconditions for negotiating that have made any offers by either side a sign of weakness and betrayal. He was facing a too common obstacle in negotiations and one that can be intractable. Something bold had to be done. Mandela launched a risky strategy especially for a leader known for his transparency and integrity.

Within a few weeks, Mandela secretly reached out to the Government by writing to Kobie Coetsee to "propose talks about talks." When he did not respond, Mandela looked for other opportunities to reach out to the Government.

He did not tell anyone in the ANC what he was doing because he thought that they would object. He justified this daring move by concluding that sometimes "a leader must move out ahead of his flock. ..."[187]

---

ently was unaware of. A good friend of Coetsee, Piet de Waal, had serendipitously become friends with Winnie Mandela. De Waal and Coetsee's friendship dates back to their days at the University of Orange Free State. They lived in the same housing and played tennis when attending the University. De Waal later persuaded Coetsee to abandon his plans to become a teacher to go to law school and then helped Coetsee secure his first law position as an articled clerk. De Waal decided to become a small-town lawyer and moved to Brandfort the same remote village that Coetsee's predecessor, Minister of Justice Kruger, later banished Winnie to. De Waal's wife and Winnie became close friends, and Piet de Waal, as the only attorney in town, reluctantly represented Winnie locally after he was told that he was ethically obligated to do so and had advised local authorities of his predicament. To protect his friend from harassment, Coetsee vouched for de Waal's integrity with Kruger. When Coetsee became Minister of Justice in 1980, de Waal began to lobby him cautiously and persistently to lift the ban on Winnie and consider releasing Nelson from prison. This was the first lobbying of a cabinet minister by anyone within the Afrikaner nationalist fold, and Coetsee admits today that it had a considerable influence on him. You could say that's where the whole process started, he says. Sparks, *supra* note 10, at 19. The second fortuitous event occurred on a plane to Cape Town when Winnie Mandela was on her way to visit her husband in the hospital. Coetsee was on the same flight. He visited Mrs. Mandela in coach class to assure her of the Government's concern for her husband's health. Winnie then marched up to business class and sat next to Coetsee; they talked for much of the two-hour flight. By the time the flight arrived, Coetsee decided to visit Mandela in the hospital. *Id.* at 14–25.

187 Mandela, *supra* note 3, at 526.

As he was making overtures to the Government and some preliminary connections, Oliver Tambo and the ANC called for the "people to render the country ungovernable."[188] The people did what they could do. The state of unrest and political violence were reaching new heights and international pressure was increasing. The Government responded by imposing a state of emergency.[189]

Concurrently, the Government made another inconceivable change in Mandela's prison life. Without any warning or explanation in 1986, prison officials started taking Mandela on short trips to see the city and countryside. He suspected that the trips were designed to entice him with the pleasures of small freedoms in order to induce him to make compromises to gain complete freedom. The trips also might have been designed to acclimate him to life in South Africa after his release.

For the first trip, he was driven around Cape Town. He became riveted watching people doing simple and normal activities of daily life and discovered how much he missed doing them. When the Colonel driving him around went into a store to buy Mandela a cold drink, he encountered another first in his twenty-two years of confinement. He was out of prison and unguarded. He anxiously envisioned the possibilities of escaping. Then, he realized that it would be unwise, irresponsible, and dangerous, and that they were probably testing him. He was relieved when the Colonel returned. Over the next several months, he visited Cape Town, the outskirts, the nearby mountains, and local beaches. No one recognized him. The last published picture of Mandela in South Africa dated back to 1962 when he was 44 years old. He was now 68 years old.[190]

Later in 1987, Mandela resumed contact with Coetsee. They met privately several times and then Coetsee made a concrete proposal to appoint a small committee of senior officials to conduct secret discussions with Mandela. Coetsee would head the committee. Although Mandela was uncomfortable with and unhappy that the chief of intelligence services, Niel Barnard, would be on the committee, he accepted the proposal.[191]

---

188 *Id.* at 529.

189 *Id.*

190 *Id.* at 525–26, 534–36.

191 National Executive Committee of the United Democratic Front, Statement of the UDF National Executive Committee on the National Launching of the UDF, *African Nat L Cong.*, http://www.anc.org.za/show.php?id=3795&t=United%20Democratic%20Front (last visited Apr. 10, 2016).

Next, Mandela consulted behind the table. He conferred with his four prison comrades, known as the High Organ (leadership) about initiating talks with the Government but he did not inform them that he had already reached out, a government committee had been formed, and he had agreed to participate. Two of his comrades objected to him initiating talks, as he feared. As these events were unfolding, he received a note from Oliver Tambo in Lusaka, Zambia about rumors that secret meetings were being held. Mandela assured him that he was only negotiating to set up a meeting between the ANC and the Government, when he was actually doing much more.

Mandela thought he had to act alone because "my colleagues ... would condemn my proposal, and that would kill my initiative even before it was born,"[192] especially when the meetings included the head of the national intelligence services. Mandela thought it was time to make some hard and risky choices. Mandela believed that "There are times when a leader must ... go off in a new direction, confident that he is leading his people the right way."[193]

The first secret meeting was held in May 1988. The meetings were initially conducted weekly, then sporadically, and eventually returned to meeting weekly, for a total of forty-seven. The early meetings, like any negotiations based on good practices, focused on parties getting acquainted and exchanging information, with Mandela spending time explaining the ANC's history and positions. Mandela astutely understood the need to build relationships and credibility with people across the table before focusing on the substantive issues.

When reaching the issues, they concentrated on four that by now were thoroughly familiar to all the participants: the ANC's continuation of the armed struggle, the ANC's alliance with the Communist Party, the goal of majority rule (which was mostly about the needs of the white minority including their fears that their private property would be nationalized), and racial reconciliation. Each issue was discussed extensively during multiple meetings.

For the most intractable issue, majority rule with protections for the white minority, Mandela avoided saying simply trust me the ANC is committed to democratic reforms that would unite all the people and races of South Africa. Mandela supported this commitment with a document he endorsed thirty years earlier, the 1955 Freedom Charter. It was prepared by the South African Congress Alliance that included the ANC. The Charter's preamble begins with,

---

192 *Id.* at 526.

193 *See id.* at 525–26, 534–36.

"South Africa belongs to all who live in it, black and white. …""[194] and the entire document is based on principles of democracy and equality. He emphasized that, "[T]he majority would need the minority. We do not want to drive you to the sea."[195]

In response to their fears that the ANC and the Freedom Charter supported blanket nationalization of the economy, Mandela indicated "we" favor more even distribution of the rewards and any nationalization would occur for some industries that are already monopolies.

He pointed out that he has not changed his mind since an article he wrote in 1956 in which he said, "the Freedom Charter was not a blueprint for socialism but for African-style capitalism."[196]

As the intense and secret meetings continued, the country was still in turmoil. The Government had re-imposed a state of emergency and domestic and international pressures continued to mount with companies leaving South Africa and the U.S. Congress passing a sanctions bill.

One evening in December 1988, Mandela was abruptly told to pack up his belongings and, without any explanation, driven for an hour to a new prison, Victor Verster. It turned out to be an upgrade in living conditions that was better than he had ever experienced in his lifetime. He was moved to his own house, a cottage, with a master bedroom and two guest rooms, swimming pool, personal cook, and no bars on the windows although the walls were topped with razor wire and guards were stationed at the entrance. He also could go for walks, welcome frequent visitors, and hold private discussions. He was told that this cottage would be his last home before becoming a free man. This upgrade poignantly reminded him of the harsh conditions under which he had been living for a quarter of a century and what he had been missing and longed for.[197]

---

194 The Congress of the People, The Freedom Charter, *African Nat L Cong.*, http://www.anc.org.za/show.php?id=72 (last visited Apr. 10, 2016).

195 Mandela, *supra* note 3, at 539.

196 *Id.* at 538. However, when you read the Freedom Charter, you can understand the Government's fears. It stated that: The national wealth of our country, the heritage of South Africans, shall be restored to the people; The mineral wealth beneath the soil, the Banks and monopoly industry shall be transferred to the ownership of the people as a whole; … Restrictions of land ownership on a racial basis shall be ended, and all the land re-divided amongst that who work it. … The Congress of the People, *supra* note 194. None of these ideas were ultimately imported into the new South Africa constitution while nearly all the other concerns in the Charter were addressed. *See id.*

197 Mandela, *supra* note 3, at 543–46.

Soon afterwards, Mandela pressed to meet personally with President Botha. Mandela prepared a memorandum to persuade Botha to meet and lay the groundwork for the meeting. Mandela again demonstrated good negotiation practices. He consulted key comrades on his side of the table because "Although I know I was going ahead of my colleagues, I did not want to go too far ahead and find that I was alone."[198] The memorandum reflected a thoughtful negotiation approach. He wanted the President to see they "were not wild-eyed terrorists, but reasonable men."[199]

He addressed the Government's preconditions for negotiations that the ANC renounce violence, break with the communist party, and abandon the call for majority rule. He explained how the first two issues were diverting both sides from what he saw as the central issue dividing them: how to reconcile two conflicting positions, (1) ANC's demand to adopt majority rule. It is now apparent that Mandela's interests in a democracy had morphed into a single position. Only when accepted, he said there would be peace and stability. Mandela described "the rejection of majority rule by the government" as "a poorly disguised attempt to preserve power"; (2) National Government's demand to address the impact of majority rule on white South Africa. The whites are insisting on "structural guarantees that majority rule will not mean domination of the white minority by blacks."[200]

He also understood how the sequencing of negotiations can affect progress when he proposed that negotiations proceed in two stages: first, conditions for negotiations must be created, and then actual negotiations can be conducted.[201]

In July 1989, Mandela was again starkly reminded of what he had sacrificed for the freedom struggle when celebrating his seventy-first birthday in prison. His entire family came to his cottage. It was the first time he was together with his wife, children, and grandchildren. He realized that, "It was a deep, deep pleasure to have my whole family around me, and the only pain was the knowledge that I had missed such occasions for so many years."[202]

Mandela finally had his meeting with President Botha. It was his only meeting, lasted less than a half hour on July 5, 1989, and was mostly cordial. Mandela described it as a breakthrough, not in terms of the substantive

198 *Id.* at 546.
199 *Id.*
200 *Id.* at 547.
201 *Id.* at 546–47.
202 *Id.* at 548.

negotiations but that Botha had finally "cross[ed] the Rubicon. ... Now I felt there was no turning back."[203]

As negotiations were proceeding in the face of these reminders of the missing personal pleasures, the unimaginable happened. President Botha resigned in August 1989, as a result of a stroke.[204] A new president and bargaining partner was sworn-in, F. W. de Klerk. Changing bargaining partners can sometimes create an opportunity to move negotiations forward.[205] Mandela, however, had no reason to think that this was a positive development. Although the negotiations had been going slowly with Botha, de Klerk was known by the ANC as a "cipher." "Nothing in his past seem[ed] to hint at a spirit of reform."[206] This change looked like a setback.

Mandela discovered that de Klerk was a pragmatist. As Mandela continued to meet with the secret negotiation committee, he tried to channel messages to de Klerk through the committee. To Mandela's great surprise, de Klerk began systematically dismantling many of the building blocks of apartheid, including dissolving many segregated facilities like beaches and restaurants. He also released unconditionally seven former Robben Island leaders including his close and long-term friend, Walter Sisulu. Mandela conveyed his appreciation to de Klerk. Mandela understood the importance of acknowledging progress in order to cultivate a positive negotiation relationship.

President de Klerk set up a personal meeting with Mandela for December 13, 1989. Mandela, like any good negotiator, planned for the meeting. He consulted extensively with a diverse range of colleagues including old friends and new leaders, and prepared a lengthy letter to send to de Klerk in advance of the meeting. The letter warrants a high grade for the way it set the tone, addressed candidly controversial issues, and framed an agenda that considered both sides priorities.[207]

He began the letter by praising President de Klerk for recently freeing political prisoners, and then quickly moved ahead to identify conditions for

203 *Id.* at 551.

204 President Botha suffered the stroke in January 1989.

205 Robert H. Mnookin, Scott R. Peppet and Andrew S. Tulumello, *Beyond Winning: Negotiating to Create Value in Deals and Disputes*, 218–20 (2000).

206 Mandela, *supra* note 3, at 551. *See also* Meredith, *supra* note 9, at 393–95 (highlighting in detail de Klerk's conservative credentials when he was elected president).

207 Padraig O Malley, "A Document to Create a Climate of Understanding; Nelson Mandela to F. W. de Klerk 12 December 1989," *Nelson Mandela Found.*, https://www.nelsonmandela.org/omalley/cis/omalley/OMalleyWeb/03lv01538/04lv0160 0/05lv01640/06lv01644.htm (last visited Apr. 10, 2016).

creating a "proper climate for negotiations." Throughout the letter, he meticulously presented his rationales for key points in contention.

The Government had persistently conditioned negotiations on ANC suspending the armed struggle. Mandela understood that he had to address the Government's priority in a way that might be acceptable to both sides. He justified the ANC's armed struggle as "purely a defensive measure against the violence of the government." He gave this issue a sense of urgency while framing it as a joint one when he stressed that," [A] mutually agreed-upon cease-fire to end hostilities ought to be the first order of business, for without that, no business could be conducted."[208]

He forewarned de Klerk how Mandela viewed the Government's proposal for group rights. He characterized it as a "disguised form of minority rule" under which whites would "hold firmly and defiantly to power and enforce racial separation." It would make meaningless all talk of reconciliation and justice.

He gave de Klerk encouragement. He labeled as "important" de Klerk's statement on reconciliation and "seeking mutually acceptable solutions" set out in his inaugural address to Parliament. He described the message as having a "formidable impact inside and outside the country." These words imbued South Africans and the rest of the world with hope for the birth of a new South Africa. Mandela repeated his primary interest when he said the "very first step toward reconciliation is obviously dismantling apartheid. …"[209]

Mandela linked de Klerk's call for reconciliation to the country's future. Mandela wrote:

> By reconciliation, in this context, was understood the situation where opponents, and even enemies for that matter, would sink their differences and lay down their arms for the purpose of working out a peaceful solution, where the injustices and grievances of the past would be buried and forgotten, and a fresh start made.[210]

He alerted de Klerk to Mandela's concern that the spirit of the inaugural speech has not been in action lately,[211] a comment that may be true as a good

---

208 Mandela, *supra* note 3, at 554. In the letter, he wrote: Equally important is the fact that there is a war between the ANC and the Government, and a cease-fire to end hostilities will have to be negotiated first, before talks to normalise the situation can begin. O Malley, *supra* note 207.

209 Mandela, *supra* note 3, at 554.

210 O Malley, *supra* note 207.

211 Mandela, *supra* note 3, at 554.

practice or posturing as a tactic. Only de Klerk can determine whether Mandela's statement can be justified or was a negotiation ploy that lacked merit.

Mandela tried to introduce an objective standard, as any good negotiator should do when facing a distributive conflict. A standard that is independent of the parties can become the basis for overcoming a conflict. Mandela cited a detailed negotiation plan formulated by the ANC and approved by the Frontline States,[212] the Non-Aligned Countries Conference, and almost all the members of the Commonwealth of Nations. The plan was known as the Harare Declaration of 1989.[213] It put the burden on the Government to eliminate negotiation obstacles that it created.[214] It recognized that peace and stability was possible only when the system of apartheid has been eradicated and South Africa has been transformed into a "united, democratic and non-racial state." It set out pre-conditions for negotiations (release prisoners, lift bans, end state of emergency, etc.) and guidelines (transition to a democratic order, free elections, etc.).[215]

At the time the negotiation plan was cited in the letter, however, it lacked the full persuasive power of an objective standard. It had not yet been adopted by a body independent of both sides. It was initially endorsed by sympathetic groups. The Harare Declaration achieved objective standard status the day after the December 13th meeting when it was adopted by the United Nations.[216] The letter was delivered to Mr. de Klerk the day before their meeting.

At the meeting, Mandela was surprised when he found de Klerk listening and trying to understand his point-of-view. He wrote, "This was a novel experience."[217] He appreciated the feeling that he was being heard a well-recognized prerequisite for moving forward in negotiations. He noted that his

212 A group of southern African states that formed a subcommittee of the Organization of African Unity, an organization of newly independent African states.

213 The Harare Declaration (first formal proposals by ANC on how to move forward to a negotiated settlement) was based on what ANC leaders learned during a dozen secret meetings between ANC leaders and Afrikaners who were deep inside the nationalist establishment. The high level meetings were primarily held in Mells, England in 1987–1990 and became known at the Mells Meetings facilitated by Mike Young, a private businessman with considerable political experience. *See* Sparks, *supra* note 10, at 87, 66–87.

214 Mandela, *supra* note 3, at 554.

215 Organisation of African Unity, Harare Declaration: Declaration of the OAU Ad-hoc Committee on Southern African on the question of South Africa, *African Nat L Cong.*, http://www.anc.org.za/show.php?id=3856 (last visited Apr. 10, 2016). *See* Enuga S. Reddy, *Road to Democracy in South Africa*: Volume 3, (2008), 41–140.

216 G. A. Res. 16/1, U.N. Doc. A/RES/S-16/1 (Dec. 14, 1980), http://www.un.org/documents/ga/res/spec/aress16-1.htm.

217 Mandela, *supra* note 3, at 554.

predecessors spent their time talking and trying to persuade rather than listening and trying to understand.

Mandela addressed one of the Government's major proposals for meeting its interests, the "group rights" proposal. Mandela clearly opposed it in his letter but he did not simply dismiss it during the meeting. He engaged in a discussion of its merits, another good negotiation practice.

He explained how the proposal that no racial or ethnic group could take precedence over any other appeared to preserve white domination. He said the ANC did not struggle against apartheid for seventy-five years to defer to a disguised form of it. He also cited for support a persuasive source independent of him. Mandela quoted an editorial in a newspaper that was a mouthpiece of the de Klerk's Nationalist Party. The editorial suggested that the group rights concept was "an attempt to bring back apartheid through the back door." Mandela said that if the paper of de Klerk's party perceived the proposal that way, he asked, rather than lectured, "[H]ow did he think we regarded it?"[218] As any accomplished negotiator knows, citing independent sources respected by the other side and asking questions to engage the other side can be more persuasive than making partisan arguments.

Mandela recognized the good negotiation practice of de Klerk when he did not argue with Mandela. Instead, de Klerk articulated the underlying interests motivating the group rights proposal while recognizing shared interests. He said, "You know my aim is no different than yours. Your memo to P. W. Botha said the ANC and the government should work together to deal with white fears of black domination, and the idea of 'group rights' is how we propose to deal with it."[219] Mandela was impressed with this thoughtful reply.

Mandela had to find a way to meet the other side's interests, to some extent, as any astute negotiator knows. When de Klerk raised shared interests in the whites being part of the country's future, Mandela was ready to work with de Klerk to jointly explore how to address this common concern, which they tried to do later when preparing an interim constitution.[220]

Mandela next brought up the question of his freedom, and it is clear that Mandela was then in a strong bargaining position to negotiate his terms of release.[221] The country was ungovernable and internationally isolated. Key political prisoners had already been released. Mandela was living in relative comfort

218 *Id.* at 555.

219 *Id.*

220 *Id.* at 555, 568.

221 Mnookin, *supra* note 2, at 126.

in his private prison cottage where he was told that this place would be his last one before being freed. If you have any doubt that the bargaining dynamic had changed, read the letter Mandela sent to de Klerk in advance of this meeting. The letter was confidently and forcefully written. He did not mince his words as he articulated conditions and terms necessary for any negotiated resolution.[222] Also, consider the unusual negotiation that took place two months later when de Klerk informed Mandela that he would be freed the next day. In what is now viewed as a historically comical exchange, Mandela, as a prisoner, tried to negotiate for another week in prison to properly prepare for his own release while de Klerk, as the jailer, wanted him to leave the next day.[223]

Mandela used this discussion about his release as an opportunity to make the case for unbanning the ANC, lifting the state of emergency, releasing political prisoners, and allowing exiles to return. If de Klerk did not unban the ANC, Mandela reminded him that Mandela would be working for an illegal organization and "you must simply re-arrest me after I walk through those gates."[224] This re-arrest reframing helped de Klerk see the dispute from an unappealing perspective. If these changes were not made, Mandela's freedom and any resulting positive world reactions would be short-lived. It evoked the unworkable status quo.

There were no surprises in the exchanges and the meeting ended as expected, as an exploratory one. President de Klerk said, "he would take all that [Mandela] said under consideration. …"[225] Mandela left the meeting thinking "Mr. de Klerk seemed to represent a true departure from … the past. … and was a man we could do business with."[226]

Less than two months later, President de Klerk stunned the country and the world on February 2, 1990, when he gave his now famous unbanning speech in which he met Mandela's key preconditions for negotiations and announced that he would be released unconditionally.[227]

222 Mandela, *supra* note 3, at 553–54.
223 *Id.* at 557–58.
224 *Id.* at 556.
225 *Id.*
226 *Id.*
227 *See supra* Part III.D.

Index